Stanley Gibbons
Commonwealth Stamp Catalogue

Canada & Provinces

8th Edition 2024

By Appointment to
Her Majesty Queen Elizabeth II
Philatelists
Stanley Gibbons
London

Published by Stanley Gibbons
Editorial, Publication and Sales Offices:
7 Parkside, Christchurch Road, Ringwood,
Hants BH24 3SH

© Stanley Gibbons 2024

Copyright Notice

The contents of this Catalogue, including the numbering system and illustrations, are fully protected by copyright. No part of this publication may be reproduced, stored in a retrieval system, or transmitted in any form or by any means, electronic, mechanical, photocopying, recording or otherwise, without the prior permission of Stanley Gibbons. Requests for such permission should be addressed to the Catalogue Editor. This Catalogue is sold on condition that it is not, by way of trade or otherwise, lent, re-sold, hired out, circulated or otherwise disposed of other than in its complete, original and unaltered form and without a similar condition including this condition being imposed on the subsequent purchaser.

British Library Cataloguing in Publication Data.
A catalogue record for this book is available from the British Library.

1st Edition - 2002
2nd Edition - 2004
3rd Edition - 2008
4th Edition - 2011
5th Edition - 2014
6th Edition - 2016
7th Edition - 2020
8th Edition - 2024

Errors and omissions excepted
the colour reproduction of stamps is only as
accurate as the printing process will allow.

ISBN-13: 978-1-8051792-0-7

Item No. R2874-24

Printed by
Sterling, Kettering

Contents

Stanley Gibbons Holdings Plc	iv
List of Catalogues	v
General Philatelic Information	vi
Prices	vi
Guarantee	vii
Condition Guide	ix
The Catalogue in General	x
Contacting the editor	xi
Technical matters	xi
Acknowledgements	xxi
Abbreviations	xxii
International Philatelic Glossary	xxiii
Guide to Entries	xxviii
The Small Queens of Canada, 1879-1897	xxx
Canada	**1**
Kiosk Label	165
Design Index	167
Stamp Booklets	175
Premium Booklets	261
Registration Stamps	262
Special Delivery Stamps	262
Official Stamps	263
Official Special Delivery Stamps	265
Postage Due Stamps	266

Stanley Gibbons Holdings Plc

Stanley Gibbons,
Stanley Gibbons Auctions
399 Strand, London WC2R 0LX
Tel: +44 (0)1425 472363
E-mail: support@stanleygibbons.com
Website: www.stanleygibbons.com
for all departments, Auction and Specialist Stamp Departments.

Open Monday–Friday 9.30 a.m. to 6 p.m.
Shop. Open Monday–Saturday 9.30 a.m. to 6 p.m.

Stanley Gibbons Publications,
Mail Order, Gibbons Stamp Monthly
7 Parkside, Christchurch Road,
Ringwood, Hampshire BH24 3SH.
Tel: +44 (0)1425 472363
E-mail: support@stanleygibbons.com

Monday–Friday 8.30 a.m. to 5 p.m.

Stanley Gibbons Publications
Overseas Representation
Stanley Gibbons Publications are represented overseas by the following

Australia
Renniks Publications PTY LTD
Unit 6, 30 Perry St, Matraville,
NSW 2036, Australia
Tel: +612 9695 7055
Website: www.renniks.com

Canada
Unitrade Associates
99 Floral Parkway, Toronto,
Ontario M6L 2C4, Canada
Tel: +1 416 242 5900
Website: www.unitradeassoc.com

Canada
F.v.H. Stamps
102-340 West Cordova Street,
Vancouver, BC, V6B 1E8, Canada
Tel: +1 604 684 8408
Website: www.fvhstamps.com

Cananda
Armstrong's
PO Bos 261,
Bright's Grove
Ontario, Canada N0N 1C0
Tel: +519 464 2688
Website: www.armstrongsstamps.ca

Denmark
Nordfrim A/S
Kvindevadet 42,
Otterup DK-5450, Denmark
Tel: +45 64 82 1256
Website: www.nordfrim.com

Japan
Japan Philatelic
PO Box 2, Suginami-Minami,
Tokyo 168-8081, Japan
Tel: +81 3330 41641
Website: www.yushu.co.jp

Netherlands
Uitgeverij Davo BV
PO Box 411, Ak Deventer, 7400
Netherlands
Tel: +3188 0284300
Website: www.davo.nl

New Zealand
Mowbray Collectables
Private Bag 63000
Wellington
New Zealand

New Zealand
Philatelic Distributors
PO Box 863
15 Mount Edgecumbe Street
New Plymouth 4615, New Zealand
Tel: +6 46 758 65 68
Website: www.stampcollecta.com

Singapore
C S Philatelic Agency
Peninsula Shopping Centre #04-29
3 Coleman Street, 179804, Singapore
Tel: +65 6337-1859
Website: www.cs.com.sg

USA
Vidiforms Company Inc
115 North Route 9W, Congers,
New York NY 10920, United States
Tel: +1 845 268 4005
Website: www.showgard.com

USA
Amos Media Company
1660 Campbell Road,
Suite A, Door #9,
Sidney OH 453652480,
United States
Tel: +1 937 498 2111
Website: www.amosmedia.com

Stanley Gibbons
Stamp Catalogues

Commonwealth & British Empire Stamps 1840–1970 (126th edition, 2024)

King George VI (9th edition, 2018)

Commonwealth Country Catalogues
Australia with Australian States & Dependencies (12th edition, 2022)
Bangladesh, Pakistan & Sri Lanka (3rd edition, 2015)
Brunei, Malaysia & Singapore (5th edition, 2017)
Canada (8th edition, 2024)
Cyprus, Gibraltar & Malta (6th edition, 2023)
East Africa with Egypt & Sudan (4th edition, 2018)
Eastern Pacific (3rd edition, 2015)
Falkland Islands (8th edition, 2019)
Hong Kong (6th edition, 2018)
India (including Convention & Feudatory States) (6th edition, 2023)
Indian Ocean (4th edition, 2022)
Ireland (8th edition, 2023)
Leeward Islands (3rd edition, 2017)
New Zealand & Dependencies (7th edition, 2022)
Northern Caribbean, Bahamas & Bermuda (4th edition, 2016)
St Helena & Dependencies (6th edition, 2017)
West Africa (2nd edition, 2012)
Western Pacific (4th edition, 2017)
Windward Islands & Barbados (3rd edition, 2015)

Stamps of the World 2024
Volume 1 — Abu Dhabi – Charkhari
Volume 2 — Chile – Georgia
Volume 3 — German Commands – Jasdan
Volume 4 — Jersey – New Republic
Volume 5 — New South Wales – Singapore
Volume 6 — Sirmoor – Zululand

Great Britain Catalogues
2024 Collect British Stamps (75th edition, 2024)
2022 Channel Islands & Isle of Man (31st edition, 2022)
2024 GB Concise (39th edition, 2024)

Great Britain Specialised
Volume 1 — Queen Victoria, Part 1 Line-engraved and Embossed Issues (1st edition, 2020)
Volume 2 — King Edward VII to King George VI (14th edition, 2015)
Volume 3 — Queen Elizabeth II Pre-decimal issues (13th edition, 2019)
Volume 4 — Queen Elizabeth II Decimal Definitive Issues – Part 1 (10th edition, 2008)
Queen Elizabeth II Decimal Definitive Issues – Part 2 (10th edition, 2010)

Foreign Countries
Arabia (1st edition, 2016)
Austria and Hungary (8th edition 2014)
Belgium & Luxembourg (1st edition, 2015)
China (12th edition, 2018)
Czech Republic and Slovakia (1st edition, 2017)
Denmark and Norway (1st edition, 2018)
Finland and Sweden (1st edition, 2017)
France, Andorra and Monaco (2nd edition, 2023)
French Colonies (1st edition, 2016)
Germany (13th edition, 2022)
Italy and Colonies (1st edition, 2022)
Middle East (1st edition, 2018)
Netherlands & Colonies (1st edition, 2017)
North East Africa (2nd edition, 2017)
Poland (2nd edition, 2023)
Portugal and Colonies (1st edition, 2022)
Southern Balkans (1st edition, 2019)
Spain and Colonies (1st edition, 2019)
Switzerland (1st edition, 2019)
United States of America (8th edition, 2015)

We have catalogues to suit every aspect of stamp collecting

Our catalogues cover stamps issued from across the globe - from the Penny Black to the latest issues. Whether you're a specialist in a certain reign or a thematic collector, we should have something to suit your needs. All catalogues include the famous SG numbering system, making it as easy as possible to find the stamp you're looking for.

STANLEY GIBBONS
THE HOME OF STAMP COLLECTING

STANLEY GIBBONS | 399 Strand | London | WC2R 0LX
www.stanleygibbons.com

/StanleyGibbonsGroup @StanleyGibbons @StanleyGibbons @StanleyGibbons1856

General Philatelic Information and Guidelines to the Scope of Stanley Gibbons Commonwealth Catalogues

These notes reflect current practice in compiling the Stanley Gibbons Commonwealth Catalogues.

The Stanley Gibbons Stamp Catalogue has a very long history and the vast quantity of information it contains has been carefully built up by successive generations through the work of countless individuals. Philately is never static and the Catalogue has evolved and developed over the years. These notes relate to the current criteria upon which a stamp may be listed or priced. These criteria have developed over time and may have differed somewhat in the early years of this catalogue. These notes are not intended to suggest that we plan to make wholesale changes to the listing of classic issues in order to bring them into line with today's listing policy, they are designed to inform catalogue users as to the policies currently in operation.

PRICES

The prices quoted in this Catalogue are the estimated selling prices of Stanley Gibbons at the time of publication. They are, unless it is specifically stated otherwise, for examples in fine condition for the issue concerned. Superb examples are worth more; those of a lower quality considerably less.

All prices are subject to change without prior notice and Stanley Gibbons may from time to time offer stamps below catalogue price. Individual low value stamps sold at 399 Strand are liable to an additional handling charge. Purchasers of new issues should note the prices charged for them contain an element for the service rendered and so may exceed the prices shown when the stamps are subsequently catalogued. Postage and handling charges are extra.

No guarantee is given to supply all stamps priced, since it is not possible to keep every catalogued item in stock. Commemorative issues may, at times, only be available in complete sets and not as individual values.

Quotation of prices. The prices in the left-hand column are for unused stamps and those in the right-hand column are for used.

A dagger (†) denotes that the item listed does not exist or is not believed to exist in that condition and a blank, or dash, that it exists, or may exist, but we are unable to quote a price.

We welcome information concerning items which are currently unpriced; such assistance may lead to them being priced in future editions.

Prices are expressed in pounds and pence sterling. One pound comprises 100 pence (£1 = 100p).

The method of notation is as follows: pence in numerals (e.g. 10 denotes ten pence); pounds and pence, up to £100, in numerals (e.g. 4·25 denotes four pounds and twenty-five pence); prices above £100 are expressed in whole pounds with the '£' sign shown.

Unused stamps. Great Britain and Commonwealth: the prices for unused stamps of Queen Victoria to King George V are for lightly hinged examples. Unused prices for King Edward VIII, King George VI and Queen Elizabeth issues are for unmounted mint or 'mint never hinged' (MNH).

Some stamps from the King George VI period are often difficult to find in unmounted mint condition. In such instances we would expect that collectors would need to pay a high proportion of the price quoted to obtain mounted mint examples. Generally speaking lightly mounted mint stamps from this reign, issued before 1945, are in considerable demand.

Used stamps. The used prices are normally for stamps fine postally used, which for the vast majority of those issued since 1900 refers to cancellation with a clear circular or oval dated postmark. It may also include stamps cancelled to order, where this practice exists, or with commemorative or 'first day' postmarks.

A pen-cancellation on early issues can sometimes correctly denote postal use. Instances are individually noted in the Catalogue in explanation of the used price given.

Prices quoted for bisects on cover or large piece are for those dated during the period officially authorised.

Stamps not sold unused to the public (e.g. some official stamps) are priced used only.

The use of 'unified' designs, that is stamps inscribed for both postal and fiscal purposes, results in a number of stamps of very high face value. In some instances these may not have been primarily intended for postal purposes, but if they are so inscribed we include them. The used prices shown refer to postally used examples, although prices for fiscally used may be shown within brackets. Collectors should be careful to avoid stamps with fiscal cancellations being offered as 'postal fiscals' and also fiscally used stamps that have had their cancellations removed and fraudulent postmarks applied.

Cover prices. To assist collectors, cover prices are quoted for issues up to 1945 at the beginning of each country.

The system gives a general guide in the form of a factor by which the corresponding used price of the basic loose stamp should be multiplied when found in fine average condition on cover.

Care is needed in applying the factors and they relate to a cover which bears a single of the denomination listed; if more than one denomination is present the most highly priced attracts the multiplier and the remainder are priced at the simple figure for used singles in arriving at a total.

The cover should be of non-philatelic origin; bearing the correct postal rate for the period and distance involved and cancelled with the markings normal to the offices concerned. **Purely philatelic items have a cover value only slightly greater than the catalogue value for the corresponding used stamps.** This applies generally to those high-value stamps used philatelically rather than in the normal course of commerce. Low-value stamps, e.g. ¼d. and ½d., are desirable when used as a single rate on cover and merit an increase in 'multiplier' value.

First day covers in the period up to 1945 are not within the scope of the system and the multiplier should not be used. As a special category of philatelic usage, with wide variations in valuation according to scarcity, they require separate treatment.

Oversized covers, difficult to accommodate on an album page, should be reckoned as worth little more than the corresponding value of the used stamps. The condition of a cover also affects its value. Except for 'wreck covers', serious damage or soiling reduce the value where the postal markings and stamps are ordinary ones. Conversely, visual appeal adds to the value and this can include freshness of appearance, important addresses, old-fashioned but legible hand-writing, historic town-names, etc.

The multipliers are a base on which further value would be added to take account of the cover's postal historical importance in demonstrating such things as unusual, scarce or emergency cancels, interesting routes, significant postal markings, combination usage, the development of postal rates, and so on.

Minimum price. The minimum catalogue price quoted is 10p. For individual stamps prices between 10p. and 95p. are provided as a guide for catalogue users. The lowest price charged for individual stamps or sets purchased from Stanley Gibbons is £1.

Set prices. Set prices are generally for one of each value, excluding shades and varieties, but including major colour changes. Where there are alternative shades, etc., the cheapest is usually included. The number of stamps in the set is always stated for clarity. The prices for sets containing *se-tenant* pieces are based on the prices quoted for such combinations, and not on those for the individual stamps.

Varieties. Where plate or cylinder varieties are priced in used condition the price quoted is for a fine used example with the cancellation well clear of the listed flaw.

Specimen stamps. The pricing of these items is explained under that heading.

Stamp booklets. Prices are for complete assembled booklets in fine condition with those issued before 1945 showing normal wear and tear. Incomplete booklets and those which have been 'exploded' will, in general, be worth less than the figure quoted.

Repricing. Collectors will be aware that the market factors of supply and demand directly influence the prices quoted in this Catalogue. Whatever the scarcity of a particular stamp, if there is no one in the market who wishes to buy, it cannot be expected to achieve a high price. Conversely, the same item actively sought by numerous potential buyers may cause the price to rise.

All the prices in this Catalogue are examined during the preparation of each new edition by the expert staff of Stanley Gibbons and repriced as necessary. They take many factors into account, including supply and demand, and are in close touch with the international stamp market and the auction world.

Commonwealth cover prices and advice on postal history material originally provided by Edward B Proud.

GUARANTEE

All stamps are guaranteed originals in the following terms:

If not as described, and returned by the purchaser, we undertake to refund the price paid to us in the original transaction. If any stamp is certified as genuine by the Expert Committee of the Royal Philatelic Society, London, or by BPA Expertising Ltd, the purchaser shall not be entitled to make any claim against us for any error, omission or mistake in such certificate.

Consumers' statutory rights are not affected by the above guarantee.

The recognised Expert Committees in this country are those of the Royal Philatelic Society, 15 Abchurch Lane, London EC4 7BW, and BPA Expertising Ltd, PO Box 1141, Guildford, Surrey GU5 0WR. They do not undertake valuations under any circumstances and fees are payable for their services.

Information and Guidelines

MARGINS ON IMPERFORATE STAMPS

| Superb | Very fine | Fine | Average | Poor |

GUM

| Unmounted | Very lightly mounted | Lightly mounted | Mounted/ large part original gum (o.g.) | Heavily mounted small part o.g. |

CENTRING

| Superb | Very fine | Fine | Average | Poor |

CANCELLATIONS

| Superb | Very fine | Fine | Average | Poor |

| Superb | Very fine |

| Fine | Average | Poor |

viii

CONDITION GUIDE

To assist collectors in assessing the true value of items they are considering buying or in reviewing stamps already in their collections, we now offer a more detailed guide to the condition of stamps on which this catalogue's prices are based.

For a stamp to be described as 'Fine', it should be sound in all respects, without creases, bends, wrinkles, pin holes, thins or tears. If perforated, all perforation 'teeth' should be intact, it should not suffer from fading, rubbing or toning and it should be of clean, fresh appearance.

Margins on imperforate stamps: These should be even on all sides and should be at least as wide as half the distance between that stamp and the next. To have one or more margins of less than this width, would normally preclude a stamp from being described as 'Fine'. Some early stamps were positioned very close together on the printing plate and in such cases 'Fine' margins would necessarily be narrow. On the other hand, some plates were laid down to give a substantial gap between individual stamps and in such cases margins would be expected to be much wider.

An 'average' four-margin example would have a narrower margin on one or more sides and should be priced accordingly, while a stamp with wider, yet even, margins than 'Fine' would merit the description 'Very Fine' or 'Superb' and, if available, would command a price in excess of that quoted in the catalogue.

Gum: Since the prices for stamps of King Edward VIII, King George VI and Queen Elizabeth are for 'unmounted' or 'never hinged' mint, even stamps from these reigns which have been very lightly mounted should be available at a discount from catalogue price, the more obvious the hinge marks, the greater the discount.

Catalogue prices for stamps issued prior to King Edward VIII's reign are for mounted mint, so unmounted examples would be worth a premium. Hinge marks on 20th century stamps should not be too obtrusive, and should be at least in the lightly mounted category. For 19th century stamps more obvious hinging would be acceptable, but stamps should still carry a large part of their original gum—'Large part o.g.'—in order to be described as 'Fine'.

Centring: Ideally, the stamp's image should appear in the exact centre of the perforated area, giving equal margins on all sides. 'Fine' centring would be close to this ideal with any deviation having an effect on the value of the stamp. As in the case of the margins on imperforate stamps, it should be borne in mind that the space between some early stamps was very narrow, so it was very difficult to achieve accurate perforation, especially when the technology was in its infancy. Thus, poor centring would have a less damaging effect on the value of a 19th century stamp than on a 20th century example, but the premium put on a perfectly centred specimen would be greater.

Cancellations: Early cancellation devices were designed to 'obliterate' the stamp in order to prevent it being reused and this is still an important objective for today's postal administrations. Stamp collectors, on the other hand, prefer postmarks to be lightly applied, clear, and to leave as much as possible of the design visible. Dated, circular cancellations have long been 'the postmark of choice', but the definition of a 'Fine' cancellation will depend upon the types of cancellation in use at the time a stamp was current—it is clearly illogical to seek a circular datestamp on a Penny Black.

'Fine', by definition, will be superior to 'Average', so, in terms of cancellation quality, if one begins by identifying what 'Average' looks like, then one will be half way to identifying 'Fine'. The illustrations will give some guidance on mid-19th century and mid-20th century cancellations of Great Britain, but types of cancellation in general use in each country and in each period will determine the appearance of 'Fine'.

As for the factors discussed above, anything less than 'Fine' will result in a downgrading of the stamp concerned, while a very fine or superb cancellation will be worth a premium.

Self-adhesive stamps: The majority of used self-adhesive stamps cannot easily be removed from postal items and are therefore best collected intact or 'on-piece'. In the latter case, we recommend that stamps are carefully trimmed from envelopes with straight, even margins all round, taking care not to cut into the stamp itself. A margin of 2mm all round is ideal.

Combining the factors: To merit the description 'Fine', a stamp should be fine in every respect, but a small deficiency in one area might be made up for in another by a factor meriting an 'Extremely Fine' description.

Some early issues are so seldom found in what would normally be considered to be 'Fine' condition, the catalogue prices are for a slightly lower grade, with 'Fine' examples being worth a premium. In such cases a note to this effect is given in the catalogue, while elsewhere premiums are given for well-centred, lightly cancelled examples.

In the 21st century many postal administrations seem to feel that there is little need for stamps to be legibly cancelled and ink-jet markings, heavy obliterations and pen cancellations are very much the order of the day, while a large proportion of stamps are left without a postal marking of any kind. Used stamps of this type are of very little value and the prices shown in this catalogue are for clear circular operational date stamps or appropriate commemorative cancellations, although the latter are also frowned upon by many collectors.

Stamps graded at less than fine remain collectable and, in the case of more highly priced stamps, will continue to hold a value. Nevertheless, buyers should always bear condition in mind.

Information and Guidelines

The Catalogue in General

Contents. The Catalogue is confined to adhesive postage stamps, including miniature sheets. For particular categories the rules are:
(a) Revenue (fiscal) stamps are listed only where they have been expressly authorised for postal duty.
(b) Stamps issued only precancelled are included, but normally issued stamps available additionally with precancel have no separate precancel listing unless the face value is changed.
(c) Stamps prepared for use but not issued, hitherto accorded full listing, are nowadays foot-noted with a price (where possible).
(d) Bisects (trisects, etc.) are only listed where such usage was officially authorised.
(e) Stamps issued only on first day covers or in presentation packs and not available separately are not listed but may be priced in a footnote.
(f) New printings are only included in this Catalogue where they show a major philatelic variety, such as a change in shade, watermark or paper. Stamps which exist with or without imprint dates are listed separately; changes in imprint dates are mentioned in footnotes.
(g) Official and unofficial reprints are dealt with by footnote.
(h) Stamps from imperforate printings of modern issues which occur perforated are covered by footnotes, but are listed where widely available for postal use.

Exclusions. The following are excluded:
(a) non-postal revenue or fiscal stamps;
(b) postage stamps used fiscally (although prices are now given for some fiscally used high values);
(c) local carriage labels and private local issues;
(d) bogus or phantom stamps;
(e) railway or airline letter fee stamps, bus or road transport company labels or the stamps of private postal companies operating under licence from the national authority;
(f) cut-outs;
(g) all types of non-postal labels and souvenirs;
(h) documentary labels for the postal service, e.g. registration, recorded delivery, air-mail etiquettes, etc.;
(i) privately applied embellishments to official issues and privately commissioned items generally;
(j) stamps for training postal officers.

Full listing. 'Full listing' confers our recognition and implies allotting a catalogue number and (wherever possible) a price quotation.

In judging status for inclusion in the catalogue broad considerations are applied to stamps. They must be issued by a legitimate postal authority, recognised by the government concerned, and must be adhesives valid for proper postal use in the class of service for which they are inscribed. Stamps, with the exception of such categories as postage dues and officials, must be available to the general public, at face value, in reasonable quantities without any artificial restrictions being imposed on their distribution.

For errors and varieties the criterion is legitimate (albeit inadvertent) sale through a postal administration in the normal course of business. Details of provenance are always important; printers' waste and deliberately manufactured material are excluded.

Certificates. In assessing unlisted items due weight is given to Certificates from recognised Expert Committees and, where appropriate, we will usually ask to see them.

Date of issue. Where local issue dates differ from dates of release by agencies, 'date of issue' is the local date. Fortuitous stray usage before the officially intended date is disregarded in listing.

Catalogue numbers. Stamps of each country are catalogued chronologically by date of issue. Subsidiary classes are placed at the end of the country, as separate lists, with a distinguishing letter prefix to the catalogue number, e.g. D for postage due, O for official and E for express delivery stamps.

The catalogue number appears in the extreme left-column. The boldface Type numbers in the next column are merely cross-references to illustrations.

A catalogue number with a suffix will normally relate to the main number, so 137a will be a variant of No. 137, unless the suffix appears as part of the number in the left-hand column such as Great Britain No. 20a, in which case it should be treated as the main number. A number with multiple suffixes will relate to the first letter or letters of that suffix, so 137ab will be a variant of 137a and 137aba a variant of 137ab. The exception is an 'aa' suffix, which will precede an 'a' and always refers to the main number, so 137aa relates to 137, not 137a.

Once published in the Catalogue, numbers are changed as little as possible; really serious renumbering is reserved for the occasions when a complete country or an entire issue is being rewritten. The edition first affected includes cross-reference tables of old and new numbers.

Our catalogue numbers are universally recognised in specifying stamps and as a hallmark of status.

'Missing' numbers. Following rewriting it is frequently the case that individual or series of numbers become redundant. Apparent gaps in the numbering, such as, New Zealand 472/543 or St Helena 102 do not indicate that a stamp or stamps are omitted, but that an earlier revision has been made to the listing.

Illustrations. Stamps are illustrated at three-quarters linear size. Stamps not illustrated are the same size and format as the value shown, unless otherwise indicated. Stamps issued only as miniature sheets have the stamp alone illustrated but sheet size is also quoted. Overprints, surcharges, watermarks and postmarks are normally actual size. Illustrations of varieties are often enlarged to show the detail. Stamp booklet covers are illustrated half-size, unless otherwise indicated.

The colour illustrations of stamps are intended as a guide only, they may differ in shade from the originals.

Designers. Designers' names are quoted where known, though space precludes naming every individual concerned in the production of a set. In particular, photographers supplying material are usually named only where they also make an active contribution in the design stage; posed photographs of reigning monarchs are, however, an exception to this rule.

CONTACTING THE CATALOGUE EDITOR

The editor is always interested in hearing from people who have new information which will improve or correct the Catalogue. As a general rule he must see and examine the actual stamps before they can be considered for listing; although a high-resolution scan, particularly if supported by a certificate provided by a reliable authority may provide sufficient evidence.

Submissions should be made in writing to the Catalogue Editor, Stanley Gibbons Publications at the Ringwood office or via email to thecatalogueeditor@stanleygibbons.com. For items submitted by post the cost of return postage would be appreciated, and this should include the registration fee if required.

Where information is solicited purely for the benefit of the enquirer, the editor cannot undertake to reply if the answer is already contained in these published notes or if return postage is omitted. Written communications are greatly preferred to enquiries by telephone or e-mail and the editor regrets that he or his staff cannot see personal callers without a prior appointment being made. Correspondence may be subject to delay during the production period of each new edition.

The editor welcomes close contact with study circles and is interested, too, in finding reliable local correspondents who will verify and supplement official information in countries where this is deficient.

> We regret we do not give opinions as to the genuineness of stamps, nor do we identify stamps or number them by our Catalogue.

TECHNICAL MATTERS

The meanings of the technical terms used in the catalogue will be found in our *Philatelic Terms Illustrated*.

References below to (more specialised) listings are to be taken to indicate, as appropriate, the Stanley Gibbons *Great Britain Specialised Catalogue* or the *Great Britain Concise Catalogue*.

1. Printing

Printing errors. Errors in printing are of major interest to the Catalogue. Authenticated items meriting consideration would include: background, centre or frame inverted or omitted; centre or subject transposed; error of colour; error or omission of value; double prints and impressions; printed both sides; and so on.

Apparent 'double prints' including overprints, on stamps printed by offset litho arising from movement of the rubber 'blanket' involved in this process are however, outside the scope of this catalogue, although they may be included in more specialised listings.

Designs *tête-bêche*, whether intentionally or by accident, are listable. *Se-tenant* arrangements of stamps are recognised in the listings or footnotes. Gutter pairs (a pair of stamps separated by blank margin) are not included in this volume. Colours only partially omitted are not listed. Stamps with embossing omitted are reserved for our more specialised listings.

Printing varieties. Listing is accorded to major changes in the printing base which lead to completely new types. In recess-printing this could be a design re-engraved; in photogravure or photolithography a screen altered in whole or in part. It can also encompass flat-bed and rotary printing if the results are readily distinguishable.

To be considered at all, varieties must be constant.

Early stamps, produced by primitive methods, were prone to numerous imperfections; the lists reflect this, recognising re-entries, retouches, broken frames, misshapen letters, and so on. Printing technology has, however, radically improved over the years, during which time photogravure and lithography have become predominant. Varieties nowadays are more in the nature of flaws and these, being too specialised for this general catalogue, are almost always outside the scope.

In no catalogue, however, do we list such items as: dry prints, kiss prints, doctor-blade flaws, colour shifts or registration flaws (unless they lead to the complete omission of a colour from an individual stamp), lithographic ring flaws, and so on. Neither do we recognise fortuitous happenings like paper creases or confetti flaws.

'Varieties of varieties'. We no longer provide individual listings for combinations of two or more varieties; thus a plate variety or overprinting error will not be listed for various watermark orientations.

Overprints (and surcharges). Overprints of different types qualify for separate listing. These include overprints in different colours; overprints from different printing processes such as litho and typo; overprints in totally different typefaces, etc. Major errors in machine-printed overprints are important and listable. They include: overprint inverted or omitted; overprint double (treble, etc.); overprint diagonal; overprint double, one inverted; pairs with one overprint omitted, e.g. from a radical shift to an adjoining stamp; error of colour; error of type fount; letters inverted or omitted, etc. If the overprint is hand-stamped, few of these would qualify and a distinction is drawn. We continue, however, to list pairs of stamps where one has a handstamped overprint and the other has not, unless it is known that such items were created deliberately at the request of purchasers (see note below Zanzibar 394/413).

Albino prints or double prints, one of them being albino (i.e. showing an uninked impression of the printing plate) are listable unless they are particularly common in this form (see the note below Travancore No. 32fa, for example). We do not, however, normally list reversed albino overprints, caused by the accidental or deliberate folding of sheets prior to overprinting (British Levant Nos. 51/8).

Varieties occurring in overprints will often take the form of broken letters, slight differences in spacing, rising spaces, etc. Only the most important would be considered for listing or footnote mention.

Sheet positions. If space permits we quote sheet positions of listed varieties and authenticated data is solicited for this purpose.

De La Rue plates. The Catalogue classifies the general plates used by De La Rue for printing British Colonial stamps as follows:

VICTORIAN KEY TYPE

Die I

1. The ball of decoration on the second point of the crown appears as a dark mass of lines.
2. Dark vertical shading separates the front hair from the bun.
3. The vertical line of colour outlining the front of the throat stops at the sixth line of shading on the neck.
4. The white space in the coil of the hair above the curl is roughly the shape of a pin's head.

Information and Guidelines

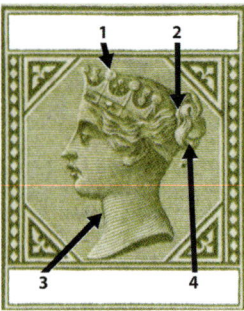

Die II

1. There are very few lines of colour in the ball and it appears almost white.
2. A white vertical strand of hair appears in place of the dark shading.
3. The line stops at the eighth line of shading.
4. The white space is oblong, with a line of colour partially dividing it at the left end.

Plates numbered 1 and 2 are both Die I. Plates 3 and 4 are Die II.

GEORGIAN KEY TYPE

Die I

A. The second (thick) line below the name of the country is cut slanting, conforming roughly to the shape of the crown on each side.
B. The labels of solid colour bearing the words 'POSTAGE' and '& REVENUE' are square at the inner top corners.
C. There is a projecting 'bud' on the outer spiral of the ornament in each of the lower corners.

Die II

A. The second line is cut vertically on each side of the crown.
B. The labels curve inwards at the top.
C. There is no 'bud' in this position.

Unless otherwise stated in the lists, all stamps with watermark Multiple Crown CA (w **8**) are Die I while those with watermark Multiple Crown Script CA (w **9**) are Die II. The Georgian Die II was introduced in April 1921 and was used for Plates 10 to 22 and 26 to 28. Plates 23 to 25 were made from Die I by mistake.

2. Paper

All stamps listed are deemed to be on (ordinary) paper of the wove type and white in colour; only departures from this are normally mentioned.

Types. Where classification so requires we distinguish such other types of paper as, for example, vertically and horizontally laid; wove and laid bâtonné; card(board); carton; cartridge; glazed; granite; native; pelure; porous; quadrillé; ribbed; rice; and silk thread.

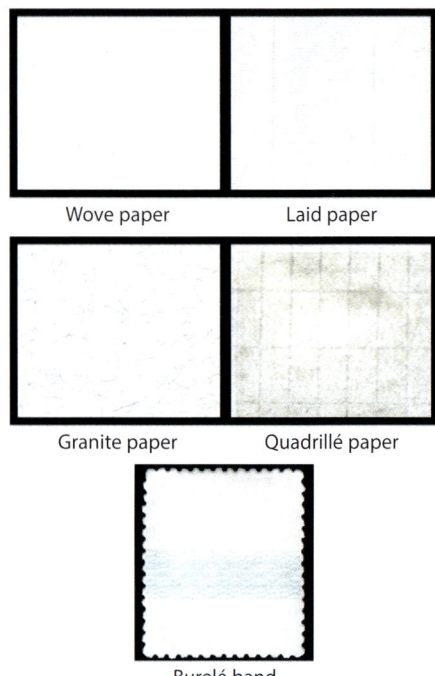

Wove paper · Laid paper

Granite paper · Quadrillé paper

Burelé band

The various makeshifts for normal paper are listed as appropriate. The varieties of double paper and joined paper are recognised. The security device of a printed burelé band on the back of a stamp, as in early Queensland, qualifies for listing.

Descriptive terms. The fact that a paper is handmade (and thus probably of uneven thickness) is mentioned where necessary. Such descriptive terms as 'hard' and 'soft'; 'smooth' and 'rough'; 'thick', 'medium' and 'thin' are applied where there is philatelic merit in classifying papers.

Coloured, very white and toned papers. A coloured paper is one that is coloured right through (front and back of the stamp). In the Catalogue the colour of the paper is given in italics, thus:

black/*rose* = black design on rose paper.

Papers have been made specially white in recent years by, for example, a very heavy coating of chalk. We do not classify shades of whiteness of paper as distinct varieties. There does exist, however, a type of paper from early days called toned. This is off-white, often brownish or buffish, but it cannot be assigned any definite colour. A toning effect brought on by climate, incorrect storage or gum staining is disregarded here, as this was not the state of the paper when issued.

'Ordinary' and 'Chalk-surfaced' papers. The availability of many postage stamps for revenue purposes made necessary some safeguard against the illegitimate re-use of stamps with removable cancellations. This was at first secured by using fugitive inks and later by printing on paper surfaced by coatings containing either chalk or china clay, both of which made it difficult to remove any form of obliteration without damaging the stamp design.

This catalogue lists these chalk-surfaced paper varieties from their introduction in 1905. Where no indication is given, the paper is 'ordinary'.

The 'traditional' method of indentifying chalk-surfaced papers has been that, when touched with a silver wire, a black mark is left on the paper, and the listings in this catalogue are based on that test. However, the test itself is now largely discredited, for, although the mark can be removed by a soft rubber, some damage to the stamp will result from its use.

The difference between chalk-surfaced and pre-war ordinary papers is fairly clear: chalk-surfaced papers being smoother to the touch and showing a characteristic sheen when light is reflected off their surface. Under good magnification tiny bubbles or pock marks can be seen on the surface of the stamp and at the tips of the perforations the surfacing appears 'broken'. Traces of paper fibres are evident on the surface of ordinary paper and the ink shows a degree of absorption into it.

Initial chalk-surfaced paper printings by De La Rue had a thinner coating than subsequently became the norm. The characteristics described above are less pronounced in these printings.

During and after the Second World War, substitute papers replaced the chalk-surfaced papers, these do not react to the silver test and are therefore classed as 'ordinary', although differentiating them without recourse to it is more difficult, for, although the characteristics of the chalk-surfaced paper remained the same, some of the ordinary papers appear much smoother than earlier papers and many do not show the watermark clearly. Experience is the only solution to identifying these, and comparison with stamps whose paper type is without question will be of great help.

Another type of paper, known as 'thin striated' was used only for the Bahamas 1s. and 5s. (Nos. 155a, 156a, 171 and 174) and for several stamps of the Malayan states. Hitherto these have been described as 'chalk-surfaced' since they gave some reaction to the silver test, but they are much thinner than usual chalk-surfaced papers, with the watermark showing clearly. Stamps on this paper show a slightly 'ribbed' effect when the stamp is held up to the light. Again, comparison with a known striated paper stamp, such as the 1941 Straits Settlements Die II 2c. orange (No. 294) will prove invaluable in separating these papers.

Glazed paper. In 1969 the Crown Agents introduced a new general-purpose paper for use in conjunction with all current printing processes. It generally has a marked glossy surface but the degree varies according to the process used, being more marked in recess-printing stamps. As it does not respond to the silver test this presents a further test where previous printings were on chalky paper. A change of paper to the glazed variety merits separate listing.

Green and yellow papers. Issues of the First World War and immediate postwar period occur on green and yellow papers and these are given separate Catalogue listing. The original coloured papers (coloured throughout) gave way to surface-coloured papers, the stamps having 'white backs'; other stamps show one colour on the front and a different one at the back. Because of the numerous variations a grouping of colours is adopted as follows:

Yellow papers

(1) The original *yellow* paper (throughout), usually bright in colour. The gum is often sparse, of harsh consistency and dull-looking. Used 1912–1920.

(2) The *white-backs*. Used 1913–1914.

(3) A bright lemon paper. The colour must have a pronounced greenish tinge, different from the 'yellow' in (1). As a rule, the gum on stamps using this lemon paper is plentiful, smooth and shiny, and the watermark shows distinctly. Care is needed with stamps printed in green on yellow paper (1) as it may appear that the paper is this lemon. Used 1914–1916.

(4) An experimental *orange-buff* paper. The colour must have a distinct brownish tinge. It is not to be confused with a muddy yellow (1) nor the misleading appearance (on the surface) of stamps printed in red on yellow paper where an engraved plate has been insufficiently wiped. Used 1918–1921.

(5) An experimental *buff* paper. This lacks the brownish tinge of (4) and the brightness of the yellow shades. The gum is shiny when compared with the matt type used on (4). Used 1919–1920.

(6) A *pale yellow* paper that has a creamy tone to the yellow. Used from 1920 onwards.

Green papers

(7) The original 'green' paper, varying considerably through shades of blue-green and yellow-green, the front and back sometimes differing. Used 1912–1916.

(8) The *white backs*. Used 1913–1914.

(9) A paper blue-green on the surface with *pale olive* back. The back must be markedly paler than the front and this and the pronounced olive tinge to the back distinguish it from (7). Used 1916–1920.

(10) Paper with a vivid green surface, commonly called *emerald-green*; it has the olive back of (9). Used 1920.

(11) Paper with *emerald-green* both back and front. Used from 1920 onwards.

3. Perforation and Rouletting

Perforation gauge. The gauge of a perforation is the number of holes in a length of 2 cm. For correct classification the size of the holes (large or small) may need to be distinguished; in a few cases the actual number of holes on each edge of the stamp needs to be quoted.

Measurement. The Gibbons *Instanta* gauge is the standard for measuring perforations. The stamp is viewed against a dark background with the transparent gauge put on top of it. Though the gauge measures to decimal accuracy, perforations read from it are generally quoted in the Catalogue to the nearest half. For example:

Just over perf 12¾ to just under 13¼ = perf 13
Perf 13¼ exactly, rounded up = perf 13½
Just over perf 13¼ to just under 13¾ = perf 13½
Perf 13¾ exactly, rounded up = perf 14

However, where classification depends on it, actual quarter-perforations are quoted.

It should be noted that there were sometimes slight variations in the spacing of the pins along the length of a perforator, giving rise to small differences in the resulting measurements. Since they come from the same perforators and the measurements are generally within the same '½' band on the Instanta gauge we ignore these differences.

Notation. Where no perforation is quoted for an issue it is imperforate. Perforations are usually abbreviated

Information and Guidelines

(and spoken) as follows, though sometimes they may be spelled out for clarity. This notation for rectangular stamps (the majority) applies to diamond shapes if 'top' is read as the edge to the top right.

P 14: perforated alike on all sides (read: 'perf 14').

P 14×15: the first figure refers to top and bottom, the second to left and right sides (read: 'perf 14 by 15'). This is a compound perforation. For an upright triangular stamp the first figure refers to the two sloping sides and second to the base. In inverted triangulars the base is first and the second figure to the sloping sides.

P 14–15 or 14 to 15: perforation measuring anything between 14 and 15: the holes are irregularly spaced, thus the gauge may vary along a single line or even along a single edge of the stamp (read: 'perf 14 to 15').

P 14 *irregular*: perforated 14 from a worn perforator, giving badly aligned holes irregularly spaced (read: 'irregular perf 14').

P *comp(ound)* 14×15: two gauges in use but not necessarily on opposite sides of the stamp. It could be one side in one gauge and three in the other; or two adjacent sides with the same gauge. (Read: 'perf compound of 14 and 15'.) For three gauges or more, abbreviated as 'P 12, 14½, 15 *or compound*' for example.

P 14, 14½: perforated approximately 14¼ (read: 'perf 14 or 14½'). It does *not* mean two stamps, one perf 14 and the other perf 14½. This obsolescent notation is gradually being replaced in the Catalogue.

Imperf: imperforate (not perforated)

Imperf×P 14: imperforate at top ad bottom and perf 14 at sides.

P 14×*imperf*: perf 14 at top and bottom and imperforate at sides.

Imperf×perf

Such headings as 'P 13×14 (*vert*) and P 14×13 (*horiz*)' indicate which perforations apply to which stamp format—vertical or horizontal.

Some stamps are additionally perforated so that a label or tab is detachable; others have been perforated for use as two halves. Listings are normally for whole stamps, unless stated otherwise.

Other terms. Perforation almost always gives circular holes; where other shapes have been used they are specified, e.g. square holes; lozenge perf. Interrupted perfs are brought about by the omission of pins at regular intervals. Perforations merely simulated by being printed as part of the design are of course ignored. With few exceptions, privately applied perforations are not listed.

In the 19th century perforations are often described as clean cut (clean, sharply incised holes), intermediate or rough (rough holes, imperfectly cut, often the result of blunt pins).

Perforation errors and varieties. Authenticated errors, where a stamp normally perforated is accidentally issued imperforate, are listed provided no traces of perforation (blind holes or indentations) remain. They must be provided as pairs, both stamps wholly imperforate, and are only priced in that form.

Note that several postal administrations and their agencies are now deliberately releasing imperforate versions of issued stamps in restricted quantities and at premium prices. These are not listable, but, where possible, their existance will be noted.

In recent years a growing number of imperforates have been released from printers' archives. These are not listable but they are so widespread that it is not practical to note all of them. Collectors are warned against confusing such releases with genuine errors.

Stamps imperforate between stamp and sheet margin are not listed in this catalogue, but such errors on Great Britain stamps will be found in the *Great Britain Specialised Catalogue*.

Pairs described as 'imperforate between' have the line of perforations between the two stamps omitted.

Imperf between (horiz pair): a horizontal pair of stamps with perfs all around the edges but none between the stamps.

Imperf between (vert pair): a vertical pair of stamps with perfs all around the edges but none between the stamps.

Imperf between (vertical pair)   Imperf horizontally (vertical pair)

Where several of the rows have escaped perforation the resulting varieties are listable. Thus:

Imperf vert (horiz pair): a horizontal pair of stamps perforated top and bottom; all three vertical directions are imperf—the two outer edges and between the stamps.

Imperf horiz (vert pair): a vertical pair perforated at left and right edges; all three horizontal directions are imperf—the top, bottom and between the stamps.

Straight edges. Large sheets cut up before issue to post offices can cause stamps with straight edges, i.e. imperf on one side or on two sides at right angles. They are not usually listable in this condition and are worth less than corresponding stamps properly perforated all round. This does not, however, apply to certain stamps, mainly from coils and booklets, where straight edges on various sides are the manufacturing norm affecting every stamp. The listings and notes make clear which sides are correctly imperf.

Malfunction. Varieties of double, misplaced or partial perforation caused by error or machine malfunction are not listable, neither are freaks, such as perforations placed diagonally from paper folds, nor missing holes caused by broken pins.

Types of perforating. Where necessary for classification, perforation types are distinguished. These include:

Line perforation from one line of pins punching single rows of holes at a time.

Comb perforation from pins disposed across the sheet in comb formation, punching out holes at three sides of the stamp a row at a time.

Harrow perforation applied to a whole pane or sheet

Information and Guidelines

at one stroke.

Rotary perforation from toothed wheels operating across a sheet, then crosswise.

Sewing machine perforation. The resultant condition, clean-cut or rough, is distinguished where required.

Pin-perforation is the commonly applied term for pin-roulette in which, instead of being punched out, round holes are pricked by sharp-pointed pins and no paper is removed.

Mixed perforation occurs when stamps with defective perforations are re-perforated in a different gauge.

Different printings of the same stamp were sometimes perforated using different machines, e.g., line or comb. Unless these involve different gauges of perforation, they are not separately listed; however, in some cases these differences can help identify listed printings, such as Falkland Islands Nos. 60/63 and 116/122.

The differences between line and comb perforations are most easily seen in blocks of four or larger, where, ideally, comb perforation will show a single perforation hole at the meeting point of four stamps, while line perforation will show a double hole at this point. Very occasionally, line perforation holes will coincide exactly, but never on all four corners of a stamp.

Care needs to be exercised where, due to a slight irregularity in the 'beat' of the machine, double holes can sometimes occur in comb perforation and, especially where there is a significant difference in the price (e.g., Jamaica 132a), accurate measurement of the perforations and reference to the relevant footnotes is essential.

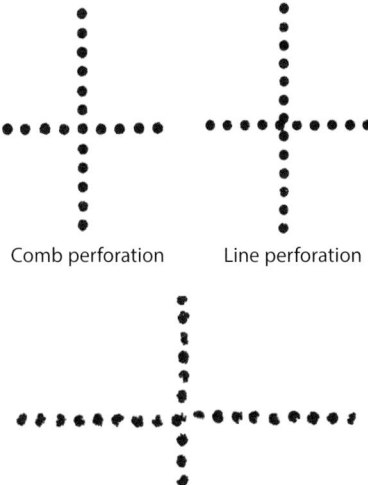

Comb perforation   Line perforation

Comb perforation. In spite of the double hole at the intersection, this cannot be line perforated as the horizontal perforations are not in a straight line

Die-cut. Self-adhesive stamps are not perforated in the traditional way, but are die-cut in order to facilitate their removal from the backing paper. Such die-cutting may be 'free-form', to match the design of the stamp, with straight edges, or, most frequently, with simulated 'perforations' or undulating edges. Such 'perforations' or undulations are measured in the same way as conventional perforations.

Punctured stamps. Perforation holes can be punched into the face of the stamp. Patterns of small holes, often in the shape of initial letters, are privately applied devices against pilferage. These (perfins) are outside the scope except for Australia, Canada, Cape of Good Hope, Papua and Sudan where they were used as official stamps by the national administration. Identification devices, when officially inspired, are listed or noted; they can be shapes, or letters or words formed from holes, sometimes converting one class of stamp into another.

Rouletting. In rouletting the paper is cut, for ease of separation, but none is removed. The gauge is measured, when needed, as for perforations. Traditional French terms descriptive of the type of cut are often used and types include:

Arc roulette (percé en arc). Cuts are minute, spaced arcs, each roughly a semicircle.

Cross roulette (percé en croix). Cuts are tiny diagonal crosses.

Line roulette (percé en ligne or en ligne droite). Short straight cuts parallel to the frame of the stamp. The commonest basic roulette. Where not further described, 'roulette' means this type.

Rouletted in colour or coloured roulette (percé en lignes colorées or en lignes de coleur). Cuts with coloured edges, arising from notched rule inked simultaneously with the printing plate.

Saw-tooth roulette (percé en scie). Cuts applied zigzag fashion to resemble the teeth of a saw.

Serpentine roulette (percé en serpentin). Cuts as sharply wavy lines.

Zigzag roulette (percé en zigzags). Short straight cuts at angles in alternate directions, producing sharp points on separation. US usage favours 'serrate(d) roulette' for this type.

Pin-roulette (originally *percé en points* and now *perforés trous d'epingle*) is commonly called pin-perforation in English.

4. Gum

All stamps listed are assumed to have gum of some kind; if they were issued without gum this is stated. Original gum (o.g.) means that which was present on the stamp as issued to the public. Deleterious climates and the presence of certain chemicals can cause gum to crack and, with early stamps, even make the paper deteriorate. Unscrupulous fakers are adept in removing it and regumming the stamp to meet the unreasoning demand often made for 'full o.g.' in cases where such a thing is virtually impossible.

The gum normally used on stamps has been gum arabic until the late 1960s when synthetic adhesives were introduced. Harrison and Sons Ltd for instance use *polyvinyl alcohol*, known to philatelists as PVA. This is almost invisible except for a slight yellowish tinge which was incorporated to make it possible to see that the stamps have been gummed. It has advantages in hot countries, as stamps do not curl and sheets are less likely to stick together. Gum arabic and PVA are not distinguished in the lists except that where a stamp exists with both forms this is indicated in footnotes. Our more specialised catalogues provide separate listing of gums for Great Britain.

Self-adhesive stamps are issued on backing paper, from which they are peeled before affixing to mail. Unused examples are priced as for backing paper intact, in which condition they are recommended to be kept. Used examples are best collected on cover or on piece.

5. Watermarks

Stamps are on unwatermarked paper except where the heading to the set says otherwise.

Detection. Watermarks are detected for Catalogue description by one of four methods: (1) holding stamps

Information and Guidelines

to the light; (2) laying stamps face down on a dark background; (3) adding a few drops of petroleum ether 40/60 to the stamp laid face down in a watermark tray; (4) by use of the Stanley Gibbons Detectamark Spectrum, or other equipment, which work by revealing the thinning of the paper at the watermark. (Note that petroleum ether is highly inflammable in use and can damage photogravure stamps.)

Listable types. Stamps occurring on both watermarked and unwatermarked papers are different types and both receive full listing.

Single watermarks (devices occurring once on every stamp) can be modified in size and shape as between different issues; the types are noted but not usually separately listed. Fortuitous absence of watermark from a single stamp or its gross displacement would not be listable.

To overcome registration difficulties the device may be repeated at close intervals *(a multiple watermark)*, single stamps thus showing parts of several devices. Similarly, a *large sheet watermark* (or *all-over watermark*) covering numerous stamps can be used. We give informative notes and illustrations for them. The designs may be such that numbers of stamps in the sheet automatically lack watermark: this is not a listable variety. Multiple and all-over watermarks sometimes undergo modifications, but if the various types are difficult to distinguish from single stamps notes are given but not separate listings.

Papermakers' watermarks are noted where known but not listed separately, since most stamps in the sheet will lack them. Sheet watermarks which are nothing more than officially adopted papermakers' watermarks are, however, given normal listing.

Marginal watermarks, falling outside the pane of stamps, are ignored except where misplacement caused the adjoining row to be affected, in which case they may be footnoted. They usually consist of straight or angled lines and double-lined capital letters, they are particularly prevalent on some Crown CC and Crown CA watermark stamps.

Watermark errors and varieties. Watermark errors are recognised as of major importance. They comprise stamps intended to be on unwatermarked paper but issued watermarked by mistake, or stamps printed on paper with the wrong watermark. Varieties showing letters omitted from the watermark are also included, but broken or deformed bits on the dandy roll are not listed unless they represent repairs.

Watermark positions. The diagram shows how watermark position is described in the Catalogue. Paper has a side intended for printing and watermarks are usually impressed so that they read normally when looked through from that printed side. However, since philatelists customarily detect watermarks by looking at the back of the stamp the watermark diagram also makes clear what is actually seen.

Illustrations in the Catalogue are of watermarks in normal positions (from the front of the stamps) and are actual size where possible.

Differences in watermark position are collectable varieties. This Catalogue now lists inverted, sideways inverted and reversed watermark varieties on Commonwealth stamps from the 1860s onwards except where the watermark position is completely haphazard or, due to the method of printing, appear in equal quantities upright and inverted (e.g. Papua Nos. 47/83) In such cases it should be assumed that the price is the same, either way.

Where a watermark comes indiscriminately in various positions our policy is to cover this by a general note: we do not give separate listings because the watermark position in these circumstances has no particular philatelic importance.

Sideways watermarks. A review of the sideways watermarks listed in this catalogue has shown that, while in Great Britain it is fair to say that the 'normal' sideways watermark shows the top of the device (as shown in its illustration) pointing to the left as seen from the front and to the right as seen from the back of the stamp, the opposite is very often the case on Crown Agents colonial issues.

We have therefore adopted the policy of clearly stating whether the normal sideways watermark points to the left or to the right for all issues up to 1970. Where the normal watermark is upright and the sideways variant constitutes a rare error it has not always been possible to confirm its orientation, so we welcome the assistance of collectors in 'filling in the gaps' in these cases.

We repeat here the watermark diagram which has appeared in these introductory notes for many years, with the caveat that, while valid for Great Britain, individual listings should be consulted for the normal orientation of other sideways watermark issues.

AS DESCRIBED (Read through front of stamp)		AS SEEN DURING WATERMARK DETECTION (Stamp face down and back examined)
GvR	Normal	ᴙvƓ
ᴙʌƓ	Inverted	ЄʌR
ᴙvƓ	Reversed	GvR
ЄʌR	Reversed and Inverted	ᴙʌƓ
GvR (rotated)	Sideways	ᴙvƧ (rotated)
GvR (rotated)	Sideways Inverted	ᴙvƓ (rotated)

Standard types of watermark. Some watermarks have been used generally for various British possessions rather than exclusively for a single colony. To avoid repetition the Catalogue classifies 11 general types, as under, with references in the headings throughout the listings being given either in words or in the form ('W w **9**') (meaning 'watermark type w **9**'). In those cases where watermark illustrations appear in the listings themselves, the respective reference reads, for example, W **153**, thus indicating that the watermark will be found in the normal sequence of illustrations as (type) **153**.

The general types are as follows, with an example of each quoted.

Information and Guidelines

W	Description	Example
w 1	Large Star	St Helena No. 1
w 2	Small Star	Turks Is. No. 4
w 2a	Small Truncated Star	Queensland No. 59
w 3	Broad (pointed) Star	Grenada No. 24
w 4	Crown (over) CC, small stamp	Antigua No. 13
w 5	Crown (over) CC, large stamp	Antigua No. 31
w 6	Crown (over) CA, small stamp	Antigua No. 21
w 7	Crown CA (CA over Crown), large stamp	Sierra Leone No. 54
w 8	Multiple Crown CA	Antigua No. 41
w 9	Multiple Script CA	Seychelles No. 158
w 9a	do. Error	Seychelles No. 158a
w 9b	do. Error	Seychelles No. 158b
w 10	V over Crown	Queensland No. 265
w 11	Crown over A	Queensland No. 282

CC in these watermarks is an abbreviation for 'Crown Colonies' and CA for 'Crown Agents'. Watermarks w **1**, w **2** and w **3** are on stamps printed by Perkins, Bacon; w **4** onwards on stamps from De La Rue and other printers.

w **4**
Crown (over) CC

w **5**
Crown (over) CC

Two *Crown (over) CC* watermarks were used: w **4** was for stamps of ordinary size and w **5** for those of larger size. It is known that the latter was sometimes used for stamps of ordinary size but since the differences are difficult to identify on single stamps we do not list them separately.

w **6**
Crown (over) CA

w **7**
CA over Crown

Two watermarks of *Crown CA* type were used, w **6** being for stamps of ordinary size. The other, w **7**, is properly described as *CA over Crown*. It was specially made for paper on which it was intended to print long fiscal stamps: that some were used postally accounts for the appearance of w **7** in the Catalogue. The watermark occupies twice the space of the ordinary Crown CA watermark, w **6**. Stamps of normal size printed on paper with w **7** watermark show it *sideways*; it takes a horizontal pair of stamps to show the entire watermark (e.g. Labuan Nos. 1/4).

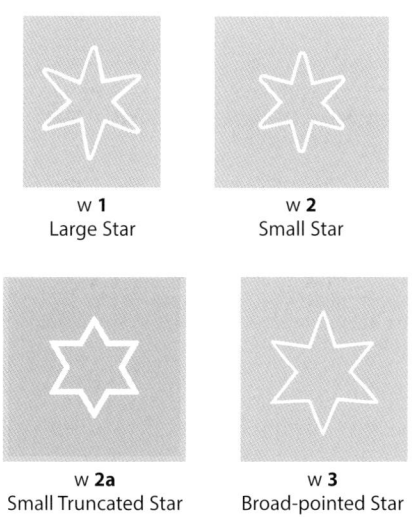

w **1**
Large Star

w **2**
Small Star

w **2a**
Small Truncated Star

w **3**
Broad-pointed Star

Watermark w **1**, *Large Star*, measures 15 to 16 mm across the star from point to point and about 27 mm from centre to centre vertically between stars in the sheet. It was made for long stamps like Ceylon 1857 and St Helena 1856.
Watermark w **2**, *Small Star* is of similar design but measures 12 to 13½mm from point to point and 24 mm from centre to centre vertically. It was for use with ordinary-size stamps such as Grenada 1863–1871.

When the Large Star watermark was used with the smaller stamps it only occasionally comes in the centre of the paper. It is frequently so misplaced as to show portions of two stars above and below and this eccentricity will very often help in determining the watermark.

Watermark w **2a**, *Small Truncated Star*, only used for Queensland stamps of 1868–1874.

Watermark w **3**, *Broad-pointed Star*, resembles w **1** but the points are broader.

w **8**
Multiple Crown CA

w **9**
Multiple Script CA

Multiple watermarks began in 1904 with w **8**, *Multiple Crown CA*, changed from 1921 to w **9**, *Multiple Script CA*. On stamps of ordinary size portions of two or three watermarks appear and on the large-sized stamps a greater number can be observed. The change to letters in script character with w **9** was accompanied by a Crown of distinctly different shape.

xvii

Information and Guidelines

It seems likely that there were at least two dandy rolls for each Crown Agents watermark in use at any one time with a reserve roll being employed when the normal one was withdrawn for maintenance or repair.

Both the Mult Crown CA and the Mult Script CA types exist with one or other of the letters omitted from individual impressions. It is possible that most of these occur from the reserve rolls as they have only been found on certain issues. The MCA watermark experienced such problems during the early 1920s and the Script over a longer period from the early 1940s until 1951.

During the 1920s damage must also have occurred on one of the Crowns on the Multiple Crowns CA paper as a substituted Crown has been found on certain issues. This is smaller than the normal and consists of an oval base joined to two upright ovals with a circle positioned between their upper ends. The upper line of the Crown's base is omitted, as are the left and right-hand circles at the top and also the cross over the centre circle (e.g. Barbados No. 201c).

in Bahamas, Perlis, St. Kitts-Nevis and Singapore and the incorrect crown likewise occurs in (Crown only) and (Crown CA) rows.

w **10**
V over Crown

w **11**
Crown over A

Resuming the general types, two watermarks found in issues of several Australian States are: w **10**, *V over Crown*, and w **11**, *Crown over A*.

Substituted Crown

The *Multiple Script CA* watermark, w **9**, is known with two errors, recurring among the 1950–1952 printings of several territories. In the first a crown has fallen away from the dandy-roll that impresses the watermark into the paper pulp. It gives w **9a**, *Crown missing*, but this omission has been found in both 'Crown only' (*illustrated*) and 'Crown CA' rows. The resulting faulty paper was used for Bahamas, Johore, Seychelles and the postage due stamps of nine colonies

w **12**
Multiple St Edward's
Crown Block CA

w **13**
Multiple PTM

The *Multiple St Edward's Crown Block CA* watermark, w **12**, was introduced in 1957 and besides the change in the Crown (from that used in Multiple Script CA, w **9**) the letters reverted to block capitals. The new watermark began to appear sideways in 1966 and these stamps are generally listed as separate sets.

The watermark w **13**, *Multiple PTM*, was introduced for new Malaysian issues in November 1961.

w **9a**: Error, Crown missing

w **14**
Multiple Crown CA Diagonal

w **9b**: Error, St Edward's Crown

When the omission was noticed a second mishap occurred, which was to insert a wrong crown in the space, giving w **9b**, St Edward's Crown. This produced varieties

By 1974 the two dandy-rolls the 'upright' and the 'sideways' for w **12** were wearing out; the Crown Agents therefore discontinued using the sideways watermark one and retained the other only as a stand-by. A new dandy-roll with the pattern of w **14**, *Multiple Crown CA Diagonal*, was introduced and first saw use with some Churchill Centenary issues.

The new watermark had the design arranged in gradually spiralling rows. It was improved in design to allow smooth passage over the paper (the gaps between letters and rows had caused jolts in previous dandy-rolls) and the sharp corners and angles, where fibres used to accumulate, were eliminated by rounding.

This watermark had no 'normal' sideways position

Information and Guidelines

amongst the different printers using it. To avoid confusion our more specialised listings do not rely on such terms as 'sideways inverted' but describe the direction in which the watermark points.

w **15**
Multiple POST OFFICE

During 1981 w **15**, *Multiple POST OFFICE* was introduced for certain issues prepared by Philatelists Ltd, acting for various countries in the Indian Ocean, Pacific and West Indies.

w **16**
Multiple Crown Script CA Diagonal

A new Crown Agents watermark was introduced during 1985, w **16**, *Multiple Crown Script CA Diagonal*. This was very similar to the previous w **14**, but showed 'CA' in script rather than block letters. It was first used on the omnibus series of stamps commemorating the Life and Times of Queen Elizabeth the Queen Mother.

w **17**
Multiple CARTOR

Watermark w **17**, *Multiple CARTOR*, was used from 1985 for issues printed by this French firm for countries which did not normally use the Crown Agents watermark.

w **18**

In 2008, following the closure of the Crown Agents Stamp Bureau, a new Multiple Crowns watermark, w **18** was introduced

In recent years the use of watermarks has, to some extent, been superseded by fluorescent security markings. These are often more visible from the reverse of the stamp (Cook Islands from 1970 onwards), but have occurred printed over the design (Hong Kong Nos. 415/430). In 1982 the Crown Agents introduced a new stock paper, without watermark, known as 'C-Kurity' on which a fluorescent pattern of blue rosettes is visible on the reverse, beneath the gum. This paper was used for issues from Gambia and Norfolk Island.

6. Colours

Stamps in two or three colours have these named in order of appearance, from the centre moving outwards. Four colours or more are usually listed as multicoloured.

In compound colour names the second is the predominant one, thus:

orange-red = a red tending towards orange;
red-orange = an orange containing more red than usual.

Standard colours used. The 200 colours most used for stamp identification are given in the Stanley Gibbons Stamp Colour Key. The Catalogue has used the Stamp Colour Key as standard for describing new issues for some years. The names are also introduced as lists are rewritten, though exceptions are made for those early issues where traditional names have become universally established.

Determining colours. When comparing actual stamps with colour samples in the Stamp Colour Key, view in a good north daylight (or its best substitute; fluorescent 'colour matching' light). Sunshine is not recommended. Choose a solid portion of the stamp design; if available, marginal markings such as solid bars of colour or colour check dots are helpful. Shading lines in the design can be misleading as they appear lighter than solid colour. Postmarked portions of a stamp appear darker than normal. If more than one colour is present, mask off the extraneous ones as the eye tends to mix them.

Errors of colour. Major colour errors in stamps or overprints which qualify for listing are: wrong colours; one colour inverted in relation to the rest; albinos (colourless impressions), where these have Expert Committee certificates; colours completely omitted, but only on unused stamps (if found on used stamps the information is footnoted) and with good credentials, missing colours being frequently faked.

Colours only partially omitted are not recognised, Colour shifts, however spectacular, are not listed.

Shades. Shades in philately refer to variations in the intensity of a colour or the presence of differing amounts of other colours. They are particularly significant when they can be linked to specific printings. In general, shades need to be quite marked to fall within the scope of this Catalogue; it does not favour nowadays listing the often numerous shades of a stamp, but chooses a single applicable colour name which will indicate particular groups of outstanding shades. Furthermore, the listings refer to colours as issued; they may deteriorate into something different through the

Information and Guidelines

passage of time. Collectors are warned against according any significance to colours which may have been altered by immersion in water or exposure to sunlight, but time, alone will sometimes cause colours to change, notably some of the letterpress De la Rue stamps of the late 19th and early 20th centuries.

Modern colour printing by lithography is prone to marked differences of shade, even within a single run, and variations can occur within the same sheet. Such shades are not listed.

Aniline colours. An aniline colour meant originally one derived from coal-tar; it now refers more widely to colour of a particular brightness suffused on the surface of a stamp and showing through clearly on the back.

Colours of overprints and surcharges. All overprints and surcharges are in black unless stated otherwise in the heading or after the description of the stamp.

7. Specimen Stamps

Originally, stamps overprinted SPECIMEN were circulated to postmasters or kept in official records, but after the establishment of the Universal Postal Union supplies were sent to Berne for distribution to the postal administrations of member countries.

During the period 1884 to 1928 most of the stamps of British Crown Colonies required for this purpose were overprinted SPECIMEN in various shapes and sizes by their printers from typeset formes. Some locally produced provisionals were handstamped locally, as were sets prepared for presentation. From 1928 stamps were punched with holes forming the word SPECIMEN, each firm of printers using a different machine or machines. From 1948 the stamps supplied for UPU distribution were no longer punctured, although receiving authorities sometimes applied SPECIMEN markings of their own.

Stamps of some other Commonwealth territories were overprinted or handstamped locally, while stamps of Great Britain and those overprinted for use in overseas postal agencies (mostly of the higher denominations) bore SPECIMEN overprints and handstamps applied by the Inland Revenue or the Post Office.

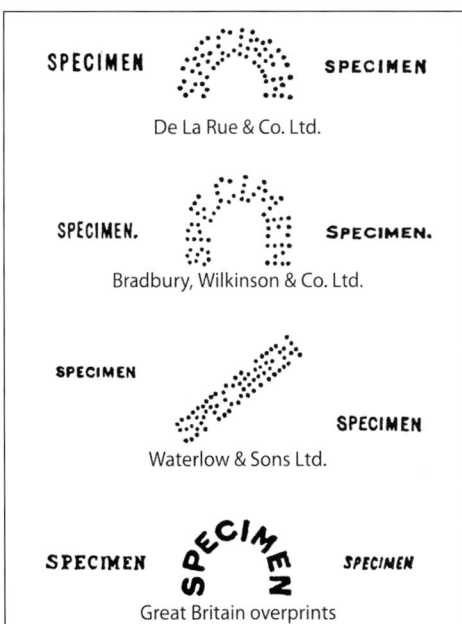

Some of the more common types of overprints or punctures are illustrated here. Collectors are warned that dangerous forgeries of the punctured types exist.

The *Stanley Gibbons Commonwealth Catalogues* record those Specimen overprints or perforations intended for distribution by the UPU to member countries and we are grateful to James Bendon, author and publisher of *UPU Specimen Stamps, 1878 - 1961*, a much expanded edition of which was published in 2015, for his assistance with these listings. The Specimen overprints of Australia and its dependent territories, which were sold to collectors by the Post Office, are also included.

All other Specimens are outside the scope of this volume.

In specifying type of specimen for individual high-value stamps, 'H/S' means handstamped, 'Optd' is overprinted and 'Perf' is punctured. Some sets occur mixed, e.g. 'Optd/Perf'. If unspecified, the type is apparent from the date or it is the same as for the lower values quoted as a set.

Prices. Prices for stamps up to £1 are quoted in sets; higher values are priced singly. Where specimens exist in more than one type the price quoted is for the cheapest. Specimen stamps have rarely survived even as pairs; these and strips of three, four or five are worth considerably more than singles.

Various Perkins Bacon issues exist obliterated with a 'CANCELLED' within an oval of bars handstamp.

Perkins Bacon 'CANCELLED' Handstamp

This was applied to six examples of those issues available in 1861 which were then given to members of Sir Rowland Hill's family. 75 different stamps (including four from Chile) are recorded with this handstamp although others may possibly exist. The unauthorised gift of these 'CANCELLED' stamps to the Hill family was a major factor in the loss of the Agent General for the Crown Colonies (the forerunner of the Crown Agents) contracts by Perkins Bacon in the following year. Where examples of these scarce items are known to be in private hands the catalogue provides a price.

For full details of these stamps see *CANCELLED by Perkins Bacon* by Peter Jaffé (published by Spink in 1998).

8. Luminescence

Machines which sort mail electronically have been introduced in recent years. In consequence some countries have issued stamps on fluorescent or phosphorescent papers, while others have marked their stamps with phosphor bands.

The various papers can only be distinguished by ultraviolet lamps emitting particular wavelengths. They are separately listed only when the stamps have some other means of distinguishing them, visible without the use of these lamps. Where this is not so, the papers are recorded in footnotes or headings.

For this catalogue we do not consider it appropriate that collectors be compelled to have the use of an ultraviolet lamp before being able to identify stamps by our listings. Some experience will also be found necessary in interpreting the results given by ultraviolet. Collectors using the lamps, nevertheless, should exercise great care in their use as exposure to their light is potentially dangerous to the eyes.

Phosphor bands are listable, since they are visible to the naked eye (by holding stamps at an angle to the light and looking along them, the bands appear dark). Stamps

Information and Guidelines

existing with or without phosphor bands or with differing numbers of bands are given separate listings. Varieties such as double bands, bands omitted, misplaced or printed on the back are not listed.

Detailed descriptions appear at appropriate places in the listings in explanation of luminescent papers; see, for example, Australia above No. 363, Canada above Nos. 472 and 611, Cook Is. above 249, etc.

For Great Britain, where since 1959 phosphors have played a prominent and intricate part in stamp issues, the main notes above Nos. 599 and 723 should be studied, as well as the footnotes to individual listings where appropriate. In general the classification is as follows.

Stamps with phosphor bands are those where a separate cylinder applies the phosphor after the stamps are printed. Issues with 'all-over' phosphor have the 'band' covering the entire stamp. Parts of the stamp covered by phosphor bands, or the entire surface for 'all-over' phosphor versions, appear matt. Stamps on phosphorised paper have the phosphor added to the paper coating before the stamps are printed. Issues on this paper have a completely shiny surface.

Further particularisation of phosphor – their methods of printing and the colours they exhibit under ultraviolet – is outside the scope. The more specialised listings should be consulted for this information.

9. Coil Stamps

Stamps issued only in coil form are given full listing. If stamps are issued in both sheets and coils the coil stamps are listed separately only where there is some feature (e.g. perforation or watermark sideways) by which singles can be distinguished. Coil stamps containing different stamps *se-tenant* are also listed.

Coil join pairs are too random and too easily faked to permit of listing; similarly ignored are coil stamps which have accidentally suffered an extra row of perforations from the claw mechanism in a malfunctioning vending machine.

10. Stamp Booklets

Stamp booklets are fully listed in this catalogue.

Single stamps from booklets are listed if they are distinguishable in some way (such as watermark or perforation) from similar sheet stamps.

Booklet panes are listed where they contain stamps of different denominations *se-tenant*, where stamp-size labels are included, or where such panes are otherwise identifiable. Booklet panes are placed in the listing under the lowest denomination present and are only priced in unused condition.

Particular perforations (straight edges) are covered by appropriate notes.

Prior to the 1970s, the majority of stamp booklets were made up from normal sheets and panes may be bound upright or inverted and booklets may be stapled or stitched at either the left or right-hand side. Unless specifically mentioned in the listings, such variations do not command a price premium.

Only items supplied pre-folded are listed as booklets. Panes supplied flat are not listed thus, even if it is clearly intended that they should be subsequently folded in order to create a 'booklet'. Such panes are included in the main listing only.

11. Miniature Sheets and Sheetlets

We distinguish between 'miniature sheets' and 'sheetlets' and this affects the catalogue numbering. An item in sheet form that is postally valid, containing a single stamp, pair, block or set of stamps, with wide, inscribed and/or decorative margins, is a miniature sheet if it is sold at post offices as an indivisable entity. As such the Catalogue allots a single **MS** number and describes what stamps make it up. The sheetlet or small sheet differs in that the individual stamps are intended to be purchased separately for postal purposes. For sheetlets, all the component postage stamps are numbered individually and the composition explained in a footnote. Note that the definitions refer to post office sale—not how items may be subsequently offered by stamp dealers.

12. Forgeries and Fakes

Forgeries. Where space permits, notes are considered if they can give a concise description that will permit unequivocal detection of a forgery. Generalised warnings, lacking detail, are not nowadays inserted, since their value to the collector is problematic.

Forged cancellations have also been applied to genuine stamps. This catalogue includes notes regarding those manufactured by 'Madame Joseph', together with the cancellation dates known to exist. It should be remembered that these dates also exist as genuine cancellations.

For full details of these see *Madame Joseph Forged Postmarks* by Derek Worboys (published by the Royal Philatelic Society London and the British Philatelic Trust in 1994) or *Madame Joseph Revisited* by Brian Cartwright (published by the Royal Philatelic Society London in 2005).

Fakes. Unwitting fakes are numerous, particularly 'new shades' which are colour changelings brought about by exposure to sunlight, soaking in water contaminated with dyes from adherent paper, contact with oil and dirt from a pocketbook, and so on. Fraudulent operators, in addition, can offer to arrange: removal of hinge marks; repairs of thins on white or coloured papers; replacement of missing margins or perforations; reperforating in true or false gauges; removal of fiscal cancellations; rejoining of severed pairs, strips and blocks; and (a major hazard) regumming. Collectors can only be urged to purchase from reputable sources and to insist upon Expert Committee certification where there is any kind of doubt.

The Catalogue can consider footnotes about fakes where these are specific enough to assist in detection.

ACKNOWLEDGEMENTS

We are grateful to individual collectors, members of the philatelic trade and specialist societies and study circles for their assistance in improving and extending the Stanley Gibbons range of catalogues.

The address of the societies relevant to this volume is:

Canadian Philatelic Society of Great Britain
Secretary — Mr. J Watson
106 Huddersfield Road, Penistone,
South Yorkshire S36 7BX
Email: john.watson1949@btinternet.com

British North America Philatelic Society
Secretary — Mr. C Livermore
288 Cook Road, East Aurora,
NY 14052, USA
Email: secretary@bnaps.org

Abbreviations

Printers

A.B.N. Co.	American Bank Note Co, New York.
B.A.B.N.	British American Bank Note Co. Ottawa
B.D.T.	B.D.T. International Security Printing Ltd, Dublin, Ireland
B.W.	Bradbury Wilkinson & Co, Ltd.
Cartor	Cartor S.A., La Loupe, France
C.B.N.	Canadian Bank Note Co, Ottawa.
Continental	Continental Bank Note Co. B.N. Co.
Courvoisier	Imprimerie Courvoisier S.A., La-Chaux-de-Fonds, Switzerland.
D.L.R.	De La Rue & Co, Ltd, London.
Enschedé	Joh. Enschedé en Zonen, Haarlem, Netherlands.
Format	Format International Security Printers Ltd., London
Harrison	Harrison & Sons, Ltd. London
J.W.	John Waddington Security Print Ltd., Leeds
L.M.G.	Lowe Martin Group, Ottawa, Canada
P.B.	Perkins Bacon Ltd, London.
Questa	Questa Colour Security Printers Ltd, London
Walsall	Walsall Security Printers Ltd
Waterlow	Waterlow & Sons, Ltd, London.

General Abbreviations

Alph	Alphabet
Anniv	Anniversary
Comp	Compound (perforation)
Des	Designer; designed
Diag	Diagonal; diagonally
Eng	Engraver; engraved
F.C.	Fiscal Cancellation
H/S	Handstamped
Horiz	Horizontal; horizontally
Imp, Imperf	Imperforate
Inscr	Inscribed
L	Left
Litho	Lithographed
mm	Millimetres
MS	Miniature sheet
N.Y.	New York
Opt(d)	Overprint(ed)
P or P-c	Pen-cancelled
P, Pf or Perf	Perforated
Photo	Photogravure
Pl	Plate
Pr	Pair
Ptd	Printed
Ptg	Printing
R	Right
R.	Row
Recess	Recess-printed
Roto	Rotogravure
Roul	Rouletted
S	Specimen (overprint)
Surch	Surcharge(d)
T.C.	Telegraph Cancellation
T	Type
Typo	Typographed
Un	Unused
Us	Used
Vert	Vertical; vertically
W or wmk	Watermark
Wmk s	Watermark sideways

(†) = Does not exist
(–) (or blank price column) = Exists, or may exist, but no market price is known.
/ between colours means 'on' and the colour following is that of the paper on which the stamp is printed.

Colours of Stamps

Bl (blue); blk (black); brn (brown); car, carm (carmine); choc (chocolate); clar (claret); emer (emerald); grn (green); ind (indigo); mag (magenta); mar (maroon); mult (multicoloured); mve (mauve); ol (olive); orge (orange); pk (pink); pur (purple); scar (scarlet); sep (sepia); turq (turquoise); ultram (ultramarine); verm (vermilion); vio (violet); yell (yellow).

Colour of Overprints and Surcharges

(B.) = blue, (Blk.) = black, (Br.) = brown, (C.) = carmine, (G.) = green, (Mag.) = magenta, (Mve.) = mauve, (Ol.) = olive, (O.) = orange, (P.) = purple, (Pk.) = pink, (R.) = red, (Sil.) = silver, (V.) = violet, (Vm.) or (Verm.) = vermilion, (W.) = white, (Y.) = yellow.

Arabic Numerals

As in the case of European figures, the details of the Arabic numerals vary in different stamp designs, but they should be readily recognised with the aid of this illustration.

0 1 2 3 4 5 6 7 8 9

International Philatelic Glossary

English	French	German	Spanish	Italian
Agate	Agate	Achat	Agata	Agata
Air stamp	Timbre de la poste aérienne	Flugpostmarke	Sello de correo aéreo	Francobollo per posta aerea
Apple Green	Vert-pomme	Apfelgrün	Verde manzana	Verde mela
Barred	Annulé par barres	Balkenentwertung	Anulado con barras	Sbarrato
Bisected	Timbre coupé	Halbiert	Partido en dos	Frazionato
Bistre	Bistre	Bister	Bistre	Bistro
Bistre-brown	Brun-bistre	Bisterbraun	Castaño bistre	Bruno-bistro
Black	Noir	Schwarz	Negro	Nero
Blackish Brown	Brun-noir	Schwärzlichbraun	Castaño negruzco	Bruno nerastro
Blackish Green	Vert foncé	Schwärzlichgrün	Verde negruzco	Verde nerastro
Blackish Olive	Olive foncé	Schwärzlicholiv	Oliva negruzco	Oliva nerastro
Block of four	Bloc de quatre	Viererblock	Bloque de cuatro	Bloco di quattro
Blue	Bleu	Blau	Azul	Azzurro
Blue-green	Vert-bleu	Blaugrün	Verde azul	Verde azzuro
Bluish Violet	Violet bleuâtre	Bläulichviolett	Violeta azulado	Violtto azzurrastro
Booklet	Carnet	Heft	Cuadernillo	Libretto
Bright Blue	Bleu vif	Lebhaftblau	Azul vivo	Azzurro vivo
Bright Green	Vert vif	Lebhaftgrün	Verde vivo	Verde vivo
Bright Purple	Mauve vif	Lebhaftpurpur	Púrpura vivo	Porpora vivo
Bronze Green	Vert-bronze	Bronzegrün	Verde bronce	Verde bronzo
Brown	Brun	Braun	Castaño	Bruno
Brown-lake	Carmin-brun	Braunlack	Laca castaño	Lacca bruno
Brown-purple	Pourpre-brun	Braunpurpur	Púrpura castaño	Porpora bruno
Brown-red	Rouge-brun	Braunrot	Rojo castaño	Rosso bruno
Buff	Chamois	Sämisch	Anteado	Camoscio
Cancellation	Oblitération	Entwertung	Cancelación	Annullamento
Cancelled	Annulé	Gestempelt	Cancelado	Annullato
Carmine	Carmin	Karmin	Carmín	Carminio
Carmine-red	Rouge-carmin	Karminrot	Rojo carmín	Rosso carminio
Centred	Centré	Zentriert	Centrado	Centrato
Cerise	Rouge-cerise	Kirschrot	Color de ceresa	Color Ciliegia
Chalk-surfaced paper	Papier couché	Kreidepapier	Papel estucado	Carta gessata
Chalky Blue	Bleu terne	Kreideblau	Azul turbio	Azzurro smorto
Charity stamp	Timbre de bienfaisance	Wohltätigkeitsmarke	Sello de beneficenza	Francobollo di beneficenza
Chestnut	Marron	Kastanienbraun	Castaño rojo	Marrone
Chocolate	Chocolat	Schokolade	Chocolate	Cioccolato
Cinnamon	Cannelle	Zimtbraun	Canela	Cannella
Claret	Grenat	Weinrot	Rojo vinoso	Vinaccia
Cobalt	Cobalt	Kobalt	Cobalto	Cobalto
Colour	Couleur	Farbe	Color	Colore
Comb-perforation	Dentelure en peigne	Kammzähnung, Reihenzähnung	Dentado de peine	Dentellatura e pettine
Commemorative stamp	Timbre commémoratif	Gedenkmarke	Sello conmemorativo	Francobollo commemorativo
Crimson	Cramoisi	Karmesin	Carmesí	Cremisi
Deep Blue	Blue foncé	Dunkelblau	Azul oscuro	Azzurro scuro
Deep bluish Green	Vert-bleu foncé	Dunkelbläulichgrün	Verde azulado oscuro	Verde azzurro scuro
Design	Dessin	Markenbild	Diseño	Disegno

International Philatelic Glossary

English	French	German	Spanish	Italian
Die	Matrice	Urstempel. Type, Platte	Cuño	Conio, Matrice
Double	Double	Doppelt	Doble	Doppio
Drab	Olive terne	Trüboliv	Oliva turbio	Oliva smorto
Dull Green	Vert terne	Trübgrün	Verde turbio	Verde smorto
Dull purple	Mauve terne	Trübpurpur	Púrpura turbio	Porpora smorto
Embossing	Impression en relief	Prägedruck	Impresión en relieve	Impressione a relievo
Emerald	Vert-eméraude	Smaragdgrün	Esmeralda	Smeraldo
Engraved	Gravé	Graviert	Grabado	Inciso
Error	Erreur	Fehler, Fehldruck	Error	Errore
Essay	Essai	Probedruck	Ensayo	Saggio
Express letter stamp	Timbre pour lettres par exprès	Eilmarke	Sello de urgencia	Francobollo per espresso
Fiscal stamp	Timbre fiscal	Stempelmarke	Sello fiscal	Francobollo fiscale
Flesh	Chair	Fleischfarben	Carne	Carnicino
Forgery	Faux, Falsification	Fälschung	Falsificación	Falso, Falsificazione
Frame	Cadre	Rahmen	Marco	Cornice
Granite paper	Papier avec fragments de fils de soie	Faserpapier	Papel con filamentos	Carto con fili di seta
Green	Vert	Grün	Verde	Verde
Greenish Blue	Bleu verdâtre	Grünlichblau	Azul verdoso	Azzurro verdastro
Greenish Yellow	Jaune-vert	Grünlichgelb	Amarillo verdoso	Giallo verdastro
Grey	Gris	Grau	Gris	Grigio
Grey-blue	Bleu-gris	Graublau	Azul gris	Azzurro grigio
Grey-green	Vert gris	Graugrün	Verde gris	Verde grigio
Gum	Gomme	Gummi	Goma	Gomma
Gutter	Interpanneau	Zwischensteg	Espacio blanco entre dos grupos	Ponte
Imperforate	Non-dentelé	Geschnitten	Sin dentar	Non dentellato
Indigo	Indigo	Indigo	Azul indigo	Indaco
Inscription	Inscription	Inschrift	Inscripción	Dicitura
Inverted	Renversé	Kopfstehend	Invertido	Capovolto
Issue	Émission	Ausgabe	Emisión	Emissione
Laid	Vergé	Gestreift	Listado	Vergato
Lake	Lie de vin	Lackfarbe	Laca	Lacca
Lake-brown	Brun-carmin	Lackbraun	Castaño laca	Bruno lacca
Lavender	Bleu-lavande	Lavendel	Color de alhucema	Lavanda
Lemon	Jaune-citron	Zitrongelb	Limón	Limone
Light Blue	Bleu clair	Hellblau	Azul claro	Azzurro chiaro
Lilac	Lilas	Lila	Lila	Lilla
Line perforation	Dentelure en lignes	Linienzähnung	Dentado en linea	Dentellatura lineare
Lithography	Lithographie	Steindruck	Litografía	Litografia
Local	Timbre de poste locale	Lokalpostmarke	Emisión local	Emissione locale
Lozenge roulette	Percé en losanges	Rautenförmiger Durchstich	Picadura en rombos	Perforazione a losanghe
Magenta	Magenta	Magentarot	Magenta	Magenta
Margin	Marge	Rand	Borde	Margine
Maroon	Marron pourpré	Dunkelrotpurpur	Púrpura rojo oscuro	Marrone rossastro
Mauve	Mauve	Malvenfarbe	Malva	Malva
Multicoloured	Polychrome	Mehrfarbig	Multicolores	Policromo
Myrtle Green	Vert myrte	Myrtengrün	Verde mirto	Verde mirto
New Blue	Bleu ciel vif	Neublau	Azul nuevo	Azzurro nuovo
Newspaper stamp	Timbre pour journaux	Zeitungsmarke	Sello para periódicos	Francobollo per giornali
Obliteration	Oblitération	Abstempelung	Matasello	Annullamento
Obsolete	Hors (de) cours	Ausser Kurs	Fuera de curso	Fuori corso
Ochre	Ocre	Ocker	Ocre	Ocra

International Philatelic Glossary

English	French	German	Spanish	Italian
Official stamp	Timbre de service	Dienstmarke	Sello de servicio	Francobollo di
Olive-brown	Brun-olive	Olivbraun	Castaño oliva	Bruno oliva
Olive-green	Vert-olive	Olivgrün	Verde oliva	Verde oliva
Olive-grey	Gris-olive	Olivgrau	Gris oliva	Grigio oliva
Olive-yellow	Jaune-olive	Olivgelb	Amarillo oliva	Giallo oliva
Orange	Orange	Orange	Naranja	Arancio
Orange-brown	Brun-orange	Orangebraun	Castaño naranja	Bruno arancio
Orange-red	Rouge-orange	Orangerot	Rojo naranja	Rosso arancio
Orange-yellow	Jaune-orange	Orangegelb	Amarillo naranja	Giallo arancio
Overprint	Surcharge	Aufdruck	Sobrecarga	Soprastampa
Pair	Paire	Paar	Pareja	Coppia
Pale	Pâle	Blass	Pálido	Pallido
Pane	Panneau	Gruppe	Grupo	Gruppo
Paper	Papier	Papier	Papel	Carta
Parcel post stamp	Timbre pour colis postaux	Paketmarke	Sello para paquete postal	Francobollo per pacchi postali
Pen-cancelled	Oblitéré à plume	Federzugentwertung	Cancelado a pluma	Annullato a penna
Percé en arc	Percé en arc	Bogenförmiger Durchstich	Picadura en forma de arco	Perforazione ad arco
Percé en scie	Percé en scie	Bogenförmiger Durchstich	Picado en sierra	Foratura a sega
Perforated	Dentelé	Gezähnt	Dentado	Dentellato
Perforation	Dentelure	Zähnung	Dentar	Dentellatura
Photogravure	Photogravure, Heliogravure	Rastertiefdruck	Fotograbado	Rotocalco
Pin perforation	Percé en points	In Punkten durchstochen	Horadado con alfileres	Perforato a punti
Plate	Planche	Platte	Plancha	Lastra, Tavola
Plum	Prune	Pflaumenfarbe	Color de ciruela	Prugna
Postage Due stamp	Timbre-taxe	Portomarke	Sello de tasa	Segnatasse
Postage stamp	Timbre-poste	Briefmarke, Freimarke, Postmarke	Sello de correos	Francobollo postale
Postal fiscal stamp	Timbre fiscal-postal	Stempelmarke als Postmarke verwendet	Sello fiscal-postal	Fiscale postale
Postmark	Oblitération postale	Poststempel	Matasello	Bollo
Printing	Impression, Tirage	Druck	Impresión	Stampa, Tiratura
Proof	Épreuve	Druckprobe	Prueba de impresión	Prova
Provisionals	Timbres provisoires	Provisorische Marken. Provisorien	Provisionales	Provvisori
Prussian Blue	Bleu de Prusse	Preussischblau	Azul de Prusia	Azzurro di Prussia
Purple	Pourpre	Purpur	Púrpura	Porpora
Purple-brown	Brun-pourpre	Purpurbraun	Castaño púrpura	Bruno porpora
Recess-printing	Impression en taille-douce	Tiefdruck	Grabado	Incisione
Red	Rouge	Rot	Rojo	Rosso
Red-brown	Brun-rouge	Rotbraun	Castaño rojizo	Bruno rosso
Reddish Lilac	Lilas rougeâtre	Rötlichlila	Lila rojizo	Lilla rossastro
Reddish Purple	Poupre-rouge	Rötlichpurpur	Púrpura rojizo	Porpora rossastro
Reddish Violet	Violet rougeâtre	Rötlichviolett	Violeta rojizo	Violetto rossastro
Red-orange	Orange rougeâtre	Rotorange	Naranja rojizo	Arancio rosso
Registration stamp	Timbre pour lettre chargée (recommandée)	Einschreibemarke	Sello de certificado lettere	Francobollo per raccomandate
Reprint	Réimpression	Neudruck	Reimpresión	Ristampa
Reversed	Retourné	Umgekehrt	Invertido	Rovesciato
Rose	Rose	Rosa	Rosa	Rosa
Rose-red	Rouge rosé	Rosarot	Rojo rosado	Rosso rosa
Rosine	Rose vif	Lebhaftrosa	Rosa vivo	Rosa vivo
Roulette	Percage	Durchstich	Picadura	Foratura
Rouletted	Percé	Durchstochen	Picado	Forato
Royal Blue	Bleu-roi	Königblau	Azul real	Azzurro reale
Sage green	Vert-sauge	Salbeigrün	Verde salvia	Verde salvia
Salmon	Saumon	Lachs	Salmón	Salmone

International Philatelic Glossary

English	French	German	Spanish	Italian
Scarlet	Écarlate	Scharlach	Escarlata	Scarlatto
Sepia	Sépia	Sepia	Sepia	Seppia
Serpentine roulette	Percé en serpentin	Schlangenliniger Durchstich	Picado a serpentina	Perforazione a serpentina
Shade	Nuance	Tönung	Tono	Gradazione de colore
Sheet	Feuille	Bogen	Hoja	Foglio
Slate	Ardoise	Schiefer	Pizarra	Ardesia
Slate-blue	Bleu-ardoise	Schieferblau	Azul pizarra	Azzurro ardesia
Slate-green	Vert-ardoise	Schiefergrün	Verde pizarra	Verde ardesia
Slate-lilac	Lilas-gris	Schierferlila	Lila pizarra	Lilla ardesia
Slate-purple	Mauve-gris	Schieferpurpur	Púrpura pizarra	Porpora ardesia
Slate-violet	Violet-gris	Schieferviolett	Violeta pizarra	Violetto ardesia
Special delivery stamp	Timbre pour exprès	Eilmarke	Sello de urgencia	Francobollo per espressi
Specimen	Spécimen	Muster	Muestra	Saggio
Steel Blue	Bleu acier	Stahlblau	Azul acero	Azzurro acciaio
Strip	Bande	Streifen	Tira	Striscia
Surcharge	Surcharge	Aufdruck	Sobrecarga	Soprastampa
Tête-bêche	Tête-bêche	Kehrdruck	Tête-bêche	Tête-bêche
Tinted paper	Papier teinté	Getöntes Papier	Papel coloreado	Carta tinta
Too-late stamp	Timbre pour lettres en retard	Verspätungsmarke	Sello para cartas retardadas	Francobollo per le lettere in ritardo
Turquoise-blue	Bleu-turquoise	Türkisblau	Azul turquesa	Azzurro turchese
Turquoise-green	Vert-turquoise	Türkisgrün	Verde turquesa	Verde turchese
Typography	Typographie	Buchdruck	Tipografia	Tipografia
Ultramarine	Outremer	Ultramarin	Ultramar	Oltremare
Unused	Neuf	Ungebraucht	Nuevo	Nuovo
Used	Oblitéré, Usé	Gebraucht	Usado	Usato
Venetian Red	Rouge-brun terne	Venezianischrot	Rojo veneciano	Rosso veneziano
Vermilion	Vermillon	Zinnober	Cinabrio	Vermiglione
Violet	Violet	Violett	Violeta	Violetto
Violet-blue	Bleu-violet	Violettblau	Azul violeta	Azzurro violetto
Watermark	Filigrane	Wasserzeichen	Filigrana	Filigrana
Watermark sideways	Filigrane couché	Wasserzeichen liegend	Filigrana acostado	Filigrana coricata
Wove paper	Papier ordinaire, Papier uni	Einfaches Papier	Papel avitelado	Carta unita
Yellow	Jaune	Gelb	Amarillo	Giallo
Yellow-brown	Brun-jaune	Gelbbraun	Castaño amarillo	Bruno giallo
Yellow-green	Vert-jaune	Gelbgrün	Verde amarillo	Verde giallo
Yellow-olive	Olive-jaunâtre	Gelboliv	Oliva amarillo	Oliva giallastro
Yellow-orange	Orange jaunâtre	Gelborange	Naranja amarillo	Arancio giallastro
Zig-zag roulette	Percé en zigzag	Sägezahnartiger Durchstich	Picado en zigzag	Perforazione a zigzag

GIBBONS Stamp MONTHLY

Dedicated to collector's interests.
Written by leading experts.

Subscribe at
gibbonsstampmonthly.com

Guide to Entries

A **Country of Issue** – When a country changes its name, the catalogue listing changes to reflect the name change, for example Namibia was formerly known as South West Africa, the stamps in the Stanley Gibbons *Southern Africa Catalogue* are all listed under Namibia, but split into South West Africa and then Namibia.

B **Country Information** – Brief geographical and historical details for the issuing country.

C **Currency** – Details of the currency, and dates of earliest use where applicable, on the face value of the stamps.

D **Illustration** – Generally, the first stamp in the set. Stamp illustrations are reduced to 75%, with overprints and surcharges shown actual size.

E **Illustration or Type Number** – These numbers are used to help identify stamps, either in the listing, type column, design line or footnote, usually the first value in a set. These type numbers are in a bold type face – **123**; when bracketed (**123**) an overprint or a surcharge is indicated. Some type numbers include a lower-case letter – **123a**, this indicates they have been added to an existing set.

F **Date of issue** – This is the date that the stamp/set of stamps was issued by the post office and was available for purchase. When a set of definitive stamps has been issued over several years the Year Date given is for the earliest issue. Commemorative sets are listed in chronological order. Stamps of the same design, or issue are usually grouped together, for example some of the New Zealand landscapes definitive series were first issued in 2003 but the set includes stamps issued to May 2007.

G **Number Prefix** – Stamps other than definitives and commemoratives have a prefix letter before the catalogue number. Their use is explained in the text: some examples are A for airmail, D for postage due and O for official stamps.

H **Footnote** – Further information on background or key facts on issues.

I **Stanley Gibbons Catalogue number** – This is a unique number for each stamp to help the collector identify stamps in the listing. The Stanley Gibbons numbering system is universally recognised as definitive.
Where insufficient numbers have been left to provide for additional stamps to a listing, some stamps will have a suffix letter after the catalogue number (for example 214a). If numbers have been left for additions to a set and not used they will be left vacant.
The separate type numbers (in bold) refer to illustrations (see **E**).

J **Colour** – If a stamp is printed in three or fewer colours then the colours are listed, working from the centre of the stamp outwards (see **R**).

K **Design line** – Further details on design variations

L **Key Type** – Indicates a design type on which the stamp is based. These are the bold figures found below each illustration, for example listed in Cameroon, in the *West Africa Catalogue*, is the Key type A and B showing the ex-Kaiser's yacht *Hohenzollern*. The type numbers are also given in bold in the second column of figures alongside the stamp description to indicate the design of each stamp. Where an issue comprises stamps of similar design, the corresponding type number should be taken as indicating the general design. Where there are blanks in the type number column it means that the type of the corresponding stamp is that shown by the number in the type column of the same issue. A dash (–) in the type column means that the stamp is not illustrated. Where type numbers refer to stamps of another country, e.g. where stamps of one country are overprinted for use in another, this is always made clear in the text.

M **Coloured Papers** – Stamps printed on coloured paper are shown – e.g. 'brown/*yellow*' indicates brown printed on yellow paper.

N **Surcharges and Overprints** – Usually described in the headings. Any actual wordings are shown in bold type. Descriptions clarify words and figures used in the overprint. Stamps with the same overprints in different colours are not listed separately. Numbers in brackets after the descriptions are the catalogue numbers of the non-overprinted stamps. The words 'inscribed' or 'inscription' (generally abbreviated as 'inscr') refer to the wording incorporated in the design of a stamp and not surcharges or overprints.

O **Face value** – This refers to the value of each stamp and is the price it was sold for at the Post Office when issued. Some modern stamps do not have their values in figures but instead it is shown as a letter, for example Great Britain use 1st or 2nd on their stamps as opposed to the actual value.

P **Catalogue Value** – Mint/Unused. Prices quoted for Queen Victoria to King George V stamps are for lightly hinged examples.

Q **Catalogue Value** – Used. Prices generally refer to fine postally used examples. For certain issues they are for cancelled-to-order.

Prices
Prices are given in pence and pounds. Stamps worth £100 and over are shown in whole pounds:

Shown in Catalogue as	Explanation
10	10 pence
1·75	£1·75
15.00	£15
£150	£150
£2300	£2300

Prices assume stamps are in 'fine condition'; we may ask more for superb and less for those of lower quality. The minimum catalogue price quoted is 10p and is intended as a guide for catalogue users. The lowest price for individual stamps purchased from Stanley Gibbons is £1.
Prices quoted are for the cheapest variety of that particular stamp. Differences of watermark, perforation, or other details, often increase the value. Prices quoted for mint issues are for single examples, unless otherwise stated. Those in *se-tenant* pairs, strips, blocks or sheets may be worth more. Where no prices are listed it is either because the stamps are not known to exist (usually shown by a †) in that particular condition, or, more usually, because there is no reliable information on which to base their value.
All prices are subject to change without prior notice and we cannot guarantee to supply all stamps as priced. Prices quoted in advertisements are also subject to change without prior notice.

R **Multicoloured** – Nearly all modern stamps are multicoloured (more than three colours); this is indicated in the heading, with a description of the stamp given in the listing.

S **Perforations** – Please see the 'Information and Guidelines' section for a detailed explanation of perforations.

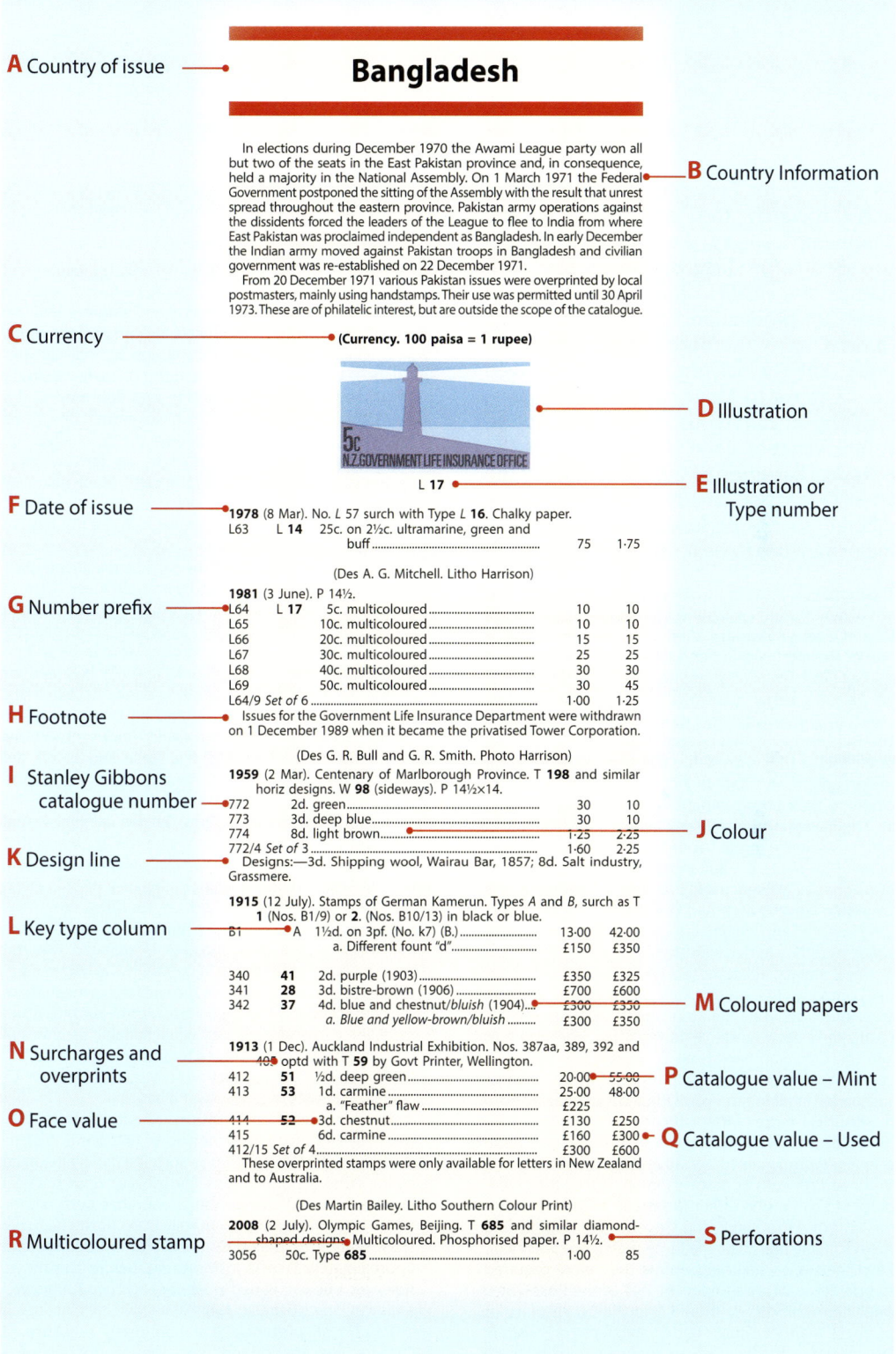

The Small Queens of Canada 1879–97
By John Hillson FRPSL FCPS

As demand for Canadian postage stamps grew towards the latter half of the nineteenth century, the current issue, the so-called 'Large Queens', was replaced with stamps of a smaller dimension in order to speed up production. The resulting 'Small Queens' were produced for more than 25 years, during which time production moved from Ottawa to Montreal and back again, resulting in numerous subtle, and not so subtle, varieties. John Hillson provides the historical backdrop to the production of the Small Queens of Canada and highlights the different shades, perforations, re-entries and major varieties to be found.

The formation of the British American Bank Note Co. was not accomplished easily. In my previous article on the Large Queens (*GSM* May 2014), it was mentioned that one of the interests, Burland L'Africaine was prepared to play dirty. For example: when Matthew Smillie and his partners began their rival printing business they called it 'The British American Bank Note Company'. The Burland group, having political influence (among other things they owned the *Montreal Gazette*), went to Parliament and had an Act passed in their favour whereby their new company was to be incorporated as 'The British American Bank Note Co. Ltd.' Similarly, when the Smillie group submitted their proposals and schedule of prices, the Burland group got hold of a copy through their influence and matched it. Eventually, the Canadian Government had the wisdom to recognise the strengths and weaknesses of both contenders and suggested they joined together.

Nevertheless, relations between Matthew Smillie, the Company's first president, and George Bull Burland, appointed general manager, could not have been particularly easy. Some years later, Mr Smillie left to join the Canadian Bank Note Engraving & Printing Co Ltd as Vice-President, a company that in 1891 almost succeeded in taking the Post Office contract away from the BABNC—more of that later.

In 1867 the new company was in business and made a series of proposals to the Government, the only one that need concern us at the moment is that they were prepared to print in either Montreal or Ottawa, but if the latter was required, the Government should find them suitable premises. The firm's preference was clear; nevertheless, as security printers they were required to operate in Ottawa under the eye of the Post Office Department and they should find their own place of business. Matthew Smillie had been offered premises in Ottawa before the two factions amalgamated and there they opened for business; the first postage stamps, the Large Queen series, being issued on 1 April 1868.

DOWNSIZING TO MEET DEMAND
It soon became clear that with a rapidly expanding postal service, a way would have to be found to speed up production of stamps and by mid-summer 1869, an advertising sheet was produced, comprising of five ½c. Large Queens, which are the same size as Small Queens, balanced by five 1c. Small Queens (*Fig 1*). The first delivery of 300,000 of this denomination was delivered to the Post Office Department (POD) in November 1869, to be followed in December by 3 million of the 3c. Small Queen (*Fig 2*). The earliest known date of use for any Small Queen is a 3c. dated 12 Jan 1870, but one can wonder if the 1c. value was used before that, since its use was largely for 4th and 5th class mail which did not require date stamping.

It had been decided that as each Large Queen plate wore out it would be replaced by a Small Queen. Then, in January 1870, there was a fire in the press room. The led to an emergency board meeting at which two resolutions were passed. First, suitable premises were to be sought in Montreal, and second, the POD was to be asked for permission for the BABNC to move operations to that city.

Note: the first did not depend on that permission being given. The steps taken in finding premises in Montreal, the signing of the lease and so on, are well documented in the Company's archives; of the permission to move printing there—not a word.

Knowing the capacity of the Ottawa printing works, probably to the last sheet, and with the likelihood that demand for postage stamps was likely to go on increasing with the expanding population, the case BABNC made out to the Post Office would be doubtless along the following lines… First, when operations were started in Ottawa such a rapid increase in demand was not anticipated by either party. Second, Ottawa had to meet a demand that it did not have the capacity to meet. Third, the company had spare capacity in Montreal which could meet the demand, no doubt while suitable premises in Ottawa were sought… so, as a temporary measure, allow us to move part of production to Montreal pro tem. Of course, the Post Office was over a barrel.

Having moved their offices to Montreal in 1871, perfectly legitimately, by the end of 1872 printing of 3c. stamps was transferred there also, to be rapidly followed by the other denominations. The most obvious physical change between the printings was that perforations which had gauged approximately 12 in Ottawa (actually 11.85, unique to that time and location) changed to approximately 11½×12 in Montreal. Before the move, however, a 6c. was issued in January 1872 (*Fig 3*), followed a month later by the 2c. (*Fig 4*).

In 1874 all pretence at a continued presence in Ottawa was abandoned with the production of a

The Small Queens of Canada 1879–97

new 10c. stamp which appeared in November. The imprints on the plate read 'British American Bank Note Co., Montreal'—previous, imprints had read 'British American Bank Note Co., Montreal & Ottawa'. So matters remained until 1887, when the POD insisted if the BABNC were to keep the contract, which was once again up for renewal, as it had been regularly every four or five years, they had to move printing back to Ottawa, as per the original contractual terms. Imprints were then changed to read 'Ottawa' instead of 'Montreal'—although none of the plates were made redundant simply because its imprint was not a current one.

THE SECOND OTTAWA PERIOD

The Company built a brand new works on the original Ottawa site, but not without problems. Completion of the new site was delayed when part of the incomplete structure collapsed. Then in 1888, before the Ottawa site was completed, the lease for the Montreal premises expired. Production was temporarily moved to the 4th floor of the Gazette Building in Montreal, owned by the Burland interest, where it remained for six months until March 1889. In May 1889, the new premises in Ottawa were officially opened.

A RIVAL BID

In 1891 the Canada Bank Note Engraving and Printing Company (CBNEPC), the company which Matthew Smillie had joined in 1880, made a bid for the Post Office contract, severely slashing prices and increasing the guaranteed capacity of each plate from the original 2½ million before repair, plus 1½ million thereafter, to 7 million before repair, and 5 million thereafter. Admittedly all plates now being made had 200 impressions instead of the original 100, but a number of the original 100 subject plates were still in use—a 6c., the 10c. and the 15c. Large Queen to instance but three. The bid nearly succeeded (*Fig 5*). Probably it did not because of the expense the BABNC had gone to in building its new premises in Ottawa. The CBNEPC had prepared a number of dies and sample plates, and the stamps were very attractive. Unfortunately, perhaps fortunately for Small Queen enthusiasts, it was decided to leave the contract with BABNC subject to their matching the competition prices, plate capacity etc.

Their competitors had spent so much time and money in trying to get the business that they went bust shortly afterwards. The BABNC then picked up their rival's tools and plates cheaply. The BABNC even used the CBNEPC 2c. design on the 1896 UPU postcard (*Fig 6*). Incidentally, very few of the major varieties described later would have existed had the bid been successful.

Fig 1 *An imprint pair of the Small Queen 1c. in the issued colour*

Fig 2 *The first printing of the 3c. Small Queen*

Fig 3 *An example of the 6c. value printed in Ottawa in 1871, prior to the move to Montreal*

Fig 4 *A 2c. value from the first Ottawa printing*

Fig 5 *A 3c. plate proof produced by the Canada Bank Note Engraving and Printing Company*

Fig 6 *The 1896 UPU postcard produced by the BABNC using the 2c. design created by the defunct CBNEPC (Reduced)*

xxxi

In 1897 came a change of government, a loss of political influence and a loss of the contract to the American Bank Note Company—not without a somewhat bitter and protracted struggle. The plates and other paraphernalia, bought for and owned by the Post Office, were not surrendered to that agency until 1903.

THE STAMPS

So much for the background; what of the stamps? As mentioned above, during the first Ottawa period just four stamps were issued: the 1c., and 3c. in 1870, and the 6c. and 2c. in 1872. The original consignment of the 1c. was in a beautiful shade of bright orange. Later consignments were shades of orange-yellow. The 3c. was originally in shades of either copper-red, or Indian-red, including a small quantity of a true perf 12½. Later deliveries were in shades of rose-red. The 2c. were in shades of delicate green, and the 6c. a medium yellow-brown. The gum was yellowish and smooth, with the occasional bits of foreign matter. Perforation in general was as described above. Shades were not dissimilar to their Large Queen predecessors. Only the 6c. sported any printing variety of note: a major re-entry, described as from position Row 7/7 from the original 1891 plate, but as no positional pieces are known, there are actually 42 other possible positions it could have come from.

MONTREAL PRINTINGS

At the end of 1872 there is evidence that production began to be transferred to Montreal, beginning with the stamp most in demand, the 3c. Covers are known from January 1873 perforated 11½×12 and in a new shade, orange-red. During 1873, probably during the early months, the three other Small Queen denomination plates were transferred along with the still current Large Queens—one plate each of the ½c., 12½c. and 15c. The 12½c. was virtually redundant at this time due to reductions in postal rates; for example the ½ ounce rate to the UK by the Allen Line was now 6c., less than half what it was in 1868. This meant no more printings were made of that value, but the other two continued in use and therefore exist perf 11½ ×12.

In November 1874 a new value, the 10c. was issued. There was no clear reason for this value at the time, though the following year saw the formation of the General Postal Union—the forerunner of the UPU—which brought with it a fall of the transatlantic rate to 5c. by any route. The new 10c. value paid the rate over ½oz up to 1oz (*Fig 7*).

At the same time a 5c. stamp was needed in a rush, so having the tools for the Large Queen 5c., which had been prepared in 1868 but never issued, a new plate was made and stamps from it issued on 1 October; the Small Queen successor appeared four months later in February 1876 in the same basic colour, olive-green (*Fig 8*). The stamp should have been printed in blue. However, as the 12½c., which was also blue, was still current it was not possible to use the same colour. Perforations between 1873 and 1876 were approximately 11½×12, 11¾×12 in 1877, and perf 12 from 1878–87.

During that last period, in 1882, the Large Queen ½c. was replaced by the smallest stamp so far produced by Canada, the Small Queen ½c. (*Fig 9*). By this time

Fig 7 *The 10c. purple introduced in November 1874*

Fig 8 *A counter block of the olive-green 5c. Small Queen*

Fig 9 *A plate proof of the 1882 ½c. Small Queen*

plates were made in a twin pane format each of 100 impressions arranged 10×10 and separated by a gutter about 1¼ inches (64 mm) wide, the panes being guillotined apart before despatch. The new ½c. plate was similar, but with a centimetre wide centre gutter perforated in each side so that when separated half the panes were still attached to it and half were not.

During the early years of printing, the paper used was of high quality. During most of the Montreal period a reasonable wove was used, which although it could vary from thin to quite stout, was generally of medium thickness. However, by 1887 the paper used to print the stamps began to get poorer in quality. At the same time perforations varied from 12×12¼, to 12¼ ×12, and even occasionally 12¼×12¼.

As already mentioned, in 1888 the lease for the Montreal premises expired before the new premises in Ottawa was completed. For six months, i.e. from September 1888 to March 1889 activities were carried out on the fourth floor of the Gazette Building where, it will be recalled, the Burland's had influence. The new Ottawa premises were officially opened in May 1889, however, there is clear evidence that work had actually started there in March. It is something of a mystery why some catalogues do not accept the facts and ascribe 2nd Ottawa printings as commencing in 1888. Even worse, the 3c rose-carmine (SG 84) is therefore described in those publications as an Ottawa printing, whereas in fact it is the one Small Queen that is known to be the product of the period the firm was temporarily operating in the *Montreal Gazette* building (*Fig 10*).

Fig 11 *An example of the 6c. deep red-brown printed during the second Ottawa period*

Fig 10 *An imprint pair of the 3c. value printed by the British American Bank Note Co at the* Montreal Gazette *building*

Fig 13 *A plate proof of the 20c. Widows Weeds in the issued colour*

Fig 12 *The 8c. value introduced in 1893 to pay the 1oz combined domestic and registration rate*

Fig 14 *50c. Widows Weeds plate proof in the issued colour*

THE SECOND OTTAWA PERIOD

The second Ottawa period in some ways is the most interesting because it was in the final years that most of the major varieties occurred, some of which are now catalogued, others remain hopefully to be included in future editions of the *Part 1* catalogue. Yet few of these varieties could have happened if the Canadian Bank Note Engraving & Printing Co. had been treated fairly.

COLOUR CHANGES

Several colour changes are seen during the second Ottawa years. The 6c. yellow-brown of the first Ottawa period changed first to chocolate, then to red-brown (*Fig 11*). The earliest known second Ottawa 6c. cover is dated December 1890 and is in a chocolate shade, but because of the habit of the POD placing new supplies when received on top of old stock, most dated chocolate copies were used in 1896 or 1897. The 5c. changed from olive-green (by 1887 a rather washed out olive-green) to greyish black. Likewise, the 2c. appeared in shades of blue-green, the 10c. in carmine-pink, brownish-red and salmon-pink, instead of the Montreal clarets and purples, and the 3c. from shades of orange-red or a dull red to bright vermilion. Most of the second Ottawa 3c. were printed using aniline ink for the first time—under UV light the backs glow yellowish. Only the ½c. and 1c. showed little change from the final Montreal printings, except for the perforations, which were now back to 12 gauge—until 1896 when 12×12¼ was the norm again.

In 1893 a new 8c. stamp was added to the range. Its main purpose was to pay the 1oz combined domestic and registration rate (*Fig 12*). Perhaps for this reason the Queen's portrait faces to the left instead of to the right as with the rest of the series. A 20c. in vermilion (*Fig 13*) and a 50c. in blue were also added (*Fig 14*). These were used primarily to pay parcel postage rates, in an adapted design based on the 1868 bill stamps, which were still current, known as the 'Widow's Weeds'.

EARLY VARIETIES

Mentioned above is the fact that if the CBNEPC had been successful, none of the, sometimes spectacular varieties that were inadvertently created in the years from 1891 would have existed. Only one major variety has been recorded from the first Ottawa years, the major re-entry on the 6c. yellow-brown from the original plate (SG 86a), and only two from Montreal, the 5c. 'straw in hair' (SG 85a) and a major re-entry to the 10c. which occurs on all printings and yet is remarkably scarce There are also a couple of instances of minor plate damage to this value; corrosion pitting in one of the value tablets, and from a different position a scratch in the other.

The Small Queens of Canada 1879–97

Fig 15 *An example of the 5c. on 6c. major re-entry*

Fig 16 *5c. on 6c. re-entry made to the 'A' pane of the 'Montreal' plate in 1892 during the second Ottawa period*

Fig 17 *A strip of three of the 6c. value showing the major re-entry at R1/7 (centre) of the 'C' pane of the 'Montreal' plate*

FINAL PERIOD VARIETIES

The situation is quite different from the final period. The best known example is perhaps the major '5c. on 6c. re-entry' (SG 107a) from pane B of the twin 'Montreal' plate (known thus because of the imprint wording on it—'Montreal', although it was only ever used in Ottawa (*Fig 15*). Less known is the fact that, while the position of this variety is known, two others, both slightly different, have been found from unknown positions. Furthermore, there are four others from an 1892 repair to the 6c. 'A' plate, which was made in the first Ottawa period and which was still in use; two of the known examples are confined to the top right half of the design, as opposed to going right across as is the case with the majors (*Fig 16*), and two are simply short lines that cut across the Queen's tiara.

The repair that gave rise to the majors, which must have taken place no earlier than late 1895 or as late as 1896, also gave birth to three huge re-entries, two from the 'C' pane and one from the 'B'. All three are notable for the entire doubling of the engraving of the face and for the distortion of the wording at the base of the design, as well as doubling of the scrollwork and in two cases to the 'CANADA POSTAGE' tablet at the top of the design (*Fig 17*). Unfortunately, I have not been able to persuade the SG catalogue editor to list them as they are as rare

The Small Queens of Canada 1879–97

Fig 18 *An example of 1c. 'Medium' 'Strand of Hair' variety*

Fig 19 *A bottom latent entry of the 2c. Small Queen*

Fig 20 *A major re-entry of the 2c. made during the second Ottawa period*

as SG 107a—but I continue to hope. The situation is somewhat complicated by the fact that the 1892 repair to the 'A' plate also gave rise to a major re-entry which is much more common than those from the 'Montreal' plate—perhaps about the same degree of scarcity as the major re-entry on the yellow-brown stamp.

The 1c. boasts a similar variety to SG 107a, and there are four of them—the so-called 'Strands of Hair'. It is unfortunate that the discoverers of varieties seemed generally to have no imagination when naming their finds—'Parting in Hair' would have been more appropriate. The 'Long' variety is illustrated in the catalogue as SG 75d but it, as with the others, a 'Medium' (*Fig 18*) and two 'Short', are all Ottawa printings, The scarcest are the 'Shorts', one of which has a good re-entry as well.

It is pretty certain that the printers were experimenting with a multi-denomination transfer roller—one could get all six of the current Small Queen normal size stamps onto one roller which was 6 inches in diameter. Two sets of impressions must have been a little too close to each other, giving rise to both the Strands and the 5c. on 6c. varieties. This was due to over-rocking when repairing plates—the varieties are only found on repaired plates. Since no such tool was sent to the POD in 1903 one can only assume the printers made it on their own account. I doubt if more than one were made.

The second Ottawa 2c. has two varieties which are on plates before any repair—the latent (or misplaced) entries. In North America they are misnamed 'Latent Re-entries' but the varieties are the original entries, laid down half a stamp too high before the mistake was realised. One shows part of the rim of the vignette below the bottom of the design, the other, part, I think, of the Queen's hair above the top of the design. They are from two different plates. The scarcer is the bottom variety and is from an unknown plate and position except it must be from the ninth horizontal row (*Fig 19*). This value also has two major re-entries recorded, one of which has similar distortion of the wording at the base of the design to the three major re-entries from the 6c. 'Montreal' plate (*Fig 20*).

The ½c. abounds in re-entries, one or two of which are major. The best known is from the right pane Row 5/9. It is relatively common. The writer has a pair of

Fig 21 *Examples of the right pane positional block of the ½c. before (left) and after (right) re-entering. The major re-entering is found at R5/9*

Fig 22 *A genuine example of an imperforate 3c. Small Queen*

matched blocks, one without and one with the re-entry; the one without is possibly the only survivor in that state (*Fig 21*).

The 50c. top row shows doubling of the top on several positions, that from position 6 is regarded as the major re-entry.

The 3c., the most prolific value of all, curiously has virtually nothing of major significance, though there are plenty of minor re-entries, which leaves just the 8c. which has one major re-entry, and since it occurs on all the catalogued shades strongly indicates only one plate was ever used in printing them, even though four were made, the Post Office even paid for two of them.

IMPERFORATES

A final word on the imperforates: From the 1897 definitive set, the Maple Leaf set, until and including the 1942 War Effort stamps, the Post Office authorised the issuing of imperforate and imperforate-between stamps (excluding most but not all of the Admirals). This bad habit began when one imperforate sheet of each of the Small Queens, Widows Weeds and the Large Queen 15c. were presented as a 'thank you' for services to a Mr Lauchlan Gibb of Montreal. Some he used in correspondence, generally in pairs. This seemed to encourage one or more employees of the BABNC occasionally to take their work home with them—not to put a fine a point on it, most imperforate Small Queens in collections and on the market were pinched. Because some of the 'legitimate' imperforates were used by Mr Gibb, it is not uncommon nowadays to see wretched used singles which have been imperforated, that is their perforation teeth have been cut off. Just very occasionally one may be offered a genuine imperforate single, although wisdom dictates they should only be bought in pairs. However, illustrated is a genuine single. In 40 years I have only seen one other in similar unused condition—a left margined 2c. (*Fig 22*).

THE END OF THE BABNC ERA

The contract was finally taken away from the British American Bank Note Co. in 1897 and awarded to the American Bank Note Co, who set up a printing works in Ottawa especially for the purpose—an offshoot that eventually became the Canadian Bank Note Co. The BABNC was very bitter about the loss of the contract and offered to match the American Bank Notes terms, but to no avail. Just how bitter the Canadian printers were can be judged by the fact that it was not until 1903 that the tools, paid for and owned by the Post Office, were finally returned to the Department for destruction. Thus ended 30 years of pretty good service.

Consign to specialists with over 150 years of auction expertise.

Contact us to
receive a free valuation

www.baldwins.co

Visit us Online for more great items

British Columbia #3 Mint OG (Store Item S007730)

www.garylyon.com

Gary J. Lyon (Philatelist) Ltd.

P.O. Box 450 - Bathurst - New Brunswick - E2A 3Z4 - Canada
Phone 1(506) 546-6363 - Toll Free 1(800) 667-8267
Email glstamps@garylyon.com - Website www.garylyon.com

Member of: ASDA - CSDA - IFSDA - PTS - APS - RPSC - BNAPS - CPSofGB - PHSC

Canada

Separate stamp issues appeared for British Columbia and Vancouver Island, Canada, New Brunswick, Newfoundland, Nova Scotia and Prince Edward Island before these colonies joined the Dominion of Canada.

BRITISH COLUMBIA & VANCOUVER ISLAND

Vancouver Island was organised as a Crown Colony in 1849 and the mainland territory was proclaimed a separate colony as British Columbia in 1858. The two colonies combined, as British Columbia, on 19 November 1866.

PRICES FOR STAMPS ON COVER	
Nos. 2/3	from × 6
Nos. 11/12	from × 2
Nos. 13/14	from × 6
Nos. 21/22	from × 10
Nos. 23/27	from × 6
Nos. 28/29	from × 10
No. 30	—
No. 31	from × 10
Nos. 32/33	—

1

(Typo D.L.R.)

1860. No wmk. Perf 14.
2	1	2½d. deep reddish rose	£450	£250
3		2½d. pale reddish rose	£450	£250

When Vancouver Island adopted the dollar currency in 1862 the 2½d. was sold at 5c. From 18 May until 1 November 1865 examples of Nos. 2/3 were used to prepay mail from Vancouver Island to British Columbia at the price of 15 cents a pair.

From 20 June 1864 to 1 November 1865, the 2½d. was sold in British Columbia for 3d. and was subsequently used for the same purpose during a shortage of 3d. stamps in 1867.

Imperforate plate proofs exist in pale dull red (*Price* £15,000 un).

VANCOUVER ISLAND

(New Currency. 100 cents = 1 dollar)

2   3

(Typo D.L.R.)

1865 (19 Sept). Wmk Crown CC.

(a) Imperf (1866).
11	2	5c. rose	£32000	£11000
12	3	10c. blue	£3500	£1000

(b) Perf 14. Perf 14.
13	2	5c. rose	£375	£275
		w. Wmk inverted	£2000	£900
		x. Wmk reversed	†	£1100
14	3	10c. blue	£325	£225
		w. Wmk inverted	£1000	£650

Medium or poor examples of Nos. 11 and 12 can be supplied at much lower prices, when in stock.

After the two colonies combined Nos. 13/14 were also used in British Columbia.

BRITISH COLUMBIA

4

(Typo D.L.R.)

1865 (1 Nov)–**67.** Wmk Crown CC. Perf 14.
21	4	3d. deep blue	£160	£110
22		3d. pale blue (19.7.67)	£170	£120
		w. Wmk inverted	£500	£350
		y. Wmk inverted and reversed	†	£550

British Columbia changed to the dollar currency on 1 January 1866. Remaining stocks of No. 21 and the supply of No. 22, when it finally arrived, were sold at 12½c. a pair.

(New Currency. 100 cents = 1 dollar)

TWO CENTS   5.CENTS.5
(5)   (6)

1868–71. T **4** in various colours. Surch as T **5** or T **6**. Wmk Crown CC.

(a) Perf 12½ (3.69). Perf 12½.
23	5c. red (Blk.)	£2250	£1300
24	10c. lake (B.)	£1500	£850
25	25c. yellow (V.)	£850	£600
26	50c. mauve (R.)	£1400	£750
27	$1 green (G.)	£1800	£1400

(b) Perf 14. Perf 14.
28	2c. brown (Blk.) (1.68)	£170	£140
29	5c. pale red (Blk.) (5.69)	£300	£200
30	10c. lake (B.)		£1500
31	25c. yellow (V.) (21.7.69)	£275	£200
	w. Wmk inverted	†	£1200
32	50c. mauve (R.) (23.2.71)	£1000	£1100
	w. Wmk inverted		£1600
33	$1 green (G.)		£1500

Nos. 30 and 33 were not issued.

British Columbia joined the Dominion of Canada on 20 July 1871.

COLONY OF CANADA

The first British post offices in what was to become the Colony of Canada were opened at Québec, Montréal and Trois Rivières during 1763. These, and subsequent, offices remained part of the British GPO system until 6 April 1851.

The two provinces of Upper Canada (Ontario) and Lower Canada (Québec) were united in 1840.

QUÉBEC

CROWNED-CIRCLE HANDSTAMPS

CC1	**CC1** QUEBEC L.C. (R.) (13.1.1842)........*Price on cover*	£160

PRICES FOR STAMPS ON COVER TO 1867	
Nos. 1/23	from × 2
Nos. 25/28	from × 3
Nos. 29/43*a*	from × 3
Nos. 44/45	from × 8

1 American Beaver (Designed by Sir Sandford Fleming)   2 Prince Albert   3

CANADA Colony of Canada

Major re-entry: Line through 'EE PEN' (Upper pane R. 5/7)

(Eng by A. Jones and recess Rawdon, Wright, Hatch and Edson, New York)

1851. Laid paper. Imperf.
1	1	3d. red (23.4)	£40000	£1100
1a		3d. orange-vermilion	£40000	£1100
		b. Major re-entry	—	£3750
2	2	6d. slate-violet (15.5)	£50000	£1400
3		6d. brown-purple	£50000	£1600
		a. Bisected (3d.) on cover	†	£38000
4	3	12d. black (14.6)	£200000	£100000

There are several re-entries on the plate of the 3d. in addition to the major re-entry listed. All re-entries occur in this stamp on all papers.

Forgeries of the 3d. are known without the full stop after 'PENCE'. They also omit the foliage in the corners, as do similar forgeries of the 6d.

4   5   6 Jacques Cartier

Re-entry (R. 10/12)

(Eng by A. Jones and recess Rawdon, Wright Hatch and Edson, New York)

1852–57. Imperf.

A. Handmade wove paper, varying in thickness (1852–1857).
5	1	3d. red	£2750	£250
		a. Bisected (1½d.) on cover (1856)	†	£38000
6		3d. deep red	£3000	£275
7		3d. scarlet-vermilion	£3500	£275
8		3d. brown-red	£3000	£275
		a. Bisected (1½d.) on cover (1856)	†	£38000
		b. Major re-entry (all shades) from	£7500	£950
9	2	6d. slate-violet	£45000	£1200
		a. Bisected (3d.) on cover	†	£20000
10		6d. greenish grey	£45000	£1400
11		6d. brownish grey	£48000	£1600
12	5	7½d. yellow-green (shades) (2.6.57)	£15000	£3500
13	6	10d. bright blue (1.55)	£14000	£2000
14		10d. dull blue	£13000	£2000
15		10d. blue to deep blue	£14000	£2000
		a. Major re-entry (all shades) from	—	£4000
16	3	12d. black	†	£150000

B. Machine-made medium to thick wove paper of a more even hard texture with more visible mesh. Clearer impressions (1857).
17	4	½d. deep rose (1.8.57)	£1100	£650
		a. Re-entry	£3500	£1500
18	1	3d. red	£3500	£450
		a. Bisected (1½d.) on cover	†	£38000
		b. Major re-entry	—	£1500
19	2	6d. grey-lilac	£48000	£2500
20	6	10d. blue to deep blue	£16000	£2250
		a. Major re-entry	£27000	£3750

C. Thin soft horizontally ribbed paper (1857).
21	4	½d. deep rose	£9500	£2250
		a. Vertically ribbed paper	£10000	£3250
22	1	3d. red	£4750	£500
		a. Major re-entry	—	£2000

D. Very thick soft wove paper (1857).
23	2	6d. reddish purple	£48000	£6000
		a. Bisected (3d.) on cover	†	£35000

Bisected examples of the 3d. value were used to make up the 7½d. Canadian Packet rate to England from May 1856 until the introduction of the 7½d. value on 2 June 1857.

The 7½d. and 10d. values can be found in wide and narrow versions. These differences are due to shrinkage of the paper, which was wetted before printing and then contracted unevenly during drying. The width of these stamps varies between 17 mm and 18 mm.

The listed major re-entry on the 10d. occurs on R. 3/5 and shows strong doubling of the top frame line and the left-hand '8d. stg.' with a line through the lower parts of 'ANAD' and 'ENCE'. Smaller re-entries occur on all values.

Examples of the 12d. on wove paper come from a proof sheet used for postal purposes by the postal authorities.

The 3d. is known perforated 14 and also *percé en scie* 13. Both are contemporary, but were unofficial.

1858–59. Perf 11¾.

A. Machine-made medium to thick wove paper with a more even hard texture.
25	4	½d. deep rose (12.58)	£4750	£1200
		a. Lilac-rose	£4750	£1200
		b. Re-entry (R. 10/10)	£9500	£2500
26	1	3d. red (1.59)	£13000	£650
		a. Major re-entry	—	£2250
27	2	6d. brownish grey (1.59)	£25000	£6000
		a. Slate-violet	£25000	£6000

B. Thin soft horizontally ribbed paper.
27b	4	½d. deep rose-red	—	£4750
28	1	3d. red	—	£2000
		a. Major re-entry		

The re-entry on the imperforate and perforated ½d. sheets was the same, but occurred on R. 10/10 of the perforated sheets because the two left-hand vertical rows were removed prior to perforation.

(New Currency. 100 cents = 1 dollar)

7   8 American Beaver   9 Prince Albert

10   11 Jacques Cartier    **5c.** Major re-entry showing as doubling of oval frame lines and lettering, particularly at the left of the design (R. 3/8)

(On 1 May 1858, Messrs. Rawdon, Wright, Hatch and Edson joined with eight other firms to form The American Bank Note Co and the 'imprint' on sheets of the following stamps has the new title of the firm with 'New York' added.)

(Recess A.B.N. Co)

1859 (1 July). Perf 12.
29	7	1c. pale rose (to rose-red)	£450	55·00
30		1c. deep rose (to carmine-rose)	£550	80·00
		a. Imperf (pair)	£4750	
		b. Imperf×perf		
31	8	5c. pale red	£450	25·00
32		5c. deep red	£450	30·00
		a. Re-entry* (R. 3/8)	£4500	£650
		b. Imperf (pair)	£18000	
		c. Bisected (2½c.) with 10c. on cover	†	£7500
33	9	10c. black-brown	£25000	£3000
		a. Bisected (5c.), on cover	†	£12000
33b		10c. deep red-purple	£4250	£750
		ba. Bisected (5c.), on cover	†	£7000
34		10c. purple (shades)	£1600	£100
		a. Bisected (5c.), on cover	†	£6500
35		10c. brownish purple	£1500	£120
36		10c. brown (to pale)	£1500	£120
		a. Bisected (5c.), on cover	†	£7500
37		10c. dull violet	£1500	£100
38		10c. bright red-purple	£1500	£100
		a. Imperf (pair)	£15000	

Colony of Canada, New Brunswick, Newfoundland CANADA

39	**10**	12½c. deep yellow-green	£1300	80·00
40		12½c. pale yellow-green	£1300	80·00
41		12½c. blue-green	£1500	90·00
		a. Imperf (pair)	£7000	
		b. Imperf between (vert pair)		
42	**11**	17c. deep blue	£1600	£110
		a. Imperf (pair)	£6500	
43		17c. slate-blue	£2000	£130
43a		17c. indigo	£1800	£100

* Slighter re-entries are worth from £40 upwards in used condition.

As there were numerous PO Dept. orders for the 10c., 12½c. and 17c. and some of these were executed by more than one separate printing, with no special care to ensure uniformity of colour, there is a wide range of shade, especially in the 10c., and some shades recur at intervals after periods during which other shades predominated. The colour-names given in the above list therefore represent groups only.

It has been proved by leading Canadian specialists that the perforations may be an aid to the approximate dating of a particular stamp, the gauge used measuring 11¾×11¾ from mid-July 1859 to mid-1863, 12×11¾ from March 1863 to mid-1865 and 12×12 from April 1865 to 1868. Exceptionally, in the 5c. value many sheets were perforated 12×12 between May and October, 1862, whilst the last printings of the 12½c. and 17c. perf 11¾×11¾ were in July 1863, the perf 12×11¾ starting towards the end of 1863.

12

(Recess A.B.N. Co)

1864 (1 Aug). Perf 12.
44	**12**	2c. rose-red	£600	£225
45		2c. bright rose	£600	£225
		a. Imperf (pair)	£3500	

The Colony of Canada became part of the Dominion of Canada on 1 July 1867.

NEW BRUNSWICK

New Brunswick, previously part of Nova Scotia, became a separate colony in June 1784. The colony became responsible for its postal service on 6 July 1851.

PRICES FOR STAMPS ON COVER	
Nos. 1/4	from × 2
Nos. 5/6	from × 3
Nos. 7/9	from × 10
Nos. 10/12	from × 30
No. 13	—
Nos. 14/17	from × 2
No. 18	from × 5
No. 19	from × 100

1 Royal Crown and Heraldic Flowers of the United Kingdom

(Recess P.B.)

1851 (5 Sept)–**60**. Blue paper. Imperf.
1	**1**	3d. bright red	£4000	£500
2		3d. dull red	£3500	£425
		a. Bisected (1½d.) (1854) (on cover)	†	£3250
2b		6d. mustard-yellow	£15000	£1600
3		6d. yellow	£10000	£950
4		6d. olive-yellow	£10000	£850
		a. Bisected (3d.) (1854) (on cover)	†	£3250
		b. Quartered (1½d.) (1860) (on cover)	†	£42000
5		1s. reddish mauve	£30000	£4500
6		1s. dull mauve	£32000	£5000
		a. Bisected (6d.) (1855) (on cover)	†	£24000
		b. Quartered (3d.) (1860) (on cover)	†	£38000

Reprints of all three values were made in 1890 on thin, hard, white paper. The 3d. is bright orange, the 6d. and 1s. violet-black.

Nos. 2a and 4b were to make up the 7½d. rate to Great Britain, introduced on 1 August 1854.

(New Currency. 100 cents = 1 dollar)

2 Locomotive   **3**    **3a** Charles Connell

4   **5**   **6** Paddle-steamer Washington

7 King Edward VII when Prince of Wales

(Recess A.B.N. Co)

1860 (15 May)–**63**. No wmk. Perf 11½, 12.
7	**2**	1c. brown-purple	85·00	65·00
8		1c. purple	70·00	50·00
9		1c. dull claret	70·00	50·00
		a. Imperf vert (horiz pair)	£650	
10	**3**	2c. orange (1863)	38·00	29·00
11		2c. orange-yellow	45·00	30·00
12		2c. deep orange	48·00	30·00
		a. Imperf horiz (vert pair)	£475	
13	**3a**	5c. brown	£10000	
14	**4**	5c. yellow-green	29·00	18·00
15		5c. deep green	29·00	18·00
16		5c. sap-green (deep yellowish green)	£300	40·00
17	**5**	10c. red	65·00	75·00
		a. Bisected (5c.) (on cover) (1860)	†	£1000
18	**6**	12½c. indigo	70·00	50·00
19	**7**	17c. black	42·00	90·00

Beware of forged cancellations.

No. 13 was not issued due to objections to the design showing Charles Connell, the Postmaster-General. Most of the printing was destroyed.

New Brunswick joined the Dominion of Canada on 1 July 1867 and its stamps were withdrawn in March of the following year.

NEWFOUNDLAND

Newfoundland became a self-governing colony in 1855 and a Dominion in 1907. In 1934 the adverse financial situation led to the suspension of the constitution, with a reversion to colonial status.

The first local postmaster, at St John's, was appointed in 1805, the overseas mails being routed via Halifax, Nova Scotia. A regular packet service was established between these two ports in 1840, the British GPO assuming control of the overseas mails at the same time.

The responsibility for the overseas postal service reverted to the colonial administration on 1 July 1851.

ST JOHN'S

CC1a

CANADA Newfoundland

CROWNED-CIRCLE HANDSTAMPS

CC1 **CC1a** ST JOHN'S NEWFOUNDLAND (R.)
(27.6.1846)..........................Price on cover £1000

PRICES FOR STAMPS ON COVER TO 1945	
No. 1	from × 30
Nos. 2/4	from × 3
No. 5	from × 20
No. 6	from × 10
No. 7	from × 3
No. 8	from × 30
No. 9	from × 8
No. 10	—
No. 11	from × 8
No. 12	from × 3
Nos. 13/14	from × 20
Nos. 15/17	—
Nos. 18/20	from × 20
No. 21	from × 15
Nos. 22/23	—
No. 25	from × 30
No. 26	from × 5
No. 27	from × 8
No. 28	from × 3
Nos. 29/30	from × 10
No. 31	from × 30
No. 32	from × 8
No. 33	from × 5
Nos. 34/39	from × 8
Nos. 40/41	from × 5
Nos. 42/43	from × 30
Nos. 44/48	from × 8
No. 49	from × 50
Nos. 50/53	from × 10
No. 54	from × 4
Nos. 55/58b	from × 10
No. 59	from × 100
No. 59a	from × 10
Nos. 60/61	from × 4
Nos. 62/65	from × 8
Nos. 65a/79	from × 3
Nos. 83/90	from × 10
Nos. 91/93	from × 2
No. 94	from × 50
Nos. 95/141	from × 3
Nos. 142/142a	from × 1½
No. 143	from × 8
Nos. 144/148f	from × 2
Nos. 149/162	from × 3
No. 163	from × 1½
Nos. 164/178	from × 2
Nos. 179/190	from × 3
No. 191	from × 1½
Nos. 192/220	from × 2
No. 221	from × 1½
Nos. 222/229	from × 3
Nos. 230/234	from × 2
No. 235	from × 1½
Nos. 236/291	from × 2
Nos. D1/D6	from × 10

5

Royal Crown and Heraldic flowers of the United Kingdom

(Recess P.B.)

1857 (1 Jan)–**64**. Thick, machine-made paper with a distinct mesh. No wmk. Imperf.

1	1	1d. brown-purple................................	£200	£250
		a. Bisected (½d.) (1864) (on cover)......	†	£40000
2	2	2d. scarlet-vermilion (15.2).....................	£25000	£6500
3	3	3d. yellowish green (H/S 'CANCELLED' in oval £12000)........................	£2250	£475
4	4	4d. scarlet-vermilion...........................	£22500	£4000
5	1	5d. brown-purple................................	£375	£550
6	4	6d. scarlet-vermilion...........................	£65000	£5500
7	5	6½d. scarlet-vermilion.........................	£5500	£5000
8	4	8d. scarlet-vermilion...........................	£425	£950
		a. Bisected (4d.) (1859) (on cover).......	†	£4250
9	2	1s. scarlet-vermilion............................	£45000	£9000
		a. Bisected (6d.) (1860) (on cover).......	†	£17000

The 6d. and 8d. differ from the 4d. in many details, as does also the 1s. from the 2d.

PERKINS BACON 'CANCELLED'. For notes on these handstamps, showing 'CANCELLED' between horizontal bars forming an oval, see Catalogue Introduction.

1860 (15 Aug–Dec). Medium, hand-made paper without mesh. Imperf.

10	2	2d. orange-vermilion...........................	£650	£750
11	3	3d. green to deep green* (H/S 'CANCELLED' in oval £11000)..........	£120	£190
12	4	4d. orange-vermilion (H/S 'CANCELLED' in oval £14000)...........	£4500	£1100
		a. Bisected (2d.) (12.60) (on cover)......	†	£20000
13	1	5d. Venetian red (H/S 'CANCELLED' in oval £13000)................................	£140	£400
14	4	6d. orange-vermilion...........................	£5500	£950
15	2	1s. orange-vermilion (H/S 'CANCELLED' in oval £17000)..........	£55000	£12000
		a. Bisected (6d.) (12.60) (on cover)......	†	£45000

* No. 11 includes stamps from the July and November 1861 printings which are very difficult to distinguish.

The 1s. on horizontally or vertically laid paper is now considered to be a proof (Price £40,000).

Stamps of this and the following issue may be found with part of the papermaker's watermark 'STACEY WISE 1858'.

BISECTS. Collectors are warned against buying bisected stamps of these issues without a reliable guarantee.

1862–64. New colours. Hand-made paper without mesh. Imperf.

16	1	1d. chocolate-brown............................	£350	£450
		a. Red-brown..................................		£12500
17	2	2d. rose-lake	£300	£500
18	4	4d. rose-lake (H/S 'CANCELLED' in oval £13000)...	50·00	£110
		a. Bisected (2d.) (1864) (on cover).......	†	£38000
19	1	5d. chocolate-brown (shades)...............	£100	£325
		a. Red-brown (shades).......................	90·00	£200
20	4	6d. rose-lake (H/S 'CANCELLED' in oval £11000)...	35·00	£100
		a. Bisected (3d.) (1863) (on cover).......	†	£9500
21	5	6½d. rose-lake (H/S 'CANCELLED' in oval £11000)...................................	£100	£450
22	4	8d. rose-lake.......................................	£130	£650
23	2	1s. rose-lake (H/S 'CANCELLED' in oval £12000)...	50·00	£300
		a. Bisected (6d.) (1863) (on cover).......	†	£22000

Nos. 16/23 come from printings made in July (2d., 4d., 6d., 6½d., and 1s. only) or November 1861 (all values), which were received in Newfoundland in January 1862. The paper used was from the same manufacturer as that for Nos. 10/15, but was of more variable thickness and texture, ranging from a relatively soft medium paper, which can be quite opaque, to a thin hard transparent paper. The rose-lake stamps also show a considerable variation in shade ranging from pale to deep. The extensive remainders of this issue were predominantly in pale shades on thin hard paper, but it is not possible to distinguish between stamps from the two printings with any certainty. Deep shades of the 2d., 4d., 6d., 6½d. and 1s. on soft opaque paper do, however, command a considerable premium.

Beware of buying used examples of the stamps which are worth much less in unused condition, as many unused stamps have been provided with faked postmarks. A guarantee should be obtained.

1   2

3   4

Newfoundland CANADA

(New Currency. 100 cents = 1 dollar)

6 Atlantic Cod

7 Common Seal on Ice Floe

8 King Edward VII when Prince of Wales

9 Queen Victoria

10 Schooner

11 Queen Victoria

(Recess A.B.N. Co, New York)

1865 (15 Nov)–**70**. Perf 12.

(a) Thin yellowish paper.

25	6	2c. yellowish green	£170	£120
		a. Bisected (1c.) (*on cover*) (1870)	†	£8500
26	7	5c. brown	£600	£200
		a. Bisected (2½c.) (*on cover*)	†	£10000
27	8	10c. black	£375	£130
		a. Bisected (5c.) (*on cover*) (1869)	†	£7000
28	9	12c. red-brown	£650	£180
		a. Bisected (6c.) (*on cover*) (1869)	†	£5000
29	10	13c. orange-yellow	£140	£150
30	11	24c. blue	55·00	45·00

(b) Medium white paper.

31	6	2c. bluish green (to deep) (1870)	£130	50·00
32	8	10c. black (1870)	£300	65·00
33	9	12c. chestnut (1870)	70·00	48·00

The inland postage rate was reduced to 3c. on 8 May, 1870. Until the 3c. value became available examples of No. 25 were bisected to provide 1c. stamps.

For the 12c. value in deep brown, see No. 61.

12 King Edward VII when Prince of Wales

14 Queen Victoria

I

II

In Type II the white oval frame line is unbroken by the scroll containing the words 'ONE CENT', the letters 'N.F.' are smaller and closer to the scroll, and there are other minor differences.

(Recess National Bank Note Co, New York)

1868 (Nov). Perf 12.

34	12	1c. dull purple (Type I)	£120	60·00

(Recess A.B.N. Co)

1868 (Nov)–**73**. Perf 12.

35	12	1c. brown-purple (Type II) (3.71)	£150	75·00
36	14	3c. vermilion (7.70)	£350	£130
37		3c. blue (1.4.73)	£300	40·00
38	7	5c. black	£350	£130
39	14	6c. rose (7.70)	25·00	32·00

1876–79. Roul 8.

40	12	1c. lake-purple (Type II) (1877)	£130	55·00
41	6	2c. bluish green (1879)	£170	50·00
42	14	3c. blue (1877)	£350	10·00
43	7	5c. blue	£225	7·50
		a. Imperf (pair)		

15 King Edward VII when Prince of Wales

16 Atlantic Cod

17

18 Common Seal on Ice Floe

(Recess British American Bank Note Co, Montréal)

1880–82. Perf 12.

44	15	1c. dull grey-brown	60·00	17·00
		a. Dull brown	60·00	17·00
		b. Red-brown	75·00	22·00
46	16	2c. yellow-green (1882)	85·00	32·00
47	17	3c. pale dull blue	£150	9·50
		a. Bright blue	95·00	6·50
48	18	5c. pale dull blue	£350	11·00

19 Newfoundland Dog (after Landseer)

20 Atlantic Brigantine

21 Queen Victoria

(Recess British American Bank Note Co, Montréal)

1887 (1 Nov). New colours and values. Perf 12.

49	19	½c. rose-red	18·00	11·00
50	15	1c. blue-green	25·00	14·00
		a. Green	10·00	4·75
		b. Yellow-green	16·00	12·00
51	16	2c. orange-vermilion	35·00	8·00
		a. Imperf (pair)	£375	
52	17	3c. deep brown	85·00	3·25
53	18	5c. deep blue	£140	7·50
54	20	10c. black	£130	75·00
49/54 *Set of 6*			£375	95·00

For re-issues in similar colours, see Nos. 62/65a.

(Recess B.A.B.N. Co)

1890 (Nov). Perf 12.

55	21	3c. deep slate	55·00	3·50
		a. Imperf (pair)		
56		3c. slate-grey (to grey)	50·00	3·75
		a. Imperf horiz (vert pair)	£550	
57		3c. slate-violet	70·00	8·00
58		3c. grey-lilac	70·00	3·75
58*a*		3c. brown-grey	75·00	9·00
58*b*		3c. purple-grey	75·00	9·00

There is a very wide range of shades in this stamp, and those given only cover the main groups.

Stamps on pink paper are from a consignment recovered from the sea and which were affected by the salt water.

CANADA Newfoundland

(Recess British American Bank Note Co, Montréal)

1894 (Aug–Dec). Changes of colour. Perf 12.

59	19	½c. black (11.94)	12·00	10·00
59a	18	5c. bright blue (12.94)	80·00	6·00
60	14	6c. crimson-lake (12.94)	40·00	29·00
61	9	12c. deep brown	90·00	90·00

The 6c. is printed from the old American Bank Note Company's plates.

1896 (Jan)–**98**. Re-issues. Perf 12.

62	19	½c. orange-vermilion	65·00	55·00
63	15	1c. deep brown	£100	65·00
63a		1c. deep green (1898)	38·00	28·00
64	16	2c. green	£120	75·00
65	17	3c. deep blue	90·00	35·00
65a		3c. chocolate-brown	£120	95·00
62/65a Set of 6			£450	£300

The above were *re-issued* for postal purposes. The colours were generally brighter than those of the original stamps.

22 Queen Victoria   **23** John Cabot   **24** Cape Bonavista

25 Caribou Hunting   **26** Mining   **27** Logging

28 Fishing   **29** *Matthew* (Cabot)   **30** Willow Grouse

31 Group of Grey Seals   **32** Salmon Fishing   **33** Seal of the Colony

34 Iceberg off St John's   **35** Henry VII

(Des R. O. Smith. Recess A.B.N. Co)

1897 (24 June). 400th Anniversary of Discovery of Newfoundland and 60th year of Queen Victoria's reign. Perf 12.

66	22	1c. green	8·50	13·00
67	23	2c. bright rose	3·00	3·00
		a. Bisected (1c.) *on cover*	†	£325
68	24	3c. bright blue	4·25	1·00
		a. Bisected (1½c.) *on cover*	†	£325
69	25	4c. olive-green	14·00	10·00
70	26	5c. violet	14·00	5·00
71	27	6c. red-brown	10·00	4·00
		a. Bisected (3c.) *on cover*	†	£350
72	28	8c. orange	25·00	10·00
73	29	10c. sepia	45·00	18·00
74	30	12c. deep blue	42·00	15·00
75	31	15c. bright scarlet	27·00	28·00
76	32	24c. dull violet-blue	32·00	40·00
77	33	30c. slate-blue	55·00	£110
78	34	35c. red	70·00	95·00
79	35	60c. black	30·00	25·00
66/79 Set of 14			£325	£325

The 60c. surcharged 'TWO—2—CENTS' in three lines is an essay made in December 1918 (*Price* £750).

ONE CENT   **ONE CENT**

(36)   (37)

ONE CENT

(38)

1897 (19 Oct). T **21** surch with Types **36/38** by the *Royal Gazette*, St John's, on stamps of various shades.

80	36	1c. on 3c. grey-purple	80·00	40·00
		a. Surch double, one diagonal	£1500	
		d. Vert pair, one without lower bar and 'ONE CENT'	£4000	
81	37	1c. on 3c. grey-purple	£200	£120
82	38	1c. on 3c. grey-purple	£600	£500

Nos. 80/82 occur in the same setting of 50 (10×5) applied twice to each sheet. T **36** appeared in the first four horizontal rows, T **37** on R. 5/1–8 and T **38** on R. 5/9 and 10.

Trial surcharges in red or red and black were not issued. (*Price* T **36** *in red* £1100, *in red and black* £1100; T **37** *in red* £3000, *in red and black* £3000; T **38** *in red* £7500, *in red and black* £8000).

These surcharges exist on stamps of various shades, but those on brown-grey are clandestine forgeries, having been produced by one of the printers at the *Royal Gazette*. On these forgeries the space between the horizontal bars is greater than on the originals.

39 Prince Edward later Duke of Windsor   **40** Queen Victoria   **41** King Edward VII when Prince of Wales

42 Queen Alexandra when Princess of Wales   **43** Queen Mary when Duchess of York   **44** King George V when Duke of York

(Recess A.B.N. Co)

1897 (7 Dec)–**1918**. Perf 12.

83	39	½c. olive (8.98)	3·50	2·50
		a. Imperf (pair)	£650	£450
84	40	1c. carmine	8·50	11·00
85		1c. blue-green (6.98)	19·00	20
		a. Yellow-green	21·00	20
		b. Imperf horiz (vert pair)	£300	
86	41	2c. orange	11·00	11·00
		a. Imperf (pair)	—	£500
87		2c. scarlet (6.98)	23·00	75
		a. Imperf (pair)	£375	£375

Newfoundland CANADA

88	42	b. Imperf between (pair).....................	£650	
		3c. orange (6.98)............................	32·00	30
		a. Imperf horiz (vert pair).................	£450	
		b. Imperf (pair)...............................	£375	£375
		c. Red-orange/bluish (6.18)................	50·00	3·50
89	43	4c. violet (21.10.01)........................	35·00	13·00
		a. Imperf (pair)...............................	£600	
90	44	5c. blue (6.99)..............................	50·00	5·00
83/90	Set of 8	....	£150	32·00

No. 88c was an emergency wartime printing made by the American Bank Note Co from the old plate, pending receipt of the then current 3c. from England.

The imperforate errors of this issue are found used, but only as philatelic 'by favour' items. It is possible that No. 86a only exists in this condition.

45 Map of Newfoundland

(Des and eng E. T. Loizeaux. Recess A.B.N. Co)

1908 (31 Aug). Perf 12.
| 94 | 45 | 2c. lake... | 38·00 | 1·00 |

46 King James I **47** Arms of Colonisation Co **48** John Guy

49 *Endeavour* (immigrant ship), 1610 **50** Cupids **51** Sir Francis Bacon

52 View of Mosquito **53** Logging Camp, Red Indian Lake **54** Paper Mills, Grand Falls

55 King Edward VII **56** King George V

1c. 'NFWFOUNDLAND' (Right pane, R. 5/1) **1c.** 'JAMRS' (Right pane, R. 5/2)

6c. (A) 'Z' in 'COLONIZATION' reversed. (B) 'Z' correct.

8c. 'MCSQUITO' for 'MOSQUITO'

(Litho Whitehead, Morris & Co Ltd)

1910 (15 Aug).

(a) Perf 12. Perf 12.
95	46	1c. green..	19·00	3·75
		a. 'NFWFOUNDLAND'............................	85·00	£110
		b. 'JAMRS'.....................................	85·00	£110
		c. Imperf between (horiz pair)................	£350	£375
96	47	2c. rose-carmine.............................	27·00	2·50
97	48	3c. olive.......................................	16·00	27·00
98	49	4c. violet......................................	27·00	21·00
99	50	5c. bright blue................................	50·00	15·00
100	51	6c. claret (A)..................................	65·00	£170
100a		6c. claret (B)..................................	40·00	£110
101	52	8c. bistre-brown...............................	70·00	£130
		a. 'MCSQUITO'.................................	£500	
102	53	9c. olive-green................................	75·00	£110
103	54	10c. purple-slate..............................	75·00	£140
104	55	12c. pale red-brown...........................	75·00	£100
		a. Imperf (pair)...............................	£350	
105	56	15c. black......................................	75·00	£130
95/105	Set of 11		£475	£700

(b) Perf 12×14. Perf 12×14.
106	46	1c. green..	9·00	18·00
		a. 'NFWFOUNDLAND'............................	70·00	£160
		b. 'JAMRS'.....................................	70·00	£160
		c. Imperf between (horiz pair)................	£700	£750
107	47	2c. rose-carmine.............................	10·00	50
		a. Imperf between (horiz pair)................	£750	
108	50	5c. bright blue (Perf 14×12).................	15·00	4·00

(c) Perf 12×11. Perf 12×11.
109	46	1c. green..	3·25	1·25
		a. Imperf between (horiz pair)................	£325	
		b. Imperf between (vert pair)................	£375	
		c. 'NFWFOUNDLAND'............................	45·00	60·00
		e. 'JAMRS'.....................................	45·00	60·00

(d) Perf 12×11½. Perf 12×11½.
| 110 | 47 | 2c. rose-carmine............................. | £500 | £350 |

(Dies eng Macdonald & Sons. Recess A. Alexander & Sons, Ltd)

1911 (7 Feb). As Types **51** to **56**, but recess printed. Perf 14.
111		6c. claret (B)..................................	20·00	50·00
112		8c. yellow-brown..............................	65·00	80·00
		a. Imperf between (horiz pair)................	£1100	
113		9c. sage-green.................................	75·00	£150
		a. Imperf between (horiz pair)................	£1100	
114		10c. purple-black..............................	90·00	£150
		a. Imperf between (horiz pair)................	£1100	
115		12c. red-brown.................................	75·00	75·00
116		15c. slate-green................................	75·00	£130
111/116	Set of 6		£350	£550

The 9c. and 15c. exist with papermaker's watermark 'E. TOWGOOD FINE'. Nos. 111/116 exist imperforate. (Price £250, unused or used, for each pair).

57 Queen Mary **58** King George V **59** Duke of Windsor when Prince of Wales **60** King George VI when Prince Albert

61 Princess Mary, the Princess Royal **62** Prince Henry, Duke of Gloucester **63** Prince George, Duke of Kent

7

CANADA Newfoundland

64 Prince John

65 Queen Alexandra

66 Duke of Connaught

67 Seal of Newfoundland

(1c. to 5c., 10c. eng and recess D.L.R.; others eng Macdonald & Co, recess A. Alexander & Sons)

1911 (19 June)–**16**. Coronation. Perf 13½×14 (comb) (1c. to 5c., 10c.) or 14 (line) (others).

117	57	1c. yellow-green	10·00	1·00
		a. Blue-green (1915)	25·00	1·00
118	58	2c. carmine	12·00	1·00
		a. Rose-red (blurred impression). Perf 14 (1916)	17·00	1·50
119	59	3c. red-brown	26·00	50·00
120	60	4c. purple	25·00	45·00
121	61	5c. ultramarine	10·00	3·00
122	62	6c. slate-grey	20·00	27·00
123	63	8c. aniline red	75·00	85·00
		a. Greenish blue	£100	£130
124	64	9c. violet-blue	40·00	55·00
125	65	10c. deep green	48·00	50·00
126	66	12c. plum	38·00	50·00
127	67	15c. lake	35·00	50·00
117/127		Set of 11	£300	£350

The 2c. rose-red, No. 118a is a poor wartime printing by Alexander & Sons.

Although No. 123 has a typical aniline appearance it is believed that the shade results from the thinning of non-aniline ink.

Nos. 117/118, 121 and 126/127 exist imperforate, without gum. (*Prices for* 1c., 2c., 5c., 12c., £275, *for* 15c. £100, *unused, per pair*).

FIRST TRANS-ATLANTIC AIR POST April, 1919.

68 Caribou (69)

(Des J. H. Noonan. Recess D.L.R.)

1919 (2 Jan). Newfoundland Contingent, 1914–1918. Perf 14.

130	68	1c. green (a) (b)	3·75	1·00
131		2c. scarlet (a) (b)	3·75	1·25
		a. Carmine-red (b)	25·00	1·50
132		3c. brown (a) (b)	8·50	1·00
		a. Red-brown (b)	16·00	1·00
133		4c. mauve (a)	13·00	1·50
		a. Purple (b)	28·00	1·25
134		5c. ultramarine (a) (b)	18·00	1·50
135		6c. slate-grey (a)	20·00	70·00
136		8c. bright magenta (a)	22·00	70·00
137		10c. deep grey-green (a)	16·00	12·00
138		12c. orange (a)	30·00	75·00
139		15c. indigo (a)	32·00	90·00
		a. Prussian blue (a)	£110	£150
140		24c. bistre-brown (a)	35·00	45·00
141		36c. sage-green (a)	30·00	55·00
130/141		Set of 12	£200	£375

Each value bears with 'Trail of the Caribou' the name of a different action: 1c. Suvla Bay; 3c. Gueudecourt; 4c. Beaumont Hamel; 6c. Monchy; 10c. Steenbeck; 15c. Langemarck; 24c. Cambrai; 36c. Combles; 2c., 5c., 8c., and 12c. inscribed 'Royal Naval Reserve-Ubique'.

Perforations. Two perforating heads were used: (*a*) comb 14×13.9; (*b*) line 14.1×14.1.

Nos. 130/141 exist imperforate, without gum. (*Price* £350 *unused, for each pair*)

1919 (12 Apr). Air. No. 132 optd with T **69**, by Robinson & Co Ltd, at the offices of the *Daily News*.

142	68	3c. brown	£25000	£12000

These stamps franked correspondence carried by Lieutenant H. Hawker on his Atlantic flight. 18 were damaged and destroyed, 95 used on letters, 11 given as presentation copies, and the remaining 76 were sold in aid of the Marine Disasters Fund.

1919 (19 Apr). Nos. 132 inscribed in 'MS'. 'Aerial Atlantic Mail. J.A.R.'

142a	68	3c. brown	£70000	£20000

This provisional was made by W. C. Campbell, the Secretary of the Postal Department, and the initials are those of the Postmaster, J. A. Robinson, for use on correspondence intended to be carried on the abortive Morgan-Raynham Trans-Atlantic flight. The mail was eventually delivered by sea.

In addition to the 25 to 30 used examples, one unused, no gum, example of No. 142a is known.

Single examples of a similar overprint on the 2c. (No. 131) and 5c. (No. 134) are known used *on cover*, the former with an unoverprinted example of the same value.

Trans-Atlantic AIR POST, 1919. ONE DOLLAR. THREE CENTS

(70) (71)

1919 (9 June). Air. No. 75 surch with T **70** by *Royal Gazette*, St John's.

143	31	$1 on 15c. bright scarlet	£130	£150
		a. No comma after 'AIR POST'	£160	£180
		b. As var a and no stop after '1919'	£375	£450
		c. As var a and 'A' of 'AIR' under 'a' of 'Trans'	£375	£450

These stamps were issued for use on the mail carried on the first successful flight across the Atlantic by Captain J. Alcock and Lieutenant A. Brown, and on other projected Trans-Atlantic flights (Alcock flown cover, *Price* £3000).

The surcharge was applied in a setting of 25 (5×5) of which 16 were normal, 7 as No. 143a, 1 as No. 143b (R. 3/4) and 1 as No. 143c (R. 5/2).

1920 (13 Sept). Nos. 75 and 77/78 surch as T **71**, by *Royal Gazette* (2c. with only one bar, at top of stamp).

A. Bars of surch 10½ mm *apart. B. Bars* 13½ mm *apart.*

144	33	2c. on 30c. slate-blue (24.9)	8·00	38·00
		a. Surch inverted	£1500	£1600
145	31	3c. on 15c. bright scarlet (A.) (13.9)	£250	£300
		a. Surch inverted	£3500	
146		3c. on 15c. bright scarlet (B.) (13.9)	40·00	42·00
147	34	3c. on 35c. red (15.9)	18·00	27·00
		a. Surch inverted	£2750	
		b. Lower bar omitted	£250	£250
		c. 'THREE' omitted	£1200	£1600

The price for No. 147b is for an example with lower bar entirely missing. The bar may be found in all stages of incompleteness, such examples being of little value (R. 3/5 in the setting of 25 (5×5)).

On No. 147c, the 'THREE' is never completley missing, with traces of the top or bottom of the letters always visible.

The 6c. T **27** surcharged 'THREE CENTS', in red or black, is an essay (*Price* £1000). The 2c. on 30c. with red surcharge is a colour trial (*Price* £1300).

AIR MAIL to Halifax, N.S. 1921.

(72)

1921 (16 Nov). Air. No. 78 optd with T **72** by *Royal Gazette*.

I. 2¾ mm *between 'AIR' and 'MAIL'*

148	34	35c. red	£150	£100
		a. No stop after '1921'	£130	90·00
		b. No stop and first '1' of '1921' below 'f' of 'Halifax'	£375	£275
		c. As No. 148, inverted	£6000	
		d. As No. 148a, inverted	£4500	
		e. As No. 148b, inverted	£25000	

II. 1½ mm *between 'AIR' and 'MAIL'*

148f	34	35c. red	£180	£120
		g. No stop after '1921'	£225	£150
		h. No stop and first '1' of '1921' below 'f' of 'Halifax'	£375	£275
		i. As No. 148f, inverted	£8000	
		k. As No. 148g, inverted	£15000	
		l. As No. 148h, inverted	£25000	

T **72** was applied as a setting of 25 which contained ten stamps as No. 148a, seven as No. 148, four as No. 148f, two as No. 148fg, one as No. 148g and one as No. 148fh.

73 Twin Hills, Tor's Cove

74 South West Arm, Trinity

75 Statue

Newfoundland CANADA

76 Humber River 77 Coast at Trinity 78 Upper Steadies, Humber River

79 Quidi Vidi, near St John's 80 Caribou Crossing Lake 81 Humber River Canyon

82 Shell Bird Island 83 Mount Moriah, Bay of Islands 84 Humber River near Little Rapids

85 Placentia 86 Topsail Falls

88 Newfoundland and Labrador 89 SS *Caribou* 90 King George V and Queen Mary

91 Duke of Windsor when Prince of Wales 92 Express Train 93 Newfoundland Hotel, St John's

94 Heart's Content 95 Cabot Tower, St John's 96 War Memorial, St John's

97 GPO, St John's 98 Vickers Vimy Aircraft 99 Parliament House, St John's

100 Grand Falls, Labrador

(Recess D.L.R.)

1923 (9 July)–**24**. Types **73**/**86**. Perf 14 (comb or line).

149	73	1c. green	2·25	1·00
150	74	2c. carmine	1·00	1·00
		a. Imperf (pair)	£200	
151	75	3c. brown	3·75	1·00
152	76	4c. deep purple	1·10	1·00
153	77	5c. ultramarine	6·50	1·75
154	78	6c. slate	13·00	20·00
155	79	8c. purple	19·00	5·00
156	80	9c. slate-green	25·00	38·00
157	81	10c. violet	18·00	11·00
		a. Purple	26·00	4·00
158	82	11c. sage-green	8·00	40·00
159	83	12c. lake	8·50	20·00
160	84	15c. Prussian blue	9·00	40·00
161	85	20c. chestnut (28.4.24)	32·00	22·00
162	86	24c. sepia (22.4.24)	75·00	£100
149/162	Set of 14		£200	£250

Perforations. Three perforating heads were used: comb 13.8×14 (all values); line 13.7 and 14, and combinations of these two (for all except 6c., 8c., 9c. and 11c.).

Nos. 149 and 151/160 also exist imperforate, but these are usually without gum. (*Price per pair from £250, unused*).

Air Mail
DE PINEDO
1927
(87)

1927 (18 May). Air. No. 79 optd with T **87**, by Robinson & Co, Ltd.

163	35	60c. black (R.)	£42000	£13000

For the mail carried by de Pinedo to Europe 300 stamps were overprinted, 230 used on correspondence, 66 presented to de Pinedo, Government Officials, etc., and four damaged and destroyed. Stamps without overprint were also used.

(Recess D.L.R.)

1928 (3 Jan)–**29**. Publicity issue. Perf 14 (1c.) 13½×13 (2c., 3c., 5c., 6c., 10c., 14c., 20c.), 13×13½ (4c.) (all comb), or 14–13½* (line) (others).

164	88	1c. deep green	5·00	1·50
165	89	2c. carmine	6·50	50
166	90	3c. brown	13·00	2·75
		a. Perf 14–13½ (line)	7·50	2·50
167	91	4c. mauve	7·50	4·50
		a. Rose-purple (1929)	16·00	14·00
168	92	5c. slate-grey	20·00	19·00
		a. Perf 14–13½ (line)	48·00	16·00
169	93	6c. ultramarine	18·00	55·00
		a. Perf 14–13½ (line)	40·00	50·00
170	94	8c. red-brown	13·00	55·00
171	95	9c. deep green	3·50	27·00
172	96	10c. deep violet	30·00	35·00
		a. Perf 14–13½ (line)	9·00	35·00
173	97	12c. carmine-lake	4·00	27·00
174	95	14c. brown-purple (8.28)	45·00	17·00
		a. Perf 14–13½ (line)	30·00	13·00
175	98	15c. deep blue	16·00	50·00
176	99	20c. grey-black	35·00	21·00
		a. Perf 14–13½ (line)	11·00	14·00
177	97	28c. deep green (11.28)	28·00	70·00
178	100	30c. sepia	12·00	25·00
164/178	Set of 15 (cheapest)		£170	£350

* Exact gauges for the various perforations are: 14 comb = 14×13.9; 13½×13 comb = 13.5×12.75; 14–13½ line = 14–13.75.
See also Nos. 179/187 and 198/208.

CANADA Newfoundland

Differences between De La Rue and Perkins Bacon Printings of Types 88–99

De La Rue	Perkins Bacon

1c. 'C. NORMAN' is below 'C.BAULD'	**1c.** 'C. NORMAN' is above 'C.BAULD'
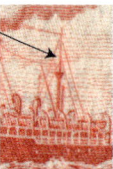	
2c. Two wires to left of rear mast	**2c.** One wire to left of rear mast

3c. The jewels in the band of the crown are colourless	**3c.** The jewels are represented by dark dashes
	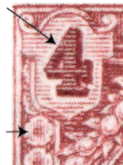
4c. The shading of the '4' is cross-hatched	**4c.** The '4' is shaded horizontally

5c. The tips of the leaves framing the value tablets are rounded	**5c.** The tips of the leaves are pointed

6c. The lower leaves in the corner ornaments do not curl upwards at the end. Full stop after 'ST. JOHNS'	**6c.** The lower leaves curl upwards at the ends. No full stop after 'ST. JOHNS'

10c. The torch at left is topped by a single flame. Full stop after 'ST. JOHNS'

10c. The torch is topped by a double flame. No full stop after 'ST. JOHNS'

15c. 'L' of 'LEAVING' under 'AI' of 'AIRPLANE' in inscription

15c. 'L' of 'LEAVING' under 'T' of 'FIRST'

20c. The points at the foot of the 'W' of 'NEWFOUNDLAND' are flattened

20c. The points of the 'W' are sharp

There are many other differences between the work of the two printers.

1929 (10 Aug)–**31**. Perkins Bacon printing. Former types re-engraved. No wmk. Perf 14 (comb) (1c.), 13½ (comb) (2c., 6c.), 14–13½ (line) (20c.) or 13½×14 (comb) (others)*.

179	**88**	1c. green (26.9.29)	8·00	1·50
		a. Perf 14–13½ (line)	8·50	1·00
		b. Imperf between (vert pair)	£250	
		c. Imperf (pair)	£160	
180	**89**	2c. scarlet	2·00	1·00
		a. Imperf (pair)	£170	
		b. Perf 14–13½ (line)	6·00	1·25
181	**90**	3c. red-brown	1·50	1·00
		a. Imperf (pair)	£170	
182	**91**	4c. reddish purple (26.8.29)	3·00	1·25
		a. Imperf (pair)	£180	
183	**92**	5c. deep grey-green (14.9.29)	14·00	5·00
184	**93**	6c. ultramarine (8.11.29)	18·00	28·00
		a. Perf 14–13½ (line)	5·00	32·00
185	**96**	10c. violet (5.10.29)	11·00	5·50
186	**98**	15c. blue (1.30)	35·00	£100
187	**99**	20c. black (1.1.31)	75·00	60·00
179/187	Set of 9		£150	£170

* Exact gauges for the various perforations are: 14 comb = 14×13.9; 13½ comb = 13.6×13.5; 14–13½ line = 14–13.75; 13½ ×14 comb = 13.6×13.8.

Trans-Atlantic AIR MAIL By B. M. "Columbia" September 1930 Fifty Cents

THREE CENTS

(101) (102)

(Surch by Messrs D. R. Thistle, St John's)

1929 (23 Aug). No. 154 surch with T **101**.

188		3c. on 6c. slate (R.)	5·00	20·00
		a. Surch inverted	£1000	£1400
		b. Surch in black	£1600	

The issued surcharge shows 3 mm space between 'CENTS' and the bar. The black surcharge also exists with 5 mm space, from a trial setting (*Price*, £900).

1930 (25 Sept). Air. No. 141 surch with T **102** by Messrs D. R. Thistle.

191	**68**	50c. on 36c. sage-green	£6000	£6000

Newfoundland CANADA

103 Aeroplane and Dog-team

104 Vickers-Vimy Biplane and Early Sailing Packet

105 Routes of Historic Transatlantic Flights

106

(Des A. B. Perlin. Recess P.B.)

1931. Air. Perf 14.

(a) Without wmk (2.1.31).

192	103	15c. chocolate	9·00	18·00
		a. Imperf between (horiz pair)	£1000	
		b. Imperf between (vert pair)	£1200	
		c. Imperf (pair)	£550	
193	104	50c. green	38·00	55·00
		a. Imperf between (horiz pair)	£1300	£1200
		b. Imperf between (vert pair)	£1700	
		c. Imperf (pair)	£850	
194	105	$1 deep blue	50·00	95·00
		a. Imperf between (horiz pair)	£1300	
		b. Imperf between (vert pair)	£1400	
		c. Imperf (pair)	£900	
192/194		Set of 3	85·00	£150

(b) Wmk W 106, (sideways*) (13.3.31).

195	103	15c. chocolate	13·00	32·00
		a. Pair, with and without wmk	42·00	
		b. Imperf between (horiz pair)	£1000	
		c. Imperf between (vert pair)	£1200	
		ca. Ditto, one without wmk (vert pair)	£1700	
		d. Imperf (pair)	£600	
		e. Wmk Cross (pair)	£160	
196	104	50c. green	35·00	75·00
		a. Imperf between (horiz pair)	£1100	
		b. Imperf between (vert pair)	£1600	
		c. Imperf (pair)	£550	
		d. Pair, with and without wmk	£900	
		w. Wmk top of shield to right	90·00	
197	105	$1 deep blue	80·00	£150
		a. Imperf between (horiz pair)	£1400	
		b. Imperf between (vert pair)	£1200	
		c. Imperf horiz (pair)	£800	
		d. Pair, with and without wmk	£900	
		e. Imperf (pair)	£800	
195/197		Set of 3	£110	£225

The normal sideways wmk on this issue shows the top of the shield to right on the 15c., but top of the shield to left on the 50c. and $1.

> **WITH AND WITHOUT WMK PAIRS** listed in the issues from No. 195a onwards must have one stamp *completely* without any trace of watermark.

1931 (25 March–July). Perkins Bacon printing (re-engraved types). W **106** (sideways on 1c., 4c., 30c.*). Perf 13½ (1c.) or 13½×14 (others), both comb**.

198	88	1c. green (7.31)	17·00	3·00
		a. Imperf between (horiz pair)	£750	
199	89	2c. scarlet (7.31)	11·00	6·00
		w. Wmk inverted	75·00	
200	90	3c. red-brown (7.31)	8·50	4·75
		w. Wmk inverted	75·00	
201	91	4c. reddish purple (7.31)	9·00	1·25
202	92	5c. deep grey-green (7.31)	7·50	23·00
203	93	6c. ultramarine	8·00	40·00
		w. Wmk inverted	90·00	
204	94	8c. chestnut (1.4.31)	48·00	55·00
		w. Wmk inverted	95·00	£110
205	96	10c. violet (1.4.31)	42·00	48·00
206	98	15c. blue (1.7.31)	35·00	85·00
207	99	20c. black (1.7.31)	60·00	27·00
208	100	30c. sepia (1.7.31)	45·00	55·00
198/208		Set of 11	£250	£300

* On the sideways watermark stamps the top of the shield is to the left, *as seen from the back of the stamp*.
** Exact gauges for the two perforations are: 13½ = 13.6×13.5; 13½×14 = 13.6×13.8.

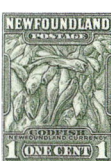
107 Atlantic Cod

108 King George V

109 Queen Mary

110 Duke of Windsor when Prince of Wales

111 Caribou

112 Queen Elizabeth II when Princess

113 Atlantic Salmon

114 Newfoundland Dog

115 Harp Seal

116 Cape Race

117 Sealing Fleet

118 Fishing Fleet

(Recess P.B.)

1932 (2 Jan). W **106** (sideways* on vert designs). Perf 13½ (comb).

209	107	1c. green	3·75	75
		a. Imperf (pair)	£225	
		b. Perf 13 (line)	23·00	55·00
		ba. Imperf between (vert pair)	£180	
		w. Wmk top of shield to right	70·00	
210	108	2c. carmine	1·50	75
		a. Imperf (pair)	£225	
		c. Perf 13 (line)	23·00	45·00
		w. Wmk top of shield to right	70·00	
211	109	3c. orange-brown	1·50	75
		a. Imperf (pair)	£100	
		c. Perf 13 (line)	27·00	55·00
		ca. Imperf between (vert pair)	£350	
		d. Perf 14 (line). Small holes	35·00	55·00
		w. Wmk top of shield to right	75·00	
212	110	4c. bright violet	13·00	2·25
		w. Wmk top of shield to right		
213	111	5c. maroon	10·00	8·00
		a. Imperf (pair)	£180	
		w. Wmk top of shield to right	75·00	
214	112	6c. light blue	14·00	16·00
215	113	10c. black-brown	1·00	65
		a. Imperf (pair)	£100	
		w. Wmk inverted	10·00	
216	114	14c. black	7·50	6·00
		a. Imperf (pair)	£180	

11

CANADA Newfoundland

217	115	15c. claret		1·25	2·00
		a. Imperf (pair)		£180	
		b. Perf 14 (line)		8·50	12·00
218	116	20c. green		2·00	1·00
		a. Imperf (pair)		£200	
		b. Perf 14 (line)		£150	£150
		w. Wmk inverted		48·00	
219	117	25c. slate		3·50	2·75
		a. Imperf (pair)		£225	
		b. Perf 14 (line)		80·00	90·00
		ba. Imperf between (vert pair)		£600	
220	118	30c. ultramarine		55·00	48·00
		a. Imperf (pair)		£750	
		b. Imperf between (vert pair)		£1600	
		c. Perf 14 (line)		£500	
209/220 Set of 12				£100	80·00

* The normal sideways watermark shows the top of the shield to left, as seen from the back of the stamp.

The Caribou shown on T **111** is taken from the monument to the Royal Newfoundland Regiment, near Beaumont Hamel, France.

Nos. 209b, 210c and 211c were only issued in stamp booklets.

For similar stamps in different perforations see Nos. 222/228c and 276/289.

TRANS-ATLANTIC
WEST TO EAST
Per Dornier DO-X
May, 1932.
One Dollar and Fifty Cents

(119)

1932 (19 May). Air. No. 197 surch as T **119**, by Messrs. D. R. Thistle. Perf 14.

221	105	$1.50 on $1 deep blue (R.)	£250	£225
		a. Surch inverted	£21000	

120 Queen Mother, when Duchess of York

121 Corner Brook Paper Mills

122 Loading Iron Ore, Bell Island

5c. Die I   **5c.** Die II

No. 225. There are two dies of the 5c., Die I only being used for No. 213 and both dies for the violet stamp. In Die II the antler pointing to the 'T' of 'POSTAGE' is taller than the one pointing to the 'S' and the individual hairs on the underside of the Caribou's tail are distinct.

(Recess P.B.)

1932 (15 Aug)–**38**. W **106** (sideways* on vert designs). Perf 13½ (comb.)

222	107	1c. grey		3·25	10
		a. Imperf (pair)		48·00	
		c. Perf 14 (line)		8·50	23·00
		d. Perf 14 (line). Small holes		30·00	55·00
		e. Pair, with and without wmk		95·00	
		w. Wmk top of shield to right		65·00	50·00
223	108	2c. green		2·50	10
		a. Imperf (pair)		40·00	
		c. Perf 14 (line)		8·50	23·00
		ca. Imperf between (horiz pair)		£275	
		d. Perf 14 (line). Small holes		23·00	50·00
		e. Pair, with and without wmk		95·00	
		w. Wmk top of shield to right		50·00	
224	110	4c. carmine (21.7.34)		7·00	40
		a. Imperf (pair)		70·00	
		b. Perf 14 (line)		8·50	16·00
		ba. Imperf between (horiz pair)		£350	
		bb. Imperf between (vert pair)		£140	
		c. Pair, with and without wmk		£100	
		w. Wmk top of shield to right		70·00	
225	111	5c. violet (Die I)		6·50	1·75
		a. Imperf (pair)		75·00	
		b. Perf 14 (line). Small holes		27·00	55·00
		c. Die II		1·00	30
		ca. Imperf (pair)		70·00	
		cb. Perf 14 (line)		25·00	50·00
		cbw. Wmk top of shield to right		80·00	
		cc. Imperf between (horiz pair)		£275	
		cd. Pair, with and without wmk		£180	
		cw. Wmk top of shield to right		75·00	
226	120	7c. red-brown		3·00	4·50
		b. Perf 14 (line)		£250	
		ba. Imperf between (horiz pair)		£650	
		c. Imperf (pair)		£190	
		w. Wmk top of shield to right		£110	
227	121	8c. brownish red		3·75	2·00
		a. Imperf (pair)		£110	
		w. Wmk inverted			
228	122	24c. bright blue		2·00	3·25
		a. Imperf (pair)		£350	
		b. Doubly printed		£1700	
		w. Wmk inverted		75·00	
228c	118	48c. red-brown (1.1.38)		15·00	14·00
		ca. Imperf (pair)		£140	
222/228c Set of 8				32·00	18·00

* The normal sideways watermark shows the top of the shield to left, as seen from the back of the stamp.

No. 223. Two dies exist of the 2c., Die I was used for No. 210 and both dies for No. 223. The differences, though numerous, are very slight.

The 2c., 4c. and 5c. (Die I) can be found with two design widths (20.5mm and 21mm), resulting from differences in printing from flat-bed presses on dampened paper and rotary presses on dry paper.

For similar stamps in a slightly larger size and perforated 12½ or 13½ (5c.) see Nos. 276/289.

(**123**) 'L. & S.'—Land and Sea

1933 (9 Feb). No. 195 optd with T **123** for ordinary postal use, by Messrs D. R. Thistle. W **106** (sideways top of shield to right from back). Perf 14.

229	103	15c. chocolate	10·00	25·00
		a. Pair, one without wmk	30·00	
		b. Opt reading up	£6000	
		c. Vertical pair, one without opt	£7000	

124 Put to Flight   **125** Land of Heart's Delight

126 Spotting the Herd   **127** News from Home

128 Labrador

(Des J. Scott. Recess P.B.)

1933 (9 June). Air. Types **124/128** and similar horiz designs. W **106** (sideways*). Perf 14 (5c., 30c., 75c.) or 11½ (10c., 60c.).

230	124	5c. red-brown		22·00	22·00
		a. Imperf (pair)		£225	
		b. Imperf between (horiz pair)		£1000	
		c. Imperf between (vert pair)		£1200	
231	125	10c. orange-yellow		20·00	35·00
		a. Imperf (pair)		£200	
232	126	30c. light blue		42·00	50·00
		a. Imperf (pair)		£750	
233	127	60c. green		50·00	£120
		a. Imperf (pair)		£750	
234	128	75c. yellow-brown		55·00	£120
		a. Imperf (pair)		£650	
		b. Imperf between (horiz or vert pair)		£6000	
		w. Wmk top of shield to left		£150	
230/234 Set of 5				£170	£325

* The normal sideways watermark shows the top of the shield to right, as seen from the back of the stamp.

Newfoundland CANADA

1933 GEN. BALBO FLIGHT. $4.50
(129)

(Surch by Robinson & Co, St John's)

1933 (24 July). Air. Balbo Transatlantic Mass Formation Flight. No. 234 surch with T **129**. W **106**. Perf 14.

235		$4.50 on 75c. yellow-brown	£275	£350
		a. Surch inverted	£90000	
		b. Surch on 10c. (No. 231)	£75000	
		w. Wmk top of shield to left	£2500	

No. 235a. When this error was discovered the stamps were ordered to be officially destroyed but four copies which had been torn were recovered and skilfully repaired. In addition, four undamaged examples exist and the price quoted is for one of these (*Price for repaired example, £20,000, unused*).

130 Sir Humphrey Gilbert

131 Compton Castle, Devon

132 Gilbert Coat of Arms

133 Eton College

134 Anchor Token

135 Gilbert Commissioned by Elizabeth I

136 Fleet Leaving Plymouth, 1583

137 Arrival at St John's

138 Annexation, 5th August, 1583

139 Royal Arms

140 Gilbert in the *Squirrel*

141 Map of Newfoundland, 1626

142 Queen Elizabeth I

143 Gilbert's Statue at Truro

(Recess P.B.)

1933 (3 Aug). 350th Anniversary of the Annexation by Sir Humphrey Gilbert. Types **130/143**. W **106** (sideways* on vert designs). Perf 13½ (comb†).

236	**130**	1c. slate	1·25	1·50
		a. Imperf (pair)	60·00	
237	**131**	2c. green	2·00	70
		a. Imperf (pair)	60·00	
		b. Doubly printed	£550	
238	**132**	3c. chestnut	2·50	1·25
		w. Wmk top of shield to right	60·00	90·00
239	**133**	4c. carmine	1·00	50
		a. Imperf (pair)	65·00	
240	**134**	5c. violet	2·00	1·00
241	**135**	7c. greenish blue	21·00	25·00
		a. Perf 14 (line)	22·00	60·00
242	**136**	8c. vermilion	11·50	25·00
		a. Brownish red	£550	
		b. Bisected (4c.) (*on cover*)	†	£425
243	**137**	9c. ultramarine	9·00	26·00
		a. Imperf (pair)	£550	
		b. Perf 14 (line)	95·00	£110
244	**138**	10c. brown-lake	9·00	21·00
		a. Imperf (pair)	£550	
		b. Perf 14 (line)	£120	£160
245	**139**	14c. grey-black	22·00	50·00
		a. Perf 14 (line)	28·00	70·00
		aw. Wmk top of shield to right	£100	
246	**140**	15c. claret	26·00	50·00
		w. Wmk top of shield to right	12·00	35·00
247	**141**	20c. grey-green	20·00	25·00
		a. Perf 14 (line)	38·00	70·00
		w. Wmk inverted	90·00	
248	**142**	24c. maroon	22·00	35·00
		a. Imperf (pair)	£250	
		b. Perf 14 (line)	42·00	55·00
		w. Wmk top of shield to right	45·00	
249	**143**	32c. olive-black	21·00	75·00
		a. Perf 14 (line)	25·00	95·00
		w. Wmk top of shield to right	30·00	80·00
236/249 Set of 14			£120	£275

* The normal sideways watermark shows the top of the shield to left, *as seen from the back of the stamp*.

† Exact gauges for the two perforations are: 13½ comb = 13.4; 14 line = 13.8.

1935 (6 May). Silver Jubilee. As Nos. 91/94 of Antigua, but printed by B.W. Perf 11×12.

250	4c. rosine	1·00	1·75
251	5c. bright violet	1·25	4·25
252	7c. blue	4·75	7·00
253	24c. olive-green	6·00	30·00
250/253 Set of 4		11·50	40·00
250s/253s Perf 'SPECIMEN' Set of 4		£225	

1937 (12 May). Coronation Issue. As Nos. 95/97 of Antigua, but name and value uncoloured on coloured background. Perf 11×11½.

254	2c. green	1·00	3·00
255	4c. carmine	1·60	4·00
256	5c. purple	2·00	4·00
254/256 Set of 3		4·00	10·00
254s/256s Perf 'SPECIMEN' Set of 3		£150	

144 Atlantic Cod

145 Map of Newfoundland

146 Caribou

147 Corner Brook Paper Mills

148 Atlantic Salmon

149 Newfoundland Dog

150 Harp Seal

151 Cape Race

CANADA Newfoundland

152 Bell Island **153** Sealing Fleet

154 The Banks Fishing Fleet

Die I   Die II

No. 258. In Die II the shading of the King's face is heavier and dots have been added down the ridge of the nose. The top frame line is thicker and more uniform.

1c. Fish-hook flaw (R. 1/7 or 3/3)   **3c.** 'Cigar stub' variety (R. 1/9)    **7c.** Re-entry to right of design (inscr oval, tree and value) (R. 4/8)

20c. Extra chimney (R. 6/5)

(Des and eng J. B. Dickinson & Co. Recess P.B.)

1937 (12 May). Additional Coronation Issue. Types **144**/**154**. W **106**. Perf 14 (line)*.

257	144	1c. grey	3·50	30
		a. Pair, with and without wmk	35·00	
		b. Fish-hook flaw	35·00	20·00
		cw. Wmk inverted	70·00	
		d. Perf 13½ (line)	5·00	1·25
		da. Pair, with and without wmk	50·00	
		db. Fish-hook flaw	45·00	32·00
		e. Perf 13 (comb)	45·00	80·00
		ea. Pair, with and without wmk		
		eb. Fish-hook flaw	£200	£425
258	145	3c. orange-brown (Die I)	38·00	7·50
		aa. Cigar Stub	£100	
		a. Pair, with and without wmk	£250	
		b. Imperf between (horiz pair)	£750	
		c. Perf 13½ (line)	38·00	11·00
		ca. Pair, with and without wmk	£250	
		cb. Imperf between (vert pair)	£650	
		cc. Imperf vert (horiz pair)		
		cd. Cigar Stub	£100	
		d. Perf 13 (comb)	22·00	4·00
		da. Cigar Stub	75·00	
		e. Die II (Perf 14, line)	18·00	14·00
		ea. Pair, with and without wmk	£225	
		ec. Perf 13½ (line)	15·00	15·00
		eca. Pair, with and without wmk	£225	
		ecb. Imperf between (vert pair)	£950	
		ed. Perf 13 (comb)	9·50	5·00
		eda. Pair, with and without wmk	£180	
259	146	7c. bright ultramarine	4·00	1·25
		a. Pair, with and without wmk	£150	
		b. Re-entry at right	85·00	85·00
		c. Perf 13½ (line)	4·25	1·75
		ca. Pair, with and without wmk	£160	
		cb. Re-entry at right	85·00	95·00
		d. Perf 13 (comb)	£1200	£800
		db. Re-entry at right	£4000	
		e. Perf compound 13½×14 (line)		
260	147	8c. scarlet	5·50	4·00
		a. Pair, with and without wmk	£130	
		b. Imperf vert, horiz pair	£1300	
		c. Imperf between (vert pair)	£1300	
		d. Imperf (pair)	£450	
		e. Perf 13½ (line)	8·00	8·50
		ea. Pair, with and without wmk	£160	
		eb. Imperf between (vert pair)		
		f. Perf 13 (comb)	24·00	29·00
261	148	10c. blackish brown	8·00	9·00
		a. Pair, with and without wmk	£170	
		b. Perf 13½ (line)	10·00	13·00
		ba. Pair, with and without wmk	£170	
		c. Perf 13 (comb)	3·25	20·00
		cw. Wmk inverted	£110	
262	149	14c. black	3·00	4·00
		a. Pair, with and without wmk	£150	
		b. Perf 13½ (line)	3·75	6·00
		ba. Pair, with and without wmk	£150	
		c. Perf 13 (comb)	£28000	£18000
		d. Perf compound 14×13½ (line)		
263	150	15c. claret	21·00	9·00
		a. Pair, with and without wmk	£180	
		bw. Wmk inverted	£150	
		c. Perf 13½ (line)	26·00	13·00
		ca. Pair, with and without wmk	£200	
		cb. Imperf between (vert pair)	£2250	
		d. Perf 13 (comb)	48·00	75·00
		da. Pair, with and without wmk	£325	
264	151	20c. green	11·00	21·00
		a. Pair, with and without wmk	£160	
		c. Extra chimney	£130	
		dw. Wmk inverted	£180	
		e. Perf 13½ (line)	11·00	23·00
		ea. Pair, with and without wmk	£250	
		eb. Imperf between (vert pair)	£2500	
		ec. Extra chimney	£140	£200
		f. Perf 13 (comb)	8·00	10·00
		fc. Extra chimney	£120	
		fw. Wmk inverted	£275	
265	152	24c. light blue	2·75	3·00
		a. Pair, with and without wmk	£275	
		c. Perf 13½ (line)	2·75	3·00
		ca. Pair, with and without wmk	£275	
		cb. Imperf between (vert pair)	£4250	
		d. Perf 13 (comb)	50·00	70·00
266	153	25c. slate	5·50	4·50
		a. Pair, with and without wmk	£225	
		b. Perf 13½ (line)	8·00	6·00
		ba. Pair, with and without wmk	£250	
		c. Perf 13 (comb)	50·00	£120
267	154	48c. slate-purple	11·00	6·50
		a. Pair, with and without wmk	£350	
		b. Imperf between (vert pair)	£3750	
		c. Perf 13½ (line)	17·00	14·00
		ca. Pair, with and without wmk	£400	
		cb. Imperf between (vert pair)	£3750	
		cw. Wmk inverted	£350	
		d. Perf 13 (comb)	65·00	£150
257/267		Set of 11	60·00	50·00

The line perforations measure 14.1 (14) or 13.7 (13½). The comb perforation measures 13.3×13.2.

The 1c. has been reported with compound perforations of 13½ and 14, but we have not seen an example.

The paper used had the watermarks spaced for smaller format stamps. In consequence, the individual watermarks are out of alignment so that for instance stamps from the second vertical column or the bottom horizontal row were sometimes without watermark.

Newfoundland CANADA

155 King George VI
156 Queen Mother

157 Queen Elizabeth II as princess
158 Queen Mary

(Recess P.B.)

1938 (12 May). Types **155**/**158**. W **106** (sideways*). Perf 13½ (comb).
268	155	2c. green	6·50	1·75
		a. Pair, with and without wmk	£250	
		b. Imperf (pair)	£130	
		w. Wmk top of shield to right	£100	
269	156	3c. carmine	2·00	1·00
		a. Perf 14 (line)	£1000	£650
		b. Pair, with and without wmk	£375	
		c. Imperf (pair)	£130	
		d. Printed double, one albino	£250	
270	157	4c. light blue	8·00	1·00
		a. Pair, with and without wmk	£150	
		b. Imperf (pair)	£120	
		w. Wmk top of shield to right	£100	
271	158	7c. deep ultramarine	2·50	12·00
		a. Pair, with and without wmk	£225	
		b. Imperf (pair)	£190	
268/271 Set of 4			18·00	14·00

* The normal sideways watermark shows the top of the shield to left, as seen from the back of the stamp.
  For similar designs, perf 12½, see Nos. 277/281.

159 King George VI and Queen Elizabeth

(Recess B.W.)

1939 (17 June). Royal Visit. No wmk. Perf 13½.
272	159	5c. deep ultramarine	5·00	1·50

 CENTS

(160)

'CENTL' (R. 5/3)

1939 (20 Nov). No. 272 surch as T **160**, at St John's.
273	159	2c. on 5c. deep ultramarine (Br.)	2·50	50
274		4c. on 5c. deep ultramarine (C.)	2·00	2·50
		a. 'CENTL'	55·00	55·00

161 Grenfell on the *Strathcona* (after painting by Gribble)
162 Memorial University College

(Recess C.B.N.)

1941 (1 Dec). 50th Anniversary of Sir Wilfred Grenfell's Labrador Mission. Perf 12.
275	161	5c. blue	30	1·50

Damaged 'A' (R. 5/9)

(Recess Waterlow)

1941 (Oct)–**44**. W **106** (sideways* on vert designs). Perf 12½ (line).
276	107	1c. grey (14.8.42)	20	2·75
		w. Wmk top of shield to right	75·00	
277	155	2c. green (11.41)	40	75
		w. Wmk top of shield to right	55·00	
278	156	3c. carmine (10.41)	50	30
		a. Pair, with and without wmk	£140	
		b. Damaged 'A'	90·00	50·00
		w. Wmk top of shield to right	55·00	
279	157	4c. blue (As No. 270) (10.41)	6·00	40
		a. Pair, with and without wmk	£250	
		w. Wmk top of shield to right	70·00	
280	111	5c. violet (Die I) (Perf 13½ comb) (10.41)	£180	
		a. Perf 12½ (line) (6.42)	3·00	1·00
		ab. Pair, with and without wmk	£225	
		ac. Printed double	£750	
		ad. Imperf vert (horiz pair)	£650	
		b. Imperf (pair)	£225	
281	158	7c. deep ultramarine (As No. 271) (3.43)	14·00	29·00
		a. Pair, with and without wmk	£350	
282	121	8c. rose-red (9.42)	2·25	4·50
		a. Pair, with and without wmk	£225	
283	113	10c. black-brown (4.43)	2·00	2·25
284	114	14c. black (1.44)	10·00	14·00
		a. Imperf between (vert pair)		
285	115	15c. claret (7.43)	6·50	8·50
286	116	20c. green (1.44)	6·50	8·50
287	122	24c. blue (4.43)	3·50	25·00
		w. Wmk inverted	90·00	
288	117	25c. slate (4.43)	11·00	21·00
289	118	48c. red-brown (1.43)	6·00	9·50
276/289 Set of 14			60·00	£110

* The normal sideways watermark shows the top of the shield to left, as seen from the back of the stamp.
  Nos. 279 and 281 were printed from the original Perkins Bacon plates. New plates were made for the other values, using the original dies of Nos. 282/287 and 289, but new (1c., 25c.) or re-engraved (2c., 3c., 5c.) dies for the remaining values.
  No. 280. For Die I see note relating to No. 225.

(Recess C.B.N.)

1943 (1 Jan). Perf 12.
290	162	30c. carmine	2·50	5·50

163 St Johns
(**164**) TWO CENTS

(Recess C.B.N.)

1943 (1 June). Air. Perf 12.
291	163	7c. ultramarine	50	2·50

1946 (21 Mar). No. 290 surch locally with T **164**.
292 **162** 2c. on 30c. carmine .... 30 3·00

165 Queen Elizabeth II when Princess
166 Cabot off Cape Bonaventa

(Recess Waterlow)
1947 (21 Apr). Princess Elizabeth's 21st Birthday. W **106** (sideways). Perf 12½.
293 **165** 4c. light blue .... 1·50 3·00
    a. Imperf vert (horiz pair) £475

(Recess Waterlow)
1947 (24 June). 450th Anniversary of Cabot's Discovery of Newfoundland. W **106** (sideways). Perf 12½.
294 **166** 5c. mauve .... 50 2·00
    a. Printed double, one albino £275
    b. Imperf between (horiz pair) ....
    w. Wmk top of shield to right .... 50·00

STAMP BOOKLETS

1926. Black on pink cover with Ayre and Sons advertisement on front. Stapled.
SB1   40c. booklet containing 8×1c. and 16×2c.
    (Nos. 149/150) in blocks of 8 .... £1900

B1

1932 (2 Jan). Black on buff cover as T **B1**. Stapled.
SB2   40c. booklet containing 4×1c., 12×2c. and 4×3c. (Nos. 209b, 210c, 211c) in blocks
    of 4 .... £500
    a. Contents as No. SB2, but containing Nos. 209b, 210 and 211c £550
    b. Contents as No. SB2, but containing Nos. 222d, 223d and 211d £500

B2

1932. Black on cream cover as T **B2**. Stapled.
SB3   40c. booklet containing 4×1c., 12×2c. and 4×3c. (Nos. 222, 223, 211) in blocks of 4 .... £550

POSTAGE DUE STAMPS

D1   'POSTAGE LUE' (R. 3/3 and 3/8)

Stop after 'E' (R. 10/1 and 10/6)

(Litho John Dickinson & Co, Ltd)
1939 (1 May)–**49**. No Wmk. Perf 10.
D1   **D1**   1c. green .... 2·50 26·00
    a. Perf 11 (1949) .... 3·25 32·00
D2   2c. vermilion .... 20·00 10·00
    a. Perf 11×9 (1946) .... 14·00 35·00
D3   3c. ultramarine .... 5·00 45·00
    a. Perf 11×9 (1949) .... 13·00 65·00
    b. Perf 9 .... £4750
D4   4c. orange .... 9·50 35·00
    a. Perf 11×9 (5.48) .... 16·00 70·00
D5   5c. brown .... 14·00 50·00
D6   10c. violet .... 13·00 35·00
    a. Perf 11 (W **106**) (1949) .... 18·00 £100
    ab. Ditto. Imperf between (vert pair) ... £1400
    ac. 'POSTAGE LUE' £150 £475
    ad. Stop after 'E' £150 £475
D1/D6 Set of 6 .... 50·00 £180

Newfoundland joined the Dominion of Canada on 31 March 1949.

NOVA SCOTIA

Organised postal services in Nova Scotia date from April 1754 when the first of a series of Deputy Postmasters was appointed, under the authority of the British GPO. This arrangement continued until 6 July 1851 when the colony assumed responsibility for its postal affairs.

AMHERST

CROWNED-CIRCLE HANDSTAMPS

CC1   **CC1** AMHERST. N.S.(R) (25.2.1845) .... *Price on cover*   £1000

ST MARGARETS BAY

CROWNED CIRCLE HANDSTAMPS

CC2   **CC1** ST MARGARETS BAY. N.S.(R) (30.6.1845)
    ....*Price on cover*   £10000

Nos. CC1/CC2 were later used during temporary shortages of stamps, struck in red or black.

PRICES FOR STAMPS ON COVER	
No. 1	from × 5
Nos. 2/4	from × 2
Nos. 5/8	from × 4
Nos. 9/10	from × 10
Nos. 11/13	from × 2
Nos. 14/15	—
No. 16	from × 4
Nos. 17/19	from × 10
Nos. 20/25	from × 2
No. 26	from × 50
Nos. 27/28	from × 4
No. 29	from × 10

NOVA SCOTIA, PRINCE EDWARD ISLAND CANADA

1    **2**

Crown and Heraldic Flowers of United Kingdom and Mayflower of Nova Scotia.

(Recess P.B.)

1851 (1 Sept)–**60**. Bluish paper. Imperf.

1	1	1d. red-brown (12.5.53)	£3250	£475
		a. Bisected (½d.) (on cover) (1857)	†	£50000
2	2	3d. deep blue	£1500	£225
		a. Bisected (1½d.) (on cover)	†	£2500
3		3d. bright blue	£1400	£200
		a. Bisected (1½d.) (on cover)	†	£2500
4		3d. pale blue (1857)	£1400	£200
		a. Bisected (1½d.) (on cover)	†	£2500
5		6d. yellow-green	£4750	£750
		a. Bisected (3d.) (on cover)	†	£3250
		b. Quartered (1½d.) (on cover) (1860)	†	£60000
6		6d. deep green (1857)	£10000	£1800
		a. Bisected (3d.) (on cover)	†	£5000
7		1s. cold violet	£30000	£6000
7c		1s. deep purple (1851)	£18000	£4500
		d. Watermarked	£25000	£7500
8		1s. purple (1857)	£18000	£4250
		a. Bisected (6d.) (on cover) (1860)	†	£38000
		b. Quartered (3d.) (on cover) (1858)	†	£90000

The watermark on No. 7d consists of the whole or part of a letter from the name 'T. H. SAUNDERS' (the papermakers).

The stamps formerly catalogued on almost white paper are probably some from which the bluish paper has been discharged.

Reprints of all four values were made in 1890 on thin, hard, white paper. The 1d. is brown, the 3d. blue, the 6d. deep green, and the 1s. violet-black.

The 3d. bisects, which were authorised on 19 October 1854, are usually found used to make up the 7½d. rate.

(New Currency. 100 cents = 1 dollar)

3   **4**   **5**

(Recess American Bank Note Co, New York)

1860–63. Perf 12.

(a) Yellowish paper.

9	3	1c. jet black	5·00	18·00
		a. Bisected (½c.) (on cover)	†	£8000
10		1c. grey-black	5·00	18·00
11		2c. grey-purple	12·00	16·00
11a		2c. purple	17·00	15·00
12		5c. blue	£475	25·00
13		5c. deep blue	£475	25·00
14	4	8½c. deep green	5·00	65·00
15		8½c. yellow-green	5·50	65·00
16		10c. scarlet	25·00	42·00
17	5	12½c. black	38·00	30·00
17a		12½c. greyish black	—	30·00

(b) White paper.

18	3	1c. black	5·00	21·00
		a. Imperf vert (horiz pair)	£200	
19		1c. grey	5·00	21·00
20		2c. dull purple	5·00	14·00
21		2c. purple	5·00	14·00
22		2c. grey-purple	5·00	14·00
		a. Bisected (1c.) (on cover)	†	£3500
23		2c. slate-purple	5·00	13·00
24		5c. blue	£550	29·00
25		5c. deep blue	£550	29·00
26	4	8½c. deep green	23·00	65·00
27		10c. scarlet	8·50	42·00
28		10c. vermilion	8·50	42·00
		a. Bisected (5c.) (on cover)	†	£750
29	5	12½c. black	60·00	32·00

Nova Scotia joined the Dominion of Canada on 1 July 1867.

PRINCE EDWARD ISLAND

Prince Edward Island, previously administered as part of Nova Scotia, became a separate colony in 1769.

PRICES FOR STAMPS ON COVER		
Nos.	1/4	from × 4
No.	5	—
No.	6	from × 5
Nos.	7/8	from × 10
Nos.	9/11	from × 8
Nos.	12/18	from × 6
Nos.	19/20	from × 10
Nos.	21/26	from × 4
Nos.	27/31	from × 8
Nos.	32/33	from × 40
Nos.	34/37	from × 8
No.	38	from × 30
Nos.	39/41	from × 20
No.	42	from × 50
Nos.	43/47	from × 8

1   **2**   **3**

4   **5**   **6**

Two Dies of 2d.:

Die I.   Left-hand frame and circle merge at centre left (all stamps in the sheet of 60 (10×6) except R. 2/5).

Die II.   Left-hand frame and circle separate at centre left (R. 2/5). There is also a break in the top frame line.

(Typo Charles Whiting, London)

1861 (1 Jan). Yellowish toned paper.

(a) Perf 9. Perf 9.

1	1	2d. rose (Die I)	£650	£225
		a. Imperf between (horiz pair)	£11000	
		b. Imperf horiz (vert pair)		
		c. Bisected (1d.) (on cover)	†	£8000
		d. Die II		
2		2d. rose-carmine (Die I)	£750	£250
		a. Die II	—	£1000
3	2	3d. blue	£1200	£550
		a. Bisected (1½d.) (on cover)	†	£8000
		b. Double print	£4000	
4	3	6d. yellow-green	£1700	£850

(b) Rouletted.

5	1	2d. rose (I)	†	£25000

The 2d. and 3d., perf 9, were authorised to be bisected and used for half their normal value.

1862–69. Yellowish toned paper.

(a) Perf 11 (1862) or 11¼ (1869). Perf 11 (1862) or 11¼ (1869).

6	4	1d. brown-orange	£120	90·00
6a		2d. rose (Die I) (1869)	†	£550
7	6	9d. bluish lilac (29.3.62)	£170	£120
8		9d. dull mauve	£170	£120

(b) Perf 11½–12 (1863–1869). Perf 11½–12.

9	4	1d. yellow-orange (1863)	55·00	70·00
		a. Bisected (½d.) (on cover)	†	£5500
		b. Imperf between (horiz pair)	£550	
10		1d. orange-buff	60·00	70·00
11		1d. yellow	70·00	70·00
12	1	2d. rose (Die I) (1863)	26·00	19·00
		a. Imperf vert (horiz pair)		
		b. Bisected (1d.) (on cover)	†	£3750
		c. Die II	£110	£100
13		2d. deep rose (Die I)	28·00	23·00
		a. Die II	£120	£110
14	2	3d. blue (1863)	50·00	32·00
		a. Imperf horiz (vert pair)		
		b. Bisected (1½d.) (on cover)	†	—
15		3d. deep blue	50·00	32·00
16	5	4d. black (8.68)	32·00	65·00

Canadian Philately at its Best!

Our award-winning auction catalogues regularly feature the best that Canadian philately has to offer.

The famous 1851 12 pence black, a superlative mint pair *ex. Dale, Nickle*.
Sold in our recent March 2024 public auction, Brigham Estate - Part III.
A Record Price for a philatelic item sold in Canada
Realized $740,625 inclusive of buyer's premium.

Canada's Most Trusted Auction House

Our expertise combined with meticulous research and descriptions have been fundamental in achieving highly successful results for our consignors. For over 40 years, the offering of numerous rarities, proofs, high-quality stamps and postal history has been the delight of serious collectors around the world. We look forward to working with you!

Eastern Auctions Ltd.

P.O. Box 250 - Bathurst - New Brunswick - E2A -3Z2 - Canada
Tel: 1(506) 548-8986 - Fax 1(506) 546-6627
Toll Free Tel: 1(800) 667-8267 - Fax 1(888) 867-8267 *(North America only)*

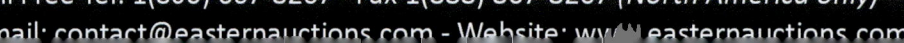

Prince Edward Island, Dominion Of Canada CANADA

		a. Imperf vert (horiz pair)..................	£350	
		b. Bisected (2d.) (on cover)...............	†	£2000
		c. Imperf between (horiz strip of 3)...	£550	
17	3	6d. yellow-green (15.12.66)............	£170	£130
		a. Bisected (3d.) (on cover)............	†	£6500
18		6d. blue-green (1868)......................	£170	£120
19	6	9d. lilac (1863)..................................	£140	£120
20		9d. reddish mauve (1863)................	£140	£120
		a. Imperf vert (horiz pair).................	£950	
		b. Bisected (4½d.) (on cover)...........	†	£6000

A new perforator, gauging exactly 11¼, was introduced in 1869. Apart from No. 6a, it was used in compound with the perf 11½–12 machine.

(c) Perf compound of 11 or 11¼ (1869) and 11½–12. Perf compound of 11 or 11¼ (1869) and 11½–12.

21	4	1d. yellow-orange............................	£250	95·00
22	1	2d. rose (Die I).................................	£225	75·00
		a. Die II		
23	2	3d. blue..	£275	80·00
24	5	4d. black...	£325	£275
25	3	6d. yellow-green.............................	£375	£325
26	6	9d. reddish mauve...........................	£475	£350

1870. Coarse, wove bluish white paper. Perf 11½–12.

27	1	2d. rose (Die I).................................	17·00	21·00
		a. Die II	95·00	£110
28		2d. rose-pink (Die I)........................	9·50	19·00
		a. Die II	70·00	85·00
		b. 'TWC' (R. 6/4)...............................	90·00	£130
		c. Imperf between (horiz pair).........	£275	
		d. Imperf horiz (vert pair)................	£275	
29	2	3d. pale blue...................................	16·00	23·00
30		3d. blue..	11·00	23·00
		a. Imperf between (horiz pair)........	£375	
31	5	4d. black...	7·00	45·00
		a. Imperf between (horiz pair)........	£225	
		b. Bisected (2d.) (on cover)............	†	£2000

(New Currency. 100 cents = 1 dollar)

7

(Recess British-American Bank Note Co., Montréal and Ottawa)

1870 (1 June). Perf 12.

32	7	4½d. (3d. stg), yellow-brown...........	80·00	90·00
33		4½d. (3d. stg), deep brown..............	80·00	95·00

8  9  10

11  12  13

(Typo Charles Whiting, London)

1872 (1 Jan).

(a) Perf 11½–12. Perf 11½–12.

34	8	1c. orange..	10·00	35·00
35		1c. yellow-orange............................	14·00	30·00
36		1c. brown-orange............................	9·00	35·00
37	10	3c. rose..	45·00	50·00
		a. Stop between 'PRINCE. EDWARD'..	90·00	£110
		b. Bisected (1½c.) (on cover)............		
		c. Imperf horiz (vert pair).................	£550	

(b) Perf 12 to 12¼ large holes. Perf 12 to 12¼ large holes.

38	9	2c. blue..	28·00	65·00
		a. Bisected (1c.) (on cover).............	†	£4000
39	11	4c. yellow-green.............................	12·00	38·00
40		4c. deep green................................	14·00	40·00
		a. Bisected (2c.) (on cover).............	†	£4750
41	12	6c. black...	10·00	40·00
		a. Bisected (3c.) (on cover).............	†	£2000
		b. Imperf between (horiz pair).........	£325	

		c. Imperf vert (horiz pair).................		
42	13	12c. reddish mauve..........................	12·00	85·00

(c) Perf 12½–13, smaller holes. Perf 12½–13, smaller holes.

43	8	1c. orange..	24·00	
44		1c. brown-orange............................	10·00	40·00
45	10	3c. rose..	42·00	50·00
		a. Stop between 'PRINCE. EDWARD'..	85·00	£130
45b	12	6c. black...	—	£275

(d) Perf compound of (a) and (c) 11½–12×12½–13. Perf compound of (a) and (c) 11½–12×12½–13.

46	8	1c. orange..	£100	75·00
47	10	3c. rose..	£130	80·00
		a. Stop between 'PRINCE. EDWARD'..	£350	£300

The Stop between 'PRINCE. EDWARD' variety listed as Nos. 37a, 45a, 47a occurred at R. 1/2 in the master block of ten clichés (5×2), which was repeated ten times to construct the plate of 100 (10×10). It therefore appears ten times in each sheet at R. 1/2, 1/7, 3/2, 3/7, 5/2, 5/7, 7/2, 7/7, 9/2 and 9/7.

Prince Edward Island joined the Dominion of Canada on 1 July 1873.

DOMINION OF CANADA

On 1 July 1867, Canada, Nova Scotia and New Brunswick were united to form the Dominion of Canada.

The provinces of Manitoba (1870), British Columbia (1871), Prince Edward Island (1873), Alberta (1905), Saskatchewan (1905), and Newfoundland (1949) were subsequently added, as were the Northwest Territories (1870) and Yukon Territory (1898).

PRICES FOR STAMPS ON COVER TO 1945	
Nos. 46/67	from × 2
Nos. 68/71	from × 10
Nos. 72/89	from × 3
Nos. 90/100	from × 2
Nos. 101/102	from × 5
Nos. 103/111	from × 3
Nos. 115/120	from × 6
Nos. 121/149	from × 3
Nos. 150/165	from × 2
Nos. 166/172	from × 3
Nos. 173/187	from × 5
Nos. 188/195	from × 2
Nos. 196/215	from × 3
Nos. 219/224b	from × 4
Nos. 225/245	from × 2
Nos. 246/255	from × 8
Nos. 256/310	from × 2
No. 312	from × 20
No. 313	from × 10
Nos. 315/318	from × 2
Nos. 319/328	from × 3
Nos. 329/340	from × 2
Nos. 341/400	from × 1
Nos. R1/R7a	from × 5
Nos. R8/R9	from × 50
Nos. R10/R11	from × 20
Nos. S1/S3	from × 8
No. S4	from × 6
No. S5	from × 5
Nos. S6/S11	from × 3
Nos. S12/S14	from × 5
Nos. D1/D8	from × 4
Nos. D9/D13	from × 5
Nos. D14/D24	from × 4

13 14 15

Large types

PRINTERS. Nos. 46/120 were recess-printed by the British American Bank Note Co at Ottawa or Montréal.

CANADIAN PHILATELY
FROM ANOTHER POINT OF VIEW

JOIN THE CANADIAN PHILATELIC SOCIETY OF GREAT BRITAIN

Founded over 70 years ago to promote and study all aspects of philately in British North America (Canada and its Provinces), the Society offers its members:-

- A quarterly award-winning full colour magazine
- Auctions each year with many hundreds of lots
- Subscriptions payable in local currency

For more information or membership details visit our website at www.canadianpsgb.org.uk or contact our Secretary, John Watson at Lyngarth, 106 Huddersfield Road, Penistone, South Yorkshire S36 7BX or by email at john.watson1949@btinternet.com

www.canadianpsgb.org.uk

DEALING IN STAMPS SINCE 1924

Exceptional selections of Canada and the Provinces plus British Commonwealth and Worldwide material

Our unreserved public auctions feature a wide variety of philatelic material, from classics to modern.

r. maresch & son
2 VATA CRT UNIT 6 AURORA ON L4G 4B6
☎ (905) 726-2197   www.maresch.com

CELEBRATING 100 YEARS OF WORLDWIDE TRADING

CANADA

(Eng A. Jones (portrait), H. Searle and W. Smillie)
1868 (1 Apr)–**90**. As Types **13/15** (various frames).

I. Ottawa printings. Perf 12(a) Thin rather transparent crisp paper. Perf 12.
46	13	½c. black (1.4.68)	£120	95·00
47	14	1c. red-brown (1.4.68)	£750	85·00
48		2c. grass-green (1.4.68)	£900	75·00
49		3c. red-brown (1.4.68)	£1600	40·00
50		6c. blackish brown (1.4.68)	£1800	£180
51		12½c. bright blue (1.4.68)	£1600	£150
52		15c. deep reddish purple	£1400	£200

In these first printings the impression is generally blurred and the lines of the background are less clearly defined than in later printings.

(b) Medium to stout wove paper (1868–1871).
53	13	½c. black	80·00	70·00
54		½c. grey-black	80·00	70·00
		a. Imperf between (pair)		
		b. Watermarked	£35000	£9500
55	14	1c. red-brown	£550	65·00
		a. Laid paper	£25000	£4500
		b. Watermarked (1868)	£3500	£450
56		1c. deep orange (1.1869)	£1600	£150
56a		1c. orange-yellow (5(?).1869)	£1100	£110
56b		1c. pale orange-yellow	£1200	£110
		ba. Imperf		
57		2c. deep green	£950	55·00
57a		2c. pale emerald-green (1871)	£1200	85·00
		ab. Bisected (1c. with 2c. to make 3c. rate) *on cover*	†	£5500
		ac. Laid paper		†£150000
57d		2c. bluish green	£1000	55·00
		da. Watermarked (1868)	£3000	£350
58		3c. brown-red	£1600	25·00
		a. Laid paper	£16000	£750
		b. Watermarked (1868)	£4000	£300
59		6c. blackish brown (*to* chocolate)	£1500	75·00
		a. Watermarked (1868)	£10000	£1500
59b		6c. yellow-brown (1870)	£1400	70·00
		ba. Bisected (3c.), *on cover*	†	£3250
60		12½c. bright blue	£1000	65·00
		a. Imperf horiz (vert pair)	†	£25000
		b. Watermarked (1868)	£5000	£350
60c		12½c. pale dull blue (milky)	£1200	95·00
61		15c. deep reddish purple	£850	75·00
61a		15c. pale reddish purple	£750	65·00
		ab. Watermarked (1868)	—	£1500
61b		15c. dull violet-grey	£250	38·00
		ba. Watermarked (1868)	£5500	£900
61c		15c. dull grey-purple	£325	38·00

The official date of issue was 1 April 1868. Scattered examples of most values can be found used in the second half of March.

The two-line watermark on the stout paper stamps consists of the words 'E & G BOTHWELL CLUTHA MILLS,' in large double-lined capitals which can be found upright, inverted or reversed. Portions of one or two letters only may be found on these stamps, which occur in the early printings of 1868.

The paper may, in most cases, be easily divided if the stamps are laid face downwards and carefully compared. The thin hard paper is more or less transparent and shows the design through the stamp; the thicker paper is softer to the feel and more opaque.

Of the 2c. laid paper No. 57ac three examples only are known.
No. 60a is only known as a vertical strip of six.

II. Montréal printings. Medium to stout wove paper(a) Perf 11½×12 or 11¾×12. Perf 11½×12 or 11¾×12.
62	13	½c. black (1873)	£110	85·00
63	15	5c. olive-green (28.9.75)	£1000	£100
		a. Perf 12	£6000	£800
64	14	15c. dull grey-purple (1874)	£1200	£250
65		15c. lilac-grey (3.77)	£1300	£250
		a. Script watermark	£28000	£4500
		b. 'BOTHWELL' watermark	†	£850
66		15c. slate	£1300	£300

(b) Perf 12. Perf 12.
67	14	15c. clear deep violet (*thick paper*) (1879)	£5000	£1000
68		15c. deep slate (1881)	£160	35·00
69		15c. slaty blue (1887)	£200	35·00
70		15c. slate-purple (*shades*) (7.88–92)	75·00	20·00

No. 63a gauges 12 or above on all four sides.

The watermark on No. 65a is part of 'Alexr Pirie & Sons' which appeared diagonally as script letters once per sheet in a small batch of the paper used for the 1877 printing.

For a description of the sheet watermark on No. 65b, see note after No. 61c.

Several used examples of the 12½c. have been reported perforated 11½×12 or 11¾×12.

The last printing of the 15c. slate-purple, No. 70, took place at Ottawa.

III. Ottawa printings. Thinnish paper of poor quality, often toned grey or yellowish. Perf 12. Perf 12.
71	14	15c. slate-violet (*shades*) (5.90)	75·00	23·00
		a. Imperf (pair). Brown-purple	£1400	

Examples of No. 71 are generally found with yellowish streaky gum.

21 *Small type*

1c. Strand of hair

5c. Straw in hair

6c. Major re-entry (Pl. A, R. 7/7)

Papers (*a*). 1870–1880. Medium to stout wove.
Papers (*b*). 1870–1872. Thin, soft, very white.
Papers (*c*). 1878–1897. Thinner and poorer quality.

1870–**90**. As T **21** (various frames). Ottawa (1870–1873) and Montréal printings. Perf 12 (or slightly under).
72	21	1c. bright orange (*a, b*) (2.1870–1873)	£225	45·00
		a. Thick soft paper (1871)	£1000	£225
73		1c. orange-yellow (*a*) (1876–1879)	95·00	7·00
74		1c. pale dull yellow (1877–1879)	70·00	4·75
75		1c. bright yellow (*a, c*) (1878–1897)	50·00	2·25
		a. Imperf (pair) (*c*)	£600	
		b. Bisected (½c.) (on *Railway News*)	†	£4500
		c. Printed both sides	£2000	
		d. Strand of hair	£1000	£350
76		1c. lemon-yellow (*c*) (1880)	£120	22·00
77		2c. deep green (*a, b*) (2.72–73 and 1876–1878)	95·00	6·00
78		2c. grass-green (*c*) (1878–1888)	65·00	2·50
		a. Imperf (pair)	£700	
		b. Bisected (1c.) *on cover*	†	£2500
		c. Stamp doubly printed	†	£5500
79		3c. Indian red (*a*) (1.70)	£2000	75·00
		a. Perf 12½ (2.70)	£20000	£1600
80		3c. pale rose-red (9.70)	£450	18·00
81		3c. deep rose-red (*a, b*) (1870–1873)	£450	18·00
		a. Thick soft paper (1.71)	£3000	£250
82		3c. dull red (*a, c*) (1876–1888)	£150	3·50
83		3c. orange-red (*shades*) (*a, c*) (1876–1888)	£125	3·00
84		3c. rose-carmine (*c*) (10.88–4.89)	£450	18·00
85		5c. olive-green (*a, c*) (2.76–88)	£550	25·00
		a. Straw in hair	£2500	£1200
86		6c. yellowish brown (*a, b, c*) (1.72–73 and 1876–1890)	£450	25·00
		a. Major re-entry	£1300	£300
		b. Bisected (3c.) *on cover*	†	£1400
		c. Perf 12×11½* (1873)	†	—
		d. Perf 12×12½	†	£2500
87		10c. pale lilac-magenta (*a*) (1876–?)	£1000	60·00

CANADA

88		10c. deep lilac-magenta (*a*, *c*) (3.76–88)	£1000	65·00
89		10c. lilac-pink (3.88)	£750	55·00

* The exact perforation measurement on No. 86c is 11.85×11.6.

Nos. 75 and 78 were printed in the same shades during the second Ottawa period.

Nos. 75a and 78a date from *circa* 1894–1895.

There are four variants of the Strand of Hair, with the strand in the same position but varying in length. R. 2/13 and R. 3/16 have been identified. The illustration shows the 'Long Strand'.

Examples of paper (*a*) can often be found showing traces of ribbing, especially on the 2c. value.

No. 79a was issued in New Brunswick and Nova Scotia.

6c. Neck flaw ('A' Plate, R. 5/1)   **27**

1873–79. Montréal printings. Medium to stout wove paper. Perf 11½×12 or 11¾×12.

90	**21**	1c. bright orange	£300	50·00
91		1c. orange-yellow (1873–1879)	£300	18·00
92		1c. pale dull yellow (1877–1879)	£300	21·00
93		1c. lemon-yellow (1879)	£325	21·00
94		2c. deep green (1873–1878)	£500	24·00
95		3c. dull red (1875–1879)	£450	24·00
96		3c. orange-red (1873–1879)	£450	24·00
97		5c. olive-green (1.2.76–79)	£650	38·00
98		6c. yellowish brown (1873–1879)	£650	55·00
		a. Neck flaw	£1800	£275
99		10c. very pale lilac-magenta (11.74)	£2500	£500
100		10c. deep lilac-magenta (1876–1879)	£1500	£225

1882–97. Montréal (to March 1889) and Ottawa printings. Thinnish paper of poor quality. Pef 12.

101	**27**	½c. black (7.82–97)	22·00	13·00
102		½c. grey-black	22·00	13·00
		ab. Imperf (pair) (1891–1893?)	£700	
		ac. Imperf between (horiz pair)	£950	

2c. Latent entries (R. 9)

2c. Latent entries (R. 10/8)

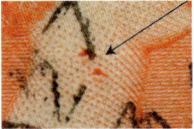

3c. 'Vampire bite'

6c. 5c. on 6c. re-entry (R. 3/5)

6c. Major re-entry (Pane B, R. 9/7)

1889–97. Ottawa printings. Thinnish paper of poor quality, often toned grey or yellowish. Perf 12.

103	**21**	2c. dull sea-green	85·00	2·50
104		2c. blue-green (7.89–91)	75·00	3·50
		a. Latent entries	£850	£300
105		3c. bright vermilion (4.89–97)	55·00	1·50
		a. Vampire bite	£550	£200
		b. Imperf (pair) (1891–1893?)	£650	
106		5c. brownish grey (5.89)	£150	2·50
		a. Imperf (pair) (1891–1893)	£700	
107		6c. deep chestnut (10.90)	80·00	22·00
		a. '5c.' re-entry*	£4500	£2000
		b. Major re-entry	£500	£180
		c. Imperf (pair) (1891–1893)	£750	
108		6c. pale chestnut	£100	25·00
109		10c. salmon-pink	£450	£120
110		10c. carmine-pink (4.90)	£450	45·00
		a. Imperf (pair) (1891–1893?)	£850	
111		10c. brownish red (1894?)	£425	45·00
		a. Imperf (pair)	£950	

On No. 107a the top portion of the 5c. design cuts across 'CANADA POSTAGE', the white circle surrounding the head, and can be seen on the top of the head itself. Lesser re-entries are visible on R. 2/10 and R. 3/1 from another plate.

There are two latent entries recognised on the 2c. The stamp with the partial image in the upper margin has been identified as being R. 10/8, that with the image in the lower margin is from a position in row 9. The plates are not known.

The 1c. showed no change in the Ottawa printings, so is not included.

The 2c. reverted to its previous grass-green shade in 1891.

28   **29**

(Recess B.A.B.N.)

1893 (17 Feb). Perf 12.

115	**28**	20c. vermilion	£300	75·00
		a. Imperf (pair)	£1700	
116		50c. blue	£300	60·00
		a. Imperf *Prussian blue* (pair)	£1800	

1893 (1 Aug). Perf 12.

117	**29**	8c. pale bluish grey	£200	15·00
		a. Imperf (pair)	£950	
118		8c. bluish slate	£180	15·00
119		8c. slate-purple	£150	15·00
120		8c. blackish purple	£140	15·00
		a. Imperf (pair)	£950	

PRINTERS. The following stamps to No. 287 were recess-printed by the American Bank Note Co, Ottawa, which in 1923 became the Canadian Bank Note Co.

CANADA

30

(Des L. Pereira and F. Brownell after portraits by A. Chalon and A. Bassano)

1897 (19 June). Jubilee issue. Perf 12.
121	30	½c. black	75·00	75·00
122		1c. orange	20·00	10·00
123		1c. orange-yellow	20·00	10·00
		a. Bisected (½c.) (on *Railway News*)	†	£5500
124		2c. green	35·00	16·00
125		2c. deep green	35·00	16·00
126		3c. carmine	18·00	4·00
127		5c. slate-blue	60·00	28·00
128		5c. deep blue	60·00	28·00
129		6c. brown	£140	£140
130		8c. slate-violet	55·00	65·00
131		10c. purple	£100	70·00
132		15c. slate	£140	£120
133		20c. vermilion	£140	£120
134		50c. pale ultramarine	£190	£130
135		50c. bright ultramarine	£200	£140
136		$1 lake	£600	£550
137		$2 deep violet	£1100	£450
138		$3 bistre	£1500	£800
139		$4 violet	£1400	£750
140		$5 olive-green	£1500	£750
121/140 *Set of 16*			£6000	£3500
133s/140s Handstamped 'SPECIMEN' *Set of 7*			£2500	

No. 123a was used on issues of the *Railway News* of 5, 6 and 8 November 1897 and must be on a large part of the original newspaper with New Glasgow postmark.

31   32

(From photograph by W. & D. Downey, London)

1897–98. Perf 12.
141	31	½c. grey-black (9.11.97)	18·00	7·50
142		½c. black	15·00	6·00
		a. Imperf (pair)	£475	
143		1c. blue-green (12.97)	30·00	1·00
		a. Imperf (pair)	£450	
144		2c. violet (12.97)	35·00	2·00
		a. Imperf (pair)	£475	
145		3c. carmine (1.98)	65·00	2·25
		a. Imperf (pair)	£800	
146		5c. deep blue/*bluish* (12.97)	70·00	6·00
		a. Imperf (pair)	£475	
147		6c. brown (12.97)	60·00	40·00
		a. Imperf (pair)	£750	
148		8c. orange (12.97)	85·00	20·00
		a. Imperf (pair)	£475	
149		10c. brownish purple (1.98)	£140	90·00
		a. Imperf (pair)	£550	
141/149 *Set of 8*			£450	£150

BOOKLET PANES. Most definitive booklets issued from 1900 onwards had either the two horizontal sides or all three outer edges imperforate. Stamps from the panes show one side or two adjacent sides imperforate.

Die 1a   Die 1b

Two types of the 2c.
Die Ia. Frame consists of four fine lines.
Die Ib. Frame has one thick line between two fine lines.

The die was retouched in 1900 for Plates 11 and 12, producing weak vertical frame lines and then retouched again in 1902 for Plates 15 to 20 resulting in much thicker frame lines. No. 155b covers both states of the retouching.

1898–1902. Perf 12.
150	32	½c. black (9.98)	12·00	1·50
		a. Imperf (pair)	£475	
151		1c. blue-green (6.98)	35·00	1·00
152		1c. deep green/*toned paper*	45·00	3·25
		a. Imperf (pair)	£1100	
153		2c. dull purple (Die Ia) (9.98)	50·00	1·25
		a. Thick paper (6.99)	£120	10·00
154		2c. violet (Die Ia)	32·00	30
154a		2c. reddish purple (Die Ia)	70·00	2·25
155		2c. rose-carmine (Die Ia) (20.8.99)	38·00	30
		a. Imperf (pair)	£475	
155b		2c. rose-carmine (Die Ib) (1900)	80·00	2·25
		ba. Booklet pane of 6 (11.6.00)	£750	
156		3c. rose-carmine (6.98)	80·00	1·00
157		5c. slate-blue/*bluish*	£110	4·00
		a. Imperf (pair)	£1000	
158		5c. Prussian blue/*bluish*	£120	4·00
159		6c. brown (9.98)	£110	65·00
		a. Imperf (pair)	£1000	
160		7c. greenish yellow (23.12.02)	80·00	32·00
161		8c. orange-yellow (10.98)	£130	48·00
162		8c. brownish orange	£130	48·00
		a. Imperf (pair)	£1000	
163		10c. pale brownish purple (11.98)	£170	22·00
164		10c. deep brownish purple	£170	22·00
		a. Imperf (pair)	£1000	
165		20c. olive-green (29.12.00)	£325	85·00
150/165 *Set of 11*			£950	£225

The 7c. and 20c. also exist imperforate, but unlike the values listed in this condition, they have no gum. (*Price*, 7c. £450, 20c. £3500 *pair, unused*).

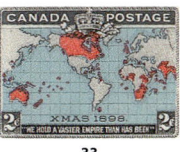

33

(Des R. Weir Crouch, G. Hahn, A. H. Howard and R. Holmes. Eng C. Skinner. Design recess, colours added by typo)

1898 (7 Dec). Imperial Penny Postage. Design in black. British possessions in red. Oceans in colours given. Perf 12.
166	33	2c. lavender	25·00	6·00
		a. Imperf (pair) (*no gum*)	£400	
167		2c. greenish blue	30·00	6·00
		a. Imperf (pair) (*no gum*)	£450	
168		2c. blue	35·00	6·50
		a. Imperf (pair) (*no gum*)	£475	

Forgeries of T **33** are without horizontal lines across the continents and have a forged Montréal postmark of 24.12.98.

1899 (4 Jan). Provisionals used at Port Hood, Nova Scotia. No. 156 divided vertically and handstamped.
169	32	'1' in blue, on ⅓ of 3c.	—	£3500
170		'2' in violet, on ⅔ of 3c.	—	£3000

Nos. 169/170 were prepared by the local postmaster during a shortage of 2c. stamps caused by a change in postage rates.

(34)   35 King Edward VII

1899. Surch with T **34**, by Public Printing Office.
171	31	2c. on 3c. carmine (8.8)	22·00	8·00
		a. Surch inverted	£450	
172	32	2c. on 3c. rose-carmine (28.7)	24·00	6·00
		a. Surch inverted	£450	

(Des King George V when Prince of Wales and J. A. Tilleard. Eng J. A. C. Harrison (portrait) and C. Skinner (layout))

1903 (1 July)–**12**. Perf 12.
173	35	1c. pale green	42·00	50
174		1c. deep green	35·00	50
175		1c. green	35·00	50

CANADA

176		2c. rose-carmine	20·00	50
	a.	Booklet pane of 6	£800	£950
177		2c. pale rose-carmine	20·00	50
	a.	Imperf (pair) (18.7.09)	30·00	45·00
178		5c. blue/*bluish*	90·00	2·75
179		5c. indigo/*bluish*	90·00	2·75
180		7c. yellow-olive	£100	5·00
181		7c. greenish bistre	£110	5·00
181*a*		7c. straw (1.12)	£120	65·00
182		10c. brown-lilac	£160	35·00
183		10c. pale dull purple	£160	35·00
184		10c. dull purple	£160	35·00
185		20c. pale olive-green (27.9.04)	£325	45·00
186		20c. deep olive-green	£325	45·00
	s.	Handstamped 'SPECIMEN'	£110	
187		50c. deep violet (19.11.08)	£500	£150
173/187 *Set of 7*			£1100	£200

The 1c., 5c., 7c. and 10c. exist imperforate but are believed to be proofs. (*Prices per pair*, 1c. £550, 5c. £1000, 7c. £650, 10c. £1000, *without gum*).

Between 1905 and 1907 experimental printings of the 2c. value were made on dry paper (see note above No. 196). The resulting stamps are slightly wider with a sharper impression.

IMPERFORATE AND PART-PERFORATED SHEETS. Prior to 1946 many Canadian issues exist imperforate, or with other perforation varieties, in the colours of the issued stamps and, usually, with gum. In the years before 1927 such examples are believed to come from imprimatur sheets, removed from the Canadian Post Office archives. From 1927 until 1946 it is known that the printers involved in the production of the various issues submitted several imperforate plate proof sheets of each stamp to the Post Office authorities for approval. Some of these sheets or part sheets were retained for record purposes, but the remainder found their way on to the philatelic market.

Part-perforated sheets also occur from 1927–1929 issues.

From 1908 until 1946 we now only list and price such varieties of this type which are known to be genuine errors, sold from post offices. Where other imperforate or similar varieties are known they are recorded in footnotes.

It is possible, and in some cases probable, that some imperforate varieties listed before 1908 may have also been removed from the archives as mentioned above, but it is far harder to be explicit over the status of this earlier material.

36 King George V and Queen Mary when Prince and Princess of Wales

37 Jacques Cartier and Samuel Champlain

38 King Edward VII and Queen Alexandra

39 Champlain's House in Québec

40 Generals Montcalm and Wolfe

41 Québec in 1700

42 Champlain's Departure for the West

43 Cartier's Arrival before Québec

½**c.** Re-entry (R. 5/4)

(Des Machado)

1908 (16 July). Québec Tercentenary. Types **36/43**. Perf 12.

188	**36**	½c. sepia	9·00	4·50
	a.	Re-entry	75·00	75·00
189	**37**	1c. blue-green	35·00	4·50
190	**38**	2c. carmine	32·00	2·50
191	**39**	5c. indigo	65·00	50·00
192	**40**	7c. olive-green	95·00	75·00
193	**41**	10c. violet	£110	£100
194	**42**	15c. brown-orange	£130	£125
195	**43**	20c. dull brown	£160	£150
188/195 *Set of 8*			£550	£450

Some values exist on both toned and white papers.
Nos. 188/195 exist imperforate. (*Price* £750, *unused, for each pair*.)

WET AND DRY PRINTINGS. Until the end of December 1922 all Canadian stamps were produced by the 'wet' method of recess-printing in which the paper was dampened before printing, dried and then gummed.

In late December 1922 the Canadian Bank Note Co. began to use the 'dry' process in which the paper was gummed before printing. Late printings of the 3c. brown were the first stamps to be produced by this method, but the changeover was not completed until January 1926. The 1c., 2c. and 3c. values In the 1932–1933 series also exist from both 'wet' and 'dry' printings from the Stickney rotary press.

'Dry' printings have a sharper appearance and can often be found with a degree of embossing showing on the reverse. Stamps from 'wet' printings shrink during drying and are narrower than 'dry' examples. In many cases the difference can be as great as 0.5 mm. On some early booklet panes the difference is in the vertical, rather than the horizontal, measurement.

On Nos. 196/215 all values only exist from 'wet' printings, except the 3c., 20c. and 50c. which come from both types of printing.

44 King George V

1c. Major re-entry

1911–22. Perf 12.

196	**44**	1c. yellow-green (22.12.11)	14·00	75
197		1c. bluish green	6·00	50
	a.	Major Re-entry	£5000	£1500
	b.	Booklet pane of 6 (1.5.13)	50·00	
198		1c. deep bluish green	8·00	50
	a.	With fine horiz lines across stamp	50·00	10·00
199		1c. deep yellow-green	8·00	1·00
	a.	Booklet pane of 6	40·00	
200		2c. rose-red (15.12.11)	12·00	50
201		2c. deep rose-red	7·50	50
	a.	Booklet pane of 6 (1.12)	35·00	
202		2c. pale rose-red	9·00	50
	a.	With fine horiz lines across stamp	26·00	18·00
203		2c. carmine	11·00	50
204		3c. brown (6.8.18)	8·50	50
205		3c. deep brown	8·50	50
	a.	Booklet pane of 4+2 labels (2.22)	55·00	
205*b*		5c. deep blue (17.1.12)	75·00	75
206		5c. indigo	£120	11·00
206*a*		5c. grey-blue	£110	5·00
206*b*		7c. straw (12.1.12)	£100	20·00
207		7c. pale sage-green (1914)	£275	55·00
208		7c. olive-yellow (1915)	30·00	4·50
209		7c. yellow-ochre (1916)	30·00	4·50
210		10c. brownish purple (12.1.12)	£120	2·75
211		10c. reddish purple	£150	7·00
212		20c. olive-green (23.1.12)	55·00	2·00
213		20c. olive	55·00	2·00
214		50c. grey-black (26.1.12)	£150	13·00
215		50c. sepia	60·00	3·75
197/215 *Set of 8*			£325	12·00

The 20c. and 50c. values exist imperforate (*Price* £3500 *unused, for each pair*).

The major re-entry on the 1c. (No. 197a) shows as a distinct doubling of the lower right corner of the stamp on Plate 12, lower right pane. R. 4/5.

1912 (Oct)–**21**. For use in coil-machines.

		(*a*) Perf 12×imperf. Perf 12×imperf.		
216	**44**	1c. yellow-green (1914)	4·00	16·00
217		1c. blue-green (1914)	28·00	28·00
	a.	Two large holes at top and bottom (vert pair) (7.18)	80·00	95·00
218		2c. deep rose-red (1914)	45·00	26·00
218*a*		3c. brown (1921)	10·00	11·00

CANADA

No. 217a has two large holes about 3½ mm in diameter in the top and bottom margins. They were for experimental use in a vending machine at Toronto in July 1918 and were only in use for two days.

The 1c. and 2c. also exist with two small 'V' shaped holes about 9.5 mm apart at top which are gripper marks due to modifications made in vending machines in 1917.

(b) Imperf×perf 8. Imperf×perf 8.

219	**44**	1c. yellow-green (10.12)	25·00	9·00
220		1c. blue-green	32·00	9·00
		a. With fine horiz lines across stamp.	75·00	
221		2c. carmine (10.12)	35·00	3·75
222		2c. rose-red	35·00	3·75
223		2c. scarlet	48·00	8·00
224		3c. brown (8.18)	15·00	2·75

(c) Perf 8×imperf. Perf 8×imperf.

224a	**44**	1c. blue-green (13.2.13)	75·00	50·00
224b		2c. carmine (15.2.13)	75·00	50·00

The stamps imperf×perf 8 were sold in coils over the counter; those perf 8×imperf were on sale in automatic machines. Varieties showing perf 12 on two or three adjacent sides and one or two sides imperf are from booklets, or the margins of sheets.

(45)   46   47

1915 (12 Feb). Optd with T **45**.

225	**44**	5c. blue	£180	£200
226		20c. olive-green	85·00	£110
227		50c. sepia (R.)	£250	£200
225/227	Set of 3		£450	£450

These stamps were intended for tax purposes, but owing to ambiguity in an official circular dated 16 April 1915, it was for a time believed that their use for postal purposes was authorised. The position was clarified by a further circular on 20 May 1916 which made clear that Nos. 225/227 were for fiscal use only.

1915. Perf 12.

228	**46**	1c. green (15.4.15)	15·00	80
229		2c. carmine-red (16.4.15)	28·00	4·00
230		2c. rose-carmine	35·00	5·00

Die I   Die II

Die I. There is a long horizontal coloured line under the foot of the 'T', and a solid bar of colour runs upwards from the '1' to the 'T'.

Die II. This solid bar of colour is absent, and there is a short horizontal line under the left side of the 'T', with two short vertical dashes and a number of dots under the right-hand side.

1916 (1 Jan). Perf 12.

231	**47**	2c.+1c. 2c.+1c. rose-red (Die I)	65·00	3·00
232		2c.+1c. bright carmine (Die I)	50·00	3·00
233		2c.+1c. scarlet (Die I)	60·00	3·50

1916 (Feb). Coil stamps. Imperf×perf 8.

234	**47**	2c.+1c. rose-red (Die I)	70·00	14·00

1916 (July). Perf 12×8.

235	**47**	2c.+1c. carmine-red (Die I)	40·00	60·00
236		2c.+1c. bright rose-red (Die I)	48·00	60·00

1916 (Aug). Perf 12.

237	**47**	2c.+1c. carmine-red (Die II)	£170	28·00

1916 (Aug). Colour changed.

(a) Perf 12. Perf 12.

238	**47**	2c.+1c. brown (Die I)	£450	27·00
239		2c.+1c. yellow-brown (Die II)	10·00	1·00
		a. Imperf (pair)	£1500	
240		2c.+1c. deep brown (Die II)	22·00	1·00

(b) Coil stamps. Imperf×perf 8. Imperf×perf 8.

241	**47**	2c.+1c. brown (Die II)	£125	16·00
		a. Pair, Nos. 241 and 243	£350	
243		2c.+1c. deep brown (Die II)	60·00	6·50

No. 239a, which is a genuine error, should not be confused with ungummed proofs of the Die I stamp, No. 238 (*Price per pair*, £140).

This value also exists Perf 12×imperf or imperf×perf 12, but was not issued with these perforations (*Price, in either instance*, £350, *unused, per pair*).

48 Québec Conference, 1864, from Painting *The Fathers of Confederation*, by Robert Harris

1917 (15 Sept). 50th Anniversary of Confederation. Perf 12.

244	**48**	3c. bistre-brown	25·00	5·00
245		3c. deep brown	30·00	6·50

No. 244 exists imperforate, without gum (*Price per pair*, £500 *unused*).

Die I (top) and II (bottom)

Die I. Space between top of 'N' and oval frame line and space between 'CENT' and lower frame line.

Die II. 'ONE CENT' appears larger so that 'N' touches oval and 'CENT' almost touches frame line. There are other differences but this is the most obvious one.

Die I (top) and II (bottom)

Die I. The lowest of the three horizontal lines of shading below the medals does not touch the three heavy diagonal lines; three complete white spaces over both 'E's of 'THREE'; long centre bar to figures '3'. Vertical spandrel lines fine.

Die II. The lowest horizontal line of shading touches the first of the three diagonal lines; two and a half spaces over first 'E' and spaces over second 'E' partly filled by stem of Maple leaf; short centre bar to figures '3'. Vertical spandrel lines thick. There are numerous other minor differences.

WET AND DRY PRINTINGS. See notes above No. 196. On Nos. 246/263 all listed items occur from both 'wet' and 'dry' printings except Nos. 246aa/246ab, 248aa, 256, 259, 260 and 262 which come 'wet' only, and Nos. 246a, 248/248a, 252/254a, 256b and 263 which are 'dry' only.

1922–31. As T **44**.

(a) Perf 12. Perf 12.

246	**44**	1c. chrome-yellow (Die I) (7.6.22)	3·50	60
		aa. Booklet pane of 4+2 labels (7.22)	60·00	
		ab. Booklet pane of 6 (12.22)	40·00	
		a. Die II (1925)	9·00	30
247		2c. deep green (6.6.22)	2·50	10
		aa. Booklet pane of 4+2 labels (7.22)	55·00	
		ab. Booklet pane of 6 (12.22)	£325	
		b. Thin paper (9.24)	3·50	6·50
248		3c. carmine (Die I) (18.12.23)	4·00	10
		aa. Booklet pane of 4+2 labels (12.23)	50·00	

CANADA

		a. Die II (11.24)	45·00	80
249		4c. olive-yellow (7.7.22)	9·00	3·50
		a. Yellow-ochre	8·00	3·50
250		5c. violet (2.2.22)	7·50	1·75
		a. Thin paper (9.24)	6·00	10·00
		b. Reddish violet (1925)	12·00	2·25
251		7c. red-brown (12.12.24)	12·00	9·00
		a. Thin paper	£170	55·00
252		8c. blue (1.9.25)	23·00	11·00
253		10c. blue (20.2.22)	18·00	3·25
254		10c. bistre-brown (1.8.25)	29·00	4·25
		a. Yellow-brown	25·00	5·00
255		$1 brown-orange (22.7.23)	55·00	10·00
246/255 Set of 10			£140	38·00

The $1 differs from T **44** in that the value tablets are oval.

Nos. 249/252 and 254/255 exist imperforate (*Prices per unused pair* 4c. to 10c. £2500 *each*, $1 £3000).

(b) Coil stamps. Imperf×perf 8. Imperf×perf 8.

256	**44**	1c. chrome-yellow (Die I) (1922)	4·00	11·00
		a. Imperf horiz (vert pair) (1924)	£180	
		b. Die II (1925)	4·50	7·00
		c. Do. Imperf horiz (vert pair) (1927)	8·00	27·00
257		2c. deep green (26.7.22)	7·00	2·25
		b. Imperf horiz (vert pair) (1927)	9·00	27·00
258		3c. carmine (Die I) (9.4.24)	70·00	19·00
		a. Imperf horiz (vert pair) (1924)	£250	
		b. Die II (1925)	£100	38·00
256/258 Set of 3			75·00	25·00

Nos. 256a, 256c, 257b and 258a come from coil printings sold in sheet form. Those issued in 1924 were from 'wet' printings and those in 1927 from 'dry'. A 'wet' printing of No. 257b, issued in 1924, also exists (*Price* £180 *mint*), but cannot be identified from that issued in 1927 except by the differences between 'wet' and 'dry' stamps.

(c) Imperf (pairs). Imperf (pairs).

259	**44**	1c. chrome-yellow (Die I) (6.10.24)	50·00	70·00
260		2c. deep green (6.10.24)	50·00	70·00
261		3c. carmine (Die I) (31.12.23)†	32·00	55·00

(d) Coil stamp. Perf 12×imperf. Perf 12×imperf.

262	**44**	2c. deep green (9.24)	65·00	65·00

(e) Perf 12×8. Perf 12×8.

263	**44**	3c. carmine (Die II) (24.6.31)	5·50	4·00

† Earliest known postmark.

Nos. 259 to 261 were on sale only at the Philatelic Branch, PO Dept, Ottawa.

No. 263 was produced by adding horizontal perforations to unused sheet stock of No. 258b. The stamps were then issued in 1931 pending the delivery of No. 293.

2 CENTS **2 CENTS**
(49) (50)

1926. No. 248 surch.

(a) With T **49**, *by the Govt Printing Bureau.*

264	**44**	2c. on 3c. carmine (12.10.26)	50·00	65·00
		a. Vert pair, one without surch	£750	
		b. On Die II	£850	

(b) With T **50**, *by the Canadian Bank Note Co.*

265	**44**	2c. on 3c. carmine (4.11.26)	20·00	35·00
		a. Surch double (partly treble)	£250	

51 Sir J. A. Macdonald   **52** The Fathers of Confederation

55 Canada, Map 1867–1927

1927 (29 June). 60th Anniversary of Confederation. Perf 12.

I. Commemorative Issue. Inscr '1867–1927 CANADA CONFEDERATION'.

266	**51**	1c. orange	2·50	1·50
267	**52**	2c. green	2·25	30
268	**53**	3c. carmine	11·00	5·50
269	**54**	5c. violet	7·00	5·00
270	**55**	12c. blue	35·00	12·00
266/270 Set of 5			50·00	22·00

Nos. 266/270 exist imperforate, imperf×perf or perf×imperf (*Prices from* £120, *unused, per pair*).

56 Darcy McGee   **57** Sir W. Laurier and Sir J. A. Macdonald

58 R. Baldwin and L. H. Lafontaine

II. Historical Issue.

271	**56**	5c. violet	3·00	3·50
272	**57**	12c. green	17·00	9·00
273	**58**	20c. carmine	28·00	19·00
271/273 Set of 3			42·00	28·00

Nos. 271/273 exist imperforate, imperf×perf or perf×imperf (*Prices from* £140, *unused, per pair*).

59

(Des H. Schwartz)

1928 (21 Sept). Air. Perf 12.

274	**59**	5c. olive-brown	8·00	6·50

No. 274 exists imperforate, imperf×perf or perf×imperf (*Price per pair*, £275, *unused*).

60 King George V   **61** Mount Hurd and Indian Totem Poles

62 Québec Bridge   **63** Harvesting with Horses

CANADA

64 *Bluenose* (fishing schooner)

65 Parliament Buildings, Ottawa

1928–29.

(a) Perf 12. Perf 12.

275	**60**	1c. orange (25.10.28)	2·75	3·00
		a. Booklet pane of 6	19·00	
276		2c. green (16.10.28)	1·50	20
		a. Booklet pane of 6	19·00	
277		3c. lake (12.12.28)	20·00	23·00
278		4c. olive-bistre (16.8.29)	14·00	13·00
279		5c. violet (12.12.28)	9·00	5·50
		a. Booklet pane of 6 (6.1.29)	£130	
280		8c. blue (21.12.28)	12·00	7·50
281	**61**	10c. green (5.12.28)	15·00	2·25
282	**62**	12c. grey-black (8.1.29)	38·00	22·00
283	**63**	20c. lake (8.1.29)	60·00	25·00
284	**64**	50c. blue (8.1.29)	£190	55·00
285	**65**	$1 olive-green (8.1.29)	£250	90·00
		a. Brown-olive	£300	£140
275/285 Set of 11			£550	£225

(b) Coil stamps. Imperf×perf 8 (5.11.28). Imperf×perf 8 (5.11.28).

286	**60**	1c. orange	30·00	27·00
287		2c. green	30·00	10·00

Slight differences in the size of many Canadian stamps, due to paper shrinkage, are to be found.

Nos. 275/285 exist imperforate, imperf×perf or perf×imperf (*Prices per unused pair, 1c. to 8c., from £120, 10c. to 20c., from £200, 50c. and $1, from £650*). Tête-bêche horizontal pairs of the 1c., 2c. and 5c. are also known from uncut booklet sheets (*Prices per pair, £325, unused*).

PRINTERS. The following stamps to No. 334 were recess-printed by the British American Bank Note Co, Ottawa.

66 King George V   **67** Parliamentary Library, Ottawa   **68** The Old Citadel, Québec

69 Harvesting with Tractor   **70** Acadian Memorial Church and Statue of *Evangeline*, Grand Pre, Nova Scotia

71 Mount Edith Cavell, Canadian Rockies   Die I   Die II

1c.
Die I. Three thick coloured lines and one thin between 'P' and ornament, at right. Curved line in ball-ornament short.
Die II. Four thick lines. Curved line longer.

Die I   Die II

2c.
Die I. Three thick coloured lines between 'P' and ornament, at left. Short line in ball.
Die II. Four thick lines. Curved line longer.

Normal

Re-entry. Plate 2, upper left pane, R. 10/6 (later retouched on 1c. green)

Normal

2c. 'Cockeyed King' (Retouch on coil stamps)

(Des . Eng C. Arlt (1c. to 8c.))

1930–31.

(a) Perf 11. Perf 11.

288	**66**	1c. orange (Die I) (17.7.30)	1·75	1·75
		a. Re-entry	80·00	70·00
289		1c. green (Die I) (6.12.30)	5·50	10
		a. Re-entry	95·00	50·00
		b. Booklet pane of 6 (21.7.31)	35·00	
		d. Die II (8.31)	4·00	10
		da. Imperf (pair)	£2000	
		db. Booklet pane of 4+2 labels (13.11.31)	£100	
290		2c. green (Die I) (6.6.30)	1·75	10
		a. Booklet pane of 6 (17.6.30)	45·00	
291		2c. scarlet (Die I) (17.11.30)	3·00	3·50
		a. Booklet pane of 6 (17.11.30)	25·00	
		b. Die II	1·00	10
292		2c. deep brown (Die I) (4.7.31)	4·25	6·50
		a. Booklet pane of 6 (23.7.31)	55·00	
		b. Die II (4.7.31)	2·00	10
		ba. Booklet pane of 4+2 labels (13.11.31)	£140	
293		3c. scarlet (13.7.31)	2·75	10
		a. Booklet pane of 4+2 labels	55·00	
294		4c. yellow-bistre (5.11.30)	15·00	4·50
295		5c. violet (18.6.30)	3·00	11·50
296		5c. deep slate-blue (13.11.30)	11·00	20
		a. Dull blue	25·00	1·50

CANADA

297		8c. blue (13.8.30)		12·00	24·00
298		8c. red-orange (5.11.30)		14·00	5·50
299	**67**	10c. olive-green (15.9.30)		23·00	2·25
		a. Imperf (pair)		£1800	
300	**68**	12c. grey-black (4.12.30)		20·00	7·00
301	**69**	20c. red (4.12.30)		35·00	2·50
302	**70**	50c. blue (4.12.30)		£120	17·00
303	**71**	$1 olive-green (4.12.30)		£180	40·00
288/303		Set of 16		£400	90·00

(b) Coil stamps. Imperf×perf 8½. Imperf×perf 8½.

304	**66**	1c. orange (Die I) (14.7.30)		13·00	21·00
305		1c. green (Die I) (4.2.31)		6·00	7·50
306		2c. green (Die I) (27.6.30)		4·00	13·00
		a. Cockeyed King		65·00	95·00
307		2c. scarlet (Die I) (19.11.30)		4·50	11·00
		a. Cockeyed King		70·00	95·00
308		2c. deep brown (Die I) (4.7.31)		9·00	1·50
		a. Cockeyed King		80·00	65·00
309		3c. scarlet (13.7.31)		14·00	2·25
304/309		Set of 6		45·00	50·00

Nos. 300/303 exist imperforate (*Prices per unused pair*, 12c. £900, 20c. £900, 50c. £950, $1 £1000).

The 'Cockeyed King' variety appears on every eighth roll, on every 48th stamp in that roll, to the left of every second inter-plate line.

Some low values in the above and subsequent issues have been printed by both Rotary and 'Flat plate' processes. The former can be distinguished by the gum, which has a striped appearance.

For 13c. bright violet, T **68**, see No. 325.

72 Mercury and Western Hemisphere **73** Sir Georges Étienne Cartier

(Des H. Schwartz)

1930 (4 Dec). Air. Perf 11.

310	**72**	5c. deep brown		26·00	30·00

1931 (30 Sept). Perf 11.

312	**73**	10c. olive-green		14·00	50

No. 312 exists imperforate (*Price per pair*, £500, *unused*).

(74)   (75)

1932 (22 Feb). Air. No. 274 surch with T **74**.

313	**59**	6c. on 5c. olive-brown		3·00	4·00

Examples of this stamp with surcharge inverted, surcharge double, surcharge triple or surcharge omitted in pair with normal are not now believed to have been regularly issued. Such 'errors' have also been forged and collectors are warned against forged examples, some of which bear unauthorised markings which purport to be the guarantee of Stanley Gibbons Ltd.

1932 (21 June). Nos. 291/291b surch with T **75**.

314	**66**	3c. on 2c. scarlet (Die I)		6·00	5·50
		a. Die II		1·00	60

76 King George V   **77** Duke of Windsor when Prince of Wales   **78** Allegory of British Empire

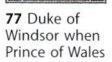

OTTAWA CONFERENCE 1932

(79)

1932 (12 July). Ottawa Conference. Perf 11.

(a) Postage stamps.

315	**76**	3c. scarlet		1·00	80
316	**77**	5c. blue		14·00	5·50
317	**78**	13c. green		14·00	6·00

*(b) Air. No. 310 surch with T **79**.*

318	**72**	6c. on 5c. deep brown (B.)		16·00	28·00
315/318		Set of 4		40·00	35·00

80 King George V   '3' level Die I (Plates 1 and 2)   '3' raised Die II (Plates 3 to 12)

1932 (1 Dec)–**33**.

(a) Perf 11. Perf 11.

319	**80**	1c. green		60	10
		a. Booklet pane of 6 (28.12.33)		16·00	
		b. Booklet pane of 4+2 labels (19.9.33)		85·00	
320		2c. sepia		70	10
		a. Booklet pane of 6 (7.9.33)		22·00	
		b. Booklet pane of 4+2 labels (19.9.33)		95·00	
321		3c. scarlet (Die I)		2·75	10
		b. Die II (29.11.32)		85	10
		ba. Booklet pane of 4+2 labels (28.8.33)		45·00	
322		4c. yellow-brown		50·00	15·00
323		5c. blue		13·00	10
		a. Imperf vert (horiz pair)		£1800	
324		8c. red-orange		45·00	4·50
325	**68**	13c. bright violet		85·00	3·50
319/325		Set of 7		£170	21·00

Nos. 319/325 exist imperforate (*Prices per unused pair*, 1c. to 8c. £225, 13c. £800).

(b) Coil stamps. Imperf×perf 8½ (1933). Imperf×perf 8½ (1933).

326	**80**	1c. green (3.11.33)		24·00	7·50
327		2c. sepia (15.8.33)		24·00	6·50
328		3c. scarlet (Die II) (16.8.33)		12·00	4·00
326/328		Set of 3		55·00	16·00

WET AND DRY PRINTINGS. See note above No. 196. Nos. 319/321 exist from both 'wet' and 'dry' printings from the Stickney rotary press.

81 Parliament Buildings, Ottawa

WORLD'S GRAIN EXHIBITION & CONFERENCE

REGINA 1933

(82)

1933 (18 May). UPU Congress Preliminary Meeting. Perf 11.

329	**81**	5c. blue		13·00	5·50

No. 329 exists imperforate (*Price per pair* £850, *unused*).

1933 (24 July). World's Grain Exhibition and Conference, Regina. No. 301 optd with T **82** in blue.

330	**69**	20c. red		25·00	19·00

No. 330 exists imperforate (*Price per pair* £850, *unused*).

83 SS *Royal William* (after S. Skillett)   **84** Jacques Cartier Approaching Land

1933 (17 Aug). Centenary of First Trans-Atlantic Steamboat Crossing. Perf 11.

331	**83**	5c. blue		20·00	8·00

No. 331 exists imperforate (*Price per pair* £850, *unused*).

1934 (1 July). 400th Anniversary of Discovery of Canada. Perf 11.

332	**84**	3c. blue		6·00	2·00

No. 332 exists imperforate (*Price per pair* £800, *unused*).

CANADA

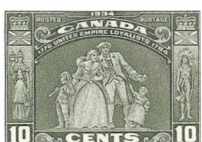 

85 UEL Statue, Hamilton   **86** Seal of New Brunswick

1934 (1 July). 150th Anniversary of Arrival of United Empire Loyalists. Perf 11.
333   85   10c. olive-green............................. 15·00   14·00
No. 333 exists imperforate (*Price per pair* £1600, *unused*)

1934 (16 Aug). 150th Anniversary of Province of New Brunswick. Perf 11.
334   86   2c. red-brown .... 2·00   3·50
No. 334 exists imperforate (*Price per pair* £850, *unused*).

PRINTERS. The following stamps were recess-printed (*except where otherwise stated*) by the Canadian Bank Note Co, Ottawa, until No. 616.

87 Queen Elizabeth II when Princess   **88** King George VI when Duke of York   **89** King George V and Queen Mary

90 King Edward VIII when Prince of Wales   **91** Windsor Castle

92 Royal Yacht *Britannia*   'Weeping Princess' (Pl 1 upper right pane R. 3/1)

'Shilling mark' (Pl 1 upper right pane R. 8/8)

1935 (4 May). Silver Jubilee. Types **87**/**92**. Perf 12.
335   87   1c. green.. 1·50   1·75
           a. Weeping Princess £160   £100
336   88   2c. brown.. 1·00   1·75
337   89   3c. carmine-red.................................. 4·50   2·25
338   90   5c. blue.. 9·00   9·00
339   91   10c. green.. 13·00 10·00
340   92   13c. blue.. 16·00 15·00
           a. Shilling mark..................................... £600   £600
335/340 Set of 6... 40·00 35·00
Nos. 335/340 exist imperforate (*Prices per unused pair*, 1c to 5c. *each* £300, 10c. *and* 13c. *each* £350).

93 King George V   **94** Royal Canadian Mounted Policeman

95 Confederation Conference, Charlottetown, 1864   **96** Niagara Falls

97 Parliament Buildings, Victoria, British Columbia   **98** Champlain Monument, Québec

 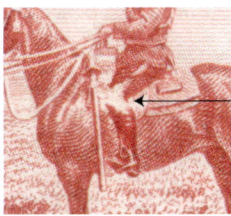

99 Daedalus   **10c.** Broken leg (Pl. 1, R. 5/8)

50c. Major re-entry (Pl. 1 upper right pane, R. 5/5)

1c. Normal   **1c.** Narrow '1'

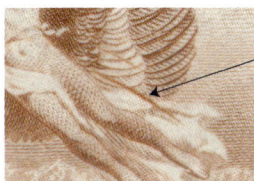

6c. Moulting wing (Pl. 1, lower right pane, R. 3/4)

29

CANADA

1935 (1 June–16 Nov). Types **93/99**.

(a) Postage(i) Perf 12. Perf 12.

341	**93**	1c. green	1·75	10
		a. Booklet pane of 6 (19.8.35)	28·00	
		b. Booklet pane of 4+2 labels (22.7.35)	70·00	
342		2c. brown	1·75	10
		a. Booklet pane of 6 (16.11.35)	29·00	
		b. Booklet pane of 4+2 labels (22.7.35)	70·00	
343		3c. scarlet	1·75	10
		a. Booklet pane of 4+2 labels	42·00	
		b. Printed on the gummed side	£325	
344		4c. yellow	3·50	3·25
345		5c. blue	3·75	10
		a. Imperf vert (horiz pair)	£225	
346		8c. orange	4·25	5·00
347	**94**	10c. carmine	6·50	50
		a. Broken leg	£2500	£1800
348	**95**	13c. purple	8·00	75
349	**96**	20c. olive-green	25·00	2·50
350	**97**	50c. deep violet	32·00	10·00
		a. Major re-entry	£150	£100
351	**98**	$1 bright blue	50·00	16·00
341/351	Set of 11		£120	32·00

(ii) Coil stamps. Imperf×perf 8. mperf×perf 8.

352	**93**	1c. green (5.11.35)	21·00	17·00
		a. Narrow '1'	80·00	65·00
353		2c. brown (14.10.35)	14·00	7·50
354		3c. scarlet (20.7.35)	9·00	2·00
352/354	Set of 3		40·00	24·00

(b) Air. Perf 12. Perf 12.

355	**99**	6c. red-brown	4·25	1·00
		a. Imperf vert (horiz pair)	£8500	
		b. Moulting wing	£110	70·00

Nos. 341/351 (*Prices per pair*, 1c. to 8c. *each* £170, 10c. to 50c. *each* £300, $1 £350, *unused*) and No. 355 (*Price per pair* £750, *unused*) exist imperforate.

100 King George VI and Queen Elizabeth

1937 (10 May). Coronation. Perf 12.

356	**100**	3c. carmine	2·00	1·50

No. 356 exists imperforate (*Price per pair* £900, *unused*).

Crease on collar (Pl 2 upper right pane R. 9/5)

(T **101**. Photograph by Bertram Park. Des H. Schwartz, 10c. to $1.)

1937–38. Types **101/107**.

(a) Postage(i) Perf 12. Perf 12.

357	**101**	1c. green (1.4.37)	2·50	10
		a. Booklet pane of 4+2 labels (14.4.37)	30·00	
		b. Booklet pane of 6 (18.5.37)	12·50	
358		2c. brown (1.4.37)	3·25	10
		a. Booklet pane of 4+2 labels (14.4.37)	60·00	
		b. Booklet pane of 6 (3.5.38)	16·00	
359		3c. scarlet (1.4.37)	1·75	10
		a. Booklet pane of 4+2 labels (14.4.37)	6·50	
		b. Crease on collar	£100	40·00
360		4c. yellow (10.5.37)	5·50	1·75
361		5c. blue (10.5.37)	8·50	10
362		8c. orange (10.5.37)	6·50	3·75
363	**102**	10c. rose-carmine (15.6.38)	7·00	60
		a. Red	5·00	10
364	**103**	13c. blue (15.11.38)	35·00	3·50
365	**104**	20c. red-brown (15.6.38)	25·00	2·75
366	**105**	50c. green (15.6.38)	50·00	16·00
367	**106**	$1 violet (15.6.38)	65·00	20·00
		a. Imperf horiz (vert pair)	£7500	
357/367	Set of 11		£180	40·00

Nos. 357/367 exist imperforate (*Prices per pair* 1c. to 8c. *each* £375, 10c. to 50c. *each* £700, $1 £900 *unused*).

(ii) Coil stamps. Imperf×perf 8. Imperf×perf 8.

368	**101**	1c. green (15.6.37)	4·50	7·00
369		2c. brown (18.6.37)	3·75	6·50
370		3c. scarlet (15.4.37)	35·00	10·00
368/370	Set of 3		38·00	14·50

(b) Air. Perf 12. Perf 12.

371	**107**	6c. blue (15.6.38)	20·00	2·25

No. 371 exists imperforate (*Price per pair* £850, *unused*).

101 King George VI

102 Memorial Chamber, Parliament Buildings, Ottawa

103 Entrance to Halifax Harbour

104 Fort Garry Gate, Winnipeg

105 Entrance, Vancouver Harbour

106 Château de Ramezay, Montréal

107 Fairchild 45-80 Sekani Seaplane over SS *Distributor* on River Mackenzie

108 Queen Elizabeth II when Princess and Princess Margaret

109 National War Memorial

110 King George VI and Queen Elizabeth

1939 (15 May). Royal Visit. Perf 12.

372	**108**	1c. black and green	3·50	25
373	**109**	2c. black and brown	3·00	2·00
374	**110**	3c. black and carmine	2·00	25
372/374	Set of 3		7·50	2·25

Nos. 372/374 exist imperforate (*Price* £850, *unused, for each pair*).

CANADA

111 King George VI in Naval Uniform **112** King George VI in Military Uniform **113** King George VI in Air Force Uniform **114** Grain Elevator

115 Farm Scene **116** Parliament Buildings **117** Ram Tank

118 Launching of Corvette HMCS *La Malbaie*, Sorel **119** Munitions Factory

120 HMS *Cossack* (destroyer) **121** Air Training Camp

1942 (1 July)–**48**. War Effort. Types **111/121** and similar designs.

(a) Postage(i) Perf 12. Perf 12.

375	111	1c. green	1·50	10
		a. Booklet pane of 4+2 labels (12.9.42)	35·00	
		b. Booklet pane of 6 (24.11.42)	7·50	
376	112	2c. brown	1·75	10
		a. Booklet pane of 4+2 labels (12.9.42)	42·00	
		b. Booklet pane of 6 (6.10.42)	32·00	
377	113	3c. carmine-lake	1·25	60
		a. Booklet pane of 4+2 labels (20.8.42)	5·50	
378		3c. purple (30.6.43)	1·75	10
		a. Booklet pane of 4+2 labels (28.8.43)	7·50	
		b. Booklet pane of 6 (24.11.47)	16·00	
379	114	4c. slate	5·50	3·75
380	112	4c. carmine-lake (9.4.43)	1·00	10
		a. Booklet pane of 6 (3.5.43)	5·00	
381	111	5c. blue	3·50	10
382	115	8c. red-brown	6·50	1·25
383	116	10c. brown	16·00	10
384	117	13c. dull green	15·00	13·00
385		14c. dull green (16.4.43)	29·00	1·00
386	118	20c. chocolate	22·00	45
387	119	50c. violet	28·00	8·00
388	120	$1 blue	50·00	18·00
375/388 *Set of 14*			£160	40·00

Nos. 375/388 exist imperforate (*Prices per pair 1c. to 8c. each £375, 10c. to 20c. each £750, 50c. and $1 each £850, unused*).

(ii) Coil stamps. Imperf×perf 8. Imperf×perf 8.

389	111	1c. green (9.2.43)	1·00	1·50
390	112	2c. brown (24.11.42)	2·25	3·50
391	113	3c. carmine-lake (23.9.42)	2·00	11·00
392		3c. purple (19.8.43)	11·00	11·00
393	112	4c. carmine-lake (13.5.43)	12·00	2·25
389/393 *Set of 5*			25·00	26·00

(iii) Booklet stamps. Imperf×perf 12 (1.9.43). Imperf×perf 12 (1.9.43).

394	111	1c. green	6·50	1·75
		a. Booklet pane of 3	18·00	
395	113	3c. purple	6·50	2·25
		a. Booklet pane of 3	18·00	
396	112	4c. carmine-lake	6·50	3·00
		a. Booklet pane of 3	18·00	
394/396 *Set of 3*			17·00	6·25

Nos. 394/396 are from booklets in which the stamps are in strips of three, imperforate at top and bottom and right-hand end.

(iv) Coil stamps. Imperf×perf 9½. Imperf×perf 9½.

397	111	1c. green (13.7.48)	4·25	5·00
397a	112	2c. brown (1.10.48)	8·00	19·00
398	113	3c. purple (2.7.48)	5·00	6·00
398a	112	4c. carmine-lake (22.7.48)	9·00	7·00
397/398a *Set of 4*			24·00	32·00

(b) Air. Perf 12. Perf 12.

399	121	6c. blue (1.7.42)	32·00	14·00
400		7c. blue (16.4.43)	5·50	50

Nos. 399/400 exist imperforate (*Price £1000, unused, for each pair*).

122 Ontario Farm Scene **123** Great Bear Lake

124 St Maurice River Power Station **125** Combine-harvester

126 Lumbering in British Columbia **127** *Abegweit* (train ferry), Prince Edward Island

128 Canada Geese in Flight **129** Alexander Graham Bell and Fame

1946 (16 Sept)–**47**. Peace Re-conversion. Types **122/128**. Perf 12.

(a) Postage.

401	122	8c. brown	3·25	4·00
402	123	10c. olive-green	3·00	10
403	124	14c. sepia	6·50	4·00
404	125	20c. slate	6·50	10
405	126	50c. green	15·00	8·00
406	127	$1 purple	30·00	8·00

(b) Air.

407	128	7c. blue	6·00	40
		a. Booklet pane of 4 (24.11.47)	20·00	
401/407 *Set of 7*			60·00	22·00

1947 (3 Mar). Birth Centenary of Bell (inventor of telephone). Perf 12.

408	129	4c. blue	15	50

130 Canadian Citizenship **131** Queen Elizabeth II when Princess

31

CANADA

1947 (1 July). Advent of Canadian Citizenship and 18th Anniversary of Confederation. Perf 12.
409	**130**	4c. blue..	10	40

(From photograph by Dorothy Wilding)

1948 (16 Feb). Princess Elizabeth's Marriage. Perf 12.
410	**131**	4c. blue..	15	30

132 Queen Victoria, Parliament Building, Ottawa, and King George VI

133 Cabot's Ship *Matthew*

1948 (1 Oct). 100 Years of Responsible Government. Perf 12.
411	**132**	4c. grey...	10	10

1949 (1 Apr). Entry of Newfoundland into Canadian Confederation. Perf 12.
412	**133**	4c. green...	30	10

134 Founding of Halifax, 1749 (C. W. Jefferys)

1949 (21 June). Bicentenary of Halifax, Nova Scotia. Perf 12.
413	**134**	4c. violet...	45	20

135 **136** **137**

138 King George VI **139** King George VI

(From photographs by Dorothy Wilding)

1949 (15 Nov)–51.

(i) Perf 12. Perf 12.
414	**135**	1c. green...	50	10
415	**136**	2c. sepia...	2·25	45
415a		2c. olive-green (25.7.51).................	1·40	10
416	**137**	3c. purple..	30	10
		a. Booklet pane of 4+2 labels (12.4.50)..	3·50	
417	**138**	4c. carmine-lake................................	20	10
		a. Booklet pane of 6 (5.5.50)............	25·00	
417b		4c. vermilion (2.6.51).......................	60	10
		ba. Booklet pane of 6.......................	8·00	
418	**139**	5c. blue..	1·50	60
414/418 Set of 7...			6·00	1·00

(ii) Coil stamps. Imperf×perf 9½. Imperf×perf 9½.
419	**135**	1c. green (18.5.50)............................	3·00	3·50
420	**136**	2c. sepia (18.5.50).............................	9·50	7·00
420a		2c. olive-green (9.10.51)..................	1·75	6·00
421	**137**	3c. purple (18.5.50)...........................	2·25	4·00
422	**138**	4c. carmine-lake (20.4.50)..............	14·00	14·00
422a		4c. vermilion (27.11.51)....................	3·25	4·00
419/422a Set of 5...			30·00	35·00

(iii) Booklet stamps. Imperf×perf 12. Imperf×perf 12.
422b	**135**	1c. green (18.5.50)............................	1·25	3·25
		ba. Booklet pane of 3.......................	4·50	
423	**137**	3c. purple (18.5.50)...........................	1·50	1·00
		a. Booklet pane of 3.........................	5·50	
423b	**138**	4c. carmine-lake (18.5.50)..............	18·00	14·00
		ba. Booklet pane of 3.......................	55·00	
423c		4c. vermilion (25.10.51)..................	13·00	14·00
		ca. Booklet pane of 3.......................	42·00	
422b/423c Set of 4..			29·00	28·00

These booklet panes are imperforate at top, bottom and right-hand end.

140 King George VI **141** Oil Wells in Alberta

(From photograph by Dorothy Wilding)

1950 (19 Jan). As Types **135/139** but without 'POSTES POSTAGE', as T **140**.

(i) Perf 12. Perf 12.
424		1c. green...	70	2·25
425		2c. sepia...	1·00	7·00
426		3c. purple..	70	1·00
427		4c. carmine-lake................................	70	30
428		5c. blue..	70	4·50
424/428 Set of 5...			3·50	13·00

(ii) Coil stamps. Imperf×perf 9½. Imperf×perf 9½.
429		1c. green...	30	2·50
430		3c. purple..	80	3·50

1950 (1 Mar). Perf 12.
431	**141**	50c. green..	7·50	1·00

142 Drying Furs **143** Fisherman

1950 (2 Oct). Perf 12.
432	**142**	10c. brown-purple............................	3·50	10

1951 (1 Feb). Perf 12.
433	**143**	$1 ultramarine.................................	35·00	7·50

144 Sir R. L. Borden **145** W. L. Mackenzie King

1951 (25 June). Prime Ministers (1st issue). Perf 12.
434		3c. blue-green....................................	30	1·50
435	**145**	4c. rose-carmine................................	80	25

See also Nos. 444/445, 475/476 and 483/484.

146 Mail Trains, 1851 and 1951 **147** SS *City of Toronto* and SS *Prince George*

148 Mail Coach and DC-4M North Star **149** Reproduction of 3d., 1851

1951 (24 Sept). Canadian Stamp Centenary. Perf 12.
436	**146**	4c. black...	75	10
437	**147**	5c. violet..	2·00	3·50
438	**148**	7c. blue..	1·00	2·25

CANADA

439	**149**	15c. scarlet		1·60	10
436/439	*Set of 4*			4·75	5·50

150 Queen Elizabeth II when Princess and Duke of Edinburgh

151 Forestry Products

1951 (26 Oct). Royal Visit. Perf 12.
440	**150**	4c. violet		20	30

(Des A. L. Pollock)

1952 (1 Apr). Perf 12.
441	**151**	20c. grey		2·75	10

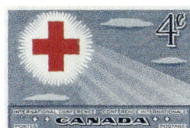
152 Red Cross Emblem

1952 (26 July). 18th International Red Cross Conference, Toronto. Design recess; cross litho. Perf 12.
442	**152**	4c. scarlet and blue		15	10

153 Canada Goose

154 Pacific Coast Indian House and Totem Pole

(Des E. Hahn)

1952 (3 Nov). Perf 12.
443	**153**	7c. blue		1·25	10

1952 (3 Nov). Prime Ministers (2nd issue). Various portraits as T **144**. Perf 12.
444		3c. reddish purple		35	75
445		4c. orange-red		25	35

Portraits: 3c. Sir John J. C. Abbott; 4c. A. Mackenzie.

(Des E. Hahn)

1953 (2 Feb). Perf 12.
446	**154**	$1 black		4·50	25

155 Polar Bear

156 Elk

157 American Bighorn

(Des J. Crosby (2c.), E. Hahn (others))

1953 (1 Apr). National Wild Life Week. Perf 12.
447	**155**	2c. blue		15	10
448	**156**	3c. sepia		15	70
449	**157**	4c. slate		15	10
447/449	*Set of 3*			40	70

158 Queen Elizabeth II

159 Queen Elizabeth II

(From photograph by Karsh, Ottawa)

1953 (1 May–3 Sept).

(a) Sheet stamps. Perf 12. Perf 12.
450	**158**	1c. purple-brown		10	10
451		2c. green		15	10
452		3c. carmine		15	15
		a. Booklet pane of 4+2 labels (17.7)		2·50	
453		4c. violet		20	10
		a. Booklet pane of 6 (6.7)		8·00	
454		5c. ultramarine		25	10
450/454	*Set of 5*			75	30

(b) Coil stamps. Imperf×perf 9½. Imperf×perf 9½.
455	**158**	2c. green (30.7)		2·25	2·00
456		3c. carmine (27.7)		2·25	1·00
457		4c. violet (3.9)		2·25	1·25
455/457	*Set of 3*			6·00	3·75

(c) Booklet stamps. Imperf×perf 12. Imperf×perf 12.
458	**158**	1c. purple-brown (12.8)		2·25	1·50
		a. Booklet pane of 3		6·50	
459		3c. carmine (17.7)		2·25	1·50
		a. Booklet pane of 3		6·50	
460		4c. violet (6.7)		2·25	1·50
		a. Booklet pane of 3		6·50	
458/460	*Set of 3*			6·00	4·00

These booklet stamps have top and bottom or top, bottom and right-hand sides imperforate.

(Des E. Hahn)

1953 (1 June). Coronation. Perf 12.
461	**159**	4c. violet		20	20

160 Textile Industry

161 Queen Elizabeth II

(Des A. L. Pollock)

1953 (2 Nov). Perf 12.
462	**160**	50c. deep bluish green		1·75	10

(From photograph by Dorothy Wilding)

1954–62.

(i) Perf 12. Perf 12.
463	**161**	1c. purple-brown (10.6.54)		10	10
		a. Booklet pane. 5 stamps plus printed label (1.6.56)		2·50	
		p. 2 phosphor bands (13.1.62)		1·00	3·75
464		2c. green (10.6.54)		20	10
		a. Pack. 2 blocks of 25 (12.61)		9·00	
		p. 2 phosphor bands (13.1.62)		1·00	4·50
465		3c. carmine (10.6.54)		1·00	10
		a. Imperf vert (horiz pair)		£1800	
		p. 2 phosphor bands (13.1.62)		1·50	3·50
466		4c. violet (10.6.54)		30	10
		a. Booklet pane of 6 (7.7.55)		6·50	
		b. Booklet pane. 5 stamps plus printed label (1.6.56)		3·50	
		p. 1 phosphor band (13.1.62)		2·25	11·00
467		5c. bright blue (1.4.54)		30	10
		a. Booklet pane. 5 stamps plus printed label (14.7.54)		3·50	
		b. Pack. 1 block of 20 (12.61)		6·00	
		c. Imperf vert (horiz pair)*		£6000	
		p. 2 phosphor bands (13.1.62)		3·50	8·00
468		6c. red-orange (10.6.54)		1·75	55
463/468	*Set of 6*			3·25	70
463p/467p	*Set of 5*			8·25	27·00

(ii) Coil stamps. Imperf×perf 9½. Imperf×perf 9½.
469	**161**	2c. green (9.9.54)		1·50	75
470		4c. violet (23.8.54)		1·50	2·00
471		5c. bright blue (6.7.54)		1·75	45
469/471	*Set of 3*			4·50	3·00

* No. 467c is from the left side of a sheet and shows perforations between the stamps and the sheet margin.

CANADA

Nos. 464a and 467b are blocks with the outer edges imperf. These come from One Dollar Plastic Packages sold at post offices.

WINNIPEG PHOSPHOR BANDS. In 1962 facer-cancelling machines were introduced in Winnipeg which were activated by phosphor bands on the stamps. Under long or short wave ultraviolet light the phosphor glows and there is also a short after-glow when the lamp is turned off. This should not be confused with the fluorescent bands introduced in Ottawa in 1971.

162 Walrus **163** American Beaver **164** Northern Gannet

(Des E. Hahn)

1954 (1 Apr). National Wild Life Week. Perf 12.
472	**162**	4c. slate-black	45	30
473	**163**	5c. ultramarine	35	10
		a. Booklet pane. 5 stamps plus 1 printed label	2·00	

(Des L. Hyde)

1954 (1 Apr). Perf 12.
474	**164**	15c. black	1·50	10

1954 (1 Nov). Prime Ministers (3rd issue). Various portraits as T **144**. Perf 12.
475		4c. violet	20	1·00
476		5c. bright blue	20	60

Portraits: 4c. Sir John Thompson; 5c. Sir Mackenzie Bowell.

165 Inuit Hunter

(Des H. Beament)

1955 (21 Feb). Perf 12.
477	**165**	10c. purple-brown	1·25	10

166 Musk Ox **167** Whooping Cranes

(Des E. Hahn (4c.), Dr W. Rowan (5c.))

1955 (4 Apr). National Wild Life Week. Perf 12.
478	**166**	4c. violet	30	10
479	**167**	5c. ultramarine	1·00	20

168 Dove and Torch **169** Pioneer Settlers

(Des W. Lohse)

1955 (1 June). Tenth Anniversary of International Civil Aviation Organisation. Perf 12.
480	**168**	5c. ultramarine	40	20

(Des L. Hyde)

1955 (30 June). 50th Anniversary of Alberta and Saskatchewan Provinces. Perf 12.
481	**169**	5c. ultramarine	20	30

170 Scout Badge and Globe **173** Ice Hockey Players

(Des L. Hyde)

1955 (20 Aug). Eighth World Scout Jamboree, Niagara-on-the-Lake. Perf 12.
482	**170**	5c. orange-brown and green	30	10

1955 (8 Nov). Prime Ministers (4th issue). Various portraits as T **144**. Perf 12.
483		4c. violet	25	70
484		5c. bright blue	25	10

Portraits: 4c. R. B. Bennett; 5c. Sir Charles Tupper.

(Des J. Simpkins)

1956 (23 Jan). Ice Hockey Commemoration. Perf 12.
485	**173**	5c. ultramarine	20	20

174 Reindeer **175** Mountain Goat

(Des E. Hahn)

1956 (12 Apr). National Wild Life Week. Perf 12.
486	**174**	4c. violet	20	15
487	**175**	5c. bright blue	20	10

176 Pulp and Paper Industry **177** Chemical Industry

(Des A. J. Casson (20c.), A. L. Pollock (25c.))

1956 (7 June). P12.
488	**176**	20c. green	75	10
489	**177**	25c. red	75	10

178

(Des A. Price)

1956 (9 Oct). Fire Prevention Week. Perf 12.
490	**178**	5c. red and black	30	10

179 Fishing **180** Swimming

(Des L. Hyde)

1957 (7 Mar). Outdoor Recreation. Types **179**/**180** and similar horiz designs. Perf 12.
491	**179**	5c. ultramarine	40	15
		a. Block of 4. Nos. 491/494	2·00	3·00
492	**180**	5c. ultramarine	40	15

CANADA

493	–	5c. ultramarine	40	15
494	–	5c. ultramarine	40	15
491/494	Set of 4		2·00	3·00

Designs: No. 493, Hunting. No. 494, Skiing. Nos. 491/494 are printed together in sheets of 50 (5×10). In the first, second, fourth and fifth vertical rows the four different designs are arranged in *se-tenant* blocks, whilst the central row is made up as follows (reading downwards): Nos. 491/494, 491/492 (or 493/494), 491/494.

183 White-billed Diver   **184** Thompson with Sextant, and North American Map

(Des L. Hyde)

1957 (10 Apr). National Wild Life Week. Perf 12.
495	183	5c. black	50	20

(Des G. A. Gundersen)

1957 (5 June). Death Centenary of David Thompson (explorer). Perf 12.
496	184	5c. ultramarine	45	30

185 Parliament Buildings, Ottawa   **186** Globe within Posthorn

(Des Carl Mangold)

1957 (14 Aug). 14th UPU Congress, Ottawa. Perf 12.
497	185	5c. grey-blue	15	10
498	186	15c. blackish blue	2·00	2·00

187 Miner   **188** Queen Elizabeth II and Duke of Edinburgh

(Des A. J. Casson)

1957 (5 Sept). Mining Industry. Perf 12.
499	187	5c. black	35	20

(From photographs by Karsh, Ottawa)

1957 (10 Oct). Royal Visit. Perf 12.
500	188	5c. black	30	10

189 'A Free Press'   **190** Microscope

(Des A. L. Pollock)

1958 (22 Jan). The Canadian Press. Perf 12.
501	189	5c. black	20	70

(Des A. L. Pollock)

1958 (5 Mar). International Geophysical Year. Perf 12.
502	190	5c. blue	20	10

191 Miner panning for Gold   **192** la Vérendrye (statue)

(Des J. Harman)

1958 (8 May). Centenary of British Columbia. Perf 12.
503	191	5c. deep turquoise-green	20	10

(Des G. Trottier)

1958 (4 June). la Vérendrye (explorer) Commemoration. Perf 12.
504	192	5c. ultramarine	20	10

193 Samuel de Champlain and the Heights of Québec   **194** Nurse

(Des G. Trottier)

1958 (26 June). 350th Anniversary of Founding of Québec. Perf 12.
505	193	5c. brown-ochre and deep green	30	10

(Des G. Trottier)

1958 (30 July). National Health. Perf 12.
506	194	5c. reddish purple	30	10

195 'Petroleum 1858–1958'   **196** Speaker's Chair and Mace

(Des A. L. Pollock)

1958 (10 Sept). Centenary of Canadian Oil Industry. Perf 12.
507	195	5c. scarlet and olive	30	10

(Des G. Trottier and C. Dair)

1958 (2 Oct). Bicentenary of First Elected Assembly. Perf 12.
508	196	5c. deep slate	20	10

197 John McCurdy's *Silver Dart* Biplane   **198** Globe showing NATO Countries

1959 (23 Feb). 50th Anniversary of First Flight of the *Silver Dart* in Canada. Perf 12.
509	197	5c. black and ultramarine	30	10

(Des P. Weiss)

1959 (2 Apr). Tenth Anniversary of North Atlantic Treaty Organisation. Perf 12.
510	198	5c. ultramarine	40	10

CANADA

199   **200** Queen Elizabeth II

(Des Helen Fitzgerald)

1959 (13 May). Associated Country Women of the World Commemoration. Perf 12.
511   **199**   5c. black and yellow-olive   15   10

(Des after painting by Annigoni)

1959 (18 June). Royal Visit. Perf 12.
512   **200**   5c. lake-red   40   20

201 Maple Leaf linked with American Eagle   **202** Maple Leaves

(Des A. L. Pollock, G. Trottier (of Canada); W. H. Buckley, A. J. Copeland, E. Metzl (of the United States))

1959 (26 June). Opening of St Lawrence Seaway. Perf 12.
513   **201**   5c. ultramarine and red   20   10
               a. Centre inverted £10000   £6500

It is believed that No. 513a occurred on two printer's sheets, each of 200 stamps. About 230 examples have been discovered, but many have slight imperfections. The prices quoted are for examples in very fine condition.

(Des P. Weiss)

1959 (10 Sept). Bicentenary of Battle of Plains of Abraham (Québec). Perf 12.
514   **202**   5c. deep green and red   20   10

203   **204** Dollard des Ormeaux

(Des Helen Fitzgerald)

1960 (20 Apr). Golden Jubilee of Canadian Girl Guides Movement. Perf 12.
515   **203**   5c. ultramarine and orange-brown   20   10

(Des P. Weiss)

1960 (19 May). Tercentenary of Battle of the Long Sault. Perf 12.
516   **204**   5c. ultramarine and light brown   20   10

205 Surveyor, Bulldozer and Compass Rose   **206** E. Pauline Johnson

(Des B. J. Reddie)

1961 (8 Feb). Northern Development. Perf 12.
517   **205**   5c. emerald and red   15   10

(Des B. J. Reddie)

1961 (10 Mar). Birth Centenary of E. Pauline Johnson (Mohawk poetess). Perf 12.
518   **206**   5c. green and red........................   15   10

207 Arthur Meighen (statesman)   **208** Engineers and Dam

1961 (19 Apr). Arthur Meighen Commemoration. Perf 12.
519   **207**   5c. ultramarine   15   10

(Des B. J. Reddie)

1961 (28 June). Tenth Anniversary of Colombo Plan. Perf 12.
520   **208**   5c. blue and brown..........................   30   10

209 'Resources for Tomorrow'   **210** 'Education'

(Des A. L. Pollock)

1961 (12 Oct). Natural Resources. Perf 12.
521   **209**   5c. blue-green and brown   15   10

(Des Helen Fitzgerald)

1962 (28 Feb). Education Year. Perf 12.
522   **210**   5c. black and orange-brown   15   10

211 Lord Selkirk and Farmer   **212** Talon bestowing Gifts on Married Couple

(Des Phillips-Gutkin Ltd)

1962 (3 May). 150th Anniversary of Red River Settlement. Perf 12.
523   **211**   5c. chocolate and green........................   20   10

(Des P. Weiss)

1962 (13 June). Jean Talon Commemoration. Perf 12.
524   **212**   5c. blue...   20   10

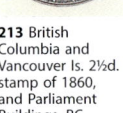

213 British Columbia and Vancouver Is. 2½d. stamp of 1860, and Parliament Buildings, BC   **214** Highway (map version) and Provincial Arms

(Des Helen Bacon)

1962 (22 Aug). Centenary of Victoria, BC. Perf 12.
525   **213**   5c. red and black............................... 30   10

(Des A. L. Pollock)

1962 (31 Aug). Opening of Trans-Canada Highway. Perf 12.
526   **214**   5c. black and orange-brown 15   20

215 Queen Elizabeth II and Wheat (Agriculture) Symbol

216 Sir Casimir Gzowski

(From drawing by Ernst Roch)

1962–64. Horiz designs as T **215** showing Queen Elizabeth II and industry symbols.

(i) Perf 12. Perf 12.

527	1c. chocolate (4.2.63)	10	10
	a. Booklet pane. 5 stamps plus 1 printed label (15.5.63)	5·00	
	p. 2 phosphor bands (15.5.63)	15	70
528	2c. green (2.5.63)	15	20
	a. Pack. 2 blocks of 25	12·00	
	p. 2 phosphor bands (15.5.63)	40	3·00
529	3c. reddish violet† (2.5.63)	15	10
	p. 2 phosphor bands (15.5.63)	40	1·00
530	4c. carmine-red (4.2.63)	20	10
	a. Booklet pane. 5 stamps plus 1 printed label (15.5.63)	5·00	
	b. Pack. 1 block of 25	11·00	
	p. 1 centre phosphor band (*narrow*)* (2.63)	50	3·25
	pa. 1 centre phosphor band (*wide*) (8.64) ...	6·00	15·00
	pb. 1 side phosphor band (12.64)	1·75	6·50
531	5c. ultramarine (3.10.62)	50	10
	a. Booklet pane. 5 stamps plus 1 printed label (5.63)	8·00	
	b. Pack. 1 block of 20	14·00	
	c. Imperf horiz (vert pair)	£750	
	p. 2 phosphor bands (31.1.63?)	50	1·75
	pa. Pack. 1 block of 20	18·00	
	pb. Imperf (pair)	£3250	
527/531	Set of 5..	1·00	25
527p/531p	Set of 5..	1·75	8·75

(ii) Coil stamps. Perf 9½×imperf. Perf 9½×imperf.

532	2c. green (2.5.63)	8·00	10·00
532a	3c. reddish violet (2.5.63)	4·75	4·00
533	4c. carmine-red (4.4.63)	3·00	4·00
	a. Imperf (vert pair)	£3250	
534	5c. ultramarine (3.10.62)	4·50	1·50
532/534	Set of 4..	18·00	18·00

Symbols: 1c. Crystals (Mining); 2c. Tree (Forestry); 3c. Fish (Fisheries); 4c. Electricity pylon (Industrial power); 5c. T **215**.

†   This is a fugitive colour which tends to become reddish on drying. In successive printings the violet colour became more and more reddish as the printer tried to match the shade of each previous printing instead of referring back to the original shade. A deep reddish violet is also known from Plate 3. As there is such a range of shades it is not practical to list them.

*   On No. 530p the band is 4 mm wide as against 8 mm on No. 530pa. No. 530pb exists with the band at either left or right side of the stamp, the bands being applied across alternate vertical perforations.

Nos. 528a, 530b, 531b and 531pa are blocks with the outer edges imperf. These come from One Dollar Plastic Packages sold at post offices.

Postal forgeries are known of the 4c. showing a coarser background and lack of shading on the Queen's face.

(Des P. Weiss)

1963 (5 Mar). 150th Birth Anniversary of Sir Casimir Gzowski (engineer). Perf 12.
535   **216**   5c. reddish purple 15   10

217 Export Trade

218 Frobisher and barque *Gabriel*

(Des A. L. Pollock)

1963 (14 June). Perf 12.
536   **217** $1 carmine .... 4·25   1·50

(Des P. Weiss)

1963 (21 Aug). Sir Martin Frobisher Commemoration. Perf 12.
537   **218**   5c. ultramarine 30   10

219 Horseman and Map   **220** Canada Geese

(Des B. J. Reddie)

1963 (25 Sept). Bicentenary of Québec–Trois-Rivieres–Montréal Postal Service. Perf 12.
538   **219**   5c. red-brown and deep green............. 20   25

(Des A. Short and P. Arthur)

1963 (30 Oct). Perf 12.
539   **220**   15c. blue... 1·00   10

221 Douglas DC-9 Airliner and Uplands Airport, Ottawa   **222** Peace on Earth

1964. Perf 12.
540   **221**   7c. blue (11.3)................................... 35   80
540a   8c. blue (18.11)................................. 50   50

1964 (8 Apr). Peace. Litho and recess. Perf 12.
541   **222**   5c. ochre, blue and turquoise-blue...... 15   10

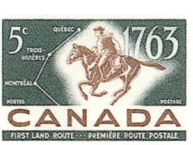

223 Maple Leaves

1964 (14 May). Canadian Unity. Perf 12.
542   **223**   5c. lake-red and light blue 10   10

224 White Trillium and Arms of Ontario   **225** Madonna Lily and Arms of Québec

226 Purple Violet and Arms of New Brunswick   **227** Mayflower and Arms of Nova Scotia

CANADA

228 Dogwood and Arms of British Columbia
229 Prairie Crocus and Arms of Manitoba

230 Lady's Slipper and Arms of Prince Edward Island
231 Wild Rose and Arms of Alberta

232 Prairie Lily and Arms of Saskatchewan
233 Pitcher Plant and Arms of Newfoundland

234 Mountain Avens and Arms of Northwest Territories
235 Fireweed and Arms of Yukon Territory

236 Maple Leaf and Arms of Canada

1964–66. Provincial Emblems. Types **224/236**. Recess (No. 555) or litho and recess (others). Perf 12.

543	224	5c. green, brown and orange (30.6.64)	35	20
544	225	5c. green, orange-brown and yellow (30.6.64)	35	20
545	226	5c. carmine-red, green and bluish violet (3.2.65)	25	20
546	227	5c. blue, red and green (3.2.65)	25	20
547	228	5c. purple, green and yellow-brown (28.4.65)	25	20
548	229	5c. red-brown, deep bluish green and mauve (28.4.65)	25	20
549	230	5c. slate-lilac, green and light reddish purple (21.7.65)	40	20
550	231	5c. green, yellow and rose-red (19.1.66)	25	20
551	232	5c. sepia, orange and green (19.1.66)	25	20
552	233	5c. black, green and red (23.2.66)	25	20
553	234	5c. drab, green and yellow (23.3.66)	25	20
554	235	5c. blue, green and rose-red (23.3.66)	25	20
555	236	5c. red and blue (30.6.66)	25	20
543/555 Set of 13			3·25	2·40

(237)
238 Fathers of the Confederation Memorial, Charlottetown

1964 (15 July). No. 540 surch with T **237**.

556	221	8c. on 7c. blue	25	30
		a. Surch omitted (left-hand stamp of horiz pair)	£11000	

(Des P. Weiss)

1964 (29 July). Centenary of Charlottetown Conference. Perf 12.

557	238	5c. black	10	10

239 Maple Leaf and Hand with Quill Pen
240 Queen Elizabeth II

(Des P. Weiss)

1964 (9 Sept). Centenary of Québec Conference. Perf 12.

558	239	5c. light red and chocolate	15	10

(Portrait by Anthony Buckley)

1964 (5 Oct). Royal Visit. Perf 12.

559	240	5c. reddish purple	15	10

241 Canadian Family
242 Co-operation

1964 (14 Oct). Christmas. Perf 12.

560	241	3c. scarlet	10	10
		a. Pack. 2 blocks of 25	7·00	
		p. 2 phosphor bands	60	2·50
		pa. Pack. 2 blocks of 25	16·00	
561		5c. ultramarine	10	10
		p. 2 phosphor bands	90	5·00

Nos. 560a and 560pa are blocks with the outer edges imperf. These come from $1.50 Plastic Packages sold at post offices.

1965 (3 Mar). International Co-operation Year. Perf 12.

562	242	5c. grey-green	35	10

243 Sir W. Grenfell
244 National Flag

1965 (9 June). Birth Centenary of Sir Wilfred Grenfell (missionary). Perf 12.

563	243	5c. deep bluish green	20	10

1965 (30 June). Inauguration of National Flag. Perf 12.

564	244	5c. red and blue	15	10

245 Sir Winston Churchill
246 Peace Tower, Parliament Buildings, Ottawa

(Des P. Weiss from photo by Karsh. Litho)

1965 (12 Aug). Churchill Commemoration. Perf 12.

565	245	5c. purple-brown	15	10

CANADA

(Des Philips-Gutkin)
1965 (8 Sept). Inter-Parliamentary Union Conference, Ottawa. Perf 12.
566 246   5c. deep green................................... 10   10

247 Parliament Buildings, Ottawa, 1865   **248** Gold, Frankincense and Myrrh

(Des G. Trottier)
1965 (8 Sept). Centenary of Proclamation of Ottawa as Capital. Perf 12.
567 247   5c. brown.. 10   10

(Des Helen Fitzgerald)
1965 (13 Oct). Christmas. Perf 12.
568 248   3c. olive-green 10   10
            a. Pack. 2 blocks of 25 .... 5·00
            p. 2 phosphor bands 10   2·00
            pa. Pack. 2 blocks of 25 .... 6·50
569   5c. ultramarine 10   10
            p. 2 phosphor bands 30   50

Nos. 568a and 568pa are blocks with the outer edges imperf. These come from $1.50 Plastic Packages sold at post offices.

249 *Alouette 2* over Canada   **250** la Salle

1966 (5 Jan). Launching of Canadian Satellite, *Alouette 2*. Perf 12.
570 249   5c. ultramarine 15   10

(Des Brigdens Ltd., Toronto)
1966 (13 Apr). 300th Anniversary of la Salle's Arrival in Canada. Perf 12.
571 250   5c. deep bluish green 15   10

251 Road Signs   **252** Canadian Delegation and Houses of Parliament

(Des Helen Fitzgerald)
1966 (2 May). Highway Safety. Invisible gum. Perf 12.
572 251   5c. yellow, blue and black 15   10

(Des P. Pederson (Brigdens Ltd.))
1966 (26 May). London Conference Centenary. Perf 12.
573 252   5c. red-brown 10   10

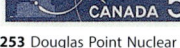

253 Douglas Point Nuclear Power Station   **254** Parliamentary Library, Ottawa

(Des A. L. Pollock)
1966 (27 July). Peaceful Uses of Atomic Energy. Perf 12.
574 253   5c. ultramarine 10   10

(Des Brigdens Ltd.)
1966 (8 Sept). Commonwealth Parliamentary Association Conference, Ottawa. Perf 12.
575 254   5c. purple 10   10

255 Praying Hands, after Dürer   **256** Flag and Canada on Globe

(Des G. Holloway)
1966 (12 Oct). Christmas. Perf 12.
576 255   3c. carmine 10   10
            a. Pack. 2 blocks of 25 .... 4·50
            p. 2 phosphor bands .... 1·25 1·50
            pa. Pack. 2 blocks of 25 .... 17·50
577   5c. orange 10   10
            p. 2 phosphor bands .... 1·25 1·50

Nos. 576a and 576pa are blocks with the outer edges imperf. These come from $1.50 Plastic Packages sold at post offices.

(Des Brigdens Ltd.)
1967 (11 Jan). Canadian Centennial. Invisible gum. Perf 12.
578 256   5c. scarlet and blue 10   10
            p. 2 phosphor bands 50   2·25

257 Northern Lights and Dog Team   **258** Totem Pole   **259** Combine-harvester and Oil Derrick

260 Ship in Lock   **261** Harbour Scene   **261a** Transport

262 *Alaska Highway* (A. Y. Jackson)   **263** *The Jack Pine* (T. Thomson)

264 *Bylot Island* (L. Harris)   **265** *Québec Ferry* (J. W. Morrice)

266 *The Solemn Land* (J. E. H. MacDonald)   **267** *Summer's Stores* (grain elevators) (J. Ensor)

CANADA

268 Oilfield (near Edmonton) (H. G. Glyde)
268a Library of Parliament

(Des H. T. Prosser (1c.–6c.), Rapid Grip and Batten Ltd (8c.–$1), Eng A. A. Carswell (8c.–50c.), Y. Baril (1c.–6c. and $1))

1967 (8 Feb)–**73**. Types **257**/**268a**.

A. Recess C.B.N.(i) Perf 12. Perf 12.

579	1c. brown		10	10
	a. Booklet pane. 5 stamps plus 1 printed label (2.67)		1·25	
	b. Printed on the gummed side		£850	
	c. White paper (10.71)		10	
	ca. White fluorescent paper (6.71)		1·00	
	p. 2 phosphor bands		1·00	1·00
	pa. Centre phosphor band (12.68)		30	2·00
	pac. Centre phosphor band, white paper (9.71)		30	
	paca. Centre phosphor band, white fluorescent paper (10.71)		3·00	
	q. 2 fluorescent bands (11.71)		60	75
580	2c. green		10	20
	a. Glazed fluorescent paper (booklets) (26.10.70)		25	
	b. Booklet pane. No. 580a×4 se-tenant with No. 581a×4 with gutter margin between		1·75	
	c. White paper (3.72)		10	
	p. 2 phosphor bands		1·50	4·25
	pa. Centre phosphor band (12.68)		30	1·00
	pac. Centre phosphor band, white paper (3.72)		60	
	q. 2 fluorescent bands (12.72)		75	1·00
581	3c. slate-purple		30	50
	a. Glazed fluorescent paper (booklets) (26.10.70)		25	
	p. 2 phosphor bands		30	3·00
	q. 2 fluorescent bands (1972?)		2·00	3·50
582	4c. red		20	10
	a. Booklet pane. 5 stamps plus 1 printed label (2.67)		1·75	
	b. Pack. 1 block of 25 (8.2.67)		13·00	
	c. White paper (5.72)		20	
	p. 1 side phosphor band		1·25	4·00
	pa. Centre phosphor band (3.69)		30	1·00
	pac. Centre phosphor band, white paper (5.72)		50	
	paca. Centre phosphor band, white fluorescent paper (1972)		2·00	
	q. 2 fluorescent bands (4.73)		55	1·75
583	5c. blue		20	10
	a. Booklet pane. 5 stamps plus 1 printed label (3.67)		6·00	
	b. Pack. 1 block of 20 (2.67)		22·00	
	c. White paper (12.71?)		40	
	ca. White fluorescent paper (12.71)		1·00	
	p. 2 phosphor bands		75	3·25
	pa. Pack. 1 block of 20 (8.2.67)		35·00	
	pb. Centre phosphor band (12.68)		30	2·50
	pbc. Centre phosphor band, white paper (4.72)		1·00	
	pbca. Centre phosphor band, white fluorescent paper (12.71)		1·00	
583r	6c. black (*white paper*) (1.72)		2·75	30
	ra. Printed on the gummed side		12·00	
	rp. Centre phosphor band (1.72)		4·75	6·50
	rq. 2 fluorescent bands (1.72)		1·25	2·00
584	8c. purple-brown		25	1·00
	c. White fluorescent paper (7.71)		12·00	
585	10c. olive-green		25	10
	c. White paper (3.71)		80	
	ca. White fluorescent paper (12.71)		80	
	p. 2 phosphor bands (9.12.69)		1·50	3·50
	pc. 2 phosphor bands, white paper (11.72)		1·00	
	pca. 2 phosphor bands, white fluorescent paper (1.72)		4·50	
	q. 2 fluorescent bands (1.72)		1·00	1·00
	qa. 2 fluorescent bands, white fluorescent paper (2.72)		4·50	
586	15c. dull purple		30	10
	c. White paper (3.72)		65	
	ca. White fluorescent paper (3.71)		2·00	
	p. 2 phosphor bands (9.12.69)		1·50	2·75
	pc. 2 phosphor bands, white paper (3.72)		2·00	
	q. 2 fluorescent bands (2.72)		1·00	2·00
587	20c. deep blue		2·00	10
	c. White paper (5.72)		1·60	
	ca. White fluorescent paper (8.71)		2·00	
	p. 2 phosphor bands (9.12.69)		2·50	6·00
	pc. 2 phosphor bands, white paper (5.72)		2·00	
588	25c. myrtle-green		2·00	10
	ca. White fluorescent paper (10.71)		2·25	
	p. 2 phosphor bands (9.12.69)		4·25	8·50
	pca. 2 phosphor bands, white fluorescent paper (12.71)		16·00	
589	50c. cinnamon		2·00	10
	c. White paper (12.71)		2·50	
	ca. White fluorescent paper (3.71)		3·00	
590	$1 scarlet		1·50	1·25
	c. White paper (12.71)		3·00	
	ca. White fluorescent paper (3.71)		3·00	
579/590 *Set of 13*			8·50	3·00
579pa/588p *Set of 10*			13·50	29·00

(ii) Coil stamps. Perf 9½×imperf. Perf 9½×imperf.

591	3c. slate-purple (3.67)		2·00	5·50
592	4c. red (3.67)		2·00	2·75
593	5c. blue (2.67)		2·00	4·00

(iii) Coil stamps. Perf 10×imperf. Perf 10×imperf.

594	6c. orange-red (1.69)		90	35
	a. Imperf (vert pair)		£250	
	c. White fluorescent paper (12.69)		11·00	
	ca. Imperf (vert pair)		£2500	
595	6c. black (*white fluorescent paper*) (8.70)		35	3·00
	a. Imperf (vert pair)		£2500	
596	7c. green (*white fluorescent paper*) (30.6.71)		40	3·00
	a. Imperf (vert pair)		£850	
597	8c. black (*white paper*) (30.12.71)		1·75	2·75
	a. Imperf (vert pair)		£425	
	q. 2 fluorescent bands (7.72)		40	40
	qa. 2 fluorescent bands, white fluorescent paper		1·00	
	qb. Imperf (vert pair)		£800	

B. Recess B.A.B.N.(i) Perf 10 (sheets (Nos. 601/601p) or booklets). Perf 10.

598	1c. brown (9.68)		30	2·50
	a. Booklet pane. No. 598b×5 se-tenant with No. 599×5 (9.68)		1·75	
	b. Booklet pane. No. 601×4 se-tenant with No. 598 plus one printed label (10.68)		2·00	
	c. White fluorescent paper (11.69)		10·00	
	cb. Booklet pane. No. 601c×4 se-tenant with No. 598c plus 1 printed label (11.69)		16·00	
599	4c. red (9.68)		20	2·50
	a. Booklet pane. 25 stamps plus 2 printed labels		6·50	
600	5c. blue (9.68)		30	2·50
	a. Booklet pane of 20		4·50	
601	6c. orange-red (10.68)		45	10
	a. Booklet pane. 25 stamps plus 2 printed labels (10.68)		10·00	
	c. White fluorescent paper (11.69)		1·50	
	p. 2 phosphor bands (1.11.68)		1·00	1·00
602	6c. black (1.70)		1·00	2·25
	a. Booklet pane. 25 stamps plus 2 printed labels		16·00	
	c. White fluorescent paper (11.69)		65·00	
	ca. Booklet pane. 25 stamps plus 2 printed labels		£1500	
603	6c. black (*re-engraved die*) (8.70)		3·50	4·50
	a. Booklet pane of 4		12·00	

(ii) Perf 12½×12 (sheets (Nos. 606/610) or booklets). Perf 12½×12.

604	1c. brown (30.6.71)		50	3·00
	a. Booklet pane. Nos. 604×4, 605×4 and 609×12 se-tenant		13·00	
	b. Booklet pane. Nos. 604/605 and 609×3 se-tenant plus 1 printed label		4·00	
	c. Booklet pane. Nos. 604×3, 608 and 610×2 se-tenant (30.12.71)		1·50	
	d. Booklet pane. Nos. 604×6, 608 and 610×11 se-tenant (30.12.71)		6·50	
	e. Booklet pane. Nos. 604×4, 608 and 610×5 se-tenant (8.72)		4·50	
	f. White fluorescent paper (30.12.71)		40	1·00
	fa. Booklet pane. No. 604f×4, 608 and 610×5 se-tenant (30.12.71)		1·75	
	q. 2 fluorescent bands (30.12.71)		40	2·25
	qc. Booklet pane. Nos. 604q×3, 608 and 610q×2 se-tenant		2·00	
	qd. Booklet pane. Nos. 604q×6, 608 and 610q×11 se-tenant		5·00	
	qe. Booklet pane. Nos. 604q×4, 608 and 610q×5 se-tenant (8.72)		4·50	
	qf. 2 fluorescent bands, white fluorescent paper (30.12.71)		40	
	qfa. Booklet pane. No. 604qfa×4, 608 and 610×5 se-tenant (30.12.71)		2·50	
605	3c. slate-purple (30.6.71)		4·75	8·50
606	6c. orange-red (3.69)		60	1·00
	f. White fluorescent paper (12.69)		17·00	
	p. 2 phosphor bands (4.69)		2·00	2·00
	pf. 2 phosphor bands, white fluorescent paper (12.69)		£850	
607	6c. black (7.1.70)		30	10

	a. Booklet pane. 25 stamps plus 2 printed labels (8.70)	20·00	
	f. White fluorescent paper (1.70)	14·00	
	p. 2 phosphor bands (1.70)	2·50	3·25
608	6c. black (re-engraved die) (9.70)	1·00	10
	a. Booklet pane of 4 (11.70)	4·00	
	f. White fluorescent paper	1·25	
	p. One centre phosphor band (9.71)	3·75	5·50
	q. 2 fluorescent bands (30.12.71)	1·75	45
	qf. 2 fluorescent bands, white fluorescent paper (12.71)	1·00	
609	7c. myrtle-green (30.6.71)	30	1·25
	p. 2 phosphor bands	1·50	3·75
610	8c. slate-black (30.12.71)	30	10
	c. White paper (7.72)	30	
	cf. White fluorescent paper (11.72)	2·75	
	p. 2 phosphor bands	60	1·00
	pf. 2 phosphor bands, white paper (7.72)	50	
	pfa. 2 phosphor bands, white fluorescent paper (11.72)	4·50	
	q. 2 fluorescent bands (30.12.71)	45	15
	qf. 2 fluorescent bands, white paper	75	
	qfa. 2 fluorescent bands, white fluorescent paper (12.72)	1·50	

No. 581q only exists as a pre-cancel.

Nos. 582b, 583b, 583pa are blocks with the outer edges imperf. These come from One Dollar Plastic Packages sold at post offices.

Following a change to metric sizing in 1968, the design sizes of Types **216a** and **268a** are slightly smaller than those of Types **257/261**.

No. 582p comes with the band to the left or right of the stamp, the phosphor having been applied across alternate vertical perforations.

Postal forgeries exist of the 6c. orange printed in lithography and perforated 12½.

Normal

Re-engraved

When the basic postal rate was changed to 6c. the C.B.N. lent their die to B.A.B.N. who made a duplicate die from it by transfer. Parts of this proved to be weak, but it was used for Nos. 601/602 and 606/607. B.A.B.N. later re-engraved their die to make fresh plates which were used for Nos. 603 and 608. No. 608 first appeared on sheets from Plate 4. The engraving is much more deeply etched and the side frame lines are noticeably thicker. The Canadian Bank Note printings, Nos. 583r and 595 are more clearly engraved than the first B.A.B.N. issue, lack the heavy side frames of the re-engraved version.

There are no records of dates of issue of the booklets, packs and coils, but supplies of these were distributed to depots in the months indicated.

IMPERF BETWEEN PAIRS FROM COIL STAMPS. Nos. 594/597 are known in blocks or horizontal pairs imperf between vertically. Coils are supplied to post offices in batches of ten coils held together by roulettes between every fourth stamp so that they can easily be split apart. If two or more unsplit coils are purchased it is possible to obtain blocks or pairs imperf between vertically.

Vertical coil stamps are also known imperf between horizontally or with some stamps apparently completely imperf. These can result from blind perforations identifiable by slight indentations.

WHITE PAPERS. Original printings of the sheet and coil stamps were made on toned paper. From the later part of 1969 experimental printings were made on white fluorescent paper, as referred to in the note below No. 620; this paper is distinct from the glazed type used for the 'Opal' booklet (see Nos. 580a and 581a).

During 1971 a further type of paper, white but non-fluorescent, was introduced. This later white (non-fluorescent) paper typically has PVA gum, readily distinguishable from the shiny 'Dextrine' gum of the white fluorescent paper. Exceptions are No. 582paca and Nos. 610/610qfa, which have PVA gum. Identification of fluorescent papers can be confirmed with the use of a UV lamp. Particular care is needed in the cases of Nos. 602c/602ca and 606pf, where the listings refer to examples on the 'hybrite' paper.

FLUORESCENT BANDS. During the second half of 1971 new sorting machines were installed in the Ottawa area which were activated by stamps bearing fluorescent bands. These differ from the Winnipeg phosphor bands in that they react green and have no after-glow. To the naked eye the fluorescent bands appear shiny when compared with the remainder of the stamp when looking along its surface. Winnipeg phosphor bands appear matt.

The experiments were successful and what was at first called 'Ottawa tagging' has since come into more general use and the Winnipeg phosphor was phased out. However, the substance at first used (known as OP-4) was found to migrate to envelopes, documents, album pages, etc. as well as to adjoining stamps. Late in 1972 this fault was cured by using another substance (called OP-2). The migrating bands were used on early printings of Nos. 604q, 608q and 610q as well as certain stamps referred to in a footnote after No. 692. It is most advisable to use plastic mounts for housing stamps with migrating bands or else clear acetate should be affixed to the album leaves.

269 Canadian Pavilion   **270** Allegory of Womanhood on Ballot Box

(Des C.B.N.)

1967 (28 Apr). World Fair, Montréal. Perf 12.
611   **269**   5c. blue and red 10   10

(Des Helen Fitzgerald. Litho)

1967 (24 May). 50th Anniversary of Women's Franchise. Perf 12.
612   **270**   5c. reddish purple and black............ 10   10

271 Queen Elizabeth II and Centennial Emblem   **272** Athlete

(Portrait from photo by Anthony Buckley)

1967 (30 June). Royal Visit. Perf 12.
613   **271**   5c. plum and orange-brown 15   10

(Des Brigdens Ltd.)

1967 (19 July). Fifth Pan-American Games, Winnipeg. Perf 12.
614   **272**   5c. rose-red 10   10

273 World News   **274** Governor-General Vanier

(Des W. McLauchlan)

1967 (31 Aug). 50th Anniversary of the Canadian Press. Perf 12.
615   **273**   5c. blue.. 10   10

(Des from photo by Karsh)

1967 (15 Sept). Vanier Commemoration. Perf 12.
616   **274**   5c. black...................................... 10   10

PRINTERS. The following were printed either by the Canadian Bank Note Co, Ottawa (C.B.N.) or the British American Bank Note Co, Ottawa (B.A.B.N.), *except where otherwise stated.*

CANADA

275 People of 1867 and Toronto, 1967   **276** Carol Singers

(Des and recess C.B.N.)

1967 (28 Sept). Centenary of Toronto as Capital City of Ontario. Perf 12.
617 275 5c. myrtle-green and vermilion 10 10

(Des and recess B.A.B.N.)

1967 (11 Oct). Christmas. Perf 12.
618 276 3c. scarlet.. 10 10
           a. Pack. 2 blocks of 25 .... 4·50
           p. 2 phosphor bands .... 20 1·75
           pa. Pack. 2 blocks of 25 .... 5·50
619   5c. emerald-green............................. 10 10
           p. 2 phosphor bands .... 70 1·75

Nos. 618a and 618pa are blocks with the outer edges imperf. These come from $1.50 Plastic Packs sold at post offices.

277 Grey Jays   **278** Weather Map and Instruments

(Des M. G. Loates. Litho C.B.N.)

1968 (15 Feb). Wild Life. Perf 12.
620 277 5c. multicoloured 30 10
See also Nos. 638/640.

WHITE FLUORESCENT PAPER. Different papers with varying degrees of whiteness have been used for Canadian stamps and it is understood that much of the paper contained a high percentage of recycled pulp. The fluorescent content of this paper varies, but during 1968–1970 a distinctive very white and highly fluorescent paper was used known by the tradename 'hybrite'; this fluoresces on the back and front. Some issues were wholly printed on this paper, and these can be used for distinguishing those which appeared on ordinary paper as well, both being listed.
See also notes following No. 610qfa.

(Des and litho B.A.B.N.)

1968 (13 Mar). Bicentenary of First Meteorological Readings. Perf 11.
621 278 5c. multicoloured 15 10
           a. White fluorescent paper................... 1·00

279 Narwhal   **280** Globe, Maple Leaf and Rain Gauge

(Des J. A. Crosby. Litho B.A.B.N.)

1968 (10 Apr). Wildlife. White fluorescent paper. Perf 11.
622 279 5c. multicoloured 25 20
           a. Ordinary paper .... 2·00

No. 622 has a background of yellow-green and pale blue but copies are known with the yellow-green apparently missing. This 'yellow-green' is produced by an overlay of yellow on the blue but we have not come across any examples where the yellow is completely missing and the wide range of colour variation is due to technical difficulties in maintaining an exact blend of the two colours.

(Des I. von Mosdossy. Litho B.A.B.N.)

1968 (8 May). International Hydrological Decade. Perf 11.
623 280 5c. multicoloured 15 10
           a. White fluorescent paper................... 40

IMPERF EDGES. On Nos. 624/654, 657 and 659 (stamps printed by the B.A.B.N. Co.) the outer edges of the sheets were guillotined to remove the imprints for PO stock so that single stamps may, therefore, be found with either one, or two adjacent sides imperforate.

281 Nonsuch   **282** Lacrosse Players

(Recess and photo B.A.B.N.)

1968 (5 June). 300th Anniversary of Voyage of the *Nonsuch*. Perf 10.
624 281 5c. multicoloured 20 20

(Des J. E. Aldridge. Recess and photo B.A.B.N.)

1968 (3 July). Lacrosse. Perf 10.
625 282 5c. black, red and lemon.................... 15 10

283 Front Page of *The Globe*, George Brown and Legislative Building   **284** H. Bourassa

(Des N. Sabolotny. Recess and photo B.A.B.N.)

1968 (21 Aug). 150th Birth Anniversary of George Brown (politician and journalist). Perf 10.
626 283 5c. multicoloured 10 10

(Des, recess and litho C.B.N.)

1968 (4 Sept). Birth Centenary of Henri Bourassa (journalist and politician). White fluorescent paper. Perf 12.
627 284 5c. black, red and pale cream 10 10

285 John McCrae, Battlefield and First Lines of *In Flanders Fields*   **286** Armistice Monument, Vimy

(Des I. von Mosdossy. Litho C.B.N.)

1968 (15 Oct). 50th Death Anniversary of John McCrae (soldier and poet). White fluorescent paper. Perf 12.
628 285 5c. multicoloured 10 10

(Des and recess C.B.N.)

1968 (15 Oct). 50th Anniversary of 1918 Armistice. Perf 12.
629 286 15c. slate-black 30 50

287 Inuit Family (carving)   **288** Mother and Child (carving)

CANADA

(Designs from Inuit carvings by Munamee (6c.) and unknown carver (5c.). Photo C.B.N.)

1968. Christmas. White fluorescent paper. Perf 12.
630	**287**	5c. black and new blue (1.11.68)	10	10
		a. Booklet pane of 10 (15.11.68)	2·25	
		p. 1 centre phosphor band	10	1·75
		pa. Booklet pane of 10 (15.11.68)	3·00	
631	**288**	6c. black and ochre (15.11.68)	10	10
		p. 2 phosphor bands	20	2·00

 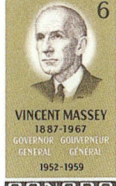

289 Curling   **290** Vincent Massey

(Des D. Eales. Recess and photo B.A.B.N.)

1969 (15 Jan). Curling. Perf 10.
632	**289**	6c. black, new blue and scarlet	15	25

(Des I. von Mosdossy. Recess and litho C.B.N.)

1969 (20 Feb). Vincent Massey, First Canadian-born Governor-General. White fluorescent paper. Perf 12.
633	**290**	6c. sepia and yellow-ochre	10	10

291 *Return from the Harvest Field* (Suzor-Côté)   **292** Globe and Tools

(Photo C.B.N.)

1969 (14 Mar). Birth Centenary of Marc Aurèle de Foy Suzor-Côté (painter). White fluorescent paper. Perf 12.
634	**291**	50c. multicoloured	1·50	3·25

(Des J. Hébert. Recess B.A.B.N.)

1969 (21 May). 50th Anniversary of International Labour Organisation. White fluorescent paper. Perf 12½×12.
635	**292**	6c. bronze-green	10	10
		a. Ordinary paper	1·00	

293 Vickers FB-27 Vimy Aircraft over Atlantic Ocean   **294** *Sir William Osler* (J. S. Sargent)

(Des R. W. Bradford. Recess and photo B.A.B.N.)

1969 (13 June). 50th Anniversary of First Non-stop Transatlantic Flight. White fluorescent paper. Perf 12.
636	**293**	15c. chocolate, bright green and pale blue	40	1·50

(Des, recess and photo B.A.B.N.)

1969 (23 June). 50th Death Anniversary of Sir William Osler (physician). Perf 12½×12.
637	**294**	6c. deep blue, light blue and chestnut	20	10
		a. White fluorescent paper	80	

295 White-throated Sparrows   **298** Flags of Winter and Summer Games

(Des M. G. Loates. Litho C.B.N.)

1969 (23 July). Birds. T **295** and similar multicoloured designs. White fluorescent paper. Perf 12.
638		6c. Type **295**	25	10
639		10c. Savannah Sparrow ('Ipswich Sparrow') (*horiz*)	35	1·75
640		25c. Hermit Thrush (*horiz*)	1·10	4·50
638/640	*Set of 3*		1·50	6·00

(Des C. McDiarmid. Recess and litho C.B.N.)

1969 (15 Aug). Canadian Games. White fluorescent paper. Perf 12.
641	**298**	6c. emerald, scarlet and blue	10	10

299 Outline of Prince Edward Island showing Charlottetown   **300** Sir Isaac Brock and Memorial Column

(Des L. Fitzgerald. Recess and photo B.A.B.N.)

1969 (15 Aug). Bicentenary of Charlottetown as Capital of Prince Edward Island. White fluorescent paper. Perf 12×12½.
642	**299**	6c. yellow-brown, black and blue	20	20
		a. Ordinary paper	80	

(Des I. von Mosdossy. Recess and litho C.B.N.)

1969 (12 Sept). Birth Bicentenary of Sir Isaac Brock. Perf 12.
643	**300**	6c. orange, bistre and bistre-brown	10	10

301 Children of the World in Prayer   **302** Stephen Butler Leacock, Mask and 'Mariposa'

(Des Rapid Grip and Batten Ltd. Litho C.B.N.)

1969 (8 Oct). Christmas. White fluorescent paper. Perf 12.
644	**301**	5c. multicoloured	10	10
		a. Booklet pane of 10	1·50	
		p. 1 centre phosphor band	10	1·75
		pa. Booklet pane of 10	2·50	
645		6c. multicoloured	10	10
		a. Black (inscr, value and frame omitted)	£1700	£1300
		p. 2 phosphor bands	20	1·75

(Des, recess and photo B.A.B.N.)

1969 (12 Nov). Birth Centenary of Stephen Butler Leacock (humorist). Perf 12×12½.
646	**302**	6c. multicoloured	10	10

CANADA

303 Symbolic Cross-roads   **304** *Enchanted Owl* (Kenojuak)

(Des K. C. Lochhead. Litho C.B.N.)

1970 (27 Jan). Centenary of Manitoba. Perf 12.
647	**303**	6c. ultramarine, lemon and vermilion	15	10
		p. 2 phosphor bands	15	1·75

(Des N. E. Hallendy and Miss S. van Raalte. Recess C.B.N.)

1970 (27 Jan). Centenary of Northwest Territories. White fluorescent paper. Perf 12.
648	**304**	6c. carmine, red and black	10	10

312 Louis Riel (Métis leader)   **313** Mackenzie's Inscription, Dean Channel

(Des R. Derreth. Photo B.A.B.N.)

1970 (19 June). Louis Riel Commemoration. Perf 12½×12.
657	**312**	6c. greenish blue and vermilion	10	10

(Design from Government Archives photo. Recess C.B.N.)

1970 (25 June). Sir Alexander Mackenzie (explorer). White fluorescent paper. Perf 12×11½.
658	**313**	6c. bistre-brown.............................	15	10

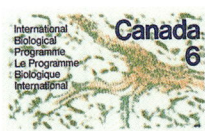 

305 Microscopic View of Inside of Leaf   **306** Expo 67 Emblem and Stylised Cherry Blossom

(Des I. Charney. Recess and photo B.A.B.N.)

1970 (18 Feb). International Biological Programme. Perf 12×12½.
649	**305**	6c. emerald, orange-yellow and ultramarine	15	10

(Des E. R. C. Bethune. Litho C.B.N.)

1970 (18 Mar). World Fair, Osaka. T **306** and similar horiz designs. Multicoloured; colour of Cherry Blossom given. Perf 12.
650		25c. red	1·50	2·25
		a. Block of 4. Nos. 650/653	5·50	10·00
		p. 2 phosphor bands	1·50	2·75
		pa. Block of 4. Nos. 650p/653p	5·50	12·00
651		25c. violet	1·50	2·25
		p. 2 phosphor bands	1·50	2·75
652		25c. green	1·50	2·25
		p. 2 phosphor bands	1·50	2·75
653		25c. blue	1·50	2·25
		p. 2 phosphor bands	1·50	2·75
		650/653 Set of 4	5·50	8·00
		650p/653p Set of 4	5·50	10·00

Designs: No. 650, T **306**; No. 651, Dogwood and stylised Cherry blossom; No. 652, White Trillium and stylised Cherry blossom; No. 653, White Garden Lily and stylised Cherry blossom.

Nos. 650/653 and 650p/653p are printed together in sheets of 50 (5×10). In the first, second, fourth and fifth vertical rows the four different designs are arranged in *se-tenant* blocks, whilst the centre row is composed as follows (reading downwards): 650(p)/653(p), 650(p)×2, 653(p), 651(p), 652(p) and 650(p).

314 Sir Oliver Mowat (statesman)   **315** *Isles of Spruce* (A. Lismer)

(Des E. Roch. Recess and photo B.A.B.N.)

1970 (12 Aug). Sir Oliver Mowat Commemoration. Perf 12×12½.
659	**314**	6c. vermilion and black	10	10

(Litho Ashton-Potter)

1970 (18 Sept). 50th Anniversary of Group of Seven (artists). Perf 11.
660	**315**	6c. multicoloured	10	10

316 Horse-drawn Sleigh (D. Niskala)   **317** Christ in Manger (C. Fortier)

(Des from children's drawings. Litho C.B.N.)

1970 (7 Oct). Christmas. Horiz designs as Types **316**/**317**, showing children's drawings. Multicoloured. White fluorescent paper. Perf 12.
661		5c. Type **316**	30	20
		a. Strip of 5. Nos. 661/665	1·40	2·50
		p. 1 centre phosphor band	55	1·25
		pa. Strip of 5. Nos. 661p/665p	2·50	5·00
662		5c. Stable and Star of Bethlehem (L. Wilson) (26×21 mm)	30	20
		p. 1 centre phosphor band	55	1·25
663		5c. Snowmen (M. Lecompte) (26×21 mm)	30	20
		p. 1 centre phosphor band	55	1·25
664		5c. Skiing (D. Durham) (26×21 mm)	30	20
		p. 1 centre phosphor band	55	1·25
665		5c. Santa Claus (A. Martin) (26×21 mm)	30	20
		p. 1 centre phosphor band	55	1·25
666		6c. Santa Claus (E. Bhattacharya) (26×21 mm)	30	20
		a. Strip of 5. Nos. 666/670	1·40	2·50
		p. 2 phosphor bands	55	1·25
		pa. Strip of 5. Nos. 666p/670p	2·50	5·00
667		6c. Christ in Manger (J. McKinney) (26×21 mm)	30	20
		p. 2 phosphor bands	55	1·25
668		6c. Toy Shop (N. Whateley) (26×21 mm)	30	20
		p. 2 phosphor bands	55	1·25
669		6c. Christmas Tree (J. Pomperleau) (26×21 mm)	30	20
		p. 2 phosphor bands	55	1·25
670		6c. Church (J. McMillan) (26×21 mm)................	30	20
		p. 2 phosphor bands	55	1·25
671		10c. Type **317**	25	30
		p. 2 phosphor bands	45	1·25
672		15c. Trees and Sledge (J. Dojcak) (35×21 mm)..	35	60
		p. 2 phosphor bands	55	1·75

310 Henry Kelsey   **311** Towards Unification

(Des D. Burton. Recess and photo B.A.B.N.)

1970 (15 Apr). 300th Birth Anniversary of Henry Kelsey (explorer). Perf 12×12½.
654	**310**	6c. multicoloured	10	10

(Des B. Fisher. Litho B.A.B.N.)

1970 (13 May). 25th Anniversary of United Nations. Perf 11.
655	**311**	10c. blue.....................................	30	1·75
		p. 2 phosphor bands	50	3·25
656		15c. magenta and bluish lilac................	50	50
		p. 2 phosphor bands	50	3·00

CANADA

661/672 Set of 12 .... 3·25 2·50
661p/672p Set of 12 .... 6·00 12·50

The designs of the 5c. and 6c. were each issued with the various designs *se-tenant* in a diamond-shaped arrangement within the sheet. This generally results in *se-tenant* pairs both vert and horiz, but due to the sheet arrangement vert and horiz pairs of the same design exist from the two centre vert and horiz rows.

328 Sir Donald A. Smith   **329** *Big Raven* (E. Carr)

(Des Dora de Pédery-Hunt. Litho C.B.N.)

1970 (4 Nov). 150th Birth Anniversary of Sir Donald Alexander Smith. Perf 12.
673   **328**   6c. yellow, brown and bronze-green .. 15 10

(Litho C.B.N)

1971 (12 Feb). Birth Centenary of Emily Carr (painter). Perf 12.
674   **329**   6c. multicoloured 20 30

330 Laboratory Equipment   **331** The Atom

(Des R. Webber. Litho B.A.B.N)

1971 (3 Mar). 50th Anniversary of Discovery of Insulin. Perf 10½.
675   **330**   6c. multicoloured 30 30

(Des R. Webber. Litho B.A.B.N)

1971 (24 Mar). Birth Centenary of Lord Rutherford (scientist). Perf 11.
676   **331**   6c. yellow, red, deep chocolate and black 20 30
              a. Black omitted £6000

332 Maple 'Keys'   **333** Louis Papineau

(Des Alma Duncan. Litho Ashton-Potter.)

1971 (14 Apr–19 Nov). The Maple Leaf in Four Seasons. T **332** and similar vert designs. Multicoloured. Perf 11.
677   6c. Type **332** (Spring) (14.4) 20 20
      a. Imperf (pair) £500
678   6c. Green leaves (Summer) (16.6) 20 20
679   7c. Autumn leaves (3.9) 20 20
      a. Grey (inscr and value) omitted £1500
680   7c. Withered leaves and snow (Winter) (19.11) 20 20
677/680 Set of 4 .... 70 70

(Des L. Marquart. Recess and photo B.A.B.N)

1971 (7 May). Death Centenary of Louis-Joseph Papineau (politician). Ordinary paper. Perf 12½×12.
681   **333**   6c. multicoloured 15 40

334 Chart of Coppermine River   **335** People and Computer Tapes

(Des L. Marquart. Recess and photo B.A.B.N)

1971 (7 May). Bicentenary of Samuel Hearne's Expedition to Coppermine River. Ordinary paper. Perf 12×12½.
682   **334**   6c. red, sepia and pale buff 40 50

(Des H. Kleefeld. Litho C.B.N)

1971 (1 June). Centenary of First Canadian Census. Perf 11½.
683   **335**   6c. blue, red and black 30 30

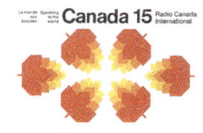 

336 Maple Leaves   **337** 'BC'

(Des B. Kramer. Litho C.B.N)

1971 (1 June). Radio Canada International. Perf 12.
684   **336**   15c. red, yellow and black .... 50 1·50
              p. Two phosphor bands .... 1·00 3·00

(Des E. R. C. Bethune. Litho C.B.N)

1971 (20 July). Centenary of British Columbia's Entry into the Confederation. Perf 12.
685   **337**   7c. multicoloured 15 10

Paul Kane   **Canada 7**

338 *Indian Encampment on Lake Huron* (Kane)   **339** Snowflake

(Des and litho B.A.B.N)

1971 (11 Aug). Death Centenary of Paul Kane (painter). Perf 12½.
686   **338**   7c. multicoloured 20 10

(Des Lisl Levinsohn. Recess (6c., 7c.) or recess and litho (others) C.B.N)

1971 (6 Oct). Christmas. T **339** and similar design. White fluorescent paper. Perf 12.
687   **339**   6c. deep blue 15 10
              o. Ordinary paper 70
              po. One centre phosphor band 30 50
              p. One centre phosphor band, ordinary paper 85 50
688   7c. deep emerald 15 10
              p. Two phosphor bands 30 50
689   –   10c. silver and cerise .... 40 1·00
              p. Two phosphor bands .... 50 1·75
690   –   15c. silver, brown-purple and lavender .... 60 1·50
              p. Two phosphor bands .... 60 2·75
687/690 Set of 4 .... 1·10 1·25
687p/690p Set of 4 .... 1·50 5·00

Design:—10c., 15c. Snowflake design similar to Type **339**, but square (26×26 mm).

CANADA

340 Pierre Laporte (Quebec Cabinet Minister)   **341** Skaters

(Des G. Gundersen. Recess and litho B.A.B.N)

1971 (20 Oct). First Anniversary of the Assassination of Pierre Laporte. Ordinary paper. Perf 12½×12.
691	**340**	7c. black/*pale buff*	15	20

(Des Design Workshop, Toronto. Litho C.B.N)

1972 (1 Mar). World Figure Skating Championships, Calgary. Perf 12.
692	**341**	8c. purple	15	25

342 J. A. Macdonald   **342a** W. Laurier   **342b** R. Borden   **342c** W. L. Mackenzie King

342d R.B. Bennett   **342e** L.B. Pearson   **342f** Louis St. Laurent   **342g** Queen Elizabeth II

343 Forest, Central Canada   **343a** American Bighorn Sheep   **343b** Prairie Landscape from the air

343c Polar Bears   **343d** Seashore, Eastern Canada

344 Vancouver

344a Quebec

Type I   Type II

Two types of 10c. (No. 702):

Type I. Light impression of green recess colour. Cross-hatching around 'Canada' clearly visible (plate 1).

Type II. Green recess colour much more deeply etched. Cross-hatching around 'Canada' entirely obscured (plates 2 and 3).

Type I

Type II

Two types of 15c.:

Type I. Trees on hillside, shown in blue, clearly detailed (plate 1).

Type II. Trees shown in solid colour (plate 2).

Type I   Type II

Two types of 25c.:

Type I. Bears' shadows evenly shaded.

Type II. Shadows have a solid central area.

(Des D. Annesley (1c. to 10c. (No. 701)), R. Derreth (others))

1972 (1 Jan)–**77**. Various designs as T **342/344a**.

(a) T **342/342g** and similar vert portraits. Recess C.B.N. (1c. to 6c.) and last ptgs of 7c. and 8c. (No. 700), B.A.B.N (7c., 8c., 10c. and booklet panes). Two fluorescent bands. Perf 12×12½ (1c. to 8c.) or 13 (10c.). (17.10.73).

693		1c. orange	10	30
		a. Booklet pane. Nos. 693×3, 698 and 700×2 (10.4.74)	75	
		b. Booklet pane. Nos. 693×6, 698 and 700×11 (17.1.75)	2·25	
		c. Booklet pane. Nos. 693×2, 694×4 and 701a×4 (1.9.76)	1·50	
		d. Printed on the gummed side	£650	
694		2c. deep green	10	10
695		3c. agate	10	70
696		4c. black	10	50

697		5c. deep magenta	10	10
698		6c. Indian red	10	50
		a. Printed on the gummed side	£120	
699		7c. reddish brown (8.4.74)	40	70
700		8c. dull ultramarine	15	10
		a. Perf 13 (12.76)	1·00	1·00
701		10c. brown-lake (1.9.76)	75	10
		a. Perf 12×12½ (booklets)	75	1·00

*(b) T **343d** and similar vert designs. Recess and photo B.A.B.N. Two fluorescent bands. Perf 12½×12 (8.9.72)*

702		10c. deep green, blue-green and yellow-orange (I)	60	10
		a. Type II (7.74)	40	15
		b. Perf 13½ (2.76)	75	10
		p. Two phosphor bands	1·00	2·00
703		15c. dull ultramarine and orange-brown (I)	1·00	15
		a. Type II (1975)	4·50	2·25
		b. Perf 13½ (2.76)	1·50	10
		p. Two phosphor bands	2·00	3·00
704		20c. pale orange, reddish violet and ultramarine	1·00	10
		a. Perf 13½ (30.1.76)	1·75	10
		p. Two phosphor bands	2·00	3·50
705		25c. deep ultramarine and pale blue (I)	1·50	10
		a. Type II (1975)	8·50	3·50
		b. Perf 13½ (2.76)	1·00	10
		p. Two phosphor bands	2·50	4·25
706		50c. blue-green, royal blue and buff	1·00	30
		a. Blue-green, ultramarine and buff (8.74)	80	20
		b. Perf 13½ (2.76)	1·75	10

*(c) T **344a** and similar horiz design. Recess B.A.B.N. and litho Ashton-Potter. No fluorescent bands. Perf 11 (17.3.72).*

707		$1 multicoloured	4·75	5·00
708		$2 multicoloured	2·00	2·00
		a. Brown (value and inscr) ptd albino	£2500	

*(d) T **344**. Recess and photo B.A.B.N. Two fluorescent bands. Perf 12½×12 (24.10.73).*

709		$1 multicoloured	2·00	1·25
		a. Perf 13½ (4.77)	85	70
		b. White fluorescent paper (8.74)	2·75	

(e) As Nos. 700/701. Recess C.B.N. Imperf×perf 10 (coil stamps).

710		8c. dull ultramarine (10.4.74)	60	20
		a. Imperf (horiz pair)	90·00	
711		10c. brown-lake (1.9.76)	30	20
		a. Imperf (horiz pair)	£110	

Stamps from booklets (Nos. SB80/SB82) exist with one or two adjacent sides imperforate.
Nos. 712/718 are vacant.

PAPER. Various papers were used for the low value stamps. Nos 693/701, most of which show some degree of fluorescence under U.V. light. The 1c., 2c., 6c., 7c. and 8c. also exist on paper which does not react. In addition all the low values, except the 3c., 5c., 7c. and 10c., occur on paper showing a ribbing effect. The medium values were printed on fluorescent paper, although the amount of fluorescence visible under UV light varies greatly between printings. A small part of the printing of the $1 (No. 707) was on a paper with a distinct textured effect. This paper was used for stamp production in error.

345 Heart   **346** Frontenac and Fort Saint-Louis, Quebec

(Des Joyce Wieland. Recess B.A.B.N.)

1972 (7 Apr). Heart Disease (World Health Day). Perf 12×12½.

719	**345**	8c. carmine	30	10
		o. Ordinary soft toned paper	1·00	1·00
		q. Two fluorescent bands	1·50	1·50
		qo. Two fluorescent bands, ordinary paper	1·25	1·50

The chemical used on No. 719q migrates.

(Des L. Marquart. Recess and photo B.A.B.N)

1972 (17 May). 300th Anniversary of Governor Frontenac's Appointment to New France. Ordinary paper. Perf 12×12½.

720	**346**	8c. brown-red, orange-brown and deep ultramarine	15	15
		q. Two fluorescent bands	15	40

The chemical used on No. 720q migrates.

347 Plains Indians' Artefacts   **347a** Buffalo Chase

347b Algonkian Artefacts   **347c** Micmac Indians

347d Pacific Coast Indiaus Artefacts   **347e** Inside of a Nootka Sound House

347f Subarctic Indians Artefacts   **347g** Dance of the Kutcha-Kutchin

347h Iriquoians' Artefacts   **347i** Iriquoian Encampment

(Des G. Beaupré. Litho Ashton-Potter (721/722, 725/726 and 729/730), B.A.B.N. (723/724), C.B.N. (727/728)))

1972 (1 Jan)–**76**. Canadian Indians. Two fluorescent bands (Nos. 723/30 and 733/40). Perf 12×12½ (721/722, 725/726), 12 (723/724), 13 (727/730), 12½×12 (731/736) or 12½ (737/740).

*(a) Horiz designs issued in se-tenant pairs as T **347/347i**.*

721		8c. multicoloured (6.7.72)	25	10
		a. Pair. Nos. 721/722	50	1·00
		q. Two fluorescent bands	25	15
		qa. Pair. Nos. 721q/722q	50	1·00
722		8c. deep brown, yellow and grey-black (6.7.72)	25	10
		q. Two fluorescent bands	25	15
723		8c. multicoloured (21.2.73)	25	10
		a. Pair. Nos. 723/724	50	1·00
724		8c. multicoloured (21.2.73)	25	10
725		8c. multicoloured (16.1.74)	25	10
		a. Pair. Nos. 725/726	50	1·25
726		8c. deep brown, yellow and grey-black (16.1.74)	25	10
727		8c. multicoloured (4.4.75)	25	10
		a. Pair. Nos. 727/728	50	1·25
		b. Imperf between (horiz pair)	£750	
728		8c. multicoloured (4.4.75)	25	10
729		10c. multicoloured (17.9.76)	25	20
		a. Pair. Nos. 729/730	50	1·00
730		10c. light stone and black (17.9.76)	25	20

CANADA

348 Thunderbird and Tribal Pattern

348a Dancer in Ceremonial Costume

348b Thunderbird

348c Algonkian couple

348d Kwatiuti house Thunderbird

348e Chief and blanket

348f Ojibwé Thunderbird

348g Kutchin ceremonial costume

348h Iriquoian Thunderbird

348i Iriquoian couple

(Des G. Beaupré. Recess and photo B.A.B.N. (Nos. 731/736). Litho and embossed Ashton-Potter (Nos. 737, 739). Litho Ashton-Potter (Nos. 738, 740)))

(b) Vert designs issued in se-tenant pairs as T 348/348i.

731	8c. light yellow-orange, rose-red and black (4.10.72)	25	15
	a. Pair. Nos. 731/732	50	1·00
	q. Two fluorescent bands	25	15
	qa. Pair. Nos. 731q/732q	50	1·00
732	8c. multicoloured (4.10.72)	25	15
	q. Two fluorescent bands	25	15
733	8c. light rose-red, violet and black (28.11.73)	25	10
	a. Pair. Nos. 733/734	50	1·00
734	8c. turquoise-green, lake-brown and black (28.11.73)	25	10
735	8c. rose-red and black (22.2.74)	25	10
	a. Pair. Nos. 735/736	50	1·00
	c. White fluorescent paper	1·25	
	ca. Pair. Nos. 735c/736c	2·50	
736	8c. multicoloured (22.2.74)	25	10
	c. White fluorescent paper	1·25	
737	8c. myrtle-green, grey-brown and black (4.4.75)	25	10
	a. Pair. Nos. 737/738	50	1·25
738	8c. multicoloured (4.4.75)	25	10
739	10c. olive-bistre, reddish orange and black (17.9.76)	25	20
	a. Pair. Nos. 739/740	50	1·00
740	10c. multicoloured (17.9.76)	25	20
721/740 Set of 10 pairs		4·50	9·50

The paper and gum of Nos. 735/736 are yellowish; on Nos 735c/736c they are white. Fluorescent paper printings of Nos. 733/734, but there is no apparent difference to the naked eye, except that the fluorescent paper is slightly more transparent.

The fluorescent bands on Nos. 721q/722q and 731q/732q migrate.

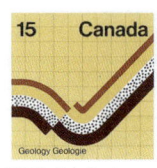
349 Earth's Crust

350 Candles

(Des Gottschalk and Ash Ltd. Litho Ashton-Potter)

1972 (2 Aug). Earth Sciences. T **349** and similar square designs. Perf 12.

741	–	15c. multicoloured	1·00 1·90
		a. Block of 4. Nos. 741/744	3·50 7·00
		q. Two fluorescent bands	1·25 2·25
		qa. Block of 4. Nos. 741q/744q	4·50 8·00
742	–	15c. pale grey, dull ultramarine and black	1·00 1·90
		q. Two fluorescent bands	1·25 2·25
743		15c. multicoloured	1·00 1·90
		q. Two fluorescent bands	1·25 2·25
744		15c. light emerald, red-orange and black	1·00 1·90
		q. Two fluorescent bands	1·25 2·25
741/744 Set of 4			3·50 7·00
741q/744q Set of 4			4·50 8·00

Designs and Events:—No. 741, Photogrammetric surveying (12th Congress of International Society of Photogrammetry); No. 742, Siegfried lines (Sixth Conference of International Cartographic Association); No. 743, Type **349** (24th International Geological Congress; No. 744, Diagram of village at road-intersection (22nd International Geographical Congress).

Nos. 741/744 were issued in sheets of 64, made up of four panes of 16, each pane having a marginal commemorative inscription. Within a pane are four copies of each design, arranged in *se-tenant* blocks of four.

(Des R. Webber. Litho Ashton-Potter)

1972 (1 Nov). Christmas. T **350** and similar designs. Perf 12½×12 (6c. and 8c.) or 11×10½ (others).

745	**350**	6c. multicoloured	10 10
		p. One centre phosphor band	25 50
		q. Two fluorescent bands	30 15
746		8c. multicoloured	15 10
		p. Two phosphor bands	30 55
		q. Two fluorescent bands	35 15
747	–	10c. multicoloured	40 1·00
		p. Two phosphor bands	1·00 1·75
		q. Two fluorescent bands	80 1·40
748	–	15c. multicoloured	45 1·50
		p. Two phosphor bands	1·25 2·50
		q. Two fluorescent bands	1·10 1·90
745/748 Set of 4			1·00 2·50
745p/748p Set of 4			2·50 4·75
745q/748q Set of 4			2·25 3·25

Designs: Horiz (36×20 mm)—10c. Candles with fruits and pine boughs; 15c. Candles with prayer-book, caskets and vase.

> **WHITE FLUORESCENT PAPER.** All issues are on white fluorescent paper, *unless otherwise stated*. From November 1972 stamps printed by lithography were produced on two types of this paper, one fluorescing on both sides, the other on one side only. Some issues exist on both papers. Those on the single-sided coating can be found with the fluorescence on the front or back of the stamp.

351 *The Blacksmith's Shop* (Krieghoff)

352 François de Montmorency-Laval

(Des and litho B.A.B.N. and Saults and Pollard Ltd., Winnipeg)

1972 (29 Nov). Death Centenary of Cornelius Krieghoff (painter). Perf 12½.
749 **351** 8c. multicoloured 30 15
    q. Two fluorescent bands 30 55

> **FLUORESCENT BANDS**. Stamps from No. 750 onwards were issued only with two fluorescent bands, *unless otherwise stated*. Examples are known with the bands omitted in error, but such varieties are outside the scope of the catalogue.

(Des M. Fog and G. Lorange. Litho Ashton-Potter)

1973 (31 Jan). 350th Birth Anniversary of Monsignor de Laval (First Bishop of Quebec). Perf 11.
750 **352** 8c. ultramarine, gold and silver............. 20 40

353 Commissioner French and Route of the March West   **354** Jeanne Mance

(Des Dallaire Morin DeVito Inc. Litho Ashton-Potter)

1973 (9 Mar). Centenary of Royal Canadian Mounted Police. T **353** and similar horiz designs. Multicoloured (except 8c.). Perf 11.
751   8c. Type **353** (deep reddish brown, dull orange and orange-vermilion) 30 20
752   10c. Spectrograph .... 45 1·00
753   15c. Mounted policeman................................ 1·50 1·60
751/753 *Set of 3*... 2·00 2·50

No. 753 is known imperforate but it is not believed that it was issued in this form.

(Des R. Bellemare. Litho Ashton-Potter)

1973 (18 Apr). 300th Death Anniversary of Jeanne Mance (nurse). Perf 11.
754 **354** 8c. multicoloured 20 40
    a. Printed on gummed side .... 55·00

355 Joseph Howe   **356** *Mist Fantasy* (MacDonald)

(Des A. Fleming. Litho Ashton-Potter)

1973 (16 May). Death Centenary of Joseph Howe (Nova Scotian politician). Perf 11.
755 **355** 8c. gold and black 20 40

(Des and litho Ashton-Potter)

1973 (8 June). Birth Centenary of J. E. H. MacDonald (artist). Perf 12½.
756 **356** 15c. multicoloured 30 55

357 Oaks and Harbour   **358** Scottish Settlers

(Des A. Mann. Recess and photo B.A.B.N)

1973 (22 June). Centenary of Prince Edward Island's Entry into the Confederation. Perf 12.
757 **357** 8c. pale orange and brown-red............. 20 30

(Des P. Swan. Litho Ashton-Potter)

1973 (20 July). Bicentennial of Arrival of Scottish Settlers at Pictou, Nova Scotia. Perf 12×12½.
758 **358** 8c. multicoloured 25 20

359 Queen Elizabeth II   **360** Nellie McClung

(Des A. Fleming from photograph by Anthony Buckley,. Eng G. A. Gundersen. Recess and photo B.A.B.N.))

1973 (2 Aug). Royal Visit and Commonwealth Heads of Government Meeting, Ottawa. Ordinary paper. Perf 12×12½.
759 **359** 8c. multicoloured 25 20
    a. White fluorescent paper................... 2·75
760   15c. red, black and bright gold................ 1·50 2·00
    a. Red, black and pale dull gold............ 1·25 2·00

(Des S. Mennie. Litho Ashton-Potter)

1973 (29 Aug). Birth Centenary of Nellie McClung (feminist). Perf 10½×11.
761 **360** 8c. multicoloured 20 50

361 Emblem of 1976 Olympics   **362** Ice-skate

(Des Wallis and Matanovic. Litho Ashton-Potter)

1973 (20 Sept). Olympic Games, Montreal (1976) (1st issue). Perf 12×12½.
762 **361** 8c. multicoloured 25 15
763   15c. multicoloured .... 45 1·25
See also Nos. 768/771, 772/774, 786/789, 798/802, 809/811, 814/816, 829/831, 833/837 and 842/844.

(Des A. Maggs. Litho Ashton-Potter)

1973 (7 Nov). Christmas. T **362** and similar vert designs. Multicoloured. Perf 12½×12 (6c., 8c.) or 11 (others).
764   6c. Type **362**... 15 10
765   8c. Bird decoration...................................... 15 10
766   10c. Santa Claus (20×36 mm)..................... 35 1·10
767   15c. Shepherd (20×36 mm)......................... 45 1·50
    a. Green (background) omitted .... †   —
764/767 *Set of 4*.. 1·00 2·50

A single used example of No. 767a is known.

363 Diving   **364** Winnipeg Signpost, 1872

(Des Hunter, Straker, Templeton Ltd. Recess C.B.N)

1974 (22 Mar). Olympic Games, Montreal (1976) (2nd issue). Summer Activities. T **363** and similar vert designs. Each deep blue. Perf 12.
768   8c. Type **363**... 30 50
    a. Block of 4. Nos. 768/771 .... 1·10 2·25
769   8c. Jogging 30 50
770   8c. Cycling 30 50
771   8c. Hiking 30 50
768/771 *Set of 4*.. 1·10 2·25

CANADA

Nos. 768/771 were printed in *se-tenant* blocks of four throughout the sheet. Each design has a second (latent) image—the Canadian Olympic Games symbol—which appears when the stamp is viewed obliquely to the light.

See also Nos. 786/789.

(Des Wallis and Matanovic. Litho Ashton-Potter)

1974 (17 Apr). Olympic Games, Montreal (1976) (3rd issue). As T **361** but smaller (20×36½ mm). Perf 12½.

772	**361**	8c.+2c. multicoloured	25	45
773		10c.+5c. multicoloured	40	1·00
774		15c.+5c. multicoloured	45	1·40
772/774 *Set of 3*			1·00	2·50

(Des J. R. MacDonald. Litho and embossed Ashton-Potter)

1974 (3 May). Winnipeg Centennial. Perf 12½×12.

775	**364**	8c. multicoloured	20	15

365 Postmaster and Customer

366 Canada's Contribution to Agriculture

(Des S. Mennie. Litho Ashton-Potter)

1974 (11 June). Centenary of Canadian Letter Carrier Delivery Service. T **365** and similar horiz designs. Multicoloured. Perf 13½.

776	8c. Type **365**	50 85
	a. Block of 6. Nos. 776/781	2·75 4·50
777	8c. Postman collecting mail	50 85
778	8c. Mail handler	50 85
779	8c. Mail sorters	50 85
780	8c. Postman making delivery	50 85
781	8c. Rural delivery by car	50 85
776/781 *Set of 6*		2·75 4·50

Nos. 776/781 were printed in *se-tenant* combinations throughout a sheet of 50, giving 6 blocks of six and 14 single stamps.

(Des M. Brett, P. Cowley-Brown, and A. McAllister. Litho Ashton-Potter)

1974 (12 July). Agricultural Education. Centenary of Ontario Agricultural College. Perf 12½×12.

782	**366**	8c. multicoloured	20	20

367 Telephone Development

368 Bicycle Wheel

(Des R. Webber. Litho Ashton-Potter)

1974 (26 July). Centenary of Invention of Telephone by Alexander Graham Bell. Perf 12½.

783	**367**	8c. multicoloured	20	20
		a. Imperf		

(Des Burns and Cooper. Recess and photo B.A.B.N)

1974 (7 Aug). World Cycling Championships, Montreal. Perf 12½×12½.

784	**368**	8c. black, rosine and silver	20	30

369 Mennonite Settlers

370 Mercury, Winged Horses and UPU Emblem

(Des W. Davies. Litho Ashton-Potter)

1974 (28 Aug). Centenary of Arrival of Mennonites in Manitoba. Perf 12½.

785	**369**	8c. multicoloured	20	20

(Des Hunter, Straker, Templeton Ltd. Recess C.B.N)

1974 (23 Sept). Olympic Games, Montreal (1976) (4th issue). Winter Activities. Horiz designs as T **363**, each rosine. Perf 13½×13.

786		8c. Snow-shoeing	45	60
		a. Block of 4. Nos. 786/789	1·60	2·25
		ab. Printed on the gummed side (block of 4)	£2250	
787		8c. Skiing	45	60
788		8c. Skating	45	60
789		8c. Curling	45	60
786/789 *Set of 4*			1·60	2·25

(Des G. Gundersen. Recess and photo B.A.B.N)

1974 (9 Oct). Centenary of Universal Postal Union. Ordinary paper. Perf 12½×12½.

790	**370**	8c. violet, red-orange and cobalt	15	15
791		15c. red-orange, violet and cobalt	50	1·00
		a. White fluorescent paper	2·50	2·50

371 The Nativity (J. P. Lemieux)

372 Marconi and St. John's Harbour, Newfoundland

(Des Wallis and Matanovic. Litho Ashton-Potter)

1974 (1 Nov). Christmas. T **371** and similar horiz designs showing paintings. Multicoloured. Perf 13½.

792	6c. Type **371**	10	10
	a. Creamy ordinary paper	6·00	2·00
793	8c. *Skaters in Hull* (H. Masson) (34×31 mm)	10	10
794	10c. *The Ice Cone, Montmorency Falls* (R. C. Todd)	30	75
795	15c. *Village in the Laurentian Mountains* (C. A. Gagnon)	35	1·10
792/795 *Set of 4*		75	1·75

(Des J. Boyle. Litho Ashton-Potter)

1974 (15 Nov). Birth Centenary of Guglielmo Marconi (radio pioneer). Perf 13.

796	**372**	8c. multicoloured	20	20

373 Merritt and Welland Canal

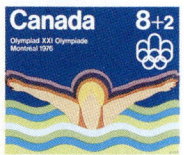
374 Swimming

(Des W. Rueter. Recess (B.A.B.N.) and litho (C.B.N.))

1974 (29 Nov). William Merritt Commemoration. Perf 13×13½.

797	**373**	8c. multicoloured	20	30

(Des Wallis and Matanovic. Litho C.B.N)

1975 (5 Feb). Olympic Games, Montreal (1976) (5th issue). T **374** and similar horiz designs. Multicoloured. Perf 13.

798	8c.+2c. Type **374**	30	55
799	10c.+5c. Rowing	40	1·10
800	15c.+5c. Sailing	45	1·40
798/800 *Set of 3*		1·00	2·75

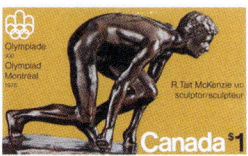
375 The Sprinter

376 Anne of Green Gables (Lucy Maud Montgomery)

CANADA

(Des A. R. Fleming. Litho and embossed Ashton-Potter)

1975 (14 Mar). Olympic Games, Montreal (1976) (6th issue). T **375** and similar multicoloured design showing sculpture by R. T. McKenzie. Perf 12½×12 ($1) or 12×12½ ($2).
801	$1 Type **375**	1·00	1·75
802	$2 The Diver (*vert*)	1·50	3·25

(Des P. Swan (No. 803), C. Gagnon (No. 804). Litho Ashton-Potter)

1975 (15 May). Canadian Writers (1st series). T **376** and similar vert design. Multicoloured. Perf 13½.
803	8c. Type **376**	30	10
	a. Pair. Nos. 803/804	60	1·00
804	8c. *Maria Chapdelaine* (Louis Hémon)	30	10

Nos. 803/804 were printed horizontally and vertically *se-tenant* throughout the sheet.

See also Nos. 846/847, 940/941 and 1085/1086.

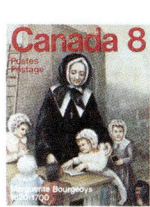 

377 Marguerite Bourgeoys (founder of the Order of Notre Dame)

378 S. D. Chown (founder of United Church of Canada)

(Des Design and Communication, Montreal. Litho Ashton-Potter (Nos. 805/806). Des W. Southern. Eng G. Gundersen. Recess and photo B.A.B.N. (Nos. 807/808)))

1975 (30 May). Canadian Celebrities. T **377**/**3788** and similar vert designs.

(a) As T **377**. Perf 12½×12.
805	8c. multicoloured	30	40
806	8c. multicoloured	30	40

(b) As T **378**. Perf 12×12½.
807	8c. sepia, flesh and light yellow	30	50
	a. Pair. Nos. 807/808	60	1·75
808	8c. sepia, flesh and light yellow	30	50
805/808 *Set of 4*		1·00	2·25

Designs: No. 805, Type **377**; No. 806, Alphonse Desjardins (leader of Credit Union movement); No. 807, Type **378**; No. 808, Dr. J. Cook (first moderator of Presbyterian Church in Canada).

Nos. 807/808 were printed together in the sheet horizontally and vertically *se-tenant*.

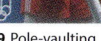

379 Pole-vaulting

380 Untamed (photo by Walt Petrigo)

(Des P. Swan. Litho Ashton-Potter)

1975 (11 June). Olympic Games, Montreal (1976) (7th issue). T **379** and similar vert designs. Multicoloured. Perf 12×12½.
809	20c. Type **379**	30	80
810	25c. Marathon-running	30	80
811	50c. Hurdling	50	1·25
	o. Creamy ordinary paper	7·00	1·50
809/811 *Set of 3*		1·00	2·25

(Des B. Reilander. Litho C.B.N)

1975 (3 July). Centenary of Calgary. Perf 12×12½.
812	**380**	8c. multicoloured	20	30

381 IWY Symbol   **382** Fencing

(Des Susan McPhee. Recess and photo B.A.B.N)

1975 (14 July). International Women's Year. Perf 13.
813	**381**	8c. light grey-brown, bistre-yellow and black	20	30

(Des J. Hill. Litho C.B.N)

1975 (6 Aug). Olympic Games, Montreal (1976) (8th issue). T **382** and similar vert designs showing combat sports. Multicoloured. Perf 13.
814	8c.+2c. Type **382**	35	75
815	10c.+5c. Boxing	45	1·50
816	15c.+5c. Judo	55	1·75
814/816 *Set of 3*		1·25	3·50

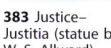

383 Justice– Justitia (statue by W. S. Allward)

384 *William D. Lawrence* (full-rigged ship)

(Des A. Fleming. Litho Ashton-Potter)

1975 (2 Sept). Centenary of Canadian Supreme Court. Perf 12½.
817	**383**	8c. multicoloured	20	30

(Des T. Bjarnason. Recess and photo B.A.B.N)

1975 (24 Sept). Canadian Ships (1st series). T **384** and similar horiz designs showing coastal ships. Perf 13.
818	8c. yellow-brown and black	45	80
	a. Block of 4. Nos. 818/821	1·75	3·00
819	8c. blue-green and black	45	80
820	8c. yellow-green and black	45	80
821	8c. yellow-brown and black	45	80
818/821 *Set of 4*		1·75	3·00

Designs: No. 819, *Neptune* (steamer). No. 820, *Beaver* (paddle-steamer). No. 821, *Quadra* (steamer).

Nos. 818/821 were printed together, *se-tenant*, in different combinations throughout the sheet, giving ten blocks of four and ten single stamps.

See also Nos. 851/854, 902/905 and 931/934.

385 Santa Claus (G. Kelly)

386 Text, Badge and Bugle

(Des B. Reilander from children's paintings. Litho Ashton-Potter)

1975 (22 Oct). Christmas. T **385** and similar multicoloured designs. Perf 13.
822	6c. Type **385**	15	10
	a. Pair. Nos. 822/823	30	40
823	6c. Skater (Bill Cawsey)	15	10
824	8c. Child (D. Hébert)	15	10
	a. Pair. Nos. 824/825	30	45
825	8c. Family (L. Caldwell)	15	10
826	10c. Gift (D. Louie)	30	50
827	15c. Trees (R. Kowalski) (*horiz*)	40	75
822/827 *Set of 6*		1·10	1·90

Nos. 822/823 and 824/825 were respectively issued together *se-tenant* in an alternate arrangement within the sheet.

CANADA

(Des R. Kavach. Recess and photo B.A.B.N)
1975 (10 Nov). 50th Anniversary of Royal Canadian Legion. Perf 12½×13.
828 **386** 8c. multicoloured 20 20

387 Basketball

(Des J. Hill. Litho Ashton-Potter)
1976 (7 Jan). Olympic Games, Montreal (9th issue). T **387** and similar vert designs. Multicoloured. Perf 13.
829   8c.+2c. Type **387** .... 1·00 60
830   10c.+5c. Gymnastics 25 80
831   20c.+5c. Soccer .... 40 1·25
829/831 *Set of 3* .... 1·50 1·40

388 Games Symbol and Snow Crystal   **389** Communications Arts

(Des R. Harder. Litho Ashton-Potter)
1976 (6 Feb). 12th Winter Olympic Games, Innsbruck. Perf 12½.
832 **388** 20c. multicoloured 20 40

(Des R. Webber. Litho C.B.N)
1976 (6 Feb). Olympic Games, Montreal (10th issue). T **389** and similar vert designs. Multicoloured. Perf 12×12½.
833   20c. Type **389** 40 25
834   25c. Handicrafts 50 75
835   50c. Performing Arts .... 70 1·60
833/835 *Set of 3* .... 1·40 2·40

390 Place Ville Marie and Notre-Dame Church

(Des J. and P. Mercier. Recess and photo B.A.B.N)
1976 (12 Mar). Olympic Games, Montreal (11th issue). T **390** and similar horiz design. Multicoloured. Perf 13.
836       $1 Type **390** .... 1·75 3·50
837       $2 Olympic Stadium and flags .... 2·50 4·50

391 Flower and Urban Sprawl   **392** Benjamin Franklin and Map

(Des I. McLeod. Litho Ashton-Potter)
1976 (12 May). UN Conference on Human Settlements (HABITAT), Vancouver. Perf 12×12½.
838 **391** 20c. multicoloured 20 30

(Des B. Reilander. Recess and photo B.A.B.N)
1976 (1 June). Bicentenary of American Revolution. Perf 13.
839 **392** 10c. multicoloured 20 35

393 Wing Parade before Mackenzie Building   **394** Transfer of Olympic Flame by Satellite

(Des W. Davies. Litho C.B.N)
1976 (1 June). Royal Military College Centenary. T **393** and similar vert design. Multicoloured. Perf 12½.
840   8c. Colour party and Memorial Arch 25 30
          a. Pair. Nos. 840/841 .... 50 1·00
          ab. Imperf (pair) £1200
841   8c. Type **393** 25 30
Nos. 840/841 were printed horizontally and vertically *se-tenant* throughout the sheet.

(Des P. Swan. Litho Ashton-Potter)
1976 (18 June). Olympic Games, Montreal (12th issue). T **394** and similar horiz designs. Multicoloured. Perf 13½.
842   8c. Type **394** 20 10
843   20c. Carrying the Olympic flag 45 60
844   25c. Athletes with medals 45 85
842/844 *Set of 3* .... 1·00 1·40

395 Archer

(Des T. Bjarnason. Litho C.B.N)
1976 (3 Aug). Olympiad for the Physically Disabled. Perf 12×12½.
845 **395** 20c. multicoloured 20 30

396 *Sam McGee* (Robert W. Service)   **397** Nativity (F. Mayer)

(Des D. Bierk (No. 846), A. Dumas (No. 847). Litho Ashton-Potter)
1976 (17 Aug). Canadian Writers (2nd series). T **396** and similar vert design. Multicoloured. Perf 13.
846   8c. Type **396** 15 40
          a. Pair. Nos. 846/847 .... 30 1·25
847   8c. *Le Survenant* (Germaine Guèvremont) .. 15 40
Nos. 846/847 were printed horizontally and vertically *se-tenant* throughout the sheet.

(Des B. Reilander. Litho Ashton-Potter)
1976 (3 Nov). Christmas. T **397** and similar vert designs showing stained-glass windows. Multicoloured. Perf 13½.
848   8c. Type **397** 10 10
849   10c. Nativity (G. Maile and Son) 10 10
850   20c. Nativity (Yvonne Williams) 20 60
848/850 *Set of 3* 30 60

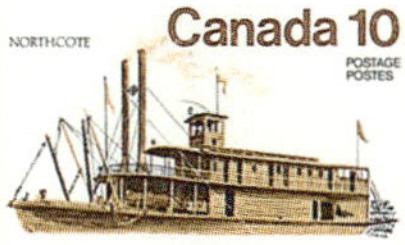

398 *Northcote* (paddle-steamer)

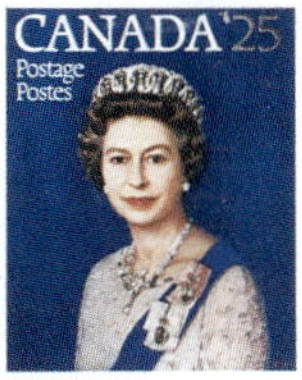

399 Queen Elizabeth II

(Des T. Bjarnason. Recess and litho C.B.N)

1976 (19 Nov). Canadian Ships (2nd series). T **398** and similar horiz designs showing inland vessels. Perf 12×12½.

851	10c. ochre, chestnut and black	40	70
	a. Block of 4. Nos. 851/854	1·40	2·50
852	10c. violet-blue and black	40	70
853	10c. bright blue and black	40	70
854	10c. apple-green, olive-green and black	40	70
851/854 *Set of 4*		1·40	2·50

Designs: No. 851, Type **398**; No. 852, *Passport* (paddle-steamer); No. 853, *Chicora* (paddle-steamer); No. 854, *Athabasca* (steamer).

Nos. 851/854 were printed together, *se-tenant*, in different combinations throughout the sheet, giving ten blocks of four and ten single stamps.

(Des K. Rodmell from photograph by P. Grugeon. Litho ('25' die-stamped) Ashton-Potter))

1977 (4 Feb). Silver Jubilee. Perf 12½×12.

855	**399**	25c. multicoloured	30	50
		a. Silver (die-stamped '25') omitted	£650	£425

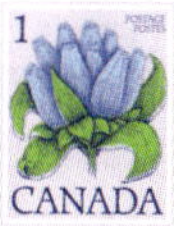

400 Bottle Gentian

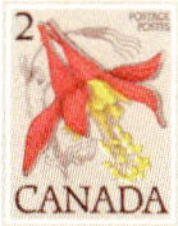

400a Red Columbine

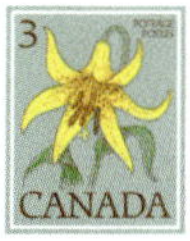

400b Canada Lily

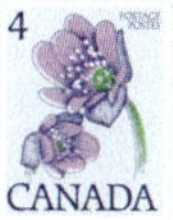

400c Hepatica

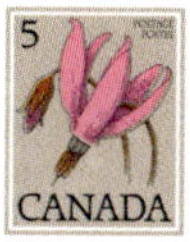

400d Shooting Star

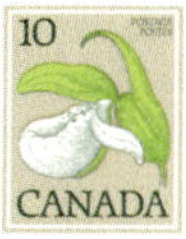

400e Franklin's Lady's Slipper Orchid

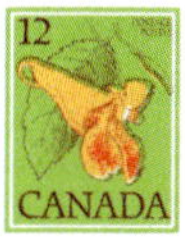

400f Jewelweed

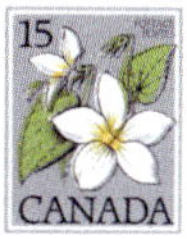

400g Canada Violet

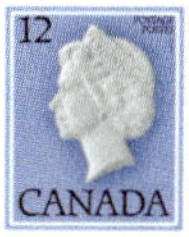

401 Queen Elizabeth II (bas-relief by J. Huta)

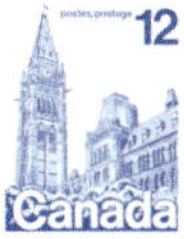

402 Houses of Parliament

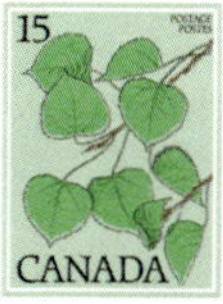

403 Trembling Aspen

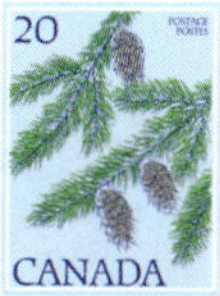

403a Douglas Fir

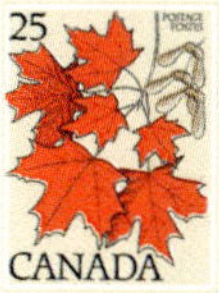

403b Sugar Maple

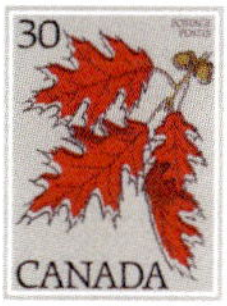

403c Red Oak

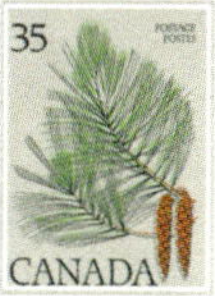

403d White Pine

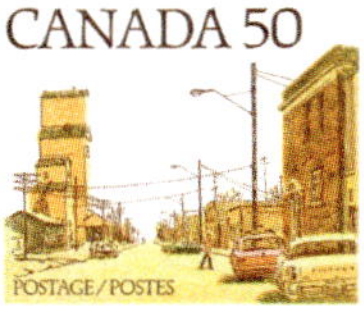

404 Prairie Town Main Street

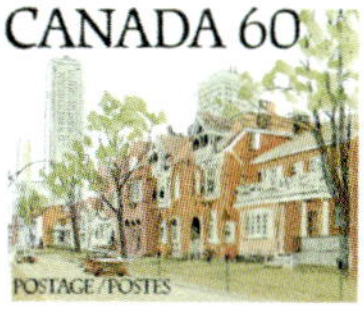

404a Ontario City Street

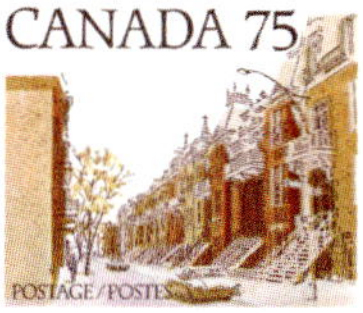

404b Eastern City Street

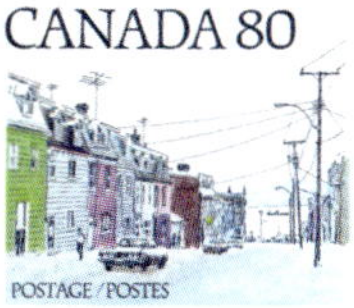

404c Maritimes Street

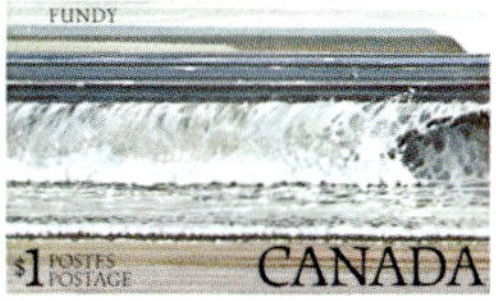

405 Fundy National Park

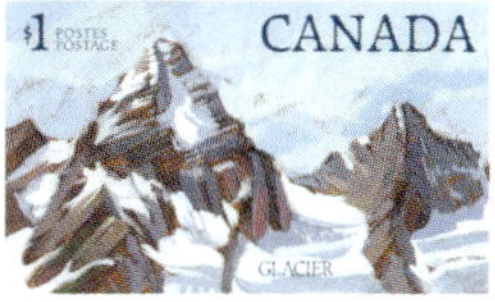

405a Glacier

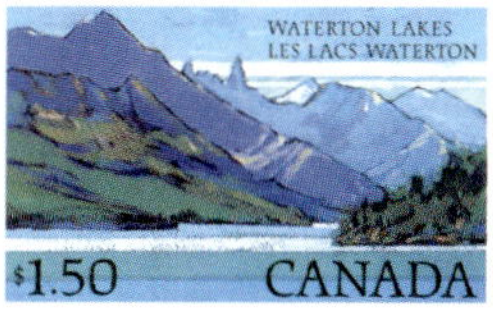

405b Waterton Lakes

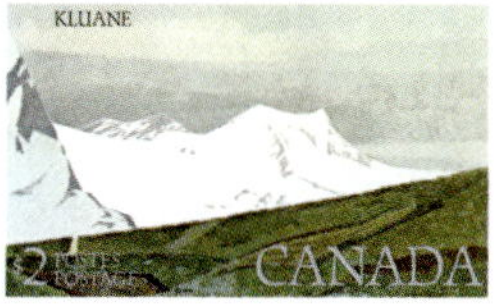

405c Kluane

CANADA

405d Banff

405e Point Pelee

405f La Mauricie

(Des R. Derreth (Nos. 870/874*d*), T. Bjarnason (No. 880/883*b*), R. Bolt (No. 884), B. Laycock and W. Tibbles (No. 884*c*), A. Collier (No. 885), W. Tibbles and G. Weber (No. 885*c*), W. Terry and W. Tibbles (No. 885*d*), L. Marois and W. Tibbles (No. 885*e*), Heather Cooper (others T **401** after plaster cast by Jaroslav Huta). Eng Y. Baril (Nos. 870/874*d* and 880/883*a*))

1977 (1 Mar)–**86**.

*(a) Vert designs as T **400/400g** showing flowers. Multicoloured. (i) Recess and litho C.B.N. Sheet stamps. Perf 12×12½.*

856	1c. Type **400** (22.4.77)................................	10	20
	a. Printed on the gummed side (pre-cancelled only)....................................	£600	
857	2c. Red Columbine (22.4.77).....................	10	10
	a. Printed on the gummed side................	£450	
858	3c. Canada Lily (22.4.77)..........................	10	10
859	4c. Hepatica (22.4.77)...............................	10	10
	a. Printed on the gummed side................	£160	
860	5c. Shooting Star (22.4.77)........................	10	10
861	10c. Franklin's Lady's Slipper Orchid (22.4.77)..	15	10
	a. Perf 13×13½ (5.10.78)...........................	70	55

(ii) Recess and photo B.A.B.N. Booklet stamps (1c., 2c.) or sheet stamps (others). Chalk-surfaced paper. Perf 12×12½ (1c., 2c.) or 13×13½ (others).

862	1c. Type **400** (1.11.77)...............................	1·00	2·50
	a. Booklet pane. Nos. 862×2 and 867a×4.	3·25	
	b. Perf 13×13½ (from sheets) (16.6.79) ...	20	1·00
863	2c. Red Columbine (1.4.78).......................	65	1·00
	a. Booklet pane. Nos. 863×4 and 868b×3 plus one printed label............................	2·75	
	b. Perf 13×13½ (from sheets) (2.8.79)......	30	30
864	3c. Canada Lily (11.4.79)...........................	20	30
864a	4c. Hepatica (3.7.79).................................	50	10
865	5c. Shooting Star (24.1.79)........................	40	10
865a	10c. Franklin's Lady's Slipper Orchid (4.10.79)..	60	10
866	12c. Jewelweed (6.7.78)...............................	15	60
866a	15c. Canada Violet (16.8.79).......................	15	15

*(b) T **401**. Recess and photo B.A.B.N. Chalk-surfaced paper. Perf 13×13½.*

867	12c. black, grey and cobalt (1.3.77)............	15	10
	a. Perf 12×12½ (from booklets) (1.11.77)..	40	1·25
868	14c. black, grey and rose-red (7.3.78).........	20	10
	a. Rose-red (background) omitted...........	£650	
	b. Perf 12×12½ (from booklets) (1.4.78)...	35	1·00
	ba. Booklet pane. No. 868a×25, plus two printed labels (13.11.78).........................	7·50	
869	17c. black, grey and yellowish green (8.3.79)...	50	10
	aa. Imperf (pair)...	£2000	
	a. Perf 12×12½ (from booklets) (28.3.79)..	35	35
	ab. Booklet pane. No. 869a×25, plus two printed labels (3.7.79)............................	8·00	
869b	30c. maroon, grey and reddish purple (11.5.82)...	70	1·25
	ba. *Maroon, grey and bright mauve* (9.83)....	2·25	1·75
869c	32c. black, grey and light blue (24.5.83)......	50	1·25
	ca. Grey printed double	†	—

*(c) T **402**. (i) Recess C.B.N. (Nos. 872a, 873/874) or B.A.B.N. (others). Booklet stamps (Nos. 870/871) or sheet stamps (others). Chalk-surfaced paper (1c., 5c., 12c.). Perf 12×12½ (1c., 5c.) or 13×13½ (others).*

870	1c. indigo (28.3.79)...................................	1·25	3·25
	a. Booklet pane. Nos. 869a×2, 870 and 871×3	2·50	
871	5c. deep rose-lilac (28.3.79)......................	50	70
872	12c. blue (chalk-surfaced paper) (3.5.77).....	70	40
	a. Printed on the gummed side	£130	
	b. *New blue* (ordinary paper) (4.78).........	70	40
873	14c. scarlet (7.3.78).....................................	15	10
	a. Printed on the gummed side	18·00	
	b. Scarlet omitted (albino impression)		
874	17c. deep green (8.3.79)..............................	30	10
	a. Printed on the gummed side	20·00	

(ii) Recess C.B.N. Coil stamps. Imperf×perf 10.

874b	12c. new blue (3.5.77).................................	75	30
	ba. Imperf (horiz pair).................................	90·00	
874c	14c. scarlet (7.3.78).....................................	60	50
	ca. Imperf (horiz pair)................................	90·00	
874d	17c. deep green (8.3.79)..............................	50	20
	da. Imperf (horiz pair)................................	£100	

*(d) Vert designs as T **403/403d** showing leaves. Multicoloured. Recess and photo B.A.B.N. Chalk-surfaced paper. Perf 13½.*

875	15c. Type **403** (8.8.77)................................	15	10
876	20c. Douglas Fir (8.8.77).............................	15	10
877	25c. Sugar Maple (8.8.77)...........................	15	10
878	30c. Red Oak (7.3.78).................................	20	10
879	35c. White Pine (8.3.79).............................	25	10

*(e) Horiz designs as T **404/404c** showing city streets. Multicoloured. Perf 13½. (i) Recess and photo B.A.B.N. Chalk-surfaced paper. No fluorescent bands (75c., 80c.) (6.7.78).*

880	50c. Type **404**	1·00	1·25
881	75c. Eastern city street	1·00	1·00
882	80c. Maritimes street..................................	85	1·00

(ii) Recess and litho C.B.N.

883	50c. Type **404** (13.12.78)............................	85	1·00
	a. Brown (recess value and inscr) omitted	£1200	
883b	60c. Ontario city street (11.5.82)................	65	80

*(f) Horiz designs as T **405/405f** showing national parks. Multicoloured. Recess and litho C.B.N. or B.A.B.N. (ptgs of Nos. 884bb, 885c and 885e from 26 Sept 1986). No. 884 with or without fluorescent bands, others only exist without. Perf 13½.*

884	$1 Type **405** (fluorescent bands) (24.1.79)	70	35
	a. No fluorescent bands (4.3.81)...............	1·10	55
	ab. Black (inscr and value) ptd albino........	£350	
884b	$1 Glacier (chalk-surfaced paper) (15.8.84)	85	45
	ba. Blue (inscr and value) omitted..............	£500	
	bb. Imperf (pair)...	£2000	
	bc. Blue double...		
	bd. Ordinary paper (12.7.85).......................	2·00	1·50
884c	$1.50 Waterton Lakes (18.6.82)...................	1·25	1·75
	ca. Black (inscr and value) omitted.............	£2000	
885	$2 Kluane (27.4.79)..................................	1·00	45
	a. Silver (inscr and value) omitted............	£300	
	b. Chalk-surfaced paper (14.12.84).........	4·25	3·00
885c	$2 Banff (21.6.85)....................................	3·75	1·75
	ca. Bottle-green (inscr and value) omitted	£600	
885d	$5 Point Pelee (10.1.83)..........................	2·50	2·00
	da. Chalk-surfaced paper (14.12.84).........	9·00	3·75
885e	$5 La Mauricie (14.3.86).........................	5·00	4·00
	ea. Deep blue (inscr and value) omitted.....	£1700	

Used examples of No. 857 are known with the purple (inscription and face value) omitted.

The main differences between No. 861a and No. 865*a* are in the background. On No. 865*a* this is toned and has the blurred edges typical of photogravure. No. 861a has a background of solid appearance with the edges clean. The B.A.B.N. version also has stronger lines on the recess part of the design.

No. 883 can be identified from 880 in that the brown printing from the recess plate of the former is deeper and the detail more defined; the registration plate of the car in the foreground can clearly be seen under a glass as '1978'. The 'hidden date' (1977) occurs alongside the grain elevator door on No. 880. Also the colours from the lithographic plates of No. 883 are much bolder than those from the photogravure cylinders of 880. In addition the paper of No. 883 has a shiny appearance.

No. 884ab shows an uninked impression of the recess-printed part of the design.

Stamps with one or two adjacent sides imperforate come from booklets Nos. SB83/SB88.

406 Puma

407 April in Algonquin Park

CANADA

(Des R. Bateman. Litho Ashton-Potter)

1977 (30 Mar). Endangered Wildlife (1st series). Perf 12½.
886 **406** 12c. multicoloured 20 20
See also Nos. 906, 936/937, 976/977 and 1006/1007.

(Litho Ashton-Potter)

1977 (26 May). Birth Centenary of Tom Thomson (painter). T **407** and similar square design. Multicoloured. Perf 12.
887 12c. Type **407** 15 25
    a. Pair. Nos. 887/888 .... 30 1·50
888 12c. *Autumn Birches* 15 25

Nos. 887/888 were printed horizontally and vertically *se-tenant* throughout the sheet.

 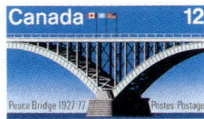

408 Crown and Lion   **409** Peace Bridge, Niagara River

(Des A. Hobbs. Litho (No. 890 also embossed) Ashton-Potter)

1977 (30 June). Anniversaries. T **408** and similar horiz design. Multicoloured. Perf 12½.
889 12c. Type **408** 15 40
890 12c. *Order of Canada* 15 40

Events:—No. 889, 25th Anniversary of first Canadian-born Governor-General; No. 890, Tenth Anniversary of Order of Canada.

(Des R. Harder. Litho Ashton-Potter)

1977 (4 Aug). 50th Anniversary of Opening of Peace Bridge. Perf 12½.
891 **409** 12c. multicoloured 15 15

410 Sir Sandford Fleming (engineer)

(Des W. Davies. Recess B.A.B.N)

1977 (16 Sept). Famous Canadians. T **410** and similar horiz design. Perf 13.
892 12c. grey-blue 30 30
    a. Pair. Nos. 892/893 .... 60 1·25
893 12c. reddish brown 30 30

Design:—No. 892, Joseph E. Bernier (explorer) and *Arctic* (survey ship). The above were printed together, horizontally and vertically *se-tenant* throughout the sheet.

 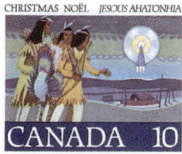

411 Peace Tower, Parliament Buildings, Ottawa   **412** Hunter Braves following Star

(Des S. Ash. Litho Ashton-Potter)

1977 (19 Sept). 23rd Commonwealth Parliamentary Conference. Perf 12½.
894 **411** 25c. multicoloured 20 30

(Des R. G. White. Litho C.B.N)

1977 (26 Oct). Christmas. T **412** and similar horiz designs depicting Canada's first Christmas carol *Jesous Ahatonhia*. Multicoloured. Perf 13½×13.
895 10c. Type **412** 10 10
    a. Printed on the gummed side £250
    b. Imperf between (horiz pair) £750
896 12c. *Angelic choir and Northern Lights* ... 10 10
    a. Imperf (vert pair) £1100
897 25c. *Christ Child and chiefs* 20 45
895/897 *Set of 3* 35 45

No. 895b also shows both stamps partly imperforate at top and bottom.

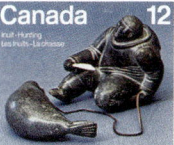 

413 Seal Hunter (soapstone sculpture)   **414** *Pinky* (fishing boat)

(Des R. Derreth. Litho Ashton-Potter)

1977 (18 Nov). Canadian Inuits (1st series). Hunting. T **413** and similar horiz designs. Multicoloured. Perf 12×12½.
898 12c. Type **413** 25 40
    a. Pair. Nos. 898/899 .... 50 80
899 12c. *Fishing with spear* 25 40
    a. Grey omitted £1500
900 12c. *Disguised archer* 25 40
    a. Pair. Nos. 900/901 .... 50 80
901 12c. *Walrus hunting* 25 40
898/901 *Set of 4* .... 1·00 1·60

Nos. 898/899 and 900/901 were each printed together, *se-tenant*, in horizontal and vertical pairs throughout the sheet.
The price for No. 889a is for the error in pair with No. 898.
See also Nos. 924/927, 958/961 and 989/992.

(Des T. Bjarnason. Recess and litho C.B.N)

1977 (18 Nov). Canadian Ships (3rd series). T **414** and similar horiz designs, showing sailing craft. Multicoloured. Perf 12×12½.
902 12c. Type **414** 20 45
    a. Block of 4. Nos. 902/905 .... 70 1·50
    ab. Block of 4, lower pair imperf..... £2000
903 12c. *Malahat* (schooner) 20 45
904 12c. *Tern schooner* 20 45
905 12c. *Mackinaw boat* 20 45
902/905 *Set of 4* .... 70 1·50

Nos. 902/905 were printed together, *se-tenant*, in different combinations throughout the sheet, giving ten blocks of four and ten single stamps.

415 Peregrine Falcon   **416** Pair of 1851 12d. Black Stamps

(Des R. Bateman. Litho Ashton-Potter)

1978 (18 Jan). Endangered Wildlife (2nd series). Perf 12½.
906 **415** 12c. multicoloured 30 20

(Des C. Brett. Recess and photo B.A.B.N)

1978 (18 Jan). CAPEX 78 International Stamp Exhibition, Toronto (1st issue). Perf 13.
907 **416** 12c. black and brownish grey 10 10
See also Nos. 914/917.

417 Games Emblem   **418** *Captain Cook* (Nathaniel Dance)

(Des S. Ash. Litho Ashton-Potter)

1978 (31 Mar). Commonwealth Games. Edmonton (1st issue). T **417** and similar horiz designs. Multicoloured. Perf 12½.
908 14c. Type **417** 10 10
909 30c. *Badminton* 20 60
See also Nos. 918/921.

(Des W. Rueter. Litho Ashton-Potter)

1978 (26 Apr). Bicentenary of Cook's Third Voyage. T **418** and similar vert design. Multicoloured. Perf 13½.
910 14c. Type **418** 20 20
    a. Pair. Nos. 910/911 .... 40 80
911 14c. *Nootka Sound* (J. Webber) 20 20

CANADA

Nos. 910/911 were printed together, *se-tenant*, in horizontal and vertical pairs throughout the sheet.

419 Hardrock Silver Mine, Cobalt, Ontario

420 Princes' Gate (Exhibition entrance)

(Des W. Davies. Litho Ashton-Potter)

1978 (19 May). Resource Development. T **419** and similar horiz design. Multicoloured. Perf 12½.
912	14c. Type **419**	15	25
	a. Pair. Nos. 912/913	30	1·50
913	14c. Giant excavators, Athabasca Tar Sands.	15	25

Nos. 912/913 were printed together, *se-tenant*, in horizontal and vertical pairs throughout the sheet.

(Des C. Brett. Eng R. Couture. Recess and photo B.A.B.N)

1978 (10 June). CAPEX 78 International Stamp Exhibition, Toronto (2nd issue). Horiz designs as T **416**. Two fluorescent bands (none on $1.25 from miniature sheet). Perf 13.
914	14c. Prussian blue, pale grey and brownish grey	15	10
915	30c. deep rose, pale grey and brownish grey	25	40
916	$1.25 slate-violet, pale grey and brownish grey	70	1·50
914/916 Set of 3		1·00	2·00
MS917 101×76 mm. Nos. 914/916		1·00	2·00

Designs: 14c. Pair of 1855 10d. Cartier stamps; 30c. Pair of 1857 ½d. deep rose stamps; $1.25, Pair of 1851 6d. Prince Albert stamps.

(Des S. Ash. Litho Ashton-Potter)

1978 (3 Aug). Commonwealth Games, Edmonton (2nd issue). Horiz designs as T **417**. Multicoloured. Perf 12½.
918	14c. Games stadium	20	20
	a. Pair. Nos. 918/919	40	80
919	14c. Running	20	20
920	30c. Alberta Legislature building	35	50
	a. Pair. Nos. 920/921	70	1·60
921	30c. Bowls	35	50
918/921 Set of 4		1·00	1·10

Nos. 918/919 and 920/921 were each printed together, *se-tenant*, in horizontal and vertical pairs throughout the sheet.

(Des T. Dimson,. Litho Ashton-Potter)

1978 (16 Aug). Centenary of National Exhibition. Perf 12½.
922	**420**	14c. multicoloured	15	30

421 Marguerite d'Youville

422 *Madonna of the Flowering Pea* (Cologne School)

(Des A. Dumas. Litho C.B.N)

1978 (21 Sept). Marguerite d'Youville (founder of Grey Nuns) Commemoration. Perf 13.
923	**421**	14c. multicoloured	15	30

(Des R. Derreth. Litho Ashton-Potter)

1978 (27 Sept). Canadian Inuits (2nd series). Travel. Horiz designs as T **413**. Multicoloured. Perf 13½.
924	14c. *Woman on foot* (painting by Pitseolak)	20	35
	a. Pair. Nos. 924/925	40	1·25
925	14c. Migration (soapstone sculpture of sailing umiak by Joe Talurinili)	20	35
926	14c. Aeroplane (stonecut and stencil print by Pudlo)	20	35
	a. Pair. Nos. 926/927	40	1·25
927	14c. Dogteam and dogsled (ivory sculpture by Abraham Kingmeatook)	20	35
924/927 Set of 4		80	1·25

Nos. 924/925 and 926/927 were each printed together, *se-tenant*, in horizontal and vertical pairs throughout the sheet.

(Des J. Morin. Litho Ashton-Potter)

1978 (20 Oct). Christmas. Paintings. T **422** and similar vert designs. Multicoloured. Perf 12½.
928	12c. Type **422**	10	10
929	14c. *The Virgin and Child with St Anthony and Donor* (detail, Hans Memling)	10	10
	a. Black omitted	£650	
930	30c. *The Virgin and Child* (Jacopo di Cione)	25	90
928/930 Set of 3		35	1·00

423 Chief Justice Robinson (paddle-steamer)

424 Carnival Revellers

(Des T. Bjarnason. Recess and litho C.B.N)

1978 (15 Nov). Canadian Ships (4th series). T **423** and similar horiz designs showing ice vessels. Multicoloured. Perf 13.
931	14c. Type **423**	40	65
	a. Block of 4. Nos. 931/934	1·40	2·40
932	14c. *St Roch* (steamer)	40	65
933	14c. *Northern Light* (steamer)	40	65
934	14c. *Labrador* (steamer)	40	65
931/934 Set of 4		1·40	2·40

Nos. 931/934 were printed together, *se-tenant*, in different combinations throughout the sheet, giving ten blocks of 4 and ten single stamps.

(Des A. Dumas. Litho Ashton-Potter)

1979 (1 Feb). Quebec Carnival. Perf 13.
935	**424**	14c. multicoloured	20	20

425 Eastern Spiny Soft-shelled Turtle (*Trionyx spinifera*)

426 Knotted Ribbon round Woman's Finger

(Des G. Lowe (17c.), R. Bateman (35c.). Litho Ashton-Potter)

1979 (10 Apr). Endangered Wildlife (3rd series). T **425** and similar horiz design. Multicoloured. Perf 12½.
936	17c. Type **425**	20	10
937	35c. Bowhead Whale (*Balaena mysticetus*)	90	90

(Des D. Haws. Litho Ashton-Potter)

1979 (27 Apr). Postal Code Publicity. T **426** and similar vert design. Multicoloured. Perf 13.
938	17c. Type **426**	20	20
	a. Pair. Nos. 938/939	30	1·25
939	17c. Knotted string round man's finger	20	20

Nos. 938/939 were printed together, *se-tenant*, in horizontal and vertical pairs throughout the sheet.

427 Scene from *Fruits of the Earth* by Frederick Philip Grove

428 Charles-Michel de Salaberry (military hero)

(Des Rosemary Kilbourne (No. 940), Monique Charbonneau (No. 941). Litho C.B.N)

1979 (3 May). Canadian Writers (3rd series). T **427** and similar horiz design. Multicoloured. Perf 13.
940	17c. Type **427**	15	15
	a. Pair. Nos. 940/941	30	1·25

CANADA

	ab. Imperf (vert pair)	£500	—
941	17c. Scene from *Le Vaisseau d'Or* by Emile Nelligan	15	15

Nos. 940/941 were printed together, *se-tenant*, in horizontal and vertical pairs throughout the sheet.

(Des T. Dimson. Litho and embossed Ashton-Potter)

1979 (11 May). Famous Canadians. T **428** and similar vert design. Multicoloured. Perf 13.

942	17c. Type **428**	20	15
	a. Pair. Nos. 942/943	40	1·25
943	17c. John By (engineer)	20	15

Nos. 942/943 were printed together, *se-tenant*, in horizontal and vertical pairs throughout the sheet.

429 Ontario

430 Paddling Kayak

(Des R. Bellemare. Litho Ashton-Potter)

1979 (15 June). Canada Day. Flags. T **429** and similar horiz designs. Multicoloured. Perf 13.

944	17c. Type **429**	25	40
	a. Sheetlet of 12. Nos. 944/955	2·75	5·00
945	17c. Quebec	25	40
946	17c. Nova Scotia	25	40
947	17c. New Brunswick	25	40
948	17c. Manitoba	25	40
949	17c. British Columbia	25	40
950	17c. Prince Edward Island	25	40
951	17c. Saskatchewan	25	40
952	17c. Alberta	25	40
953	17c. Newfoundland	25	40
954	17c. Northwest Territories	25	40
955	17c. Yukon Territory	25	40
944/955 Set of 12		2·75	5·00

Nos. 944/955 were printed together, *se-tenant*, in sheetlets of 12.

(Des J. Eby. Litho Ashton-Potter)

1979 (3 July). Canoe-Kayak Championships. Perf 12½.

956	**430**	17c. multicoloured	15	30

431 Hockey Players

432 Toy Train

(Des J. Eby. Litho Ashton-Potter)

1979 (16 Aug). Women's Field Hockey Championships, Vancouver. Perf 12½.

957	**431**	17c. black, yellow and emerald	15	30

(Des R. Derreth. Litho Ashton-Potter)

1979 (13 Sept). Canadian Inuits (3rd series). Shelter (Nos. 958/959) and Community (Nos. 960/961). Horiz designs as T **413**. Multicoloured. Perf 13.

958	17c. Summer Tent (print by Kiakshuk)	15	40
	a. Pair. Nos. 958/959	30	1·25
959	17c. Five Eskimos building an Igloo (soapstone sculpture by Abraham)	15	40
960	17c. The Dance (print by Kalvak)	15	40
	a. Pair. Nos. 960/961	30	1·25
961	17c. Inuit drum dance (soapstone sculptures by Madeleine Isserkut and Jean Mapsalak)	15	40
958/961 Set of 4		60	1·40

Nos. 958/959 and 960/961 were each printed together, *se-tenant*, in horizontal and vertical pairs throughout the sheet.

(Des A. Maggs. Litho C.B.N)

1979 (17 Oct). Christmas. T **432** and similar multicoloured designs showing toys. Fluorescent frame (35c.) or two fluorescent bands (others). Perf 13.

962	15c. Type **432**	10	10
963	17c. Hobby-horse	10	10
964	35c. Rag-doll (*vert*)	25	1·00
	a. Gold omitted	£500	
962/964 Set of 3		35	1·00

433 Child watering Tree of Life (painting by Marie-Annick Viatour)

434 Canadair CL-215

(Des J. Morin. Litho Ashton-Potter)

1979 (24 Oct). International Year of the Child. Perf 13.

965	**433**	17c. multicoloured	15	30

(Des R. Bradford and J. Charette. Litho Ashton-Potter)

1979 (15 Nov). Canadian Aircraft (1st series). Flying Boats. T **434** and similar horiz designs. Multicoloured. Perf 12½.

966	17c. Type **434**	20	20
	a. Pair. Nos. 966/967	40	70
967	17c. Curtiss HS-2L	20	20
968	35c. Vickers Vedette	35	65
	a. Pair. Nos. 968/969	70	1·25
969	35c. Consolidated PBY-5A Canso	35	65
966/969 Set of 4		1·00	2·00

Nos. 966/967 and 968/969 were each printed together, *se-tenant*, in horizontal and vertical pairs throughout the sheet.

See also Nos. 996/969, 1026/1029 and 1050/1053.

435 Map of Arctic Islands

436 Skiing

(Des Gottschalk and Ash Ltd. Litho Ashton-Potter)

1980 (23 Jan). Centenary of Arctic Islands Acquisition. Perf 13.

970	**435**	17c. multicoloured	15	30

(Des C. Malenfant. Litho C.B.N)

1980 (23 Jan). Winter Olympic Games, Lake Placid, USA. Perf 13.

971	**436**	35c. multicoloured	30	70

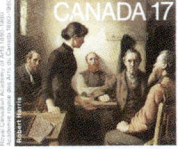

437 *A Meeting of the School Trustees* (painting by Robert Harris)

438 Canadian Whitefish (*Coregonus canadenis*)

(Des J. Morin. Litho Ashton-Potter)

1980 (6 Mar). Centenary of Royal Canadian Academy of Arts. T **437** and similar horiz designs. Multicoloured. Perf 13.

972	17c. Type **437**	15	25
	a. Pair. Nos. 972/973	30	75
973	17c. Inspiration (sculpture by Philippe Hébert)	15	25
974	35c. *Sunrise on the Saguenay* (Lucius O'Brien)	25	65
	a. Pair. Nos. 974/975	50	1·50
975	35c. Sketch of design for original Parliament Buildings by Thomas Fuller	25	65
972/975 Set of 4		70	1·60

Nos. 972/973 and 974/975 were each printed together, *se-tenant*, in horizontal and vertical pairs throughout the sheet.

(Des M. Dumas (No. 976), R. Bateman (No. 977). Litho Ashton-Potter)

1980 (6 May). Endangered Wildlife (4th series). T **438** and similar horiz design. Multicoloured. Perf 12½.

976	17c. Type **438**	20	15
977	17c. Prairie Chicken (*Tympanuchus cupido pinnatus*)	30	15

CANADA

439 Garden Flowers **440** Helping Hand

(Des Heather Cooper. Litho Ashton-Potter)

1980 (29 May). International Flower Show, Montreal. Perf 13.
978 **439** 17c. multicoloured 15 20

(Des R. Harder. Litho and embossed Ashton-Potter)

1980 (29 May). Rehabilitation. Perf 12½.
979 **440** 17c. gold and ultramarine 15 20

441 Opening Bars of O Canada **442** John G. Diefenbaker

(Des F. Peter. Litho Ashton-Potter)

1980 (6 June). Centenary of O Canada (national song). T **441** and similar horiz design. Multicoloured. Perf 12½.
980   17c. Type **441** 15 15
         a. Pair. Nos. 980/981 .... 30 50
981   17c. Calixa Lavallee (composer), Adolphe-Basile Routhier (original writer) and Robert Stanley Weir (writer of English version) 15 15
Nos. 980/981 were printed together, *se-tenant*, in horizontal and vertical pairs throughout the sheet.

(Des B. Reilander. Eng Y. Baril. Recess C.B.N)

1980 (20 June). John G. Diefenbaker (former Prime Minister) Commemoration. Perf 13½×13.
982 **442** 17c. deep ultramarine 15 20

443 Emma Albani (singer) **444** Alberta

(Des C. Webster (No. 985), H. Brown (others). Litho Ashton-Potter)

1980 (4 July). Famous Canadians. T **443** and similar multicoloured designs. Perf 13.
983   17c. Type **443** 15 25
         a. Pair. Nos. 983/984 .... 30 1·50
984   17c. Healey Willan (composer) 15 25
985   17c. Ned Hanlan (oarsman) (*horiz*) 15 15
983/985 Set of 3 .... 40 60
Nos. 983/984 were printed together, *se-tenant*, in horizontal and vertical pairs throughout the sheet.

(Des G. Hunter and C. Yaneff. Litho Ashton-Potter)

1980 (27 Aug). 75th Anniversary of Alberta and Saskatchewan Provinces. T **444** and similar horiz design. Multicoloured. Perf 13.
986   17c. Type **444** 15 15
987   17c. Saskatchewan 15 15

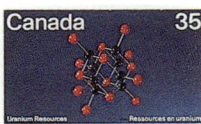 

445 Uraninite Molecular Structure **446** Christmas Morning (J. S. Hallam)

(Des J. Charette. Litho C.B.N)

1980 (3 Sept). Uranium Resources. Perf 13.
988 **445** 35c. multicoloured 30 30
         a. Printed on the gummed side £550

(Des R. Derreth. Litho C.B.N)

1980 (25 Sept). Canadian Inuits (4th series). Spirits. Horiz designs as T **413**. Multicoloured. Perf 13½.
989   17c. Return of the Sun (print by Kenojouak).. 15 15
         a. Pair. Nos. 989/990 .... 30 75
990   17c. Sedna (sculpture by Ashoona Kiawak) .. 15 15
991   35c. Shaman (print by Simon Tookoome) 25 55
         a. Pair. Nos. 991/992 .... 50 1·40
992   35c. Bird Spirit (sculpture by Doris Hagiolok) 25 55
989/992 Set of 4 .... 70 1·25
Nos. 989/990 and 991/992 were each printed together, *se-tenant*, in horizontal and vertical pairs throughout the sheet.

(Des Yvon Laroche. Litho Ashton-Potter)

1980 (22 Oct). Christmas. Paintings. T **446** and similar vert designs. Multicoloured. Perf 12½×12.
993   15c. Type **446** 10 10
994   17c. Sleigh Ride (Frank Hennessy) 15 10
995   35c. McGill Cab Stand (Kathleen Morris) .... 30 1·40
993/995 Set of 3 .... 50 1·40

447 Avro (Canada) CF-100 Canuck Mk 5

(Des R. Bradford and J. Charette. Litho C.B.N)

1980 (10 Nov). Canadian Aircraft (2nd series). T **447** and similar horiz designs. Multicoloured. Perf 13.
996   17c. Type **447** 30 20
         a. Pair. Nos. 996/997 .... 60 60
997   17c. Avro Type 683 Lancaster 30 20
998   35c. Curtiss JN-4 Canuck 40 65
         a. Pair. Nos. 998/999 .... 80 1·25
999   35c. Hawker Hurricane Mk 1 .... 40 65
996/999 Set of 4 .... 1·25 1·60
Nos. 996/997 and 998/999 were each printed together, *se-tenant*, in horizontal and vertical pairs throughout the sheet.

448 Emmanuel-Persillier Lachapelle **449** Mandora Instrument (18th-century)

(Des J. Morin. Litho Ashton-Potter)

1980 (5 Dec). Dr. Emmanuel-Persillier Lachapelle (founder of Notre-Dame Hospital, Montreal) Commemoration. Perf 13½.
1000 **448** 17c. cobalt, chocolate and brown 15 15

(Des C. Webster. Litho Ashton-Potter)

1981 (19 Jan). The Look of Music Exhibition, Vancouver. Perf 12½.
1001 **449** 17c. multicoloured 15 15
No. 1001 is known with gold omitted and printed on the gummed side of the paper.

CANADA

450 Henrietta Edwards

451 Vancouver Marmot (*Marmota vancouverensis*)

(Des Muriel Wood and D. Goddard. Litho C.B.N)

1981 (4 Mar). Feminists. T **450** and similar horiz designs. Multicoloured. Perf 13.
1002	17c. Type **450**	15	30
	a. Block of 4. Nos. 1002/1005	55	1·00
1003	17c. Louise McKinney	15	30
1004	17c. Idola Saint-Jean	15	30
1005	17c. Emily Stowe	15	30
1002/1005 Set of 4		55	1·00

Nos. 1002/1005 were printed together, *se-tenant*, in different combinations throughout the sheet, giving ten blocks of four and ten single stamps.

(Des M. Dumas (17c.), R. Bateman (35c.). Litho C.B.N.)

1981 (6 Apr). Endangered Wildlife (5th series). T **451** and similar horiz design. Multicoloured. Perf 13.
1006	17c. Type **451**	15	10
1007	35c. American Bison (*Bison bison athabascae*)	35	30

452 Kateri Tekakwitha

453 *Self Portrait* (Frederick H. Varley)

(Des L. Marquart. Litho Ashton-Potter)

1981 (24 Apr). 17th-century Canadian Catholic Women. Statues by Emile Brunet. T **452** and similar vert design. Perf 12½.
1008	17c. red-brown and pale grey-olive	15	20
	a. Pair. Nos. 1008/1009	30	1·00
1009	17c. steel blue and new blue	15	20

Designs: No. 1008, Type **452**; No. 1009, Marie de l'Incarnation.
Nos. 1008/1009 were printed together, *se-tenant*, in horizontal and vertical pairs throughout the sheet.

(Des P. Fontaine. Litho Ashton-Potter (17c. both)), B.A.B.N. (35c.))

1981 (22 May). Canadian Paintings. T **453** and similar multicoloured designs. Perf 12½ (17c. (both)) or 13×13½ (35c.).
1010	17c. Type **453**	15	10
1011	17c. *At Baie Saint-Paul* (Marc-Aurele Fortin) (horiz)	15	10
1012	35c. *Untitled No 6* (Paul-Emile Borduas)	30	45
1010/1012 Set of 3		55	60

454 Canada in 1867

455 Frère Marie-Victorin

(Des R. Bellemare. Litho B.A.B.N)

1981 (30 June). Canada Day. Maps showing evolution of Canada from Confederation to present day. T **454** and similar horiz designs. Multicoloured. Perf 13½.
1013	17c. Type **454**	15	20
	a. Horiz strip of 4. Nos. 1013/1016	55	1·25
1014	17c. Canada in 1873	15	20
1015	17c. Canada in 1905	15	20
1016	17c. Canada since 1949	15	20
1013/1016 Set of 4		55	1·25

Nos. 1013/1016 were printed together, *se-tenant*, in horizontal strips of four throughout the sheet.

(Des R. Hill. Litho and embossed Ashton-Potter)

1981 (22 July). Canadian Botanists. T **455** and similar vert design. Multicoloured. Perf 12½×12.
1017	17c. Type **455**	20	30
	a. Pair. Nos. 1017/1018	40	1·40
1018	17c. John Macoun	20	30

Nos. 1017/1018 were printed together, *se-tenant*, in horizontal and vertical pairs throughout the sheet.

456 The Montreal Rose

457 Drawing of Niagara-on-the-Lake

(Des J.-P. Beaudin, J. Morin and T. Yakobina. Litho C.B.N.)

1981 (22 July). Montreal Flower Show. Perf 13½.
1019	**456**	17c. multicoloured	15	20

(Des J. Mardon. Recess and litho B.A.B.N)

1981 (31 July). Bicentenary of Niagara-on-the-Lake (town). Perf 13×13½.
1020	**457**	17c. multicoloured	15	20

458 Acadian Community

459 Aaron R. Mosher

(Des N. DeGrâce. Litho Ashton-Potter)

1981 (14 Aug). Centenary of first Acadia (community) Convention. Perf 13½.
1021	**458**	17c. multicoloured	15	20

(Des R. Hill. Litho Ashton-Potter)

1981 (8 Sept). Birth Centenary of Aaron R. Mosher (founder of Canadian Labour Congress). Perf 13½.
1022	**459**	17c. multicoloured	15	20

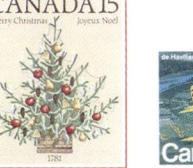

460 Christmas Tree, 1781

461 de Havilland DH.82C Tiger Moth

(Des Anita Kunz and W. Tibbles. Litho Ashton-Potter)

1981 (16 Nov). Christmas. Bicentenary of First Illuminated Christmas Tree in Canada. T **460** and similar vert designs. Multicoloured. Perf 13½.
1023	15c. Type **460**	20	15
1024	15c. Christmas Tree, 1881	20	15
1025	15c. Christmas Tree, 1981	20	15
1023/1025 Set of 3		55	40

(Des R. Bradford and J. Charette. Litho Ashton-Potter)

1981 (24 Nov). Canadian Aircraft (3rd series). T **461** and similar horiz designs. Multicoloured. Perf 12½.
1026	17c. Type **461**	25	15
	a. Pair. Nos. 1026/1027	50	80
1027	17c. Canadair CL-41 Tutor	25	15
1028	35c. Avro (Canada) CF-102 jet airliner	45	40

CANADA

	a. Pair. Nos. 1028/1029		90	1·50
1029	35c. de Havilland DHC-7 Dash Seven		45	40
1026/1029 Set of 4			1·25	2·25

The two designs of each value were printed together, *se-tenant*, in horizontal and vertical pairs throughout the sheet.

462 Canadian Maple Leaf Emblem   **463** 1851 3d. Stamp

(Des R. Bellemare. Recess B.A.B.N. No. 1030), C.B.N. (others)))

1981 (29 Dec). Ordinary paper.

(a) Sheet stamp. Perf 13×13½

1030	**462**	A bright scarlet		
		(30c.)	20	45
		a. Printed on the gummed side	£425	
		b. *Carmine-red*, chalk-surfaced paper	20	45

(b) Coil stamp. Imperf×perf 10.

1031	**462**	A bright scarlet		
		(30c.)	30	1·00
		a. Imperf (pair)	£300	£150

Nos. 1030/1031 were printed before a new first class domestic letter rate had been agreed, 'A' representing the face value of the stamp later decided at 30c. Because of UPU regulations these stamps were only intended for use within Canada.

(Recess, or recess and photo (Nos. 1032/1032), B.A.B.N. (Nos. 1032/1035) or C.B.N. (Nos. 1036/1036)))

1982 (1 Mar)–84. Designs as Nos. 1030/1031 but including face values.

(a) Sheet stamps. Ordinary paper (Nos. 1032, 1032b) or from booklets (Nos. 1032a, 1032ba). Chalk-surfaced paper. Perf 13×13½

1032	**462**	30c. vermilion, slate-blue and azure (11.5.82)	30	60
		a. Perf 12×12½ (from booklets) (30.6.82)	70	1·40
		ab. Booklet pane. No. 1032a×20 plus one printed label	15·00	
1032b		32c. vermilion, orange-brown and stone (10.2.83)	45	45
		a. Stone omitted	£500	—
		c. Perf 12×12½ (from booklets) (8.4.83)	75	1·50
		ca. Booklet pane. No. 1032ba×25 plus two printed labels	16·00	
		cb. Ordinary paper (15.2.84)	1·00	1·25
		cc. Booklet pane. No. 1032bc×25 plus two printed labels	22·00	

(b) Booklet stamps. Ordinary paper. Perf 12×12½*.

1033	**462**	5c. maroon	10	20
		a. Booklet pane. Nos. 1033×2, 1034 and 1035 plus two printed labels in bottom row	3·00	
		ab. Ditto. Printed labels in top row (10.82)	3·50	
		b. Chalk-surfaced paper (8.82)	40	1·25
		ba. Booklet pane. Nos. 1033b×2, 1034a and 1035a plus two printed labels in bottom row	9·00	
		bb. Ditto. Printed labels in top row (10.82)	9·00	
		c. Booklet pane. Nos. 1033×2, 1033d and 1035b plus two printed labels (15.2.83)	4·00	
1033d		8c. indigo (15.2.83)	2·25	2·75
1034		10c. bottle green	1·50	2·75
		a. Chalk-surfaced paper	4·00	4·25
1035		30c. carmine-red	1·50	2·50
		a. Chalk-surfaced paper	4·00	4·25
1035b		32c. Indian red (15.2.83)	2·50	3·00

(c) Coil stamps. Ordinary paper. Imperf×perf 10.

1036	**462**	30c. bright scarlet (20.5.82)†	35	40
		a. Imperf (pair)	£200	
1036b		32c. Indian red (10.2.83)	1·00	2·25
		ba. Imperf (pair)	£100	

*The 30c. and 32c. values are perforated on two sides, the other values on three.

†The 30c. coil stamp was originally intended for release on 11 May, but, due to production difficulties, it was not placed on sale until 20 May; First day covers, however, carry the 11 May postmark.

(Des Gottschalk and Ash Ltd. Litho C.B.N)

1982 (11 Mar–20 May). Canada 82 International Philatelic Youth Exhibition, Toronto. Stamps on Stamps. T **463** and similar horiz designs. Multicoloured. Perf 13½.

1037	30c. Type **463**	30	30
1038	30c. 1908 Centenary of Quebec 15c. commemorative (20.5.82)	30	30
1039	35c. 1935 10c. R.C.M.P.	30	50
1040	35c. 1928 10c. (20.5.82)	30	50
1041	60c. 1929 50c. (20.5.82)	60	1·00
1037/1041 Set of 5		1·60	2·40
MS1042 159×108 mm. Nos. 1037/1041 (20.5.82)		1·60	2·75

464 Jules Léger   **465** Stylized Drawing of Terry Fox

(Des P. Fontaine from photograph by M. Bedford. Litho Ashton-Potter)

1982 (2 Apr). Jules Léger (politician) Commemoration. Perf 13½.

1043	**464**	30c. multicoloured	20	20

(Des F. Peter. Litho Ashton-Potter)

1982 (13 Apr). Cancer-victim Terry Fox's Marathon of Hope (Trans-Canada fund-raising run) Commemoration. Fluorescent frame. Perf 12½.

1044	**465**	30c. multicoloured	20	20

466 Stylised Open Book

(Des F. Peter. Litho Ashton-Potter)

1982 (16 Apr). Patriation of Constitution. Perf 12×12½.

1045	**466**	30c. multicoloured	20	20

467 1880's Male and Female Salvationists with Street Scene   **468** The Highway near Kluane Lake (Yukon Territory) (Jackson)

(Des T. Dimson. Litho C.B.N)

1982 (25 June). Centenary of the Salvation Army in Canada. Perf 13½.

1046	**467**	30c. multicoloured	20	20

(Des J. Morin and P. Sasseville. Litho Ashton-Potter)

1982 (30 June). Canada Day. Paintings of Canadian Landscapes. T **468** and similar horiz designs. Multicoloured. Perf 12½×12.

1047a	30c. Type **468**	35	40
	ab. Sheetlet of 12. Nos. 1047a/1047l	3·75	5·50
1047b	30c. *Street Scene, Montreal* (Quebec) (Hébert)	35	50
1047c	30c. *Breakwater* (Newfoundland) (Pratt)	35	50
1047d	30c. *Along Great Slave Lake* (Northwest Territories) (Richard)	35	50
1047e	30c. *Till Hill* (Prince Edward Island) (Lamb)	35	50
1047f	30c. *Family and Rain-storm* (Nova Scotia) (Colville)	35	50
1047g	30c. *Brown Shadows* (Saskatchewan) (Knowles)	35	50
1047h	30c. *The Red Brick House* (Ontario) (Milne)	35	50
1047i	30c. *Campus Gates* (New Brunswick) (Bobak)	35	50
1047j	30c. *Prairie Town—Early Morning* (Alberta) (Kerr)	35	50

CANADA

1047k	30c. *Totems at Ninstints* (British Columbia) (Plaskett)		35	50
1047l	30c. *Doc Snider's House* (Manitoba) (FitzGerald)		35	50
1047a/1047l	*Set of 12*		3·75	5·50

Nos. 1047a/1047l were printed together, *se-tenant*, in sheetlets of 12.

469 Regina Legislature Building

470 Finish of Race

(Des Kim Martin and R. Russell. Litho Ashton-Potter)

1982 (3 Aug). Regina Centenary. Perf 13½×13.

1048	469	30c. multicoloured	20	20

(Des B. Reilander. Litho Ashton-Potter)

1982 (4 Aug). Centenary of Royal Canadian Henley Regatta. Perf 12½.

1049	470	30c. multicoloured	20	25

471 Fairchild FC-2W1

(Des R. Bradford. Litho Ashton-Potter)

1982 (5 Oct). Canadian Aircraft (4th series). Bush Aircraft. T **471** and similar horiz designs. Multicoloured. Perf 12½.

1050		30c. Type **471**	35	20
		a. Pair. Nos. 1050/1051	70	1·25
1051		30c. de Havilland DHC-2 Beaver	35	20
1052		60c. Fokker Super Universal	65	85
		a. Pair. Nos. 1052/1053	1·25	2·00
1053		60c. Noorduyn Norseman	65	85
1050/1053	*Set of 4*		1·90	3·00

Nos. 1050/1051 and 1052/1053 were each printed together, *se-tenant*, in horizontal and vertical pairs throughout the sheet.

472 Decoy

472a Fishing Spear

472b Stable Lantern

472c Bucket

472d Weathercock

472e Skates

472f Butter Stamp

472g Plough

472h Settle-bed

472i Linen Chest

472j Cradle

472k Sleigh

472l Iron Kettle

472m Kitchen Stove

472n Spinning Wheel

472o Hand-drawn Cart

(Des J.-P. Beaudin and J. Morin. Litho C.B.N. (Nos. 1054b/1054ba, 1055b/1055bc, 1056b, 1057b/1057ba, 1058b) or Ashton-Potter (others))

1982 (19 Oct)–**87**. Heritage Artifacts. T **472/472o** and similar designs. No fluorescent bands (1c. to 5c.). Chalk-surfaced paper (25c., 42c., 50c., 72c.). Perf 12×12½ (37c. to 72c.) or 14×13½ (others).

1054	472	1c. black, grey-brown and brown	10	10
		a. Chalk-surfaced paper (4.7.86)	20	70
		b. Perf 13×13½ (10.1.85)	40	45
		ba. Chalk-surfaced paper (6.8.85)	1·50	1·00
1055	472a	2c. black, pale turquoise-blue and deep blue-green	10	10
		a. Chalk-surfaced paper (4.7.86)	30	65
		b. Perf 13×13½ (10.2.84)	30	50
		ba. Imperf (horiz pair)	£950	
		bb. Printed on the gummed side	35·00	
		bc. Ordinary paper (23.1.86)	10	70
1056	472b	3c. black, dull violet-blue and chalky blue	10	10
		a. Chalk-surfaced paper (4.7.86)	1·25	1·00
		b. Perf 13×13½ (10.1.85)	1·25	1·00
1057	472c	5c. black, flesh and chestnut	10	10
		a. Chalk-surfaced paper (15.8.86)	30	10
		b. Perf 13×13½ (*chalk-surfaced paper*) (6.7.84)	20	20
		ba. Ordinary paper (1.3.85)	20	30
1058	472d	10c. black, light blue and deep turquoise-blue	10	10
		a. Chalk-surfaced paper (22.8.86)	50	50
		b. Perf 13×13½ (15.3.85)	70	30
1059	472e	20c. black, brownish grey and sepia	20	10
		aa. Sepia omitted	£250	
		a. Chalk-surfaced paper (4.7.86)	50	50
1060	472f	25c. multicoloured (6.5.87)	1·25	10
1061	472g	37c. grey-black, deep yellow-green and sage-green (8.4.83)	45	1·25
		a. Chalk-surfaced paper (18.5.84)	1·00	1·60
1062	472h	39c. brownish black, violet-grey and slate-violet (1.8.85)	1·75	2·50
1063	472i	42c. multicoloured (6.5.87)	2·25	1·75
1064	472j	48c. blackish brown, red-brown and pale pink (8.4.83)	50	40
		a. Chalk-surfaced paper (19.12.83)	80	1·25
1065	472k	50c. black, dull turquoise-blue and turquoise-blue (1.8.85)	1·75	20
1066	472l	55c. multicoloured (6.5.87)	2·00	30
1067	472m	64c. grey-black, black and pale grey (8.4.83)	60	35
		a. Chalk-surfaced paper (29.6.84)	1·50	1·40
1068	472n	68c. black, pale brown and reddish brown (1.8.85)	2·25	50
1069	472o	72c. multicoloured (6.5.87)	2·00	35
		a. Imperf (pair)	£500	
1054/1069	*Set of 16*		13·50	7·00

No. 1058b has a fluorescent frame instead of bands.
Nos. 1070/1079 are vacant.

CANADA

475 Mary, Joseph and Baby Jesus **476** Globes forming Symbolic Designs

(Des J. Eby. Litho C.B.N)

1982 (3 Nov). Christmas. Nativity Scenes. T **475** and similar vert designs. Multicoloured. Perf 13.
1080		30c. Type **475**	20	10
1081		35c. The Shepherds	25	60
1082		60c. The Three Wise Men	45	1·50
1080/1082 Set of 3			80	2·00

(Des R. Bellemare. Litho Ashton-Potter)

1983 (10 Mar). World Communications Year. Fluorescent frame. Perf 12×12½.
1083	**476**	32c. multicoloured	30	30

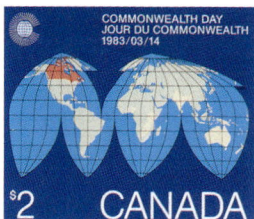

477 Map of World showing Canada

(Des R. Harder. Litho Ashton-Potter)

1983 (14 Mar). Commonwealth Day. Without fluorescent bands. Perf 12½.
1084	**477**	$2 multicoloured	1·25	2·75

 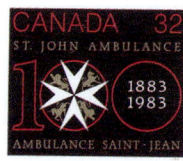

478 Scene from Novel *Angéline de Montbrun* by Laure Conan (Félicité Angers) **479** St John Ambulance Badge and '100'

(Des R. Milot (No. 1085), Claire Pratt (No. 1086), adapted W. Tibbles. Litho C.B.N.))

1983 (22 Apr). Canadian Writers (4th series). T **478** and similar horiz design. Multicoloured. Perf 13.
1085		32c. Type **478**	50	90
		a. Pair. Nos. 1085/1086	1·00	1·75
1086		32c. Woodcut illustrating Sea-gulls (poem by E. J. Pratt)	50	90

Nos. 1085/1086 were printed together, *se-tenant*, in horizontal and vertical pairs throughout the sheet.

(Des L. Fishauf. Litho Ashton-Potter)

1983 (3 June). Centenary of St John Ambulance in Canada. Perf 13.
1087	**479**	32c. bright rose-red, gold and deep chocolate	30	30

480 Victory Pictogram **481** Fort William, Ontario

(Des Krista Huebner, D. Kilvert and P.-Y. Pelletier. Litho C.B.N)

1983 (28 June). Universiade 83 World University Games, Edmonton. Perf 13.
1088	**480**	32c. multicoloured	25	15
		a. Printed on the gummed side	£500	
1089		64c. multicoloured	50	70

(Des R. Harder. Litho Ashton-Potter)

1983 (30 June). Canada Day. Forts (1st series). T **481** and similar horiz designs. Multicoloured. Perf 12½×13.
1090		32c. Fort Henry, Ontario (44×22 mm)	40	70
		a. Booklet pane. Nos. 1090/1099	3·50	
1091		32c. Type **481**	40	70
1092		32c. Fort Rodd Hill, British Columbia	40	70
1093		32c. Fort Wellington, Ontario (28×22 mm)	40	70
1094		32c. Fort Prince of Wales, Manitoba (28×22 mm)	40	70
1095		32c. Halifax Citadel, Nova Scotia (44×22 mm)	40	70
1096		32c. Fort Chambly, Quebec	40	70
1097		32c. Fort No. 1, Point Levis, Quebec	40	70
1098		32c. Coteau-du-Lac Fort, Quebec (28×22 mm)	40	70
1099		32c. Fort Beausejour, New Brunswick (28×22 mm)	40	70
1090/1099 Set of 10			3·50	6·50

Nos. 1090/1099 were only available from $3.20 stamp booklets, No. SB93, containing the *se-tenant* pane, No. 1090a.

See also Nos. 1163/1172.

482 Scouting Poster by Marc Fournier (aged 12) **483** Cross Symbol

(Des F. Dallaire. Litho Ashton-Potter)

1983 (6 July). 75th Anniversary of Scouting in Canada and 15th World Scout Jamboree, Alberta. Perf 13.
1100	**482**	32c. multicoloured	30	30

(Des G. Tsetsekas. Recess and photo B.A.B.N)

1983 (22 July). Sixth Assembly of the World Council of Churches, Vancouver. Perf 13.
1101	**483**	32c. blue-green and grey-lilac	30	20

484 Sir Humphrey Gilbert (founder) **485** NICKEL Deposits

(Des R. Hill. Litho C.B.N)

1983 (3 Aug). 400th Anniversary of Newfoundland. Perf 13.
1102	**484**	32c. multicoloured	30	30

(Des J. Capon. Litho (' NICKEL' die-stamped) C.B.N)

1983 (12 Aug). Centenary of Discovery of Sudbury Nickel Deposits. Perf 13.
1103	**485**	32c. multicoloured	30	30
		a. Silver ('NICKEL') omitted	£500	

486 Josiah Henson and Escaping Slaves

487 Robert Stephenson's Locomotive *Dorchester*, 1836

(Des T. Kew and J. Hamel. Litho B.A.B.N)

1983 (16 Sept). 19th-century Social Reformers. T **486** and similar horiz design. Multicoloured. Perf 13×13½ (No. 1104) or 13 (No. 1105).

1104	32c. Type **486**	35	50
1105	32c. Father Antoine Labelle and rural village (32×26 mm)	35	50

(Des E. Roch. Litho Ashton-Potter)

1983 (3 Oct). Railway Locomotives (1st series). T **487** and similar horiz designs. Multicoloured. Perf 12½×13.

1106	32c. Type **487**	75	1·00
	a. Pair. Nos. 1106/1107	1·50	2·00
1107	32c. Locomotive *Toronto*, 1853	75	1·00
1108	37c. Timothy Hackworth's locomotive *Samson*, 1838	75	1·00
1109	64c. Western Canadian Railway locomotive *Adam Brown*, 1855	1·25	2·50
1106/1109	Set of 4	3·25	5·00

Nos. 1106/1107 were printed together, *se-tenant*, in horizontal and vertical pairs throughout the sheet.

See also Nos. 1132/**MS**1136, 1185/1188 and 1223/1226.

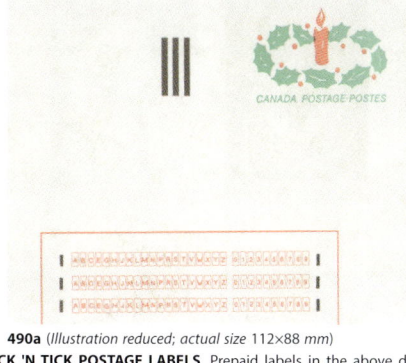

490a (*Illustration reduced; actual size* 112×88 *mm*)

STICK 'N TICK POSTAGE LABELS. Prepaid labels in the above design, printed in a combination of red, green and black, were tested by the Canadian Post Office in Winnipeg, Manitoba, between 21 November and 17 December 1983. These self-adhesive labels were sold to the public in kits of 12 or 25, at a saving of 35c. or $1.11 on the normal postage. They were primarily intended for use on Christmas cards and were only valid on mail posted to Canadian addresses. The label was affixed to normally addressed envelopes, but the user was then required to mark the postal code on the three lines at the foot. It was hoped that this incentive would increase the use of the postal codes and so speed automatic mail sorting. The system was extended to seven other cities in 1984. The second version had separate postage paid and Postal Code labels, being available from 5 November until 17 December 1984.

488 School Coat of Arms

489 City Church

491 Gold Mine in Prospecting Pan

492 Montreal Symphony Orchestra

(Des Denise Saulnier. Litho C.B.N)

1983 (28 Oct). Centenary of Dalhousie Law School. Perf 13.

1110	**488**	32c. multicoloured	30	40

(Des C. Simard. Litho Ashton-Potter)

1983 (3 Nov). Christmas. Churches. T **489** and similar horiz designs. Multicoloured. Perf 13.

1111	32c. Type **489**	30	10
1112	37c. Family walking to church	40	90
1113	64c. Country chapel	1·00	2·00
1111/1113	Set of 3	1·50	2·75

(Des K. Hughes. Litho Ashton-Potter)

1984 (15 Mar). 50th Anniversary of Yellowknife. Perf 13½.

1116	**491**	32c. multicoloured	30	30

(Des J. Delisle and P. Kohler. Litho Ashton-Potter)

1984 (24 Mar). 50th Anniversary of Montreal Symphony Orchestra. Perf 12½.

1117	**492**	32c. multicoloured	35	30

490 Royal Canadian Regiment and British Columbia Regiment

493 Jacques Cartier

494 *Eagle* (US Coastguard cadet ship)

(Des W. Southern and R. Tibbles. Litho C.B.N)

1983 (10 Nov). Canadian Army Regiments. T **490** and similar vert design. Multicoloured. Fluorescent frame. Perf 13.

1114	32c. Type **490**	65	1·25
	a. Pair. Nos. 1114/1115	1·25	2·50
1115	32c. Royal Winnipeg Rifles and Royal Canadian Dragoons	65	1·25

Nos. 1114/1115 were printed together, *se-tenant*, in horizontal and vertical pairs throughout the sheet.

(Des Y. Paquin, Engraved C. Haley. Recess French Govt Ptg Wks, Perigueux)

1984 (20 Apr). 450th Anniversary of Jacques Cartier's Voyage to Canada. Perf 13.

1118	**493**	32c. multicoloured	40	50

(Des O. Schenk. Litho Ashton-Potter)

1984 (18 May). Tall Ships Visit. Fluorescent frame. Perf 12×12½.

1119	**494**	32c. multicoloured	35	45

CANADA

495 Service Medal   **496** Oared Galleys

(Des W. Tibbles and C. Webster. Litho Ashton-Potter)

1984 (28 May). 75th Anniversary of Canadian Red Cross Society. Perf 13½.
1120	**495**	32c. multicoloured	35	40

(Des P. Dorn. Photo and recess B.A.B.N)

1984 (18 June). Bicentenary of New Brunswick. Perf 13½.
1121	**496**	32c. multicoloured	35	30

497 St. Lawrence Seaway

(Des E. Barenscher. Litho C.B.N)

1984 (26 June). 25th Anniversary of St Lawrence Seaway. Fluorescent frame. Perf 13.
1122	**497**	32c. multicoloured	45	50

498 New Brunswick   **499** Loyalists of 1784

(Des J. Morin and T. Yakobina. Litho C.B.N)

1984 (29 June). Canada Day. Paintings by Jean Paul Lemieux. T **498** and similar multicoloured designs. Perf 13.
1123a		32c. Type **498**	45	60
	ab.	Sheetlet of 12. Nos. 1123a/1123l	4·75	8·00
1123b		32c. British Columbia	45	60
1123c		32c. 'Northwest Territories'	45	60
1123d		32c. Quebec	45	60
1123e		32c. Manitoba	45	60
1123f		32c. Alberta	45	60
1123g		32c. Prince Edward Island	45	60
1123h		32c. Saskatchewan	45	60
1123i		32c. Nova Scotia (vert)	45	60
1123j		32c. 'Yukon Territory'	45	60
1123k		32c. Newfoundland	45	60
1123l		32c. Ontario (vert)	45	60
1123a/1123l Set of 12			4·75	8·00

Nos. 1123a/1123l were printed, *se-tenant*, in sheetlets of 12.

The captions on the Northwest Territories and Yukon Territory paintings were transposed at the design stage. No. 1123c actually shows Yukon Territory and No. 1123j Northwest Territories.

(Des W. Davies. Litho B.A.B.N)

1984 (3 July). Bicentenary of Arrival of United Empire Loyalists. Perf 13×13½.
1124	**499**	32c. multicoloured	30	30

500 St John's Basilica   **501** Coat of Arms of Pope John Paul II

(Des J. Morin and R. Ethier. Litho C.B.N)

1984 (17 Aug). Bicentenary of Roman Catholic Church in Newfoundland. Perf 13½.
1125	**500**	32c. multicoloured	30	25

(Des L. Rivard. Litho Ashton-Potter)

1984 (31 Aug). Papal Visit. Perf 12½.
1126	**501**	32c. multicoloured	40	20
1127		64c. multicoloured	85	1·10

502 Louisbourg Lighthouse, 1734

(Des D. Noble and K. Rodmell. Litho Ashton-Potter)

1984 (21 Sept). Canadian Lighthouses (1st series). T **502** and similar horiz designs. Multicoloured. Perf 12½.
1128		32c. Type **502**	1·75	1·40
	a.	Block of 4. Nos. 1128/1131	6·25	5·00
1129		32c. Fisgard Lighthouse, 1860	1·75	1·40
1130		32c. Ile Verte Lighthouse, 1809	1·75	1·40
1131		32c. Gibraltar Point Lighthouse, 1808	1·75	1·40
1128/1131 Set of 4			6·25	5·00

Nos. 1128/1131 were printed together, *se-tenant*, in different combinations throughout the sheet, giving ten blocks of four and ten single stamps.

See also Nos. 1176/**MS**1180.

503 Great Western Railway Locomotive, *Scotia*, 1860

(Des E. Roch. Litho Ashton-Potter)

1984 (25 Oct). Railway Locomotives (2nd series). T **503** and similar horiz designs. Multicoloured. Perf 12½×13.
1132		32c. Type **503**	1·10	1·40
	a.	Pair. Nos. 1132/1133	2·10	2·75
1133		32c. Northern Pacific Railroad locomotive *Countess of Dufferin*, 1872	1·10	1·40
1134		37c. Grand Trunk Railway Class E3 locomotive, 1886	1·10	1·60
1135		64c. Canadian Pacific Class D10a steam locomotive	1·60	2·75
1132/1135 Set of 4			5·00	7·00
MS1136 153×104 mm. As Nos. 1132/1135, but with background colour changed from pale green to pale grey-blue			5·00	7·00

Nos. 1132/1133 were issued together, *se-tenant*, in horizontal and vertical pairs throughout the sheet.

No. **MS**1136 commemorates CANADA 84 National Stamp Exhibition, Montreal.

See also Nos. 1185/1188 and 1223/1226.

504 The Annunciation (Jean Dallaire)   **505** Pilots of 1914–1918, 1939–1945 and 1984

(Des J. Morin and T. Yakobina. Litho Ashton-Potter)

1984 (2 Nov). Christmas. Religious Paintings. T **504** and similar horiz designs. Multicoloured. Perf 13½.
1137		32c. Type **504**	35	10
1138		37c. *The Three Kings* (Simone Bouchard)	45	85
1139		64c. *Snow in Bethlehem* (David Milne)	55	1·60
1137/1139 Set of 3			1·25	2·25

(Des W. Southern and R. Tibbles. Litho Ashton-Potter)

1984 (9 Nov). 60th Anniversary of Royal Canadian Air Force. Fluorescent frame. Perf 12×12½.
| 1140 | **505** | 32c. multicoloured | 35 | 30 |

506 Trefflé Berthiaume (editor) **507** Heart and Arrow

(Des P.-Y. Pelletier. Litho Ashton-Potter)

1984 (16 Nov). Centenary of *La Presse* (newspaper). Fluorescent frame. Perf 13×13½.
| 1141 | **506** | 32c. agate, vermilion and pale grey-brown | 35 | 30 |

(Des F. Dallaire. Litho Ashton-Potter)

1985 (8 Feb). International Youth Year. Perf 12½.
| 1142 | **507** | 32c. multicoloured | 30 | 30 |

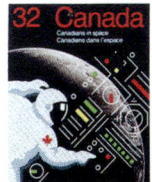

508 Astronaut in Space, and Planet Earth   **509** Emily Murphy

(Des L. Holloway. Litho Ashton-Potter)

1985 (15 Mar). Canadian Space Programme. Perf 13½.
| 1143 | **508** | 32c. multicoloured | 40 | 30 |

(Des Muriel Wood and R. Tibbles. Litho Ashton-Potter)

1985 (17 Apr). Women's Rights Activists. T **509** and similar horiz design. Multicoloured. Perf 13½.
1144		32c. Type **509**	40	75
		a. Horiz pair. Nos. 1144/1145	60	1·50
1145		32c. Thérèse Casgrain	30	75

Nos. 1144/1145 were printed together, *se-tenant*, in horizontal pairs throughout the sheet.

510 Gabriel Dumont (Métis leader) and Battle of Batoche, 1885

(Des R. Derreth. Litho Ashton-Potter)

1985 (6 May). Centenary of the North-West Rebellion. Perf 14×13½.
| 1146 | **510** | 32c. blue, carmine and grey | 30 | 30 |

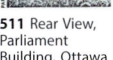

511 Rear View, Parliament Building, Ottawa   **512** Queen Elizabeth II   **512a** Queen Elizabeth II in 1984 (from photo by Karsh)

(Des R. Bellemare. Eng R. Couture (Nos. 1161/1162). Des T. Yakobina and C. Candlish (Nos. 1162a/1162h), R. Harder (others)))

1985 (21 June)–**00**. No fluorescent bands (1c. to 6c.) or fluorescent frame (34c., 36c., 39c., 40c., 42c., 43c., 45c., 46c., 47c.).

(a) T **511** and similar horiz designs. (i) Booklet stamps. Recess B.A.B.N. Chalk-surfaced paper (6c. (No. 1150b), 37c., 38c.) or ordinary paper (others). Perf 12½×12.

1147	–	1c. grey-olive (30.3.87)	1·00	2·50
		a. Booklet pane. Nos. 1147×2, 1150×2, 1152 and label	9·00	
		b. Chalk-surfaced paper (1.10.87)	1·00	1·50
		ba. Booklet pane. Nos. 1147b×2, 1150a×2,1152a and label	7·50	
		bb. Booklet pane. Nos. 1147b, 1150a×3, 1153 and two labels (3.2.88)	3·25	
1148	–	2c. bottle green	25	1·50
		a. Booklet pane. Nos. 1148×3, 1149×2 and 1151	4·00	
		b. Chalk-surfaced paper (18.1.89)	30	40
		ba. Booklet pane. Nos. 1148b×3, 1150b, 1154 and label	5·50	
1149	–	5c. sepia	75	1·75
1150	–	6c. chestnut (30.3.87)	1·50	2·75
		a. Chalk-surfaced paper (1.10.87)	1·00	70
1150b		6c. blackish purple (18.1.89)	2·50	1·00
1151	**511**	34c. blue-black	3·00	3·25
1152		36c. reddish purple (30.3.87)	4·50	6·00
		a. Chalk-surfaced paper (1.10.87)	4·50	6·00
1153		37c. dull ultramarine (3.2.88)	2·00	30
1154		38c. deep blue (18.1.89)	3·50	1·25

(ii) Litho C.B.N. (Nos. 1155 (from sheets), 1156/1157c), B.A.B.N. (No. 1155 (from booklets) or Ashton-Potter (Nos. 1155b, 1156a, 1157a/1157ba, 1157ca/1157cb). Chalk-surfaced paper (Nos. 1155b/1155ba, 1156, 1156b/1156bb and 1157c/1157cb). Perf 13×13½ (No. 1157c) or 13½×13 (others).

1155	**511**	34c. multicoloured	60	10
		a. Booklet pane. No. 1155×25 (1.8.85)	13·00	
		b. Perf 13½×14 (4.7.86)	1·25	1·75
		ba. Booklet pane. No. 1155b×25	26·00	
1156		36c. multicoloured (30.3.87)	1·25	30
		a. Ordinary paper	30	45
		b. Perf 13½×14	1·40	1·75
		ba. Booklet pane. No. 1156a×10	12·00	
		bb. Booklet pane. No. 1156a×25 (19.5.87)	27·00	
		c. Imperf (pair)	£500	
1157	–	37c. multicoloured (30.12.87)	85	10
		a. Perf 13½×14 (5.1.88)	1·00	1·00
		ab. Booklet pane. No. 1157a×10	13·00	
		ac. Booklet pane. No. 1157a×25 (2.5.88)	15·00	
		ad. Chalk-surfaced paper (5.1.88)	1·50	1·00
		ae. Booklet pane. No. 1157ad×25	27·00	
1157c	–	38c. multicoloured (29.12.88)	65	10
		ca. Booklet pane. No. 1157c×10 and two labels	6·00	
		cb. Booklet pane. No. 1157c×25 and two labels	15·00	
		cc. Printed on the gummed side	45·00	

(iii) Coil stamps. Recess C.B.N. Perf 10×imperf.

1158	**511**	34c. purple-brown (1.8.85)	1·75	3·00
		a. Imperf (pair)	95·00	
1159		36c. carmine-vermilion (19.5.87)	1·75	55
		a. Imperf (pair)	£150	
1160		37c. deep ultramarine (22.2.88)	1·00	40
		a. Imperf (pair)	£110	
1160b		38c. bottle green (1.2.89)	50	30
		ba. Imperf (pair)	£225	

(b) Recess and photo B.A.B.N. Perf 13×13½.
| 1161 | **512** | 34c. black and cobalt (12.7.85) | 1·40 | 30 |
| 1162 | | 36c. reddish purple (1.10.87) | 2·75 | 1·10 |

(c) Litho B.A.B.N. (Nos. 1162a/1162c), Ashton-Potter (Nos. 1162bc, 1162ca, 1162d/1162e, 1162fa), C.B.N. (Nos. 1162f/1162g, 1162i) or Ashton-Potter Canada (No. 1162l). Chalk-surfaced paper (40c. to 47c.). Perf 13½×13 (Nos. 1162a, 1162h/1162i), 13×12½ (No. 1162b) or 13×13½ (Nos. 1162c, 1162d/1162g).

1162a	**512a**	37c. multicoloured (30.12.87)	3·50	10
1162b		38c. multicoloured (29.12.88)	1·50	20
		ba. Imperf (horiz pair)	£300	
		bb. Imperf at top and sides (horiz pair)	£250	
		bc. Perf 13×13½. Chalk-surfaced paper	70	80
		bd. Booklet pane. No. 1162bc×10 and two labels	6·50	
		be. Imperf between (horiz pair) (from pane No. 1162bd)	£600	
1162c		39c. multicoloured (12.1.90)	1·00	20
		ca. Chalk-surfaced paper	2·00	80
		cb. Booklet pane. No. 1162ca×10 and two labels	19·00	
		cc. Perf 13×12½ (2.90)	7·00	1·00

CANADA

1162d	40c. multicoloured (28.12.90)		1·00	20
	da. Booklet pane. No. 1162d×10 and two labels		13·00	
	db. Ordinary paper (24.5.91)		1·25	20
1162e	42c. multicoloured (27.12.91)		1·00	40
	eaa. Imperf (pair)		£450	
	ea. Booklet pane. No. 1162e×10		15·00	
1162f	43c. multicoloured (30.12.92)		1·75	1·00
	faa. Imperf (pair)		£450	
	fa. Booklet pane. No. 1162f×10		16·00	
1162g	45c. multicoloured (31.7.95)		2·75	1·00
	ga. Booklet pane. No. 1162g×10		23·00	
1162h	46c. multicoloured (28.12.98)		1·00	1·00
1162i	47c. multicoloured (28.12.00)		1·00	1·25
	ia. Imperf (pair)		£350	

Designs: 1c., 5c., 6c. (No. 1150b) East Block, Parliament Building; 2c., 6c. (No. 1150) West Block, Parliament Building; 38c. (No. 1157c) Side view, Parliament Building.

Stamps from booklet panes Nos. 1147a, 1147ba/1147bb and 1148a/1148b have one or two adjacent sides imperforate. Stamps from the first and last vertical columns of booklet panes Nos. 1155a, 1155ba, 1156ba/1156bb, 1157ab/1157ac, 1157ae, 1157ca/1157cb, 1162bd, 1162cb, 1162da 1162ea, 1162fa and 1162ga are imperforate at left or right. Those from the bottom row of No. 1157ac are also imperforate at foot.

Nos. 1157c and 1162b/1162i have a slightly larger design image 21×17 mm.

Printings of booklet pane No. 1162fa from booklet No. SB164 were initially by Ashton-Potter. On 7 January 1994 the printer changed to C.B.N. and the booklet cover to Type **B37**. This booklet is listed as No. SB177. There were further printings by C.B.N. before production reverted to Ashton-Potter Canada for supplies released on 27 March 1995.

Nos. 1162g/1162ga were reissued on 6 October 1995 showing a change of printer to Ashton-Potter Canada. There are no listable differences between these stamps and the previous printings.

No. 1162ca has been reported both imperforate and in imperf between pairs. The status of both is inknown.

(Des R. Harder. Litho Ashton-Potter)

1985 (28 June). Canada Day. Forts (2nd series). Horiz designs as T **481**. Multicoloured. Perf 12½×13.

1163	34c. Lower Fort Garry, Manitoba (44×22 mm)	35	55
	a. Booklet pane. Nos. 1163/1172	3·25	
1164	34c. Fort Anne, Nova Scotia	35	55
1165	34c. Fort York, Ontario	35	55
1166	34c. Castle Hill, Newfoundland (28×22 mm)	35	55
1167	34c. Fort Whoop Up, Alberta (28×22 mm)	35	55
1168	34c. Fort Erie, Ontario (44×22 mm)	35	55
1169	34c. Fort Walsh, Saskatchewan	35	55
1170	34c. Fort Lennox, Quebec	35	55
1171	34c. York Redoubt, Nova Scotia (28×22 mm)	35	55
1172	34c. Fort Frederick, Ontario (28×22 mm)	35	55
1163/1172 Set of 10		3·25	5·00

Nos. 1163/1172 were only available from $3.40 stamp booklets (No. SB96) containing the *se-tenant* pane, No. 1163a.

513 Louis Hébert (apothecary)

514 Parliament Buildings and Map of World

515 Guide and Brownie Saluting

(Des C. Malenfant. Litho Ashton-Potter)

1985 (30 Aug). 45th International Pharmaceutical Sciences Congress of Pharmaceutical Federation, Montreal. Fluorescent frame. Perf 12½.

1173	**513**	34c. multicoloured	45	45

(Des E. Barenscher. Litho Ashton-Potter)

1985 (3 Sept). 74th Conference of Inter-Parliamentary Union, Ottawa. Perf 13½.

1174	**514**	34c. multicoloured	45	45

(Des Barbara Griffin. Recess and photo B.A.B.N)

1985 (12 Sept). 75th Anniversary of Girl Guide Movement. Fluorescent frame. Perf 13½×13.

1175	**515**	34c. multicoloured	45	35

516 Sisters Islets Lighthouse

517 Santa Claus in Reindeer-drawn Sleigh

(Des B. Reilander (No. 1180), L. Rivard (others). Litho Ashton-Potter))

1985 (3 Oct). Canadian Lighthouses (2nd series). T **516** and similar horiz designs. Multicoloured. Perf 13½.

1176	34c. Type **516**	2·00	1·50
	a. Block of 4. Nos. 1176/1179	7·00	7·50
1177	34c. Pelee Passage Lighthouse	2·00	1·50
1178	34c. Haut-fond Prince Lighthouse	2·00	1·50
1179	34c. Rose Blanche Lighthouse, Cains Island.	2·00	1·50
1176/1179 Set of 4		7·00	7·50
MS1180 109×90 mm. Nos. 1176/1179		2·50	7·00

Nos. 1176/1179 were printed together, *se-tenant*, in different combinations throughout the sheet, giving ten blocks of 4 and ten single stamps.

No. **MS**1180 publicises Capex 87 International Stamp Exhibition, Toronto.

(Des Barbara Carroll and C. Yaneff. Litho Ashton-Potter)

1985 (23 Oct). Christmas. Santa Claus Parade. T **517** and similar horiz designs. Multicoloured. Perf 13½.

1181	32c. Canada Post's parade float	50	85
	a. Booklet pane. No. 1181×10	4·25	
1182	34c. Type **517**	50	10
1183	39c. Acrobats and horse-drawn carriage	60	90
1184	68c. Christmas tree, pudding and goose on float	1·00	2·00
1181/1184 Set of 4		2·50	3·50

No. 1181 was only available from $3.20 stamp booklets, No. SB98, which had the upper and lower edges of the pane imperforate. This value was intended for use on greeting cards posted on or before 31 January 1986, and represented a 2c. saving of postage. After this date these stamps could be used for any postal purpose in conjunction with other values.

(Des E. Roch. Litho Ashton-Potter)

1985 (7 Nov). Railway Locomotives (3rd series). Horiz designs as T **503**. Multicoloured. Perf 12½×13.

1185	34c. Grand Trunk Railway Class K2 steam locomotive	1·25	1·75
	a. Pair. Nos. 1185/1186	2·50	3·50
1186	34c. Canadian Pacific Class P2a steam locomotive	1·25	1·75
1187	39c. Canadian Northern Class 010a steam locomotive	1·25	1·50
1188	68c. Canadian Government Railway Class H4D steam locomotive	2·00	3·25
1185/1188 Set of 4		5·25	7·50

Nos. 1185/1186 were printed together, *se-tenant*, in horizontal and vertical pairs throughout the sheet.

518 Naval Personnel of 1910, 1939–1945 and 1985

519 The Old Holton House, Montreal (James Wilson Morrice)

(Des W. Southern and R. Tibbles. Litho C.B.N)

1985 (8 Nov). 75th Anniversary of Royal Canadian Navy. Fluorescent frame. Perf 13½×13.

1189	**518**	34c. multicoloured	65	65

(Des L. Parent and J. Morin. Litho C.B.N)

1985 (15 Nov). 125th Anniversary of Montreal Museum of Fine Arts. Perf 13½.

1190	**519**	34c. multicoloured	40	50

CANADA

520 Map of Alberta showing Olympic Sites

(Des P.-Y. Pelletier. Litho Ashton-Potter)

1986 (13 Feb). Winter Olympic Games, Calgary (1988) (1st issue). Fluorescent frame. Perf 12½×13.
1191	**520**	34c. multicoloured	40	50

See also Nos. 1216/1217, 1236/1237, 1258/1259 and 1281/1284.

525 Great Blue Heron **526** Railway Rotary Snowplough

(Des P. Fontaine and J.-L. Grondin. Litho Ashton-Potter)

1986 (22 May). Birds of Canada. T **525** and similar horiz designs. Multicoloured. Perf 13½.
1199	34c. Type **525**	1·60	2·25
	a. Block of 4. Nos. 1199/1202	5·75	9·00
1200	34c. Snow Goose	1·60	2·25
1201	34c. Great Horned Owl	1·60	2·25
1202	34c. Spruce Grouse	1·60	2·25
1199/1202 Set of 4		5·75	9·00

Nos. 1199/1202 were printed together, *se-tenant*, in different combinations throughout the sheet, giving ten blocks of four and ten single stamps.

(Des R. Hill. Litho C.B.N)

1986 (27 June). Canada Day. Science and Technology. Canadian Inventions (1st series). T **526** and similar vert designs. Multicoloured. Perf 13½.
1203	34c. Type **526**	1·25	2·00
	a. Block of 4. Nos. 1203/1206	4·50	7·25
1204	34c. Space shuttle *Challenger* launching satellite with Canadarm	1·25	2·00
1205	34c. Pilot wearing anti-gravity flight suit and Supermarine Spitfire	1·25	2·00
1206	34c. Variable-pitch propeller and Avro 504 aeroplane	1·25	2·00
1203/1206 Set of 4		4·50	7·25

Nos. 1203/1206 were printed together, *se-tenant*, in blocks of four throughout the sheet.
See also Nos. 1241/1244 and 1292/1295.

521 Canada Pavilion **522** Molly Brant

(Des Debbie Adams. Recess and photo B.A.B.N)

1986 (7 Mar). Expo '86 World Fair Vancouver (1st issue). T **521** and similar horiz design. Multicoloured. Fluorescent frame. Perf 13×13½.
1192		34c. Type **521**	75	50
1193		39c. Early telephone, dish aerial and satellite	1·25	3·00

No. 1192 has been reported with 'CANADA 34' omitted.
See also Nos. 1196/1197.

(Des Sara Tyson. Litho Ashton-Potter)

1986 (14 Apr). 250th Birth Anniversary of Molly Brant (Iroquois leader). Perf 13½.
1194	**522**	34c. multicoloured	40	50

527 CBC Logos over Map of Canada **528** Ice Age Artefacts, Tools and Settlement

(Des R. Mah and G. Tsetsekas. Litho Ashton-Potter)

1986 (23 July). 50th Anniversary of Canadian Broadcasting Corporation. Perf 12½.
1207	**527**	34c. multicoloured	40	50

(Des F. Hagan. Litho Ashton-Potter)

1986 (29 Aug)–**00**. Exploration of Canada (1st series). Discoverers. T **528** and similar horiz designs. Multicoloured. Perf 12½×13.
1208	34c. Type **528**	1·00	1·75
	a. Block of 4. Nos. 1208/1211	3·50	6·25
1209	34c. Viking ships	1·00	1·75
1210	34c. John Cabot's *Matthew*, 1497, compass and Arctic Char (fish)	1·00	1·75
1211	34c. Henry Hudson cast adrift, 1611	1·00	1·75
1208/1211 Set of 4		3·50	6·25
MS1212 119×84 mm. Nos. 1208/1211 (1.10)		4·00	7·00

Nos. 1208/1211 were printed together, *se-tenant*, in different combinations throughout the sheet, giving ten blocks of four and ten single stamps.

No. **MS**1212 publicises Capex '87 International Stamp Exhibition, Toronto.
See also Nos. 1232/1235, 1285/1288 and 1319/1322.

523 Philippe Aubert de Gaspé and Scene from *Les Anciens Canadiens* **524** Canadian Field Post Office and Cancellation, 1944

(Des P. Fontaine and Y. Paquin. Litho Ashton-Potter)

1986 (14 Apr). Birth Bicentenary of Philippe Aubert de Gaspé (author). Fluorescent frame. Perf 12½.
1195	**523**	34c. multicoloured	40	50

(Des Debbie Adams. Recess and photo B.A.B.N)

1986 (28 Apr). Expo '86 World Fair, Vancouver (2nd issue). Multicoloured designs as T **521**. Fluorescent frame. Perf 13½×13 (34c.) or 13×13½ (68c.).
1196		34c. Expo Centre, Vancouver (*vert*)	70	50
1197		68c. Early and modern trains	1·40	3·25

(Des J. DesRosiers. Litho Ashton-Potter)

1986 (9 May). 75th Anniversary of Canadian Forces Postal Service. Perf 13½.
1198	**524**	34c. multicoloured	60	60

529 Crowfoot (Blackfoot Chief) and Indian Village **530** Peace Dove and Globe

CANADA

(Des Wanda Lewicka and J. Morin. Litho C.B.N)

1986 (5 Sept). Founders of the Canadian West. T **529** and similar horiz design. Multicoloured. Perf 13×13½.
1213	34c. Type **529**	65	1·00
	a. Pair. Nos. 1213/1214	1·25	2·00
1214	34c. James Macleod of the North West Mounted Police and Fort Macleod	65	1·00

Nos. 1213/1214 were printed together, *se-tenant*, in horizontal and vertical pairs throughout the sheet.

(Des Carole Jeghers. Litho and embossed Ashton-Potter)

1986 (16 Sept). International Peace Year. Perf 13½.
1215	**530** 34c. multicoloured	60	60

531 Ice Hockey   **532** Angel with Crown

(Des P.-Y. Pelletier. Litho C.B.N)

1986 (15 Oct). Winter Olympic Games, Calgary (1988) (2nd issue). T **531** and similar vert design. Multicoloured. Perf 13½×13.
1216	34c. Type **531**	1·40	1·90
	a. Pair. Nos. 1216/1217	2·75	3·75
1217	34c. Biathlon	1·40	1·90

Nos. 1216/1217 were printed together, *se-tenant*. in horizontal and vertical pairs throughout the sheet.
See also Nos. 1236/1237, 1258/1259 and 1281/1284.

(Des T. Dimson. Litho Ashton-Potter)

1986 (29 Oct). Christmas. T **532** and similar multicoloured designs. Fluorescent frame (34c. to 68c.). Perf 13½×imperf (29c.) or 12½ (others).
1218	29c. Angel singing carol (36×22 mm)	50	35
	a. Booklet pane. No. 1218×10	4·50	
	b. Perf 12½×imperf	5·50	2·50
	ba. Booklet pane. No. 1218b×10	50·00	
1219	34c. Type **532**	50	10
1220	39c. Angel playing lute	60	1·25
1221	68c. Angel with ribbon	1·10	2·50
1218/1221 Set of 4		2·50	3·75

Nos. 1218/1218b were only available from $2.90 stamp booklets, Nos. SB99/SB99a, which had the sides of the pane imperforate. In addition to the design each stamp in the pane included an integral horizontal label showing a bar code. This value was intended for use on greeting cards posted on or before 31 January 1987, and represented a 5c. saving when used in conjunction with special postcoded envelopes. These stamps were valid for normal postal purposes after 31 January when used with other values.

533 John Molson with Theatre Royal, Montreal, *Accommodation* (paddle-steamer) and Railway Train

534 Toronto's First Post Office

(Des C. Malenfant. Litho Ashton-Potter)

1986 (4 Nov). 150th Death Anniversary of John Molson (businessman). Perf 12½.
1222	**533** 34c. multicoloured	1·00	1·00

(Des E. Roch. Litho Ashton-Potter)

1986 (21 Nov). Railway Locomotives (4th series). Horiz designs as T **503**, but size 60×22 mm. Multicoloured. Perf 12½×13.
1223	34c. Canadian National Class V-1-a diesel locomotive No. 9000	1·75	1·90
	a. Pair. Nos. 1223/1224	3·50	3·75
1224	34c. Canadian Pacific Class T1a steam locomotive No. 9000	1·75	1·90
1225	39c. Canadian National Class U-2-a steam locomotive	1·75	1·00
1226	68c. Canadian Pacific Class H1c steam locomotive No. 2850	2·00	3·50
1223/1226 Set of 4		6·50	7·50

Nos. 1223/1224 were issued together, *se-tenant*, in horizontal and vertical pairs throughout the sheet.

(Des J. Mardon (stamps) and B. Reilander (sheet). Recess and litho B.A.B.N)

1987 (16 Feb–12 June). Capex '87 International Stamp Exhibition, Toronto. T **534** and similar horiz designs showing Post Offices. Fluorescent frame. Perf 13×13½.
1227	34c. Type **534**	60	20
1228	36c. Nelson-Miramichi, New Brunswick (12.6)	65	45
1229	42c. Saint-Ours, Quebec (12.6)	70	65
1230	72c. Battleford, Saskatchewan (12.6)	1·00	1·25
1227/1230 Set of 4		2·75	2·25
MS1231 155×92 mm. 36c. As No. 1227 and Nos. 1228/1230, but main inscription in bright green (12.6)		3·25	4·50

535 Étienne Brûlé exploring Lake Superior

(Des J. Britton and F. Hagan. Litho Ashton-Potter)

1987 (13 Mar). Exploration of Canada (2nd series). Pioneers of New France. T **535** and similar horiz designs. Multicoloured. Perf 12½×13.
1232	34c. Type **535**	1·25	1·75
	a. Block of 4. Nos. 1232/1235	4·50	6·25
1233	34c. Radisson and des Groseilliers with British and French flags	1·25	1·75
1234	34c. Jolliet and Father Marquette on the Mississippi	1·25	1·75
1235	34c. Jesuit missionary preaching to Indians	1·25	1·75
1232/1235 Set of 4		4·50	6·25

Nos. 1232/1235 were printed together, *se-tenant*, in different combinations throughout the sheet, giving ten blocks of four and ten single stamps.

(Des P.-Y. Pelletier. Litho C.B.N)

1987 (3 Apr). Winter Olympic Games, Calgary (1988) (3rd issue). Vert designs as T **531**. Multicoloured. Perf 13½×13.
1236	36c. Speed skating	50	40
1237	42c. Bobsleighing	75	60

536 Volunteer Activities   **537** Canadian Coat of Arms

(Des W. Davies. Litho Ashton-Potter)

1987 (13 Apr). National Volunteer Week. Perf 12½×13.
1238	**536** 36c. multicoloured	30	35

(Des R. Tibbles. Litho Ashton-Potter)

1987 (15 Apr). Fifth Anniversary of Canadian Charter of Rights and Freedoms. Fluorescent frame. Perf 14×13½.
1239	**537** 36c. multicoloured	75	35
	a. Imperf (pair)	£800	

CANADA

538 Steel Girder, Gear Wheel and Microchip
539 R. A. Fessenden (AM Radio)

(Des L. Holloway, R. Kerr and Nita Wallace. Litho Ashton-Potter)

1987 (19 May). Centenary of Engineering Institute of Canada. Perf 12½×13.
1240	**538**	36c. multicoloured	75	40

(Des R. Hill. Litho C.B.N)

1987 (25 June). Canada Day. Science and Technology. Canadian Inventors (2nd series). T **539** and similar vert designs. Multicoloured. Perf 13½.
1241		36c. Type **539**	75	1·25
		a. Block of four. Nos. 1241/1244	2·75	4·50
1242		36c. C. Fenerty (newsprint pulp)	75	1·25
1243		36c. G.-E. Desbarats and W. Leggo (half-tone engraving)	75	1·25
1244		36c. F. N. Gisborne (first North American undersea telegraph)	1·75	1·25
1241/1244	Set of 4		2·75	4·50

Nos. 1241/1244 were printed together, *se-tenant*, in blocks of four throughout the sheet.

 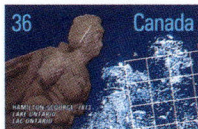

540 Segwun
541 Figurehead from *Hamilton*, 1813

(Des D. Champion. Litho C.B.N)

1987 (20 July). Canadian Steamships. T **540** and similar multicoloured design. Perf 13.
1245		36c. Type **540**	1·50	2·25
		a. Horiz pair. Nos. 1245/1246	3·00	4·50
1246		36c. *Princess Marguerite* (52×22 mm)	1·50	2·25

Nos. 1245/1246 were printed together horizontally, *se-tenant*, throughout the sheet of 25, with No. 1245 occurring in columns 1, 3 and 5 and No. 1246 in columns 2 and 4.

(Des L.-A. Rivard. Litho Ashton-Potter)

1987 (7 Aug). Historic Shipwrecks. T **541** and similar horiz designs. Multicoloured. Perf 13½×13.
1247		36c. Type **541**	1·25	1·75
		a. Block of four. Nos. 1247/1250	4·50	6·25
1248		36c. Hull of *San Juan*, 1565	1·25	1·75
1249		36c. Wheel from *Breadalbane*, 1853	1·25	1·75
1250		36c. Bell from *Ericsson*, 1892	1·25	1·75
1247/1250	Set of 4		4·50	6·25

Nos. 1247/1250 were printed together, *se-tenant*, in different combinations throughout the sheet, giving ten blocks of four and ten single stamps.

 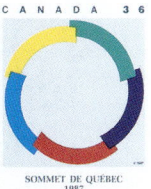

542 Air Canada Boeing 767-200 and Globe
543 Summit Symbol

(Des Debbie Adams and D. Carter. Litho C.B.N)

1987 (1 Sept). 50th Anniversary of Air Canada. Perf 13½.
1251	**542**	36c. multicoloured	1·00	35

(Des C. Gaudreau. Litho Ashton-Potter)

1987 (2 Sept). Second International Francophone Summit, Quebec. Fluorescent frame. Perf 13×12½.
1252	**543**	36c. multicoloured	30	35

544 Commonwealth Symbol
545 Poinsettia

(Des G. Tsetsekas. Litho Ashton-Potter)

1987 (13 Oct). Commonwealth Heads of Government Meeting, Vancouver. Fluorescent frame. Perf 13×12½.
1253	**544**	36c. multicoloured	35	40

(Des C. Simard. Litho Ashton-Potter)

1987 (2 Nov). Christmas. Christmas Plants. T **545** and similar multicoloured designs. Fluorescent frame. Perf 12½×13 (31c.) or 13½ (others).
1254		31c. Decorated Christmas tree and presents (36×20 mm)	90	50
		a. Booklet pane. No. 1254×10	8·00	
		b. Imperf between (horiz pair) (from booklet)	£1800	
1255		36c. Type **545**	40	20
1256		42c. Holly wreath	1·00	50
1257		72c. Mistletoe and decorated tree	1·40	80
1254/1257	Set of 4		2·75	1·75

On No. 1254 the left-hand third of the design area is taken up by a bar code which has fluorescent bands between the bars. This value was only available from $3.10 stamp booklets, No. SB103, which had the sides of the pane imperforate. This value was intended for use on greeting cards posted on or before 31 January 1988 and represented a 5c. saving when used in conjunction with special postcoded envelopes.

(Des P.-Y. Pelletier. Litho C.B.N)

1987 (13 Nov). Winter Olympic Games, Calgary (1988) (4th issue). Vert designs as T **531**. Multicoloured. Fluorescent frame. Perf 13½×13.
1258		36c. Cross-country skiing	75	75
		a. Pair. Nos. 1258/1259	1·50	1·50
1259		36c. Ski-jumping	75	75

Nos. 1258/1259 were printed together, *se-tenant*, in horizontal and vertical pairs throughout the sheet.

546 Football, Grey Cup and Spectators

(Des L. Holloway. Litho Ashton-Potter)

1987 (20 Nov). 75th Grey Cup Final (Canadian football championship), Vancouver. Fluorescent frame. Perf 12½.
1260	**546**	36c. multicoloured	35	40

547 Flying Squirrel **547a** Porcupine **547b** Muskrat

547c Varying Hare **547d** Red Fox **547e** Striped Skunk

69

CANADA

547f American Beaver

548 Lynx

548a Walrus

548b Pronghorn

548c Wolverine

548d Killer Whale

548e Musk Ox

548f Wolf

548g Harbour Porpoise

548h Wapiti

548i Brown Bear

548j White Whale

548k Peary Caribou

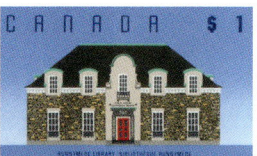
548l Runnymede Library, Toronto

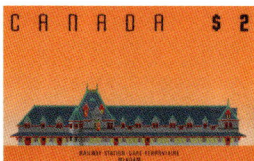
548m McAdam Railway Station, New Brunswick

548n Bonsecours Market, Montréal

(Des Gottschalk and Ash International (1c. to 25c.), B. Tsang (43c. to 80c.), R. Bellemare ($1, $2, $5). Litho Ashton-Potter (1c. to 80c.), Recess and litho B.A.B.N. to June 1992, thereafter C.B.N. ($1, $2, $5))

1988 (18 Jan)–93. Canadian Mammals and Architecture. Multicoloured. Fluorescent frame (10c. and 43c. to 80c.).

(a) Horiz designs as T 547/547f. Chalk-surfaced paper. Perf 13×13½.

1261	547	1c. Flying Squirrel (3.10.88)	10	10
		aa. Imperf (pair)	£500	
		a. Perf 13×12½ (1.92)	3·50	3·50
1262	547a	2c. Porcupine (3.10.88)	10	10
		a. Imperf (pair)	£400	
1263	547b	3c. Muskrat (3.10.88)	10	10
		a. Imperf (pair)	£500	
1264	547c	5c. Varying Hare (3.10.88)	10	10
		a. Imperf (pair)	£1000	
1265	547d	6c. Red Fox (3.10.88)	10	10
		a. Imperf (pair)	£1400	
1266	547e	10c. Striped Skunk (3.10.88)	10	10
		aa. Imperf (pair)	£400	
		a. Perf 13×12½ (2.91)	3·75	1·50
		b. No fluorescent frame (25.10.91)	75	10
1267	547f	25c. American Beaver (3.10.88)	30	15
		a. No fluorescent frame (22.4.92)	2·25	55

(b) Horiz designs as T 548/548k. Chalk-surfaced paper (45c., 46c., 57c., 61c., 63c., 78c., 80c.) or ordinary paper (others). Perf 12×12½ (43c., 57c., 74c.) or 14½×14 (others).

1268	548	43c. Lynx (26×20 mm)	1·00	1·40
1269	548a	44c. Walrus (18.1.89)	1·40	20
		a. Perf 12½×13. Chalk-surfaced paper	1·40	55
		ab. Booklet pane. No. 1269a×5 and label with margins all round	5·50	
		b. Chalk-surfaced paper (9.6.89)	4·25	1·50
		c. Perf 13½×13. Chalk-surfaced paper (11.89)	£300	25·00
1270	548b	45c. Pronghorn (12.1.90)	50	40
		aa. Imperf (pair)	£550	
		a. Perf 12½×13	2·00	40
		ab. Booklet pane. No. 1270a×5 and label with margins all round	9·00	
		b. Perf 13 (6.90)	14·00	50
1270c	548c	46c. Wolverine (28.12.90)	1·75	2·00
		ca. Perf 13	3·75	3·25
		cb. Perf 12½×13	2·75	50
		cc. Booklet pane. No. 1270cb×5 and label with margins all round	12·00	
1271	548d	57c. Killer Whale	2·00	55
		a. Ordinary paper (26.9.88)	3·75	2·00
1272	548e	59c. Musk Ox (18.1.89)	3·50	3·25
		a. Chalk-surfaced paper (1.11.89)	9·00	6·00
		b. Perf 13. Chalk-surfaced paper (1.11.89)	6·00	6·00
1273	548f	61c. Wolf (12.1.90)	70	1·60
		a. Perf 13 (7.90)	32·00	4·50
1273b	548g	63c. Harbour Porpoise (28.12.90)	2·00	3·50
		ba. Perf 13	12·00	5·00
1274	548h	74c. Wapiti	1·60	50
		a. Chalk-surfaced paper	£500	8·00
1275	548h	76c. Brown Bear (18.1.89)	2·50	50
		a. Perf 12½×13. Chalk-surfaced paper	1·75	70
		ab. Booklet pane. No. 1275a×5 and label with margins all round	8·50	
		b. Chalk-surfaced paper (25.8.89)	7·50	3·50
		c. Perf 13. Chalk-surfaced paper (1989)	26·00	10·00
1276	548j	78c. White Whale (12.1.90)	1·00	55
		aa. Imperf (pair)	£500	
		a. Perf 12½×13	2·25	70
		ab. Booklet pane. No. 1276a×5 and label with margins all round	11·00	
		b. Perf 13 (4.90)	40·00	6·00
1276c	548k	80c. Peary Caribou (28.12.90)	1·00	60
		ca. Perf 13	6·00	1·00
		cb. Perf 12½×13	1·90	60
		cc. Booklet pane. No. 1276cb×5 and label with margins all round	10·00	

(c) Horiz designs as T 548l/548n. Chalk-surfaced paper ($5) or ordinary paper (others). Perf 13½.

1277	548l	$1 Runnymede Library, Toronto (brown roof) (5.5.89)	1·25	30
		a. Chalk-surfaced paper (28.8.92)	6·00	1·10
		ab. Black (recess inscr) inverted	£6500	
		ac. Imperf (pair)	£800	

CANADA

1278	548m	ad. Black roof (1993)		10·00	1·25
		$2 McAdam Railway Station, New Brunswick (5.5.89)		1·75	50
		a. Chalk-surfaced paper (29.7.92)		12·00	2·40
		ab. Imperf (pair)		£550	
1279	548n	$5 Bonsecours Market, Montreal (28.5.90)		4·75	4·00
1261/1279 Set of 22				24·00	16·00

The later issues of the mammal series are slightly larger than the original three, measuring 27×21 mm.

Nos. 1269a, 1270a, 1270cb, 1275a, 1276a and 1276cb were only issued in stamp booklets, Nos. SB110, SB124, SB134, SB113, SB126 and SB136.

Nos. 1277a/1277ac and 1278a were printed by C.B.N. There was also a printing of the $5 by C.B.N. in September 1992, but this does not differ from the B.A.B.N. version. All C.B.N. printings are on thinner paper, less crisp than the initial printings.

No. 1277ad appears to be from new plates. In addition to the differences in the roof colour it shows a less solid blue background around the building.

For further designs as Type **548l**, but in a changed format, see Nos. 1479/1481.

No. 1280 is vacant.

(Des P-Y. Pelletier. Litho Ashton-Potter)

1988 (12 Feb). Winter Olympic Games, Calgary (1988) (5th issue). Vert designs as T **531**. Multicoloured. Fluorescent frame. Perf 12×12½ (37c.) or 12½ (others).

1281		37c. Slalom skiing	70	50
		a. Pair. Nos. 1281/1282	1·40	1·00
1282		37c. Curling	70	50
1283		43c. Figure skating	70	45
1284		74c. Luge	1·25	80
1281/1284 Set of 4			3·00	2·00

Nos. 1281/1282 were printed together, *se-tenant*, in horizontal and vertical pairs throughout the sheet.

549 Trade Goods, Blackfoot Encampment and Page from Anthony Henday's Journal

(Des F. Hagan. Litho Ashton-Potter)

1988 (17 Mar). Exploration of Canada (3rd series). Explorers of the West. T **549** and similar horiz designs. Multicoloured. Fluorescent frame. Perf 12½×13.

1285		37c. Type **549**	1·00	1·00
		a. Block of 4. Nos. 1285/1288	3·50	4·50
1286		37c. *Discovery* and map of George Vancouver's voyage	1·00	1·00
1287		37c. Simon Fraser's expedition portaging canoes	1·00	1·00
1288		37c. John Palliser's surveying equipment and view of prairie	1·00	1·00
1285/1288 Set of 4			3·50	4·50

Nos. 1285/1288 were printed together, *se-tenant*, in different combinations throughout the sheet, giving ten blocks of four and ten single stamps.

550 *The Young Reader* (Ozias Leduc)

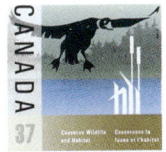

551 Mallard landing on Marsh

(Des P-Y. Pelletier. Eng G. Prosser. Recess and photo B.A.B.N.)

1988 (20 May). Canadian Art (1st series). No fluorescent bands. Perf 13×13½.

1289	**550**	50c. multicoloured	70	1·00

No. 1289 was issued in sheets of 16 with descriptive texts on the margins.

See also Nos. 1327, 1384, 1421, 1504, 1539, 1589, 1629, 1681, 1721, 1825, 1912, 2011, 2097 and 2133.

(Des J. Gault and T. Telmet. Litho C.B.N)

1988 (1 June). Wildlife and Habitat Conservation. T **551** and similar horiz design. Multicoloured. Fluorescent frame. Perf 13×13½.

1290		37c. Type **551**	75	50
		a. Pair. Nos. 1290/1291	1·50	2·00
1291		37c. Moose feeding in marsh	75	50

Nos. 1290/1291 were printed together, *se-tenant*, in horizontal and vertical pairs throughout the sheet.

552 Kerosene Lamp and Diagram of Distillation Plant

553 *Papilio brevicauda*

(Des R. Hill. Litho Ashton-Potter)

1988 (17 June). Canada Day. Science and Technology. Canadian Inventions (3rd series). T **552** and similar vert designs. Multicoloured. Fluorescent frame. Perf 12½×13.

1292		37c. Type **552**	75	1·00
		a. Block of 4. Nos. 1292/1295	2·75	3·50
1293		37c. Ears of Marquis wheat	75	1·00
1294		37c. Electron microscope and magnified image	75	1·00
1295		37c. Patient under 'Cobalt 60' cancer therapy	75	1·00
1292/1295 Set of 4			2·75	3·50

Nos. 1292/1295 were printed together, *se-tenant*, in blocks of four throughout the sheet.

(Des Heather Cooper. Litho Ashton-Potter)

1988 (4 July). Canadian Butterflies. T **553** and similar vert designs. Multicoloured. Fluorescent frame. Perf 12×12½.

1296		37c. Type **553**	85	1·25
		a. Block of four. Nos. 1296/1299	3·00	4·50
1297		37c. *Lycaeides idas*	85	1·25
1298		37c. *Oeneis macounii*	85	1·25
1299		37c. *Papilio glaucus*	85	1·25
1296/1299 Set of 4			3·00	4·50

Nos. 1296/1299 were printed together, *se-tenant*, in different combinations throughout the sheet, giving ten blocks of four and ten single stamps.

554 St John's Harbour Entrance and Skyline

555 Club Members working on Forestry Project and Rural Scene

(Des L.-A. Rivard. Litho Ashton-Potter)

1988 (22 July). Centenary of Incorporation of St John's, Newfoundland. Fluorescent frame. Perf 13½×13.

1300	**554**	37c. multicoloured	35	40

(Des Debbie Adams. Litho Ashton-Potter)

1988 (5 Aug). 75th Anniversary of 4 H Clubs. Fluorescent frame. Perf 13½×13.

1301	**555**	37c. multicoloured	35	40

556 Saint-Maurice Ironworks

557 Tahltan Bear Dog

CANADA

(Des Michèle Cayer and Hélène Racicot. Eng. Y. Baril. Recess and litho C.B.N)

1988 (19 Aug). 250th Anniversary of Saint-Maurice Ironworks, Québec. Fluorescent frame. Perf 13½.

| 1302 | **556** | 37c. black, pale orange and cinnamon. | 40 | 40 |

(Des Mia Lane and D. Nethercott. Litho Ashton-Potter)

1988 (26 Aug). Canadian Dogs. T **557** and similar horiz designs. Multicoloured. Fluorescent frame. Perf 12½×12.

1303		37c. Type **557**	1·40	1·40
		a. Block of 4. Nos. 1303/1306	5·00	5·00
1304		37c. Nova Scotia Duck Tolling Retriever	1·40	1·40
1305		37c. Canadian Eskimo Dog	1·40	1·40
1306		37c. Newfoundland	1·40	1·40
1303/1306		Set of 4	5·00	5·00

Nos. 1303/1306 were printed together, *se-tenant*, in different combinations throughout the sheet, giving ten blocks of four and ten single stamps.

558 Baseball, Glove and Pitch

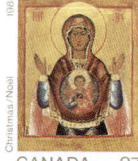
559 Virgin with Inset of Holy Child

(Des L. Holloway. Litho C.B.N)

1988 (14 Sept). 150th Anniversary of Baseball in Canada. Fluorescent frame. Perf 13½×13.

| 1307 | **558** | 37c. multicoloured | 35 | 40 |

(Des E. Roch and T. Yakobina. Litho Ashton-Potter)

1988 (27 Oct). Christmas. Icons. T **559** and similar multicoloured designs. Fluorescent frame. Perf 12½×13 (32c.) or 13½ (others).

1308		32c. Holy Family (36×21 mm)	35	55
		a. Booklet pane. No. 1308×10	2·50	
1309		37c. Type **559**	40	15
1310		43c. Virgin and Child	45	50
1311		74c. Virgin and Child (*different*)	70	1·00
1308/1311		Set of 4	1·75	2·00

On No. 1308 the left-hand third of the design area is taken up by a bar code which has fluorescent bands between the bars. This value was only available from $3.20 stamp booklets, No. SB109, which had the sides and bottom of the pane imperforate. It was intended for use on greeting cards posted on or before 31 January 1989.

No. 1309 also commemorates the Millennium of Ukrainian Christianity.

560 Bishop Inglis and Nova Scotia Church

561 Frances Ann Hopkins and 'Canoe manned by Voyageurs'

(Des S. Slipp and K. Sollows. Litho Ashton-Potter)

1988 (1 Nov). Bicentenary of Consecration of Charles Inglis (first Canadian Anglican bishop) (1987). Fluorescent frame. Perf 12½×13.

| 1312 | **560** | 37c. multicoloured | 35 | 40 |

(Des D. Nethercott. Litho Ashton-Potter)

1988 (18 Nov). 150th Birth Anniversary of Frances Ann Hopkins (artist). Fluorescent frame. Perf 13½×13.

| 1313 | **561** | 37c. multicoloured | 35 | 40 |

562 Angus Walters and *Bluenose* (yacht)

563 Chipewyan Canoe

(Des R. Hill. Litho Ashton-Potter)

1988 (18 Nov). 20th Death Anniversary of Angus Walters (yachtsman). Fluorescent frame. Perf 13½.

| 1314 | **562** | 37c. multicoloured | 40 | 40 |

(Des B. Leduc and L.-A. Rivard. Litho Ashton-Potter)

1989 (1 Feb). Small Craft of Canada (1st series). Native Canoes. T **563** and similar horiz designs. Multicoloured. Fluorescent frame. Perf 13½×13.

1315		38c. Type **563**	75	80
		a. Block of 4. Nos. 1315/1318	2·75	3·00
1316		38c. Haida canoe	75	80
1317		38c. Inuit kayak	75	80
1318		38c. Micmac canoe	75	80
1315/1318		Set of 4	2·75	3·00

Nos. 1315/1318 were printed together, *se-tenant*, throughout the sheet, giving ten blocks of four and ten single stamps.

See also Nos. 1377/1380 and 1428/1431.

564 Matonabbee and Hearne's Expedition

565 Construction of Victoria Bridge, Montreal and William Notman

(Des F. Hagan. Litho Ashton-Potter)

1989 (22 Mar). Exploration of Canada (4th series). Explorers of the North. T **564** and similar horiz designs. Multicoloured. Fluorescent frame. Perf 12½×13.

1319		38c. Type **564**	1·25	75
		a. Block of 4. Nos. 1319/1322	4·50	5·00
1320		38c. Relics of Franklin's expedition and White Ensign	1·25	75
1321		38c. Joseph Tyrrell's compass, hammer and fossil	1·25	75
1322		38c. Vilhjalmur Stefansson, camera on tripod and sledge dog team	1·25	75
1319/1322		Set of 4	4·50	5·00

Nos. 1319/1322 were printed together, *se-tenant*, in different combinations throughout the sheet, giving ten blocks of four and ten single stamps.

(Des J. Morin and T. Yakobina. Litho Ashton-Potter)

1989 (23 June). Canada Day. 150 Years of Canadian Photography. T **565** and similar horiz designs, each showing early photograph and photographer. Multicoloured. Perf 12½×12.

1323		38c. Type **565**	50	70
		a. Block of 4. Nos. 1323/1326	1·75	2·50
1324		38c. Plains Indian village and W. Hanson Boorne	50	70
1325		38c. Horse-drawn sleigh and Alexander Henderson	50	70
1326		38c. Quebec street scene and Jules-Ernest Livernois	50	70
1323/1326		Set of 4	1·75	2·50

Nos. 1323/1326 were printed together, *se-tenant*, in blocks of four throughout the sheet.

CANADA

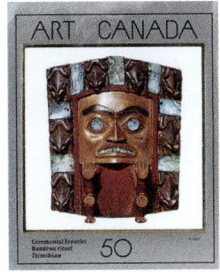

566 Tsimshian Ceremonial Frontlet, c 1900

567 Canadian Flag and Forest

(Des P-Y. Pelletier. Litho and die-stamped Ashton-Potter)

1989 (29 June). Canadian Art (2nd series). No fluorescent bands. Perf 12½×13.
1327	**566**	50c. multicoloured	70	60

No. 1327 was issued in a similar sheet format to No. 1289.

(Des Gottschalk and Ash International,. Litho Ashton-Potter)

1989 (30 June)–**93**. T **567** and similar horiz designs. Multicoloured. Fluorescent frame. Self-adhesive. Die-cut.
1328	38c. Type **567**		1·50	3·00
	aa. Blue omitted		£850	
	ab. Yellow omitted		£500	
	a. Booklet pane. No. 1328×12		14·00	
1328b	39c. Canadian flag and prairie (8.2.90)		1·50	3·00
	ba. Booklet pane. No. 1328b×12		14·00	
1328c	40c. Canadian flag and sea (11.1.91)		1·75	1·75
	ca. Booklet pane. No. 1328c×12		16·00	
1328d	42c. Canadian flag and mountains (28.1.92)		2·00	3·25
	da. Booklet pane. No. 1328d×12		22·00	
1328e	43c. Canadian flag over lake (15.2.93)		1·50	2·25
	ea. Booklet pane. No. 1328e×12		14·00	
1328/1328e Set of 5			7·50	12·00

Nos. 1328, 1328b, 1328c, 1328d and 1328e were only available from self-adhesive booklets, Nos. SB116, SB127, SB139, SB153 and SB168, in which the backing card forms the booklet cover.

568 Archibald Lampman

569 *Clavulinopsis fusiformis*

(Des R. Milot. Litho Ashton-Potter)

1989 (7 July). Canadian Poets. T **568** and similar horiz design. Multicoloured. Fluorescent frame. Perf 13½.
1329	38c. Type **568**		1·00	1·40
	a. Pair. Nos. 1329/1330		2·00	2·75
1330	38c. Louis-Honoré Fréchette		1·00	1·40

Nos. 1329/1330 were printed together, *se-tenant*, in horizontal and vertical pairs throughout the sheet.

(Des E. Roch. Litho Ashton-Potter)

1989 (4 Aug). Mushrooms. T **569** and similar vert designs. Multicoloured. Fluorescent frame. Perf 13½.
1331	38c. Type **569**		60	1·00
	a. Block of 4. Nos. 1331/1334		3·25	3·50
1332	38c. *Boletus mirabilis*		60	1·00
1333	38c. *Cantharellus cinnabarinus*		60	1·00
1334	38c. *Morchella esculenta*		60	1·00
1331/1334 Set of 4			2·25	3·50

Nos. 1331/1334 were printed together, *se-tenant*, in different combinations throughout the sheet, giving ten blocks of 4 and ten single stamps.

570 Night Patrol, Korea

571 Globe in Box

(Des N. Fontaine, J. Gault and T. Telmet. Eng Y. Baril. Recess and litho C.B.N)

1989 (8 Sept). 75th Anniversaries of Canadian Regiments. T **570** and similar horiz design. Multicoloured. Fluorescent frame. Perf 13.
1335	38c. Type **570** (Princess Patricia's Canadian Light Infantry)		1·40	2·00
	a. Vert pair. Nos. 1335/1336		2·75	4·00
1336	38c. Trench raid, France, 1914–1918 (Royal 22e Régiment)		1·40	2·00

Nos. 1335/1336 were printed together, *se-tenant*, in vertical pairs throughout the sheet.

(Des L. Holloway and Nita Wallace. Litho Ashton-Potter)

1989 (2 Oct). Canada Export Trade Month. Fluorescent frame. Perf 13½×13.
1337	**571**	38c. multicoloured	40	45

572 Film Director

573 'Snow II' (Lawren S. Harris)

(Des W. Tibbles from paper sculptures by J. Milne. Litho Ashton-Potter)

1989 (14 Oct). Arts and Entertainment. T **572** and similar vert designs. Fluorescent frame. Perf 13×13½.
1338	38c. grey-brown, blackish brown and bright reddish violet		55	75
	a. Block of 4. Nos. 1338/1341		2·00	2·75
1339	38c. grey-brown, blackish brown and bright green		55	75
1340	38c. grey-brown, blackish brown and bright magenta		55	75
1341	38c. grey-brown, blackish brown and new blue		55	75
1338/1341 Set of 4			2·00	2·75

Designs: No. 1339, Actors; No. 1340, Dancers; No. 1341, Musicians.
Nos. 1338/1341 were printed together, *se-tenant*, in different combinations throughout the sheet, giving ten blocks of four and ten single stamps.

(Des D. Nethercott and Viviane Warburton. Litho Ashton-Potter)

1989 (26 Oct). Christmas. Paintings of Winter Landscapes. T **573** and similar multicoloured designs. Fluorescent frame. Perf 12½×13 (33c.), 13×13½ (38c.) or 13½ (others).
1342	33c. *Champ-de-Mars, Winter* (William Brymner) (35×21 mm)		1·00	65
	a. Booklet pane. No. 1342×10		9·00	
	b. Imperf between (horiz pair) (from booklet)		£1200	
1343	38c. *Bend in the Gosselin River* (Marc-Aurèle Suzor-Coté) (21×35 mm)		40	25
	a. Perf 13×12½		3·50	1·25
	ab. Booklet pane. No. 1343a×10		32·00	
1344	44c. Type **573**		50	50
	a. Booklet pane. No. 1344×5 plus one printed label		13·00	
1345	76c. *Ste. Agnès* (A. H. Robinson)		90	85
	a. Booklet pane. No. 1345×5 plus one printed label		22·00	
1342/1345 Set of 4			2·50	2·00

On No. 1342 the left-hand third of the design area is taken up by a bar code which has fluorescent bands between the bars. This value was only available from $3.30 stamp booklets, No. SB118, which had the sides and bottom of the pane imperforate. It was intended for use on greeting cards posted on or before 31 January 1990.

No. 1343a was only issued in $3.80 stamp booklets, SB119.

Booklet pane No. 1343ab has the outer edges of the pane imperforate while Nos. 1344a and 1345a (from SB117 and SB120) have the vertical edges imperforate.

574 Canadians listening to Declaration of War, 1939

CANADA

(Des J.-P. Armanville and P.-Y. Pelletier. Litho C.B.N)

1989 (10 Nov). 50th Anniversary of Second World War (1st issue). T **574** and similar horiz designs. Fluorescent frame. Perf 13½.

1346	38c. black, silver and slate-purple	1·40	1·40
	a. Block of 4. Nos. 1346/1349	5·00	5·00
1347	38c. black, silver and olive-grey	1·40	1·40
1348	38c. black, silver and grey-green	1·40	1·40
1349	38c. black, silver and azure	1·40	1·40
1346/1349	Set of 4	5·00	5·00

Designs: No. 1347, Army mobilization; No. 1348, British Commonwealth air crew training; No. 1349, North Atlantic convoy.

Nos. 1346/1349 were printed together, *se-tenant*, in different combinations throughout the sheet, giving four blocks of four.

See also Nos. 1409/1412, 1456/1459, 1521/1524, 1576/1579, 1621/1624 and 1625/1628.

575 Canadian Flag   **575a**   **575b**

576 Flag over clouds   **576a** Flag over forest   **576b** Flag over mountains

576c Flag over pairie   **576d** Flag and skyscraper   **576e** Flag and icebergs

576f   **576g** Flag and inukshuk (Inuit cairn)   **576h** Flag and Canada Post Headquarters, Ottawa

576i Flag and Edmonton   **576j** Flag and Broadway Bridge, Saskatoon   **576k** Flag and Durrell, South Twillingate Island

576l Flag and Shannon Falls, Squamish   **576m** Flag and Church of St Hilaire, Quebec   **576n** Flag and Toronto skyline   **576o** Flag and winter scene

576p Flag and Bouctouche, New Brunswick   **576q** Flag and wind turbines   **576r** Flag and Fort Garry   **576s** Flag and dogsled

1989 (28 Dec)–**2005**. No fluorescent bands (1c., 5c.) or fluorescent frame (39c., 40c., 42c., 43c., 45c., 46c., 47c., 48c., 49c., 50c., 51c.).

(a) Booklet stamps. T **575** and similar horiz designs, each showing Canadian flag. Litho Ashton-Potter. Chalk-surfaced paper. Perf 13½×14.

1350	575	1c. multicoloured (12.1.90)	20	1·00
		a. Booklet pane. Nos. 1350, 1351×2 and 1352	1·40	
		b. Perf 12½×13	18·00	19·00
		ba. Booklet pane. Nos. 1350b, 1351a×2 and 1352a	40·00	
		c. Booklet pane. Nos. 1350×2, 1351 and 1353 (28.12.90)	2·00	
		ca. Imperf pane	£500	
1351	575a	5c. multicoloured (12.1.90)	40	30
		a. Perf 12½×13	9·00	11·00
1352	575b	39c. multicoloured (12.1.90)	2·00	2·25
		a. Perf 12½×13	18·00	19·00
1353		40c. multicoloured (28.12.90)	2·50	3·25

(b) Litho (for printers see below). Chalk-surfaced paper. Perf 14½ (45c.), 13×13½ (46c.) or 13½×13 (others).

1354	576	39c. multicoloured	70	10
		aa. Imperf (pair)	£300	
		a. Booklet pane. No. 1354×10 and two labels	11·00	
		b. Booklet pane. No. 1354×25 and two labels	24·00	
		c. Perf 12½×13 (2.90)	15·00	5·50
		ca. Imperf between (horiz pair)	£300	
1355	576a	40c. multicoloured (28.12.90)	80	10
		a. Booklet pane. No. 1355×10 and two labels	12·00	
		b. Booklet pane. No. 1355×25 and two labels	26·00	
1356	576b	42c. multicoloured (27.12.91)	1·00	15
		aa. Imperf (pair)	£400	
		aab. Imperf between (vert pair)	£500	
		a. Booklet pane. No. 1356×10	15·00	
		b. Booklet pane. No. 1356×25 and two labels	27·00	
		c. Booklet pane. No. 1356×50 and two labels	60·00	
1357	576c	43c. multicoloured (30.12.92)	1·00	1·75
		aa. Imperf (pair)	£400	
		a. Booklet pane. No. 1357×10	12·00	
		b. Booklet pane. No. 1357×25 and two labels	27·00	
		c. Perf 14½ (18.1.94)	1·75	2·25
		ca. Booklet pane. No. 1357c×10	15·00	
		cb. Booklet pane. No. 1357c×25 and two labels	29·00	
		cc. Imperf between (vert pair)	£550	
1358	576d	45c. mult (17×21 mm) (31.7.95)	80	1·50
		a. Booklet pane. No. 1358×10	8·00	
		b. Booklet pane. No. 1358×25 and two labels	16·00	
		c. Perf 13½×13 (6.10.95)	1·40	1·50
		ca. Booklet pane. No. 1358c×10	12·00	
		cb. Booklet pane. No. 1358c×25 and two labels	27·00	
		d. Perf 13×13½ (16×20 mm) (2.2.98)	1·25	1·50
		daa. Imperf (pair)	£400	
		da. Booklet pane. No. 1358d×10	11·00	
		db. Booklet pane. No. 1358d×30 (two blocks of 15 (5×3) separated by vertical gutter)	26·00	
1359	576e	46c. mult (16×20 mm) (28.12.98)	80	1·25
		a. Booklet pane. No. 1359×10	7·00	

*(c) Coil stamps. Designs as T **575**, but different folds in flag. Recess C.B.N. Perf 10×imperf.*

1360	576f	39c. deep purple (8.2.90)	60	75
		a. Imperf (pair)	£100	
1361		40c. indigo (28.12.90)	40	60
		a. Imperf (pair)	£160	
1362		42c. scarlet-vermilion (27.12.91)	40	60
		a. Imperf (pair)	75·00	
1363		43c. deep olive (30.12.92)	1·50	2·25
		a. Imperf (pair)	65·00	
1364		45c. bluish green (31.7.95)	1·00	1·75
		a. Imperf (pair)	65·00	
1365		46c. carmine-red (28.12.98)	80	1·75
		a. Imperf (pair)	75·00	

(d) Self-adhesive booklet stamps. Litho Ashton-Potter Canada (Nos. 1366/1366a, 1367b, 1368), C.B.N. (Nos. 1367a and 1370/1374e), Ashton-

Potter, C.B.N. or Lowe-Martin (Nos. 1369/1369a). Chalk-surfaced paper. Die-cut perf 9 (48c.) or die cut (others).

1366	**576e**	46c. multicoloured (28.12.98)	80	75
		a. Imperf (pair)	£250	
		b. Booklet pane. No. 1366×30	25·00	
1367	**576g**	47c. multicoloured (28.12.00)	1·25	1·00
		a. Booklet pane. No. 1367×10	11·00	
		b. Booklet pane. No. 1367×30	30·00	
1368	**576h**	48c. multicoloured (2.1.02)	1·25	1·50
		a. Blue omitted	£200	
		b. Booklet pane. No. 1368×10	11·00	
1369	**576i**	49c. multicoloured (19.12.03)	1·25	1·75
		a. Imperf (pair)	70·00	
		ab. Printed on the gummed side	6·00	
		b. Booklet pane. No. 1369×10	11·00	
1370	**576j**	50c. multicoloured (20.12.04)	2·00	2·50
		a. Booklet pane. Nos. 1370/1374, each×2	15·00	
		ab. Printed on the gummed side	60·00	
1371	**576k**	50c. multicoloured (20.12.04)	2·00	2·50
1372	**576l**	50c. multicoloured (20.12.04)	2·00	2·50
1373	**576m**	50c. multicoloured (20.12.04)	2·00	2·50
1374	**576n**	50c. multicoloured (20.12.04)	2·00	2·50

(e) Self-adhesive booklet stamps. Litho CBN. Fluorescent frame. Die-cut.

1374a	**576o**	51c. multicoloured (19.12.05)	1·40	2·25
		ab. Booklet pane. Nos. 1374a/1374e, each×2	12·00	
1374b	**576p**	51c. multicoloured (19.12.05)	1·40	2·25
1374c	**576q**	51c. multicoloured (19.12.05)	1·40	2·25
1374d	**576r**	51c. multicoloured (19.12.05)	1·40	2·25
1374e	**576s**	51c. multicoloured (19.12.05)	1·50	2·25

Booklet panes Nos. 1350a/1350b, 1356a/1356c, 1357ca/1357cb, 1358a/1358b, 1358ca/1358cb, 1358da/1358db and 1359a have the vertical edges of the panes imperforate and each shows a margin at foot. Booklet panes Nos. 1354a/1354b, 1355a/1355b and 1357a/1357b are imperforate at top and bottom.

Booklet pane No. 1368a was printed in two vertical strips of three and one of four with the stamps within each strip separated by the die-cut perforations and the surplus self-adhesive backing paper around the stamps removed.

Due to changes in the Canada Post contracts the printing history of Nos. 1354/1359 is very complex. Details are provided below with Ashton-Potter Ltd. printings shown as AP, Canadian Bank Note Co as CBN, Leigh-Mardon Ltd as LM and Ashton-Potter Canada Ltd. as APC.

The C.B.N. printings of the 45c. (No. 1358c) show the copyright date on flag changed from '1990' to '1995'.

Postal forgeries of Nos. 1359 and 1362 exist showing heavier printing across the foot of the design.

For similar designs inscribed 'P' instead of a face value, see Nos. 2434/**MS**2450.

39c. (No. 1354) CBN (28.12.89), AP (14.2.90)
(No. 1354a/1354b) AP (28.12.89)
(No. 1354c) AP (2.90)
40c. (No. 1355) CBN (28.12.90)
(Nos. 1355a/1355b) AP (28.12.90)
42c. (No. 1356) CBN (27.12.91)
43c. (Nos. 1357/1357b) AP (30.12.92), CBN (14.11.94)
(Nos. 1357c/1357cb) LM (18.1.94)
45c. (No. 1358/1358b) LM (31.7.95)
(No. 1358c/1358cb) CBN (6.10.95)
(No. 1358d) CBN (2.2.98)
(No. 1358da) APC (2.2.98)
(No. 1358db) APC (2.2.96)
46c. (No. 1359) CBN (28.12.98)

577 Norman Bethune in 1937, and performing Operation, Montreal

578 Maple Leaf Mosaic

(Des Wanda Lewicka, J. Morin and Liu Xiang Ping. Eng Hu Zhenyuan and Yan Bingwu. Recess and litho C.B.N)

1990 (2 Mar). Birth Centenary of Dr. Norman Bethune (surgeon). T **577** and similar horiz design. Multicoloured. Fluorescent frame. Perf 13×13½.

1375		39c. Type **577**	1·75	2·25
		a. Pair. Nos. 1375/1376	3·50	4·50
1376		39c. Bethune in 1939, and treating wounded Chinese soldiers	1·75	2·25

Nos. 1375/1376 were printed together, *se-tenant*, in horizontal and vertical pairs throughout the sheet.

China issued a similar set on 3 March.

(Des B. Leduc and L.-A. Rivard. Litho Ashton-Potter)

1990 (15 Mar). Small Craft of Canada (2nd series). Early Work Boats. Horiz designs as T **563**. Multicoloured. Fluorescent frame. Perf 13½×13.

1377		39c. Fishing dory	1·10	1·50
		a. Block of 4. Nos. 1377/1380	4·00	5·50
1378		39c. Logging pointer	1·10	1·50
1379		39c. York boat	1·10	1·50
1380		39c. North canoe	1·10	1·50
1377/1380 Set of 4			4·00	5·50

Nos. 1377/1380 were printed together, *se-tenant*, throughout the sheet, giving ten blocks of four and ten single stamps.

(Des F. Peter. Recess and litho C.B.N)

1990 (5 Apr). Multiculturalism. Perf 13.

1381	**578**	39c. multicoloured	35	40
		a. Black omitted	£750	

579 Mail Van (facing left)

580 Amerindian and Inuit Dolls

(Des J. Morin and A. Rochon. Litho Ashton-Potter)

1990 (3 May). Moving the Mail. T **579** and similar horiz design. Multicoloured. Fluorescent frame. Perf 13½.

1382		39c. Type **579**	75	75
		a. Booklet pane. Nos. 1382/1383, each×4	7·00	
		b. Booklet pane. Nos. 1382×5, 1383×4 and 3 labels	17·00	
1383		39c. Mail van (facing right)	75	75

Nos. 1382/1383 were only issued in $9.75 stamp booklets No. SB128.

(Des P.-Y. Pelletier. Litho and die-stamped Ashton-Potter)

1990 (3 May). Canadian Art (3rd series). Vert design as T **550**. Multicoloured. No fluorescent bands. Perf 12½×13.

1384		50c. *The West Wind* (Tom Thomson)	1·00	1·25

No. 1384 was issued in a similar sheet format to No. 1289.

(Des Nita Wallace. Litho Ashton-Potter)

1990 (8 June). Dolls. T **580** and similar horiz designs. Multicoloured. Fluorescent frame. Perf 12½×12.

1385		39c. Type **580**	1·00	1·40
		a. Block of 4. Nos. 1385/1388	3·50	5·00
1386		39c. 19th-century settlers' dolls	1·00	1·40
1387		39c. Commercial dolls, 1917–1936	1·00	1·40
1388		39c. Commercial dolls, 1940–1960	1·00	1·40
1385/1388 Set of 4			3·50	5·00

Nos. 1385/1388 were printed together, *se-tenant*, in different combinations throughout the sheet, giving ten blocks of 4 and ten single stamps.

 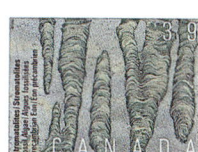

581 Canadian Flag and Fireworks

582 *Stromatolites* (fossil algae)

(Des C. Malenfant. Litho Ashton-Potter)

1990 (1 July). Canada Day. Fluorescent frame. Perf 13×12½.

1389	**581**	39c. multicoloured	50	50
		a. Silver (inscr and value) omitted	£1500	

No. 1389 was issued in sheets of 16 with descriptive texts on the coloured margins.

*First day covers of No. 1389 are postmarked 29 June 1990. The stamp was available from two temporary post offices in Ottawa on Sunday 1 July, but was not sold throughout Canada until 3 July.

(Des R. Harder. Eng Y. Baril. Recess and litho C.B.N)

1990 (12 July). Prehistoric Canada (1st series). Primitive Life. T **582** and similar horiz designs. Multicoloured. Fluorescent frame. Perf 13×13½.

1390		39c. Type **582**	1·25	1·50
		a. Block of 4. Nos. 1390/1393	4·50	5·50
1391		39c. *Opabinia regalis* (soft invertebrate)	1·25	1·50
1392		39c. *Paradoxides davidsi* (Trilobite)	1·25	1·50

CANADA

1393	39e. *Eurypterus remipes* (Sea Scorpion)		1·25	1·50
1390/1393	Set of 4		4·50	5·50

Nos. 1390/1393 were printed together, *se-tenant*, in different combinations throughout the sheet, giving four blocks of four and four single stamps.

See also Nos. 1417/1420, 1568/1571 and 1613/1616.

583 Acadian Forest **584** Clouds and Rainbow

(Des M. and Jan Waddell. Litho Ashton-Potter)

1990 (7 Aug). Canadian Forests. T **583** and similar horiz designs. Multicoloured. Fluorescent frame. Perf 12½×13.

1394	39c. Type **583**	80	90
	a. Block of 4. Nos. 1394/1397	2·75	3·00
1395	39c. Great Lakes–St. Lawrence forest	80	90
1396	39c. Pacific Coast forest	80	90
1397	39c. Boreal forest	80	90
1394/1397	Set of 4	2·75	3·00

Nos. 1394/1397 were printed together, *se-tenant*, in different combinations throughout the sheet, giving four blocks of four and four single stamps.

Nos. 1394/1397 also exist as blocks of four of the same design surrounded by margins. Such blocks were not available from post offices, but could be obtained for $1 each at Petro-Canada filling stations by using a previously-distributed voucher in conjunction with the purchase of 25 litres of petrol. They could also be obtained, at face value, from the Canadian Philatelic Service by post (*Price £6.50 per block*).

(Des D. L'Allier and Dominique Trudeau. Litho Ashton-Potter)

1990 (5 Sept). 150th Anniversary of Weather Observing in Canada. Fluorescent frame. Perf 12½×13½.

1398	**584**	39c. multicoloured	60	50

No. 1398 has a break in the lower vertical sides of the fluorescent frame to allow the clouds to run on to the margins.

585 'Alphabet' Bird **586** Sasquatch

(Des Debbie Adams. Recess and litho C.B.N)

1990 (7 Sept). International Literacy Year. Fluorescent frame. Perf 13½×13.

1399	**585**	39c. multicoloured	40	50

(Des A. Cormack, Deborah Drew-Brook and R. Tibbles. Litho Ashton-Potter)

1990 (1 Oct). Legendary Creatures. T **586** and similar horiz designs. Multicoloured. Fluorescent frame. Perf 12½×13½.

1400	39c. Type **586**	1·25	1·50
	a. Block of 4. Nos. 1400/1403	4·50	5·50
	b. Perf 12½×12	8·00	3·00
	ba. Block of 4. Nos. 1400b/1403b	40·00	25·00
	bab. Imperf (block of 4)	£1000	
1401	39c. Kraken	1·25	1·50
	b. Perf 12½×12	8·00	3·00
1402	39c. Werewolf	1·25	1·50
	b. Perf 12½×12	8·00	3·00
1403	39c. Ogopogo	1·25	1·50
	b. Perf 12½×12	8·00	3·00
1400/1403	Set of 4	4·50	5·50

Nos. 1400/1403 were printed together, *se-tenant*, in different combinations throughout the sheet, giving ten blocks of four and ten single stamps.

Stamps perforated 12½×12 come from a small percentage of the 'non-philatelic" stock without imprints. Examples have also been found on official First Day Covers included in Presentation Packs.

587 Agnes Macphail **588** *Virgin Mary with Christ Child and St John the Baptist* (Norval Morrisseau)

(Des M. and Jan Waddell. Litho Ashton-Potter)

1990 (9 Oct). Birth Centenary of Agnes Macphail (first woman elected to Parliament). Fluorescent frame. Perf 13×13½.

1404	**587**	39c. multicoloured	40	50

(Des C. Malenfant. Litho Ashton-Potter)

1990 (25 Oct). Christmas. Native Art. T **588** and similar designs. Fluorescent frame. Perf 12½×13 (34c.) or 13½ (others).

1405	34c. multicoloured (35×21 mm)	65	55
	a. Booklet pane. No. 1405×10	6·00	
1406	39c. multicoloured	30	20
	a. Booklet pane. No. 1406×10	8·00	
1407	45c. multicoloured	35	45
	a. Booklet pane. No. 1407×5 plus one printed label	4·25	
1408	78c. black, bright scarlet and violet-grey	70	75
	a. Booklet pane. No. 1408×5 plus one printed label	9·00	
1405/1408	Set of 4	1·75	1·75

Designs: 34c. *Rebirth* (Jackson Beardy); 45c. Mother and Child (Inuit sculpture, Cape Dorset); 78c. *Children of the Raven* (Bill Reid).

On No. 1405 the left-hand third of the design area is taken up by a bar code which has fluorescent bands between the bars. This value was only available from $3.40 stamp booklets, No. SB130, which had the sides and bottom of the pane imperforate. It was intended for use on greeting cards posted on or before 31 January 1991.

Booklet panes Nos. 1406a, 1407a and 1408a (from Nos. SB129 and SB131/SB132) also have the side and bottom edges imperforate.

(Des J.-P. Armanville and P.-Y. Pelletier. Litho Ashton-Potter)

1990 (9 Nov). 50th Anniversary of Second World War (2nd issue). Horiz designs as T **574**. Fluorescent frame. Perf 12½×12.

1409	39c. black, silver and grey-olive	2·00	2·25
	a. Block of 4. Nos. 1409/1412	7·25	8·00
1410	39c. black, silver and red-brown	2·00	2·25
1411	39c. black, silver and bistre-brown	2·00	2·25
1412	39c. black, silver and dull mauve	2·00	2·25
1409/1412	Set of 4	7·25	8·00

Designs: No. 1409, Canadian family at home, 1940; No. 1410, Packing parcels for the troops; No. 1411, Harvesting; No. 1412, Testing anti-gravity flying suit.

Nos. 1409/1412 were printed together, *se-tenant*, in different combinations throughout the sheet, giving four blocks of 4.

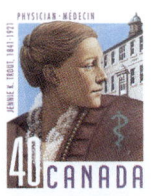
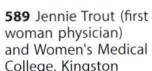 

589 Jennie Trout (first woman physician) and Women's Medical College, Kingston **590** Blue Poppies and Butchart Gardens, Victoria

(Des R. Milot. Litho Ashton-Potter)

1991 (15 Mar). Medical Pioneers. T **589** and similar vert designs. Multicoloured. Fluorescent frame. Perf 13½.

1413	40c. Type **589**	1·10	1·00
	a. Block of 4. Nos. 1413/1416	4·00	3·50
1414	40c. Wilder Penfield (neurosurgeon) and Montreal Neurological Institute	1·10	1·00
1415	40c. Frederick Banting (discoverer of insulin) and University of Toronto medical faculty	1·10	1·00
1416	40c. Harold Griffith (anesthesiologist) and Queen Elizabeth Hospital, Montreal	1·10	1·00
1413/1416	Set of 4	4·00	3·50

Nos. 1413/1416 were printed together, *se-tenant*, in different combinations throughout the sheet, giving ten blocks of four and ten single stamps.

(Des R. Harder. Eng L. Bloss. Recess and litho Ashton-Potter)

1991 (5 Apr). Prehistoric Canada (2nd series). Primitive Vertebrates. Horiz designs as T **582**. Multicoloured. Fluorescent frame. Perf 12½×13½.
1417	40c. Foord's Crossopt (*Eusthenopteron foordi*) (fish fossil)	1·75	2·00
	a. Block of 4. Nos. 1417/1420	6·25	7·25
1418	40c. *Hylonomus lyelli* (land reptile)	1·75	2·00
1419	40c. Fossil Conodonts (fossil teeth)	1·75	2·00
1420	40c. *Archaeopteris halliana* (early tree)	1·75	2·00
1417/1420 Set of 4		6·25	7·25

Nos. 1417/1420 were printed together, *se-tenant*, in different combinations throughout the sheet, giving four blocks of four and four single stamps.

(Des P-Y. Pelletier. Litho and die-stamped Ashton-Potter)

1991 (7 May). Canadian Art (4th series). Vert design as T **550**. Multicoloured. No fluorescent bands. Perf 12½×13½.
1421	50c. Forest, British Columbia (Emily Carr)	1·25	2·00

No. 1421 was issued in a similar sheet format to No. 1289.

(Des G. Gauci and D. Wyman. Litho Ashton-Potter)

1991 (22 May). Public Gardens. T **590** and similar vert designs. Multicoloured. Fluorescent frame. Perf 13×12½.
1422	40c. Type **590**	50	70
	a. Booklet pane. Nos. 1422/1426, each×2	4·50	
1423	40c. Marigolds and International Peace Garden, Boissevain	50	70
1424	40c. Lilac and Royal Botanical Gardens, Hamilton	50	70
1425	40c. Roses and Montreal Botanical Gardens	50	70
1426	40c. Rhododendrons and Halifax Public Gardens	50	70
1422/1426 Set of 5		2·25	3·25

Nos. 1422/1426 were only available from $4 stamp booklets (No. SB140) containing No. 1422a, which is imperforate at top and bottom.

593 Leaving Europe

594 Ski Patrol rescuing Climber

(Des J. Gault and T. Telmet. Litho C.B.N)

1991 (29 Aug). Centenary of Ukrainian Immigration. Panels from *The Ukrainian Pioneer* by William Kurelek. T **593** and similar vert designs. Multicoloured. Fluorescent frame. Perf 13½×13.
1437	40c. Type **593**	80	85
	a. Block of 4. Nos. 1437/1440	2·75	3·00
1438	40c. Canadian Winter	80	85
1439	40c. Clearing the Land	80	85
1440	40c. Harvest	80	85
1437/1440 Set of 4		2·75	3·00

Nos. 1437/1440 were printed together, *se-tenant*, in different combinations throughout the sheet, giving four blocks of four and four single stamps.

(Des Suzanne Duranceau. Litho C.B.N)

1991 (23 Sept). Emergency Services. T **594** and similar vert designs. Multicoloured. Fluorescent frame. Perf 13½.
1441	40c. Type **594**	2·25	2·25
	a. Block of 4. Nos. 1441/1444	8·00	9·00
1442	40c. Police at road traffic accident	2·25	2·25
1443	40c. Firemen on extending ladder	2·25	2·25
1444	40c. Boeing-Vertol CH-147 Chinook rescue helicopter and *Spindrift* (lifeboat)	2·25	2·25
1441/1444 Set of 4		8·00	9·00

Nos. 1441/1444 were printed together, *se-tenant*, in different combinations throughout the sheet, giving ten blocks of four and ten single stamps.

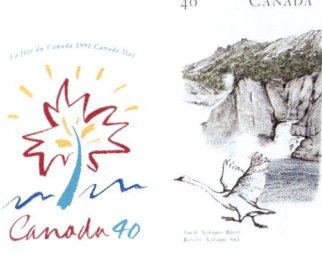

591 Maple Leaf   592 South Nahanni River

(Des Lisa Miller, R. Séguin and J.-P. Veilleux. Litho C.B.N)

1991 (28 June). Canada Day. Fluorescent frame. Perf 13½×13.
1427	**591**	40c. multicoloured	50	60

No. 1427 was issued in sheets of 20 with inscribed and decorated margins.

(Des B. Leduc and L.-A. Rivard. Litho Ashton-Potter)

1991 (18 July). Small Craft of Canada (3rd series). Horiz designs as T **563**. Multicoloured. Fluorescent frame. Perf 13½×13.
1428	40c. Verchère rowboat	1·25	1·40
	a. Block of 4. Nos. 1428/1431	4·50	5·00
1429	40c. Touring kayak	1·25	1·40
1430	40c. Sailing dinghy	1·25	1·40
1431	40c. Cedar strip canoe	1·25	1·40
1428/1431 Set of 9		4·50	5·00

Nos. 1428/1431 were printed together, *se-tenant*, throughout the sheet, giving ten blocks of four and ten single stamps.

(Des M. and Jan Waddell. Litho Ashton-Potter)

1991 (20 Aug). Canadian Rivers (1st series). T **592** and similar vert designs. Multicoloured. Fluorescent frame. Perf 13×12½.
1432	40c. Type **592**	70	1·25
	a. Booklet pane. Nos. 1432/1436, each×2 with margins all round	6·00	
1433	40c. Athabasca River	70	1·25
1434	40c. Boundary Waters, Voyageur Waterway	70	1·25
1435	40c. Jacques-Cartier River	70	1·25
1436	40c. Main River	70	1·25
1432/1436 Set of 5		3·25	5·50

Nos. 1432/1436 were only issued in $4 stamp booklets, No. SB141. See also Nos. 1492/1496, 1558/1562 and 1584/1588.

595 'he Witched Canoe'

596 Grant Hall Tower

(Des A. Cormack, Deborah Drew-Brook and R. Tibbles. Litho Ashton-Potter)

1991 (1 Oct). Canadian Folktales. T **595** and similar vert designs. Multicoloured. Fluorescent frame. Perf 13½×12½.
1445	40c. Type **595**	1·10	95
	a. Block of 4. Nos. 1445/1448	4·00	3·50
1446	40c. 'The Orphan Boy'	1·10	95
1447	40c. 'Chinook'	1·10	95
1448	40c. 'Buried Treasure'	1·10	95
1445/1448 Set of 4		4·00	3·50

Nos. 1445/1448 were printed together, *se-tenant*, in different combinations throughout the sheet, giving ten blocks of four and ten single stamps.

(Des L. Holloway and R. Kerr. Litho Ashton-Potter)

1991 (16 Oct). 150th Anniversary of Queen's University, Kingston. Fluorescent frame. Perf 13×12½.
1449	**596**	40c. multicoloured	80	1·00
		a. Booklet pane. No. 1449×10 plus two printed labels with margins all round	6·50	

No. 1449 was only issued in $4 stamp booklets, No. SB142.

CANADA

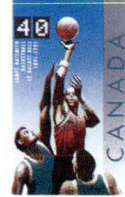

597 North American Santa Claus
598 Players jumping for Ball

(Des S. Slipp. Litho Ashton-Potter)

1991 (23 Oct). Christmas. T **597** and similar multicoloured designs. Fluorescent frame. Perf 12½×13 (35c.) or 13½ (others).

1450	35c. British Father Christmas (35×21 mm)	1·00	1·00
	a. Booklet pane. No. 1450×10	8·00	
1451	40c. Type **597**	1·00	20
	a. Booklet pane. No. 1451×10	8·00	
1452	46c. French Bonhomme Noel	1·40	1·60
	a. Booklet pane. No. 1452×5 plus one printed label	6·25	
1453	80c. Dutch Sinterklaas	2·00	3·75
	a. Booklet pane. No. 1453×5 plus one printed label	8·00	
1450/1453 Set of 4		4·75	6·00

On No. 1450 the left-hand third of the design area is taken up by a bar code which has fluorescent bands between the bars. This value was only available from $3.50 stamp booklets, No. SB144, which had the edges of the pane imperforate. It was intended for use on greeting cards posted on or before 31 January 1992.

Nos. 1451a, 1452a and 1453a (from Nos. SB143 and SB145/SB146) also have the vertical edges of the panes imperforate.

No. 1453 has been reported imperforate, its status is unknown.

(Des J. Gault, C. Reynolds and T. Telmet. Litho Ashton-Potter)

1991 (25 Oct). Basketball Centenary. T **598** and similar vert designs. Multicoloured. Fluorescent frame. Perf 13×13½.

1454	40c. Type **598**	1·50	75
MS1455	155×90 mm. 40c. Type **598**, but with shorter inscr below face value; 46c. Player taking shot; 80c. Player challenging opponent	7·50	6·50

(Des J.-P. Armanville and P.-Y. Pelletier. Litho C.B.N)

1991 (8 Nov). 50th Anniversary of Second World War (3rd issue). Horiz designs as T **574**. Fluorescent frame. Perf 13½.

1456	40c. black silver and greenish blue	2·00	2·00
	a. Block of 4. Nos. 1456/1459	7·25	7·25
1457	40c. black, silver and brown	2·00	2·00
1458	40c. black, silver and lilac	2·00	2·00
1459	40c. black, silver and ochre	2·00	2·00
1456/1459 Set of 4		7·25	7·25

Designs: No. 1456, Women's services, 1941; No. 1457, Armament factory; No. 1458, Cadets and veterans; No. 1459, Defence of Hong Kong.

Nos. 1456/1459 were printed together, *se-tenant*, in different combinations throughout the sheet, giving four blocks of four.

599 Blueberry
600 McIntosh Apple

600a Court House, Yorkton

(Des Tania Craan and D. Noble (1c. to 25c.), C. Malenfant (48c. to 90c.), R. Bellemare ($1, $2, $5))

1991 (27 Dec)–**96**. Multicoloured. Chalk-surfaced paper.

*(a) Edible Berries. Litho (for printers see below). T **599** and similar horiz designs. No fluorescent frame. Perf 13×13½ (5.8.92).*

1460	1c. Type **599**	10	10
	a. Imperf (pair)	£400	
1461	2c. Wild Strawberry	10	10
	a. Imperf (pair)	£400	
1462	3c. Black Crowberry	50	10
	a. Imperf (pair)	£400	
1463	5c. Rose Hip	10	10
	a. Imperf (pair)	£400	
1464	6c. Black Raspberry	10	10
	a. Imperf (pair)	£400	
1465	10c. Kinnikinnick	10	10
	a. Imperf (horiz pair)	£400	
1466	25c. Saskatoon Berry	25	25
	a. Imperf (pair)	£400	

*(b) Fruit and Nut Trees. Litho (for printers see below). T **600** and similar horiz designs. Three fluorescent bands (90c.) or fluorescent frame (others). Perf 13.*

1467	48c. Type **600**	50	35
	aa. Imperf (pair)	£450	
	a. Perf 14½×14	2·00	1·00
	ab. Booklet pane. No. 1467a×5 and label	8·00	
1468	49c. Delicious Apple (30.12.92)	2·50	1·00
	a. Booklet pane. No. 1468×5 and label (7.1.94)	11·00	
	b. Perf 14½×14	2·00	1·75
	ba. Booklet pane. No. 1468b×5 and label	9·00	
1469	50c. Snow Apple (25.2.94)	1·00	1·00
	a. Booklet pane. No. 1469×5 and label	7·50	
	b. Perf 14½×14 (27.3.95)	4·50	2·00
	ba. Booklet pane. No. 1469b×5 and label	15·00	
1470	52c. Gravenstein Apple (31.7.95)	1·60	1·50
	a. Booklet pane. No. 1470×5 and label	7·00	
	b. Perf 14½×14 (6.10.95)	4·50	1·00
	ba. Booklet pane. No. 1470b×5 and label	13·00	
1471	65c. Black Walnut	1·75	50
	a. Imperf (pair)	£1000	
1472	67c. Beaked Hazelnut (30.12.92)	1·75	1·25
	a. Imperf (pair)	£900	
1473	69c. Shagbark Hickory (25.2.94)	2·75	2·00
1474	71c. American Chestnut (31.7.95)	3·00	2·50
	a. Perf 14½×14 (6.10.95)	50·00	10·00
1475	84c. Stanley Plum	1·00	75
	aa. Imperf (pair)	£900	
	a. Perf 14½×14	3·00	1·50
	ab. Booklet pane. No. 1475a×5 and label	13·00	
1476	86c. Bartlett Pear (30.12.92)	2·75	1·00
	a. Booklet pane. No. 1476×5 and label (7.1.94)	12·00	
	b. Perf 14½×14	6·00	4·50
	ba. Booklet pane. No. 1476b×5 and label	18·00	
1477	88c. Westcot Apricot (25.2.94)	1·75	1·60
	a. Booklet pane. No. 1477×5 and label	11·00	
	b. Three fluorescent bands (14.11.94)	4·00	4·50
	ba. Booklet pane. No. 1477b×5 and label	17·00	
	c. Perf 14½×14. Three fluorescent bands (27.3.95)	4·50	6·00
	ca. Booklet pane. No. 1477c×5 and label	19·00	
1478	90c. Elberta Peach (31.7.95)	1·60	1·00
	a. Booklet pane. No. 1478×5 and label	7·00	
	b. Perf 14½×14 (6.10.95)	7·00	6·00
	ba. Booklet pane. No. 1478b×5 and label	19·00	

*(c) Architecture. Recess and litho Leigh-Mardon Ltd, Melbourne (Nos. 1479/1480) or C.B.N. (Nos. 1479a, 1480a, 1481). T **600a** and similar horiz designs. Perf 14½×14 ($1, $2) or 13½×13 ($5).*

1479	$1 Type **600a** (21.2.94)	2·00	60
	a. Deep turquoise-blue (recess inscr) omitted	£1000	
	b. Perf 13½×13 (20.2.95)	4·00	60
	ba. Deep turquoise-blue (recess inscr) omitted	£1000	
1480	$2 Provincial Normal School, Truro (21.2.94)	2·50	1·50
	a. Deep turquoise-blue (recess inscr) omitted	£650	
	b. Perf 13½×13 (20.2.95)	6·00	1·25
	ba. Deep turquoise-blue (recess inscr) omitted	£900	
	bb. Deep turquoise-blue (recess inscr) inverted	£4250	
1481	$5 Public Library, Victoria (29.2.96)	7·00	3·25
1460/1481 Set of 22		30·00	18·00

Nos. 1460/1466 were so printed that each horizontal row formed a composite design.

Nos. 1467a, 1468b, 1469b, 1475a, 1476b and 1477c were only issued in stamp booklets.

Booklet panes Nos. 1467ab, 1468a, 1468ba, 1475ab, 1476a, 1476ab, 1477a and 1477ba each have the vertical edges of the pane imperforate and margins at top and bottom.

CANADA

Due to changes in the Canada Post contracts the printing history of Nos. 1460/1480 is very complex. Details are provided below with Ashton-Potter Ltd printings shown as AP, Canadian Bank Note Co as CBN, Leigh-Mardon Ltd as LM and Ashton-Potter Canada Ltd as APC.

1c. No. 1460 AP (5.8.92), CBN (19.8.94), APC (3.4.95)
2c. No. 1461 AP (5.8.92), CBN (22.4.94), APC (1.8.95)
3c. No. 1462 AP (5.8.92), CBN (22.4.94), APC (2.5.97)
5c. No. 1463 AP (5.8.92), CBN (11.3.94), APC (20.9.95)
6c. No. 1464 AP (5.8.92), CBN (11.3.94)
10c. No. 1465 AP (5.8.92), CBN (11.3.94), APC (1.9.95)
25c. No. 1466 AP (5.8.92), CBN (22.4.94), APC (1.5.96)
48c. No. 1467/ab AP (27.12.91)
49c. No. 1468 AP (30.12.92), CBN (7.1.94); No. 1468a CBN (7.1.94); Nos. 1468b/1468ba AP (30.12.92)
50c. No. 1469 CBN (25.2.94), APC (10.4.95); No. 1469a CBN (25.2.94); Nos. 1469b/1469ba APC (27.3.95)
52c. No. 1470 CBN (31.7.95), APC (6.10.95); No. 1470a CBN (31.7.95), APC (1997); Nos. 1470b/1470ba APC (6.10.95)
65c. No. 1471 AP (27.12.91)
67c. No. 1472 AP (27.12.91)
69c. No. 1473 CBN (25.2.94), APC (10.4.95)
71c. No. 1474 CBN (31.7.95), APC (6.10.95); No. 1474a APC (6.10.95)
84c. Nos. 1475/1475ab AP (27.12.91)
86c. No. 1476 AP (30.12.92), CBN (7.1.94); No. 1476a CBN (7.1.94); Nos. 1476b/1476ba AP (30.12.92)
88c. Nos. 1477/1477a CBN (25.2.94); No. 1477b CBN (14.11.94), APC (10.4.95); Nos. 1477ba CBN (14.11.94); No. 1477c/1477ca APC (27.3.95)
90c. No. 1478 CBN (31.7.95), APC (6.10.95); No. 1478a CBN (31.7.95), APC (1997); Nos. 1478b/1478ba APC (6.10.95)
$1 No. 1479 LM (21.2.94); No. 1479a LM (20.2.95)
$2 No. 1480 LM (21.2.94); No. 1480a LM (20.2.95)
$5 No. 1481 CBN (29.2.96)

601 Ski Jumping

(Des Gottschalk and Ash International. Litho Ashton-Potter)

1992 (7 Feb). Winter Olympic Games, Albertville. T **601** and similar horiz designs. Multicoloured. Fluorescent frame. Perf 12½×13.

1482	42c. Type **601**	80	1·25
	a. Booklet pane. Nos. 1482/1486, each×2 with margins all round	7·00	
1483	42c. Figure skating	80	1·25
1484	42c. Ice hockey	80	1·25
1485	42c. Bobsleighing	80	1·25
1486	42c. Alpine skiing	80	1·25
1482/1486 Set of 5		3·50	5·50

Nos. 1482/1486 were only available from $4.20 stamp booklets, No. SB154.

602 Ville-Marie in 17th Century **603** Road Bed Construction and Route Map

(Des Suzanne Duranceau and P.-Y. Pelletier. Litho C.B.N)

1992 (25 Mar). CANADA 92 International Youth Stamp Exhibition, Montreal. T **602** and similar horiz designs. Multicoloured. Fluorescent frame. Perf 13½.

1487	42c. Type **602**	1·50	2·00
	a. Pair. Nos. 1487/1488	3·00	4·00
1488	42c. Modern Montreal	1·50	2·00
1489	48c. Compass rose, snow shoe and crow's nest of Cartier's ship *Grande Hermine*	2·75	1·25
1490	84c. Atlantic map, Aztec 'calendar stone' and navigational instrument	4·25	4·75
1487/1490 Set of 4		9·00	9·00
MS1491 181×120 mm. Nos. 1487/1490		11·00	13·00

Nos. 1487/1488 were printed together, *se-tenant*, in horizontal and vertical pairs throughout the sheet.

No. **MS**1491 also exists showing the facsimile signature of Paul Chomedy de Maisonneuve printed at bottom right. These miniature sheets were prepared in connection with CANADA '92, but were not sold by the Canadian Post Office. Forgeries of this sheet are known.

(Des M. and Jan Waddell. Litho Ashton-Potter)

1992 (22 Apr). Canadian Rivers (2nd series). Multicoloured designs as T **592**, but horiz. Fluorescent frame. Perf 12½×13.

1492	42c. Margaree River	1·50	1·50
	a. Booklet pane. Nos. 1492/1496, each×2	13·00	
1493	42c. West (Eliot) River	1·50	1·50
1494	42c. Ottawa River	1·50	1·50
1495	42c. Niagara River	1·50	1·50
1496	42c. South Saskatchewan River	1·50	1·50
1492/1496 Set of 5		6·75	6·75

Nos. 1492/1496 were only issued in $4.20 stamp booklets, No. SB155. Booklet pane No. 1492a has the horizontal edges of the pane imperforate.

(Des J. Charette and Vivian Laliberté. Litho C.B.N)

1992 (15 May). 50th Anniversary of Alaska Highway. Fluorescent frame. Perf 13½.

1497	**603**	42c. multicoloured	1·50	70

(Des Gottschalk and Ash International. Litho Ashton-Potter)

1992 (15 June). Olympic Games, Barcelona. Horiz designs as T **601**. Multicoloured. Fluorescent frame. Perf 12½×13.

1498	42c. Gymnastics	1·00	1·25
	a. Booklet pane. Nos. 1498/1502 each×2 with margins all round	9·00	
1499	42c. Athletics	1·00	1·25
1500	42c. Diving	1·00	1·25
1501	42c. Cycling	1·00	1·25
1502	42c. Swimming	1·00	1·25
1498/1502 Set of 5		4·50	5·50

Nos. 1498/1502 were only available from $4.20 stamp booklets, No. SB156.

604 *Quebec, Patrimoine Mondial* (A. Dumas) **605** Jerry Potts (scout)

(Des P.-Y. Pelletier. Litho Ashton-Potter)

1992 (29 June). Canada Day. Paintings. T **604** and similar diamond-shaped designs. Multicoloured. Fluorescent frame. Perf 13×12½.

1503a	42c. Type **604**	1·90	2·00
	ab. Sheetlet. Nos. 1503a/1503l	19·00	22·00
1503b	42c. *Christie Passage, Hurst Island, British Columbia* (E. J. Hughes)	1·90	2·00
1503c	42c. *Torono Landmarks of Time* (Ontario) (V. McIndoe)	1·90	2·00
1503d	42c. *Near the Forks* (Manitoba) (S. Gouthro)	1·90	2·00
1503e	42c. *Off Cape St Francis* (Newfoundland) (R. Shepherd)	1·90	2·00
1503f	42c. *Crowd at City Hall* (New Brunswick) (Molly Bobak)	1·90	2·00
1503g	42c. *Across the Tracks to Shop* (Alberta) (Janet Mitchell)	1·90	2·00
1503h	42c. *Cove Scene* (Nova Scotia) (J. Norris)	1·90	2·00
1503i	42c. *Untitled* (Saskatchewan) (D. Thauberger)	1·90	2·00
1503j	42c. *Town Life* (Yukon) (T. Harrison)	1·90	2·00
1503k	42c. *Country Scene* (Prince Edward Island) (Erica Rutherford)	1·90	2·00
1503l	42c. *Playing on an Igloo* (Northwest Territories) (Agnes Nanogak)	1·90	2·00
1503a/1503l Set of 12		20·00	22·00

No. 1503 is vacant.

(Des P.-Y. Pelletier. Litho and die-stamped Ashton-Potter)

1992 (29 June). Canadian Art (5th series). Vert design as T **550**. Multicoloured. No fluorescent bands. Perf 12½×13.

1504	50c. *Red Nasturtiums* (David Milne)	1·25	1·40

No. 1504 was issued in a similar sheet format to No. 1289.

(Des A. Cormack, Deborah Cormack and R. Tibbles. Litho Ashton-Potter)

1992 (8 Sept). Folk Heroes. T **605** and similar vert designs. Multicoloured. Fluorescent frame. Perf 12½.

1505	42c. Type **605**	1·25	1·50
	a. Block of 4. Nos. 1505/1508	4·50	5·50
1506	42c. Captain William Jackman and wreck of *Sea Clipper*, 1867	1·25	1·50
1507	42c. Laura Secord (messenger)	1·25	1·50

CANADA

	1508 42c. Jos Montferrand (lumberjack)	1·25	1·50
1505/1508 Set of 4		4·50	5·50

Nos. 1505/1508 were printed together, *se-tenant*, in different combinations throughout the sheet, giving ten blocks of four and ten single stamps.

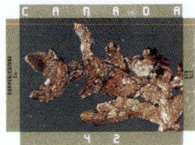 

606 Copper   **607** Satellite and Photographs from Space

(Des R. Bellemare. Litho Ashton-Potter)

1992 (21 Sept). 150th Anniversary of Geological Survey of Canada. Minerals. T **606** and similar horiz designs. Multicoloured. Fluorescent frame. Perf 12½.

1509	42c. Type **606**	1·75	2·00
	a. Booklet pane. Nos. 1509/1513, each×2 with margins all round	15·00	
1510	42c. Sodalite	1·75	2·00
1511	42c. Gold	1·75	2·00
1512	42c. Galena	1·75	2·00
1513	42c. Grossular	1·75	2·00
1509/1513 Set of 5		8·00	9·00

Nos. 1509/1513 were only issued in $4.20 stamp booklets, No. SB157.

(Des Debbie Adams. Litho C.B.N)

1992 (1 Oct). Canadian Space Programme. T **607** and similar horiz design. Multicoloured. Fluorescent frame. Perf 13.

1514	42c. Type **607**	1·25	1·75
	a. Horiz pair. Nos. 1514/1515	2·50	3·50
	b. Silver omitted	£1600	
1515	42c. Space Shuttle over Canada (hologram) (32×26 mm)	1·25	1·75
	a. Hologram omitted	£1200	

Nos. 1514/1515 were printed together, *se-tenant*, in horizontal pairs throughout the sheet of 20 with No. 1514 occurring on the first and fourth vertical rows and No. 1515 on the second and third.

608 Babe Siebert, Skates and Stick   **609** Companion of the Order of Canada Insignia

(Des L. Holloway and R. Kerr. Litho Ashton-Potter)

1992 (9 Oct). 75th Anniversary of National Ice Hockey League. T **608** and similar horiz designs. Multicoloured. Fluorescent frame. Perf 13×12½.

1516	42c. Type **608**	1·60	1·75
	a. Booklet pane. No. 1516×8 plus one printed label with margins all round	11·50	
1517	42c. Claude Provost, Terry Sawchuck and team badges	1·60	1·75
	a. Booklet pane. No. 1517×8 plus one printed label with margins all round	11·50	
1518	42c. Hockey mask, gloves and modern player	1·60	1·75
	a. Booklet pane. No. 1518×9 with margins all round	13·00	
1516/1518 Set of 3		4·25	4·75

Nos. 1516/1518 were only issued in $10.50 stamp booklets, No. SB158. Booklet pane Nos. 1516a/1518a only exist folded between the first and second vertical rows.

(Des Tania Craan. Litho Ashton-Potter)

1992 (21 Oct). 25th Anniversary of the Order of Canada and Daniel Roland Michener (former Governor-General) Commemoration. T **609** and similar vert design. Multicoloured. Fluorescent frame. Perf 12½.

1519	42c. Type **609**	1·40	2·00
	a. Pair. Nos. 1519/1520	2·75	4·00
1520	42c. Daniel Roland Michener	1·40	2·00

Nos. 1519/1520 were printed together, *se-tenant*, within the sheet of 25 (5×5) with 16 examples of No. 1519 (R. 1/1-5, 2/1, 2/5, 3/1, 3/5, 4/1, 4/5, 5/1-5) and nine of No. 1520 (R. 2/2-4, 3/2-4, 4/2-4).

(Des J.-P. Armanville and P.-Y. Pelletier. Litho C.B.N)

1992 (10 Nov). 50th Anniversary of Second World War (4th issue). Horiz designs as T **574**. Fluorescent frame. Perf 13½.

1521	42c. black, silver and sepia	2·50	2·75
	a. Block of 4. Nos. 1521/1524	9·00	10·00
1522	42c. black, silver and dull blue-green	2·50	2·75
1523	42c. black, silver and brown	2·50	2·75
1524	42c. black, silver and light blue	2·50	2·75
1521/1524 Set of 4		9·00	10·00

Designs: No. 1521, Reporters and soldiers, 1942; No. 1522, Consolidated Liberator bombers over Newfoundland; No. 1523, Dieppe raid; No. 1524, U-boat sinking merchant ship.

Nos. 1521/1524 were printed together, *se-tenant*, in different combinations throughout the sheet, giving four blocks of four.

610 Estonian Jouluvana   **611** Adelaide Hoodless (women's movement pioneer)

(Des R. MacDonald (37c.), Anita Kunz (42c.), J. Bennett (48c.), S. Ng (84c.), adapted L. Fishauf and Stephanie Power. Litho Ashton-Potter.)

1992 (13 Nov). Christmas. T **610** and similar multicoloured designs. Fluorescent frame. Perf 12½×imperf (37c.), 12½ (42c.) or 13½ (others).

1525	37c. North American Santa Claus (35×21 mm)	1·10	80
	a. Booklet pane. No. 1525×10	10·00	
1526	42c. Type **610**	40	20
	a. Perf 13½	1·25	75
	ab. Booklet pane. No. 1526a×10	11·00	
1527	48c. Italian La Befana	1·50	2·25
	a. Booklet pane. No. 1527×5 plus one printed label	9·00	
1528	84c. German Weihnachtsmann	2·25	3·25
	a. Booklet pane. No. 1528×5 plus one printed label	11·00	
1525/1528 Set of 4		4·75	6·00

On No. 1525 the left-hand third of the design area is taken up by a bar code which has fluorescent bands between the bars. This value was only available from $3.70 stamp booklets (No. SB160) which had the vertical edges of the pane imperforate. It was intended for use on greeting cards posted on or before 31 January 1993.

No. 1526a was only issued in $4.20 stamp booklets, No. SB161. Nos. 1526ab, 1527a and 1528a have the vertical edges of the panes imperforate.

No. 1528 is known imperforate, but it is not believed that it was issued in this form.

(Des Heather Cooper. Litho Ashton-Potter)

1993 (8 Mar). Prominent Canadian Women. T **611** and similar vert designs. Multicoloured. Fluorescent frame. Perf 12½.

1529	43c. Type **611**	85	1·40
	a. Block of 4. Nos. 1529/1532	3·00	5·00
1530	43c. Marie-Josephine Gérin-Lajoie (social reformer)	85	1·40
1531	43c. Pitseolak Ashoona (Inuit artist)	85	1·40
1532	43c. Helen Kinnear (lawyer)	85	1·40
1529/1532 Set of 4		3·00	5·00

Nos. 1529/1532 were printed together, *se-tenant*, in different combinations throughout the sheet, giving ten blocks of four and ten single stamps.

612 Ice Hockey Players with Cup   **613** Coverlet, New Brunswick

(Des F. Dallaire and Lise Giguère. Litho C.B.N)

1993 (16 Apr). Centenary of Stanley Cup. Fluorescent frame. Perf 13½.

1533	**612**	43c. multicoloured	1·00	60

(Des P. Adam. Litho Ashton-Potter)

1993 (30 Apr). Hand-crafted Textiles. T **613** and similar square designs. Multicoloured. Fluorescent frame. Perf 13×12½.
1534	43c. Type **613**	70	1·10
	a. Booklet pane. Nos. 1534/1538, each×2	6·50	
1535	43c. Pieced quilt, Ontario	70	1·10
1536	43c. Doukhobor bedcover, Saskatchewan ...	70	1·10
1537	43c. Ceremonial robe, Kwakwaka'wakw	70	1·10
1538	43c. Boutonné coverlet, Quebec	70	1·10
1534/1538	Set of 5	3·25	5·00

Nos. 1534/1538 were only available from $4.30 stamp booklets, No. SB169.
Booklet pane No. 1534a has the horizontal edges of the pane imperforate and margins at both left and right.

(Des P.-Y. Pelletier. Litho and die-stamped Ashton-Potter)

1993 (17 May). Canadian Art (6th series). Vert design as T **550**. Multicoloured. Fluorescent frame. Perf 12½×13.
1539	86c. *The Owl* (Kenojuak Ashevak)................	2·25	3·25

No. 1539 was issued in a similar sheet format to No. 1289.

614 Empress Hotel, Victoria

615 Algonquin Park, Ontario

(Des G. Tsetsekas. Litho Ashton-Potter)

1993 (14 June). Historic Hotels. T **614** and similar horiz designs. Multicoloured. Fluorescent frame. Perf 13½.
1540	43c. Type **614**	50	90
	a. Booklet pane. Nos. 1540/1544, each×2	4·50	
1541	43c. Banff Springs Hotel	50	90
1542	43c. Royal York Hotel, Toronto	50	90
1543	43c. Le Chateau Frontenac, Quebec	50	90
1544	43c. Algonquin Hotel, St. Andrews	50	90
1540/1544	Set of 5	2·25	4·00

Nos. 1540/1544 were only issued in $4.30 stamp booklets, No. SB170.
Booklet pane No. 1540a has the horizontal edges of the pane margins imperforate and margins at both left and right.

(Des M. and Jan Waddell. Litho C.B.N)

1993 (30 June). Canada Day. Provincial and Territorial Parks. T **615** and similar horiz designs. Multicoloured. Fluorescent frame. Perf 13.
1545	43c. Type **615**	70	1·10
	a. Sheetlet of 12. Nos. 1545/1556	7·50	12·00
1546	43c. De La Gaspésie Park, Quebec	70	1·10
1547	43c. Cedar Dunes Park, Prince Edward Island	70	1·10
1548	43c. Cape St Mary's Seabird Reserve, Newfoundland	70	1·10
1549	43c. Mount Robson Park, British Columbia ..	70	1·10
1550	43c. Writing-on-Stone Park, Alberta	70	1·10
1551	43c. Spruce Woods Park, Manitoba	70	1·10
1552	43c. Herschel Island Park, Yukon	70	1·10
1553	43c. Cypress Hills Park, Saskatchewan	70	1·10
1554	43c. The Rocks Park, New Brunswick	70	1·10
1555	43c. Blomidon Park, Nova Scotia	70	1·10
1556	43c. Katannilik Park, Northwest Territories ...	70	1·10
1545/1556	Set of 12	7·50	12·00

Nos. 1545/1556 were printed together, *se-tenant*, in sheetlets of 12, which come with or without a large illustrated and inscribed margin at top.

616 Toronto Skyscrapers

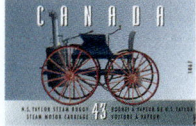
617 Taylor's Steam Buggy, 1867

(Des R. Heeney and V. McIndoe. Litho C.B.N)

1993 (6 Aug). Bicentenary of Toronto. Fluorescent frame. Perf 13½×13.
1557	**616**	43c. multicoloured	1·00	70

(Des M. and Jan Waddell. Litho Ashton-Potter)

1993 (10 Aug). Canadian Rivers (3rd series). Vert designs as T **592**. Multicoloured. Fluorescent frame. Perf 13×12½.
1558	43c. Fraser River	70	1·10
	a. Booklet pane. Nos. 1558/1562, each×2	6·00	
1559	43c. Yukon River	70	1·10
1560	43c. Red River	70	1·10
1561	43c. St Lawrence River	70	1·10
1562	43c. St John River	70	1·10
1558/1562	Set of 5	3·25	5·00

Nos. 1558/1562 were only issued in $4.30 stamp booklets, No. SB171.

(Des J. Gault, T. Telmet and C. Wykes. Litho C.B.N)

1993 (23 Aug). Historic Automobiles (1st series). Sheet, 177×125 mm, containing T **617** and similar horiz designs. Multicoloured. Fluorescent frame. Perf 12½×13.
MS1563	43c. Type **617**; 43c. Russel 'Model L' touring car, 1908; 49c. Ford 'Model T' touring car, 1914 (43×22 mm); 49c. Studebaker 'Champion Deluxe Starlight' coupe, 1950 (43×22 mm); 86c. McLaughlin-Buick '28-496 special', 1928 (43×22 mm); 86c. Gray-Dort '25 SM' luxury sedan, 1923 (43×22 mm)...	6·50	9·00

See also Nos. **MS**1611, **MS**1636 and **MS**1683/1684.

618 The Alberta Homesteader

619 Polish Swiety Mikolaj

(Des Deborah Cormack, A. Cormack and R. Tibbles. Litho Ashton-Potter)

1993 (7 Sept). Folk Songs. T **618** and similar horiz designs. Multicoloured. Fluorescent frame. Perf 12½.
1564	43c. Type **618**	70	1·00
	a. Block of 4. Nos. 1564/1567	2·50	3·50
1565	43c. *Les Raftmans* (Quebec)	70	1·00
1566	43c. *I'se the B'y that Builds the Boat* (Newfoundland)	70	1·00
1567	43c. *Onkwa:ri Tenhanonniahkwe* (Mohawk Indian)	70	1·00
1564/1567	Set of 4	2·50	3·50

Nos. 1564/1567 were printed together, *se-tenant*, in different combinations throughout the sheet, giving ten blocks of four and ten single stamps.

(Des R. Harder. Litho Ashton-Potter)

1993 (1 Oct). Prehistoric Canada (3rd series). Dinosaurs. Horiz designs as T **582**, but 40×28 mm. Multicoloured. Fluorescent frame. Perf 13½.
1568	43c. Massospondylus	80	80
	a. Block of 4. Nos. 1568/1571	2·75	2·75
1569	43c. Stryacosaurus	80	80
1570	43c. Albertosaurus	80	80
1571	43c. Platecarpus	80	80
1568/1571	Set of 4	2·75	2·75

Nos. 1568/1571 were printed together, *se-tenant*, in different combinations throughout the sheet, giving four blocks of four and four single stamps.

(Des J. Bennett (38c.), J. Jackson (43c.), B. Dawson (49c.), B. Blitt (86c.), adapted L. Fishauf and Stephanie Power. Litho C.B.N)

1993 (4 Nov). Christmas. T **619** and similar multicoloured designs. Fluorescent frame. Perf 13×imperf (38c.) or 13½ (others).
1572	38c. North American Santa Claus (35×22 mm)	70	70
	a. Booklet pane. No. 1572×10	6·00	
1573	43c. Type **619**	55	20
	a. Booklet pane. No. 1573×10	6·50	
	b. Imperf between (horiz pair).................	£500	
1574	49c. Russian Ded Moroz	1·00	1·40
	a. Booklet pane. No. 1574×5 plus one printed label	4·50	
1575	86c. Australian Father Christmas..................	1·50	2·25
	a. Booklet pane. No. 1575×5 plus one printed label	6·50	
1572/1575	Set of 4	3·25	4·00

On No. 1572 the left-hand third of the design area is taken up by a barcode which has fluorescent bands between the bars. This value was only available from $3.80 stamp booklets (No. SB173) which had the vertical edges of the pane imperforate. It was intended for use on greeting cards posted before 31 January 1994.
Nos. 1573a/1575a are from Nos. SB172 and SB174/SB175 and have the vertical edges of the panes imperforate.

CANADA

No. 1573b appears to originate from the incorrect use of the booklet pane perforation on ordinary sheet stock.

(Des J.-P. Armanville and P.-Y. Pelletier. Litho C.B.N)

1993 (8 Nov). 50th Anniversary of Second World War (5th issue). Horiz designs as T **574**. Fluorescent frame. Perf 13½.
1576		43c. black, silver and brown-olive	2·50	2·50
	a.	Block of 4. Nos. 1576/1579	9·00	9·00
1577		43c. black, silver and slate-blue	2·50	2·50
1578		43c. black, silver and dull-violet blue	2·50	2·50
1579		43c. black, silver and chestnut	2·50	2·50
1576/1579 Set of 4			9·00	9·00

Designs: No. 1576, Loading munitions for Russia, 1943; No. 1577, Loading bombs on Avro Type 683 Lancaster; No. 1578, Escorts attacking U-boat; No. 1579 Infantry advancing, Italy.

Nos. 1576/9 were printed together, *se-tenant* in different combinations throughout the sheet, giving four blocks of four.

620 (face value at right)

(Des Tarzan Communication Graphique. Litho Leigh-Mardon Ltd, Melbourne)

1994 (28 Jan). Greetings stamps. T **620** and similar horiz design. Multicoloured. Inscriptions behind face value and 'CANADA' show names of family events. Fluorescent outline. Self-adhesive. Die-cut.
1580		43c. Type **620**	55	1·00
	a.	Booklet pane. Nos. 1580/1581, each×5, and 35 circular greetings labels	5·00	
1581		43c. As Type **620**, but face value at left	55	1·00

Nos. 1580/1581 were only available from $4.50 self-adhesive booklets, No. SB181, in which the backing card formed the cover. It was intended that the sender should insert the appropriate greetings label into the circular space on each stamp before use.

For 45c. values in this design see Nos. 1654/1655.

621 Jeanne Sauvé   **622** Timothy Eaton, Toronto Store of 1869 and Merchandise

(Des J. Morin and T. Yakobina. Litho C.B.N)

1994 (8 Mar). Jeanne Sauvé (former Governor-General) Commemoration. Fluorescent frame. Perf 12½×13.
1582	**621**	43c. multicoloured	60	60

No. 1582 was printed in sheets of 20 (4×5), the horizontal rows containing four stamps, each with a differently-inscribed 6×22½ mm *se-tenant* label. These are at the right of the stamps on rows 1, 3 and 5 and at left on rows 2 and 4.

(Des L. Fishauf. Litho C.B.N)

1994 (17 Mar). 125th Anniversary of T. Eaton Company Ltd (department store group). Fluorescent frame. Perf 13½×13.
1583	**622**	43c. multicoloured	55	75
	a.	Booklet pane. No. 1583×10 and 2 labels with margins all round	5·00	

No. 1583 was only available from $4.30 stamp booklets, No. SB184.

(Des M. and Jan Waddell. Litho C.B.N)

1994 (22 Apr). Canadian Rivers (4th series). Horiz designs as T **592**. Multicoloured. Fluorescent frame. Perf 13½×13.
1584		43c. Saguenay River	55	90
	a.	Booklet pane. Nos. 1584/1588 each×2	5·00	
1585		43c. French River	55	90
1586		43c. Mackenzie River	55	90
1587		43c. Churchill River	55	90
1588		43c. Columbia River	55	90
1584/1588 Set of 5			2·50	4·00

Nos. 1584/1588 were only issued in $4.30 stamp booklets, No. SB185. Booklet pane No. 1584a has the vertical edges of the pane imperforate.

(Des P.-Y. Pelletier. Litho and die-stamped Leigh-Mardon Ltd, Melbourne)

1994 (6 May). Canadian Art (7th series). Vert design as T **550**. Multicoloured. Fluorescent frame. Perf 14×14½.
1589		88c. *Vera* (detail) (Frederick Varley)	1·25	1·75

No. 1589 was issued in a similar sheet format to No. 1289.

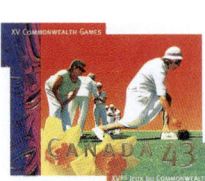

623 Lawn Bowls   **624** Mother and Baby

(Des D. Coates and R. Roodenburg. Litho and die-stamped Leigh-Mardon Ltd, Melbourne)

1994 (20 May–5 Aug). 15th Commonwealth Games. Victoria. T **623** and similar horiz designs. Multicoloured. Fluorescent frame. Perf 14.
1590		43c. Type **623**	50	70
	a.	Pair. Nos. 1590/1591	1·00	1·40
1591		43c. Lacrosse	50	70
1592		43c. Wheelchair race (5.8)	50	70
	a.	Pair. Nos. 1592/1593	1·00	1·40
1593		43c. High jumping (5.8)	50	70
1594		50c. Diving (5.8)	50	55
	a.	Gold omitted	£750	
1595		88c. Cycling (5.8)	2·25	2·00
	a.	Gold omitted	£950	
1590/1595 Set of 6			4·25	4·75

Nos. 1590/1591 and 1592/1593 were printed together, *se-tenant*, in horizontal and vertical pairs throughout the sheets.

(Des Suzanne Duranceau. Litho Leigh-Mardon Ltd, Melbourne)

1994 (2 June). International Year of the Family. Sheet 178×134 mm, containing T **624** and similar vert designs. Multicoloured. Fluorescent paper. Perf 14×14½.
MS1596	43c. Type **624**; 43c. Family outing; 43c. Grandmother and granddaughter; 43c. Computer class; 43c. Play group, nurse with patient and female lawyer	3·25	4·00

625 Big Leaf Maple Tree   **626** Billy Bishop (fighter ace) and Nieuport 17

(Des D. Noble. Litho C.B.N)

1994 (30 June). Canada Day. Maple Trees. T **625** and similar horiz designs. Multicoloured. Fluorescent frame. Perf 13×13½.
1597		43c. Type **625**	75	95
	a.	Sheetlet of 12. Nos. 1597/1608	8·00	10·50
1598		43c. Sugar Maple	75	95
1599		43c. Silver Maple	75	95
1600		43c. Striped Maple	75	95
1601		43c. Norway Maple	75	95
1602		43c. Manitoba Maple	75	95
1603		43c. Black Maple	75	95
1604		43c. Douglas Maple	75	95
1605		43c. Mountain Maple	75	95
1606		43c. Vine Maple	75	95
1607		43c. Hedge Maple	75	95
1608		43c. Red Maple	75	95
1597/1608 Set of 12			8·00	10·50

Nos. 1597/1608 were printed together, *se-tenant*, in sheetlets of 12, which come with or without a large illustrated and inscribed margin at top.

(Des P. Fontaine and B. Leduc. Litho C.B.N)

1994 (12 Aug). Birth Centenaries. T **626** and similar horiz design. Multicoloured. Fluorescent frame. Perf 13½.
1609		43c. Type **626**	1·00	1·25
	a.	Pair. Nos. 1609/1610	2·00	2·50
1610		43c. Mary Travers ('La Bolduc') (singer) and musicians	1·00	1·25

Nos. 1609/1610 were printed together, *se-tenant*, in horizontal and vertical pairs throughout the sheet.

(Des J. Gault, T. Telmet, and C. Wickes. Litho C.B.N)

1994 (19 Aug). Historic Automobiles (2nd issue). Sheet 177×125 mm, containing horiz designs as T **617**. Multicoloured. Fluorescent frame. Perf 12½×13.

MS1611 43c. Ford 'Model F60L-AMB' military ambulance, 1942–43; 43c. Winnipeg police wagon, 1925; 50c. Sicard snowblower, 1927 (43×22 mm); 50c. Bickle 'Chieftain' fire engine, 1936 (43×22 mm); 88c. St John Railway Company tramcar No. 40, 1894 (51×22 mm); 88c. Motor Coach Industries 'Courier 50 Skyview' coach, 1950 (51×22 mm).......... 8·50 10·00

No. **MS**1611 was sold in a protective pack.

627 Symbolic Aircraft, Radar Screen and Clouds

628 Carol Singing around Christmas Tree

(Des Gottschalk and Ash International, Katalin Kovats and S. Napoleone. Litho C.B.N)

1994 (16 Sept). 50th Anniversary of International Civil Aviation Organization. Fluorescent frame. Perf 13.
1612 **627** 43c. multicoloured .... 1·00 70

(Des R. Harder. Litho C.B.N)

1994 (26 Sept). Prehistoric Canada (4th series). Mammals. Multicoloured designs as T **582**, but 40×28 mm. Fluorescent frame. Perf 13½.
1613	43c. Coryphodon	1·50	1·50
	a. Block of 4. Nos. 1613/1616	5·50	6·50
1614	43c. Megacerops	1·50	1·50
1615	43c. Arctodus simus (Bear)	1·50	1·50
1616	43c. Mammuthus primigenius (Mammoth)	1·50	1·50
1613/1616 Set of 4		5·50	6·50

Nos. 1613/1616 were printed together, *se-tenant*, in different combinations throughout the sheet, giving four blocks of four and four single stamps.

(Des Nina Berkson, Diti Katona and J. Pylypczak. Litho C.B.N)

1994 (3 Nov). Christmas. T **628** and similar multicoloured designs. Fluorescent frame. Perf 13×imperf (No. 1617) or 13½ (others).
1617	(38c.) Carol singer (35×21 mm)	50	65
	a. Booklet pane. No. 1617×10	4·50	
1618	43c. Type **628**	55	20
	a. Booklet pane. No. 1618×10	5·00	
1619	50c. Choir (*vert*)	90	1·40
	a. Booklet pane. No. 1619×5 plus one printed label	4·00	
1620	88c. Couple carol singing in snow (*vert*)	1·50	2·75
	a. Booklet pane. No. 1620×5 plus one printed label	5·00	
1617/1620 Set of 4		3·00	4·50

No. 1617 was only available from $3.80 stamp booklets, No. SB187, with the vertical edges of the pane imperforate. The stamp is without face value, but was intended for use as a 38c. on internal greetings cards posted before 31 January 1995. The design shows a barcode at left with fluorescent bands between the bars.

Nos. 1617a/1620a are from booklets, Nos. SB186/SB189, and have the vertical edges of the panes imperforate.

Stamps as Nos. 1618/1620, but with face values of 45c., 52c. and 90c. were prepared, but not issued. Examples of the 52c. and 90c. are known.

(Des J.-P. Armanville and P.-Y. Pelletier. Litho C.B.N)

1994 (7 Nov). 50th Anniversary of Second World War (6th issue). Horiz designs as T **574**. Fluorescent frame. Perf 13½.
1621	43c. black, silver and dull green	2·50	2·50
	a. Block of 4. Nos. 1621/1624	9·00	9·00
1622	43c. black, silver and Venetian red	2·50	2·50
1623	43c. black, silver and light blue	2·50	2·50
1624	43c. black, silver and violet-grey	2·50	2·50
1621/1624 Set of 4		9·00	9·00

Designs: No. 1621, D-Day landings, Normandy; No. 1622, Canadian artillery, Normandy; No. 1623, Hawker Typhoons on patrol; No. 1624, Canadian infantry and disabled German self-propelled gun, Walcheren.

Nos. 1621/1624 were printed together, *se-tenant*, in different combinations throughout the sheet, giving four blocks of four.

(Des J.-P. Armanville and P.-Y. Pelletier. Litho C.B.N)

1995 (20 Mar). 50th Anniversary of Second World War (7th issue). Horiz designs as T **574**. Fluorescent frame. Perf 13½.
1625	43c. black, silver and reddish purple	2·50	2·50
	a. Block of 4. Nos. 1625/1628	9·00	9·00
1626	43c. black, silver and yellow-brown	2·50	2·50
1627	43c. black, silver and dull yellowish green	2·50	2·50
1628	43c. black, silver and light greenish blue	2·50	2·50
1625/1628 Set of 4		9·00	9·00

Designs: No. 1625, Returning troopship; No. 1626, Canadian POW's celebrating freedom; No. 1627, Canadian tank liberating Dutch town; No. 1628, Parachute drop in support of Rhine Crossing.

Nos. 1625/1628 were printed together, *se-tenant*, in different combinations throughout the sheet, giving four blocks of four.

(Des P.-Y. Pelletier. Litho and die-stamped C.B.N)

1995 (21 Apr). Canadian Art (8th series). Vert design as T **550**. Multicoloured. Fluorescent frame. Perf 13×13½.
1629	88c. *Floraison* (Alfred Pellan)	1·50	2·25
	a. Gold (frame) omitted	£1000	

No. 1629 was issued in a similar sheet format to No. 1289.

629 Flag and Lake

630 Louisbourg Harbour

(Des Gottschalk and Ash International. Litho C.B.N)

1995 (1 May). 30th Anniversary of National Flag. Fluorescent frame. Perf 13½×13.
1630	**629**	(43c.) multicoloured	1·00	50

No. 1630 is without any indication of face value, but was sold for 43c.

PRINTER. Following a change in ownership, and the awarding of a further Canada Post contract, the previous Ashton-Potter Ltd was known as Ashton Potter Canada Ltd from 1995. The imprint reverted to Ashton Potter at the beginning of 1998. From mid-2001 many Ashton Potter issues were printed in the USA.

(Des R. Harder. Litho Ashton-Potter Canada)

1995 (5 May). 275th Anniversary of Fortress of Louisbourg. T **630** and similar horiz designs. Multicoloured. 'All-over' fluorescent. Perf 12½×13.
1631		(43c.) Type **630**	55	80
		a. Booklet pane. Nos. 1631/1635 each×2 with margins all round	5·00	
1632		(43c.) Barracks (32×29 mm)	55	80
1633		(43c.) King's Bastion (40×29 mm)	55	80
1634		(43c.) Site of King's Garden, convent and hospital (56×29 mm)	55	80
1635		(43c.) Site of coastal fortifications	55	80
1631/1635 Set of 5			2·50	3·50

Nos. 1631/1635 are without any indication of face value, but were sold in booklets of ten (No. SB190) for $4.30.

(Des J. Gault, T. Telmet and C. Wykes. Litho C.B.N)

1995 (26 May). Historic Automobiles (3rd issue). Sheet 177×25 mm, containing horiz designs as T **617**. Multicoloured. Fluorescent frame. Perf 12½×13.

MS1636 43c. Cockshutt '30' farm tractor, 1950; 43c. Bombardier 'Ski-Doo Olympique 335' snowmobile, 1970; 50c. Bombardier 'B-12 CS' multi-passenger snowmobile, 1948 (43×22 mm); 50c. Gotfredson 'Model 20' farm truck, 1924 (43×22 mm); 88c. Robin-Nodwell 'RN 110' tracked carrier, 1962 (43×22 mm); 88c. Massey-Harris 'No. 21' self-propelled combine harvester, 1942 (43×22 mm)..... 6·00 9·00

No. **MS**1636 was sold in a protective pack.

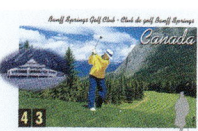

631 Banff Springs Golf Club, Alberta

CANADA

(Des P. Adam. Litho Ashton-Potter Canada)

1995 (6 June). Centenaries of Canadian Amateur Golf Championship and of the Royal Canadian Golf Association. T **631** and similar horiz designs. Fluorescent frame. Perf 13½×13.

1637	43c. Type **631**	65	80
	a. Booklet pane. Nos. 1637/1641 each×2	6·00	
1638	43c. Riverside Country Club, New Brunswick	65	80
1639	43c. Glen Abbey Golf Club, Ontario	65	80
1640	43c. Victoria Golf Club, British Columbia	65	80
1641	43c. Royal Montreal Golf Club, Quebec	65	80
1637/1641	Set of 5	3·00	3·50

Nos. 1637/1641 were only issued in $4.30 stamp booklets, No. SB191. Booklet pane No. 1637a has the vertical edges of the pane imperforate.

632 *October Gold* (Franklin Carmichael)   **633** Academy Building and Ship Plan

(Des A. Leduc. Litho C.B.N)

1995 (29 June). Canada Day. 75th Anniversary of 'Group of Seven' (artists). Miniature sheets, each 180×80 mm, containing T **632** and similar square designs. Multicoloured. Fluorescent paper. Perf 13.

MS1642a	43c. Type **632**; 43c. *From the North Shore, Lake Superior* (Lawren Harris); 43c. *Evening, Les Eboulements, Quebec* (A. Jackson)	2·50	3·50
MS1642b	43c. *Serenity, Lake of the Woods* (Frank Johnston); 43c. *A September Gale, Georgian Bay* (Arthur Lismer); 43c. *Falls, Montreal River* (J. E. H. MacDonald); 43c. *Open Window* (Frederick Varley)	2·50	3·50
MS1642c	43c. *Mill Houses* (Alfred Casson); 43c. *Pembina Valley* (Lionel FitzGerald); 43c. *The Lumberjack* (Edwin Holgate)	2·50	3·50

The three sheets were sold together in an envelope which also includes a small descriptive booklet.

(Des B. Mackay-Lyons and S. Slipp. Litho C.B.N)

1995 (29 June). Centenary of Lunenburg Academy. Fluorescent frame. Perf 13.

1643	**633** 43c. multicoloured	50	45

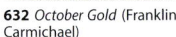

634 Aspects of Manitoba   **635** Monarch Butterfly

(Des T. Gallagher and S. Rosenberg. Litho Ashton-Potter Canada)

1995 (14 July). 125th Anniversary of Manitoba as Canadian Province. Fluorescent frame. Perf 13½×13.

1644	**634** 43c. multicoloured	50	45

Two Types of Belted Kingfisher design:
Type I. Inscr 'aune migratrice' in error.
Type II. Inscr corrected to 'faune migratrice'.

(Des Debbie Adams. Litho C.B.N)

1995 (15 Aug)–**00**. Migratory Wildlife. T **635** and similar vert designs. Fluorescent paper. Perf 13×12½.

1645	45c. Type **635**	1·10	1·40
	a. Block of 4. Nos. 1645/1646, 1648/1649	4·25	5·00
	b. Block of 4. Nos. 1647/1649 (26.9)	4·25	5·00
1646	45c. Belted Kingfisher (I)	1·10	1·40
1647	45c. Belted Kingfisher (II) (26.9)	1·10	1·40
1648	45c. Pintail	1·10	1·40
1649	45c. Hoary Bat	1·10	1·40
1645/1649	Set of 5	5·00	6·25

The inscription error on No. 1646 was corrected in a new printing issued 26 September 1995.

The four different designs were printed together, *se-tenant*, throughout the sheet, giving four blocks of four and four single stamps, showing an overall background design of migration routes.

636 Quebec Railway Bridge   **637** Mountain, Baffin Island, Polar Bear and Caribou

(Des J. Gault, T. Telmet and C. Wykes. Litho Ashton-Potter Canada)

1995 (1 Sept). 20th World Road Congress, Montreal. Bridges. T **636** and similar horiz designs. Multicoloured. Fluorescent paper. Perf 12½×13.

1650	45c. Type **636**	2·50	2·50
	a. Block of 4. Nos. 1650/1653	9·00	9·00
1651	45c. 401-403-410 Interchange, Mississauga	2·50	2·50
1652	45c. Hartland Bridge, New Brunswick	2·50	2·50
1653	45c. Alex Fraser Bridge, British Columbia	2·50	2·50
1650/1653	Set of 4	9·00	9·00

Nos. 1650/1653 were printed together, *se-tenant*, throughout the sheet, giving four blocks of four and four single stamps.

Two Types of Background to Nos. 1654/1655:

Type I. Inscriptions behind face value and 'CANADA' show names of Canadian Provinces.

Type II. Inscription behind face value and 'CANADA' show names of family events.

(Des Tarzan Communication Graphique. Litho Ashton-Potter Canada (Nos. 1654/5) or Leigh-Mardon Ltd, Melbourne (Nos. 1654b/1655b)))

1995 (1 Sept)–**96**. Greetings stamps. Horiz designs as T **620**. Multicoloured. Fluorescent outline. Self-adhesive. Die-cut.

1654	45c. Face value at right (I)	50	75
	a. Booklet pane. Nos. 1654/1655, each×5	4·75	
	b. Type II (15.1.96)	80	80
	ba. Booklet pane. Nos. 1654b and 1655b each×5	5·50	
1655	45c. Face value at left (I)	50	75
	b. Type II (15.1.96)	60	80

Nos. 1654/1655 were only available from $4.70 self-adhesive booklets, Nos. SB197 and SB205, in which the backing card formed the cover. Booklets containing Nos. 1654/1655 also include a separate pane of 15 self-adhesive labels which it was intended the sender should insert in the circular space on each stamp before use. Booklets containing Nos. 1654b/1655b included 35 circular greetings labels on the same pane as the stamps.

(Des Eskind Waddell. Litho C.B.N)

1995 (15 Sept). 50th Anniversary of Arctic Institute of North America. T **637** and similar horiz designs. Multicoloured. Fluorescent paper. Perf 13×12½.

1656	45c. Type **637**	75	1·10
	a. Booklet pane. Nos. 1656/1660, each×2, with margins all round	6·50	
1657	45c. Arctic poppy, Auyuittuq National Park and cargo canoe	75	1·10
1658	45c. Inuk man and igloo	75	1·10
1659	45c. Ogilvie Mountains, dog team and ski-equipped aeroplane	75	1·10
1660	45c. Inuit children	75	1·10
1656/1660	Set of 5	3·25	5·00

Nos. 1656/1660 were only issued in $4.50 stamp booklets, No. SB199.

638 Superman   **639** Prime Minister MacKenzie King signing UN Charter, 1945

(Des L. Fishauf. Litho Ashton-Potter Canada)

1995 (2 Oct). Comic Book Superheroes. T **638** and similar vert designs. Multicoloured. Fluorescent frame. Perf 13×12½.

1661	45c. Type **638**	50	70
	a. Booklet pane. Nos. 1661/1665, each×2, with margins all round	4·50	
1662	45c. Johnny Canuck	70	80
1663	45c. Nelvana	70	80

1664		45c. Captain Canuck	70	80
1665		45c. Fleur de Lys	70	80
1661/1665 Set of 5			2·25	3·25

Nos. 1661/1665 were only issued in $4.50 stamp booklets, No. SB200.

(Des L. Holloway and R. Kerr. Litho and die-stamped C.B.N)

1995 (24 Oct). 50th Anniversary of United Nations. Fluorescent frame. Perf 13½.

| 1666 | **639** | 45c. multicoloured | 75 | 50 |

No. 1666 was issued in sheets of ten with a large illustrated and inscribed margin at top.

640 'The Nativity'   **641** World Map and Emblem

(Des F. Dallaire. Litho Ashton-Potter Canada (40c.) or C.B.N. (others))

1995 (2 Nov). Christmas. T **640** and similar multicoloured designs showing sculptured capitals from Ste.-Anne-de-Beaupré Basilica designed by Emilé Brunet (Nos. 1668/70). Fluorescent frames. Perf 12½×13 (40c.) or 13½ (others).

1667		40c. Sprig of holly (35×22 mm)	85	70
		a. Booklet pane. No. 1667×10	8·00	
1668		45c. Type **640**	40	20
		a. Booklet pane. No. 1668×10	10·00	
1669		52c. The Annunciation	1·25	1·60
		a. Booklet pane. No. 1669×5 plus one printed label	7·25	
1670		90c. The Flight to Egypt	1·75	2·25
		a. Booklet pane. No. 1670×5 plus one printed label	10·00	
1667/1670 Set of 4			3·75	4·25

On No. 1667 the left-hand third of the design area is taken up by a barcode which has fluorescent bands between the bars. This value was only available from $4 stamp booklets, No. SB202, which had the vertical edges of the pane imperforate. It was intended for use on greetings cards posted before 31 January 1996.

Nos. 1668a/1670a (from Nos. SB201 and SB203/SB204) have the vertical edges of the panes imperforate.

(Des A. Leduc. Litho Ashton-Potter Canada)

1995 (6 Nov). 25th Anniversary of La Francophonie and The Agency for Cultural and Technical Co-operation. Fluorescent frame. Perf 13×13½.

| 1671 | **641** | 45c. multicoloured | 60 | 50 |

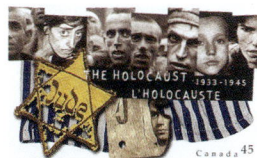

642 Concentration Camp Victims, Uniform and Identity Card

(Des Q30 Design. Litho Ashton-Potter Canada)

1995 (9 Nov). 50th Anniversary of the End of The Holocaust. Fluorescent paper. Perf 12½×13.

| 1672 | **642** | 45c. multicoloured | 70 | 50 |

Horizontal strips of No. 1672 form a continuous design which is carried over on to the vertical sheet margins.

643 American Kestrel   **644** Louis R. Desmarais (tanker), Three-dimensional Map and Radar Screen

(Des R. Bellemare and P. Leduc. Litho C.B.N)

1996 (9 Jan). Birds (1st issue). T **643** and similar horiz designs. Multicoloured. Fluorescent frame. Perf 13½.

1673		45c. Type **643**	1·60	1·60
		a. Horiz strip of 4. Nos. 1673/1676	5·75	5·75
1674		45c. Atlantic Puffin	1·60	1·60
1675		45c. Pileated Woodpecker	1·60	1·60
1676		45c. Ruby-throated Hummingbird	1·60	1·60
1673/1676 Set of 4			5·75	5·75

Nos. 1673/1676 were printed together, *se-tenant*, in panes of 12 (4×3) containing three examples of No. 1673a. Those panes intended for philatelic sale had inscribed margins so arranged as to produce a diamond-shaped format.

See also Nos. 1717/1720, 1779/1782, 1865/1872, 1974/1881 and 2058/2065.

(Des Q30 Design Inc. Litho C.B.N)

1996 (15 Feb). High Technology Industries. T **644** and similar horiz designs. Multicoloured. Fluorescent paper. Perf 13½.

1677		45c. Type **644**	45	85
		a. Booklet pane. Nos. 1677/1680, each×3	4·75	
1678		45c. Canadair Challenger 601-3R, jet engine and navigational aid	45	85
1679		45c. Map of North America and eye	45	85
1680		45c. Genetic engineering experiment and Canola (plant)	45	85
1677/1680 Set of 4			1·60	3·00

Nos. 1677/1680 were only available from $5.40 stamp booklets, No. SB206, which had the vertical edges of the pane imperforate.

(Des P-Y. Pelletier. Litho and die-stamped Ashton-Potter Canada)

1996 (30 Apr). Canadian Art (9th series). Vert design as T **550**. Multicoloured. Fluorescent paper. Perf 12½×13.

| 1681 | | 90c. *The Spirit of Haida Gwaii* (sculpture) (Bill Reid) | 1·00 | 2·00 |

No. 1681 was issued in a similar sheet format to No. 1289.

645 One World, One Hope (Joe Average)

(Des G. Tsetsekas. Litho Ashton Potter Canada)

1996 (8 May). 11th International Conference on AIDS, Vancouver. Fluorescent frame. Perf 13½.

| 1682 | **645** | 45c. multicoloured | 70 | 70 |

(Des J. Gault, T. Telmet and C. Wickes. Litho C.B.N)

1996 (8 June). Historic Automobiles (4th issue). Sheet 177×125 mm, containing horiz designs as T **617**. Multicoloured. Fluorescent frame. Perf 12½×13.

| **MS**1683 | 45c. Still Motor Co. electric van, 1899; 45c. Waterous Engine Works steam roller, 1914; 52c. International 'D.35' delivery truck, 1938; 52c. Champion road grader, 1936; 90c. White 'Model WA 122' articulated lorry, 1947 (51×22 mm); 90c. Hayes 'HDX 45-115' logging truck, 1975 (51×22 mm) | 7·50 | 9·00 |

No. **MS**1683 also includes the CAPEX '96 International Stamp Exhibition logo on the sheet margin and was sold in a protective pack.

CANADA

(Des J. Gault, T. Telmet and C. Wickes. Litho C.B.N)

1996 (8 June). CAPEX '96 International Stamp Exhibition, Toronto. Sheet, 368×182 mm, containing horiz designs as Nos. **MS**1563, **MS**1611, **MS**1636, **MS**1683, but with different face values and one new design (45c.). Fluorescent frame (45c.). Perf 12½×13.

MS1684 5c. Bombardier 'Ski-Doo Olympique 335' snowmobile, 1970; 5c. Cockshutt '30' farm tractor, 1950; 5c. Type **617**; 5c. Ford 'Model F160L-AMB' military ambulance, 1942; 5c. Still Motor Co electric van, 1895; 5c. International 'D.35' delivery truck, 1936; 5c. Russel 'Model L' touring car, 1908; 5c. Winnipeg police wagon, 1925; 5c. Waterous Engine Works steam roller, 1914; 5c. Champion road grader, 1936; 10c. White 'Model WA 122" articulated lorry, 1947 (51×22 mm); 10c. St. John Railway Company tramcar, 1894 (51×22 mm); 10c. Hayes 'HDX 45-115' logging truck, 1975 (51×22 mm); 10c. Motor Coach Industries 'Courier 50 Skyview' coach, 1950 (51×22 mm); 20c. Ford 'Model T' touring car, 1914 (43×22 mm); 20c. McLaughlin-Buick '28-496 special', 1928 (43×22 mm); 20c. Bombardier 'B-12 CS' multi-passenger snowmobile, 1948 (43×22 mm); 20c. Robin-Nodwell 'RN 110' tracked carrier, 1962 (43×22 mm); 20c. Studebaker 'Champion Deluxe Starlight' coupe, 1950 (43×22 mm); 20c. Gray-Dort '25 SM' luxury sedan, 1923 (43×22 mm); 20c. Gotfredson 'Model 20' farm truck, 1924 (43×22 mm); 20c. Massey-Harris 'No. 21' self-propelled combine-harvester, 1942 (43×22 mm); 20c. Bickle 'Chieftain' fire engine, 1936 (43×22 mm); 20c. Sicard snowblower, 1927 (43×22 mm); 45c. Bricklin 'SV-1' sports car, 1975 (51×22 mm)...... 8·00 10·00

No. **MS**1684 was sold folded within a special pack at $3.75, a premium of 40c. over the face value. It was only possible to obtain an unfolded example by purchasing an uncut press sheet, containing three miniature sheets, of which only 25000 were made available. The price quoted for No. **MS**1684 is for a folded example.

646 Skookum Jim Mason and Bonanza Creek   **647** Patchwork Quilt Maple Leaf

(Des S. Slipp. Litho and gold die-stamped Ashton-Potter Canada)

1996 (13 June). Centenary of Yukon Gold Rush. T **646** and similar horiz designs. Multicoloured. Fluorescent paper. Perf 13½.
1685	45c. Type **646**........	1·10	1·10
	a. Horiz strip of 5. Nos. 1685/1689	5·00	6·50
1686	45c. Prospector and boats on Lake Laberge.....	1·10	1·10
1687	45c. Superintendent Sam Steele (N.W.M.P.) and USA–Canada border	1·10	1·10
1688	45c. Dawson saloon..........	1·10	1·10
1689	45c. Miner with rocker box and sluice..........	1·10	1·10
1685/1689 Set of 5............		5·00	6·50

Nos. 1685/1689 were printed together, *se-tenant*, in sheetlets of ten, containing two examples of No. 1685a.

(Des R. Bellemare. Litho Ashton-Potter Canada)

1996 (28 June). Canada Day. Self-adhesive. Fluorescent frame. Die-cut.
1690	**647**	45c. multicoloured	1·00	60

No. 1690 was printed in sheets of 12 with each stamp separate on the backing paper.

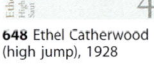

648 Ethel Catherwood (high jump), 1928   **649** Indian Totems, City Skyline, Forest and Mountains

(Des M. Koudys. Litho and die-stamped Ashton-Potter Canada)

1996 (8 July). Canadian Olympic Gold Medal Winners. T **648** and similar vert designs. Multicoloured. Fluorescent paper. Perf 13×12½.
1691	45c. Type **648**................	60	80
	a. Booklet pane. Nos. 1691/1695, each×2 with margins all round	8·50	
1692	45c. Etienne Desmarteau (56lb weight throw), 1904	60	80
1693	45c. Fanny Rosenfeld (400 metres relay), 1928	60	80
1694	45c. Gerald Ouellette (small bore rifle, prone), 1956	60	80
1695	45c. Percy Williams (100 and 200 metres), 1928	60	80
1691/1695 Set of 5............		2·75	3·50

Nos. 1691/1695 were only issued in $4.50 stamp booklets, No. SB207.

(Des M. Warburton. Litho Ashton-Potter Canada)

1996 (19 July). 125th Anniversary of British Columbia. Fluorescent paper. Perf 13×12½.
1696	**649**	45c. multicoloured	50	50

650 Canadian Heraldic Symbols   **651** *L'Arrivee d'un Train en Gare* (1896)

(Des D. Sarty and R. Gaynor. Litho Ashton-Potter Canada)

1996 (19 Aug). 22nd International Congress of Genealogical and Heraldic Sciences, Ottawa. Fluorescent paper. Perf 12½.
1697	**650**	45c. multicoloured	50	50

(Des P.-Y. Pelletier. Litho C.B.N)

1996 (22 Aug). Centenary of Cinema. Two sheets, each 180×100 mm containing T **651** and similar vert designs. Multicoloured. Self-adhesive. Fluorescent paper. Die-cut.

MS1698a 45c. Type **651**; 45c. *Back to God's Country* (1919); 45c. *Hen Hop!* (1942); 45c. *Pour la Suite du Monde* (1963); 45c. *Goin' Down the Road* (1970)........ 2·75 4·50

MS1698b 45c. *Mon Oncle Antoine* (1971); 45c. *The Apprenticeship of Duddy Kravitz* (1974); 45c. *Les Ordres* (1974); 45c. *Les Bons Debarras* (1980); 45c. *The Grey Fox* (1982)...................... 2·75 4·50

The two sheets of No. **MS**1698 were sold together in an envelope with a descriptive booklet.

652 Interlocking Jigsaw Pieces and Hands   **653** Edouard Montpetit and Montreal University

(Des Debbie Adam. Litho Ashton-Potter Canada)

1996 (9 Sept). Literacy Campaign. Fluorescent paper. Perf 13×12½.
1699	**652**	45c.+5c. multicoloured	60	1·00
		a. Booklet pane. No. 1699×10 with margins all round............	5·50	

No. 1699 has one piece of the jigsaw removed by die-cutting and was only issued in $5 stamp booklet, No. SB208.

(Des J. Beauchesne. Litho Ashton-Potter Canada)

1996 (26 Sept). Edouard Montpetit (academic) Commemoration. Fluorescent frame. Perf 12×12½.
1700	**653**	45c. multicoloured	50	50

CANADA

 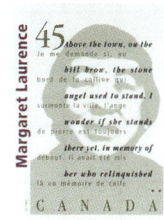

654 Winnie and Lt. Colebourn, 1914

655 Margaret Laurence

(Des Wai Poon. Litho Ashton-Potter Canada)

1996 (1 Oct). Stamp Collecting Month. Winnie the Pooh. T **654** and similar horiz designs. Multicoloured. Fluorescent frame. Perf 12½×13.
1701	45c. Type **654**		1·75	1·75
	a. Double sheetlet of 16. Nos. 1701/1704 each×4		25·00	
1702	45c. Christopher Robin Milne and teddy bear, 1925		1·75	1·75
1703	45c. Illustration from *Winnie the Pooh*, 1926		1·75	1·75
1704	45c. Winnie the Pooh at Walt Disney World, 1996		1·75	1·75
1701/1704 Set of 4			6·25	6·25
MS1705 152×112 mm. Nos. 1701/1704			6·25	6·50

Nos. 1701/1704 were printed together, *se-tenant*, as blocks of four in double sheetlets, used as a cover to 'The True Story of Winnie the Pooh" booklet.

(Des A. Leduc. Recess and litho C.B.N)

1996 (10 Oct). Canadian Authors. T **655** and similar vert designs. Fluorescent paper. Perf 13½×13.
1706	45c. multicoloured	60	1·10
	a. Booklet pane. Nos. 1706/1710 each×2	5·50	
1707	45c. black, greenish grey and scarlet-vermilion	60	1·10
1708	45c. multicoloured	60	1·10
1709	45c. multicoloured	60	1·10
1710	45c. multicoloured	60	1·10
1706/1710 Set of 5		3·00	5·00

Designs: No. 1706 Type **655**; No. 1707 Donald G. Creighton; No. 1708, Gabrielle Roy; No. 1709, Felix-Antoine Savard; No. 1710, Thomas C. Haliburton.

Nos. 1706/1710 were only issued in $4.50 stamp booklets, No. SB209, with the horizontal edges of the pane imperforate and margins at left and right.

656 Children tobogganing

657 Head of Ox

(Des T. Harrison (45c.), Pauline Paquin (52c.), Joan Bacquie (90c.). Litho C.B.N. (45c.) or Ashton Potter Canada (others))

1996 (1 Nov). Christmas. 50th Anniversary of UNICEF. T **656** and similar vert designs. Multicoloured. Fluorescent frame. Perf 13½ (45c.) or 12½×12 (others).
1711	45c. Type **656**	50	20
	a. Booklet pane. No. 1711×10	5·50	
1712	52c. Father Christmas skiing	70	1·00
	a. Perf 13½	1·00	1·00
	ab. Booklet pane. No. 1712a×5 plus one printed label	4·50	
1713	90c. Couple ice-skating	1·25	2·00
	a. Perf 13½	1·00	2·00
	ab. Booklet pane. No. 1713a×5 plus one printed label	4·50	
1711/1713 Set of 3		2·25	2·75

Nos. 1712a and 1713a were only issued in stamp booklets.
Nos. 1711a, 1712ab and 1713ab come from booklets, Nos. SB210/SB212, and have the vertical edges of the panes imperforate and margins at top and bottom.

(Des Ivy Li and Liu Xiang-Ping. Litho Ashton-Potter Canada)

1997 (7 Jan). Chinese New Year ('Year of the Ox'). Fluorescent frame. Perf 13×12½.
1714	**657**	45c. multicoloured	1·00	1·00
MS1715 155×75 mm*. No. 1714×2			2·00	2·50

*No. **MS**1715 is an extended fan shape with overall measurements as quoted.
Three examples of No. 1714, taken from the miniature sheet, have been found with the gold ('Canada, 45', etc.) omitted.

1997 (7 Jan). HONG KONG '97 International Stamp Exhibition. As No. **MS**1715, but with exhibition logo added to the sheet margin in gold. Fluorescent frame. Perf 13×12½.
MS1716 155×75 mm. No. 1714×2	7·00	9·50

(Des R. Bellemare and P. Leduc. Litho Ashton-Potter Canada)

1997 (10 Jan). Birds (2nd series). Horiz designs as T **643**. Multicoloured. Fluorescent frame. Perf 12½×13.
1717	45c. Mountain Bluebird	1·25	1·40
	a. Block of 4. Nos. 1717/1720	4·50	5·00
1718	45c. Western Grebe	1·25	1·40
1719	45c. Northern Gannet	1·25	1·40
1720	45c. Scarlet Tanager	1·25	1·40
1717/1720 Set of 4		4·50	5·00

Nos. 1717/1720 were printed together, *se-tenant*, in different combinations throughout the sheet, giving four blocks of four and four single stamps.

(Des P-Y. Pelletier. Litho and die-stamped Ashton-Potter Canada)

1997 (17 Feb). Canadian Art (10th series). Vert design as T **550**. Multicoloured. Fluorescent paper. Perf 12½×13½.
1721	90c. *York Boat on Lake Winnipeg, 1930* (Walter Phillips)	2·00	2·50

No. 1721 was issued in a similar sheet format to No. 1289.

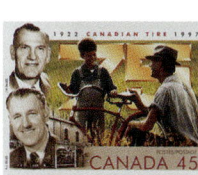 

658 Man and Boy with Bike, and A. J. and J. W. Billes (company founders)

659 Abbé Charles-Emile Gadbois

(Des Fuel Design. Litho Ashton-Potter Canada)

1997 (3 Mar). 75th Anniversary of Canadian Tire Corporation. Fluorescent frame. Perf 13×13½.
1722	**658**	45c. multicoloured	80	70

No. 1722 was printed in sheets of 12 which were supplied in special envelopes each with a pamphlet on the history of the company.

(Des Marie Lessard. Litho C.B.N)

1997 (20 Mar). Abbé Charles-Emile Gadbois (musicologist) Commemoration. Fluorescent frame. Perf 13½×13.
1723	**659**	45c. multicoloured	60	50

660 Blue Poppy

661 Nurse attending Patient

(Des C. Simard. Litho Ashton-Potter Canada)

1997 (4 Apr). Quebec in Bloom International Floral Festival. Fluorescent frame. Perf 13×12½.
1724	**660**	45c. multicoloured	50	55
		a. Booklet pane. No. 1724×12	5·50	

No. 1724 was only issued in $5.40 booklets, No. SB213. No. 1724a has the horizontal edges of the pane imperforate and margins at left and right.

(Des Margaret Issenman. Litho Ashton Potter Canada)

1997 (12 May). Centenary of Victorian Order of Nurses. Fluorescent frame. Perf 12½×13.
1725	**661**	45c. multicoloured	1·25	1·00

CANADA

662 Osgoode Hall and Seal of Law Society

663 Great White Shark

(Des L. Holloway. Litho C.B.N)

1997 (23 May). Bicentenary of Law Society of Upper Canada. Fluorescent frame. Perf 13½×13.
1726	**662**	45c. multicoloured	75	50

(Des Q30 Design. Litho Ashton-Potter Canada)

1997 (30 May). Ocean Fish. T **663** and similar horiz designs. Multicoloured. Fluorescent frame. Perf 12½×13.
1727		45c. Type **663**	1·00	1·25
		a. Block of 4. Nos. 1727/1730	3·50	4·50
1728		45c. Pacific Halibut	1·00	1·25
1729		45c. Common Sturgeon	1·00	1·25
1730		45c. Blue-finned Tuna	1·00	1·25
1727/1730 Set of 4			3·50	4·50

Nos. 1727/1730 were printed together, *se-tenant*, throughout the sheet giving four blocks of four and four single stamps.

664 Lighthouse and Confederation Bridge

(Des C. Burke and J. Hudson. Litho C.B.N)

1997 (31 May). Opening of Confederation Bridge, Northumberland Strait. T **664** and similar horiz design. Multicoloured. Fluorescent frame. Perf 12½×13.
1731		45c. Type **664**	1·40	1·00
		a. Horiz pair. Nos. 1731/1732 and centre label	2·75	2·75
1732		45c. Confederation Bridge and Great Blue Heron	1·40	1·00

Nos. 1731/1732 were printed together, horizontally *se-tenant*, in sheets of 20 (4×5) with labels measuring 16×23½ mm between vertical rows 1 and 2 and 3 and 4 which link the two designs.

665 Gilles Villeneuve in Ferrari T-3

666 Globe and the *Matthew*

(Des J. Gault and N. Skinner. Litho C.B.N)

1997 (12 June). 15th Death Anniversary of Gilles Villeneuve (racing car driver). T **665** and similar horiz design. Multicoloured. Fluorescent frame. Perf 12½×13.
1733		45c. Type **665**	75	50
1734		90c. Villeneuve in Ferrari T-4	1·25	2·00
MS1735	203×115 mm. Nos. 1733/1734 each×4		7·00	9·00

No. **MS**1735 was sold in an illustrated folder.

(Des Susan Warr. Litho Ashton-Potter Canada)

1997 (24 June). 500th Anniversary of John Cabot's Discovery of North America. Fluorescent paper. Perf 12½×13.
1736	**666**	45c. multicoloured	1·00	55

667 Sea to Sky Highway, British Columbia, and Skier

(Des L. Cable. Litho C.B.N)

1997 (30 June). Scenic Highways (1st series). T **667** and similar horiz designs. Multicoloured. Fluorescent frame. Perf 12½×13.
1737		45c. Type **667**	1·25	1·40
		a. Block of 4. Nos. 1737/1740	4·50	5·00
1738		45c. Cabot Trail, Nova Scotia, and rug-making	1·25	1·40
1739		45c. Wine route, Ontario, and glasses of wine	1·25	1·40
1740		45c. Highway 34, Saskatchewan, and cowboy	1·25	1·40
1737/1740 Set of 4			4·50	5·00

Nos. 1737/1740 were printed together, *se-tenant*, in sheets of 20 containing four blocks of four and four single stamps.

See also Nos. 1810/1813 and 1876/1879.

668 Kettle, Ski-bike, Lounger and Plastic Cases

(Des F. Dallaire. Litho C.B.N)

1997 (23 July). 20th Congress of International Council of Societies for Industrial Design. Fluorescent frame. Perf 12½×13.
1741	**668**	45c. multicoloured	60	50

No. 1741 was printed in sheets of 24 (4×6), the horizontal rows containing four stamps each with a different 11½×24 mm *se-tenant* label showing examples of Canadian industrial design. These labels are on the right of the stamps in rows 1, 3 and 5 and to the left in rows 2, 4 and 6.

669 Caber Thrower, Bagpiper, Drummer and Highland Dancer

670 Knights of Columbus Emblem

(Des F. Ross. Litho C.B.N)

1997 (1 Aug). 50th Anniversary of Glengarry Highland Games, Ontario. Fluorescent frame. Perf 12½×13.
1742	**669**	45c. multicoloured	1·00	50

(Des A. Leduc. Litho C.B.N)

1997 (5 Aug). Centenary of Knights of Columbus (welfare charity) in Canada. Fluorescent frame. Perf 13.
1743	**670**	45c. multicoloured	50	50

671 Postal and Telephone Workers with P.T.T.I. Emblem

CANADA

672 C.Y.A.P. Logo

676 Grizzly Bear

673 Paul Henderson
celebrating Goal

(Des Epicentre. Litho C.B.N)

1997 (18 Aug). 28th World Congress of Postal, Telegraph and Telephone International Staff Federation, Montreal. Fluorescent frame. Perf 13.
1744	**671**	45c. multicoloured	50	50

(Des K. Fung. Litho C.B.N)

1997 (25 Aug). Canada's Year of Asia Pacific. Fluorescent frame. Perf 13½.
1745	**672**	45c. multicoloured	1·00	50

(Des C. Vinh. Litho Ashton-Potter Canada)

1997 (20 Sept). 25th Anniversary of Canada–USSR. Ice Hockey Series. T **673** and similar horiz design. Multicoloured. Fluorescent frame. Perf 12½×13.
1746		45c. Type **673**	80	1·25
		a. Booklet pane. Nos. 1746/1747, each×5 with margins all round	7·00	
1747		45c. Canadian team celebrating	80	1·25

Nos. 1746/1747 were only issued in $4.50 stamp booklets, No. SB214, with a partial fluorescent frame around each stamp.

Examples of the booklet pane, No. 1746a, exist overprinted 'SERIES OF THE CENTURY 97-09-28 Anniversaire 25 Anniversary LA SERIE DU SIECLE' and player Paul Henderson's signature. These come from Collector Gift Sets which also included a sweatshirt, puck and print.

674 Martha Black   675 Vampire and Bat

(Des S. Hepburn. Litho C.B.N)

1997 (26 Sept). Federal Politicians. T **674** and similar vert designs. Multicoloured. Fluorescent frame. Perf 13½×13.
1748	45c. Type **674**	55	75
	a. Block of 4. Nos. 1748/1751	2·00	2·75
1749	45c. Lionel Chevrier	55	75
1750	45c. Judy LaMarsh	55	75
1751	45c. Réal Caouette	55	75
1748/1751 Set of 4		2·00	2·75

The four different designs were printed together, *se-tenant*, throughout the sheet, giving four blocks of 4 and four single stamps.

(Des L. Fishauf, J. Bennett, B. Drawson, T. Hunt, S. Ng. Litho Ashton-Potter Canada)

1997 (1 Oct). The Supernatural. Centenary of Publication of Bram Stoker's *Dracula*. T **675** and similar square designs. Multicoloured. Fluorescent paper. Perf 12½×13.
1752	45c. Type **675**	65	1·00
	a. Block of 4. Nos. 1752/1755	2·40	3·50
1753	45c. Werewolf	65	1·00
1754	45c. Ghost	65	1·00
1755	45c. Goblin	65	1·00
1752/1755 Set of 4		2·40	3·50

Nos. 1752/1755 were printed together, *se-tenant*, in blocks of four throughout the sheet.

(Des R.-R. Carmichael and Steven Slipp (No. 1756), Xerxes Irani (No. 1757), Pierre Leduc (No. 1758), Steven Slipp and B. Townsend (No. 1759), Dwayne Harty (No. 1760), Parable Communications (No. 1761), Jorge and Rodrigo Peral (No. 1761*a*), David Preston-Smith and Steven Slipp (No. 1762), A. Leduc (No. 1762*b*), Suzanne Duranceau and Fugazi (No. 1762*c*). Eng. M. Morck (No. 1759), Jorge Peral (others). Eng Martin Morck (1769), Jorge Peral (others). Recess and litho CBN)

1997 (15 Oct)–**2018**. Fauna. T **676** and similar horiz designs. Multicoloured. Fluorescent frames (1757/1758, 1760/1761, **MS**1762*d*). Perf 13½×13 (1756, 1759), 12½×13½ (1757/1758, 1760/1761, **MS**1762*d*) or 12½×13 (1761*a*, 1762/1762*c*).
1756	$1 Great Northern Diver ('Loon') (47×39 mm) (27.10.98)	1·75	1·50
	a. Chalk-surfaced paper (4.2.03)	2·75	1·25
1757	$1 White-tailed Deer (47×39 mm) (20.10.05)	2·00	2·00
	a. Pair. Nos. 1757/1758	4·00	4·00
1758	$1 Atlantic Walrus (47×39 mm) (20.10.05)	2·00	2·00
1759	$2 Polar Bear (47×39 mm) (27.10.98)	2·75	2·00
	a. Chalk-surfaced paper (4.2.03)	5·00	5·00
1760	$2 Peregrine Falcon (47×39 mm) (19.12.05)	3·50	3·50
	a. Pair. Nos. 1760/1761	7·00	7·00
1761	$2 Sable Island Horse (mare and foal) (47×39 mm) (19.12.05)	3·50	3·50
1761*a*	$4 Rocky Mountain Bighorn Sheep (47×39 mm) (10.10.18)	9·00	6·50
1762	$5 Moose (19.12.03)	11·00	8·50
	a. Brown (Moose) ptd albino	£3500	
1762*b*	$8 Type **676**	14·00	10·00
1762*c*	$10 Blue Whale (128×49 mm) (4.10.2010)	17·00	16·00
1756/1762*c* Set of 9		55·00	48·00
MS1762*d* Two sheets, each 155×130 mm. (a) Nos. 1757/1758, each×2. (b) Nos. 1760/1761, each×2 Set of 2 sheets		18·00	24·00

Nos. 1757/1758 and 1760/1761 were each printed together, *se-tenant*, in horizontal and vertical pairs in sheets of 16 stamps.

677 Our Lady of the Rosary (detail, Holy Rosary Cathedral, Vancouver)

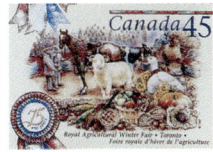

678 Livestock and Produce

(Des G. Nincheri (45c.), Ellen Simon (52c.), C. Wallis (90c.). Litho Ashton-Potter Canada)

1997 (3 Nov). Christmas. Stained Glass Windows. T **677** and similar horiz designs. Multicoloured. Fluorescent frame. Perf 12½×13.
1763	45c. Type **677**	40	20
	a. Perf 12½×imperf	50	40
	ab. Booklet pane. No. 1763×10	4·75	
1764	52c. Nativity (detail, Leith United Church, Ontario)	60	65
	a. Perf 12½×imperf	85	70
	ab. Booklet pane. No. 1764×5	3·75	
1765	90c. Life of the Blessed Virgin (detail, St Stephen's Ukrainian Catholic Church, Calgary)	1·00	1·40
	a. Perf 12½×imperf	1·00	1·25

CANADA

	ab. Booklet pane. No. 1765a×5		4·75	
1763/1765	Set of 3		1·75	2·00

Nos. 1763a/1765a were only issued in stamp booklets, Nos. SB215/SB217, with the vertical edges of the panes imperforate and margins at top and bottom.

(Des Heather Lafleur and Shelagh Armstrong. Litho C.B.N)

1997 (6 Nov). 75th Anniversary of Royal Agricultural Winter Fair, Toronto. Fluorescent frame. Perf 12½×13.

1766	678	45c. multicoloured	1·50	55

679 Tiger

680 John Robarts (Ontario, 1961–1971)

(Des R. Mah. Litho Ashton-Potter Canada)

1998 (8 Jan). Chinese New Year. Year of the Tiger. Fluorescent frame. Perf 13½×12½.

1767	679	45c. multicoloured	60	50
MS1768	130×110 mm. As No. 1767×2. Perf 13×12½		1·25	1·50

No. **MS**1768 is diamond-shaped with overall measurements as quoted. As originally issued the miniature sheet was surrounded by a plain gold margin. Examples from the 'Lunar New Year' pack issued on 28 January were additionally inscribed with design and printing information on this gold margin at foot.

(Des R. Bellemare. Litho C.B.N)

1998 (18 Feb). Canadian Provincial Premiers. T **680** and similar horiz designs. Multicoloured. Fluorescent frame. Perf 13½.

1769	45c. Type **680**	65	90
	a. Sheetlet of 10. Nos. 1769/1778	5·75	9·00
1770	45c. Jean Lesage (Quebec, 1960–1966)	65	90
1771	45c. John McNair (New Brunswick, 1940–1952)	65	90
1772	45c. Tommy Douglas (Saskatchewan, 1944–1961)	65	90
1773	45c. Joseph Smallwood (Newfoundland, 1949–1972)	65	90
1774	45c. Angus MacDonald (Nova Scotia, 1933–1940, 1945–1954)	65	90
1775	45c. W. A. C. Bennett (British Columbia, 1960–1966)	65	90
1776	45c. Ernest Manning (Alberta, 1943–1968)	65	90
1777	45c. John Bracken (Manitoba, 1922–1943)	65	90
1778	45c. J. Walter Jones (Prince Edward Island, 1943–1953)	65	90
1769/1778	Set of 10	5·75	9·00

Nos. 1769/1778 were printed together, *se-tenant*, in sheetlets of ten with illustrated margins.

(Des R. Bellemare and P. Leduc. Litho C.B.N)

1998 (13 Mar). Birds (3rd series). Horiz designs as T **643**. Multicoloured. Fluorescent frame. Perf 13×13½.

1779	45c. Hairy Woodpecker	1·40	1·25
	a. Block of 4. Nos. 1779/1782	5·00	4·50
1780	45c. Great Crested Flycatcher	1·40	1·25
1781	45c. Eastern Screech Owl	1·40	1·25
1782	45c. Gray-crowned Rosy-finch	1·40	1·25
1779/1782	Set of 4	5·00	4·50

Nos. 1779/1782 were printed together *se-tenant* in different combinations throughout the sheet, giving four blocks of four and four single stamps.

681 Maple Leaf

682 Coquihalla Orange Fly

(Des Gottschalk and Ash. Litho Avery Dennison, USA)

1998 (14 Apr). Self-adhesive. Automatic Cash Machine Stamp. Fluorescent paper. Die-cut.

1783	681	45c. multicoloured	45	1·00

No. 1783 was issued, in sheets of 18 (3×6), from bank automatic cash machines and philatelic centres.

For stamps in this design, but without 'POSTAGE POSTES' at top left see Nos. 1836/1840.

(Des P. Brunelle. Litho Ashton Potter Canada)

1998 (16 Apr). Fishing Flies. T **682** and similar horiz designs. Multicoloured. Fluorescent frame. Perf 12½×13.

1784	45c. Type **682**	60	75
	a. Booklet pane. Nos. 1784/1789, each×2	6·00	
1785	45c. Steelhead Bee	60	75
1786	45c. Dark Montréal	60	75
1787	45c. Lady Amherst	60	75
1788	45c. Coho Blue	60	75
1789	45c. Cosseboom Special	60	75
1784/1789	Set of 6	3·25	4·00

Nos. 1784/1789 were only issued in stamp booklets, No. SB220, containing pane No. 1784a which incorporates an inscribed margin at left.

683 Mineral and Petroleum Excavation and Pickaxe

684 1898 2c. Imperial Penny Postage Stamp and Postmaster General Sir William Mulock

(Des Monique Dufour and Sophie Lafortune. Litho Ashton Potter Canada)

1998 (4 May). Centenary of Canadian Institute of Mining, Metallurgy and Petroleum. Fluorescent frame. Perf 12½.

1790	683	45c. multicoloured	70	50

(Des F. Dallaire. Litho C.B.N)

1998 (29 May). Centenary of Imperial Penny Postage. Fluorescent frame. Perf 12½×13.

1791	684	45c. multicoloured	1·00	1·00

No. 1791 was printed in sheets of 14 stamps with a label showing the Imperial State Crown appearing in the centre of the sheet.

685 Two Sumo Wrestlers

686 St Peters Canal, Nova Scotia

(Des G. Takeuchi and S. Dittberner. Litho and embossed Ashton Potter Canada)

1998 (5 June). First Canadian Sumo Basho (tournament), Vancouver. T **685** and similar horiz design. Multicoloured. Fluorescent frame. Perf 12½×13.

1792	45c. Type **685**	65	75
	a. Pair. Nos. 1792/1793	1·25	1·50
1793	45c. Sumo wrestler in ceremonial ritual	65	75
MS1794	84×152 mm. Nos. 1792/1793	3·50	4·00

On Nos. 1792/1794 the outlines of the wrestlers are embossed.

Nos. 1792/1793 were printed together, *se-tenant*, both horizontally and vertically in sheets of 20 (4×5). The horizontal rows include labels 7×30 mm either side of each stamp with that on the left inscribed in English and that on the right in Japanese.

(Des V. McIndoe, G. George and D. Martin. Litho Ashton-Potter Canada)

1998 (17 June). Canadian Canals. T **686** and similar vert designs. Multicoloured. Fluorescent frame. Perf 12½.

1795	45c. Type **686**	80	1·40
	a. Booklet pane. Nos. 1795/1804 and 10 stamp-size labels	7·00	
1796	45c. St Ours Canal, Quebec	80	1·40
1797	45c. Port Carling Lock, Ontario	80	1·40
1798	45c. Lock on Rideau Canal, Ontario	80	1·40
1799	45c. Towers and platform of Peterborough Lift Lock, Trent–Severn Waterway, Ontario	80	1·40
1800	45c. Chambly Canal, Quebec	80	1·40
1801	45c. Lachine Canal, Quebec	80	1·40
1802	45c. Rideau Canal in winter, Ontario	80	1·40
1803	45c. Boat on Big Chute incline railway, Trent–Severn Waterway, Ontario	80	1·40

1804	45c. Sault Ste Marie Canal, Ontario		80	1·40
1795/1804 Set of 10			7·00	12·50

Nos. 1795/1804 were only issued in $4.50 stamp booklets, No. SB221, with the ten labels in the pane providing a location map for the canals depicted.

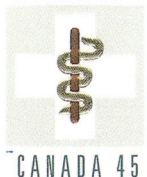 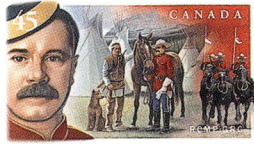

687 Staff of Aesculapius and Cross

688 Policeman of 1873 and Visit to Indian Village

(Des P.-Y. Pelletier. Typo (embossed) and litho Ashton-Potter Canada)

1998 (25 June). Canadian Health Professionals. Fluorescent paper. Perf 12½.

1805	**687**	45c. multicoloured	1·00	1·00

(Des A. Valko and Circle Design. Litho (No. 1808 also embossed) Ashton-Potter Canada)

1998 (3 July). 125th Anniversary of Royal Canadian Mounted Police. T **688** and similar horiz design. Multicoloured. Fluorescent frame. Perf 12½×13.

1806		45c. Type **688**	90	90
	a. Horiz pair. Nos. 1806/1807 with label....		1·75	1·75
1807		45c. Policewoman of 1998 and aspects of modern law enforcement	90	90
MS1808 160×102 mm. Nos. 1806/1807			1·75	1·90

Nos. 1806/1807 were printed together, *se-tenant*, in pairs both horizontally and vertically, throughout the sheet of 20 (4×5). The horizontal rows include labels, 15×26 mm, on either side of each stamp. There are two label designs, one showing the R.C.M.P. crest and the other the Musical Ride which continues the design shown on the two stamps.

No. **MS**1808 also exists from a limited printing with the facsimile signature of Lieut-Col. G. A. French, the first commissioner, added to the bottom margin.

No. **MS**1808 was also issued overprinted with the logos of 'Portugal 98' or 'Italia 98' for sale at these International Stamp Exhibitions.

 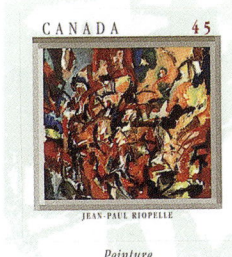

689 William J. Roue (designer) and *Bluenose* (schooner)

690 Painting (Jean-Paul Riopelle)

(Des L. Herbert. Recess and litho C.B.N)

1998 (24 July). William James Roue (naval architect) Commemoration. Fluorescent frame. Perf 13.

1809	**689**	45c. multicoloured	70	50

(Des L. Cable. Litho Ashton-Potter Canada)

1998 (28 July). Scenic Highways (2nd series). Horiz designs as T **667**. Multicoloured. Fluorescent frame. Perf 12½×13.

1810		45c. Dempster Highway, Yukon, and caribou	65	75
	a. Block of 4. Nos. 1810/1813		2·40	3·50
1811		45c. Dinosaur Trail, Alberta, and skeleton.....	65	75
1812		45c. River Valley Drive, New Brunswick, and fern	65	75
1813		45c. Blue Heron Route, Prince Edward Island, and lobster	65	75
1810/1813 Set of 4			2·50	3·50

Nos. 1810/1813 were printed together, *se-tenant*, in sheets of 20 containing four blocks of four and four single stamps.

CANADA

(Des R. Bellemare. Litho C.B.N)

1998 (7 Aug). 50th Anniversary of *Refus Global* (manifesto of The Automatistes group of artists). T **690** and similar multicoloured designs. Self-adhesive. Fluorescent frame. Die-cut.

1814		45c. Type **690**	80	1·25
	a. Booklet pane. Nos. 1814/1820		5·00	
1815		45c. La dernière campagne de Napoléon (Fernand Leduc) (37×31½ mm)	80	1·25
1816		45c. Jet fuligineux sur noir torture (Jean-Paul Mousseau)	80	1·25
1817		45c. Le fond du garde-robe (Pierre Gauvreau) (29½×42 mm)	80	1·25
1818		45c. Joie lacustre (Paul-Emile Borduas).........	80	1·25
1819		45c. Seafarers Union (Marcelle Ferron) (36×34 mm)	80	1·25
1820		45c. Le tumulte à la mâchoire crispée (Marcel Barbeau) (36×34 mm)	80	1·25
1814/1820 Set of 7			5·00	8·00

Nos. 1814/1820 were only available from $3.15 self-adhesive booklets, No. SB222, in which the backing card formed the cover.

691 Napoléon Alexandre Comeau (naturalist)

692 Indian Wigwam

(Des Catherine Bradbury and D. Bartsch. Litho C.B.N)

1998 (15 Aug). Legendary Canadians. T **691** and similar vert designs. Multicoloured. Fluorescent frame. Perf 13½.

1821		45c. Type **691**	45	60
	a. Block of 4. Nos. 1821/1824		1·60	2·25
1822		45c. Phyllis Munday (mountaineer)	45	60
1823		45c. Bill Mason (film-maker)	45	60
1824		45c. Harry Red Foster (sports commentator)	45	60
1821/1824 Set of 4			1·60	2·25

Nos. 1821/1824 were printed together, *se-tenant*, in sheets of 20 containing four blocks of four and four single stamps.

(Des P.-Y. Pelletier. Litho and die-stamped Ashton Potter Canada)

1998 (8 Sept). Canadian Art (11th series). Vert design as T **550**. Multicoloured. Fluorescent frame. Perf 12½×13.

1825		90c. *The Farmer's Family* (Bruno Bobak)	1·00	2·00

No. 1825 was issued in a similar sheet format to No. 1289.

(Des C. Gibson and P. Scott. Litho Ashton Potter Canada)

1998 (23 Sept). Canadian Houses. T **692** and similar horiz designs. Multicoloured. Fluorescent frame. Perf 12½×13.

1826		45c. Type **692**	70	1·00
	a. Sheetlet of 9. Nos. 1826/1834		5·50	9·00
1827		45c. Settler sod hut	70	1·00
1828		45c. Maison Saint-Gabriel (17th-century farmhouse), Quebec	70	1·00
1829		45c. Queen Anne style brick house, Ontario	70	1·00
1830		45c. Terrace of town houses	70	1·00
1831		45c. Prefabricated house	70	1·00
1832		45c. Veterans' houses	70	1·00
1833		45c. Modern bungalow	70	1·00
1834		45c. Healthy House, Toronto	70	1·00
1826/1834 Set of 9			5·50	9·00

Nos. 1826/1834 were printed together, *se-tenant*, in sheetlets of nine with additional side margins carrying design descriptions.

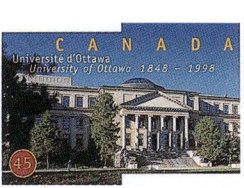 

693 University of Ottawa

694 Performing Animals

CANADA

(Des Harris Design Associates. Litho C.B.N)

1998 (25 Sept). 150th Anniversary of University of Ottawa. Fluorescent frame. Perf 13½.
1835	**693**	45c. multicoloured	50	50

1998 (30 Sept–28 Dec). As T **681**, but without 'POSTAGE POSTES' at top left.

(a) Litho Ashton Potter Canada. Fluorescent frame. Perf 13×13½.
1836	**681**	55c. multicoloured (28.12)	1·75	2·00
		a. Booklet pane. No. 1836×5 plus printed label	8·00	
1837		73c. multicoloured (28.12)	1·25	1·25
1838		95c. multicoloured (28.12)	2·50	2·75
		a. Booklet pane. No. 1838×5 plus printed label	11·00	

(b) Coil stamp. Litho and die-stamped (gold) Ashton Potter Canada. Fluorescent frame. Perf 13.
1839	**681**	45c. multicoloured	1·25	1·25

(c) Self-adhesive automatic cash machine stamp. Litho Avery Dennison, USA. Fluorescent paper. Die-cut.
1840	**681**	46c. multicoloured (28.12)	1·10	1·25

Booklet panes Nos. 1836a and 1838a come from SB229/SB230 and have the vertical edges of the panes imperforate and margins at top and bottom.

No. 1839 was available in rolls of 100 on which the surplus self-adhesive paper around each stamp was removed.

No. 1840 was issued in sheets of 18 (3×6), from bank automatic cash machines and philatelic centres.

(Des Monique Dufour, Sophie Lafortune and Paule Thibault. Litho Ashton-Potter Canada)

1998 (1 Oct). Canadian Circus. T **694** and similar vert designs, each incorporating a different clown. Multicoloured. Fluorescent frame. Perf 13.
1851	45c. Type **694**	80	1·10
	a. Booklet pane. Nos. 1851/1854, each×3	8·50	
1852	45c. Flying trapeze and acrobat on horseback	80	1·10
1853	45c. Lion tamer	80	1·10
1854	45c. Acrobats and trapeze artists	80	1·10
1851/1854 Set of 4		3·00	4·00
MS1855 133×133 mm. Nos. 1851/1854		4·25	5·00

Nos. 1851/1854 only exist from $5.40 booklets, No. SB223, in which the upper and lower edges of the pane are imperforate.

The fluorescent frames on Nos. 1851/1854 are broken at various points where the designs encroach onto the margins.

695 John Peters Humphrey (author of original Declaration draft)

(Des J. Hudson. Litho C.B.N)

1998 (7 Oct). 50th Anniversary of Universal Declaration of Human Rights. Fluorescent frame. Perf 13×13½.
1856	**695**	45c. multicoloured	50	50

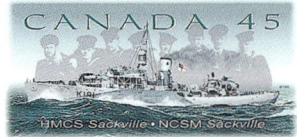

696 HMCS *Sackville* (corvette)

(Des T. Hawkins and D. Page. Litho C.B.N)

1998 (4 Nov). 75th Anniversary of Canadian Naval Reserve. T **696** and similar horiz design. Multicoloured. Fluorescent frame. Perf 12½×13.
1857	45c. Type **696**	80	1·00
	a. Pair. Nos. 1857/1858	1·60	2·00
1858	45c. HMCS *Shawinigan* (coastal defence vessel)	80	1·00

Nos. 1857/1858 were printed together, *se-tenant*, in horizontal and vertical pairs throughout the sheet.

 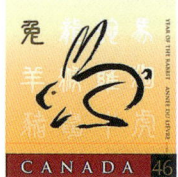

697 Angel blowing Trumpet   **698** Rabbit

(Des Anita Zeppetelli. Litho Ashton Potter Canada)

1998 (6 Nov). Christmas. Statues of Angels. T **697** and similar vert designs. Multicoloured. Fluorescent frame. Perf 13 (45c.) or 13×13½ (others).
1859	45c. Type **697**	50	20
	a. Booklet pane. No. 1859×10	7·00	
	b. Perf 13×13½	1·75	1·40
	ba. Booklet pane. No. 1859b×10	16·00	
1860	52c. Adoring Angel	1·40	1·50
	a. Booklet pane. No. 1860×5 plus one printed label	7·50	
	b. Perf 13	1·75	75
	ba. Booklet pane. No. 1860b×5 plus one printed label	3·75	
1861	90c. Angel at prayer	3·25	3·50
	a. Booklet pane. No. 1861×5 plus one printed label	15·00	
	b. Perf 13	2·00	2·00
	ba. Booklet pane. No. 1861b×5 plus one printed label	7·50	
1859/1861 Set of 3		2·40	2·50

Nos. 1860b and 1861b only come from stamp booklets. Sheets of the 45c. are known in either perforation, but sheet stamps in the 13×13½ gauge are rare (*Price £300 mint for example with perforations on all four sides*).

The booklet panes come from Nos. SB224/SB226a and show vertical edges of the panes imperforate and margins at top and bottom.

(Des K. Koo and K. Fung. Litho Ashton-Potter Canada)

1999 (8 Jan). Chinese New Year. Year of the Rabbit. Fluorescent frame. Perf 13½.
1862	**698**	46c. multicoloured	50	50
		a. Red omitted	£500	
MS1863 Circular 100 mm diameter. **698** 95c. multicoloured (40×40 mm). Perf 12½×13			1·75	2·25

No. **MS**1863 also exists with the CHINA '99 World Stamp Exhibition, Beijing, logo overprinted in gold on the top of the margin.

The omission of the colour causes the background to appear yellow rather than orange.

No. **MS**1863 has also been reported with the red omitted.

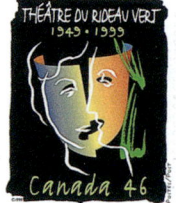 

699 Stylized Mask and Curtain   **700** *The Raven and the First Men* (B. Reid) and The Great Hall

(Des Y. Paquin and Marie Rouleau. Litho C.B.N)

1999 (16 Feb). 50th Anniversary of Le Théâtre du Rideau. Fluorescent frame. Perf 13×12½.
1864	**699**	46c. multicoloured	50	50

(Des R. Bellemare and P. Leduc. Litho Ashton-Potter Canada)

1999 (24 Feb). Birds (4th series). Horiz designs as T **643**. Multicoloured. Fluorescent frame.

(a) Perf 12½×13.
1865	46c. Northern Goshawk	85	1·00
	a. Block of 4. Nos. 1865/1868	3·00	3·50
1866	46c. Red-winged Blackbird	85	1·00
1867	46c. American Goldfinch	85	1·00
1868	46c. Sandhill Crane	85	1·00
1865/1868 Set of 4		3·00	3·50

(b) Self-adhesive. Perf 11½.
1869	46c. Northern Goshawk	1·25	1·50
	b. Booklet pane. Nos. 1869/1872, each×3, with margins all round	10·00	
1870	46c. Red-winged Blackbird	1·25	1·50
1871	46c. American Goldfinch	1·25	1·50

1872		46c. Sandhill Crane	1·25	1·50
1869/1872		Set of 4	4·50	5·50

Nos. 1865/1868 were printed together *se-tenant* in different combinations throughout the sheet, giving four blocks of four and four single stamps.

Nos. 1869/1872 were only issued in $5.52 stamp booklets, No. SB231, on which the surplus self-adhesive paper was retained.

(Des Barbara Hodgson. Litho C.B.N)

1999 (9 Mar). 50th Anniversary of University of British Columbia Museum of Anthropology. Fluorescent frame. Perf 13½.

1873	**700**	46c. multicoloured	50	50

701 *Marco Polo* (full-rigged ship)   **702** Inuit Children and Landscape

(Des J. Franklin Wright. Litho Ashton-Potter Canada)

1999 (19 Mar). Canada–Australia Joint Issue. *Marco Polo* (emigrant ship). Multicoloured. Fluorescent frame. Perf 13×12½.

1874		46c. Type **701**	70	50
MS1875		160×95 mm. 85c. As No. 1728 of Australia. Perf 13; 46c. Type **701**. Perf 13½ (No. **MS**1875 was sold at $1.25 in Canada)	2·00	2·75

No. **MS**1875 includes the Australia '99 emblem on the sheet margin and was postally valid in Canada to the value of 46c.

The same miniature sheet was also available in Australia.

(Des L. Cable. Litho Ashton-Potter Canada)

1999 (31 Mar). Scenic Highways (3rd series). Horiz designs as T **667**. Multicoloured. Fluorescent frame. Perf 12½×13.

1876		46c. Route 132, Quebec, and hang-glider	75	1·00
		a. Block of 4. Nos. 1876/1879	2·75	3·50
1877		46c. Yellowhead Highway, Manitoba, and Bison	75	1·00
1878		46c. Dempster Highway, Northwest Territories, and Indian village elder	75	1·00
1879		46c. The Discovery Trail, Newfoundland, and whale's tailfin	75	1·00
1876/1879		Set of 4	2·75	3·50

Nos. 1876/1879 were printed together, *se-tenant*, in sheets of 20 comprising four blocks of four and four single stamps.

(Des Susan Point and Bonne Zabolotney. Litho Ashton-Potter Canada)

1999 (1 Apr). Creation of Nunavut Territory. Fluorescent frame. Perf 12½×13.

1880	**702**	46c. multicoloured	50	50

703 Elderly Couple on Country Path   **704** Khanda (Sikh symbol)

(Des Sheila Armstrong-Hodgson, P. Hodgson and S. Peters. Litho C.B.N)

1999 (12 Apr). International Year of Older Persons. Fluorescent frame. Perf 13½.

1881	**703**	46c. multicoloured	50	50

(Des S. Zabolotney. Litho C.B.N)

1999 (19 Apr). Tercentenary of the Khalsa Panth (Sikh order). Interrupted fluorescent frame. Perf 13.

1882	**704**	46c. multicoloured	1·00	50

705 *Arethusa bulbosa* (orchid)   **706** Bookbinding

(Des Marlene Wou, Poon Kuen Chow and Y. Lai. Litho Ashton-Potter Canada)

1999 (27 Apr). 16th World Orchid Conference, Vancouver. T **705** and similar vert designs. Multicoloured. Fluorescent frame. Perf 13×12½.

1883		46c. Type **705**	60	85
		a. Booklet pane. Nos. 1883/1886, each×3, with margins all round	6·50	
1884		46c. *Amerorchis rotundifolia*	60	85
1885		46c. *Cypripedium pubescens*	60	85
1886		46c. *Platanthera psycodes*	60	85
1883/1886		Set of 4	2·25	3·00

Nos. 1883/1886 were initially only issued in $5.52 stamp booklets, No. SB232, but later appeared in No. **MS**1917.

(Des Monique Dufour and Sophie Lafortune. Litho Ashton-Potter Canada or C.B.N (1c., 5c., 10c., 25c.) or Ashton-Potter Canada (others))

1999 (29 Apr)–**02**. Traditional Trades. T **706** and similar vert designs. Multicoloured.

(a) No fluorescent frame. Perf 13×13½.

1887		1c. Type **706**	10	20
1888		2c. Decorative ironwork	10	20
1889		3c. Glass-blowing	10	20
1890		4c. Oyster farming	10	20
		a. Imperf (pair)	£500	
1891		5c. Weaving	10	20
1892		9c. Quilting	15	20
1893		10c. Wood carving	15	20
		a. Imperf (pair)	£750	
1894		25c. Leatherworking	40	25
1887/1894		Set of 8	1·00	1·50

(b) Self-adhesive. Chalk-surfaced paper. Fluorescent frame. Die-cut perf 9×imperf.

1895		65c. Jewellery making (*horiz*) (2.1.02)	50	65
		a. Pane of 6	2·50	
1896		77c. Basket-weaving (*horiz*) (2.1.02)	1·50	1·75
1897		$1.25 Wood-carving (*horiz*) (2.1.02)	1·00	1·40
		a. Pane of 6	5·50	
1895/1897		Set of 3	2·75	3·50

Nos. 1895/1897 were issued in coils of 50, with the surplus self-adhesive paper between each stamp removed, or as panes of 6 (65c., $1.25 only) where the surplus paper was retained.

Nos. 1898/1902 are vacant.

707 Northern Dancer (racehorse)   **708** Logo engraved on Limestone

(Des P.-Y. Pelletier. Litho Ashton-Potter Canada)

1999 (2 June). Canadian Horses. T **707** and similar horiz designs. Multicoloured. Fluorescent frame.

(a) Perf 13×13½.

1903		46c. Type **707**	80	1·10
		a. Block of 4. Nos. 1903/1906	3·00	4·00
1904		46c. Kingsway Skoal (rodeo horse)	80	1·10
1905		46c. Big Ben (show jumper)	80	1·10
1906		46c. Armbro Flight (trotter)	80	1·10
1903/1906		Set of 4	3·00	4·00

(b) Self-adhesive. Perf 11½×11.

1907		46c. Type **707**	70	90
		a. Booklet pane. Nos. 1907/1910, each×3, with margins all round	6·50	
1908		46c. Kingsway Skoal (rodeo horse)	70	90

CANADA

1909		46c. Big Ben (show jumper)		70	90
1910		46c. Armbro Flight (trotter)		70	90
1907/1910 Set of 4				2·50	3·25

Nos. 1903/1906 were printed together, *se-tenant*, in blocks of four throughout sheets of 16.

Nos. 1907/1910 were only issued in $5.52 stamp booklets, No. SB233, on which the surplus self-adhesive paper was retained.

(Des P. Fontaine. Litho C.B.N)

1999 (3 June). 150th Anniversary of Barreau du Québec (Quebec lawyers' association). Fluorescent frame. Perf 13½.

1911	708	46c. multicoloured		50	50

(Des P.-Y. Pelletier. Litho and die-stamped Ashton-Potter Canada)

1999 (3 July). Canadian Art (12th series). Vert design as T 550. Multicoloured. Fluorescent inner frame. Perf 12½×13.

1912		95c. Coq licorne (Jean Dallaire)		1·25	1·75
		a. Silver omitted		£1300	

No. 1912 was issued in a similar sheet format to No. 1289.

709 Athletics

(Des Circle Design. Litho Ashton-Potter Canada)

1999 (12 July). 13th Pan-American Games, Winnipeg. T **709** and similar square designs. Multicoloured. Fluorescent frame. Perf 13½.

1913		46c. Type **709**		85	90
		a. Block of 4. Nos. 1913/1916		3·00	3·25
1914		46c. Cycling		85	90
1915		46c. Swimming		85	90
1916		46c. Football		85	90
1913/1916 Set of 4				3·00	3·25

Nos. 1913/1916 were printed together, *se-tenant*, as blocks of four in sheets of 16.

(Des Chris Dahl Design, Poon Kuen Chow and Y. Lai. Litho Ashton-Potter Canada)

1999 (21 Aug). China '99 International Stamp Exhibition, Beijing. Sheet 78×133 mm, containing Nos. 1883/1886. Multicoloured. Fluorescent frame. Perf 13×12½.

MS1917	46c. Type **705**; 46c. *Amerorchis rotundifolia*; 46c. *Cypripedium pubescens*; 46c. *Platanthera psycodes*		2·25	4·00

710 Female Rower

(Des P. Haslip and A. Lum. Litho Ashton-Potter Canada)

1999 (22 Aug). 23rd World Rowing Championships, St. Catharines. Fluorescent frame. Perf 12½×13.

1918	710	46c. multicoloured		50	50

711 UPU Emblem and World Map

(Des P.-Y. Pelletier. Litho C.B.N)

1999 (26 Aug). 125th Anniversary of Universal Postal Union. Fluorescent frame. Perf 12½×13.

1919	711	46c. multicoloured		75	50

712 de Havilland Mosquito F.B. VI

(Des T. Telmet, M. Barac and G. Lay. Litho C.B.N)

1999 (4 Sept). 75th Anniversary of Canadian Air Force. T **712** and similar horiz designs. Multicoloured. Fluorescent frame. Perf 12½×13.

1920		46c. Type **712**	1·00	1·00
		a. Sheetlet of 16. Nos. 1920/1935	13·00	16·00
1921		46c. Sopwith F.1 Camel	1·00	1·00
1922		46c. de Havilland Canada DHC-3 Otter	1·00	1·00
1923		46c. de Havilland Canada CC-108 Caribou	1·00	1·00
1924		46c. Canadair CL-28 Argus Mk 2	1·00	1·00
1925		46c. Canadair (North American) F-86 Sabre 6	1·00	1·00
1926		46c. McDonnell Douglas CF-18	1·00	1·00
1927		46c. Sopwith 5.F.1 Dolphin	1·00	1·00
1928		46c. Armstrong Whitworth Siskin IIIA	1·00	1·00
1929		46c. Canadian Vickers (Northrop) Delta II	1·00	1·00
1930		46c. Sikorsky CH-124A Sea King helicopter	1·00	1·00
1931		46c. Vickers-Armstrong Wellington Mk II	1·00	1·00
1932		46c. Avro Anson Mk I	1·00	1·00
1933		46c. Canadair (Lockheed) CF-104G Starfighter	1·00	1·00
1934		46c. Burgess-Dunne	1·00	1·00
1935		46c. Avro 504K	1·00	1·00
1920/1935 Set of 16			13·00	16·00

Nos. 1920/1935 were printed together, *se-tenant*, in sheetlets of 16.

713 Fokker DR-1

(Des T. Telmet and M. Barac. Litho C.B.N)

1999 (4 Sept). 50th Anniversary of Canadian International Air Show. T **713** and similar horiz designs. Multicoloured. Fluorescent frame. Perf 12½×13.

1936		46c. Type **713**	1·10	1·25
		a. Sheetlet of 4. Nos. 1936/1939	4·00	5·50
1937		46c. H101 Salto glider	1·10	1·25
1938		46c. de Havilland DH100 Vampire Mk III	1·10	1·25
1939		46c. Wing-walker on Stearman A-75	1·10	1·25
1936/1939 Set of 4			4·00	5·50

Nos. 1936/1939 were printed together, *se-tenant*, in sheetlets of four forming a composite design which includes a nine-plane 'snowbird' formation of Canadair CT114 Tutor in the background.

714 NATO Emblem and National Flags

(Des Bonnie Ross and F. Ross. Litho Ashton Potter Canada)

1999 (21 Sept). 50th Anniversary of North Atlantic Treaty Organization. Fluorescent frame. Perf 12½×13.

1940	714	46c. multicoloured		1·00	50

715 Man ploughing on open Book

716 Master Control Sports Kite

CANADA

(Des Q30 Design. Litho C.B.N)

1999 (24 Sept). Centenary of Frontier College (workers' education organization). Fluorescent frame. Perf 13×13½.
1941	**715**	46c. multicoloured	50	50

The fluorescent frame on No. 1941 is incomplete as there are breaks at one, two or three corners.

(Des Debbie Adams. Litho Ashton-Potter Canada)

1999 (1 Oct). Stamp Collecting Month. Kites. T **716** and similar multicoloured designs. Die-cut perforations.
1942	46c. Type **716**	55	75
	a. Booklet pane. Nos. 1942/1945×2	4·00	
1943	46c. Indian Garden Flying Carpet (*irregular rectangle*, 35×32 mm)	55	75
1944	46c. Gibson Girl box kite (*horiz*, 38½×25 mm)	55	75
1945	46c. Dragon Centipede (*oval*, 39×29 mm)	55	75
1942/1945 Set of 4		2·00	2·75

Nos. 1942/1945 were only issued in stamp booklets, No. SB234, containing pane No. 1942a.

No. 1942 has been reported printed on the gummed side.

717 Boy holding Dove

718 Angel playing Drum

(Des P.-Y. Pelletier (46c.), Monique Dufour and Sophie Lafortune (55c.), J. Peral (95c.))

1999 (12 Oct). New Millennium. Three sheets, each 108×108 mm, containing T **717** and similar square designs in blocks of 4.

(a) Litho Ashton-Potter Canada (hologram by Crown Canada). Self-adhesive. Die-cut.
MS1946	46c.×4 multicoloured	2·00	3·50

(b) Litho Ashton-Potter Canada. Perf 13½.
MS1947	55c.×4 multicoloured	2·50	5·00

(c) Recess C.B.N. Perf 13.
MS1948	95c.×4 red-brown	2·25	5·00

Designs: 46c. Holographic image of dove in flight; 95c. Dove with olive branch.

Designs as Nos. **MS**1946/**MS**1948 also exist in similar-sized miniature sheets each containing one stamp. These were only available in the Canada Post 'Official Millennium Keepsake' which presented them in a tin box, together with a certificate and a medallion, for $8.99.

(Des Tannis Hopkins, K. Tsetsekas and Bonne Zabolotney. Litho C.B.N)

1999 (4 Nov). Christmas. Victorian Angels. T **718** and similar vert designs. Multicoloured. Fluorescent frame. Perf 13½.
1949	46c. Type **718**	60	20
	a. Booklet pane. No. 1949×10	6·50	
1950	55c. Angel with toys	80	50
	a. Booklet pane. No. 1950×5 plus one printed label	5·50	
1951	95c. Angel with star	1·40	2·50
	a. Booklet pane. No. 1951×5 plus one printed label	6·50	
1949/1951 Set of 3		2·40	3·00

Nos. 1949a/1951a come from booklet Nos. SB235/SB237 and show the vertical edges of the panes imperforate and have margins at top and bottom.

Nos. 1949 and 1951 have been reported in imperf-between pairs.

719 Portia White (singer)

720 Millennium Partnership Programme Logo

(Des F. and B. Ross, A. Dunkelman, R. Willms and Y. Laroche (No. 1952); J. Michaud, P. Haslip, Geneviève Caron and C. Malenfant (1953); T. Gregorashchuk, M. Serre, D. Fortin, G. Fok and Alexis Brothers, Sheri Hancock and Hélène L'Heureux (2) (1954); K. Tsetsekas and G. Kehrig, H. Chung, D. Corriveau, P. Scott and Glenda Rissman, B. Canning and M. Waddell (1955). Litho Ashton-Potter Canada)

1999 (17 Dec). Millennium Collection (1st series). Entertainment and Arts. Miniature sheets, each 108×112 mm, containing T **719** and similar vert designs. Multicoloured. Fluorescent frame. Perf 13½.
MS1952 46c. Type **719**; 46c. Glenn Gould (pianist); 46c. Guy Lombardo (conductor of 'Royal Canadians'); 46c. Félix Leclerc (musician, playwright and actor)	2·25 5·00
MS1953 46c. Artists looking at painting (Royal Canadian Academy of Arts); 46c. Cloud, stave and pencil marks (The Canada Council); 46c. Man with video camera (National Film Board of Canada); 46c. News-reader (Canadian Broadcasting Corporation)	2·25 5·00
MS1954 46c. Calgary Stampede; 46c. Circus performers; 46c. Ice hockey (Hockey Night); 46c. Goalkeeper (Ice hockey live from The Forum)	3·75 5·50
MS1955 46c. IMAX cinema; 46c. Computer image (Softimage); 46c. Ted Rogers Sr ('Plugging in the Radio'); 46c. Sir William Stephenson (inventor of radio facsimile system)	2·75 5·50
MS1952/1955 Set of 4 sheets	10·00 19·00

In addition to Nos. **MS**1952/**MS**1955, these designs were also available in a presentation album showing two stamps per page.

On stamps from the presentation date the copyright date is 2 mm long, but only 1.75 mm long on those from miniature sheets.

See also Nos. **MS**1959/**MS**1962, **MS**1969/**MS**1973 and **MS**1982/**MS**1985.

(Des karacters design group. Litho C.B.N)

2000. Canada Millennium Partnership Programme. Fluorescent frame. Perf 13×12½.
1956	**720**	46c. bright red, myrtle-green and light grey-blue	50	50

721 Chinese Dragon

(Des K. Fun and K. Koo using illustrations by S. Tseng. Litho and embossed Ashton-Potter Canada)

2000 (5 Jan). Chinese New Year. Year of the Dragon. Fluorescent frame. Perf 12½.
1957	**721**	46c. multicoloured	50	50
MS1958	150×85 mm. **721** 95c. multicoloured. Perf 13½×13		1·25	2·00

No. **MS**1958 has been reported with red omitted and orange omitted.

(Des R. Tibbles, P.-Y. Pelletier, Koo Creative Group Inc, and L. Cable (No. 1959); L. Fishauf, Louise Delisle and J.-C. Guénette, Stéphane Huot, and T. Yakobina (No. 1960); R. Bellemare, Margaret Issenman and Bonnie Ross, Letterbox Design Group, and Circle Design Incorporated (No. 1961); F. Blais, Orange, F. Dallaire and B. Leduc, and Gaynor and D. Sarty (No. 1962). Litho Ashton-Potter Canada)

2000 (17 Jan). Millennium Collection (2nd series). Charities, Medical Pioneers, Peace-keepers and Social Reforms. Miniature sheets, each 108×112 mm, containing vert designs as T **719**. Multicoloured. Fluorescent frame. Perf 13½.
MS1959 46c. Providing equipment (Canadian International Development Agency); 46c. Dr. Lucille Teasdale (medical missionary); 46c. Terry Fox (Marathon of Hope); 46c. Delivering meal (Meals on Wheels)	3·00 5·50
MS1960 46c. Sir Frederick Banting (discovery of insulin); 46c. Armand Frappier (developer of BCG vaccine); 46c. Dr. Hans Selye (research into stress); 46c. 'Dr. Maude Abbott" (pathologist) (M. Bell Eastlake)	3·00 5·50
MS1961 46c. Senator Raoul Dandurand (diplomat); 46c. Pauline Vanier and Elizabeth Smellie (nursing pioneers); 46c. Lester B. Pearson (diplomat); 46c. One-legged man (Ottawa Convention on Banning Landmines)	3·00 5·50
MS1962 46c. Nun and surgeon (medical care); 46c. Women are Persons (sculpture by Barbara Paterson) (Appointment of women senators); 46c. Alphonse and Doriméne Desjardins (People's bank movement); 46c. Father Moses Coady (Adult education pioneer)	3·00 5·50
MS1959/1962 Set of 4 sheets	11·00 20·00

In addition to Nos. **MS**1959/**MS**1962, these designs were also available in a presentation album showing two stamps per page.

CANADA

722 Wayne Gretzky (ice-hockey player)

723 Judges and Supreme Court Building

(Des D. Fell and V. McIndoe. Litho C.B.N)

2000 (5 Feb). National Hockey League. All-Star Game Players (1st series). T **722** and similar square designs. Multicoloured. Fluorescent circular frame around central design. Perf 13.

1963	46c. Type **722**	80	1·25
	a. Sheetlet. Nos. 1963/1968	4·25	6·50
1964	46c. Gordie Howe (No. 9 in white jersey)	80	1·25
1965	46c. Maurice Richard (No. 9 in blue and red jersey)	80	1·25
1966	46c. Doug Harvey (No. 2)	80	1·25
1967	46c. Bobby Orr (No. 4)	80	1·25
1968	46c. Jacques Plante (No. 1)	80	1·25
1963/1968 Set of 6		4·25	4·25

Nos. 1963/1968 were printed together, *se-tenant*, in sheetlets of six with portraits of the players shown on the sheet margins alongside the individual stamps.

See also Nos. 2052/2057, 2118/2123, 2178/2183 and 2250/2256f.

(Des R. Harder, S. Bhandari and G. Khayat, J. Skipp and J. Evans and S. Slipp (No. 1969); I. Drolet, B. Tsang, P. Fontaine, and Zabolotney Graphic Design (1970); Susan Warr, H. Deppe and F. Ross, B. Kierstead, K. Sollows and G. Tuck and L. Holloway (1971); D. Bartsch, P. Fontaine, Lise Giguère and G. Ludwig (1972); Debbie Adams, D. Page and T. Hawkins, T. Nokes and R. Harder (1973). Litho Ashton-Potter Canada)

2000 (17 Feb). Millennium Collection (3rd series). First Inhabitants, Great Thinkers, Culture and Literary Legends, and Charitable Foundations. Miniature sheets, each 108×112 mm, containing vert designs as T **719**. Multicoloured. Fluorescent frame. Perf 13½.

MS1969	46c. Pontiac (Ottawa chief); 46c. Tom Longboat (long-distance runner); 46c. Inuit Shaman (sculpture by Paul Toolooktook); 46c. Shaman and patient (Indian medicine)	2·75	5·00
MS1970	46c. Professor Marshall McLuhan (media philosopher); 46c. Northrop Frye (literary critic); 46c. Roger Lemelin (novelist); 46c. Prof. Hilda Marion Neatby (educator)	2·75	5·00
MS1971	46c. Bow of Viking longship (L'Anse aux Meadows World Heritage Site); 46c. Immigrant family (Pier 21 monument); 46c. Neptune mask (Neptune Theatre, Halifax); 46c. Auditorium and actor (The Stratford Festival)	2·75	5·00
MS1972	46c. W. O. Mitchell (writer); 46c. Gratien Gélinas (actor, producer and play-wright); 46c. Text and fountain pen (Cercle du Livre de France); 46c. Harlequin and roses (Harlequin Books)	2·75	5·00
MS1973	46c. Hart Massey (Massey Foundation); 46c. Izaak Walton Killam and Dorothy Killam; 46c. Eric Lafferty Harvie (Glenbow Foundation); 46c. Macdonald Stewart Foundation	2·75	5·00
MS1969/1973 Set of 5 sheets		12·00	22·00

In addition to Nos. **MS**1969/**MS**1973, these designs were also available in a presentation album showing two stamps per page.

(Des P. Leduc and R. Bellemare. Litho Ashton-Potter Canada)

2000 (1 Mar). Birds (5th series). Horiz designs as T **643**. Multicoloured. Fluorescent frame.

(a) Perf 12½×13.

1974	46c. Canadian Warbler	1·10	1·10
	a. Block of 4. Nos. 1974/1977	4·00	5·00
1975	46c. Osprey	1·10	1·10
1976	46c. Pacific Loon	1·10	1·10
1977	46c. Blue Jay	1·10	1·10
1974/1977 Set of 4		4·00	5·00

(b) Self-adhesive. Perf 11½.

1978	46c. Canadian Warbler	80	80
	a. Booklet pane. Nos. 1978/1981, each×3	7·50	
1979	46c. Osprey	80	80
1980	46c. Pacific Loon	80	80
1981	46c. Blue Jay	80	80
1978/1981 Set of 4		3·00	3·25

Nos. 1974/1977 were printed together *se-tenant* in different combinations throughout the sheet, giving four blocks of 4 and four single stamps.

Nos. 1978/1981 were only available from $5.52 stamp booklets, No. SB238.

(Des Taylor/Sprules Corporation and P. Sayers, M. Koudis, D. Preston Smith and P.-M. Brunelle and J. Hudson (No. 1982); Susan Scott, N. Smith, Monique Dufour and Sophie LaFortune and Doreen Colonello and S. Ash (1983); T. Telmet and M. Barac, S. Slipp and D. Preston Smith, J. LeBlanc and Bonnie Ross and Michèle Cayer and T. Kapas (1984); K. van der Leek and A. McKinley, E. Roch, T. Yakobina and N. Skinner, J. Gault and N.C.K. Engineering (1985). Litho Ashton-Potter Canada)

2000 (17 Mar). Millennium Collection (4th series). Canadian Agriculture, Commerce and Technology. Miniature sheets, each 108×112 mm, containing vert designs as T **719**. Multicoloured. Fluorescent frame. Perf 13½.

MS1982	46c. Sir Charles Saunders (developer of Marquis wheat); 46c. Baby (Pablum baby food); 46c. Dr. Archibald Gowanlock Huntsman (frozen fish pioneer); 46c. Oven chips and field of potatoes (McCain Frozen Foods)	4·00	6·50
MS1983	46c. Early trader and Indian (Hudson's Bay Company); 46c. Satellite over earth (Bell Canada Enterprises); 46c. Jos. Louis biscuits and Vachon family (Vachon Family Bakery); 46c. Bread and eggs (George Weston Limited)	4·00	6·50
MS1984	46c. George Klein and cog wheels (inventor of electric wheelchair and microsurgical staple gun); 46c. Abraham Gesner (developer of kerosene); 46c. Alexander Graham Bell (inventor of telephone); 46c. Joseph-Armand Bombardier (inventor of snowmobile)	4·00	6·50
MS1985	46c. Workers and steam locomotive (Rogers Pass rail tunnel); 46c. Manic 5 dam (Manicouagan River hydro-electric project); 46c. Mobile Servicing System for International Space Station (Canadian Space Program); 46c. CN Tower (World's tallest building)	4·00	6·50
MS1982/1985 Set of 4 sheets		14·00	23·00

In addition to Nos. **MS**1982/**MS**1985, these designs were also available in a presentation album showing two stamps per page.

(Des C. Le Sauter. Litho C.B.N)

2000 (10 Apr). 125th Anniversary of Supreme Court of Canada. Fluorescent frame. Perf 12½×13.

1986	**723**	46c. multicoloured	50	50

724 Lethbridge Bridge, Synthetic Rubber Plant, X-ray of Heart Pacemaker and Microwave Radio System

725 Picture frame

(Des D. Freeman. Litho Ashton-Potter Canada)

2000 (25 Apr). 75th Anniversary of Ceremony for Calling of an Engineer. Fluorescent frame. Perf 12½×13.

1987	**724**	46c. multicoloured	50	50
		a. Tête-bêche (vert pair)	1·00	1·50

No. 1987 was printed in sheets of 16 (4×4), with a central horizontal gutter, showing rows 2 and 4 *tête-bêche*. Each vertical pair completes the engineer's ring as shown on Type **724**.

No. 1987 has been reported with silver omitted.

(Des S. Spazuk. Litho Ashton-Potter Canada)

2000 (28 Apr). Picture Postage Greetings Stamps. Self-adhesive. Fluorescent frame. Perf 11½.

1988	**725**	46c. multicoloured	55	50
		a. Booklet pane. No. 1988×5, and 5 rectangular greetings labels	2·50	

No. 1988 was either available from $2.30 booklets, No. SB239, including appropriate greetings labels which could be inserted into the rectangular space on each stamp, or from sheets of 25 issued in connection with a mail order scheme which provided frames and personalised labels for $24.95 a sheet.

See also Nos. 2020 and 2045/2049.

726 Coastal-style Mailboxes in Autumn

CANADA

(Des R. Bellemare and M. Côté. Litho Ashton-Potter Canada)

2000 (28 Apr). Traditional Rural Mailboxes. T **726** and similar horiz designs. Multicoloured. Fluorescent frame. Perf 12½×13.

1989		46c. Type **726**	65	80
	a.	Booklet pane. Nos. 1989/1992, each×3	6·50	
1990		46c. House and cow-shaped mailboxes in Spring	65	80
1991		46c. Tractor-shaped mailbox in Summer	65	80
1992		46c. Barn and duck-shaped mailboxes in Winter	65	80
1989/1992 *Set of 4*			2·40	3·00

Nos. 1989/1992 were only available from $5.52 stamp booklets (No. SB240) as a *se-tenant* pane of 12, containing three of each design, with margins at top and bottom and imperforate vertical edges.

727 Gorge and Fir Tree

(Des Mia Mattes and Maximage Design. Litho Ashton Potter Canada)

2000 (23 May). Canadian Rivers and Lakes. T **727** and similar horiz designs. Multicoloured. Fluorescent frame. Self-adhesive. Die-cut serpentine roul.

1993		55c. Type **727**	60	1·25
	a.	Booklet pane. Nos. 1993/1997	2·75	
1994		55c. Lake and water lilies	60	1·25
1995		55c. Glacier and reflected mountains	60	1·25
1996		55c. Estuary and aerial view	60	1·25
1997		55c. Waterfall and forest edge	60	1·25
1998		95c. Iceberg and mountain river	95	1·50
	a.	Booklet pane. Nos. 1998/2002	4·25	
1999		95c. Rapids and waterfall	95	1·50
2000		95c. Moraine and river	95	1·50
2001		95c. Shallows and waves on lake	95	1·50
2002		95c. Forest sloping to waters edge and tree	95	1·75
1993/2002 *Set of 10*			7·00	12·00

Nos. 1993/1997 and 1998/2002 were only available from $2.75 or $4.75 booklets, Nos. SB241/SB242, on which the self-adhesive paper formed the booklet covers.

728 Queen Elizabeth the Queen Mother with Roses

729 Teenager with Two Children

(Des Gottschalk and Ash. Litho C.B.N)

2000 (23 May). Queen Elizabeth the Queen Mother's 100th Birthday. Fluorescent frame. Perf 13×12½.

2003	**728**	95c. multicoloured	1·00	1·40
		a. Imperf (pair)		
		b. Sheetlet of 9	8·00	

No. 2003 was printed in sheetlets of nine, with enlarged inscribed right margin, for which an illustrated presentation folder was provided.

(Des Gottschalk and Ash. Litho C.B.N)

2000 (1 June). Centenary of Boys and Girls Clubs of Canada. Fluorescent frame. Perf 13.

2004	**729**	46c. multicoloured	50	50

730 Clouds over Rockies and Symbol

731 Space Travellers and Canadian Flag (Rosalie Anne Nardelli)

(Des Malcolm Waddell Associates. Litho Ashton-Potter Canada)

2000 (29 June). 57th General Conference Session of Seventh-day Adventist Church, Toronto. Fluorescent frame. Perf 13½×13.

2005	**730**	46c. multicoloured	50	50

(Litho C.B.N)

2000 (1 July). Stampin' the Future (children's stamp design competition). T **731** and similar horiz designs. Multicoloured. Fluorescent frame. Perf 13½.

2006		46c. Type **731**	45	70
	a.	Strip or block of 4. Nos. 2006/2009	1·60	2·50
2007		46c. Travelling to the Moon (Sarah Lutgen)	45	70
2008		46c. Astronauts in shuttle (Andrew Wright)	45	70
2009		46c. Children completing Canada as jigsaw (Christine Weera)	45	70
2006/2009 *Set of 4*			1·60	2·50
MS2010 114×90 mm. Nos. 2006/2009			1·60	3·00

Nos. 2006/2009 were printed together, *se-tenant*, as horizontal or vertical strips of four in sheets of 16.

(Des P.-Y. Pelletier. Litho and die-stamped Ashton-Potter Canada)

2000 (7 July). Canadian Art (13th series). Vert design as T **550**. Multicoloured. Fluorescent inner frame. Perf 12½×13.

2011		95c. *The Artist at Niagara, 1858* (Cornelius Krieghoff)	1·25	1·75

No. 2011 was issued in a similar sheet format to No. 1289.

732 Tall Ships, Halifax Harbour

(Des F. Ross and Bonnie Ross. Litho Ashton-Potter Canada)

2000 (19 July). Tall Ships Race. T **732** and similar horiz design. Multicoloured. Self-adhesive. Fluorescent frame. Die-cut serpentine roul.

2012		46c. Type **732**	50	90
	a.	Booklet pane. Nos. 2012/2013, each×5	4·50	
2013		46c. Tall Ships, Halifax Harbour (face value top right)	50	90

Nos. 2012/2013 were only issued in $4.60 stamp booklets, No. SB243, on which the surplus self-adhesive paper was retained. The stamps are arranged as five *se-tenant* pairs on a background photograph of Halifax Harbour.

733 Workers, Factory and Transport

734 Petro-Canada Sign, Oil Rig and Consumers

(Des P. Hodgson and Sandra Dionisi. Litho C.B.N)

2000 (1 Sept). Centenary of Department of Labour. Fluorescent frame. Perf 12½×13.

2014	**733**	46c. multicoloured	50	50

(Des D. L'Allier and R. Gendron. Litho C.B.N)

2000 (13 Sept–4 Oct). 25th Anniversary of Petro-Canada (oil company). Self-adhesive. Fluorescent frame. Die-cut with central zigzag showing two points at right and foot, one point at top and left.

2015	**734**	46c. multicoloured	75	50
		a. Booklet pane. No. 2015×12	7·00	
		ab. Imperf		
		b. With two points at top and left, one point at right and foot (4.10)	4·00	7·50

No. 2015 was only available in $5.52 stamp booklets, No. SB245, on which the surplus self-adhesive paper was retained. The die-cutting does not separate the backing paper.

No. 2015ab occurred when the booklet pane was fed into the die-cutter upside-down, resulting in the cuts appearing in the souvenir section of the pane, leaving all 12 stamps imperforate.

No. 2015b comes from various packs issued by Canada Post at the end of 2000. The die-cutting device was reversed and used to cut through the backing paper to create single stamps.

CANADA

735 Narwhal (*Monodon manoceros*)

(Des K. Martin. Litho Ashton Potter)

2000 (2 Oct). Whales. T **735** and similar horiz designs. Multicoloured. Fluorescent frame. Perf 12½×13.
2016		46c. Type **735**	1·40	1·40
		a. Block of 4. Nos. 2016/2019	5·00	6·00
2017		46c. Blue Whale (*Balaenoptera musculus*)	1·40	1·40
2018		46c. Bowhead Whale (*Balaena mysticetus*)	1·40	1·40
2019		46c. White Whales (*Delphinapterus leucas*)	1·40	1·40
2016/2019	*Set of 4*		5·00	6·00

Nos. 2016/2019 were printed together, as *se-tenant* blocks of four, in sheets of 16 with the backgrounds forming an overall composite design.

736 Picture Frame   **737** The Nativity (Susie Matthias)

(Des S. Spazuk. Litho Ashton-Potter Canada)

2000 (5 Oct). Picture Postage Christmas Greetings. Self-adhesive. Fluorescent frame. Perf 11½.
2020	**736**	46c. multicoloured	55	50
		a. Booklet pane. No. 2020×5 plus 5 Christmas labels	2·50	

No. 2020, which could be used in either a horizontal or vertical format, was either available from $2.30 self-adhesive booklets, No. SB246, which included five Christmas labels so that the sender could complete the design, or in panes of 25 available by mail order as part of a personalised labels offer.

(Des L. and Kelly Burke. Litho Ashton-Potter Canada)

2000 (3 Nov). Christmas. Religious Paintings by Mouth and Foot Artists. T **737** and similar vert designs. Multicoloured. Fluorescent frame. Perf 13½.
2021		46c. Type **737**	50	20
		a. Booklet pane. No. 2021×10	5·50	
2022		55c. The Nativity and Christmas Star (Michael Guillemette)	65	1·00
		a. Booklet pane. No. 2022×6	4·00	
2023		95c. Mary and Joseph journeying to Bethlehem (David Allan Carter)	1·25	2·00
		a. Booklet pane. No. 2023×6	7·00	
2021/2023	*Set of 3*		2·10	3·00

Nos. 2021a/2023a show the vertical edges of the panes imperforate and have margins at top and bottom.

738 Lieutenant-Colonel Sam Steele, Lord Strathcona's Horse   **739** Red Fox

(Des P.-Y. Pelletier. Litho C.B.N)

2000 (11 Nov). Canadian Regiments. T **738** and similar vert design. Multicoloured. Fluorescent frame. Perf 13½×13.
2024		46c. Type **738**	75	1·00
		a. Pair. Nos. 2024/2025	1·50	2·00
2025		46c. Drummer, Voltigeurs de Québec	75	1·00

Nos. 2024/2025 were printed together, *se-tenant*, as horizontal or vertical pairs in sheets of 16.

(Des P.-Y. Pelletier and R. Milot. Litho Ashton-Potter Canada)

2000 (28 Dec). Wildlife. T **739** and similar horiz designs. Multicoloured. Self-adhesive. Chalk-surfaced paper. Fluorescent frame. Perf 9×imperf.
2026		60c. Type **739**	65	85
		a. Pane of 6	3·50	
2027		75c. Grey Wolf	1·50	1·75
2028		$1.05 White-tailed Deer	1·10	1·75
		a. Pane of 6	6·00	
2026/2028	*Set of 3*		3·00	4·00

Nos. 2026/2028 were only issued as coils (all three values) or as small panes of 6 (2×3) (60c., $1.05). On the coils the surplus self-adhesive paper between each stamp was removed, but this was retained on the two panes. The horizontal pairs on the panes are separated by die-cutting.

Postal forgeries of Nos. 2028/a are known.

740 Maple Leaves   **740a** Maple Leaves and Key   **740b** Red Maple Leaf and Stem

(Des P.-Y. Pelletier (47c., 48c.), J. Gault (49c.), Monique Dufour and Sophie Lafortune (80c., $1.40). C.B.N. (No. 2031a),. Litho Ashton-Potter Canada or Lowe-Martin (80c., $1.40), Ashton-Potter Canada (others))

2000 (28 Dec)–**04**. Ordinary paper (Nos. 2031a, 2032a, 2033a) or Chalk-surfaced paper (others). Fluorescent frame.

(a) Self-adhesive coil stamps. Perf 9×imperf (47c., 48c.), 8×imperf (49c.) or imperf×8 (80c., $1.40).
2029	**740**	47c. multicoloured	1·00	1·25
		a. Blue (country name and value) omitted	£400	
2030	-	48c. multicoloured (2.1.02)	1·00	1·00
2031	**740a**	49c. multicoloured (19.12.03)	1·00	1·25
		a. Imperf (pair) (9.2004)		
2032	**740b**	80c. multicoloured (19.12.03)	1·10	1·60
		a. Perf 8×imperf (9.2004)	1·10	1·60
		a. Perf 8×imperf (9.2004)	2·00	2·75
		ab. Imperf (pair)		

(b) Self-adhesive booklet stamps. Die-cut.
		a. Pane. No. 2035×6	6·50	
2036	-	$1.40 multicoloured (19.12.03)	1·90	2·75
		a. Pane. No. 2036×6	11·00	

Designs: 48c. As Type **740** but leaves in three shades of green; $1.40 As Type **740b** but green leaf.

On Nos. 2029/2030 the surplus self-adhesive paper between each stamp was removed, but on Nos. 2031/2036 it was retained.

No. 2034 has been left for additions to this series.

Nos. 2035/2036 were only issued in $4.80 or $8.40 panes of six stamps. Originally printed by Ashton Potter Canada, they were reprinted by Lowe-Martin from 2 July 2004.

Postal forgeries of Nos. 2036/2036a are known.

(Des. S. Spazuk. Litho Ashton-Potter Canada)

2000 (28 Dec). Picture Postage Greetings Stamps. T **725**, **736** and similar horiz frames. Multicoloured. Self-adhesive. Fluorescent frame. Perf 11½.
2045		47c. Type **725**	55	1·00
		a. Booklet pane. Nos. 2045/2049 plus 5 rectangular greetings labels	2·50	
2046		47c. Type **736**	55	1·00
2047		47c. Roses frame	55	1·00
2048		47c. Mahogany frame	55	1·00
2049		47c. Silver frame	55	1·00
2045/2049	*Set of 5*		2·50	4·50

Nos. 2037/2044 are vacant.

Nos. 2045/2049, which could be used in either a horizontal or vertical format, were either available from $2.35 self-adhesive booklets, SB252, which included five greetings labels so that the sender could complete the design, or in panes of twenty-five of one design which could only be obtained by mail order as part of a personalised labels offer.

For designs as Nos. 2045/2047 and 2049, but inscr 'Domestic Lettermail Postes-lettres du régime intérieur' see also Nos. 2099/2103.

CANADA

741 Green Jade Snake

(Des Marlene Wou. Litho and embossed Ashton-Potter Canada)

2001 (5 Jan). Chinese New Year. Year of the Snake. T **741** and similar horiz design. Multicoloured. Two fluorescent bands. Perf 13½.
2050	47c. Type **741**		50	50
	a. Gold omitted		£750	
MS2051	112×75 mm. $1.05, Brown jade snake		1·25	1·60

(Des S. Huot and C. Vinh. Litho Ashton-Potter Canada)

2001 (18 Jan). National Hockey League. All-Star Game Players (2nd series). Square designs as T **722**. Multicoloured. Fluorescent circular frame around central design. Perf 12½×13.
2052	47c. Jean Bèliveau (wearing No. 4)	75	1·00
	a. Sheetlet of 6. Nos. 2052/2057	4·00	5·00
	b. Blue (circle and text) omitted (*vert strip of three**)		
2053	47c. Terry Sawchuk (on one knee)	75	1·00
2054	47c. Eddie Shore (wearing No. 2)	75	1·00
2055	47c. Denis Potvin (wearing No. 5)	75	1·00
	b. Blue (circle and text) omitted		
2056	47c. Bobby Hull (wearing No. 9)	75	1·00
2057	47c. Syl Apps (in Toronto jersey)	75	1·00
	b. Blue (circle and text) omitted		
2052/2057	Set of 6	4·00	5·00

* No. 2052b is a strip of three (Nos. 2052, 2054 and 2056) all missing the blue circle and text.

Nos. 2052/2057 were printed together, *se-tenant*, in sheetlets of 6 containing two vertical strips of three separated by labels featuring further portraits of the players shown on the stamps. Nos. 2052, 2054 and 2056 are imperforate at left and the others imperforate at right.

(Des R. Bellemare and P. Leduc. Litho Ashton-Potter Canada)

2001 (1 Feb). Birds (6th series). Horiz design as T **643**. Multicoloured. Fluorescent frame.

(a) Perf 12½×13.
2058	47c. Golden Eagle	75	80
	a. Block of 4. Nos. 2058/2061	2·75	3·00
2059	47c. Arctic Tern	75	80
2060	47c. Rock Ptarmigan	75	80
2061	47c. Lapland Longspur	75	80
2058/2061	Set of 4	2·75	3·00

(b) Self-adhesive. Perf 11½.
2062	47c. Golden Eagle	65	80
	a. Booklet pane. Nos. 2062/2065, each×3	7·00	
2063	47c. Arctic Tern	65	80
2064	47c. Rock Ptarmigan	65	80
2065	47c. Lapland Longspur	65	80
2062/2065	Set of 4	2·40	3·00

Nos. 2058/2061 were printed together *se-tenant* in different combinations throughout the sheet, giving four blocks of four and four single stamps.

Nos. 2062/2065 were only issued in $5.64 stamp booklets, No. SB253, on which the surplus self-adhesive paper was retained.

742 Highjumping

(Des C. Malenfant. Litho C.B.N)

2001 (28 Feb). Fourth Francophonie Games. T **742** and similar vert design. Multicoloured. Fluorescent frame. Perf 13½.
2066	47c. Type **742**	70	90
	a. Horiz pair. Nos. 2066/2067	1·40	1·75
2067	47c. Folk dancing	70	90

Nos. 2066/2067 were printed together, *se-tenant*, as horizontal pairs throughout the sheet.

743 Ice Dancing

744 Three Pence Beaver Stamp of 1851

(Des Barbara Hodgson. Litho C.B.N)

2001 (19 Mar). World Figure Skating Championships, Vancouver. T **743** and similar horiz designs. Multicoloured. Fluorescent frame. Perf 13×12½.
2068	47c. Type **743**	80	90
	a. Block of 4. Nos. 2068/2071	3·00	3·25
2069	47c. Pairs	80	90
2070	47c. Men's singles	80	90
2071	47c. Women's singles	80	90
2068/2071	Set of 4	3·00	3·25

Nos. 2068/2071 were printed together, *se-tenant*, as blocks of four in sheets of 16 (two panes 4×2).

(Des T. Yakobina. Recess and litho C.B.N)

2001 (6 Apr). 150th Anniversary of the Canadian Postal Service. Fluorescent frame around centre. Perf 12½.
2072	**744**	47c. multicoloured	1·00	1·50

No. 2072 was only available in sheets of eight (2×4) in a special folder with a commemorative leaflet.

745 Toronto Blue Jay Emblem, Maple Leaf and Baseball

746 North and South America on Globe

(Des P. Haslip. Litho Ashton-Potter Canada)

2001 (9 Apr). 25th Season of the Toronto Blue Jays (baseball team). Fluorescent outline. Self-adhesive. Die-cut.
2073	**745**	47c. multicoloured	50	1·00
		a. Booklet pane of 8	3·50	

No. 2073 was only available from $3.76 stamp booklets No. SB254.

(Des D. L'Allier. Litho Ashton-Potter Canada)

2001 (20 Apr). Summit of the Americas, Quebec. Fluorescent frame. Perf 13.
2074	**746**	47c. multicoloured	1·00	1·00

747 Butchart Gardens, British Columbia

748 Christ on Palm Sunday and Khachkar (stone cross)

(Des Bradbury Design. Litho C.B.N)

2001 (11 May). Tourist Attractions (1st series). T **747** and similar horiz designs. Multicoloured. Fluorescent frame. Self-adhesive. Perf 11 (die-cut).
2075	60c. Type **747**	95	1·40
	a. Booklet pane of 5. Nos. 2075/2079	4·25	
2076	60c. Apple Blossom Festival, Nova Scotia	95	1·40
2077	60c. White Pass and Yukon Route	95	1·40
2078	60c. Sugar Bushes, Quebec	95	1·40

CANADA

2079	60c. Court House, Niagara-on-the-Lake, Ontario		95	1·40
2080	$1.05 The Forks, Winnipeg, Manitoba		1·40	2·00
	a. Booklet pane of 5. Nos. 2080/2084		6·25	
2081	$1.05 Barkerville, British Columbia		1·40	2·00
2082	$1.05 Canadian Tulip Festival, Ontario		1·40	2·00
2083	$1.05 Auyuittuq National Park, Nunavut		1·40	2·00
2084	$1.05 Signal Hill, St John's, Newfoundland		1·40	2·00
2075/2084 Set of 10			10·50	15·00

Nos. 2075/2079 and 2080/2084 were only available in $3 or $5.25 stamp booklets, Nos. SB255/SB256.

See also Nos. 2143/2052, 2205/2014 and 2257/2061.

(Des Debbie Adams. Litho Ashton-Potter Canada)

2001 (16 May). 1700th Anniversary of Armenian Church. Fluorescent frame. Perf 13×12½.

| 2085 | **748** | 47c. multicoloured | 60 | 1·00 |

No. 2085 was printed in sheets of 16 containing four blocks of four separated by vertical and horizontal gutters showing an Armenian manuscript.

749 Cadets, Mackenzie Building and Military Equipment

(Des J. Hudson. Litho C.B.N)

2001 (1 June). 125th Anniversary of Royal Military College of Canada. Fluorescent frame. Perf 12½×13.

| 2086 | **749** | 47c. multicoloured | 1·00 | 1·00 |

750 Pole-vaulting   **751** Pierre Trudeau (Myfanwy Pavelic)

(Des T. Nokes. Litho Ashton-Potter Canada)

2001 (25 June). Eighth International Amateur Athletic Federation World Championships, Edmonton. T **750** and similar vert design. Multicoloured. Fluorescent frame. Perf 12½.

2087		47c. Type **750**	80	1·25
		a. Pair. Nos. 2087/2088	1·60	2·50
2088		47c. Sprinting	80	1·25

Nos. 2087/2088 were printed together, *se-tenant*, both vertically and horizontally in sheets of 16.

(Des T. Yakobina. Litho Ashton-Potter Canada)

2001 (1 July). Pierre Trudeau (former Prime Minister) Commemoration. Fluorescent frame. Perf 13×12½.

| 2089 | **751** | 47c. multicoloured | 60 | 60 |
| MS2090 128×155 mm. No. 2089×4 | | | 2·00 | 2·75 |

No. MS2090 was sold in a commemorative folder.

752 'Morden Centennial' Rose

(Des G. Takeuchi. Litho Ashton-Potter Canada)

2001 (1 Aug). Canadian Roses. T **752** and similar horiz designs. Multicoloured. Fluorescent frame.

(a) Self-adhesive. Die-cut.

2091		47c. Type **752**	80	1·25
		a. Booklet pane. Nos. 2091/2094, each×3	7·50	
2092		47c. Agnes	80	1·25
2093		47c. Champlain	80	1·25
2094		47c. Canadian White Star	80	1·25
2091/2094 Set of 4			3·00	5·00

(b) PVA gum. Perf 12½×13.

| MS2095 145×90 mm. Nos. 2091/2094 | | 3·50 | 5·00 |

Nos. 2091/2094 were only issued in $5.64 stamp booklets, No. SB257, on which the surplus self-adhesive paper was retained.

753 Ottawa Chief Hassaki addressing Peace Delegates

(Des N. Tessier and F. Back. Litho Ashton-Potter Canada)

2001 (3 Aug). 300th Anniversary of Great Peace Treaty of Montréal between Indians and New France. Fluorescent frame. Perf 12½×13.

| 2096 | **753** | 47c. multicoloured | 60 | 1·00 |

No. 2096 was printed in sheets of 16 containing a block of eight (2×4) with a vertical strip of four on either side separated by a narrow vertical gutter showing pictographs.

(Des P-Y Pelletier. Litho and die-stamped C.B.N)

2001 (24 Aug). Canadian Art (14th series). Vert design as T **550**. Multicoloured. Fluorescent inner frame. Perf 13×13½.

| 2097 | | $1.05 *The Space Between Columns 21* (Italian) (Jack Shadbolt) | 2·00 | 2·25 |

No. 2097 was issued in a similar sheet format to No. 1289.

754 Clown juggling with Crutches and Handicapped Boy   **755** Toys and Flowers

(Des Monique Dufour and Sophie Lafortune. Litho C.B.N)

2001 (19 Sept). The Shriners (charitable organisation) Commemoration. Fluorescent frame. Perf 13½×13.

| 2098 | **754** | 47c. multicoloured | 60 | 1·00 |

(Des S. Spazuk. Litho Ashton-Potter Canada)

2001 (21 Sept). Picture Postage Greetings Stamps. T **755** and horiz frames as Nos. 2045/2047 and 2049, but each inscr *'Domestic Lettermail Postes-lettres du régime intérieur'*. Multicoloured. Self-adhesive. Fluorescent frame. Perf 11½.

2099		(–) As Type **725**	60	1·25
		a. Booklet pane. Nos. 2099/2103 plus 5 rectangular greetings labels	2·75	
2100		(–) As Type **736**	60	1·25
2101		(–) As Type **755**	60	1·25
2102		(–) Roses frame	60	1·25
2103		(–) Silver frame	60	1·25
2099/2103 Set of 5			2·75	5·50

Nos. 2099/2103, which could be used in either a horizontal or a vertical format, were either available from stamp booklets (No. SB258), initially sold at $2.35, which included five greetings labels so that the sender could complete the design, or in panes of 25 of one design which could only be obtained by mail order as part of a personalised labels offer.

756 Jean Gascon and Jean-Louis Roux (founders of Théâtre du Nouveau Monde, Montreal)

(Des Graphème of Montreal. Litho Ashton-Potter Canada)

2001 (28 Sept). Theatre Anniversaries. T **756** and similar horiz design. Multicoloured. Fluorescent frame. Perf 12½.
2104	47c. Type **756** (50th anniversary)		65	80
	a. Horiz pair. Nos. 2104/2105		1·25	1·60
2105	47c. Ambrose Small (founder of Grand Theatre, London, Ontario) (centenary)		65	80

Nos. 2104/2105 were printed together, *se-tenant*, in horizontal pairs throughout the sheets of 16.

757 Hot Air Balloons

(Des Lise Giguère and D. Fell. Litho C.B.N)

2001 (1 Oct). Stamp Collecting Month. Hot Air Balloons. T **757** and similar triangular designs. Multicoloured, background colours different below. Self-adhesive. Fluorescent frame. Die-cut.
2106	47c. Type **757** (green background)		70	1·00
	a. Booklet pane. Nos. 2106/2109, each×2		5·00	
2107	47c. Balloons with lavender background		70	1·00
2108	47c. Balloons with mauve background		70	1·00
2109	47c. Balloons with bistre background		70	1·00
2106/2109 Set of 4			3·00	3·50

Nos. 2106/2109 were only available in $3.76 stamp booklets, No. SB259.

758 Horse-drawn Sleigh and Christmas Lights

759 Pattern of Ys Logo

(Des Circle Design Incorporated. Litho C.B.N)

2001 (1 Nov). Christmas. Festive Lights. T **758** and similar horiz designs. Multicoloured. Fluorescent frame. Perf 12½×13.
2110	47c. Type **758**		70	20
	a. Booklet pane. No. 2110×10 with margins all round		6·50	
2111	60c. Ice skaters and Christmas lights		1·00	1·00
	a. Booklet pane. No. 2111×6 with margins all round		5·50	
2112	$1.05 Children with snowman and Christmas lights		1·25	2·25
	a. Booklet pane. No. 2112×6 with margins all round		6·75	
2110/2112 Set of 3			2·75	3·00

(Des Hélène L'Heureux. Litho C.B.N)

2001 (8 Nov). 150th Anniversary of YMCA in Canada. Fluorescent frame. Perf 13½.
2113	**759**	47c. multicoloured	70	60

760 Statues from Canadian War Memorial, Ottawa, and Badge

(Des N. Smith. Litho C.B.N)

2001 (11 Nov). 75th Anniversary of Royal Canadian Legion. Fluorescent frame. Perf 12½×13.
2114	**760**	47c. multicoloured	80	60

 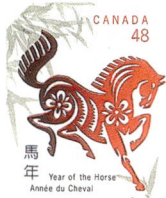

761 Queen Elizabeth II and Maple Leaf

762 Horse and Bamboo Leaves

(Des Gottschalk and Ash. Litho Ashton-Potter Canada)

2002 (2 Jan). Golden Jubilee. Chalk-surfaced paper. Fluorescent frame. Perf 13×12½.
2115	**761**	48c. multicoloured	70	60
		a. Imperf (pair)	£850	

See also No. 2203.

(Des Up Inc. Litho and embossed Ashton-Potter Canada)

2002 (3 Jan). Chinese New Year. Year of the Horse. T **762** and similar vert design. Multicoloured. Fluorescent frame. Perf 13½ (with one diamond-shaped hole on each vertical side).
2116		48c. Type **762**	1·00	60
MS2117	102×102 mm. (octagonal). $1.25, Horse and peach blossom		1·40	2·50

No. 2116, which is an octagonal design, was printed in sheets of 25, with small red diamond-shaped labels at each corner surrounded by perforations and bisected horizontally and vertically by roulettes. The design within No. **MS**2117 is in normal vertical format.

A pane of 25 has been reported with the horse omitted.

(Des S. Huot, C. Vinn and P. Rousseau. Litho C.B.N)

2002 (12 Jan). National Hockey League. All-Star Game Players (3rd series). Square designs as T **722**. Multicoloured. Fluorescent circular frame around central design. Perf 12½×13.
2118	48c. Tim Horton (wearing Maple Leaf No. 7 jersey)	1·00	1·00
	a. Sheetlet of 6. Nos. 2118/2123	5·50	5·50
2119	48c. Guy Lafleur (wearing Canadiens No. 10 jersey)	1·00	1·00
2120	48c. Howie Morenz (wearing Canadiens jersey and brown gloves)	1·00	1·00
2121	48c. Glenn Hall (wearing Chicago Blackhawks jersey)	1·00	1·00
2122	48c. Red Kelly (wearing Maple Leaf No. 4 jersey)	1·00	1·00
2123	48c. Phil Esposito (wearing Boston Bruins No. 7 jersey)	1·00	1·00
2118/2123 Set of 6		5·50	5·50

Nos. 2118/2123 were printed together, *se-tenant*, in sheetlets of six containing two vertical strips of three separated by labels featuring further portraits of the players shown on the stamps. Nos. 2118, 2120 and 2121 are imperforate at left, and the others at right.

 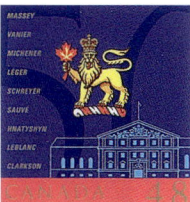

763 Speed Skating

764 Lion Symbol of Governor-General and Rideau Hall, Ottawa

(Des Bahandari and Plater. Litho Ashton-Potter Canada)

2002 (25 Jan). Winter Olympic Games, Salt Lake City. T **763** and similar vert designs. Multicoloured. Fluorescent frame. Perf 13.
2124	48c. Type **763**	1·00	1·00
	a. Block of 4. Nos. 2124/2127	3·50	4·00
2125	48c. Curling	1·00	1·00
2126	48c. Aerial skiing	1·00	1·00
2127	48c. Women's ice hockey	1·00	1·00
2124/2127 Set of 4		3·50	4·00

Nos. 2124/2127 were printed together, *se-tenant*, as blocks and strips of four in sheets of 16. The Olympic symbol appears in varnish on each stamp and the yellow ink is fluorescent.

(Des N. Smith. Litho Ashton-Potter Canada)

2002 (1 Feb). 50th Anniversary of First Canadian Governor-General. Fluorescent frame. Perf 13×12½.
2128	**764**	48c. multicoloured	60	60

CANADA

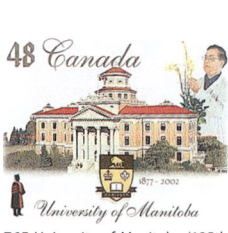
765 University of Manitoba (125th Anniversary)

766 City of Vancouver Tulip and Vancouver Skyline

(Des S. Slipp. Litho Ashton-Potter Canada)

2002 (28 Feb–27 May). Canadian Universities' Anniversaries (1st issue). T **765** and similar horiz designs. Multicoloured. Fluorescent frame. Perf 13½.

2129	48c. Type **765**	65	1·00
	a. Booklet pane. No. 2129×8 with margins all round	4·75	
2130	48c. Université Laval, Quebec (150th anniv of charter) (4.4)	65	1·00
	a. Booklet pane. No. 2130×8 with margins all round	4·75	
2131	48c. Trinity College, Toronto (150th anniversary of foundation) (30.4)	65	1·00
	a. Booklet pane. No. 2131×8 with margins all round	4·75	
2132	48c. Saint Mary's University, Halifax (bicentenary) (27.5)	65	1·00
	a. Booklet pane. No. 2132×8 with margins all round	4·75	
2129/2132	Set of 4	2·50	3·50

Nos. 2129/2132 were only available in four separate $3.84 stamp booklets, Nos. SB264/SB267.

See also Nos. 2190/2194, 2271/2272, 2333, 2419, 2487/2488 and 2544/2545.

(Des P-Y Pelletier. Litho and die-stamped Ashton-Potter Canada)

2002 (22 Mar). Canadian Art (15th series). Vert design as T **550**. Multicoloured. Fluorescent inner frame. Perf 12½×13.

2133	$1.25 *Church and Horse* (Alex Colville)	1·60	2·00
	a. Colour (centre) omitted	£1400	
	b. Imperf (pair)	£700	

No. 2133 was issued in a similar sheet format to No. 1289.

(Des Monique Dufour and Sophie Lafortune. Litho Lowe-Martin)

2002 (3 May). 50th Canadian Tulip Festival, Ottawa. Tulips. T **766** and similar vert designs. Multicoloured. Self-adhesive. Fluorescent frame. Die-cut.

2134	48c. Type **766**	70	85
	a. Booklet pane. Nos. 2134/2137, each×2	5·00	
2135	48c. Monte Carlo and Dows Lake tulip beds	70	85
2136	48c. Ottawa and National War Memorial	70	85
2137	48c. The Bishop and Ottawa Hospital	70	85
2134/2137	Set of 4	2·50	3·00

Nos. 2134/2137 were only available in $3.84 stamp booklets, No. SB268. For Nos. 2134/2137 in miniature sheet see No. **MS**2157.

767 *Dendronepthea gigantea* and *Dendronepthea* (Corals)

(Des B. Kwan (Nos. 2138/9), Signals Design Group (others). Litho Lowe-Martin)

2002 (19 May). Canada–Hong Kong Joint Issue. Corals. T **767** and similar horiz designs. Multicoloured. Fluorescent frame. Perf 12½×13.

2138	48c. Type **767**	70	90
	a. Block of 4. Nos. 2138/2141	2·50	3·25
2139	48c. *Tubastrea, Echinogorgia* and island	70	90
2140	48c. North Atlantic Pink Tree Coral, Pacific Orange Cup and North Pacific Horn Coral	70	90
2141	48c. North Atlantic Giant Orange Tree Coral and Black Coral	70	90
2138/2141	Set of 4	2·50	3·25
MS2142	161×87 mm. Nos. 2138/2141. Perf 13½×13	2·25	3·50

Nos. 2138/2141 were printed together, *se-tenant*, as blocks of four throughout the sheets.

(Des Bradbury Design. Litho C.B.N)

2002 (1 June). Tourist Attractions (2nd series). Horiz designs as T **747**. Multicoloured. Self-adhesive. Fluorescent frame. Perf 11.

2143	65c. Yukon Quest Sled Dog Race	80	1·40
	a. Booklet pane. Nos. 2143/2147	3·50	
2144	65c. Icefields Parkway, Alberta	80	1·40
2145	65c. Train in Agawa Canyon, Northern Ontario	80	1·40
2146	65c. Old Port, Montreal	80	1·40
2147	65c. Saw mill, Kings Landing, New Brunswick	80	1·40
2148	$1.25 Northern Lights, Northwest Territories	1·25	2·50
	a. Booklet pane. Nos. 2148/2152	5·50	
2149	$1.25 Stanley Park, British Columbia	1·25	2·50
2150	$1.25 Head-Smashed-In Buffalo Jump, Alberta	1·25	2·50
2151	$1.25 Saguenay Fjord, Quebec	1·25	2·50
2152	$1.25 Lighthouse, Peggy's Cove, Nova Scotia	1·25	2·50
2143/2152	Set of 10	9·00	17·00

Nos. 2143/2147 and 2148/2152 were only available in $3.25 or $6.25 stamp booklets, Nos. SB269/70.

768 *Embâcle* (Charles Daudelin)

(Des Suzanne Morin. Litho C.B.N)

2002 (10 June). Sculptures. T **768** and similar horiz design. Multicoloured. Fluorescent frame. Perf 13½.

2153	48c. Type **768**	60	90
	a. Pair. Nos. 2153/2154	1·10	1·75
2154	48c. Lumberjacks (Leo Mol)	60	90

Nos. 2153/2154 were printed together, *se-tenant*, as horizontal and vertical pairs throughout the sheet.

769 1899 Queen Victoria 2c. Stamp, Stonewall Post Office and Postmark

770 World Youth Day Logo

(Des C. Candlish. Litho C.B.N)

2002 (5 July). Centenary of Canadian Postmasters and Assistants Association. Fluorescent frame. Perf 13½×12½.

2155	**769**	48c. multicoloured	75	1·00

No. 2155 was printed in sheets of 16 with the horizontal rows separated by 8 mm gutters into which the 2c. stamp and the postmark intrude. The fluorescent frame around each stamp is broken where these features cross the perforations.

(Des Lise Giguère. Litho Ashton-Potter Canada)

2002 (23 July). 17th World Youth Day, Toronto. Self-adhesive. Fluorescent frame. Die-cut.

2156	**770**	48c. multicoloured	60	70
		a. Booklet pane. No. 2156×8	4·25	

The die-cutting on No. 2156 forms the shape of a cross which is followed by the fluorescent frame.

No. 2156 was only available in $3.84 stamp booklets, No. SB271.

(Des Monique Dufour and Sophie Lafortune. Litho Lowe-Martin)

2002 (30 Aug). Amphilex 2002 International Stamp Exhibition, Amsterdam. Phosphor frame. Perf 13×12½.

MS2157	160×97 mm. As Nos. 2134/2137, but PVA gum	2·25	3·75

771 Hands gripping Rope and P.S.I. Logo

(Des D. L'Allier. Litho Lowe-Martin)

2002 (4 Sept). Public Services International World Congress, Ottawa. Fluorescent frame. Perf 12½×13.
2158 **771** 48c. multicoloured 60 75
The fluorescent frame around each stamp is broken by the PSI logo.

776 Sir Sandford Fleming, Map of Canada and *Iris* (cable ship)

777 Genesis (painting by Daphne Odjig)

(Des Susan Warr. Litho Lowe-Martin)

2002 (31 Oct). Communications Centenaries. T **776** and similar vert design. Multicoloured. Fluorescent frame. Perf 13×12½.
2170 48c. Type **776** (opening of Pacific Cable)...... 75 1·00
      a. Horiz pair. Nos. 2170/2171 .... 1·50 2·00
2171 48c. Guglielmo Marconi, Map of Canada and wireless equipment (first Transatlantic radio message)................. 75 1·00
Nos. 2170/2171 were printed together, *se-tenant*, as horizontal pairs in sheets of 16 (8×2).

772 Tree in Four Seasons

(Des Debbie Adams. Litho C.B.N)

2002 (10 Sept). 75th Anniversary of Public Pensions. Fluorescent frame. Perf 13½.
2159 **772** 48c. multicoloured .... 60 1·00

(Des Signals Design Group. Litho C.B.N)

2002 (4 Nov). Christmas. Aboriginal Art. T **777** and similar vert designs. Multicoloured. Fluorescent frame. Perf 12½×13.
2172 48c. Type **777** 55 20
      a. Booklet pane of 10 with margins all round................................. 5·50
2173 65c. Winter Travel (painting by Cecil Youngfox) 70 75
      a. Booklet pane of 6 with margins all round................................. 4·25
2174 $1.25 Mary and Child (sculpture by Irene Katak Angutitaq)............................. 1·25 2·00
      a. Booklet pane of 6 with margins all round................................. 6·75
2172/2174 *Set of 3* .... 2·25 2·75

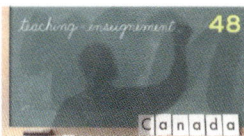

773 Mount Elbrus, Russia   **774** Teacher writing on Board

(Des Q30 Design. Litho Lowe-Martin)

2002 (1 Oct). International Year of Mountains. T **773** and similar mountain-shaped designs. Multicoloured. Self-adhesive. Fluorescent frame. Die-cut.
2160 48c. Type **773** .... 95 1·40
      a. Sheetlet of 8. Nos. 2160/2167 .... 7·00 10·00
2161 48c. Puncak Jaya, Indonesia........................ 95 1·40
2162 48c. Mount Everest, Nepal.......................... 95 1·40
2163 48c. Mount Kilimanjaro, Tanzania .... 95 1·40
2164 48c. Vinson Massif, Antarctica .... 95 1·40
2165 48c. Mount Aconcagua, Argentina............. 95 1·40
2166 48c. Mount McKinley, USA........................... 95 1·40
2167 48c. Mount Logan, Canada........................... 95 1·40
2160/2167 *Set of 8*... 7·00 10·00
Nos. 2160/2167 were only available in circular sheetlets of eight with the stamps arranged individually around the circumference. Each design forms a rectangle with a *se-tenant* inscribed label which includes a separate small circular illustration showing wildlife. Philatelic stocks were sold in a card folder.

(Des M. Koudis. Litho C.B.N)

2002 (4 Oct). World Teachers' Day. Fluorescent frame. Perf 12½×13.
2168 **774** 48c. multicoloured 60 60

778 Conductor's Hands and Original Orchestra

(Des Monique Dufour and Sophie Lafortune. Litho Lowe-Martin)

2002 (17 Nov). Centenary of Quebec Symphony Orchestra. Fluorescent frame. Perf 12½×13.
2175 **778** 48c. multicoloured .... 1·00 70

775 Frieze from Toronto Stock Exchange and Globe

(Des I. Novotny, J. Taylor and P. Sayers. Litho C.B.N)

2002 (24 Oct). 150th Anniversary of Toronto Stock Exchange. Fluorescent frame. Perf 12½×13.
2169 **775** 48c. multicoloured .... 60 1·00

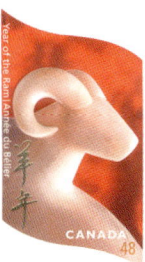
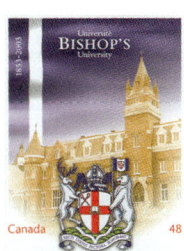

779 Sculpture of Ram's Head

779a Bishop's University, Quebec (150th anniversary of university status)

CANADA

(Des Rosina Li from sculptures by C. Reid. Litho Lowe-Martin (foil embossing and die-cutting by Gravure Choquet)

2003 (3 Jan). Chinese New Year. Year of the Ram. T **779** and similar vert design. Multicoloured. Fluorescent frame. Perf 13*.
2176	48c. Type **779**	60	1·00
	a. Gold omitted	£300	
MS2177	125×103 mm. $1.25 Sculpture of goat's head (33×57 mm)	1·25	2·25

*The horizontal perforations of Nos. 2176/2177 are arranged as a wavy line. On the vertical perforations there are 10 mm gaps at the top left and bottom right of each stamp where the separation is by straight die-cutting.
The top of No. **MS**2177 is die-cut in the shape of a ram's horn with a small barcode label attached to the bottom right hand corner.
No. 2176 has been reported imperforate.

(Des S. Huot, C. Vinh and P. Rousseau. Litho C.B.N)

2003 (18 Jan). National Hockey League. All-Star Game Players (4th series). Square designs as T **722**. Multicoloured. Fluorescent frame.

(a) PVA gum. Perf 12½×13.
2178	48c. Frank Mahovlich (wearing Maple Leaf No. 27 jersey)	80	1·50
	a. Sheetlet of 6. Nos. 2178/2183	4·25	8·00
2179	48c. Raymond Bourque (wearing Boston Bruins No. 77 jersey)	80	1·50
2180	48c. Serge Savard (wearing Canadiens No. 18 jersey)	80	1·50
2181	48c. Stan Mikita (wearing Chicago Blackhawks No. 21 jersey)	80	1·50
2182	48c. Mike Bossy (wearing New York Islanders No. 22 jersey)	80	1·50
2183	48c. Bill Durnan (wearing Canadiens jersey and brown gloves)	80	1·50
2178/2183 Set of 6		4·25	8·00

(b) Self-adhesive. Die-cut.
2184	48c. Frank Mahovlich (wearing Maple Leaf No. 27 jersey)	8·00	12·00
	a. Pane. Nos. 2184/2189	45·00	65·00
2185	48c. Raymond Bourque (wearing Boston Bruins No. 77 jersey)	8·00	12·00
2186	48c. Serge Savard (wearing Canadiens No. 18 jersey)	8·00	12·00
2187	48c. Stan Mikita (wearing Chicago Blackhawks No. 21 jersey)	8·00	12·00
2188	48c. Mike Bossy (wearing New York Islanders No. 22 jersey)	8·00	12·00
2189	48c. Bill Durnan (wearing Canadiens jersey and brown gloves)	8·00	12·00
2184/2189 Set of 6		45·00	65·00

Nos. 2178/2183 were printed together, *se-tenant*, in sheetlets of six containing two vertical strips of three separated by labels featuring further portraits of the players shown on the stamps. Nos. 2178, 2180 and 2182 are imperforate at left, and the others at right.

Nos. 2184/2189 were only available as $2.88 panes on which the surplus self-adhesive paper around each stamp was retained. The additional photographs, shown on the central labels of Nos. 2178/83, appear on the reverse of the backing paper of the self-adhesive versions.

(Des Denis L'Allier. Litho C.B.N)

2003 (28 Jan–4 Sept). Canadian Universities' Anniversaries (2nd issue). T **779a** and similar vert designs. Multicoloured. Fluorescent frame. Perf 13½.
2190	48c. Type **779a** (150th anniversary of university status)	70	1·00
	a. Booklet pane. No. 2190×8 with margins all round	6·00	
2191	48c. University of Western Ontario, London (150th anniversary) (19.3)	70	1·00
	a. Booklet pane. No. 2191×8 with margins all round	6·00	
2192	48c. St Francis Xavier University, Nova Scotia (150th anniversary) (4.4)	70	1·00
	a. Booklet pane. No. 2192×8 with margins all round	6·00	
2193	48c. Macdonald Institute, University of Guelph, Ontario (centenary) (20.6)	70	1·00
	a. Booklet pane. No. 2193×8 with margins all round	6·00	
2194	48c. University of Montréal (125th anniversary) (4.9)	70	1·00
	a. Booklet pane. No. 2194×8 with margins all around	6·00	
2190/2194 Set of 5		3·25	4·50

Nos. 2190/2194 were only available in $3.84 stamp booklets, Nos. SB275/SB279.

780 Leach's Storm Petrel

(Des R. Harder. Litho Lowe-Martin)

2003 (21 Feb). Bird Paintings by John J. Audubon (1st series). T **780** and similar multicoloured designs. Fluorescent frame.

(a) PVA gum. Perf 13×12½.
2195	48c. Type **780**	1·00	1·00
	a. Block of 4. Nos. 2195/2198	3·50	4·00
2196	48c. Brent Goose ('Brant')	1·00	1·00
2197	48c. Great Cormorant	1·00	1·00
2198	48c. Common Murre	1·00	1·00
2195/2198 Set of 4		3·50	4·00

(b) Self-adhesive. Die-cut.
2199	65c. Gyrfalcon (*vert*)	2·00	2·75
	a. Booklet pane. No. 2199×6	11·00	

Nos. 2195/2198 were printed together, *se-tenant*, as blocks of four throughout the sheet.
No. 2199 was only available in $3.90 stamp booklets, No. SB280, on which the surplus self-adhesive paper around each stamp was retained. See also Nos. 2274/2278 and 2340/2344.

781 Ranger looking through Binoculars   **782** Greek Figure with Dove

(Des O. Hill and D. Page. Litho Lowe-Martin)

2003 (3 Mar). 60th Anniversary of Canadian Rangers. Fluorescent frame. Perf 12½×13.
2200	**781**	48c. multicoloured	70	75

(Des K. Tsetsekas and J. Belisle. Litho C.B.N)

2003 (25 Mar). 75th Anniversary of American Hellenic Educational Progressive Association in Canada. Fluorescent frame. Perf 12½×13.
2201	**782**	48c. multicoloured	70	75

783 Firefighter carrying Boy and Burning Buildings   **784** Queen Elizabeth II and Maple Leaf

(Des F. Dallaire. Litho C.B.N)

2003 (30 May). Volunteer Firefighters. Fluorescent frame. Perf 13½.
2202	**783**	48c. multicoloured	1·25	75

(Des Saskia van Kampen. Litho Lowe-Martin)

2003 (2 June). 50th Anniversary of Coronation. Fluorescent frame. Perf 13×12½.
2203	**784**	48c. multicoloured	1·00	75

785 Québec City (c. 1703) Seal and Excerpt from Letter

(Des C. Malenfant. Litho C.B.N)

2003 (6 June). Pedro da Silva (first official courier of New France). Fluorescent frame. Perf 13.
2204	**785**	48c. multicoloured	70	75

(Des Bradbury Design. Litho Ashton-Potter)

2003 (12 June). Tourist Attractions (3rd series). Horiz designs as T **747**. Multicoloured. Self-adhesive. Fluorescent frame. Perf 11½.
2205	65c. Wilberforce Falls, Nunavut	1·10	1·50
	a. Booklet pane of 5. Nos. 2205/2209	5·00	
2206	65c. Inside Passage, British Columbia	1·10	1·50
2207	65c. Royal Canadian Mounted Police Depot Division, Regina, Saskatchewan	1·10	1·50
2208	65c. Casa Loma, Toronto	1·10	1·50
2209	65c. Gatineau Park, Québec	1·10	1·50
2210	$1.25 Dragon boat race, Vancouver	1·75	2·00
	a. Booklet pane of 5. Nos. 2210/2214	8·00	
2211	$1.25 Polar bear, Churchill, Manitoba	1·75	2·00
2212	$1.25 Niagara Falls, Ontario	1·75	2·00
2213	$1.25 Magdalen Islands, Québec	1·75	2·00
2214	$1.25 Province House, Charlottetown, Prince Edward Island	1·75	2·00
2205/2214 Set of 10		13·00	16·00

Nos. 2205/2209 and 2210/2214 were only available in $3.25 or $6.25 stamp booklets, Nos. SB281/SB282.

Vancouver **2010**

(786) **787** Mountains and Sea

2003 (11 July). Vancouver's Successful Bid for Winter Olympic Games, 2010. No. 1368 optd with T **786** in red.
2215	48c. multicoloured	1·00	1·25
	a. Booklet pane. No. 2215×10	9·00	

2003 (19 July). Canada–Alaska Cruise Picture Postage. T **787** and similar horiz design. Multicoloured. Litho. Self-adhesive. Die-cut.
2216	($1.25) Type **787**	6·00	10·00
2217	($1.25) Tail fin of whale, mountains and sea	6·00	10·00

Nos. 2216/2217 were issued in sheets of ten containing five of each of the two designs and three stamp-size Picture Post labels. The stamps were inscribed 'POSTAGE PAID PORT PAYÉ' and could be used as postage from Canada to anywhere in the world. The sheets of ten were sold at $12.50 and could only be purchased by cruise guests or through the National Philatelic Centre (*Price £50, mint*).

788 Assembly Logo

(Des P. Fontaine. Litho Lowe-Martin)

2003 (21 July). Tenth Lutheran World Federation Assembly, Winnipeg. Fluorescent frame. Perf 12½×13.
2218	**788**	48c. multicoloured	70	1·00

789 Canadian F-86 Sabre Fighter Plane, sailors and Infantrymen

(Des S. Slipp. Litho C.B.N)

2003 (25 July). 50th Anniversary of Signing of Korea Armistice. Fluorescent frame. Perf 13.
2219	**789**	48c. multicoloured	1·00	1·00

790 Anne Herbert

(Des Katalin Kovats. Litho C.B.N)

2003 (8 Sept). 50th Anniversary of National Library of Canada. Booklet stamps. T **790** and similar horiz designs showing authors and portions of their handwritten text. Multicoloured. Fluorescent frame. Perf 13×12½.
2220	48c. Type **790**	70	1·00
	a. Booklet pane of 8. Nos. 2220/2223×2	5·00	
2221	48c. Hector de Saint-Denys Garneau	70	1·00
2222	48c. Morley Callaghan	70	1·00
2223	48c. Susanna Moodie and Catharine Parr Traill	70	1·00
2220/2223 Set of 4		2·50	3·50

Nos. 2220/2223 were only issued in $3.84 booklets, No. SB284.

791 Cyclists in Road Race

(Des Doreen Colonello. Litho C.B.N)

2003 (10 Sept). World Road Cycling Championships, Hamilton, Ontario. Booklet stamp. Fluorescent frame. Perf 12½×13.
2224	**791**	48c. multicoloured	1·10	1·00
		a. Booklet pane. No. 2224×8	8·00	

No. 2224 was only issued in $3.84 booklets, No. SB285.

792 Marc Garneau **793** Maple Leaves, Canada

(Des P.-Y. Pelletier. Litho Lowe-Martin)

2003 (1 Oct). Stamp Collecting Month. Canadian Astronauts. T **792** and similar circular designs. Multicoloured. Self-adhesive. Fluorescent frame. Die-cut.
2225	48c. Type **792**	70	1·00
	a. Pane. Nos. 2225/2232	5·00	8·00
2226	48c. Roberta Bondar	70	1·00
2227	48c. Steve MacLean	70	1·00
2228	48c. Chris Hadfield	70	1·00
2229	48c. Robert Thirsk	70	1·00
2230	48c. Bjarni Tryggvason	70	1·00
2231	48c. Dave Williams	70	1·00
2232	48c. Julie Payette	70	1·00
2225/2232 Set of 8		5·00	8·00

Nos. 2225/2232 were only available as $3.84 panes on which the surplus self-adhesive paper around each stamp was retained.

(Des R. Bellemare (No. 2231) or Veena Chantanatat (No. 2232). Litho Ashton-Potter)

2003 (4 Oct). National Emblems. T **793** and similar vert design. Multicoloured. Fluorescent frame. Perf 12½.
2233	48c. Type **793**	1·25	1·40
	a. Pair. Nos. 2233/2234	2·50	2·75
	ab. Imperf (pair)	£500	
2234	48c. *Cassis fistula* flowers, Thailand	1·25	1·40
MS2235 120×96 mm. Nos. 2233/2234		4·00	6·00
	a. Imperf	£850	

Nos. 2233/2234 were printed together, *se-tenant*, in horizontal and vertical pairs in sheets of 16.

No. **MS**2235 commemorates Bangkok 2003 International Stamp Exhibition, Thailand.

Stamps of the same designs were issued by Thailand.

CANADA

794 White Birds

(Des S. Spazuk. Litho Lowe-Martin)

2003 (7 Oct). 80th Birth Anniversary of Jean-Paul Riopelle (painter and sculptor). T **794** and similar horiz designs showing details from fresco 'L'Hommage à Rosa Luxemburg'. Multicoloured. Fluorescent frame. Perf 12½×13.

MS2236	178×244 mm. 48c. Type **794**; 48c. Two white herons and white birds; 48c. Flying bird, flower and three white birds in cameo; 48c. Grouse on moor, white bird and sun; 48c. Two flying white birds in cameo and silhouette of falcon; 48c. Two white birds and cameo of flying duck........................	4·00	6·50
MS2237	159×95 mm. $1.25 Eggs and bird silhouette. Perf 13..	2·50	4·00

797 Monkey King on Cloud **798** Bonhomme (Snowman), Quebec Winter Carnival

(Des Anita Kunz and Louis Fishauf. Litho and embossed C.B.N)

2004 (8 Jan). Chinese New Year. Year of the Monkey. T **797** and similar vert design showing scenes from 'Journey to the West' by Wu Ch'eng-en. Multicoloured. Fluorescent frame. Perf 13×12½.

2247	49c. Type **797**...	1·00	1·00
MS2248	115×82 mm. $1.40 Monkey on road to India......	1·90	3·00

No. **MS**2248 has a barcode tab attached at right.

2004 (8 Jan). Hong Kong 2004 International Stamp Exhibition. No. **MS**2248 optd 'Hong Kong Stamp Expo 2004' and exhibition emblem in gold on sheet margin.

MS2249	115×82 mm. $1.40 Monkey on road to India......	1·90	2·75

(Des Stéphane Huot, Charles Vinh and Pierre Rousseau. Litho Lowe-Martin)

2004 (24 Jan). National Hockey League. All-Star Game Players (5th series). Square designs as T **722**. Multicoloured. Fluorescent frame.

(a) PVA gum. Perf 12½×13.

2250	49c. Larry Robinson (wearing Canadiens jersey)..	1·40	1·50
	a. Sheetlet. Nos. 2250/2255............................	7·50	8·00
2251	49c. Marcel Dionne (wearing Los Angeles Kings jersey)...	1·40	1·50
2252	49c. Ted Lindsay (wearing Detroit Red Wings jersey)..	1·40	1·50
2253	49c. Johnny Bower (wearing Toronto Maple Leafs goal keeper kit).............................	1·40	1·50
2254	49c. Brad Park (wearing New York Rangers jersey)..	1·40	1·50
2255	49c. Milt Schmidt (wearing Boston Bruins jersey)..	1·40	1·50
2250/2255 Set of 6...		7·50	8·00

(b) Self-adhesive. Die-cut.

2256	49c. Larry Robinson (wearing Canadiens jersey)..	1·10	1·25
	a. Panc. Nos. 2256/2256f..................................	6·00	6·75
2256b	49c. Marcel Dionne (wearing Los Angeles Kings jersey)...	1·10	1·25
2256c	49c. Ted Lindsay (wearing Detroit Red Wings jersey)..	1·10	1·25
2256d	49c. Johnny Bower (wearing Toronto Maple Leafs goal keeper kit).............................	1·10	1·25
2256e	49c. Brad Park (wearing New York Rangers jersey)..	1·10	1·25
2256f	49c. Milt Schmidt (wearing Boston Bruins jersey)..	1·10	1·25
2256/2256f Set of 6...		6·00	6·75

Nos. 2250/2255 were printed together, *se-tenant*, in sheetlets of six containing two vertical strips of three separated by labels featuring further portraits of the players shown on the stamps. Nos. 2250, 2252 and 2254 are imperforate at left, and the others at right.

Nos. 2256/2256f were only available as $2.94 panes on which the surplus self-adhesive paper around each stamp was retained. The additional photographs, shown on the central labels of Nos. 2250/2255, appear on the reverse of the backing paper of the self-adhesive versions.

795 Ice Skates and Wrapped Presents **796** Queen Elizabeth II, 2002

(Des P. David. Litho Lowe-Martin)

2003 (4 Nov). Christmas. Self-adhesive booklet stamps. T **795** and similar square designs. Multicoloured. Fluorescent frame. Die-cut.

2238	48c. Type **795**...	70	55
	aa. Imperf (pair)...	£250	
	a. Booklet pane. No. 2238×12.........................	7·50	
2239	65c. Teddy bear and wrapped presents........	1·25	1·50
	aa. Imperf (pair)...	£250	
	a. Booklet pane. No. 2239×6...........................	6·75	
2240	$1.25 Toy duck on wheels and wrapped presents..	1·90	2·75
	aa. Imperf (pair)...	£250	
	a. Booklet pane. No. 2240×6...........................	10·00	
2238/2240 Set of 3..		3·50	4·25

Nos. 2238/2240 were only available in separate $3.90, $5.76 or $7.50 booklets, Nos. SB286/SB288.

(Des Saskia van Kampen (49c.) or Gottschalk and Ash International (50c.). Litho C.B.N)

2003 (19 Dec)–**04**. Self-adhesive booklet stamps. Fluorescent frame. Die-cut.

2241	**796** 49c. black, dull mauve and scarlet............	1·10	1·00
	a. Booklet pane. No. 2241×10.........................	10·00	
2242	50c. multicoloured (20.12.04)...................	1·10	1·00
	a. Booklet pane. No. 2242×10.........................	10·00	

Nos. 2241/2242 were only issued in seperate booklets, Nos. SB292 and SB313.

Examples of No. 2241 have been reported printed on the wrong side of the paper, so that the self-adhesive gum is on the backing paper rather than the stamps.

Postal forgeries of Nos. 2241/2241a are known.

Nos. 2243/2246 are vacant.

(Des Bradbury Branding and Design. Litho Lowe-Martin)

2004 (29 Jan–19 July). Tourist Attractions (4th series). T **798** and similar horiz designs. Multicoloured. Fluorescent frame. Self-adhesive. Imperf.

2257	49c. Type **798**...	1·00	1·60
	a. Booklet pane. No. 2257×6...........................	5·50	
2258	49c. St. Joseph's Oratory (2.4)...........................	1·00	1·60
	a. Booklet pane. No. 2258×6...........................	5·50	
2259	49c. Audience at International Jazz Festival, Montreal (1.6)..	1·00	1·60
	a. Booklet pane. No. 2259×6...........................	5·50	
2260	49c. People watching Traversée Internationale du Lac St-Jean (18.6).........	1·00	1·60
	a. Booklet pane. No. 2260×6...........................	5·50	
2261	49c. People at Canadian National Exhibition and Prince's Gate (19.7).........	1·00	1·60
	a. Booklet pane. No. 2261×6...........................	5·50	
2257/2261 Set of 5..		4·50	8·50

Nos. 2257/2261 were only available in five separate $2.94 stamp booklets, Nos. SB293/SB297.

799 Governor General Ramon Hnatyshyn

800 *Fram* (polar research ship)

(Des Susan Mavor. Litho Lowe-Martin)

2004 (16 Mar). 70th Birth Anniversary of Governor General Ramon Hnatyshyn. Fluorescent frame. Perf 12½×13.
2262	**799**	49c. multicoloured	70	1·00

(Des and. Eng Martin Mörck. Recess and litho Posts and Telegraph Office, Copenhagen, Denmark)

2004 (26 Mar). 150th Birth Anniversary of Otto Sverdrup (polar explorer). T **800** and similar vert design. Each blackish purple and buff. Perf 13.
2263	49c. Type **800**	1·50	1·00
MS2264	166×60 mm. $1.40 As No. 2263 plus two labels	2·50	3·50

No. **MS**2264 was issued with two stamp-size labels showing stamp designs of Greenland and Norway.

Stamps of similar designs were issued by Greenland and Norway.

801 Silhouettes of Cadets

(Des André Perro. Litho C.B.N)

2004 (26 Mar). 125th Anniversary of Royal Canadian Army Cadets. Fluorescent frame. Self-adhesive. Imperf.
2265	**801**	49c. multicoloured	1·25	1·50
		a. Booklet pane. No. 2265×8	8·00	

No. 2265 was only available in $3.92 self-adhesive stamp booklets, No. SB298.

802 Subway Train, Toronto

(Des Debbie Adams. Litho C.B.N)

2004 (30 Mar). Light Rail Urban Transit. T **802** and similar horiz designs. Multicoloured. Fluorescent frame. Perf 12½×13.
2266	49c. Type **802**	1·50	1·50
	a. Vert strip of 4. Nos. 2266/2269	5·50	5·50
2267	49c. TransLink SkyTrain, Vancouver	1·50	1·50
2268	49c. Métro train, Montréal	1·50	1·50
2269	49c. CTrain, Calgary	1·50	1·50
2266/2269	Set of 4	5·50	5·50

Nos. 2266/2269 were printed together, *se-tenant*, in vertical strips of four stamps in sheets of 16. The designs of the stamps provide a horizontal illusion of motion throughout the strips.

803 Canadian Map and Employee

(Des Ron Mugford. Litho Lowe-Martin)

2004 (19 Apr). 40th Anniversary of Home Hardware (co-operative business). Fluorescent frame. Self-adhesive. Perf 11.
2270	**803**	49c. multicoloured	90	1·00
		a. Booklet pane. No. 2270×10 plus central label	8·00	

No. 2270 was only available in $4.90 stamp booklets, No. SB299.

(Des Dennis L'Allier. Litho C.B.N)

2004 (4–8 May). Canadian Universities' Anniversaries (3rd issue). Vert designs as T **779a**. Multicoloured. Fluorescent frame. Perf 13½.
2271	49c. University of Sherbrooke (50th anniversary)	80	1·25
	a. Booklet pane. No. 2271×8	5·50	
2272	49c. University of Prince Edward Island (bicentenary)	80	1·25
	a. Booklet pane. No. 2272×8	5·50	

Nos. 2271/2272 were only available in two separate $3.92 stamp booklets, Nos. SB300/SB301.

804 Teddy Bears

805 Ruby-crowned Kinglet

(Des Monique Dufour and Sophie Lafortune. Litho Lowe-Martin)

2004 (6 May). Centenary of Montreal Children's Hospital. Fluorescent frame. Self-adhesive. Perf 9½×10½.
2273	**804**	49c. multicoloured	90	1·25
		a. Booklet pane. No. 2273×8	6·50	

No. 2273 was only available in $3.92 stamp booklets, No. SB302.

(Des Rolf Harder. Litho Lowe-Martin)

2004 (14 May). Bird Paintings by John J. Audubon (2nd series). T **805** and similar vert designs. Multicoloured. Fluorescent frame.

(a) PVA Gum. Perf 12½×13.
2274	49c. Type **805**	85	1·00
	a. Block of 4. Nos. 2274/2277	3·00	3·50
2275	49c. White-winged Crossbill	85	1·00
2276	49c. Bohemian Waxwing	85	1·00
2277	49c. Boreal Chickadee	85	1·00
2274/2277	Set of 4	3·00	3·50

(b) Self-adhesive. Imperf.
2278	80c. Lincoln's Sparrow	2·00	2·50
	a. Booklet pane. No. 2278 ×6	11·00	

Nos. 2274/2277 were printed together, *se-tenant*, as blocks of four stamps in sheets of 16.

No. 2278 was only available in $4.80 stamp booklets (No. SB303) in which the surplus self-adhesive paper around each stamp was retained.

806 Sir Samuel Cunard

806a Butterfly on Flower

CANADA

(Des Oliver Hill and Dennis Page. Litho Lowe-Martin)

2004 (28 May). Sir Samuel Cunard and Sir Hugh Allan (founders of transatlantic mail service) Commemorations. T **806** and similar horiz design. Multicoloured. Fluorescent frame. Self-adhesive. Perf 13×12½.
2279	49c. Type **806**	1·25	1·50
	a. Horiz pair. Nos. 2279/2280	2·50	3·00
2280	49c. Sir Hugh Allan	1·25	1·50

Nos. 2279/2280 were printed together, *se-tenant*, as horiz pairs in sheets of 16, each pair forming a composite design and also breaking up the fluorescent frame.

2004 (31 May). 'Write me...Ring me' Greetings Stamps. T **806a** and similar horiz designs. Multicoloured. Fluorescent frame. Self-adhesive. Perf 11½×12.
2280*a*	(49c.) Type **806a**	11·00	15·00
2280*b*	(49c.) Two young children at beach	11·00	15·00
2280*c*	(49c.) Red rose	11·00	15·00
2280*d*	(49c.) Pug (dog)	11·00	15·00
2280*a*/2280*d* Set of 4		40·00	55·00

Nos. 2280*a*/2280*d* are inscribed 'Domestic Lettermail' (initial value was 49c.), and were each issued in panes of two. Each pane was sold in a $5.99 greeting card which also contained a phone card.

807 Soldiers storming Juno Beach, Normandy

808 Pierre Dugua de Mons

(Des Derwyn Goodall. Litho Lowe-Martin)

2004 (6 June). 60th Anniversary of D-Day Landings. Fluorescent frame. Perf 13×12½.
2281	**807**	49c. multicoloured	1·25	1·00

(Des Rejearz Myette and Suzanne Duranceau. Eng André Lavergne. Recess and litho C.B.N)

2004 (26 June). French Settlement in North America (1st issue). 400th Anniversary of First French Settlement in Acadia, St Croix Island. Fluorescent frame. Perf 13×12½.
2282	**808**	49c. ochre, royal blue and orange	1·00	1·00

See also Nos. 2361, 2400/**MS**2401, 2508 and 2550.

809 Spyros Louis (Greek athlete) and Marathon Runner

(Des Pierre-Yves Pelletier. Litho C.B.N)

2004 (28 July). Olympic Games, Athens, Greece. T **809** and similar horiz design. Multicoloured. Fluorescent frame. Perf 12½×13.
2283	49c. Type **809**	1·50	1·50
	a. Horiz pair. Nos. 2283/2284	3·00	3·00
2284	49c. Girls playing football	1·50	1·50

Nos. 2283/2284 were printed together, *se-tenant*, in horizontal pairs throughout sheets of 16.

810 Golfer and Trophy from Early Tournament

811 Segmented Heart

(Des Q30 Design Inc. Litho and embossed Lowe-Martin and Choquet Engraving Inc)

2004 (12 Aug). Canadian Open Golf Championship. T **810** and similar circular design. Multicoloured. Self-adhesive. Fluorescent frame. Die-cut.
2285	49c. Type **810**	1·00	1·40
	a. Pane. Nos. 2285/2286, each×4	7·25	10·00
2286	49c. Golfer and trophy from modern tournament	1·00	1·40

Nos. 2285/2286 were only available as $3.92 panes of eight stamps presented in illustrated portfolios. The surplus self-adhesive paper around each stamp is retained.

(Des Guénette and Delisle Design. Litho Lowe-Martin)

2004 (15 Sept). 50th Anniversary of Montréal Heart Institute. Self-adhesive. Fluorescent frame. Perf 13½.
2287	**811**	49c. multicoloured	80	1·00
		a. Booklet pane. No. 2287×8	5·75	

No. 2287 was only available from $3.92 stamp booklets (No. SB306) on which the surplus self-adhesive backing paper was retained.

812 Goldfish in Bowl

(Des Isabelle Toussaint. Litho Lowe-Martin)

2004 (1 Oct). Pets. T **812** and similar horiz designs. Multicoloured. Fluorescent frame. Self-adhesive. Imperf.
2288	49c. Type **812**	1·10	1·40
	a. Booklet pane. Nos. 2288/2291 each×2	8·00	
2289	49c. Two cats on chair	1·10	1·40
2290	49c. Child with rabbit	1·10	1·40
2291	49c. Child with dog	1·10	1·40
2288/2291 Set of 4		4·00	5·00

Nos. 2288/2291 were only available in $3.92 stamp booklets, No. SB307.

813 Gerhard Herzberg (Chemistry, 1971)

(Des HM and E Design and Communications. Litho Lowe-Martin)

2004 (4 Oct). Nobel Prize Winners. T **813** and similar horiz design. Multicoloured. Fluorescent frame and imprint date. Perf 12½×13.
2292	49c. Type **813**	90	1·25
	a. Pair. Nos. 2292/2293	1·75	2·50
2293	49c. Michael Smith (Chemistry, 1993)	90	1·25

Nos. 2292/2293 were printed together, *se-tenant*, in horizontal and vertical pairs in sheets of 16. The designs in the silhouettes are overprinted with blue fluorescent ink.

Nos. 2292/2293 also have a hidden imprint date visible only under U.V. light.

814 Maple Leaf in Photo Album Frame

815 Victoria Cross (embossed)

CANADA

(Des Steven Spazuk and Jean-Francois Renaud. Litho C.B.N)

2004 (8 Oct). Picture Postage. T **814** and similar horiz design. Multicoloured. Fluorescent frame. Self-adhesive. Perf 12½×13.

2294	49c. Type **814**	90	1·00
	a. Pane. No. 2294×20	16·00	
2295	49c. Maple leaf in silver frame	90	1·00
	a. Pane. No. 2295×20	16·00	

Nos. 2294/2295 were both inscribed 'Domestic Postage Paid' and sold for 49c.

Nos. 2294/2295 were both only available of panes of 20 stamps including a 'keepsake' stamp and enlarged image, or panes of 40 stamps.

(Des Pierre-Yves Pelletier. Litho and embossed C.B.N. and Choquet Engraving Inc)

2004 (21 Oct). 150th Anniversary of First Canadian Recipient of the Victoria Cross. T **815** and similar vert design. Multicoloured. Fluorescent frame. Perf 13×12½.

2296	49c. Type **815**	1·10	1·25
	a. Sheetlet of 16. Nos. 2296/2297 both×8	16·00	
2297	49c. Victoria Cross and signature of Queen Elizabeth II	1·10	1·25

Nos. 2296/2297 were printed together *se-tenant* in sheetlets of 16 around a central illustration and listing of 94 Canadians who have received the Victoria Cross.

Nos. 2296/2297 also have a hidden imprint date visible only under U.V. light.

816 'Self-portrait', 1974

817 Santa in his Sleigh and Reindeer

(Des Gottschalk and Ash International. Litho Lowe-Martin)

2004 (22 Oct). Art Canada. Birth Centenary of Jean Paul Lemieux. T **816** and similar multicoloured designs. Fluorescent frame. Perf 13.

2298	49c. Type **816**	1·00	1·25
MS2299	150×86 mm. 49c. Type **816**; 80c. 'A June Wedding', 1972 (53×34 mm); $1.40 'Summer', 1959 (64×31 mm)	3·50	6·00

(Des Saskia van Kampen and Tim Zeltner. Litho C.B.N)

2004 (2 Nov). Christmas. Self-adhesive booklet stamps. T **817** and similar horiz designs. Multicoloured. Fluorescent frame. Perf 7×imperf.

2300	49c. Type **817**	1·00	45
	a. Booklet pane. No. 2300×12	11·00	
2301	80c. Santa driving a Cadillac and towing a house	1·60	2·25
	a. Pane. No. 2301×6	8·75	
2302	$1.40 Santa driving a train	2·50	3·50
	a. Pane. No. 2302×6	13·50	
2300/2302 Set of 3		4·75	5·50

Nos. 2300/2302 were only available in No. SB309, $5.88 or $8.40 panes of six, all with the surplus self-adhesive paper around each stamp retained.

818 Red Calla Lily

819 Rooster facing East (right)

(Des Monique Dufour and Sophie LaFortune (51c., 89c., $1.05, $1.49 from illustrations by Sigmond Pifco). Litho Lowe-Martin)

2004 (20 Dec)–**05**. Flowers (1st series). T **818** and similar vert designs. Multicoloured. Fluorescent frame. Self-adhesive.

(a) Coil stamps. Perf 8½×imperf (50c., 85c., $1.45) or 7×imperf (others).

2303	50c. Type **818**	1·00	1·00
	a. Imperf (pair)	45·00	
	b. Perf 7×Imperf (2.05)	1·00	1·00
2304	51c. Red Bergamot (19.12.05)	80	60
2305	85c. Yellow Calla Lily	1·00	2·50
	a. Perf 7×Imperf (2.05)	1·00	1·75
2306	89c. Lady's Slipper Orchids (19.12.05)	1·25	1·75
2307	$1.05 Pink Fairy Slipper Orchids (19.12.05)	1·50	2·00
2308	$1.45 Purple Dutch Iris	2·75	2·50
	a. Imperf (pair)	2·75	2·50
	b. Perf 7×Imperf (2.05)	2·75	2·50
2309	$1.49 Himalayan Blue Poppies (19.12.05)	2·00	2·50
2303/2309 Set of 7		9·25	11·00

(b) Booklet stamps. Imperf.

2310	85c. Yellow Calla Lily	1·25	2·00
	aa. Black omitted	£300	
	a. Pane. No. 2310×6	6·00	
2311	89c. Lady's Slipper Orchids (19.12.05)	1·25	1·75
	a. Pane. No. 2311×6	6·00	
2312	$1.05 Pink Fairy Slipper Orchids (19.12.05)	1·40	2·00
	a. Pane. No. 2312×6	7·50	
2313	$1.45 Purple Dutch Iris	2·00	2·75
	a. Pane. No. 2313×6	10·00	
2313*b*	$1.49 Himalayan Blue Poppies (19.12.05)	2·00	2·75
	ba. Pane. No. 2313×6	8·25	
2310/2313*b* Set of 5		7·00	10·00

Nos. 2310/2313*b* were issued in separate $5.10, $5.34, $6.30, $8.70 or $8.94 panes of six.

See also Nos. 2470/**MS**2477, 2530/**MS**2537 and 2645/**MS**2652.

(Des Hélène L'Heureux. Litho and embossed C.B.N)

2005 (7 Jan). Chinese New Year. Year of the Rooster. 35th Anniversary of Diplomatic Relations with China (No. **MS**2315b). T **819** and similar multicoloured designs. Perf 13½ (50c.) or 12½×13 ($1.45).

2314	50c. Type **819**	1·00	1·00
	a. Red omitted	£1100	
MS2315	Two sheets, each 105×82 mm. (a) $1.45 Rooster facing west (left) (40×41 mm). (b) $1.45 As No **MS**2315a Set of 2 sheets	2·50	4·00

Nos. **MS**2315a/**MS**2315b both have a barcode tab attached at foot.
No. **MS**2315b is optd with the flags of Canada and China and the dates '1970' and '2005' in gold foil on the margin.

(Des Stéphane Huot, François Escalmel and Pierre Rousseau. Litho C.B.N)

2005 (24 Jan). National Hockey League. All-Star Game Players (6th series). Square designs as T **722**. Multicoloured. Fluorescent frame.

(a) PVA gum. Perf 12½×13.

2316	50c. Henri Richard (wearing Habs jersey)	1·50	1·50
	a. Sheetlet of 6. Nos. 2316/2321	8·00	9·00
2317	50c. Grant Fuhr (wearing Oilers goal keeper kit)	1·50	1·50
2318	50c. Allan Stanley (wearing Toronto Maple Leafs jersey)	1·50	1·50
2319	50c. Pierre Pilote (wearing Chicago Black Hawks jersey)	1·50	1·50
2320	50c. Bryan Trottier (wearing New York Islanders jersey)	1·50	1·50
2321	50c. John Bucyk (wearing Boston Bruins jersey)	1·50	1·50
2316/2321 Set of 6		8·00	9·00

(b) Self-adhesive. Die-cut.

2322	50c. Henri Richard (wearing Habs jersey)	1·00	1·40
	a. Pane. Nos. 2322//2327	5·50	7·50
2323	50c. Grant Fuhr (wearing Oilers goal keeper kit)	1·00	1·40
2324	50c. Allan Stanley (wearing Toronto Maple Leafs jersey)	1·00	1·40
2325	50c. Pierre Pilote (wearing Chicago Black Hawks jersey)	1·00	1·40
2326	50c. Bryan Trottier (wearing New York Islanders jersey)	1·00	1·40
2327	50c. John Bucyk (wearing Boston Bruins jersey)	1·00	1·40
2322/2327 Set of 6		5·50	9·00

Nos. 2316/2321 were printed together, *se-tenant*, in sheetlets of six containing two vertical strips of three separated by labels featuring further portraits of the players shown on the stamps. Nos. 2316, 2318 and 2320 are imperforate at left, and the others at right.

Nos. 2322/2327 were only available as $3 panes on which the surplus self-adhesive paper around each stamp was retained. The additional photographs, shown on the central labels of Nos. 2316/21, appear on the reverse of the backing paper of the self-adhesive versions.

820 Alevin Fishing Fly

CANADA

(Des Circle Design and Alain Massicotte. Litho C.B.N)

2005 (4 Feb). Fishing Flies. T **820** and similar horiz designs. Multicoloured. Fluorescent frame.

(a) PVA gum. Perf 12½×13.

MS2328 190×112 mm. 50c.×4 Type **820**; Jock Scott; P.E.I. Fly; Mickey Finn		3·00	5·00

(b) Self-adhesive. Straight-edge and Perf 10.

2329	50c. Type **820**	1·10	1·50
	a. Booklet pane. Nos. 2329/2332, each×2	8·00	
2330	50c. Jock Scott	1·10	1·50
2331	50c. Mickey Finn	1·10	1·50
2332	50c. P.E.I. Fly	1·10	1·50
2329/2332 Set of 4		4·00	5·50

Nos. 2329/2332 were only issued in $4 stamp booklets (No. SB316) which contained two panes of No. 2329a and an additional pane inscribed with information about the flies and photographs of the tiers.

(Des Denis L'Allier. Litho Lowe-Martin)

2005 (14 Feb). Canadian Universities' Anniversaries (4th series). Vert design as T **779a** (No. 2190). Multicoloured. Fluorescent frame. Perf 13.

2333	50c. Nova Scotia Agricultural College	80	1·00
	a. Booklet pane. No. 2333×8	5·75	

No. 2333 was only available in $4 stamp booklets (No. SB317).
No. 2334 is vacant.

821 Inukshuk of Five Rocks

822 Yellow Daffodils

(Des Paul Haslip. Litho C.B.N)

2005 (4 Mar). Expo 2005 International Exhibition, Aichi, Japan. Fluorescent frame. Perf 13½.

2335	**821**	50c. multicoloured	70	50

No. 2335 has been reported imperforate, its status is unknown.

(Des Isabelle Toussaint. Litho Lowe-Martin)

2005 (10 Mar). Daffodils. T **822** and similar horiz design. Multicoloured. Fluorescent frame.

(a) Self-adhesive. Perf 10.

2336	50c. Type **822**	90	1·10
	a. Booklet pane. Nos. 2336/2337, each×5	8·00	
2337	50c. White daffodils with yellow trumpets	90	1·10

(b) PVA gum. Perf 13½.

MS2338 120×80 mm. Nos. 2336/2337		1·25	1·75

Nos. 2336/2337 were only available in $5 booklets, No. SB319, in which the surplus self-adhesive paper around each stamp was retained.

No. **MS**2338 also commemorates Pacific Explorer 2005 World Stamp Expo Exhibition, Sydney, Australia.

823 TD Bank Building of c.1900, Cashier and TD Tower, Toronto

824 Horned Lark

(Des q30 design inc. Litho Lowe-Martin)

2005 (18 Mar). 150th Anniversary of TD Bank Financial Group. Fluorescent frame. Self-adhesive. P 11½.

2339	**823**	50c. multicoloured	80	1·00
		a. Booklet pane. No. 2339×10	7·00	

No. 2339 was only issued in $5 booklets, No. SB320.

(Des Rolf Harder. Litho Lowe-Martin)

2005 (23 Mar). Bird Paintings by John Audubon (3rd series). T **824** and similar horiz designs. Multicoloured. Fluorescent frame.

(a) PVA gum. Perf 12½×13½.

2340	50c. Type **824**	1·50	1·50
	a. Block of 4. Nos. 2340/2343	5·50	5·50
2341	50c. Piping Plover	1·50	1·50
2342	50c. Stilt Sandpiper	1·50	1·50
2343	50c. Willow Ptarmigan	1·50	1·50
2340/2343 Set of 4		5·50	5·50

(b) Size 45×35 mm. Self-adhesive. Imperf.

2344	85c. Double-crested Cormorant	2·00	2·50
	a. Booklet pane. No. 2344×6	12·00	

Nos. 2340/2343 were printed together, *se-tenant*, as blocks of 4 in sheets of 16.

No. 2344 was only available in $5.10 booklets, No. SB321, in which the surplus self-adhesive paper around each stamp was retained.

825 Jacques Cartier Bridge, Montreal, Quebec

(Des Smith-Boake Designwerke Inc. Litho C.B.N)

2005 (2 Apr). Bridges. T **825** and similar horiz designs. Multicoloured. Fluorescent frame. Self-adhesive. Perf 12½×13½.

2345	50c. Type **825**	75	1·00
	a. Block or strip of 4. Nos. 2345/2348	2·75	3·50
2346	50c. Souris Swinging Bridge, Manitoba	75	1·00
2347	50c. Angus L. Macdonald Bridge, Halifax, Nova Scotia	75	1·00
2348	50c. Canso Causeway, Nova Scotia	75	1·00
2345/2348 Set of 4		2·75	3·50

Nos. 2345/2348 were printed together, *se-tenant*, in different combinations in sheets of 16, giving four blocks of four or four horizontal and vertical strips of four.

Nos. 2345/2348 have been reported imperforate.

The backing paper shows further illustrations of these bridges.

826 Magazine Covers of 1911, 1954, 1962 and 1917

827 Saskatoon Berries and Osprey, Waterton Lakes National Park, Alberta, Canada

(Des 52 Pick-up Inc. Litho Lowe-Martin)

2005 (12 Apr). Centenary of *Maclean's Magazine*. Fluorescent frame. Perf 12½×13½.

2349	**826**	50c. multicoloured	60	1·00

(Des Xerxes Irani and Jeff Spokes (No. 2350) or Finbarr O'Connor (No. 2351). Litho Lowe-Martin)

2005 (22 Apr). Biosphere Reserves. T **827** and similar horiz design. Multicoloured. Fluorescent frame. Perf 12½×13½.

2350	50c. Type **827**	1·25	1·25
	a. Pair. Nos. 2350/2351	2·50	2·50
2351	50c. Red Deer stags, Killarney National Park, Ireland	1·25	1·25
MS2352 120×70 mm. Nos. 2350/2351		2·50	3·25

Nos. 2350/2351 were printed together, *se-tenant*, in horizontal and vertical pairs in sheets of 16.

Stamps in similar designs were issued by Ireland.

CANADA

828 Sailor Lookout, Canadian Navy Corvette and Survivors in Lifeboat

(Des Derek Sarty. Litho Lowe-Martin)

2005 (29 Apr). 60th Anniversary of Battle of the Atlantic. Fluorescent frame. Perf 12½×13½.
2353   **828**   50c. multicoloured ....   1·25   1·00

829 Candle, Silhouettes, Memorial Cross GRV and New Museum Building

(Des Tiit Telmet and Marko Barac. Litho Lowe-Martin)

2005 (6 May). Opening of New Canadian War Museum Building, Ottawa. Fluorescent frame. Self-adhesive. Perf 8.
2354   **829**   50c. multicoloured ....   1·00   1·00
           a. Booklet pane. No. 2354×8 ....   7·00

No. 2354 was only issued in $4 booklets, No. SB322.

830 *Down in the Laurentides*

(Des Hélène L'Heureux. Litho Lowe-Martin)

2005 (27 May). Art Canada. 150th Birth Anniversary of Homer Watson (artist). T **830** and similar horiz design showing his paintings. Multicoloured. Fluorescent frame. Perf 13½.
2355   50c. Type **830**   70   1·00
MS2356 150×87 mm. 50c. Type **830** (Perf 13½); 85c. *The Flood Gate* (53×39 mm) (Perf 13½×13) ....   1·60   2·50

No. **MS**2356 also commemorates the 125th anniversary of the National Gallery of Canada.

831 Volunteer with Search Dog, Crashed Aircraft and Satellite

832 Ellen Fairclough and Parliament Buildings, Ottawa

(Des François Dallaire. Litho Lowe-Martin)

2005 (13 June). Search and Rescue. Sheet 260×170 mm containing T **831** and similar vert designs. Multicoloured. Fluorescent frame. Perf 13×13½.
MS2357 50c.×2 Type **831**; 50c.×2 Rescuers, crew in life raft and sinking ship; 50c.×2 Seaman winched into helicopter and float plane; 50c.×2 Mountain rescue team with stretcher and satellite ....   7·50   10·00

No. **MS**2357 contains two strips of the four designs with the strips arranged *tête-bêche*.

(Des Katalin Kovats. Litho C.B.N)

2005 (21 June). Birth Centenary of Ellen Fairclough (first woman federal cabinet minister). Fluorescent frame. Perf 13½×12½.
2358   **832**   50c. multicoloured   70   1·00

833 Diver spinning in mid-air

834 Port-Royal, 1605 (from drawing by Samuel de Champlain)

(Des Fugazi. Litho Lowe-Martin)

2005 (5 July). 11th FINA (Fédération Internationale de Natation) World Championships, Montreal. T **833** and similar multicoloured design. Fluorescent frame. Perf 13½.
2359   50c. Type **833**   75   1·00
           a. Pair. Nos. 2359/2360 ....   1·50   2·00
2360   50c. Swimmer in butterfly stroke   75   1·00

Nos. 2359/2360 were printed together, *se-tenant*, in pairs in sheetlets of eight. Both stamps can be oriented either vertically or horizontally.

(Des Fugazi and. Eng Martin Côté. Recess and litho C.B.N)

2005 (16 July). French Settlement in North America (2nd issue). 400th Anniversary of Founding of Port-Royal, Nova Scotia. Fluorescent frame. Perf 13×12½.
2361   **834**   50c. multicoloured   70   1·00

835 Chemicals Plant, Calgary Skyline, Mount Grassi and Railway Line

836 Woman with Arms outstretched, Sunflowers and Legislature Building, Regina

(Des Matthias Reinicke. Litho Lowe-Martin)

2005 (21 July). Centenary of Alberta Province. Fluorescent frame. Self-adhesive. Perf 12½×13½.
2362   **835**   50c. multicoloured   70   1·00

The backing paper is illustrated with four different scenes, each running across two stamps: Calgary Stampede; Jasper Avenue, Edmonton, 1963; Lake Minnewanka, Banff; and oil refinery of *c*. 1912.

(Des Bradbury. Litho C.B.N)

2005 (2 Aug). Centenary of Saskatchewan. Fluorescent frame. Perf 13×12½.
2363   **836**   50c. multicoloured   70   1·00

CANADA

837 1930 50c. Acadian Memorial Church Stamp and Acadian Flag

(Des Pierre-Yves Pellietier. Litho C.B.N)

2005 (15 Aug). 250th Anniversary of Deportation of French Settlers from Acadia (Nova Scotia) to British Colonies of North America. Fluorescent frame. Perf 13×12½.
2364   **837**   50c. multicoloured 80   1·00

838 Oscar Peterson   **839** Children playing and discarded Leg Braces

(Des Tiit Telmet. Litho C.B.N)

2005 (15 Aug). 80th Birthday of Oscar Peterson (jazz composer and musician). Fluorescent frame. Perf 13½×12½.
2365   **838**   50c. multicoloured 65   1·00
MS2366 112×116 mm. No. 2365×4..................... 2·25   4·25

(Des Debbie Adams. Litho C.B.N)

2005 (2 Sept). 50th Anniversary of Mass Polio Vaccination in Canada. Fluorescent frame. Perf 12½×13.
2367   **839**   50c. multicoloured 70   1·00

840 Wall climbing   **841** *Puma concolor* (Cougar)

(Des Circle Design. Litho Lowe-Martin)

2005 (1 Oct). Youth Sports. T **840** and similar multicoloured designs. Fluorescent frames. Self-adhesive. Imperf×P 10.
2368   50c. Type **840** 65   75
     a. Booklet pane. Nos. 2368/2371, each×2   4·50
2369   50c. Skateboarding 65   75
2370   50c. Mountain biking 65   75
2371   50c. Snowboarding 65   75
2368/2371 *Set of 4* .... 2·40   2·75
Nos. 2368/2371 were only issued in $4 booklets, SB322.
Nos. 2368/2371 can be oriented either horizontally or vertically. The outer edges of the stamps are die-cut in irregular shapes around the design. The two inner edges each have one set of nine teeth.

(Des Keith Martin and Liu Jibiao. Litho Lowe-Martin)

2005 (13 Oct). 35th Anniversary of Canada-China Diplomatic Relations. Carnivores. T **841** and similar horiz design. Multicoloured. Fluorescent frame. Perf 13½.
2372   50c. Type **841** 75   1·00
     a. Horiz pair. Nos. 2372/2373 .... 1·50   2·00
2373   50c. *Panthera pardus orientalis* (Amur Leopard) 75   1·00
MS2374 108×58 mm. Nos. 2372/2373.................... 1·50   2·25

Nos. 2372/2373 were printed together, *se-tenant*, in horizontal pairs in sheets of 16 stamps, each *se-tenant* pair having one 'maple-leaf' perforation.
Stamps of the same design were issued by China (People's Republic).

842 Snowman   **843** Crèche by Michel Forest

(Des Hélène L'Heureux. Litho with holographic stamping Lowe-Martin)

2005 (2 Nov). Christmas (1st issue). Self-adhesive booklet stamps. Fluorescent frame. Perf 8½×imperf.
2375   **842**   50c. multicoloured 70   50
     a. Booklet pane. No. 2375×12............. 7·50
No. 2375 was only available from $6 stamp booklets, No. SB323.

(Des Israël Charney. Litho Lowe-Martin)

2005 (2 Nov). Christmas (2nd issue). T **843** and similar vert designs showing Christmas crèches. Self-adhesive booklet stamps. Fluorescent frame. Perf 7×imperf.
2376   50c. Type **843** 70   50
     a. Booklet pane. No. 2376×12............. 7·50
2377   85c. Crèche with aboriginal figures by Keena (31×39 mm)............................ 1·75   2·25
     a. Pane. No. 2377×6............................ 9·00
2378 $1.45 Crèche by Sylvia Daoust (27×40 mm) .... 2·75   3·50
     a. Pane. No. 2378×6............................ 14·00
2376/2378 *Set of 3* .... 4·75   5·50
No. 2376 was only available from $6 stamp booklets, Nos. SB325.
Nos. 2377/2378 were issued in panes of six.

844 Chow   **845** Queen Elizabeth II, Ottawa, 2002

(Des Joseph Gault and Suzanne Duranceau. Litho and embossed Lowe-Martin)

2006 (6 Jan). Chinese New Year. Year of the Dog. T **844** and similar vert design. Multicoloured. Fluorescent frame. Perf 13½.
2379   51c. Type **844** 60   1·00
MS2380 129×106 mm. $1.49 Chow with puppy............. 2·50   3·25
No. 2379 has a slightly arched top representing a temple gate. It was printed in sheets of 25 stamps with narrow horizontal labels with elliptical perforation holes at each vertical side above each stamp.
The stamp within **MS**2380 also has a slightly arched top and a single elliptical perforation hole above each vertical side, representing a temple gate.
The foot of No. **MS**2380 is cut in an arch with a barcode tab attached in the centre.

(Des q30 design inc. Litho C.B.N)

2006 (12 Jan). 80th Birthday of Queen Elizabeth II (1st issue). Fluorescent frame. Self-adhesive. Perf 10.
2381   **845**   51c. multicoloured 70   1·00
     aa. Imperf (pair).................................. £180
     a. Booklet pane. No. 2381×10 and10 stickers.. 8·00
No. 2381 was only issued in $5.10 booklets, No. SB331, in which the surplus self-adhesive paper was retained.
Booklet pane No. 2381a also included ten floral stickers in two different designs.
See also No. **MS**2392.

CANADA

846 Team Pursuit Speed Skating

(Des Metaform Communication Design. Litho Lowe-Martin)

2006 (3 Feb). Winter Olympic Games, Turin, Italy. T **846** and similar horiz design. Multicoloured. Fluorescent frame. Perf 12½×13½.
2382		51c. Type **846**	75	1·00
	a.	Horiz pair. Nos. 2382/2383	1·50	2·00
2383		51c. Skeleton (sled)	75	1·00

Nos. 2382/2383 were printed together, *se-tenant*, in horizontal pairs in sheets of 16 stamps.

847 Trilliums and Black-throated Blue Warbler (Shade Garden)

848 Balloons

(Des Debbie Adams and Jeffrey Domm. Litho Lowe-Martin)

2006 (8 Mar). Gardens. T **847** and similar vert designs. Multicoloured. Fluorescent frame. Self-adhesive. Perf 10 (interrupted at corners).
2384		51c. Type **847**	1·40	1·50
	a.	Booklet pane. Nos. 2384/2387, each×2	10·00	
2385		51c. Purple Coneflowers and American Painted Lady Butterfly (flower garden)	1·40	1·50
2386		51c. Water Lilies and Green Darner dragonfly	1·40	1·50
2387		51c. Rock garden and Blue-spotted Salamander	1·40	1·50
2384/2387		*Set of 4*	5·00	5·50

Nos. 2384/2387 were only issued in $4.08 booklets, No. SB332.

(Des Designwerke Inc. Litho Lowe-Martin)

2006 (3 Apr). Greetings Stamp. Fluorescent frame. Self-adhesive. Perf 7×imperf.
2388	**848**	51c. multicoloured	75	75
	a.	Pane. No. 2388×6	4·25	

No. 2388 was issued in panes of six.

849 The Field of Rapeseed

850 Hands enclosing Globe

(Des Hélène L'Heureux. Litho Lowe-Martin)

2006 (7 Apr). Art Canada. Paintings by Dorothy Knowles. T **849** and similar multicoloured design. Fluorescent frame. Perf 13×12½.
2389		51c. Type **849**	75	1·00
MS2390		150×87 mm. 51c. Type 849 (Perf 13×12½); 89c. North Saskatchewan River (42×51 mm) (Perf 13)	2·25	3·25

(Des Steven Spazuk. Litho C.B.N)

2006 (20 Apr). 50th Anniversary of Canadian Labour Congress. Fluorescent frame. Perf 13½.
2391	**850**	51c. multicoloured	70	1·00

(Des q30 design inc. Litho C.B.N)

2006 (21 Apr). 80th Birthday of Queen Elizabeth II (2nd issue). Sheet 125×75 mm. Multicoloured. Fluorescent frame. PVA gum. Perf 12½×13.
MS2392	$1.49×2 As Type **845** but 39×31 mm	3·00	4·50

851 Colophon emerging from Book

852 Mid 19th-Century Transformation Mask and Other Exhibits

(Des James Roberts. Litho Lowe-Martin)

2006 (26 Apr). Centenary of McClelland and Stewart (publishing house). Fluorescent frame. Self-adhesive. Perf 11½×11.
2393	**851**	51c. slate-blue and silver	1·40	1·50
	a.	Booklet pane. No. 2393×8 and 8 labels	10·00	

No. 2393 was only issued in $4.10 booklets, No. SB334. Booklet pane No. 2393a also included eight small stickers showing the McClelland and Stewart colophon and '100'.

(Des Neville Smith. Litho Lowe-Martin)

2006 (11 May). 150th Anniversary of Canadian Museum of Civilization, Gatineau, Quebec. Fluorescent frame. Self-adhesive. Perf 8 (interrupted)×straight edge.
2394	**852**	89c. multicoloured	1·75	2·50
	a.	Booklet pane. No. 2394×8	12·00	

No. 2394 was only issued in $7.12 booklets, No. SB335.
The two horizontal edges each have a set of seven perforations.

853 Lorne Greene

854 Champlain's Ship

(Des Neal Armstrong, John Belisle and Kosta Tsetsekas. Litho Lowe-Martin)

2006 (26 May). Canadians in Hollywood (1st series). T **853** and similar vert designs. Multicoloured. Fluorescent frame.

(a) Self-adhesive. Perf 10.
2395		51c. Type **853**	75	85
	a.	Booklet pane. Nos. 2395/2398, each×2	6·00	
2396		51c. Fay Wray	75	85
2397		51c. Mary Pickford	75	85
2398		51c. John Candy	75	85
2395/2398		*Set of 4*	2·75	3·00

(b) PVA gum. Perf 13×12½.
MS2399	180×63 mm. As Nos. 2395/2398	2·75	3·75

Nos. 2395/2398 were only issued in $4.08 booklets, Nos. SB336/SB336c, in which the surplus self-adhesive paper around each stamp was retained. Booklet pane No. 2395a also included eight small stickers. It exists in four versions which differ in the order of the stamps within the two blocks of four which form the booklet pane.
See also Nos. 2560/2564.

113

CANADA

(Des Francis Back, Martin Côté and Fugazi. Recess and litho C.B.N. (No. 2400) or Ashton-Potter (2401))

2006 (28 May). French Settlement in North America (3rd issue). 400th Anniversary of Samuel de Champlain's Survey of East Coast of North America. Fluorescent frame (Canada stamps). Perf 13×12½.

2400		51c. Type **854**	1·00	1·00

MS2401 204×146 mm. 51c. Type **854**; 39c.×2 As Type

2879	of USA. Perf 11.	2·50	3·75

No. **MS**2401 also commemorates Washington 2006 International Stamp Exhibition. A self-adhesive stamp in the same design and an identical miniature sheet were also issued by the United States.

855 Girl watching Beluga Whale

(Des Kevin van der Leek. Litho Lowe-Martin)

2006 (15 June). 50th Anniversary of Vancouver Aquarium. Fluorescent frame. Self-adhesive. Perf 10.

2402	**855**	51c. multicoloured	70	1·00
		a. Booklet pane. No. 2402×10	6·25	

No. 2402 was only issued in $5.10 booklets, No. SB337.

856 Pilot and Snowbirds

(Des Wade Stewart and Tiit Telmet. Litho C.B.N)

2006 (28 June). 35th Anniversary of Snowbirds Demonstration Team (431 Squadron). T **856** and similar horiz design. Multicoloured. Fluorescent frame. Perf 12½×13.

2403		51c. Type **856**	1·25	1·25
		a. Horiz pair. Nos. 2403/2404	2·50	3·00
2404		51c. Snowbirds and emblem	1·25	1·25

MS2405 130×65 mm. Nos. 2403/2404 .... 2·50   3·00

Nos. 2403/2404 were printed together, *se-tenant*, in horizontal pairs in sheets of 16 stamps.

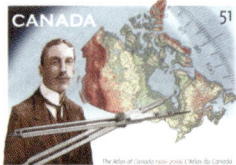

857 James White (Chief Geographer), Proportional Dividers and Modern Map

(Des Ivan Murphy and Karen Smith. Litho Lowe-Martin)

2006 (30 June). Centenary of The Atlas of Canada. Fluorescent frame. Perf 13½×12½.

2406	**857**	51c. multicoloured	1·25	1·00

No. 2406 was printed in sheets of 16 containing 2×2 rows of four stamps separated by an illustrated gutter.

858 Player and Event Tickets

859 Early and Modern Climbers

(Des Yvan Meunier and Tom Yakobina. Litho Lowe-Martin)

2006 (6 July). World Lacrosse Championships, London, Ontario. Fluorescent frame. Self-adhesive. Perf 12×imperf.

2407	**858**	51c. multicoloured	70	1·00
		a. Pane. No. 2407×8	5·00	

No. 2407 was issued in $4.08 panes of eight.

(Des Xerxes Irani. Litho Lowe-Martin)

2006 (19 July). Centenary of the Alpine Club of Canada. Fluorescent frame. Self-adhesive. Perf 12½×13.

2408	**859**	51c. multicoloured	1·00	1·00
		a. Booklet pane. No. 2408×8	7·00	

No. 2408 was only issued in $4.08 booklets, No. SB339.

860 Barrow's Goldeneye

861 'g' as Beaver enclosing '50'

(Des Oliver Hill, Dennis Page and Pierre Leduc. Litho C.B.N)

2006 (3 Aug). Duck Decoys. T **860** and similar vert designs. Multicoloured. Fluorescent frame. Perf 13×12½.

2409		51c. Type **860**	1·10	1·10
		a. Block of 4. Nos. 2409/2412	4·00	4·00
2410		51c. Mallard (decoy with white ring around neck)	1·10	1·10
2411		51c. Black Duck (plain brown decoy)	1·10	1·10
2412		51c. Red-breasted Merganser (black and white decoy with red bill)	1·10	1·10

2409/2412 Set of 4 .... 4·00   4·00
MS2413 130×145 mm. Nos. 2409/2412 .... 4·00   4·50

Nos. 2409/2412 were printed together, *se-tenant*, as blocks of four in sheets of 16.

(Des Ion Design Inc. Litho Lowe-Martin)

2006 (16 Aug). 50th Anniversary of the Society of Graphic Designers of Canada. Fluorescent frame. Perf 12½×13½.

2414	**861**	51c. multicoloured	70	1·00

862 Glasses of Wine

(Des Derwyn Goodall. Litho Lowe-Martin)

2006 (23 Aug). Canadian Wine and Cheese. T **862** and similar multicoloured designs. Fluorescent frame. Self-adhesive. Die-cut.

2415		51c. Type **862**	85	95
		a. Booklet pane. Nos. 2415/2418, each×2	6·00	
2416		51c. Wine taster (horiz as Type **862**)	85	95
2417		51c. Canadian cheeses (wedge-shaped, 36×38 mm)	85	95
2418		51c. Serving cheese platter at fromagerie (wedge-shaped, 36×38 mm)	85	95

2415/2418 Set of 4 .... 3·00   4·00

Nos. 2415/2418 were only issued in $4.08 booklets, No. SB340.

(Des Denis L'Allier. Litho Lowe-Martin)

2006 (26 Sept). Canadian Universities' Anniversaries (5th series). Vert design as T 779a (No. 2190). Multicoloured. Fluorescent frame. Self-adhesive. Perf 13×13½.

2419		51c. Macdonald College, Sainte-Anne-de-Bellevue, Quebec (centenary)	1·00	1·00
		a. Booklet pane. No. 2419×8	7·00	

No. 2419 was only available in $4.08 stamp booklets, No. SB341.

863 Newfoundland Marten

(Des Doug Martin, David Sacha and Karen Satok. Litho Lowe-Martin)

2006 (29 Sept). Endangered Species (1st series). T **863** and similar horiz designs. Multicoloured. Fluorescent frame.

(a) Self-adhesive. Die-cut.

2420	51c. Type **863**	1·10	1·10
	a. Pane. Nos. 2420/2423, each×2	7·00	
2421	51c. Blotched Tiger Salamander	1·10	1·10
2422	51c. Blue Racer	1·10	1·10
2423	51c. Swift Fox	1·10	1·10
2420/2423	Set of 4	4·00	4·00

(b) PVA gum. Size 48×24 mm. Perf 13½.

MS2424 160×74 mm. Nos. 2420/2423 .... 4·00 4·50

Nos. 2420/2423 were issued in panes of eight, containing two of each design.

See also Nos. 2511/**MS**2515 and Nos. 2569/**MS**2573.

864 Maureen Forrester and Place des Arts, Montréal

(Des Alanna Cavanagh, Paul Haslip and Judith Lacerte. Litho C.B.N)

2006 (17 Oct). Canadian Opera Singers. T **864** and similar horiz designs. Multicoloured. Fluorescent frame. Perf 12½×13½.

2425	51c. Type **864**	1·40	1·40
	a. Vert strip of 5. Nos. 2425/2429	6·25	6·25
2426	51c. Raoul Jobin and Palais Garnier, Paris	1·40	1·40
2427	51c. Léopold Simoneau, Pierrette Alarie and Opéra-Comique, France	1·40	1·40
2428	51c. Jon Vickers and La Scala, Milan	1·40	1·40
2429	51c. Edward Johnson and Metropolitan Opera Company, New York	1·40	1·40
2425/2429	Set of 5	6·25	6·25

Nos. 2425/2429 were printed together, *se-tenant*, as vertical strips of five in sheetlets of ten.

865 Madonna and Child (detail) (Antoine-Sébastien Falardeau)

866 Snowman (Yvonne McKague Housser)

(Des Pierre Fontaine. Litho Lowe-Martin)

2006 (1 Nov). Christmas (1st issue). Self-adhesive booklet stamps. Fluorescent frame. Die-cut.

2430	**865**	51c. multicoloured	85	55
		a. Booklet pane. No. 2430×12	9·50	

No. 2430 was only available from $6.12 stamp booklets, No. SB343.

(Des Peter Steiner. Litho C.B.N)

2006 (1 Nov). Christmas (2nd issue). T **866** and similar vert designs showing Christmas cards from 1931 Painters of Canada series. Self-adhesive booklet stamps. Fluorescent frame. Perf 13½×imperf.

2431	51c. Type **866**	85	55
	a. Booklet pane. No. 2431×12	9·50	
2432	89c. Winter Joys (J. E. Sampson)	1·75	2·25
	a. Pane. No. 2432×6	6·25	
2433	$1.49 Contemplation (Edwin Holgate)	2·25	3·25
	a. Pane. No. 2433×6	12·50	
2431/2433	Set of 3	4·25	5·50

No. 2431 was only available from $5.34 booklets, No. SB344.
Nos. 2432/2433 were issued in separate panes of six.

867 Ice Fields and Fjord, Sirmilik National Park, Nunavut

867a Coast and Ancient Trees, Chemainus, British Columbia

867b Polar Bears, Churchill, Manitoba

867c Lighthouse at Bras d'Or Lake, Nova Scotia

867d Tuktut Nogait National Park, Northwest Territories

867e Sambro Island Lighthouse, Nova Scotia

867f Point Clark Lighthouse, Ontario

867g 876g Cap-des-Rosiers Lighthouse, Manitoba

867h Warren Landing Lighthouse, Manitoba

867i Pachena Point Lighthouse, British Columbia

867j Watson's Mill, Manotick, Ontario

867k Keremeos Grist Mill, British Columbia

867l Old Stone Mill National Historic Site, Delta, Ontario

867m Riordon Grist Mill, Caraquet, New Brunswick

867n Cornell Mill, Stanbridge East, Québec

(Des Gottschalk+Ash International. Litho C.B.N)

2006 (16 Nov)–**10**. T **867** and similar vert designs inscr 'P' instead of face value, each showing Canadian flag. Multicoloured. Fluorescent frame.

(a) Self-adhesive booklet stamps. Die-cut (Nos. 2434/2438) or die-cut perf 13½ (Nos. 2439/2449).

2434	**867**	(51c.) Ice Fields and Fjord, Sirmilik National Park, Nunavut	1·10	1·40
		a. Booklet pane. Nos. 2434/2438, each×2	10·00	
		b. Booklet pane. Nos. 2434/2438, each×6	29·00	
2435	**867a**	(51c.) Coast and ancient trees, Chemainus, British Columbia	1·10	1·40
2436	**867b**	(51c.) Polar Bears, Churchill, Manitoba	1·10	1·40
2437	**867c**	(51c.) Lighthouse at Bras d'Or lake, Nova Scotia	1·10	1·40
2438	**867d**	(51c.) Tuktut Nogait National Park, Northwest Territories	1·10	1·40
2439	**867e**	(52c.) Sambro Island lighthouse, Nova Scotia (27.12.07)	1·60	1·60
		a. Pane. Nos. 2439/2443, each×2	14·00	
		b. Booklet pane. Nos. 2439/2442 and 2444, each×6 (1.5.08)	42·00	
		c. Pane. Nos. 2439/2442 and 2444, each×2 (2.7.08)	14·00	
2440	**867f**	(52c.) Point Clark lighthouse, Ontario (27.12.07)	1·60	1·60

CANADA

2441	867g	(52c.) Cap-des-Rosiers lighthouse, Quebec (27.12.07)		1·60	1·60
2442	867h	(52c.) Warren Landing lighthouse, Manitoba (27.12.07)		1·60	1·60
2443	867i	(52c.) Pachena Point lighthouse, British Columbia (27.12.07)		1·60	1·60
2444	867i	(52c.) Pachena Point lighthouse and part of Keeper's house (at right) (1.5.08)		1·60	1·60
2445	867j	(52c.) Watson's Mill (three storey stone building), Manotick, Ontario (11.1.2010)		1·75	1·75
		a. Pane. Nos. 2445/2449, each×2		15·00	
		b. Booklet pane. Nos. 2445/2449, each×6		45·00	
2446	867k	(57c.) Keremeos Grist Mill (wooden building with waterwheel at left), British Columbia (11.1.2010)		1·75	1·75
2447	867l	(57c.) Old Stone Mill National Historic Site (four storey stone building with red doors), Delta, Ontario (11.1.2010)		1·75	1·75
2448	867m	(57c.) Riordon Grist Mill (two storey stone building), Caraquet, New Brunswick (11.1.2010)		1·75	1·75
2449	867n	(57c.) Cornell Mill (weir at right), Stanbridge East, Quebec (11.1.2010)		1·75	1·75
2434/2449 Set of 16				21·00	22·00

(b) *Ordinary gum. Fluorescent frame. Perf 13×13½.*

MS2450	130×70 mm. As Nos. 2445/2449 (11.1.2010)		7·50	8·50

Nos. 2434/2438 were only available in $5.10 (No. SB347) or $15.30 (No. SB348) booklets. They were all inscribed 'P' and initially sold for 51c. each. Nos. 2439/2444 were all inscr 'P' and initially sold for 52c. Nos. 2439/2443 were first issued in panes of ten stamps. Subsequently Nos. 2439/2442 together with No. 2444 were issued in panes of ten and booklets of 30, No. SB378, which was originally sold for $15.60. Nos. 2445/2449 were all inscribed 'P' and initially sold for 57c. They were available in panes of ten sold for $5.70 and booklets of 30 (No. SB405) sold for $17.10.

Nos. 2451/2463 are left for possible additions to these definitive stamps.

868 Queen Elizabeth II, 2005

868a Queen Elizabeth II, Saskatoon

868b Queen Elizabeth II

868c Queen Elizabeth II

868d Queen Elizabeth II, Mi'kmaq Cultural Village

868e Queen Elizabeth II

(Des q30 design inc (No. 2464), Steven Slipp (No. 2469) or Gottschalk+Ash International (others). Litho q30 design inc (No. 2464) or Gottschalk+Ash International (others). Litho Lowe-Martin (No. 2468) or C.B.N. (others))

2006 (16 Nov)–16. Self-adhesive booklet stamps. Multicoloured. Fluorescent frame. Multicoloured. Fluorescent frame. Die-cut (No. 2464) or die-cut perf 13½ (others).

2464	868	(51c.) Queen Elizabeth II, 2005		90	1·25
		a. Pane. No. 2464×10		8·00	
2465	868a	(52c.) Queen Elizabeth II, Saskatoon, 2005 (27.12.07)		1·00	1·40
		a. Pane. No. 2465×10		9·00	
2466	868b	(54c.) Queen Elizabeth in Canada, 19 May 2005 (red background) (12.1.09)		1·75	1·90
		a. Pane. No. 2466×10		14·00	
2467	868c	(57c.) Queen Elizabeth II (wearing deep blue jacket and hat) (11.1.10)		1·40	1·75
		a. Pane. No. 2467×10		12·50	
2468	868d	(63c.) Queen Elizabeth II (wearing cream hat with yellow ribbon) at Mi'kmaq Cultural Village, June 28 2010 (14.1.13)		1·40	1·75
		a. Pane. No. 2468×10		12·50	
2468b	868d	63c. As No. 2468		1·25	1·25
		a. Pane. 2469×10		13·00	
		ba. Pane. No. 2468b×10		1·50	1·75

2469	868e	(85c.) Queen Elizabeth II at Buckingham Palace, 2014 (wearing pearl necklace) (black/white photo for 88th birthday) (11.1.16)		2·00	2·25
2469b		(90c.) Queen Elizabeth II (wearing purple hat), 2017 (14.1.19) (*horiz*)		1·50	1·75
		ba. Pane. No. 2469b×10		16·00	1·75
2464/9 Set of 6				7·00	8·50

No. 2464/2468 were all inscribed 'P' and issued in separate panes of ten stamps. They were initially valid for 51c. (No. 2464), 52c. (No. 2465), 54c. (No. 2466), 57c. (No. 2467) or 63c. (No. 2468).

No. 2469 is left for possible additions to these definitive stamps.

No. 2464 has been reported imperforate.

869 Spotted Coralroot

(Des Sigmond Pifco, Monique Dufour and Sophie Lafortune. Litho Lowe-Martin)

2006 (16 Nov–19 Dec). Flowers (2nd series). Multicoloured. Fluorescent frame.

(a) *Self-adhesive coil stamps. Perf 9½×imperf (No. 2470) or 8½×imperf (others).*

2470	(51c.) Spotted Coralroot		60	35
2471	93c. Flat-leaved Bladderwort (19.12.06)		1·10	1·40
2472	$1.10 Marsh Skullcap (19.12.06)		1·25	1·75
2473	$1.55 Little Larkspur (19.12.06)		1·75	2·50
2470/2473 Set of 4			4·25	5·50

(b) *Self-adhesive booklet stamps. Die-cut.*

2474	93c. Flat-leaved Bladderwort (19.12.06)		1·10	1·40
	a. Pane. No. 2474×6		6·50	
2475	$1.10 Marsh Skullcap (19.12.06)		1·25	1·75
	a. Pane. No. 2475×6		7·50	
2476	$1.55 Little Larkspur (19.12.06)		1·75	2·50
	a. Pane. No. 2476×6		10·50	

(c) *PVA gum. Perf 13½×13.*

MS2477	120×72 mm. As Nos. 2470/2473 (19.12.06)		6·00	7·50

No. 2470 was inscribed 'P' and initially sold for 51c. each.

Nos. 2474/2476 were issued in separate panes of six.

See also Nos. 2645/**MS**2652.

> **POSTAL FORGERIES.** During 2010 postal forgeries of three different panes were detected. In all cases the print quality is poorer than the genuine panes and forgeries do not have fluorescent bands. The panes concerned are Nos. 2439c, 2466a and 2584a.

870 Pig

(Des John Belisle and Kosta Tsetsekas. Litho and embossed Lowe-Martin)

2007 (5 Jan). Chinese New Year. Year of the Pig. T **870** and similar horiz design. Multicoloured. Fluorescent frame. Perf 13½.

2478		52c. Type **870**		1·25	1·00
		a. Gold (flowers) omitted		£100	
MS2479	98×97 mm. $1.55 Pig (running to right)			2·25	3·50

No. 2479 is cut in a lantern shape.

871 Ribbons and Confetti   872 King Eider (*Somateria spectabilis*)

(Des Karen Smith. Litho Lowe-Martin)

2007 (15 Jan). Greetings Stamp. Fluorescent frame. Self-adhesive. Perf 7½×imperf.

2480	871	52c. multicoloured		85	1·00
		a. Pane. No. 2480×6		4·50	

No. 2480 was only issued in $3.12 panes of six stamps.

(Des q30 design inc. Litho Lowe-Martin)

2007 (12 Feb). International Polar Year. T **872** and similar horiz design. Multicoloured. Fluorescent frame*. Perf 13½.
2481	52c. Type **872**	1·75	1·75
	a. Horiz pair. Nos. 2481/2482	3·50	3·50
2482	52c. *Crossota millsaeare* (Deep-sea Jellyfish)	1·75	1·75
MS2483	105×70 mm. Nos. 2481/2482	4·00	4·50

Nos. 2481/2482 were printed together, *se-tenant*, as horizontal pairs in sheetlets of 16, containing two blocks of eight stamps separated by a narrow vertical gutter. Each *se-tenant* pair (including the stamps within **MS**2483) has one 'maple-leaf' perforation.

*Nos. 2481/2482 and the stamps within **MS**2483 have a fluorescent frame around the horizontal pair, giving No. 2481 a fluorescent frame at top, left and bottom and No. 2482 a fluorescent frame at top, right and bottom.

873 *Syringa vulgaris* 'Princess Alexandra'

874 Jelly Shelf

(Des Isabelle Toussaint. Litho C.B.N)

2007 (1 Mar). Lilacs. T **873** and similar horiz design. Multicoloured. Fluorescent frame.
(a) Self-adhesive. Die-cut.
2484	52c. Type **873**	90	1·00
	a. Booklet pane. Nos. 2484/2485, each×5	8·00	
2485	52c. *Syringa×prestoniae* 'Isabella'	90	1·00

(b) PVA gum. Perf 13.
MS2486	128×80 mm. As Nos. 2484/2485	1·75	2·00

Nos. 2484/2485 were only issued in $5.20 booklets, No. SB354, in which the surplus self-adhesive paper around each stamp was retained. Booklet pane No. 2484a also included ten small stickers.

(Des Denis L'Allier. Litho Lowe-Martin)

2007 (12 Mar–3 Apr). Canadian Universities' Anniversaries (6th issue). Vert design as T **779a** (No. 2190). Multicoloured. Fluorescent frame. Self-adhesive. Perf 13×13½.
2487	52c. HEC (École des hautes études commerciales), Montréal (centenary)	85	1·00
	a. Booklet pane. No. 2487×8	6·25	
2488	52c. University of Saskatchewan (3.4)	85	1·00
	a. Booklet pane. No. 2488×8	6·25	

Nos. 2487/2488 were only issued in separate $4.16 stamp booklets, Nos. SB355/SB356.

(Des Hélène L'Heureux. Litho C.B.N)

2007 (15 Mar). Art Canada. Paintings by Mary Pratt. T **874** and similar horiz design. Multicoloured. Fluorescent frame. Perf 13×12½.
2489	52c. Type **874**	1·50	1·00
MS2490	150×87 mm. 52c. Type **874**; $1.55 *Iceberg in the North Atlantic* (62×40 mm)	3·50	4·50

875 Parliament Buildings, Ottawa, 2007 and Lumberers Regatta, 1860

(Litho (with embossing on $1.55) Lowe-Martin)

2007 (3 May). 150th Anniversary of Ottawa as Capital of Canada. Fluorescent frame.
(a) Self-adhesive. Perf 7½×imperf.
2491	**875**	52c. multicoloured	1·00	1·25
		a. Booklet pane. No. 2491×8	7·25	

(b) PVA gum. Perf 13.
MS2492	102×102 mm. 52c. As No. 2491; $1.55 As No. 2491	3·50	4·00

876 University of Lethbridge (Arthur Erickson), 1971

(Des Ivan Novotny. Litho Lowe-Martin)

2007 (9 May). Centenary of Royal Architectural Institute of Canada. T **876** and similar horiz designs. Multicoloured. Fluorescent frame. Perf 13.
2493	52c. Type **876**	1·00	1·25
	a. Vert strip of 4. Nos. 2493/2496	3·50	4·50
2494	52c. St Mary's Church (Douglas Cardinal), 1969	1·00	1·25
2495	52c. Ontario Science Centre (Raymond Moriyama), 1969	1·00	1·25
2496	52c. National Gallery of Canada (Moshe Safdie), 1988	1·00	1·25
2493/2496	Set of 4	3·50	4·50

Nos. 2493/2496 were printed together, *se-tenant*, as vertical strips of four in sheetlets of eight stamps. The sheetlets also contain eight *se-tenant* half stamp-size labels which form composite designs with the stamps. The four labels at left show the original sketches for the buildings and those at right the architects.

877 Captain George Vancouver

878 Official U-20 World Cup Football and Canadian Team in Action

(Des Niko Potton. Litho and embossed Lowe-Martin)

2007 (22 June). 250th Birth Anniversary of Captain George Vancouver (explorer of west coast of North America). Fluorescent frame. Perf 13×12½.
2497	**877**	$1.55 multicoloured	2·50	3·00
MS2498	70×120 mm. **877** $1.55 multicoloured. Perf 13		2·50	3·25

(Des Debbie Adams. Litho C.B.N)

2007 (26 June). FIFA U-20 World Cup, Canada. Partial fluorescent frame. Perf 12½×13.
2499	**878**	52c. multicoloured	1·00	1·00

The fluorescent frame on No. 2499 is broken at lower left and right sides of the stamp.

879 Gordon Lightfoot

880 Sunrise over Alexander Bay, Terra Nova National Park, Newfoundland

(Des Circle Design Inc. Litho Lowe-Martin)

2007 (29 June). Canadian Recording Artists (1st series). T **879** and similar square designs. Multicoloured. Fluorescent frame.
(a) Self-adhesive. Perf 13½.
2500	52c. Type **879**	1·00	1·25
	a. Booklet pane. Nos. 2500/2503, each×2	8·50	

CANADA

2501	52c. Joni Mitchell		1·00	1·25
2502	52c. Anne Murray		1·00	1·25
2503	52c. Paul Anka		1·00	1·25
2500/2503 Set of 4			3·50	4·50

(b) PVA gum. Perf 12½×13.

MS2504 Circular 105×105 mm. As Nos. 2500/2503...... 3·25 4·50

Nos. 2500/2503 were only issued in $4.16 stamp booklets, No. SB358/SB358c, in which the surplus self-adhesive paper around each stamp was retained. Booklet pane 2500a also included eight small stickers. It exists in four versions which differ in the order of the stamps within the two blocks of four which form the booklet pane.

See also Nos. 2618/**MS**2621, 2798/**MS**2806 and 2954/**MS**2958.

(Des Saskia van Kampen. Litho Lowe-Martin)

2007 (6 July). 50th Anniversary of Terra Nova National Park, Newfoundland. Fluorescent frame. Self-adhesive. Perf 13½.

2505	**880**	52c. multicoloured	1·00	1·25
		a. Booklet pane. No. 2505×10	10·00	

The fluorescent frame on No. 2505 is broken at lower left. It was only issued in $5.20 stamp booklets, No. SB359.

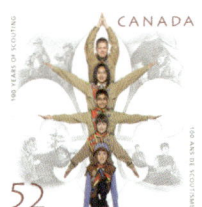

881 Jasper National Park

882 Scouts forming Emblem

(Des Saskia van Kampen. Litho Lowe-Martin)

2007 (20 July). Centenary of Jasper National Park, Alberta. Fluorescent frame. Self-adhesive. Fluorescent frame. Perf 13½.

2506	**881**	52c. multicoloured	1·00	1·25
		a. Booklet pane. No. 2506×10	10·00	

The fluorescent frame on No. 2506 is broken at lower left. It was only issued in $5.20 stamp booklets, No. SB360.

(Des Matthias Reinicke. Litho Lowe-Martin)

2007 (25 July). Centenary of Scouting. Fluorescent frame. Self-adhesive. Perf 13½.

2507	**882**	52c. multicoloured	1·00	1·25
		a. Booklet pane. No. 2507×8	7·25	

No. 2507 was only issued in $4.16 stamp booklets, No. SB361.

883 Membertou (Grand Chief of the Mi'kmaq) and French Settlement, Port Royal

884 Founding Members and Registry Roll

(Des Suzanne Duranceau and Fugazi. Eng Jorge Peral. Litho and recess C.B.N)

2007 (26 July). French Settlement in North America (4th issue). Chief Membertou. Fluorescent frame. Perf 13×12½.

2508	**883**	52c. multicoloured	1·00	1·00

(Des Bradbury Branding Design Inc. Litho C.B.N)

2007 (13 Sept). Centenary of the Law Society of Saskatchewan. Fluorescent frame. Perf 13.

2509	**884**	52c. multicoloured	1·00	1·00

No. 2509 was printed in sheets containing eight stamps and eight stamp-size labels.

885 Books, Photograph of James Muir (first President) and Gavel

886 *Hippodamia convergens* (Convergent Lady Beetle)

(Des Xerxes Irani. Litho Lowe-Martin)

2007 (13 Sept). Centenary of the Law Society of Alberta. Fluorescent frame. Perf 12½×13.

2510	**885**	52c. multicoloured	1·00	1·00

(Des Doug Martin, David Sacha and Karen Satok. Litho Lowe-Martin)

2007 (1 Oct). Endangered Species (2nd series). Horiz designs as T **863**. Multicoloured. Fluorescent frame.

(a) Self-adhesive. Die-cut.

2511		52c. North Atlantic Right Whale	1·75	1·75
		a. Pane. Nos. 2511/2514, each×2	10·00	10·00
2512		52c. Northern Cricket Frog	1·75	1·75
2513		52c. White Sturgeon	1·75	1·75
2514		52c. Leatherback Turtle	1·75	1·75
2511/2514 Set of 4			6·25	7·00

(b) PVA gum. Size 48×24 mm. Perf 13½.

MS2515 160×75 mm. As Nos. 2511/2514...... 6·25 7·00

Nos. 2511/2514 were issued in $4.16 panes of eight stamps containing two of each design.

886 *Hippodamia convergens* (Convergent Lady Beetle)

(Des Keith Martin. Litho C.B.N)

2007 (12 Oct)–**14**. Beneficial Insects. T **886** and similar vert designs. Multicoloured. Perf 13×13½.

2516		1c. Type **886**	10	20
2517		2c. *Danaus plexippus* (Monarch Caterpillar) (22.4.09)	10	20
2518		3c. *Chrysopa oculata* (Golden-eyed Lacewing)	10	20
		aa. No space between 'Canada' and Latin inscription (R. 1-4/4)	2·00	2·00
2518a		4c. *Polistes fuscatus* (Paper Wasp) (19.10.10)	10	20
2519		5c. *Bombus polaris* (Northern Bumblebee)	10	20
2519a		6c. *Zelus luridus* (Assassin Bug) (19.10.10)	15	20
2519b		7c. *Oncopeltus fasciatus* (Large Milkweed Bug) (19.10.10)	20	20
2519c		8c. *Chauliognathus marginatus* (Margined Leatherwing) (19.10.10)	25	20
2519d		9c. *Chrysochus auratus* (Dogbane Beetle) (19.10.10)	25	20
2520		10c. *Aeshna canadensis* (Canada Darner Dragonfly)	25	20
2521		22c. *Danaus plexippus* (Monarch Butterfly) (31.3.14)	50	10
2522		25c. *Hyalophora cecropia* (Cecropia Moth)	50	50
2516/2522 Set of 12			2·25	2·75
MS2523 133×58 mm. Nos. 2516, 2518, 2519, 2520 and 2522			1·25	1·75
MS2524 133×58 mm. Nos. 2518a and 2519a/2519d (19.10.10)			1·25	1·75

No. 2525 is vacant.

887 Reindeer

888 Nativity ('HOPE')

(Des Hélène L'Heureux. Litho Lowe-Martin)

2007 (1 Nov). Christmas (1st issue). Self-adhesive booklet stamps. Fluorescent frame. Perf 9×imperf.

2526	**887**	(52c.) multicoloured	1·00	50
		aa. Imperf (pair)	£250	
		a. Booklet pane. No. 2526×12	11·00	

No. 2526 was inscribed 'P' and initially sold for 52c. It was only available from $6.24 stamp booklets, No. SB363.

(Des Stephanie Carter, Steve Hepburn, Jonathon Milne and Tandem Design. Litho Lowe-Martin)

2007 (1 Nov). Christmas (2nd issue). T **888** and similar square designs. Multicoloured. Self-adhesive booklet stamps. Fluorescent frame. Perf 13½.

2527	(52c.) Type **888**	1·00	60
	a. Booklet pane. No. 2527×12	11·00	
2528	93c. Angel playing trumpet ('JOY')	2·00	2·75
	a. Pane. No. 2528×6	10·50	
2529	$1.55 Dove ('PEACE')	2·75	4·25
	a. Pane. No. 2529×6	14·50	
2527/2529	Set of 3	5·25	7·00

No. 2527 was inscribed 'P' and initially sold for 52c. It was only available from booklets of 12, No. SB365, originally sold for $6.24.

Nos. 2528/2529 were issued in separate $5.58 or $9.30 panes of six stamps.

889 Odontioda Island Red

890 Rat Bride

(Des Sigmond Pifco, Monique Dufour and Sophie Lafortune. Litho Lowe-Martin)

2007 (27 Dec). Flowers (3rd series). Canadian Hybrid Orchids. T **889** and similar horiz designs. Multicoloured. Fluorescent frame and security markings.

(a) Coil stamps. Perf 9×imperf.

2530	(52c.) Type **889**	1·00	1·00
	a. Perf 9½×imperf	1·00	1·00
2531	96c. Potinara Janet Elizabeth 'Fire Dancer'	1·75	2·25
2532	$1.15 Laeliocattleya Memoria Evelyn Light	1·90	2·50
2533	$1.60 Masdevallia Kaleidoscope 'Conni'	2·75	3·50
2530/2533	Set of 4	6·50	8·50

(b) Stamps from self-adhesive panes. Imperf.

2534	96c. As No. 2531	1·75	2·00
	a. Pane. No. 2534×6	9·75	
2535	$1.15 As No. 2532	2·25	2·75
	a. Pane. No. 2535×6	12·00	
2536	$1.60 As No. 2533	2·75	3·75
	a. Pane. No. 2536×6	15·00	
2534/2536	Set of 3	6·00	7·75

(c) PVA gum. Perf 13½×13.

MS2537 120×72 mm. As Nos. 2530/2533 .... 7·50 10·00

No. 2530 was inscribed 'P' and sold for 52c. It was issued in vertical coils with the perforated top and bottom edges of the stamps meeting each other.

No. 2530a was issued in horizontal coils with the backing paper around each stamp removed, the stamps being spaced along the backing paper.

Nos. 2534/2536 were issued in separate $5.76, $6.90 or $9.60 panes of six stamps.

(Des Harvey Chan and Tandem Design Associates Ltd. Litho and embossed Lowe-Martin)

2008 (8 Jan). Chinese New Year. Year of the Rat. T **890** and similar vert design. Multicoloured. Fluorescent frame. Perf 13½.

2538	52c. Type **890**	1·25	1·00
MS2539	130×100 mm. $1.60 Rat groom	2·75	4·00

No. 2538 was printed in sheets of 25 stamps with narrow vertical labels at the side of each stamp.

891 Fireworks

892 *Paeonia lactiflora* 'Elgin'

(Des Michael Zavacky. Litho Lowe-Martin)

2008 (15 Jan). Greetings Stamp. Fluorescent frame. Self-adhesive. Perf 13½×imperf.

2540	**891**	(52c.) multicoloured	1·25	1·00
		a. Pane. No. 2540×6	6·75	

No. 2540 was inscribed 'P' and initially sold for 52c. It was issued in panes of six stamps sold for $3.12.

(Des Isabelle Toussaint. Litho Lowe-Martin, Canada)

2008 (3 Mar). Peonies. T **892** and similar horiz design. Multicoloured.

(a) Self-adhesive. Perf 13½.

2541	52c. Type **892**	1·00	1·25
	aa. Imperf (pair)	£300	
	a. Booklet pane. Nos. 2541/2542, each×5	9·00	
2542	52c. *Paeonia lactiflora* 'Coral 'n Gold'	1·00	1·25

(b) PVA gum. Perf 13×13½.

MS2543 120×84 mm. As Nos. 2541/2542 .... 2·00 2·75

Nos. 2541/2542 were only issued in $5.20 stamp booklets, No. SB373, in which the surplus self-adhesive paper around each stamp was retained. Booklet pane No. 2541a also included ten small stickers.

893 Dentistry Building, University of Alberta (centenary)

894 Ice Hockey Players

(Des Metaform Communication Design. Litho Lowe-Martin)

2008 (7 Mar). Canadian Universities' Anniversaries (7th issue). T **893** and similar horiz design. Multicoloured. Fluorescent frame. Self-adhesive. Perf 13½.

2544	52c. Type **893**	1·00	1·00
	a. Pane. No. 2544×8	7·00	
2545	52c. Walter C. Koerner Library, University of British Columbia (centenary)	1·00	1·00
	a. Pane. No. 2545×8	7·00	

No. 2544/2545 were issued in separate $4.16 panes of eight stamps.

Nos. 2544/2548 were also issued cut so as to give strips of four each of Nos. 2544/2545 separated by a vertical gutter.

These were only available from Canada Post Natural Philatelic Centre.

(Des Ho Che Anderson, Lionel Gadoury and Dave Hurds. Litho Lowe-Martin)

2008 (3 Apr). International Ice Hockey Federation World Championship, Halifax and Québec. Fluorescent frame. Self-adhesive. Perf 13½.

2546	**894**	52c. multicoloured	1·00	1·00
		aa. Imperf (pair)	£225	
		a. Booklet pane. No. 2546×10	9·00	

No. 2546 was only issued in $5.20 stamp booklets, Nos. SB376/SB376a.

895 Guide Dog at Work

896 Welder working on Pipeline

(Des Designwerke Inc. Litho Lowe-Martin)

2008 (21 Apr). Guide Dogs. Fluorescent frame. Self-adhesive. Perf 13½×13.

2547	**895**	52c. multicoloured	1·40	1·40
		a. Booklet pane. No. 2547×10	12·00	

No. 2547 was only issued in $5.20 stamp booklets, No. SB377. It has the face value in Braille.

CANADA

(Des Tim Nokes. Litho Lowe-Martin)

2008 (2 May). Oil and Gas Industry. T **896** and similar horiz design. Multicoloured. Fluorescent frame. Self-adhesive. Perf 13½.
2548	52c. Type **896**	1·10	1·40
	a. Booklet pane. Nos. 2548/2549, each×5	10·00	
2549	52c. James Miller Williams (drilled first Canadian oil well, 1858) and Charles Tripp (developed bitumen deposits of southwest Ontario, 1850s)	1·10	1·40

Nos. 2548/2549 were only issued in $5.20 stamp booklets, No. SB378.

901 Anne

902 Athlete and Canadian Flag

(Des Dennis Page and Oliver Hill, illustrations Ben Stahl (No. 2557) and Christopher Kovacs (No. 2558). Litho Lowe-Martin)

2008 (20 June). Centenary of Publication of *Anne of Green Gables* by Lucy Maud Montgomery. T **901** and similar horiz design. Multicoloured. Fluorescent frame*.

(a) Self-adhesive. Perf 13½×13.
2557	52c. Type **901**	1·00	1·25
	a. Booklet pane. Nos. 2557/2558, each×5	9·00	
2558	52c. Green Gables (house), Cavendish, Prince Edward Island	1·00	1·25

(b) PVA gum. Perf 13½.
MS2559	124×72 mm. As Nos. 2557/2558	1·75	2·25

Nos. 2557/2558 were only issued in $5.20 booklets, No. SB381. Booklet pane No. 2557a also included ten small flower design stickers.

Nos. 2557/2558 and the stamps within **MS**2559 have a fluorescent frame around the horizontal pair, giving No. 2557 a fluorescent frame at top, left and bottom, and No. 2558 a fluorescent frame at top, right and bottom. The pair of stamps within No. **MS**2559 have one 'maple leaf' perforation.

897 Samuel de Champlain's Ship, Native Canoe and New Settlement of Québec, 1608

898 Self-portrait

(Des Francis Back and Fugazi. Eng Jorge Peral. Recess and litho C.B.N)

2008 (16 May). French Settlement in North America (5th issue). 400th Anniversary of City of Québec. Fluorescent frame. Perf 13×13½.
2550	**897**	52c. multicoloured	1·50	1·00

A stamp in a similar design was issued by France. France also issued a miniature sheet including the Canadian stamp, but with minor differences.

(Des Hélène L'Heureux. Litho Lowe-Martin)

2008 (21 May). Art Canada. Birth Centenary of Yousuf Karsh (portrait photographer). T **898** and similar vert designs. Multicoloured. Fluorescent frame.

(a) PVA gum. Perf 13×12½.
2551	52c. Type **898**	1·00	90
MS2552	150×87 mm. 52c. Type **898**; 96c. Audrey Hepburn; $1.60 Winston Churchill	6·00	7·00

(b) Self-adhesive. Die-cut.
2553	96c. Audrey Hepburn	2·00	3·00
	a. Booklet pane. No. 2553×8	14·00	
2554	$1.60 Winston Churchill	3·50	4·50
	a. Booklet pane. No. 2554×8	25·00	

Nos. 2553/2554 were only available in stamp booklets, Nos. SB379/SB380.

(Des Neal Armstrong, John Belisle and Kosta Tsetsekas. Litho Lowe-Martin)

2008 (30 June). Canadians in Hollywood (2nd series). Vert designs as T **853**. Multicoloured. Fluorescent frame.

(a) Self-adhesive. Perf 13½.
2560	52c. Norma Shearer	1·25	1·40
	a. Booklet pane. Nos. 2560/2563, each×2	9·00	
2561	52c. Chief Dan George	1·25	1·40
2562	52c. Marie Dressler	1·25	1·40
2563	52c. Raymond Burr	1·25	1·40
2560/2563	Set of 4	4·50	5·00

(b) PVA gum. Perf 13×12½.
MS2564	136×77 mm. As Nos. 2560/2563	4·50	5·00

Nos. 2560/2563 were only issued in $4.16 booklets, Nos. SB382/SB382c. Booklet pane No. 2560a also included eight small stickers. It exists in four versions which differ in the order of the stamps within the two blocks of four which form the booklet pane.

(Des Laurie Lafrance and q30 design inc. Litho Lowe-Martin)

2008 (18 July). Olympic Games, Beijing. Fluorescent frame. Self-adhesive. Perf 13½.
2565	**902**	52c. multicoloured	1·40	1·40
		a. Booklet pane. No. 2565×10	12·00	

No. 2565 was only issued in $5.20 booklets, No. SB385.

903 Lifeguard and Water Rescue

(Des Derwyn Goodall. Litho Lowe-Martin)

2008 (25 July). Centenary of Lifesaving Society. Fluorescent frame. Self-adhesive. Perf 13½×13.
2566	**903**	52c. multicoloured	1·00	1·25
		a. Booklet pane. No. 2566×10	9·00	

No. 2566 was only issued in $5.20 booklets, No. SB386.

899 50 Cent Coin, 1908

900 Nurse

(Des Stéphane Huot. Litho and embossed Lowe-Martin)

2008 (4 June). Centenary of the Royal Canadian Mint. Fluorescent frame. Perf 13×13½.
2555	**899**	52c. multicoloured	1·25	1·00

(Des Gottschalk+Ash International. Litho C.B.N)

2008 (16 June). Centenary of Canadian Nurses Association. Fluorescent frame. Self-adhesive. Perf 13½.
2556	**900**	52c. multicoloured	1·10	1·25
		a. Booklet pane. No. 2556×10	10·00	

No. 2556 was only issued in $5.20 stamp booklets, No. SB381.

904 Panning for Gold

CANADA

(Des Adam Rogers and Subplot Design Inc. Litho Lowe-Martin)

2008 (1 Aug). 150th Anniversary of British Columbia. Fluorescent frame. Perf 12½×13.

| 2567 | **904** | 52c. multicoloured | 1·90 | 1·25 |

No. 2567 is perforated through the backing paper, which is illustrated with eight historic photographs, each running across several stamps.

905 McLaughlin Buick, c. 1912 and Sam McLaughlin

906 Woman with Megaphone

(Litho Lowe-Martin)

2008 (8 Sept). Sam McLaughlin (founder of McLaughlin Motor Car Company and philanthropist) Commemoration. Fluorescent frame. Perf 12½×13.

| 2568 | **905** | 52c. multicoloured | 1·00 | 85 |

The fluorescent frame on No. 2568 is broken along the lower left side.

(Des David Sacha and Karen Satok. Litho Lowe-Martin)

2008 (1 Oct). Endangered Species (3rd series). Horiz designs as T **863**. Multicoloured. Fluorescent frame.

(a) Self-adhesive. Die-cut.

2569		52c. Prothonotary Warbler	2·25	2·00
		a. Pane. Nos. 2569/2572, each×2	12·00	
2570		52c. Taylor's Checkerspot (butterfly)	2·25	2·00
2571		52c. Roseate Tern	2·25	2·00
2572		52c. Burrowing Owl	2·25	2·00
2569/2572 Set of 4			8·00	8·00

(b) PVA gum. Size 48×24 mm. Perf 13½.

| MS2573 160×75 mm. As Nos. 2569/2572 | 8·00 | 7·50 |

Nos. 2569/2572 were issued in $4.18 panes of eight stamps, containing two of each design.

(Des Paul Haslip. Litho Lowe-Martin)

2008 (6 Oct). Mental Health. Fluorescent frame. Self-adhesive. Perf 13½.

| 2574 | **906** | (52c.)+10c. multicoloured | 1·25 | 1·75 |
| | | a. Booklet pane. No. 2574×10 | 11·00 | |

No. 2574 was inscribed 'P+10' and initially sold for 52c. plus a 10c. surcharge for the Canada Post Foundation for Mental Health.
No. 2574 was only issued in booklets, No. SB388, sold for $6.20.

907 Québec City Skyline

908 Infant Jesus (crèche figure by Antonio Caruso)

(Des Ian Drolet. Litho C.B.N)

2008 (15 Oct). 12th Francophone Summit, Quebec. Fluorescent frame. Perf 12½×13.

| 2575 | **907** | 52c. multicoloured | 1·00 | 1·00 |

(Des Joseph Gault. Litho Lowe-Martin)

2008 (3 Nov). Christmas (1st issue). Self-adhesive booklet stamps. Fluorescent frame. Perf 13½.

| 2576 | **908** | (52c.) multicoloured | 1·10 | 85 |
| | | a. Booklet pane. No. 2576×12 | 12·00 | |

No. 2576 was inscribed 'P' and was initially valid for 52c. It was only available from stamp booklets, No. SB389.

909 Child making Snow Angels

910 Ox

(Des Susan Scott. Litho Lowe-Martin)

2008 (3 Nov). Christmas (2nd issue). Winter Fun. T **909** and similar vert designs showing children. Fluorescent frame. Perf 13½.

(a) Self-adhesive.

2577		(52c.) Type **909**	1·10	85
		a. Pane. No. 2577×12	10·00	
2578		96c. Child skiing	1·60	2·50
		a. Pane. No. 2578×6	8·50	
2579		$1.60 Child tobogganing	2·50	4·00
		a. Pane. No. 2579×6	13·00	
2577/2579 Set of 3			4·50	6·50

(b) PVA gum.

| MS2580 102×72 mm. As Nos. 2577/2579 | 4·50 | 7·00 |

No. 2577 was inscribed 'P' and was initially valid for 52c.
Nos. 2577 was only available from $6.24 stamp booklets, No. SB391.
Nos. 2578/2579 were issued in separate $5.76 and $9.60 panes of six.

(Des Ivan Novotny. Litho and embossed Lowe-Martin)

2009 (8 Jan). Chinese New Year. Year of the Ox. T **910** and similar square design. Multicoloured. Fluorescent frame. Perf 12½.

| 2581 | | (54c.) Type **910** | 1·40 | 1·00 |
| MS2582 40×140 mm. $1.65 Earthenware cooking pot by Shu-Hwei Kao | | | 3·25 | 4·00 |

No. 2581 was inscribed 'P' and initially sold for 54c. It has a background flower pattern which extends over the stamps and sheet margins.
The stamp within No. **MS**2582 has a partial fluorescent frame, which is absent from the upper left and top of the stamp.

2009 (8 Jan). China 2009 World Stamp Exhibition. No. **MS**2582 optd with CHINA 2009 logo in gold on the sheet margin.

| MS2583 40×140 mm. $1.65 Earthenware cooking pot by Shu-Hwei Kao | | | 3·25 | 5·00 |

911 Freestyle Skiing

912 Vancouver 2010 Winter Olympic Games Emblem

(Des John Belisle and Kosta Tsetsekas. Litho C.B.N)

2009 (12 Jan). Winter Olympic Games, Vancouver, 2010 (1st issue). Olympic Sports. T **911** and similar horiz designs. Multicoloured. Fluorescent frame. Perf 13.

(a) Self-adhesive.

2584		(54c.) Type **911**	1·40	1·50
		a. Pane. Nos. 2584/2588, each×2	12·00	
		b. Booklet pane. Nos. 2584/2588, each×6	35·00	
2585		(54c.) Snowboarding	1·40	1·50
2586		(54c.) Ice sledge hockey	1·40	1·50
2587		(54c.) Bobsleigh	1·40	1·50
2588		(54c.) Curling	1·40	1·50
2584/2588 Set of 5			6·25	6·75

(b) Ordinary gum.

| MS2589 140×82 mm. As Nos. 2584/2588 | 5·75 | 6·75 |
| a. 'VANCOUVER 2010' in silver | 15·00 | 15·00 |

Nos. 2584/2588 and stamps from **MS**2589 were all inscribed 'P' and initially sold for 54c. each.
Nos. 2584/2588 were issued in panes of ten and booklets of 30, No. SB393.
No. **MS**2589a, together with **MS**2598a and **MS**2655a, were originally sold in silver, bronze and gold 'collectors sets', also containing commemorative coins, lapel pins and a booklet at $49.95 each. However, the three sheets were subsequently made available in a souvenir pack at face value ($8.73).
See also Nos. 2590/**MS**2598, 2653/**MS**2655, 2658/**MS**2659 and 2660/**MS**2662.

CANADA

(Des Meomi and VANOC/COVAN (emblems) Naomi Broudo and Violet Finvers (mascots). Litho Lowe-Martin)

2009 (12 Jan–12 Feb). Winter Olympic Games, Vancouver, 2010 (2nd issue). Emblems and Mascots. T **912** and similar horiz designs. Multicoloured. Fluorescent frame with security markings.

(a) Self-adhesive coil stamps. Die-cut perf 9½×imperf (No. 2590) or 8×imperf (others).

2590	(54c.) Type **912**	1·00	1·50
	a. Vert pair. Nos. 2590/2591	2·00	3·00
2591	(54c.) Vancouver 2010 Paralympic Games emblem	1·00	1·50
2592	98c. Miga skiing	2·00	2·50
2593	$1.18 Sumi curling (12.2.09)	2·25	3·00
2594	$1.65 Quatchi playing ice hockey	3·25	4·25
2590/2594 Set of 5		8·50	11·50

(b) Self-adhesive stamps from panes of six. Die-cut perf 9×imperf.

2595	98c. As No. 2592	2·25	2·75
	a. Pane. No. 2595×6	12·00	
2596	$1.18 As No. 2593 (12.2.09)	2·50	3·25
	a. Pane. No. 2596×6	13·00	
2597	$1.65 As No. 2594	3·50	4·50
	a. Pane. No. 2597×6	19·00	

(c) Ordinary gum. Perf 13.

MS2598 140×82 mm. As Nos. 2590/2594 (12 Feb)		9·00	11·00
a. 'VANCOUVER 2010' in bronze		15·00	15·00

Nos. 2590/2591 were initially sold for 54c. each. They were printed together, *se-tenant*, as vertical pairs in rolls of 100.

Nos. 2592/2594 were printed in separate rolls of 50.

Nos. 2595/2597 were issued in separate panes of six, sold for $5.88, $7.08 and $9.90.

For note regarding No. **MS**2598a see below No. **MS**2589.

913 Stylized Ribbons, Fireworks and Confetti bursting from Envelope

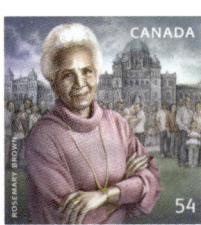

914 Rosemary Brown (civil rights campaigner) and B.C. Legislative Building

(Des Debbie Adams. Litho Lowe-Martin)

2009 (2 Feb). Greetings Stamp. 'Celebrate'. Fluorescent frame. Self-adhesive. Die-cut perf 13×imperf.

2599	**913**	(54c.) multicoloured	1·10	1·25
		a. Pane. No. 2599×6	6·00	

No. 2599, inscribed 'P', was initially sold for 54c. It was issued in panes of six.

(Des Suzanne Duranceau and Lara Minja. Litho C.B.N)

2009 (2 Feb). Black History Month. T **914** and similar square design. Multicoloured. Fluorescent frame. Perf 13×12½.

2600	54c. Type **914**	1·00	1·25
	a. Pair. Nos. 2600/2601	2·00	2·50
2601	54c. Abraham Doras Shadd holding lantern and runaway slaves	1·00	1·25

Nos. 2600/2601 were printed together, *se-tenant*, as horizontal and vertical pairs in sheets of 16.

915 Flight of *Silver Dart*, Bras d'Or Lake, Nova Scotia, 23 February 1909

(Des Michael Little, Crystal Oicle and Dennis Page. Litho Lowe-Martin)

2009 (23 Feb). Centenary of First Powered Flight in Canada. Fluorescent frame. Self-adhesive. Perf 12½×13.

2602	**915**	(54c.) multicoloured	2·00	2·00

The backing paper is illustrated with five different scenes.

916 White Rhododendron with Pink Buds

917 'Striped Column" (Jack Bush), 1964

(Des Isabelle Toussaint. Litho Lowe-Martin)

2009 (13 Mar). Rhododendrons. T **916** and similar horiz design. Multicoloured. Fluorescent frame.

(a) Self-adhesive. Perf 13½×12½.

2603	54c. Type **916**	1·10	1·40
	a. Booklet pane. Nos. 2603/2604, each×5	10·00	
2604	54c. Deep pink rhododendron	1·10	1·40

(b) Ordinary gum. Perf 13.

MS2605 120×74 mm. As Nos. 2603/2604	2·00	2·75

Nos. 2603/2604 were only issued in $5.40 booklets, No. SB394, in which the surplus self-adhesive paper around each stamp was retained.

Booklet pane No. 2603a also includes ten small stickers.

The top edge of No. **MS**2605 is cut around the shapes of the rhododendron flowers and foliage.

(Des Hélène L'Heureux. Litho Lowe-Martin)

2009 (20 Mar). Art Canada. Birth Centenary of Jack Bush (artist). T **917** and similar multicoloured design showing paintings. Fluorescent frame. Perf 13 (No. 2606) or 12½×13 (No. **MS**2607).

2606	54c. Type **917**	1·00	1·00
MS2607 150×87 mm. 54c. Type **917**; $1.65 'Chopsticks', 1977 (57×23 mm)		4·00	5·50

918 Horsehead Nebula and Dominion Astrophysical Observatory, Saanich, BC

919 Polar Bear

(Des Keith Martin. Litho Lowe-Martin)

2009 (2 Apr). International Year of Astronomy. T **918** and similar vert design. Multicoloured. Fluorescent frame. Perf 13.

(a) Self-adhesive.

2608	54c. Type **918**	1·10	1·40
	a. Booklet pane. Nos. 2608/2609, each×5	10·00	
2609	54c. Eagle Nebula and Canada-France-Hawaii Telescope, Mauna Kea, Hawaii...	1·10	1·40

(b) Ordinary gum.

MS2610 101×90 mm. As Nos. 2608/2609 but 30×40 mm	2·25	3·00
a. With fluorescent overprint		

Nos. 2608/2609 were only issued in $5.40 booklets, No. SB395, in which the surplus self-adhesive paper around each stamp was retained. Booklet pane No. 2608a also included ten small stickers.

The fluorescent overprint on No. **MS**2610a appears above the left-hand stamp, depicts an adult and child, and appears red under UV light.

(Des Tiit Telmet and Wade Stewart. Litho Lowe-Martin)

2009 (9 Apr). Preserve the Polar Regions and Glaciers. T **919** and similar horiz design. Multicoloured. Fluorescent frame. Perf 13.

2611	54c. Type **919**	2·00	2·00
	a. Pair. Nos. 2611/2612	4·00	4·50
2612	54c. Arctic Tern	2·00	2·00
MS2613 120×80 mm. Nos. 2611/2612		4·00	5·00

Nos. 2611/2612 were printed together, *se-tenant*, as horizontal and vertical pairs in sheetlets of 16 stamps.

CANADA

920 Canadian Horse   **921** Canadian Flag and Globe

(Des Wilco Design. Litho Lowe-Martin)

2009 (15 May). Canadian Horse and Newfoundland Pony. T **920** and similar horiz design. Multicoloured. Fluorescent frame. Self-adhesive. Die-cut perf 13.

2614	54c. Type **920**	2·00	2·00
	a. Booklet pane. Nos. 2614/2615, each×5	15·00	
2615	54c. Newfoundland Pony	2·00	2·00

Nos. 2614/2615 were only issued in $5.40 stamp booklets, No. SB396. Nos. 2614/2615 form a composite background design.

(Des Parable Communications and Cartesia. Litho Lowe-Martin)

2009 (1 June). Centenary of Department of Foreign Affairs and International Trade. Fluorescent frame. Perf 13.

2616	**921**	54c. multicoloured	1·25	1·00

922 Niagara Falls in 1909 and 2009   **923** Robert Charlebois

(Des Paul Haslip. Litho Lowe-Martin)

2009 (12 June). Centenary of the Boundary Waters Treaty. Fluorescent frame. Perf 13.

2617	**922**	54c. multicoloured	1·25	1·00

(Des CIRCLE. Litho Lowe-Martin)

2009 (2 July). Canadian Recording Artists (2nd series). T **923** and similar square designs. Multicoloured. Fluorescent frame.

(a) Self-adhesive. Die-cut perf 13½.

2618	54c. Type **923**	80	1·00
	a. Booklet pane. Nos. 2618/2621, each×2	7·00	
2619	54c. Edith Butler	80	1·00
2620	54c. Stompin' Tom Connors	80	1·00
2621	54c. Bryan Adams	80	1·00
2618/2621	Set of 4	3·00	3·50

(b) Ordinary gum. Perf 12½×13.

MS2622 Circular 105×105 mm. As Nos. 2618/2621............ 4·00   5·00

Nos. 2618/2621 were only issued in $4.32 booklets, Nos. SB397/SB397c. The circular booklet pane No. 2618a also included eight small stickers. It exists in four versions which differ in the order of the stamps within the two blocks of four which form the booklet pane.

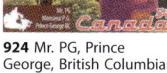

924 Mr. PG, Prince George, British Columbia   **925** Captain Bartlett with Sextant and *Roosevelt* in the Canadian Arctic

(Bonnie Ross and Fraser Ross. Litho Lowe-Martin)

2009 (6 July). Roadside Attractions (1st series). T **924** and similar multicoloured designs. Fluorescent frame.

(a) Self-adhesive. Die-cut perf 13½ (3 sides).

2623	54c. Type **924**	1·40	1·50
	a. Booklet pane. Nos. 2623/2626, each×2	10·00	
2624	54c. Sign Post Forest, Watson Lake, Yukon ...	1·40	1·50
2625	54c. Inukshuk (stone giant), Hay River, Northwest Territories	1·40	1·50
2626	54c. Pysanka (giant Easter egg), Vegreville, Alberta	1·40	1·50
2623/2626	Set of 4	5·00	5·50

(b) Ordinary gum. Perf 13.

MS2627 98×109 mm. As Nos. 2623/6............ 4·00   5·00

Nos. 2623/2626 have irregularly shaped tops to the stamps. They are perforated on three sides and imperforate at top.

Nos. 2623/2626 were only issued in $4.32 stamp booklets, No. SB398, in which the surplus self-adhesive paper around each stamp was retained. Booklet pane No. 2623a also included eight small stickers.

See also Nos. 2688/**MS**2692 and 2807/**MS**2811.

(Des Karen Smith Design. Litho Lowe-Martin)

2009 (10 July). Captain Robert Abram 'Bob' Bartlett (Arctic explorer, ice captain and scientist) Commemoration. Perf 13.

2628	**925**	54c. multicoloured	1·50	1·10

No. 2628 commemorates the centenary of Captain Bartlett's attempt to reach the North Pole.

926 Five-pin Bowling   **927** Tree and River inside Human Head and Sun breaking through Clouds

(Des q30design inc. Litho Lowe-Martin)

2009 (10 Aug). Canadian Inventions. Sports. T **926** and similar vert designs. Multicoloured. Fluorescent frame. Self-adhesive. Die-cut perf 13½.

2629	54c. Type **926**	1·50	1·50
	a. Booklet pane. Nos. 2629/2632, each×2	10·00	
2630	54c. Ringette	1·50	1·50
2631	54c. Lacrosse	1·50	1·50
2632	54c. Basketball	1·50	1·50
2629/2632	Set of 4	5·50	5·50

Nos. 2629/2632 were only issued in $4.32 stamp booklets, No. SB399. Booklet pane No. 2629a also included eight small stickers showing sports shoes.

(Des Signals Design Group. Litho Lowe-Martin)

2009 (14 Sept). Mental Health. Fluorescent frame. Self-adhesive. Die-cut perf 13.

2633	**927**	(54c.) +10c. multicoloured	1·25	1·75
		a. Booklet pane. No. 2633×10	12·00	

No. 2633 was inscr 'P+10' and was initially valid for 54c. plus a 10c. surcharge for the Canada Post Foundation for Mental Health.

No. 2633 was only issued in booklets of ten, No. SB400, initially sold for $6.40.

928 Detail from Maurice Richard's Hockey Sweater   **929** Maurice Richard, 19 October 1957

(Des Stéphane Huot. Litho and lenticular (2635) Lowe-Martin)

2009 (17 Oct). Centenary of Montreal Canadiens (ice hockey team). Multicoloured. Self-adhesive.

(a) Fluorescent frame. Die-cut perf 13.

2634	**928**	(54c.) multicoloured	1·25	1·25
		a. Booklet pane. No. 2634×10	11·00	

*(b) T **929** and similar horiz designs showing 500th goals of famous players. Perf 13.*

MS2635 $3 Type **929**; Jean Béliveau, 11 February 1971; Guy Lafleur, 20 December 1983................ 14·00   22·00

No. 2634 was inscribed 'P' and originally valid for 54c. It was only issued in booklets of ten, No. SB401, initially sold for $5.40.

The stamps within No. **MS**2635 are based on digital clips and use Motionstamp technology to show action replays of goals.

CANADA

930 Two Soldiers (detail from National War Memorial, Ottawa)   **931** Madonna and Infant Jesus

(Des Lionel Gadoury and Michael Wandelmaier. Litho Lowe-Martin)

2009 (19 Oct). 'Lest We Forget'. Fluorescent frame.

(a) Self-adhesive. Die-cut perf 13.

2636	930	(54c.) multicoloured	1·25	1·25
		a. Booklet pane. No. 2636×10	12·00	

(b) Ordinary gum. Perf 12½.

MS2637 108×60 mm. As Type **930**×2................ 2·50   3·25

No. 2636 and the stamps within **MS**2637 were all inscr 'P' and were originally valid for 54c.

No. 2636 was only issued in booklets of ten, No. SB402, initially sold for $5.40.

MS2637 was originally sold for $1.08.

(Des Joseph Gault. LItho Lowe-Martin)

2009 (2 Nov). Christmas (1st issue). T **931** and similar vert designs showing crèche figures by Antonio Caruso. Multicoloured. Fluorescent frame.

(a) Self-adhesive. Die-cut perf 13½.

2638		(54c.) Type **931**	1·10	95
		a. Booklet pane. No. 2638×12	12·00	
2639		98c. Magi with gift	2·25	3·00
		a. Pane. No. 2639×6	11·00	
2640		$1.65 Shepherd carrying lamb	3·25	4·50
		a. Pane. No. 2640×6	18·00	
2638/2640 Set of 3			6·00	7·75

(b) Ordinary gum. Perf 13×12½.

MS2641 150×100 mm. As Nos. 2576 and 2638/2640....... 7·00   8·50

No. 2638 was inscr 'P' and was originally valid for 54c. It was issued in booklets of 12 stamps, No. SB403, initially sold for $6.48.

Nos. 2639/2640 were issued in separate panes of six.

They were also available in $15.78 panes containing six of each design separated by a gutter.

932 Christmas Tree   **933** Tiger Seal

(Des Hélène L'Heureux. Litho and holographic foil Lowe-Martin)

2009 (2 Nov). Christmas (2nd issue). Self-adhesive booklet stamps. Fluorescent frame. Die-cut perf 9×imperf.

2642	932	(54c.) multicoloured	1·10	85
		a. Booklet pane. No. 2642×12	12·00	

No. 2642 was inscribed 'P' and was initially valid for 54c. It was only available from booklets of 12, No. SB404, originally sold for $6.48.

(Des Wilco Design. Litho and embossed Lowe-Martin)

2010 (8 Jan). Chinese New Year. Year of the Tiger. Fluorescent frame. Perf 12½.

2643		(57c.) Type **933**	1·25	1·00
MS2644 40×140 mm. 170c. Tiger's head seal..................			3·50	4·00

The fluorescent frame on **MS**2644 is on three sides, at the left, right and bottom of the stamp.

No. 2643 was inscr 'P' and initially sold for 57c.

934 Striped Coralroot (*Corallorhiza striata*)   **935** Whistler, British Columbia

(Monique Dufour and Sophie Lafortune. Litho Lowe-Martin)

2010 (11 Jan). Flowers (4th series). Wild Orchids. T **934** and similar horiz designs. Multicoloured. Fluorescent frame.

(a) Self-adhesive stamps from vert coils. Perf 8×imperf.

2645	(57c.) Type **934**	1·10	95
2646	$1 Giant Helleborine (*Epipactis gigantea*)..	2·25	2·50
2647	$1.22 Rose Pogonia (*Pogonia ophioglossoides*)	2·40	3·50
2648	$1.70 Grass Pink (*Calopogon tuberosus*)	3·50	4·50
2645/2648 Set of 4		8·25	10·50

(b) Self-adhesive stamps from horiz coils. Perf 9×imperf.

2648a	(57c.) Type **934**	1·10	1·10

(c) Self-adhesive stamps from panes of six. Perf 9½×imperf.

2649	$1 As No. 2646	2·50	3·00
	a. Pane. No. 2649×6	13·00	
2650	$1.22 As No. 2647	2·75	3·50
	a. Pane. No. 2650×6	15·00	
2651	$1.70 As No. 2648	4·00	4·75
	a. Pane. No. 2651×6	22·00	
2649/2651 Set of 3		8·25	10·00

(d) Ordinary gum. Perf 13.

MS2652 120×72 mm. As Nos. 2645/2648......................... 9·25   10·00

No. 2645 was inscribed 'P' and originally sold for 57c.

Perforations are variable on Nos. 2645/2648 but consistently 9·25 on No. 2648a. The latter may be identified by its rounded 'perf' tips whereas those on No. 2645 are pointed ('saw tooth').

Nos. 2649/51 were only available in separate panes of ten stamps.

(Des Tandem Design Associates Ltd. Litho Lowe-Martin)

2010 (12 Jan). Olympic Winter Games, Vancouver (3rd issue). T **935** and similar horiz design. Multicoloured. Fluorescent frame.

(a) Self-adhesive. Die-cut perf 13½.

2653	57c. Type **935**	1·40	1·60
	a. Booklet pane. Nos. 2653/2654, each×5	12·50	
2654	57c. Vancouver	1·40	1·60

(b) Ordinary gum. Perf 13½.

MS2655 141×83 mm. As Nos. 2653/2654........................ 2·75   3·25
  a. 'VANCOUVER 2010' in gold .... 9·00   9·50

Nos. 2653/2654 were only issued in $5.70 booklets, No. SB406.

For note regarding No. **MS**2655a see below **MS**2589.

936 William Hall, V.C. in 1900 and HMS *Shannon*   **937** *Roméo LeBlanc* (Christan Nicholson)

(Des Suzanne Duranceau and Lara Minja. Litho Lowe-Martin)

2010 (1 Feb). Black History Month. Fluorescent frame. Perf 12½.

2656	936	57c. multicoloured	2·25	1·40

(Des Dennis Page and Oliver Hill. Litho Lowe-Martin)

2010 (8 Feb). Roméo LeBlanc (former Minister of Fisheries and Governor General of Canada 1995–1999) Commemoration. Fluorescent frame. Perf 12½.

2657	937	57c. multicoloured	1·25	1·10

938 Vancouver 2010 Olympic Gold Medal   **939** Child with Painted Face, Bobsleigh and Speed Skaters

(Des Tandem Design Associates Ltd. Litho Lowe-Martin)

2010 (14 Feb). Olympic Winter Games, Vancouver (4th issue). Canada's First Olympic Gold on Canadian Soil. Fluorescent frame.

(a) Self-adhesive. Die-cut perf 13½.

2658	938	57c. multicoloured	1·40	1·25
		a. Booklet pane. No. 2658×10	12·50	

(b) Ordinary gum. Perf 12½.

MS2659 150×60 mm. As Type **938**×2.......................... 2·50   3·00

No. 2658 was only issued in $5.70 booklets, No. SB407.

CANADA

(Des Signals Design Group. Litho Lowe-Martin)

2010 (22 Feb). Olympic Winter Games, Vancouver (5th issue). T **939** and similar horiz design. Multicoloured. Partial fluorescent frame.

(a) Self-adhesive. Die-cut perf 13½.

2660	57c. Type **939**	1·40	1·60
	a. Booklet pane. Nos. 2660/2661, each×5	12·50	
2661	57c. Child with painted face, Chandra Crawford with gold medal (Turin 2006) and skiers	1·40	1·60

(b) Ordinary gum. Perf 13.

MS2662 134×60 mm. As Nos. 2660/2661.................. 2·50 3·00

Nos. 2660/2661 were only issued in $5.70 booklets, No. SB408.

The fluorescent frames were on three sides, being at top, right and foot of the stamp on Type **939**, and at top, left and foot of the stamp on No. 2661. The stamps within the miniature sheet have fluorescent frames as Nos. 2660/2661.

940 African Violet 'Decelles' Avalanche' **941** Figures forming Maple Leaf and Star of David

(Des Isabelle Toussaint. Litho Lowe-Martin)

2010 (3 Mar). African Violets. T **940** and similar vert design. Multicoloured. Fluorescent frame.

(a) Self-adhesive. Die-cut perf 13½.

2663	(57c.) Type **940**	1·40	1·60
	a. Booklet pane. Nos. 2663/2664, each×5	12·50	
2664	(57c.) African Violet 'Picasso' (violet and white flowers)	1·40	1·60

(b) Ordinary gum. Perf 13.

MS2665 120×82 mm. As Nos. 2663/2664................... 2·50 3·00

Nos. 2663/2664 and the stamps within **MS**2665 were all inscr 'P' and were originally valid for 57c.

Nos. 2663/2664 were only issued in booklets of ten, No. SB409, originally sold for $5.70. Booklet pane 2663a also contains ten small stickers. No. **MS**2665 was originally sold for $1.14.

The top left portion of **MS**2665 is cut around the flowers.

(Des Yarek Waszul and q30design inc. Litho Lowe-Martin)

2010 (14 Apr). Canada–Israel, 60 Years of Friendship. Fluorescent frame. Self-adhesive. Die-cut perf 13.

2666	**941**	$1.70 rosine, new blue and brownish grey	4·25	5·00
		a. Booklet pane. No. 2666×6	25·00	

No. 2666 was only issued in $10.20 booklets, No. SB410.

942 Tee Yee Neen Ho Ga Row **943** HMCS *Niobe* and Sailor, *c.* 1910

(Des Sputnik Design Partners Inc. Litho Lowe-Martin)

2010 (19 Apr). *Four Indian Kings* paintings by John Verelst. T **942** and similar vert designs. Multicoloured. Fluorescent frame. Perf 12½.

2667	57c. Type **942**	1·75	1·75
	a. Strip of 4. Nos. 2667/2670	6·25	6·25
2668	57c. Sa Ga Yeath Qua Pieth Tow	1·75	1·75
2669	57c. Ho Nee Yeath Taw No Row	1·75	1·75
2670	57c. Etow Oh Koam	1·75	1·75
2667/2670	Set of 4	6·25	7·50
MS2671 168×75 mm. Nos. 2667/2670		6·25	6·25

Nos. 2667/2670 were printed together, *se-tenant*, as horizontal and vertical strips of four in sheetlets of 16.

The portraits show representatives of the Iroquois and Algonquin nations who travelled to London in 1710 for an audience with Queen Anne.

2010 (19 Apr). London 2010 Festival of Stamps. No. **MS**2671 optd with 'LONDON 2010 FESTIVAL OF STAMPS' logo on the sheet margin.

MS2672 168×75 mm. Nos. 2667/70.................... 5·00 7·00

(Des Designwerke Inc. Litho Lowe-Martin)

2010 (4 May). Centenary of the Canadian Navy. T **943** and similar horiz design. Multicoloured. Fluorescent frame.

(a) Self-adhesive. Die-cut perf 13×13½.

2673	57c. Type **943**	1·90	1·90
	a. Booklet pane. Nos. 2673/2674, each×5	15·00	
2674	57c. HMCS *Halifax* (modern frigate) and Wren	1·90	1·90

(b) Ordinary gum. Perf 12½.

MS2675 108×64 mm. As Nos. 2673/2674................... 3·50 3·75

Nos. 2673/2674 were only issued in $5.70 booklets, No. SB411.

944 Harbour Porpoise (*Phocoena phocoena*) **945** *Selasphorus rufus* (Hummingbird) (Wing Yan Tam)

(Des Martin Mörck. Eng Lars Sjööblom. Recess and litho Sweden Post)

2010 (13 May). Marine Life: Sea Otter and Harbour Porpoise. T **944** and similar horiz design. Fluorescent frame. Each black, dull ultramarine and turquoise-blue. Perf 13×12½ (with one double elliptical perforation at right (No. 2676) or left (No. 2677), or 'maple leaf' perforation (No. **MS**2678).

2676	57c. Type **944**	1·60	1·60
	a. Booklet pane. Nos. 2676/2677, each×4	11·50	
2677	57c. Sea Otter (*Enhydra lutris*)	1·60	1·60
MS2678 105×69 mm. As Nos. 2676/2677		2·75	3·25

Nos. 2676/2677 were only issued in $4.56 stamp booklets, No. SB412. Stamps of a similar design were issued by Sweden.

(Des Susan Scott. Litho C.B.N)

2010 (22 May). Canadian Geographic's Wildlife Photography of the Year. T **945** and similar multicoloured designs showing winning entries. Fluorescent frame. Die-cut perf 13.

(a) Self-adhesive. Die-cut perf 13.

2679	57c. Type **945**	1·75	2·00
	a. Booklet pane. Nos. 2679/2683, each×2	14·00	
2680	57c. *Tachycineta bicolor* (Tree Swallows) (Mark Bradley)	1·75	2·00
2681	57c. *Tettigoniidae* (Katydid) (Julie Bazinet) (vert)	1·75	2·00
2682	57c. *Ardea herodias* (Great Blue Heron) (Martin Cooper) (vert)	1·75	2·00
2683	57c. *Vulpes vulpes* (Red Fox) (Ben Boulter) (vert)	1·75	2·00
2679/2683	Set of 5	8·00	9·00

(b) Ordinary gum. Perf 12½×13.

MS2684 150×100 mm. As Nos. 2679/2683................... 7·00 8·50

Nos. 2679/2683 were only issued in $5.70 booklets, No. SB413.

946 Man wearing Rotary Vest **947** 'Rollande', 1929

(Des Xerxes Irani. Litho Lowe-Martin)

2010 (18 June). Centenary of Rotary International. Self-adhesive. Fluorescent frame. Die-cut perf 13½×13.

2685	**946**	57c. multicoloured	1·40	1·60
		a. Booklet pane. No. 2685×8	10·00	

No. 2685 was only issued in $4.56 booklets, No. SB414.

CANADA

947 Rollande, 1929

(Des Hélène L'Heureux. Litho Lowe-Martin)

2010 (2 July). Art Canada. Paintings by Prudence Heward. T **947** and similar multicoloured design. Multicoloured. Fluorescent frame. Perf 13.
2686		57c. Type **947**	1·25	1·10
MS2687	150×87 mm. 57c. Type **947**; $1.70 'At the Theatre', 1928 (42×40 mm)		5·50	6·50

(Des Bonnie Ross and Fraser Ross. Litho Lowe-Martin)

2010 (5 July). Roadside Attractions (2nd series). Multicoloured designs as T **924**. Fluorescent frame.

(a) Self-adhesive. Die-cut perf 13½ (3 sides).
2688	(57c.) The Coffee Pot, Davidson, SK	1·75	2·00
	a. Booklet pane. Nos. 2688/2691, each×2	11·00	
2689	(57c.) Happy Rock, Gladstone, Manitoba	1·75	2·00
2690	(57c.) Goose, Wawa, Ontario	1·75	2·00
2691	(57c.) Puffin, Longue-Pointe-de-Mingan, Quebec	1·75	2·00
2688/2691 Set of 4		6·25	7·25

(b) Ordinary gum. Perf 13.
MS2692	99×109 mm. As Nos. 2688/2691	6·25	7·25

Nos. 2688/2691 have irregularly shaped tops to the stamps. They are perforated on three sides and imperforate at top.

Nos. 2688/2691 and the stamps within **MS**2692 were all inscr 'P' and were originally valid for 57c.

Nos. 2688/2691 were only issued in booklets of eight, No. SB415, originally sold for $4.56. Booklet pane No. 2688a included eight small stickers.

948 Guides   **949** Coins, Glass and Amber Trading Beads and 17th-century Map of Avalon Peninsula, Newfoundland

(Des Derwyn Goodall. Litho Lowe-Martin)

2010 (8 July). Centenary of Girl Guides of Canada. Fluorescent frame. Self-adhesive. Die-cut perf 13½.
2693	**948**	(57c.) multicoloured	1·40	1·40
		a. Booklet pane. No. 2693×10	12·50	

No. 2693 was inscr 'P' and was originally valid for 57c. It was only issued in booklets of ten, No. SB416, originally sold for $5.70. Booklet pane No. 2693a also included ten small stickers.

949 Coins, Glass and Amber Trading Beads and 17th-century Map of Avalon Peninsula, Newfoundland   **950** Immigrant Boy, Boy ploughing and SS *Sardinian*

(Des Steven Slipp. Litho Lowe-Martin)

2010 (17 Aug). 400th Anniversary of Cupids, Newfoundland (first English settlement in Canada). Fluorescent frame. Perf 12½.
2694	**949**	57c. multicoloured	2·00	1·50

(Des Debbie Adams. Litho Lowe-Martin)

2010 (1 Sept). 'Home Children' (British orphaned and abandoned children sent to Canada). Fluorescent frame. Perf 12½.
2695	**950**	57c. multicoloured	1·50	1·50

951 Mental Health Patient on Road to Recovery

(Des Paprika. Litho Lowe-Martin)

2010 (7 Sept). Mental Health. Fluorescent frame. Die-cut perf 13.
2696	**951**	(57c.)+10c. multicoloured	1·40	2·00
		a. Booklet pane. No. 2696×10	12·50	

No. 2696 was inscr 'P+10' and was initially valid for 57c. plus a 10c. surcharge for the Canada Post Foundation for Mental Health.

No. 2696 was only issued in booklets of ten, No. SB417, initially sold for $6.70.

952 'Our Lady of the Night' (sculpture by Antonio Caruso)   **953** Red Baubles

(Des Joseph Gault. Litho Lowe-Martin)

2010 (1 Nov). Christmas (1st issue). Self-adhesive booklet stamp. Fluorescent frame. Die-cut perf 13½.
2697	**952**	(57c.) multicoloured	1·25	1·10
		a. Booklet pane. No. 2697×12	15·00	

No. 2697 was inscribed 'P' and was initially valid for 57c. It was only available from booklets of 12, No. SB418, originally sold for $6.84.

953 Red Baubles

(Des Michael Zavacky. Litho Lowe-Martin)

2010 (1 Nov). Christmas (2nd issue). Baubles. T **953** and similar square designs. Multicoloured. Fluorescent frame.

(a) Self-adhesive. Die-cut perf 13½.
2698	(57c.) Type **953**	1·25	1·10
	a. Booklet pane. No. 2698×12	15·00	
2699	$1 Blue baubles	2·40	2·75
	a. Pane. No. 2699×6	14·00	
2700	$1.70 Pink baubles	3·75	4·50
	a. Pane. No. 2700×6	22·00	
2698/2700 Set of 3		6·75	7·50

(b) Ordinary gum. Perf 12½.
MS2701	116×60 mm. As Nos. 2698/2700	7·50	8·50

No. 2698 was inscr 'P' and was originally valid for 57c. It was issued in booklets of 12 stamps, No. SB419, initially sold for $6.84.

Nos. 2699/2700 were each issued in separate panes of six.

They were also available together in $16.20 panes containing six of each design separated by a gutter.

CANADA

954 Rabbit

955 Arctic Hares

(Des Tracy Walker, Tan Chao Chang, Paul Haslip and Lauren Rand. Litho and embossed Lowe-Martin and Gravure Choquet)

2011 (7 Jan). Chinese New Year. Year of the Rabbit. T **954** and similar square design. Multicoloured. Fluorescent frame. Perf 12½.

2702	(59c.) Type **954**	1·75	1·10
MS2703	140×40 mm. $1.75 Two rabbits (on medallion)..	4·75	4·75

No. 2702 was inscribed 'P' and initially sold for 59c.

The stamp within **MS**2703 has a fluorescent frame on three sides, at top, left and foot of the stamp.

(Des Monique Dufour and Sophie Lafortune. Litho Lowe-Martin)

2011 (17 Jan)–**14**. Young Wildlife. T **955** and similar horiz designs. Multicoloured. Fluorescent frame.

(a) Self-adhesive coil stamps. Die-cut perf 9×imperf (2705/6), 13½ (2706d) or 8½×imperf (others).

2704	(59c.) Type **955**	1·25	1·10
	a. Perf 9×imperf	1·25	1·10
2705	(61c.) Three young Raccoons (16.1.12)	1·50	1·50
	a. Perf 9×imperf	1·50	1·50
2706	(63c.) Four baby Woodchucks (14.1.13)	1·40	1·40
	a. Perf 9½×imperf	1·40	1·40
2706b	63c. Four baby Woodchucks (31.3.14)	1·40	1·40
	ba. Perf 9×imperf	1·40	1·40
2706c	(85c.) Adult and baby Beaver (31.3.14)	1·50	1·50
	ca. Perf 9×imperf	1·50	1·50
2706d	$1 Three Burrowing Owl chicks	2·25	2·10
2707	$1.03 Red Fox cub	2·25	2·40
2708	$1.05 Two Caribou calves (16.1.12)	2·25	2·25
2709	$1.10 Young Porcupine (14.1.13)	2·25	2·25
2709b	$1.20 Mountain Goat kid (31.3.14)	2·50	2·25
2710	$1.25 Two Canada Geese goslings	2·75	3·00
2711	$1.29 Loon and two chicks (16.1.12)	2·75	3·00
2712	$1.34 Deer fawn (14.1.13)	2·50	2·25
2713	$1.75 Polar Bear cub	3·75	4·50
2714	$1.80 Two young Moose (16.1.12)	3·75	3·50
2714b	$1.80 Adult Puffin and chick (31.3.14)	3·25	3·00
2715	$1.85 Black Bear cub (14.1.13)	3·25	3·00
2715b	$2.50 Wapiti calf (31.3.14)	4·50	4·50
2704/2715b	Set of 17	38·00	38·00

(b) Self-adhesive stamps from panes of six. Die-cut perf 9×imperf.

2716	$1.03 As No. 2707	2·25	3·00
	a. Pane. No. 2716×6	12·00	
2717	$1.05 As No. 2708 (16.1.12)	2·25	2·10
	a. Pane. No. 2717×6	12·00	
2718	$1.10 As No. 2709 (14.1.13)	2·25	2·10
	a. Pane. No. 2718×6	12·00	
2718b	$1.20 As No. 2709b (31.3.14)	2·50	2·25
	ba. Pane. No. 2718b×6	13·00	
2719	$1.25 As No. 2710	2·75	3·00
	a. Pane. No. 2719×6	14·00	
2720	$1.29 As No. 2711 (16.1.12)	2·75	3·00
	a. Pane. No. 2720×6	14·00	
2721	$1.34 As No. 2712 (14.1.13)	2·75	3·00
	a. Pane. No. 2721×6	14·00	
2722	$1.75 As No. 2713	3·75	4·50
	a. Pane. No. 2722×6	18·00	
2723	$1.80 As No. 2714 (16.1.12)	3·50	3·50
	a. Pane. No. 2723×6	17·00	
2723b	$1.80 As No. 2714b (31.3.14)	3·00	3·00
	ba. Pane. No. 2723b×6	15·00	
2724	$1.85 As No. 2715 (14.1.13)	3·00	3·00
	a. Pane. No. 2724×6	15·00	
2724b	$2.50 As No. 2715b (31.3.14)	4·50	4·50
	ba. Pane. No. 2724b×6	22·00	
2716/2724b	Set of 12	30·00	32·00

(c) Ordinary gum. Perf 13.

MS2725	120×72 mm. As Nos. 2704, 2707, 2710 and 2713	10·00	12·00
MS2726	120×72 mm. As Nos. 2705, 2708, 2711 and 2714 (16.1.12)	10·00	12·00
MS2727	120×72 mm. As Nos. 2706, 2709, 2712 and 2715 (14.1.13)	10·00	12·00
MS2727a	144×72 mm. As Nos. 2706b/c, 2709b, 2714b and 2715b (31.3.14)	12·00	15·00

Nos. 2704/2706a and 2706c were inscribed 'P' and originally sold for 59c. (No. 2704), 61c. (No. 2705), 63c. (Nos. 2706/2706a) or 85c. (No. 2706c).

No. 2704a/2706ca and 2706d are from horizontal coils with the stamps spaced along the backing paper, the others are vertical coils.

No. 2706d has been reported with yellow omitted.

956 Canadian Flag on Soldier's Uniform and Helicopter lifting Supplies

956a CCGS Louis S. St Laurent (icebreaker and Coast Guard flagship)

956b Muskoka Chairs with Maple Leaf Design on Lakeside Jetty

(Des Lionel Gadoury and Terry Popik (Nos. 2728/2732), Gottschalk+Ash International (Nos. 2733/2737) or Karen Smith Design (Nos. 2738/2747). Litho Lionel Gadoury and Terry Popik (Nos. 2728/2732), Gottschalk+Ash International (Nos. 2733/2737) or Karen Smith Design (Nos. 2738/2742). Litho Lowe-Martin (Nos. 2738/2742, 2749) or C.B.N. (others))

2011 (17 Jan)–**13**. 'Canadian Pride'. Vert designs as T **956** (No. 2728/2732), T **956a** (Nos. 2733/2737) or T **956b** (Nos. 2738/2747) showing Canadian flag. Multicoloured. Fluorescent frame (Nos. 2738/2747) or fluorescent bars (others).

(a) Self-adhesive booklet stamps. Die-cut perf 13½.

2728	(59c.) Type **956**	1·25	1·40
	a. Pane. Nos. 2728/2732, each×2	11·00	
	b. Booklet pane. Nos. 2728/2732, each ×6	35·00	
2729	(59c.) Canadian flag on hot air balloon	1·25	1·40
2730	(59c.) Canadian flag on search and rescue uniform and ship	1·25	1·40
2731	(59c.) Canadian flag on Canadarm	1·25	1·40
2732	(59c.) Canadian flag on backpack and Colosseum, Rome	1·25	1·40
2733	(61c.) Type **956a** (16.1.12)	1·50	1·40
	a. Pane. Nos. 2733/2737, each×2	13·50	
	b. Booklet pane. Nos. 2733/2737, each ×6	45·00	
2734	(61c.) Vintage van with Canadian flag in rear window (16.1.12)	1·50	1·40
2735	(61c.) Nicolas Gill carrying Canadian flag, Olympic Games, Athens, 2004 (16.1.12)	1·50	1·40
2736	(61c.) Pierre Lueders (inscr 'Leuders') in bobsled with Canadian flag (16.1.12)	1·50	1·40
	a. Inscr 'Lueders' (28.9.12)	1·50	1·40
2737	(61c.) Young Inuit child waving Canadian flag (16.1.12)	1·50	1·40
2738	(63c.) Type **956a** (14.1.13)	1·50	1·40
	a. Pane. Nos. 2738/2742, each×2	13·50	
	b. Booklet pane. Nos. 2738/2742, each×6	45·00	
2739	(63c.) Maple leaf on hay bale (14.1.13)	1·50	1·40
2740	(63c.) Maple leaf on yacht spinnaker (14.1.13)	1·50	1·40
2741	(63c.) Canadian people forming maple leaf flag, Canada Day, Winnipeg (14.1.13)	1·50	1·40
2742	(63c.) Maple leaf on fishing hut on frozen Lake Scugog, Ontario (14.1.13)	1·50	1·40
2743	63c. Type **956b**	1·50	1·50
	a. Pane. Nos. 2743/7, each ×2	13·50	
2744	63c. Maple leaf on hay bale	1·50	1·50
2745	63c. Maple leaf on yacht spinnaker	1·50	1·50
2746	63c. Canadian people forming maple leaf flag, Canada Day, Winnipeg	1·50	1·50
2747	63c. Maple leaf on fishing hut on frozen Lake Scugog, Ontario	1·50	1·50
2728/2742	Set of 20	26·00	26·00

(b) Ordinary gum. Perf 13.

MS2749	148×70 mm. As Nos. 2728/2732	6·25	7·50
MS2749a	130×71 mm. As Nos. 2733/2737 (16.1.12)	7·50	8·50
MS2749b	130×71 mm. As Nos. 2738/2742 (14.1.13)	7·50	8·50

Nos. 2728/2742 and the stamps within No. **MS**2749/**MS**2749b were all inscr 'P' and were originally valid for 59c. (Nos. 2728/2732, **MS**2749), 61c. (Nos. 2733/2737, **MS**2749a) or 63c. (Nos. 2738/2742, **MS**2749b) each.

Nos. 2728/42 and the stamps within **MS**2749/b were all inscr 'P' and were originally sold for 59c. (2728/32, **MS**2749), 61c. (2733/7, **MS**2749a) or 63c. (2738/42, **MS**2749b) each.

Nos. 2728/2732, 2733/2737 and 2738/2742 were each issued in panes of ten and booklets of 30, Nos. SB420, SB445 and SB483.

Nos. 2728/2732 and the stamps within **MS**2749 all have fluorescent bars at left and right, fluorescent maple leaf markings on the white circles which appear red under UV light and fluorescent printing at top and foot of the stamp: 'THE TRUE NORTH STRONG AND FREE!' and 'TON HISTOIRE EST UN ÉPOPÉE DES PLUS BRILLIANTS EXPLOITS'. Nos. 2733/7 and the stamps within **MS**2749a all have fluorescent bars at left and right, fluorescent printing at top and foot of the stamp reading 'PERMANENT STAMPS/TIMBRES PERMANENTS', and red fluorescent printing at top right with stamp descriptions.

On No. 2736 the microprinting to the right of the bobsled gives the incorrect spelling of Pierre Lueders' name. This was corrected on No. 2736a.

A postal forgery of No. 2731 has been reported.

Nos. 2743/2748 are left for possible additions to this definitive series.

CANADA

957 Carrie Best (journalist and civil rights campaigner)   **958** Wrapped Gift

(Des Lara Minja. Litho Lowe-Martin)

2011 (1 Feb). Black History Month. T **957** and similar horiz design. Multicoloured. Self-adhesive. Fluorescent frame. Die-cut perf 13½.

2750	59c. Type **957**	1·25	1·40
	a. Booklet pane. No. 2750×10	11·00	
2751	59c. Fergie (Ferguson) Jenkins (baseball pitcher)	1·25	1·40
	a. Booklet pane. No. 2751×10	11·00	

Nos. 2750/2751 were issued in separate booklets of ten, Nos. SB421/SB422.

(Des Debbie Adams. Litho C.B.N)

2011 (7 Feb). Greetings Stamp. 'Celebration'. Self-adhesive. Fluorescent frame. Die-cut perf 13×imperf.

2752	**958**	(59c.) multicoloured	1·25	1·25
		a. Pane. No. 2752×6	6·75	

No. 2752, inscribed 'P', was initially valid for 59c. It was issued in panes of six, originally sold for $3.54.

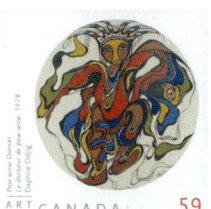

959 Pow-wow Dancer, 1978

(Des Hélène L'Heureux. Litho Lowe-Martin)

2011 (21 Feb). Art Canada. Paintings by Daphne Odjig. T **959** and similar multicoloured designs. Fluorescent frame.

(a) Ordinary gum. Perf 12½.

2753	59c. Type **959**	2·00	1·25
MS2754	150×87 mm. 59c. Type **959**; $1.03 'Pow-wow', 1969 (32×39 mm); $1.75 'Spiritual Renewal', 1984 (55×39 mm)	11·00	12·00

(b) Self-adhesive. Die-cut perf 13½×13.

2755	$1.03 'Pow-wow', 1969 (32×39 mm)	2·75	3·25
	a. Booklet pane. No. 2755×6	14·00	
2756	$1.75 'Spiritual Renewal', 1984 (55×39 mm)	4·25	5·00
	a. Booklet pane. No. 2756×6	22·00	

Nos. 2755/2756 were only available in $6.18 or $10.50 stamp booklets, Nos. SB423/SB424.

960 Sunflower 'Prado Red'   **961** Sunflower 'Sunbright'

(Des Isabelle Toussaint. Litho Lowe-Martin)

2011 (3 Mar). Sunflowers (*Helianthus annuus*). Multicoloured designs as T **960**/**961**. Fluorescent frame.

*(a) Coil stamps. Horiz designs as T **960**. Self-adhesive. Die-cut perf 8½×imperf.*

2757	(59c.) Type **960**	1·40	1·75
	a. Vert pair. Nos. 2757/2758	2·75	3·50
2758	(59c.) Sunflower 'Sunbright'	1·40	1·75

*(b) Booklet stamps. Vert designs as T **961**. Self-adhesive. Die-cut perf 13½.*

2759	(59c.) Sunflower 'Prado Red'	1·40	1·75
	a. Booklet pane. Nos. 2759/2760, each×5	12·50	
2760	(59c.) Type **961**	1·40	1·75

*(c) Ordinary gum. Sheet 120×84 mm containing T **961** and similar vert design. Perf 13.*

MS2761	(59c.) Sunflower 'Prado Red'; (59c.) As Type **961**	2·50	3·00

Nos. 2757/2760 and the stamps within MS2761 were all inscr 'P' and were originally valid for 59c.

Nos. 2757/2758 come from rolls of 50 with the two designs alternating throughout.

Nos. 2759/2760 were only issued in booklets of ten, No. SB425, originally sold for $5.90.

The top left portion of MS2761 is cut around in the shape of a sunflower.

962 Ram's Head

(Des Paprika. Litho Lowe-Martin)

2011 (21 Mar)–**13**. Signs of the Zodiac. T **962** and similar square designs. Multicoloured. Fluorescent frame.

(a) Self-adhesive. Die-cut perf 13½.

2762	(59c.) Type **962**	1·40	1·50
	a. Booklet pane. No. 2762×10	12·00	
2763	(59c.) Taurus (21.4.11)	1·40	1·50
	a. Booklet pane. No. 2763×10	12·00	
2764	(59c.) Gemini (20.5.11)	1·40	1·50
	a. Booklet pane. No. 2764×10	12·00	
2765	(59c.) Cancer (22.6.11)	1·40	1·50
	a. Booklet pane. No. 2765×10	12·00	
2766	(61c.) Leo (23.7.12)	1·40	1·50
	a. Booklet pane. No. 2766×10	12·00	
2767	(61c.) Virgo (23.7.12)	1·40	1·50
	a. Booklet pane. No. 2767×10	12·00	
2768	(61c.) Libra (23.7.12)	1·40	1·50
	a. Booklet pane. No. 2768×10	12·00	
2769	(61c.) Scorpio (23.7.12)	1·40	1·50
	a. Booklet pane. No. 2769×10	12·00	
2770	(63c.) Sagittarius (20.2.13)	1·40	1·50
	a. Booklet pane. No. 2770×10	12·00	
2771	(63c.) Capricorn (20.2.13)	1·40	1·50
	a. Booklet pane. No. 2771×10	12·00	
2772	(63c.) Aquarius (20.2.13)	1·40	1·50
	a. Booklet pane. No. 2772×10	12·00	
2773	(63c.) Pisces (20.2.13)	1·40	1·50
	a. Booklet pane. No. 2773×10	12·00	
2762/73	Set of 12	15·00	16·00

(b) Ordinary gum. Perf 12½×13 (No. MS2776a) or 12½ (others).

MS2774	128×128 mm. As Nos. 2762/2765 (22.6.11)	5·00	7·00
MS2775	128×128 mm. As Nos. 2766/2769 (23.7.12)	5·00	7·00
MS2776	128×128 mm. As Nos. 2770/2773 (20.2.13)	5·00	7·00
MS2776a	156×188 mm. As Nos. 2762/2773 (20.2.13)	15·00	20·00

Nos. 2762/2773 and the stamps within MS2774/MS2776a were all inscr 'P' and were originally valid for 59c. (Nos. 2762/2765, MS2774), 61c. (Nos. 2766/2769, MS2775) or 63c. (Nos. 2770/2773, MS2776/MS2776a).

Nos. 2762/2773 were each issued in separate booklets of ten, Nos. SB426/SB429, originally sold for $5.90, Nos. SB461/SB464, originally sold for $6.10, and Nos. SB487/SB490, originally sold for $6.30.

963 Tree

(Des S. Gibson, M. Clark and Subplot Design Inc. Litho Lowe-Martin)

2011 (21 Apr). International Year of Forests. T **963** and similar vert design. Multicoloured. Fluorescent frame.

(a) Self-adhesive. Die-cut perf 13.

2777	(59c.) Type **963**	1·75	2·00
	a. Booklet pane. Nos. 2777/2778, each×4	12·00	
2778	(59c.) Forest floor with fungi	1·75	2·00

(b) Ordinary gum. Perf 13½×13.

MS2779	70×125 mm. As Nos. 2777/2778	3·00	4·00

Nos. 2777/2778 and the stamps within MS2779 form a composite design showing forest trees and undergrowth.

Nos. 2777/2778 and the stamps within MS2779 were all inscr 'P' and were originally valid for 59c.

CANADA

Nos. 2777/2778 and the stamps within **MS**2779 have a fluorescent frame around the vertical pair, giving No. 2777 a fluorescent frame at top, left and right, and No. 2778 a fluorescent frame at left, right and foot.

Nos. 2777/2778 were only issued in booklets of eight, No. SB430, originally sold for $4.72.

964 Prince William and Miss Catherine Middleton, November 2010

(Des Isabelle Toussaint. Litho Lowe-Martin)

2011 (29 Apr). Royal Wedding (1st issue). T **964** and similar vert design. Multicoloured. Fluorescent frame.

(a) Ordinary paper. Perf 12½×13½.
2780	(59c.) Type **964**	2·50	2·25
	a. Horiz pair. Nos. 2780/2781	6·25	6·00
2781	$1.75 Prince William and Miss Catherine Middleton embracing, November 2010	3·75	3·75
MS2782 120×83 mm. Nos. 2780/2781		6·25	7·00
MS2783 As No. **MS**2782 but with gold crown on upper left sheet margin		7·00	8·00

(b) Self-adhesive. Die-cut perf 13x13½.
2784	(59c.) As Type **964**	2·50	2·25
	a. Booklet pane. No. 2784×10	20·00	
2785	$1.75 As No. 2768	6·25	6·50
	a. Booklet pane. No. 2785×10	48·00	

See also Nos. 2795/**MS**2797.

Nos. 2780/2781 were printed together, *se-tenant*, as horizontal pairs in sheetlets of 16 stamps.

Nos. 2780 and 2784 were both inscr 'P' and originally valid for 59c.

No. 2784 was only issued in booklets of ten, SB431, originally sold for $5.90.

No. 2785 was only issued in $17.50 booklets, No. SB432.

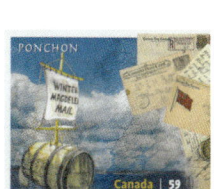 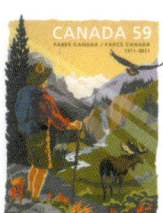

965 Mail Barrel rigged with Sail and Rudder, Magdalen Islands, 1910

966 Hiker, Moose and Eagle in Mountain Landscape

(Des Janice Kun and Karen Smith Design. Litho Lowe-Martin)

2011 (13 May). Methods of Mail Delivery. T **965** and similar horiz design. Multicoloured. Fluorescent frame. Perf 12½.
2786	59c. Type **965**	2·25	2·00
	a. Horiz pair. Nos. 2786/2787	4·50	4·00
2787	59c. Dog sled carrying mail in winter, northern Canada	2·25	2·00

Nos. 2786/2787 were printed together, *se-tenant*, as horizontal pairs in sheetlets of 16, each pair forming a composite design.

Nos. 2786/2787 had a fluorescent frame around the horizontal pair, giving No. 2786 fluorescent frame at top, left and foot, and No. 2787 a fluorescent frame at top, right and foot.

(Des Tim Nokes. Litho C.B.N)

2011 (19 May). Centenary of Parks Canada. Self-adhesive. Fluorescent frame. Die-cut perf 13.
2788	**966**	59c. multicoloured	1·75	1·50
		a. Booklet pane. No. 2788×10	15·00	

No. 2788 was issued in $5.90 booklets, No. SB433.

967 Concrete Tower of Burrard Bridge, Vancouver

(Des Ivan Novotny. Litho Lowe-Martin)

2011 (9 June). Art Déco. T **967** and similar vert designs. Multicoloured. Self-adhesive. Fluorescent frame (at top, right and foot).

(a) Self-adhesive. Die-cut perf 13½.
2789	(59c.) Type **967**	1·50	1·60
	a. Booklet pane. Nos. 2789/2793, each×2	13·00	
2790	(59c.) Wall of Cormier House with stone carving, Montreal	1·50	1·60
2791	(59c.) R. C. Harris Water Treatment Plant, Toronto	1·50	1·60
2792	(59c.) Detail from Supreme Court of Canada, Ottawa	1·50	1·60
2793	(59c.) Dominion Building, Regina	1·50	1·60
2789/2793 Set of 5		7·00	7·25

(b) Ordinary gum. Perf 13×12½.
MS2794 127×84 mm. As Nos. 2789/2793	7·00	7·25

No. 2789/2793 and the stamps within **MS**2794 were all inscr 'P' and were originally valid for 59c.

No. 2789/2793 were issued in booklets of ten, No. SB434, originally sold for $5.90.

968 Duke and Duchess of Cambridge in State Landau

(Des Isabelle Toussaint Design graphique. Litho Lowe-Martin)

2011 (22 June). Royal Wedding (2nd issue). Fluorescent frame.

(a) Self-adhesive. Die-cut perf 13.
2795	**968**	(59c.) multicoloured	2·00	1·50
		a. Booklet pane. No. 2795×10	16·00	

(b) Ordinary gum. Perf 12½×13.
MS2796 120×84 mm. As Type **968**×2 (sheet margin showing Westminster Abbey)	4·00	5·00
MS2797 120×84 mm. As Type **968**×2 (sheet margin showing Parliament Buildings, Canada and optd with gold maple leaf and 'Royal Tour 2011 From June 30 to July 8' in English and French)	4·00	5·00

No. 2795 and the stamps within **MS**2796/7 were inscr 'P' and were originally valid for 59c.

No. 2795 was issued in booklets of ten, No. SB435, originally sold for $5.90.

969 Ginette Reno

(Des CIRCLE. Litho Lowe-Martin)

2011 (30 June). Canadian Recording Artists (3rd series). T **969** and similar square designs. Multicoloured. Fluorescent frame.

(a) Self-adhesive. Die-cut perf 13½.
2798	(59c.) Type **969**	1·40	1·50
	a. Booklet pane. Nos. 2798/2801, each×2	10·00	
2799	(59c.) Bruce Cockburn	1·40	1·50

CANADA

2800	(59c.) Robbie Robertson................		1·40	1·50
2801	(59c.) Kate and Anna McGarrigle		1·40	1·50

(b) Ordinary gum. Perf 12½×13 (No. MS2806) or 12½ (others).

2802	(59c.) As Type **969**		1·40	1·50
2803	(59c.) As No. 2799		1·40	1·50
2804	(59c.) As No. 2800		1·40	1·50
2805	(59c.) As No. 2801		1·40	1·50
2798/2805 Set of 8			10·00	11·00
MS2806 Circular 105×105 mm. As Nos. 2802/2805.........			5·00	5·50

Nos. 2798/2805 and the stamps within **MS**2806 were all inscr 'P' and were originally valid for 59c.

Nos. 2802/2805 were each issued in separate sheetlets of 16 with enlarged illustrated margins.

Nos. 2798/2801 were issued in booklets of eight, No. SB436/SB436c, originally sold for $4.72. The circular booklet pane No. 2798a also included eight small stickers. It exists in four versions which differ in the order of the stamps within the two blocks of four which form the booklet pane.

(Des Bonnie Ross and Fraser Ross. Litho Lowe-Martin)

2011 (7 July). Roadside Attractions (3rd series). Multicoloured designs as T **924**. Multicoloured. Fluorescent frame.

(a) Self-adhesive. Die-cut perf 13½ (3 sides).

2807	(59c.) The World's Largest Lobster, Shediac, New Brunswick...............		1·75	2·00
	a. Booklet pane. Nos. 2807/2810, each×2		12·00	
2808	(59c.) The Wild Blueberry, Oxford, Nova Scotia....................		1·75	2·00
2809	(59c.) The Big Potato, O'Leary, Prince Edward Island....................		1·75	2·00
2810	(59c.) The Giant Squid, Glover's Harbour, Newfoundland...............		1·75	2·00
2807/2810 Set of 4			6·25	7·25

(b) Ordinary gum. Perf 12½.

MS2811 98×109 mm. As Nos. 2807/10................ 6·25 7·25

Nos. 2807/2810 have irregularly shpaed tops to the stamps. They are perforated on three sides and imperforate at top.

Nos. 2807/2810 were only issued in booklets of eight, No. SB437, originally sold for $4.72. Booklet pane No. 2807a included eight small stickers.

Nos. 2807/2810 and the stamps within **MS**2811 were all inscr 'P' and were originally valid for 59c.

970 Miss Supertest III

(Des Ivan Novotny. Litho Lowe-Martin)

2011 (8 Aug). *Miss Supertest III* (hydroplane, winner of Harmsworth Trophy 1959, 1960 and 1961). T **970** and similar horiz design. Multicoloured. Fluorescent frame.

(a) Self-adhesive. Die-cut perf 13×imperf.

2812	(59c.) Type **970**.......................		1·75	1·25
	a. Booklet pane. No. 2812×10..........		14·00	

(b) Ordinary gum. Perf 13.

MS2813 132×70 mm. As Type **970**; $1.75 *Miss Supertest III* in race............................ 5·00 6·50

No. 2812 and the left-hand stamp within **MS**2813 were inscr 'P' and were originally valid for 59c.

No. 2812 was issued in booklets of ten, No. SB438, originally sold for $5.90.

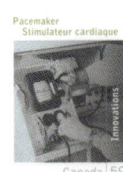 

971 Cardiac Pacemaker **972** 'The Puzzle' (Miriane Majeau)

(Des q30 design inc. Litho Lowe-Martin)

2011 (17 Aug). Canadian Innovations. T **971** and similar vert designs. Multicoloured. Self-adhesive. Fluorescent frame. Die-cut perf 13½.

2814	59c. Type **971**........................		1·60	1·60
	a. Booklet pane. Nos. 2814/2817, each ×2		11·00	
2815	59c. BlackBerry........................		1·60	1·60
2816	59c. Electric oven.....................		1·60	1·60
2817	59c. Electric wheelchair...............		1·60	1·60
2814/2817 Set of 4			5·75	5·75

Nos. 2814/2817 were issued in $4.72 stamp booklets, No. SB439.

(Des Anne Tardif and Kosta Tsetsekas/Signals. Litho Lowe-Martin)

2011 (6 Sept). Mental Health. Fluorescent frame.

(a) Self-adhesive. Die-cut perf 13×13½.

2818	(59c.)+10c. Type **972**.................		1·50	1·40
	a. Booklet pane. No. 2818×10........		14·00	

(b) Ordinary gum. Perf 12½×13.

MS2819 118×100 mm. As Type **972**×2................ 3·25 3·50

No. 2818 and the stamps within **MS**2819 were inscr 'P+10' and were initially valid for 59c. plus a 10c. surcharge for the Canada Foundation for Mental Health.

No. 2818 was issued in booklets of ten, No. SB440, initially sold for $6.90.

973 Dr. John Charles Polanyi (Nobel Prize for Chemistry, 1986) **974** Angel appearing to Joseph

(Des q30 design inc. Litho Lowe-Martin)

2011 (3 Oct). International Year of Chemistry. Fluorescent frame. Die-cut perf 13½.

2820	**973**	(59c.) multicoloured	1·25	1·10
		a. Booklet pane. No. 2820×10........	12·00	

No. 2820 was inscr 'P' and was originally valid for 59c. It was issued in booklets of ten, No. SB441, originally sold for $5.90.

(Des Andrew Perro. Litho Lowe-Martin)

2011 (1 Nov). Christmas (1st issue). Stained-glass Windows from the Cathedral of the Immaculate Conception, Kingston, Ontario. T **974** and similar vert designs. Multicoloured. Fluorescent frame.

(a) Self-adhesive. Die-cut perf 13.

2821	(59c.) Type **974**........................		1·25	1·10
	a. Booklet pane. No. 2821×12............		14·00	
2822	$1.03 Nativity		2·25	2·50
	a. Pane. No. 2822×6..................		13·00	
2823	$1.75 Epiphany		3·75	4·00
	a. Pane. No. 2823×6..................		22·00	
2821/3 Set of 3			6·50	7·00

(b) Ordinary gum. Perf 13×12½.

MS2824 105×60 mm. As Nos. 2821/2823............... 7·25 7·50

No. 2821 was inscr 'P' and was originally valid for 59c. It was issued in booklets of 12 stamps, No. SB442, initially sold for $7.08.

Nos. 2822/2823 were each issued in separate panes of six, sold for $6.18 (No. 2822) or $10.50 (No. 2823). They were also available together in $16.68 panes containing six of each design separated by a gutter.

975 Holly

(Des Hélène L'Heureux. Litho Lowe-Martin)

2011 (1 Nov). Christmas (2nd issue). Self-adhesive. Fluorescent frame. Die-cut perf 8½×imperf.

2825	**975**	(59c.) multicoloured	1·25	1·10
		a. Booklet pane. No. 2825×12........	14·00	

No. 2825 was inscr 'P' and was originally valid for 59c. It was issued in booklets of 12 stamps, No. SB443, initially sold for $7.08.

976 Dragon **977** Dragon's Head

CANADA

(Des Louis Fishauf, Charles Vinh and James Tan. Litho (2829) or litho and embossed (others) Lowe-Martin and Gravure Choquet)

2012 (10 Jan). Chinese New Year. Year of the Dragon.
(a) Ordinary paper. Perf 12½.
2826	(61c.) Type **976**	1·50	1·40
MS2827	118×90 mm. \$1.75 Two white rabbits (Year of the Rabbit); \$1.80 Type **977** (transition to Year of the Dragon)	7·25	7·50
MS2828	140×41 mm. \$1.80 Type **977**	5·00	6·00
	a. Booklet pane. No. 2829×6	16·00	

(b) Self-adhesive. Die-cut perf 13½.
2829	\$1.80 Type **977**	2·75	3·25
	a. Booklet pane. No. 2829×6	16·00	

No. 2826 has a complete fluorescent frame. The Year of the Rabbit stamp within **MS**2827 has a fluorescent frame on three sides, at left and foot of the stamp. The other stamps have a fluorescent frame broken at top left and centre foot of stamp.

No. 2826 was inscr 'P' and originally sold for 61c.
No. 2829 was issued in \$10.80 booklets, No. SB444.

978 Queen Elizabeth II   **979** 1953 Coronation Stamp (as Type **159**)

(Des Gottschalk+Ash International. Litho C.B.N)

2012 (16 Jan). Diamond Jubilee (1st issue). Self-adhesive. Fluorescent frame (broken at left). Perf 13½.
2830	**978**	(61c.) multicoloured	1·75	1·50
		a. Booklet pane. No. 2830×10	18·00	

No. 2830 was inscr 'P' and was initially valid for 61c. It was issued in booklets of ten, No. SB446, originally sold for \$6.10.
See also Nos. **MS**2831/**MS**2836 and **MS**2858.

(Des Colagene Illustration Clinic and Gottschalk+Ash International. Litho Lowe-Martin)

2012 (16 Jan–1 June). Diamond Jubilee (2nd issue). Sheets, 124×136 mm, containing T **979** and similar square designs. Multicoloured. Fluorescent frame (broken at left on No. **MS**2836). Perf 13 (No. **MS**2836) or 13½ (others)
MS2831	(61c.) Type **979**×4	6·00 6·50
MS2832	(61c.) 1967 Royal Visit 5c. stamp (as Type **271**)×4 (6.2)	6·00 6·50
MS2833	(61c.) 1977 Silver Jubilee 25c. stamp (as Type **399**)×4 (6.3)	6·00 6·50
MS2834	(61c.) 1990 Queen Elizabeth II 40c. definitive stamp (No. 1162d)×4 (10.4)	6·00 6·50
MS2835	(61c.) 2002 Golden Jubilee 48c. stamp (as Type **761**)×4 (7.5)	6·00 6·50
MS2836	(61c.) As Type **978** (32×40 mm) ×4 (1.6)	6·00 6·50

980 John Ware   **981** Smoothly She Shifted

(Des Lara Minja. Litho Lowe-Martin)

2012 (1 Feb). Black History Month. John Ware (cowboy and rancher) and Viola Desmond (civil rights campaigner). Self-adhesive. Fluorescent frame. Die-cut perf 13½×13.
2837	(61c.) Type **980**	1·10	1·40
	a. Booklet pane. No. 2837×10	10·00	
2838	(61c.) Viola Desmond	1·10	1·40
	a. Booklet pane. No. 2838×10	10·00	

Nos. 2837/2838 were inscr 'P' and were initially valid for 61c. each. They were issued in separate booklets of ten, Nos. SB447/SB448, each originally sold for \$6.10.

(Des Hélène L'Heureux. Litho Lowe-Martin)

2012 (23 Feb). Art Canada. Sculptures by Joe Fafard.
(a) Ordinary gum. Perf 12½.
2839	(61c.) Type **981**	1·50	1·25
MS2840	150×87 mm. (61c.) Type **981**; \$1.05 Dear Vincent (Van Gogh seated in chair) (32×39 mm); \$1.80 Capillery (three lasercut steel and bronze horses) (65×32 mm)	7·50	9·00

(b) Self-adhesive. Die-cut perf 13½ (No. 2841) or 13×13½ (No. 2842).
2841	\$1.05 Dear Vincent (Van Gogh seated in chair) (32×39 mm)	2·00	2·50
	a. Pane. No. 2841×6	11·00	
2842	\$1.80 Capillery (three lasercut steel and bronze horses) (65×32 mm)	3·25	4·25
	a. Booklet pane. No. 2842×6	17·00	

Type **981** was inscr 'P' and was originally valid for 61c.
No. 2841 was issued in \$6.30 panes of six.
No. 2842 was issued in \$10.80 booklets, No. SB449.

982 Daylily 'Louis Lorrain'

(Des Isabelle Toussaint Design graphique. Litho Lowe-Martin)

2012 (1 Mar). Daylilies. T **982** and similar horiz design. Multicoloured. Fluorescent frame.
(a) Coil stamp. Die-cut perf 8×imperf.
2843	(61c.) Type **982**	1·50	1·75
	a. Vert pair. Nos. 2843/2844	3·00	3·50
2844	(61c.) Common orange Daylily (*Hemerocallis fulva*)	1·50	1·75

(b) Booklet stamps. Size 32×25 mm. Die-cut perf 13½.
2845	(61c.) Common orange Daylily (*Hemerocallis fulva*)	1·75	2·00
	a. Booklet pane. Nos. 2845/2856, each ×5	15·00	
2846	(61c.) Type **982**	1·75	2·00

(c) Ordinary gum. Sheet 120×84 mm. Perf 13.
MS2847	120×84 mm. As Nos. 2845/2846	3·00	3·50

Nos. 2843/2846 and the stamps within **MS**2847 were all inscr 'P' and were originally sold for 61c. Nos. 2843/2844 come from rolls of 50 with the two designs alternating throughout.
Nos. 2843/2844 come from rolls of 50 with the two designs alternating throughout.
Nos. 2845/2846 were issued in booklets of ten, No. SB450, originally sold for \$6.10. Booklet pane 2845a also contains ten small stickers.

983 Bow of *Titanic* (left portion) and Map showing Halifax

(Des Mike Little, Dennis Page and Oliver Hill. Litho Lowe-Martin)

2012 (5 Apr). Centenary of the Sinking of the *Titanic*. Fluorescent frame.
*(a) Ordinary gum. Perf 12½ (2848/2851) or 13 (**MS**2852).*
2848	(61c.) Type **983**	2·25	2·00
	a. Block of 4. Nos. 2848/2851	8·00	7·25
2849	(61c.) Bow of *Titanic* (right portion) and map showing Southampton	2·25	2·00
2850	(61c.) Stern of *Titanic* (left portion) and propeller	2·25	2·00
2851	(61c.) Stern of *Titanic* (right portion) and propeller	2·25	2·00
2848/2851	Set of 4	8·00	7·25
MS2852	114×72 mm. \$1.80 *Titanic* (84×36 mm)	6·50	6·50

(b) Self-adhesive. Die-cut perf 13½×13 (Nos. 2853/2854) or 13½ (No. 2855).
2853	(61c.) As Type **983**	2·25	2·50
	a. Booklet pane. Nos. 2853/2854, each ×5	16·00	
2854	(61c.) As No. 2849	2·25	2·50
2855	\$1.80 *Titanic* (84×36 mm) (as stamp within **MS**2852)	6·50	7·00
	a. Booklet pane. No. 2855×6	32·00	

CANADA

Nos. 2848/2851 were printed together, *se-tenant*, as blocks of four stamps in sheetlets of 16 containing 2 panes 2×4 separated by a vertical gutter. Nos. 2848/2849 and 2850/2851 form composite designs showing the bow (2848/2849) or stern (2850/2851) of the *Titanic*.

Nos. 2848/2849 and 2850/2851 had a fluorescent frame around the horizontal pairs, giving Nos. 2848 and 2850 a fluorescent frame at top, left and bottom and Nos. 2849 and 2851 a fluorescent frame at top, right and bottom.

Nos. 2848/2851 and 2853/2854 were inscr 'P' and were originally sold for 61c. each.

Nos. 2853/2854 were issued in booklets of ten, No. SB451, originally sold for $6.10.

No. 2855 was issued in $10.80 booklets, No. SB452.

984 Thomas Douglas, 5th Earl of Selkirk (settlement founder), Settlers, Local Trapper and Métis (oil painting by Mark Heine)

985 Queen Elizabeth II in 1953 and 2012

(Des Susan Mavor. Litho C.B.N)

2012 (3 May). Bicentenary of the Red River Settlement. Fluorescent frame. Perf 13½.
| 2856 | **984** | (61c.) multicoloured | 2·00 | 1·25 |

No. 2856 was inscr 'P' and was originally sold for 61c.

(Des Parable Communications. Eng Jorge Peral and Rodrigo Peral. Recess C.B.N)

2012 (7 May). Diamond Jubilee (3rd issue). Perf 11½.
| 2857 | **985** | $2 deep lilac | 4·25 | 5·00 |
| **MS**2858 | 124×136 mm. No. 2857 | | 4·25 | 6·00 |

986 Franklin and Beaver

(Des q30 design inc. Litho Lowe-Martin)

2012 (11 May). Children's Literature. Franklin the Turtle (character from books by Paulette Bourgeois). Illlustrations by Brenda Clark. Fluorescent frame.

(a) Self-adhesive. Die-cut perf 13½.
2859	(61c.) Type **986**	1·25	1·50
	a. Booklet pane. Nos. 2859/2862, each×3	13·00	
2860	(61c.) Franklin with young sister Harriet	1·25	1·50
2861	(61c.) Franklin and Snail	1·25	1·50
2862	(61c.) Franklin, Bear and goldfish in bowl	1·25	1·50
2859/2862 Set of 4		5·00	4·50

(b) Ordinary gum. Perf 13×12½.
| **MS**2863 | 150×100 mm. As Nos. 2859/2862 | 5·50 | 6·00 |

Nos. 2859/2862 and the stamps within No. **MS**2863 were all inscr 'P' and were originally valid for 61c.

Nos. 2859/2862 were issued in booklets of 12, No. SB453, originally sold for $7.32.

987 Saddled Horse

(Des Xerxes Irani. Litho Lowe-Martin)

2012 (17 May). Centenary of the Calgary Stampede. Fluorescent frame.

(a) Self-adhesive. Die-cut perf 13.
2864	(61c.) Type **987**	1·40	1·25
	a. Booklet pane. No. 2864×10	13·00	
2865	$1.05 Centenary belt buckle	2·00	2·75
	a. Booklet pane. No. 2865×10	18·00	

(b) Ordinary gum. Perf 13×13½.
| **MS**2866 | 117×70 mm. As Nos. 2864/2865 | 3·75 | 4·50 |

No. 2864 was inscr 'P' and was originially valid for 61c. Nos. 2864 was issued in booklets of ten, No. SB454, originally sold for $6.10.

No. 2865 was issued in $10.50 booklets, No. SB455.

988 Louise Arbour

(Des Paprika. Litho Lowe-Martin)

2012 (22 May). Difference Makers. T **988** and similar square designs. Fluorescent frame.

(a) Self-adhesive. Die-cut perf 13½.
2867	(61c.) bright reddish violet, silver and vermilion	1·10	1·50
	a. Booklet pane. No. 2867×10	10·00	
2868	(61c.) new blue, silver and vermilion	1·10	1·50
	a. Booklet pane. No. 2868×10	10·00	
2869	(61c.) turquoise-green, silver and vermilion	1·10	1·50
	a. Booklet pane. No. 2869×10	10·00	
2870	(61c.) bright green, silver and vermilion	1·10	1·50
	a. Booklet pane. No. 2870×10	10·00	
2867/2870 Set of 4		4·00	5·50

(b) Ordinary gum. Perf 12½.
| **MS**2871 | 96×96 mm. As Nos. 2867/2870 | 5·50 | 6·00 |

Designs: 2867, Type **988** (prosecutor of war crimes at International Criminal Tribunal for Rwanda and Yugoslavia and President of International Crisis Group); 2868, Rick Hansen (campaigner for people with spinal injuries); 2869, Sheila Watt-Cloutier (campaigner for aboriginal rights); 2870, Michael J. Fox (actor and campaigner for Parkinson's disease research).

Nos. 2867/2870 and the stamps within **MS**2871 were all inscr 'P' and were originally valid for 61c.

Nos. 2867/2870 were issued in separate booklets of ten, Nos. SB456/SB459, originally sold for $6.10 each.

989 Major-General Sir Isaac Brock (leader of British Forces in Canada)

990 Rowers in Double-Scull Boat and Maple Leaf

(Des Suzanne Duranceau and Susan Scott. Litho Lowe-Martin)

2012 (15 June). Bicentenary of War of 1812 between United States and Britain (1st issue). T **989** and similar horiz design. Multicoloured. Fluorescent frame (on three sides)*. Perf 13×12½.
2872	(61c.) (61c.) Type **989**	1·75	1·75
	a. Horiz pair. Nos. 2872/2873	3·50	3·50
2873	(61c.) Shawnee War Chief Tecumseh (leader of Ohio Native Nations Confederation)	1·75	1·75

Nos. 2872/2873 were printed together, *se-tenant*, as horizontal pairs in sheets of 16, each pair forming a composite background design of a Niagara Peninsula landscape.

*Nos. 2872/2873 had a fluorescent frame around the horizontal pair, giving No. 2872 a fluorescent frame at top, left and bottom and No. 2873 a fluorescent frame at top, right and bottom. Stamps in similar designs were issued by Guernsey.

See also Nos. 2949/2950.

(Des Keith Martin, Mike Savage and Kosta Tsetsekas. Litho Lowe-Martin)

2012 (27 June). Olympic Games, London. Self-adhesive. Fluorescent frame. Die-cut perf 8.
| 2874 | **990** | (61c.) multicoloured | 1·10 | 1·25 |
| | | a. Booklet pane. No. 2874×10 | 10·00 | |

No. 2874 was inscr 'P' and was originally valid for 61c. It was only issued in booklets of ten, No. SB460, originally sold for $6.10.

991 BC Lions Logo

CANADA

(Des Filip Mroz, David Rosenberg and Bensimon Byrne. Litho Lowe-Martin)

2012 (29 June). CFL (Canadian Football League) Team Logos. T **991** and similar horiz designs. Fluorescent frame.

(a) Self-adhesive coil stamps. Die-cut perf 8×imperf.

2875	(61c.) black and orange-red	1·10	1·25
2876	(61c.) bottle-green, orange-yellow and black	1·10	1·25
2877	(61c.) black and rosine	1·10	1·25
2878	(61c.) black, pale green and deep emerald	1·10	1·25
2879	(61c.) deep ultramarine, gold and black	1·10	1·25
2880	(61c.) black, orange-yellow and bright scarlet	1·10	1·25
2881	(61c.) deep violet-blue, cobalt and black	1·10	1·25
2882	(61c.) multicoloured	1·10	1·25
2875/2882 Set of 8		8·00	9·00

(b) Ordinary gum. Perf 13.

MS2883 130×69 mm. As Nos. 2875/2882........... 8·00 10·00

Nos. 2875/2882 and the stamps within **MS**2883 were all inscr 'P' and were originally valid for 61c.

Designs: No. 2875 T **991**; 2876 Edmonton Eskimos; No. 2877 Calgary Stampeders; No. 2878 Saskatchewan Roughriders; No. 2879 Winnipeg Blue Bombers; No. 2880 Hamilton Tiger-Cats; No. 2881 Toronto Argonauts; No. 2882 Alouettes de Montréal.

992 Tommy Douglas   **993** BC Lions

(Des James Turner and Derwyn Goodall. Litho Lowe-Martin)

2012 (29 June). Tommy Douglas (politician and founder of Medicare) Commemoration. Fluorescent frame. Perf 12½.

2884	**992**	(61c.) multicoloured	1·40	1·25

No. 2884 was inscr 'P' and originally sold for 61c.

(Des Ron Dollekamp, Filip Mroz, David Rosenberg, Bensimon Byrne and Lara Minja. Recess and litho (2894) or litho (others) Lowe-Martin)

2012 (16 Aug). 100th Grey Cup Game. T **993** and similar vert designs. Multicoloured. Fluorescent frame.

(a) Self-adhesive. Die-cut perf 13½×13.

2885	(61c.) Grey Cup and two players	1·00	1·40
	a. Booklet pane. No. 2885×10	8·00	
2886	(61c.) Type **993**	1·00	1·40
	a. Booklet pane. No. 2886×10	8·00	
2887	(61c.) Edmonton Eskimos	1·00	1·40
	a. Booklet pane. No. 2887×10	8·00	
2888	(61c.) Calgary Stampeders	1·00	1·40
	a. Booklet pane. No. 2888×10	8·00	
2889	(61c.) Saskatchewan Roughriders	1·00	1·40
	a. Booklet pane. No. 2889×10	8·00	
2890	(61c.) Winnipeg Blue Bombers	1·00	1·40
	a. Booklet pane. No. 2890×10	8·00	
2891	(61c.) Hamilton Tiger-Cats	1·00	1·40
	a. Booklet pane. No. 2891×10	8·00	
2892	(61c.) Toronto Argonauts	1·00	1·40
	a. Booklet pane. No. 2892×10	8·00	
2893	(61c.) Alouettes de Montréal	1·00	1·40
	a. Booklet pane. No. 2893×10	8·00	
2885/2893 Set of 9		8·00	11·00

(b) Ordinary gum. Perf 12½.

MS2894 137×225 mm. As Nos. 2885/2893........... 8·00 11·00

Nos. 2885/2893 were all inscr 'P' and were originally valid for 61c. They were issued in separate booklets of ten stamps, Nos. SB465/SB473, each originally sold for $6.10.

Nos. 2885/93 were all inscr 'P' and were originally valid for 61c. They were issued in separate booklets of ten stamps, Nos. SB465/73, each originally sold for $6.10.

994 Heart and Circle of Children's Handprints   **995** The Black Watch of Canada

(Des Debbie Adams. Litho Lowe-Martin)

2012 (17 Sept). Canada Post Community Foundation. Self-adhesive. Fluorescent frame. Die-cut perf 13×13½.

2895	**994**	(61c.)+10c. multicoloured	1·10	1·25
		a. Booklet pane. No. 2895×10	10·00	

No. 2895 was inscr 'P+10' and was initially valid for 61c. plus a 10c. surcharge for the Canada Post Community Foundation. It was only issued in booklets of ten, No. SB474, initially sold for $6.10.

(Des Sharif Tarabay and Sputnik Design Partners Inc. Litho Lowe-Martin)

2012 (11 Oct). 150th Anniversary of the Black Watch of Canada, the Royal Hamilton Light Infantry and the Royal Regiment of Canada. T **995** and similar horiz designs. Multicoloured. Fluorescent frame.

(a) Self-adhesive. Die-cut perf 13½×13.

2896	(61c.) The Black Watch (RHR) of Canada	1·60	1·60
	a. Booklet pane. No. 2896×10	14·00	
2897	(61c.) The Royal Hamilton Light Infantry (Wentworth Regiment)	1·60	1·60
	a. Booklet pane. No. 2897×10	14·00	
2898	(61c.) The Royal Regiment of Canada	1·60	1·60
	a. Booklet pane. No. 2898×10	14·00	
2896/2898 Set of 3		4·25	4·25

(b) Ordinary gum. Perf 13×13½.

MS2899 160×75 mm. As Nos. 2896/2898........... 4·25 5·50

Nos. 2896/2898 and the stamps within **MS**2899 were all inscr 'P' and were initially valid for 61c.

Nos. 2896/2898 were issued in separate booklets of ten, Nos. SB475/SB477, each originally sold for $6.10.

996 Madonna and Child (stained-glass window, St. Mary's Cathedral, Kingston, Ontario)   **997** Gingerbread Man and Woman

(Des Andrew Perro. Litho Lowe-Martin)

2012 (15 Oct). Christmas (1st issue). Self-adhesive booklet stamps. Fluorescent frame. Die-cut perf 13½×13.

2900	**996**	(61c.) multicoloured	1·40	1·25
		a. Booklet pane. No. 2900×10	13·00	

No. 2900 was inscr 'P' and was initially valid for 61c. It was only available from booklets of 12, No. SB478, originally sold for $7.32.

(Des Hélène L'Heureux. Litho Lowe-Martin)

2012 (15 Oct). Christmas (2nd issue). Gingerbread Cookies. T **997** and similar vert designs. Multicoloured. Fluorescent frame.

(a) Self-adhesive. Die-cut perf 13.

2901	(61c.) Type **997**	1·40	1·25
	a. Booklet pane. No. 2901×12	16·00	
2902	$1.05 Gingerbread stars	2·25	2·50
	a. Booklet pane. No. 2902×6	13·00	
2903	$1.80 Gingerbread snowflake	2·75	3·50
	a. Booklet pane. No. 2903×6	16·00	
2901/2903 Set of 3		5·75	6·50

(b) Ordinary gum. Perf 13½×13.

MS2904 85×54 mm. As Nos. 2901/3........... 6·00 8·00

No. 2901 was inscr 'P' and was originally valid for 61c. It was issued in booklets of 12 stamps, No. SB480, initially sold for $7.32.

Nos. 2902/2903 were issued in $6.30 or $10.80 booklets, Nos. SB479 and SB481.

(Des Keith Martin. Litho C.B.N)

2012 (16 Oct). 125th Anniversary of the Royal Philatelic Society of Canada. Sheet 133×58 mm containing designs as Nos. 2518/2518a and 2519c. Perf 13½.

MS2905 3c. *Chrysopa oculata* (Golden-eyed Lacewing); 4c. *Polistes fuscatus* (Paper Wasp); 8c. *Chauliognathus marginatus* (Margined Leatherwing)........... 1·00 1·25

(Litho)

2012 (5 Nov). Picture Post. Predominantly white stamps with decorations as described. Grey (Nos. 2905a/2905b, 2905j), grey and red (No. 2905c), grey and black (No. 2905i) or multicoloured (others). Self-adhesive. Die-cut perf 13.

2905a	(61c.) Dots	2·50	2·50
2905b	(61c.) Frame	2·50	2·50

CANADA

2905c	(61c.) Hearts	2·50	2·50
2905d	(61c.) Creatures	2·50	2·50
2905e	(61c.) Butterflies	2·50	2·50
2905f	(61c.) Maple leaves	2·50	2·50
2905g	(61c.) Flowers	2·50	2·50
2905h	(61c.) Snowflakes	2·50	2·50
2905i	(61c.) Wedding bells	2·50	2·50
2905j	(61c.) Doves and flowers	2·50	2·50
2905k	(61c.) Balloons, stars and party hat	2·50	2·50
2905l	(61c.) Holly	2·50	2·50
2905a/2905l Set of 12		27·00	27·00

Nos. 2905a/2905l were all inscr 'P' and were originally valid for 61c. (63c. from 14 January 2013). They were sold in a Collectors Pack containing the 12 designs for $7.32.

Stamps as Nos. 2905a/2905l were also avaiblae with personalised photographs in the image area. These stamps in vaious denominations and with vertical or horizontal orientations, were sold at a premium.

(997a) **998** Water Snake

2012 (28 Nov). Victory of Toronto Argonauts in 100th Grey Cup Game. No. 2885 optd with T **997a**. Self-adhesive. Fluorescent frame. Die-cut perf 13½×13.

2905m	(61c.) Grey Cup and two players	1·10	1·50
	ma. Booklet pane. No. 2905m×10	10·00	

No. 2905m was inscr 'P' and was originally valid for 61c.
No. 2905m was issued in booklets of ten, No. SB481a, originally sold for $6.10.

(Des Joseph Gault and Avi Dunkelman (Mix Design Group). Calligraphy by Tan Chao Chang. Litho (No. 2909) or litho and embossed (others) Lowe-Martin and Gravure Choquet (foil stamping and embossing))

2013 (8 Jan). Chinese New Year. Year of the Snake. Partial fluorescent frame ($1.85 stamp) or broken fluorescent frame (others).

(a) Ordinary gum. Perf 12½.

2906	(61c.) Type **998**	1·40	1·25
MS2907	90×117 mm. $1.80 Dragon's head; $1.85 Jade snake (transition to Year of the Snake)	5·50	6·00
MS2908	40×140 mm. $1.85 Jade snake	3·00	3·00

(b) Self-adhesive. Die-cut perf 13½.

2909	$1.85 Jade snake	2·75	3·25
	a. Booklet pane. No. 2909×6	16·00	

No. 2906 was inscr 'P' and originally sold for 61c.
No. 2909 was issued in $11.10 booklets, No. SB482.

999 Raoul Wallenberg in 1944, Hungarian Jews and Schutz Pass   **1000** Joe Fortes

(Des q30 design inc. Litho Lowe-Martin)

2013 (17 Jan). Raoul Wallenberg (Second World War rescuer of Jews) Commemoration. Fluorescent frame. Die-cut perf 13×13½.

2910	**999**	$1.85 multicoloured	2·75	3·50
		a. Booklet pane. No. 2910×6	16·00	

No. 2910 was issued in $11.10 booklets, No. SB484.

(Des Lara Minja (Lime Design Inc). Litho Lowe-Martin)

2013 (1 Feb). Black History Month. Joe Fortes. Self-adhesive. Fluorescent frame. Die-cut perf 13.

2911	**1000**	(63c.) multicoloured	1·10	1·25
		a. Booklet pane. No. 2911×10	10·00	

No. 2911 was inscr 'P' and was originally valid for 63c. It was issued in booklets of ten, No. SB485, originally sold for $6.30.

1001 Oliver Jones   **1002** Magnolia 'Eskimo'

(Des Lara Minja (Lime Design Inc). Litho Lowe-Martin)

2013 (1 Feb). Black History Month. Oliver Jones (jazz musician). Fluorescent frame. Die-cut perf 13½×13.

2912	**1001**	(63c.) multicoloured	1·10	1·25
		a. Booklet pane. No. 2912×10	10·00	

No. 2912 was inscr 'P' and was originally valid for 63c. It was issued in booklets of ten, No. SB486, originally sold for $6.30.

(Des Isabelle Toussaint design graphique. Litho Lowe-Martin)

2013 (4 Mar). Magnolias. T **1002** and similar horiz design. Multicoloured. Fluorescent frame.

(a) Self-adhesive coil stamps. Size 24×20 mm. Die-cut perf 8½×imperf.

2913	(63c.) Type **1002**	1·40	1·50
	a. Vert pair. Nos. 2913/2914	2·75	3·00
2914	(63c.) Magnolia 'Yellow Bird'	1·40	1·50

(b) Self-adhesive booklet stamps. Size 32×26 mm. Die-cut perf 13½.

2915	(63c.) Magnolia 'Yellow Bird'	1·40	1·50
	a. Booklet pane. Nos. 2915/2916, each×5	13·00	
2916	(63c.) As Type **1002**	1·40	1·50

(c) Ordinary gum. Sheet 120×84 mm. Perf 13.

MS2917 As Nos. 2915/2916	2·75	3·00

Nos. 2913/2916 and the stamps within **MS**2917 were all inscr 'P' and originally valid for 63c.
Nos. 2915/2916 were issued in booklets of ten, No. SB491, originally sold for $6.30.
Nos. 2913/2914 were issued in rolls of 50 with the two designs in sequence.
Booklet pane 2915a included ten small stickers.

1003 Hot Properties #1 (Jim Breukelman), 1987

(Des Stephane Huot. Litho Lowe-Martin)

2013 (22 Mar). 150 Years of Photography. T **1003** and similar multicoloured designs. Fluorescent frame.

(a) Self-adhesive. Die-cut perf 13½.

2918	(63c.) Type **1003**	1·40	2·00
	a. Booklet pane. Nos. 2918/2922, each×2	11·00	
2919	(63c.) Louis-Joseph Papineau (Thomas Coffin Doane), 1852 (vert)	1·40	2·00
2920	(63c.) The Kitchen Sink (Margaret Watkins), 1919 (vert)	1·40	2·00
2921	(63c.) Andor Pasztor (Gabor Szilasi), 1978	1·40	2·00
2922	(63c.) Koo-tuck-tuck (Geraldine Moodie), 1903–1905 (vert)	1·40	2·00
2923	$1.10 Small Basement Camera Shop, circa 1937 (Rodney Graham), 2011	2·00	2·50
	a. Booklet pane. No. 2923×6	10·00	
2924	$1.85 Yousuf Karsh, from the series 48 Views (Arnaud Maggs), 1981 (shows 12 views)	2·75	3·00
	a. Booklet pane. No. 2924×6	15·00	
2918/2924 Set of 7		10·50	11·00

(b) Ordinary gum. Perf 13.

MS2925	150×75 mm. As Nos. 2919/2920 and 2922	4·00	4·50
MS2926	150×75 mm. As Nos. 2918, 2921 and 2923/2924	7·50	8·00

Nos. 2918/2922 were inscr 'P' and were originally valid for 63c. They were issued in booklets of ten, No. SB492, originally sold for $6.30.
No. 2923 was issued in $6.60 booklets, No. SB493.
See also Nos. 3052/**MS**3060, 3112/**MS**3120, 3190/**MS**3197 and 3392/**MS**3299.
No. 2924 was issued in $11.10 booklets, No. SB494. The horiz stamp designs within No. **MS**2926 are laid vertically within the miniature sheet.

CANADA

1004 Soldiers from 1890, First World War, Second World War and 2013

1005 'Punky' (one year old cat)

(Des Sharif Tarabay and Sputnik Design Partners Inc. Litho Lowe-Martin)

2013 (9 Apr). 150th Anniversary of the Princess of Wales' Own Regiment. Fluorescent frame. Die-cut perf 13½×13.

2927	**1004**	(63c.) multicoloured	1·40	1·25
		a. Booklet pane. No. 2927×10	13·00	

(Des Monica Melnychuk and Subplot Design Inc. Litho Lowe-Martin)

2013 (22 Apr). 'Adopt a Pet'. Animals from Toronto Humane Society Shelter and Toronto Parrot Sanctuary. T **1005** and similar multicoloured designs. Partial fluorescent frame (3 sides, broken at foot).

(a) Self-adhesive. Die-cut perf 13×13½ (Nos. 2928, 2932), 13 (No. 2929) or 13×13½ (Nos. 2930/2931).

2928		(63c.) Type **1005**	2·00	1·75
		a. Booklet pane. Nos. 2928/2932, each×2	17·00	
2929		(63c.) Buddy (parrot) (24×24 mm)	2·00	1·75
2930		(63c.) Captain (80% pug crossbreed dog)	2·00	1·75
2931		(63c.) Wrinkles (dog) (40×40 mm)	2·00	1·75
2932		(63c.) Mickey (black cat)	2·00	1·75
2928/2932 Set of 5			9·00	8·00

(b) Ordinary gum. Perf 12½ (Cats), 13½ (Parrot) or 12½×13 (Dogs).

MS2933	152×100 mm. As Nos. 2928/2932	7·50	8·00

Nos. 2928/2932 and the stamps within **MS**2933 were all inscr 'P' and were originally valid for 63c.

Nos. 2928/2932 were issued in booklets of ten, No. SB496, originally sold for $6.30.

1006 Zhong Hua Men Archway, Chinatown East, Toronto

(Des Harvey Chan, Charles Vinh, Renyl Lantano, Gabe Wong, Janice Wu, Normand Cousineau, Albert Ng, Mark Heine and Hélène L'Heureux. Litho Lowe-Martin and Gravure Choquet)

2013 (1 May). Chinatown Gates. T **1006** and similar square designs. Multicoloured. Fluorescent frame.

(a) Self-adhesive. Die-cut perf 13½.

2934	(63c.) Type **1006**	1·40	1·50
	a. Booklet pane. Nos. 2934/2941	10·00	
2935	(63c.) North Gate, Montréal, 1999	1·40	1·50
2936	(63c.) Chinatown Gate (pedestrian overpass linking Dynasty and Mandarin buildings), Winnipeg, 1987	1·40	1·50
2937	(63c.) Millennium Gate, Vancouver, 2002	1·40	1·50
2938	(63c.) Chinese Gate, Edmonton, 1987	1·40	1·50
2939	(63c.) Chinatown Gateway, Ottawa, 2010	1·40	1·50
2940	(63c.) Timber gate at entrance to Missisauga Chinese Centre	1·40	1·50
2941	(63c.) Gate of Harmonious Interest, Victoria, 1981	1·40	1·50
2934/2941 Set of 8		10·00	11·00

(b) Ordinary gum. Perf 12½.

MS2942 Circular 150 mm diameter. As Nos. 2934/2941... 9·50   11·50

Nos. 2934/2941 were issued in booklets of eight, No. SB497, originally sold for $5.04.

Nos. 2934/2941 and the stamps within **MS**2942 were all inscr 'P' and were originally valid for 63c.

No. **MS**2942 is a circular miniature sheet with a near stamp-size cut-out in the centre of the sheet.

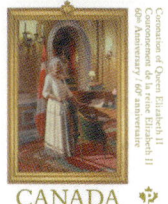 

1007 Diamond Jubilee Portrait by Philip James Richards

1008 Profiles of Girl and Woman Mentor

(Des Entro, Doreen Colonello. Litho C.B.N)

2013 (8 May). 60th Anniversary of the Coronation. Self-adhesive. Fluorescent frame. Die-cut perf 13½.

2943	**1007**	(63c.) multicoloured	1·40	1·25
		a. Booklet pane. No. 2943×10	13·00	

No. 2943 was inscr 'P' and was originally valid for 63c.

No. 2943 was issued in booklets of ten, No. SB498, originally sold for $6.30.

(Des Mike Little (illustration), Dennis Page and Oliver Hill. Litho Lowe-Martin)

2013 (14 May). Centenary of Big Brothers Big Sisters of Canada. Self-adhesive. Fluorescent frame. Die-cut perf 13×13½.

2944	**1008**	(63c.) multicoloured	1·10	1·25
		a. Booklet pane. No. 2944×10	10·00	

No. 2944 was inscr 'P' and was originally valid for 63c.

No. 2944 was issued in booklets of ten, No. SB499, originally sold for $6.30.

1009 CCM (Canadian Cycle and Motor Company) Lightweight Motorcycle, 1908

(Des Mark Pilon (illustration) and Matthew Warburton (Emdoubleyu Design). Litho C.B.N)

2013 (5 June). Motorcycles. T **1009** and similar square design. Multicoloured. Fluorescent frame (broken at foot of stamp).

(a) Self-adhesive. Die-cut perf 13½.

2945	(63c.) Type **1009**	1·40	1·50
	a. Booklet pane. Nos. 2945/2946, each×5	13·00	
2946	(63c.) Indian motorcycle, 1914	1·40	1·50

(b) Ordinary gum. Perf 12½×13.

MS2947 116×84 mm. As Nos. 2945/2946................ 2·75   3·00

Nos. 2945/2946 and the stamps within **MS**2947 were inscr 'P' and were originally valid for 63c.

Nos. 2945/2946 were issued in booklets of ten, No. SB500, originally sold for $6.30.

1010 Benjamin Franklin (postmaster for British North America, opened first Canadian post office)

(Des Andrew Perro. Eng Thomas Hipschen. Litho Lowe-Martin)

2013 (10 June). 250 Years of Postal History. Fluorescent frame. Die-cut perf 13½.

2948	**1010**	(63c.) multicoloured	1·60	1·25
		a. Booklet pane. No. 2948×10	14·00	

No. 2948 was inscr 'P' and was originally valid for 63c. It was issued in booklets of ten, No. SB501, originally sold for $6.30.

CANADA

(Des Suzanne Duranceau and Susan Scott. Litho C.B.N)

2013 (20 June). Bicentenary of War of 1812 between United States and Britain (2nd issue). Horiz designs as T **989**. Multicoloured. Fluorescent frame (on three sides)*. Perf 13×12½.

2949	(63c.) Lieutenant-Colonel Charles de Salaberry	1·75	1·50
	a. Horiz pair. Nos. 2949/2950	3·50	3·00
2950	(63c.) Laura Secord (warned British Canadian and First Nation forces of American attack plans)	1·75	1·50

Nos. 2949/2950 were printed together, *se-tenant*, as horizontal pairs in sheets of 16, each pair forming a composite background design of a Canadian landscape.

*Nos. 2949/2950 had a fluorescent frame around the horizontal pair, giving No. 2949 a fluorescent frame at top, left and bottom and No. 2950 a fluorescent frame at top, right and bottom.

1013 Robertson Davies (photo by Yousuf Karsh)

(Des Steven Slipp and Tan Chao Chang (calligraphy). Litho Lowe-Martin)

2013 (28 Aug). Birth Centenary of Robertson Davies (writer). Self-adhesive. Fluorescent frame. Die-cut perf 13.

2959	**1013**	63c. multicoloured	1·10	1·25
		a. Booklet pane. No. 2959×10	10·00	

No. 2959 was issued in $6.30 booklets, No. SB507.

1011 Stella hanging upside-down from Tree

(Des Q30 design Inc. Litho Lowe-Martin)

2013 (5 July). Children's Literature. Stella (characater from books written and illustrated by Marie-Louise Gay). T **1011** and similar square design. Multicoloured. Fluorescent frame.

(a) Self-adhesive. Die-cut perf 13½

2951	(63c.) Type **1011**	1·10	1·50
	a. Booklet pane. Nos. 2951/2952, each ×5	10·00	
2952	(63c.) Stella and little brother Sam reading book	1·10	1·50

(b) Ordinary gum. Perf 12½

MS2953 150×100 mm. Nos. 2951/2952	2·75	3·00

Nos. 2951/2952 and the stamps within **MS**2953 were all inscr 'P' and were originally valid for 63c.

Nos. 2951/2952 were issued in booklets of ten, No. SB502, originally sold for $6.30.

1014 Vancouver Canucks Logo **1015** Vancouver Canucks Jersey

(Des Ron Dollecamp (illustrations) and Avi Dunkelman and Joseph Gault, MIX Design Group. Litho or recess and litho (2975) Lowe-Martin)

2013 (3 Sept). NHL (National Hockey League) Team Logos and Jerseys. T **1014/1015** and similar horiz designs. Multicoloured. Fluorescent frames.

*(a) As T **1014** showing team logos.*
(i) Self-adhesive coil stamps. Die-cut perf 8½×imperf.

2960	63c. Type **1014**	1·40	1·50
2961	63c. Edmonton Oilers	1·40	1·50
2962	63c. Toronto Maple Leafs	1·40	1·50
2963	63c. Montreal Canadiens	1·40	1·50
2964	63c. Calgary Flames	1·40	1·50
2965	63c. Winnipeg Jets	1·40	1·50
2966	63c. Ottawa Senators	1·40	1·50
2960/2966 Set of 7		8·75	9·50

(ii) Ordinary gum. Perf 13.

MS2967 127×70 mm. As Nos. 2960/2966	8·75	10·00

*(b) As T **1015** showing team jerseys.*
(i) Self-adhesive booklet stamps. Die-cut perf 13×13½.

2968	63c. Type **1015**	1·10	1·50
	a. Booklet pane. No. 2968×10	10·00	
2969	63c. Montreal Canadiens	1·10	1·50
	a. Booklet pane. No. 2969×10	10·00	
2970	63c. Edmonton Oilers	1·10	1·50
	a. Booklet pane. No. 2970×10	10·00	
2971	63c. Ottawa Senators	1·10	1·50
	a. Booklet pane. No. 2971×10	10·00	
2972	63c. Calgary Flames	1·10	1·50
	a. Booklet pane. No. 2972×10	10·00	
2973	63c. Winnipeg Jets	1·10	1·50
	a. Booklet pane. No. 2973×10	10·00	
2974	63c. Toronto Maple Leafs	1·10	1·50
	a. Booklet pane. No. 2974×10	10·00	
2968/2974 Set of 7		7·00	9·50

(ii) Ordinary gum. Perf 12½.

MS2975 160×160 mm. As Nos. 2968/2974 with two stamp-size labels	8·75	10·00

Nos. 2968/2974 were issued in separate $6.30 booklets, Nos. SB508/SB514.

1012 The Tragically Hip

(Des Tan Chao Chang (calligraphy) and Louis Gagnon, Paprika. Litho Lowe-Martin and Gravure Choquet)

2013 (19 July). Canadian Recording Artists (4th series). T **1012** and similar multicoloured designs. Multicoloured. Fluorescent frame.

(a) Self-adhesive. Die-cut perf 13×13½ (Nos. 2954, 2956) or 13½ (Nos. 2955, 2957).

2954	(63c.) Type **1012**	1·10	1·50
	a. Booklet pane. No. 2954×10	10·00	
2955	(63c.) Rush (cover of album 2112) (32×32 mm)	1·10	1·50
	a. Booklet pane. No. 2955×10	10·00	
2956	(63c.) Beau Dommage	1·10	1·50
	a. Booklet pane. No. 2956×10	10·00	
2957	(63c.) The Guess Who (logo) (32×32 mm)	1·10	1·50
	a. Booklet pane. No. 2957×10	10·00	
2954/7 Set of 4		4·00	6·00

(b) Ordinary gum. Perf 12½.

MS2958 Circular 105×105 mm. As Nos. 2954/2957	5·50	6·00

Nos. 2954/2957 and the stamps within **MS**2958 were all inscr 'P' and originally valid for 63c.

Nos. 2954/2957 were issued in separate booklets of ten stamps, Nos. SB503/SB506, each booklet originally sold for $6.30.

1016 S Logo (from *Man of Steel #1* (John Byrne, 1986) **1017** Superman

CANADA

(Des Kosta Tsetsekas and Jasper Murphy, Signals. Litho Lowe-Martin)

2013 (10 Sept). 75th Anniversary of Superman. T **1016/1017** and similar vert designs. Multicoloured. Fluorescent frame.

*(a) T **1016**. Self-adhesive coil stamps. Die-cut perf 13½.*
2976	(63c.) Type **1016**		1·60	1·25

*(b) As T **1017**.*
(i) Self-adhesive booklet stamps. Die-cut perf 13½×13.
2977	(63c.) Type **1017**		1·60	1·50
	a. Booklet pane. Nos. 2977/2981, each×2	14·00		
2978	(63c.) Superman flying (dark grey upper background)		1·60	1·50
2979	(63c.) Superman and lightning		1·60	1·50
2980	(63c.) Superman breaking chains		1·60	1·50
2981	(63c.) Superman flying and Daily Planet building		1·60	1·50
2977/2981	Set of 5		7·25	6·75

(ii) Ordinary gum. Perf 12½.
MS2982	177×82 mm. As Nos. 2977/2981	7·00	8·00

Nos. 2977/2981 were issued in booklets of ten, Nos. SB515/SB515d, each booklet originally sold for $6.30.

Nos. 2976/2981 and the stamps within No. **MS**2982 were all inscr 'P' and were originally valid for 63c.

1018 'Floating Adrift' (plasticine on board, Ezra Peters)

1019 'Assault on Assoro' (Ted Zuber) and Poppies

(Des Parable Communications. Litho C.B.N)

2013 (30 Sept). Canada Post Community Foundation. Winning Entry in Children's Art Competition. Self-adhesive. Fluorescent frame. Die-cut perf 13×12½.
2983	**1018**	63c.+10c. multicoloured	1·40	1·50
		a. Booklet pane. No. 2983×10	13·00	

No. 2983 was issued in $7.30 booklets, No. SB516.

(Des Sharif Tarabay (illustration) and Sputnik Design Partners Inc. Litho Lowe-Martin)

2013 (18 Oct). 150th Anniversary of the Hastings and Prince Edward Regiment. Self-adhesive. Fluorescent frame.
2984	**1019**	(63c.) multicoloured	1·60	1·50
		a. Booklet pane. No. 2984×10	14·00	

No. 2984 was inscr 'P' and was originally valid for 63c. It was issued in booklets of ten, No. SB517, originally sold for $6.30.

1020 Duke and Duchess of Cambridge with Prince George

(Des Isabelle Toussaint Design Graphique. Litho Lowe-Martin)

2013 (22 Oct). Birth of Prince George of Cambridge. Fluorescent frame.
(a) Self-adhesive. Die-cut perf 13½.
2985	**1020**	(63c.) multicoloured	1·60	1·25
		a. Booklet pane. No. 2985×10	14·00	

(b) Ordinary gum. Perf 12½.
MS2986	120×84 mm. As Nos. 2985×2	3·00	3·50

No. 2985 and the stamps within **MS**2986 were inscr 'P' and were originally valid for 63c.

No. 2985 was issued in booklets of ten, No. SB518, originally sold for $6.30.

1021 Saint Anne with the Christ Child (Georges de La Tour)

1022 French Horn

(Des Louise Méthé. Litho Lowe-Martin)

2013 (22 Oct). Christmas (1st issue). Self-adhesive. Fluorescent frame. Die-cut perf 13½.
2987	**1021**	63c. multicoloured	1·40	1·25
		a. Booklet pane. No. 2987×12	16·00	

No. 2987 was issued in $7.56 booklets, No. SB519.

(Des Hélène L'Heureux. Litho Lowe-Martin)

2013 (22 Oct). Christmas (2nd issue). Embroidery. T **1022** and similar vert designs. Multicoloured.

(a) Self-adhesive. Die-cut perf 13.
2988		63c. Type **1022**	1·40	1·25
		a. Booklet pane. No. 2988×12	16·00	
2989		$1.10 Flying reindeer	2·25	2·10
		a. Booklet pane. No. 2989×6	13·00	
2990		$1.85 Christmas tree	2·75	3·25
		a. Booklet pane. No. 2990×6	16·00	
2988/2990	Set of 3		6·00	6·00

(b) Ordinary gum. Perf 13½×13.
MS2991	85×54 mm. As Nos. 2988/2990	6·25	6·50

Nos. 2988/2990 were issued in $6.60, $7.56 or $11.10 booklets, Nos. SB520/SB522.

1023 Horse

(Des Paprika. No. 2995) or litho and embossed (others) Lowe-Martin and Gravure Choquet (foil stamping and embossing)

2014 (13 Jan). Chinese New Year. Year of the Horse. Multicoloured. Partial fluorescent frame ($1.85 stamp from **MS**2994) or broken fluorescent frame (others).

(a) Ordinary gum. Perf 12½.
2992	63c. Type **1023**	1·40	1·25
MS2993	119×90 mm. $1.85 Gold horse; $1.85 Jade snake (transition to Year of the Horse)	5·50	6·00
MS2994	41×140 mm. $1.85 Gold horse	2·75	3·50

(b) Self-adhesive. Die-cut perf 13½.
2995	$1.85 Gold horse	2·75	3·25
	a. Booklet pane. No. 2995×6	16·00	
	ab. Gold (horse) omitted		

No. 2995 was issued in $11.10 booklets, No. SB523.

1024 Nora Hendrix, Fielding William Spotts Jr and Hogan's Alley, Vancouver

1025 Barbara Ann Scott (figure skater, 1928–2012)

(Des Janice Kun (illustration) and Karen Smith Design. Litho Lowe-Martin)

2014 (30 Jan). Black History Month. Africville and Hogan's Alley. T **1024** and similar square designs. Multicoloured. Self-adhesive. Fluorescent frame. Die-cut perf 13½.
2996	63c. Seven young girls and Africville, Nova Scotia	1·10	1·50
	a. Booklet pane. No. 2996×10	10·00	

2997	63c. Type **1024**		1·10	1·50
	a. Booklet pane. No. 2997×10		10·00	

Nos. 2996/2997 were issued in separate $6.30 booklets, Nos. SB524/SB525.

(Des Louis Hébert (illustration) and Paprika. Litho Lowe-Martin)

2014 (3 Feb). Pioneers of Winter Sports. T **1025** and similar square designs. Multicoloured. Fluorescent frame.

(a) Self-adhesive. Die-cut perf 13½.

2998	63c. Type **1025**		1·10	1·50
	a. Booklet pane. No. 2998×10		10·00	
2999	63c. Sandra Schmirler (curling, 1963–2000)		1·10	1·50
	a. Booklet pane. No. 2999×10		10·00	
3000	63c. Sarah Burke (freestyle skier, 1982–2012)		1·10	1·50
	a. Booklet pane. No. 3000×10		10·00	
2998/3000	Set of 3		3·00	4·00

(b) Ordinary gum. Perf 13.

MS3001	126×90 mm. As Nos. 2998/3000	4·00	5·00

Nos. 2998/3000 were issued in separate $6.30 booklets, Nos. SB526/SB528.

1027 Shiva Nataraja Sculpture, Mummified Cat and Bison

(Des Entro. Litho Lowe-Martin)

2014 (14 Apr). Centenary of the Royal Ontario Museum, Toronto. T **1027** and similar vert design. Multicoloured. Fluorescent frame.

(a) Self-adhesive. Die-cut perf 13½×13.

3020	(85c.) Type **1027**		1·60	1·60
	a. Booklet pane. Nos. 3020/3021, each×5		13·00	
3021	(85c.) Parasaurolophis walkeri and Luohan figure		1·60	1·60

(b) Ordinary gum. Perf 12½.

MS3022	127×70 mm. As Nos. 3020/3021	3·00	4·50

Nos. 3020/3021 were inscr 'P' and were originally valid for 85c. They were issued in booklets of ten, No. SB530, originally sold for $8.50.

1026 Gros Morne National Park

(Des Lime Design. Litho Lowe-Martin (3007/3011, **MS**3018) or CBN (others))

2014 (31 Mar)–17. UNESCO World Heritage Sites. T **1026** and similar horiz designs. Multicoloured. Fluorescent frame.

(a) Self-adhesive. Die-cut perf 13 (Nos. 3002/3006, 3012/3016) or 13½ (Nos. 3007/3011).

3002	(85c.) Type **1026**		1·60	1·60
	a. Pane. Nos. 3002/3006, each×2		13·00	13·00
	b. Booklet pane. Nos. 3002/3006, each×6		38·00	
3003	(85c.) Virginia Falls, Nahanni National Park, Northwest Territories		1·60	1·60
3004	(85c.) Joggins Fossil Cliffs, Nova Scotia (red sandstone cliff and rocky beach)		1·60	1·60
3005	(85c.) Miguasha National Park, Gaspé Peninsula, Quebec (cliff and shingle beach)		1·60	1·60
3006	(85c.) Climber on snowy peak, Rocky Mountains		1·60	1·60
3007	(85c.) The Landscape of Grand Pré, Nova Scotia (11.1.16)		1·60	1·60
	a. Pane. Nos. 3007/3011, each×2		13·00	13·00
	b. Booklet pane. Nos. 3007/3011, each×6		38·00	
3008	(85c.) The Rideau Canal, Ontario (11.1.16)		1·60	1·60
3009	(85c.) Haida memorial poles, Sgang Gwaay, British Columbia (11.1.16)		1·60	1·60
3010	(85c.) Head-Smashed-In Buffalo Jump, Alberta (11.1.16)		1·60	1·60
3011	(85c.) Old Town, Lunenburg, Nova Scotia (11.1.16)		1·60	1·60
3012	(85c.) Dinosaur Provincial Park		1·60	1·60
	a. Pane. Nos. 3012/16, each ×2		13·00	13·00
	b. Booklet pane. Nos. 3012/16, each ×6		38·00	
3013	(85c.) Mistaken Point		1·60	1·60
3014	(85c.) Historic District of Old Québec		1·60	1·60
3015	(85c.) L'Anse aux Meadows National Historic Site		1·60	1·60
3016	(85c.) Red Bay Basque Whaling Station		1·60	1·60
3002/3011	Set of 10		22·00	22·00

(b) Ordinary gum. Perf 13½×13.

MS3017	130×71 mm. As Nos. 3002/3006	7·00	8·00
MS3018	130×71 mm. As Nos. 3007/3011 (11.1.16)	7·00	8·00
MS3019	130×71 mm. As Nos. 3012/3016 (16.1.17)	7·00	8·00

Nos. 3002/3016 and the stamps within Nos. **MS**3017/**MS**3019 were all inscr 'P' and were originally valid for 85c. each.

Nos. 3002/3006, 3007/3011 and 3012/3016 were each issued in panes of ten originally sold for $8.50 and booklets of 30 (Nos. SB529, SB583 and SB602) originally sold for $25.50.

For similar designs to Nos. 3007/3011 see Nos. 3035/**MS**3040.

1028 Rose 'Maid of Honour'

(Des Isabelle Toussaint Design graphique. Litho Lowe-Martin)

2014 (23 Apr). Roses. T **1028** and similar multicoloured design. Multicoloured. Fluorescent frame.

(a) Coil stamps. Die-cut perf 8×imperf.

3023	(85c.) Type **1028**		1·60	1·60
	a. Vert pair. Nos. 3023/3024		3·00	3·00
3024	(85c.) Red rose 'Konrad Henkel'		1·60	1·60

(b) Booklet stamps. Size 26×32 mm. Die-cut perf 13½.

3025	(85c.) Red rose 'Konrad Henkel'		1·60	1·60
	a. Booklet pane. Nos. 3025/3026, each×5		13·00	
3026	(85c.) White rose 'Maid of Honour'		1·60	1·60

(c) Ordinary gum. Sheet 120×83 mm.

MS3027	As Nos. 3025/3026	3·00	4·00

Nos. 3023/3024 come from rolls of 50 with the two designs alternating throughout.

Nos. 3023/3026 and the stamps within **MS**3027 were all inscr 'P' and were originally sold for 85c.

Nos. 3025/3026 were issued in booklets of ten, No. SB531, originally sold for $8.50.

Booklet pane No. 3025a also contains ten small stickers.

1029 Passengers and Steamship *Komagata Maru*

1030 Flamenco at 5.15 (director Cynthia Scott, 1983)

(Des Paprika and Mark Summers (illustration). Litho C.B.N)

2014 (1 May). Centenary of the *Komagata Maru* Incident (British Indian Immigrants turned away from Canada). Self-adhesive. Fluorescent frame. Die-cut perf 13×12½.

3028	**1029**	$2.50 multicoloured	4·50	5·00
		a. Booklet pane. No. 3028×6	23·00	

No. 3028 was issued in $15 booklets, No. SB532.

CANADA

(Des Paprika. Litho C.B.N)

2014 (2 May). 75th Anniversary of NFB (National Film Board of Canada). T **1030** and similar square designs. Multicoloured. Fluorescent frame.

(a) Self-adhesive. Die-cut perf 13.

3029	(85c.) Type **1030**	1·60	1·60
	a. Booklet pane. Nos. 3029/3033, each×2	13·00	
3030	(85c.) The Railrodder (director Gerald Potterton, 1965)...	1·60	1·60
3031	(85c.) Mon Oncle Antoine (director Claude Jutra, 1971)...	1·60	1·60
3032	(85c.) Log Driver's Waltz (director John Weldon, 1979)..	1·60	1·60
3033	(85c.) Neighbours (director Norman McLaren, 1952)..	1·60	1·60
3029/33 *Set of 5*..		7·00	7·00

(b) Ordinary gum. Perf 13×12½.

MS3034 93×103 mm. As Nos. 3029/3033........................ 7·00 7·50

Nos. 3029/3033 and the stamps within **MS**3034 were all inscr 'P' and were originally valid for 85c.

Nos. 3029/3033 were issued in booklets of ten, No. SB533, originally sold for $8.50.

1031 Old Town, Lunenburg, Nova Scotia

(Des Lime Design. Litho Lowe-Martin)

2014 (16 May). UNESCO World Heritage Sites. T **1031** and similar horiz designs. Multicoloured. Fluorescent frame.

(a) Self-adhesive. Die-cut perf 13×13½.

3035	$1.20 Type **1031**	2·25	2·50
	a. Booklet pane. Nos. 3035/3037, each ×2	11·00	
3036	$1.20 Head-Smashed-In Buffalo Jump, Alberta..	2·25	2·50
3037	$1.20 The Landscape of Grand Pré, Nova Scotia...	2·25	2·50
3038	$2.50 Haida memorial poles, Sgang Gwaay, British Columbia...	4·25	4·50
	a. Booklet pane. Nos. 3038/3039, each×3	22·00	
3039	$2.50 The Rideau Canal, Ontario.........................	4·25	4·50
3035/9 *Set of 5*...		13·00	15·00

(b) Ordinary gum. Perf 12½.

MS3040 130×100 mm. As Nos. 3035/3039........................ 13·00 15·00

Nos. 3035/3039 were issued in $7.20 and $15 booklets, Nos. SB534/SB535.

1032 *Empress of Ireland*

(Des Isabelle Toussaint (No. 3041/3042) or Susan Scott (No. 3043). Litho Lowe-Martin)

2014 (29 May). Centenary of the Sinking of Liner *Empress of Ireland*. T **1032** and similar multicoloured designs. Multicoloured. Fluorescent frame.

(a) Self-adhesive. Die-cut perf 13½.

3041	(85c.) Type **1032**	1·75	1·60
	a. Booklet pane. No. 3041×10........................	15·00	

*(b) Ordinary gum. Perf 12½ (No. 3042) or 13 (No. **MS**3043).*

3042	(85c.) As Type **1032**.......................................	1·75	1·60
MS3043 114×72 mm. $2.50 *Empress of Ireland* (Aristides Balanos) (84×36 mm)...		5·50	6·00

No. 3042 were inscr 'P' and were originally valid for 85c.

No. 3041 was issued in booklets of ten, No. SB536, originally sold for $8.50.

1033 Ghost Bride and Fairmont Banff Springs Hotel, Alberta

(Des Lionel Gadoury and Terry Popik and Sam Weber and C.H.J. Snider (illustration). Litho Lowe-Martin)

2014 (13 June). Haunted Canada (1st series). T **1033** and similar square designs. Multicoloured. Fluorescent frame.

(a) Self-adhesive. Die-cut perf 13½.

3044	(85c.) Type **1033**	1·60	1·60
	a. Booklet pane. Nos. 3044/3048, each×2	13·00	
3045	(85c.) Phantom ship, Northumberland Strait, Nova Scotia...	1·60	1·60
3046	(85c.) Ghost train, St. Louis, Saskatchewan	1·60	1·60
3047	(85c.) Louis de Buade, Count of Frontenac, Fairmont Le Château Frontenac, Quebec...	1·60	1·60
3048	(85c.) Ghost soldiers, Fort George, Niagara-on-the-Lake, Ontario...................................	1·60	1·60
3044/3048 *Set of 5*...		7·00	7·00

(b) Ordinary gum. Perf 12½.

MS3049 127×74 mm. As Nos. 3044/3048........................ 7·00 7·00

Nos. 3044/3048 and the stamps within **MS**3049 were inscr 'P' and were originally valid for 85c.

Nos. 3044/3048 were issued in booklets of ten, No. SB537, originally sold for $8.50.

See also Nos. 3158/**MS**3163 and 3221/**MS**3226.

1034 Ottawa Redblacks Team Logo

1035 Roughriders Quarterback Russ Jackson and New Redblacks Stadium

(Des Bensimon Byrne. Litho Lowe-Martin (No. 3050), C.B.N. (No. 3051))

2014 (19 June). 'Ottawa Redblacks the CFL returns to Ottawa'. New Canadian Football League Team. Self-adhesive. Fluorescent frame.

*(a) Self-adhesive coil stamp as T **1034**. Die-cut perf 8×imperf.*

3050	**1034**	(85c.) multicoloured	1·60	1·60

*(b) Self-adhesive booklet stamp as T **1035**. Die-cut perf 13.*

3051	**1035**	(85c.) multicoloured	1·25	1·60
		a. Booklet pane. No. 3051×10.............	11·00	

Nos. 3050/3051 were inscr 'P' and were originally valid for 85c.

No. 3051 was issued in booklets of ten (No. SB538) originally sold for $8.50.

(Des Stephane Huot. Litho Lowe-Martin)

2014 (7 July). 150 Years of Photography (2nd issue). Multicoloured designs as T **1003**. Fluorescent frame.

(a) Self-adhesive. Die-cut perf 13½.

3052	(85c.) Bogner's Groccry (Frcd Herzog), 1960 ..	1·60	1·60
	a. Booklet pane. Nos. 3052/3056, each×2	12·00	
3053	(85c.) St Joseph's Convent School (Michel Lambeth), 1960 (*vert*).................................	1·60	1·60
3054	(85c.) La ville de Québec en hiver (L. P. Vallée), c. 1894...	1·60	1·60
3055	(85c.) Untitled (Lynne Cohen), 1970	1·60	1·60
3056	(85c.) Unidentified Chinese man (C. D. Hoy), c. 1912 (*vert*)...	1·60	1·60
3057	$1.20 Sitting Bull and Buffalo Bill (William Notman), Montreal, 1885..........................	2·00	2·25
	a. Booklet pane. No. 3057×6	11·00	
3058	$2.50 Railcuts: #1 (Edward Burtynsky), 1985 ..	3·75	4·25
	a. Booklet pane. No. 3058×6	20·00	
3052/3058 *Set of 7*...		12·00	13·00

(b) Ordinary gum. Perf 13.

MS3059 150×75 mm. As Nos. 3052, 3054/3055 and 3058.. 8·00 9·00

MS3060 150×75 mm. As Nos. 3053, 3056 and 3057.......... 4·75 6·00

CANADA

Nos. 3052/3056 were inscr 'P' and were originally valid for 85c. They were issued in booklets of ten, No. SB540, originally sold for $8.50.
No. 3057 was issued in $7.20 booklets, No. SB539.
No. 3058 was issued in $15 booklets, No. SB541.
The horiz stamp designs within **MS**3059 are laid vertically within the miniature sheet.

1036 Hank Snow

(Des Sabrina McAllister and Xerxes Irani (Nos. 3061/3063) or Roy White, Subplot Design Inc (Nos. 3064/3065). Litho Lowe-Martin)

2014 (31 July). Canadian Country Artists. T **1036** and similar horiz designs. Multicoloured. Fluorescent frame.

(a) Self-adhesive. Die-cut perf 13×13½.
3061	(85c.) Type **1036**	1·40	1·60
	a. Booklet pane. No. 3061×10	11·00	
3062	(85c.) Renée Martel	1·40	1·60
	a. Booklet pane. No. 3062×10	11·00	
3063	(85c.) Shania Twain	1·40	1·60
	a. Booklet pane. No. 3063×10	11·00	
3064	(85c.) Tommy Hunter	1·40	1·60
	a. Booklet pane. No. 3064×10	11·00	
3065	(85c.) k.d. lang	1·40	1·60
	a. Booklet pane. No. 3065×10	11·00	
3061/6 Set of 5		6·00	7·00

(b) Ordinary gum. Perf 12½.
MS3066 140×110 mm. As Nos. 3061/3065 .... 7·00 7·50

Nos. 3061/3065 and the stamps within **MS**3066 were all inscr 'P' and originally valid for 85c.
Nos. 3061/3065 were issued in separate booklets of ten stamps, Nos. SB540/SB544, each booklet originally sold for $8.50.

1037 Canadian Museum for Human Rights, Winnipeg

(Des Adrian Shum, Circle. Litho Lowe-Martin)

2014 (20 Aug). Canadian Museum for Human Rights, Winnipeg. Self-adhesive. Fluorescent frame. Die-cut perf 13.
3067	**1037** (85c.) multicoloured	1·40	1·60
	a. Booklet pane. No. 3067×10	11·00	

No. 3067 was inscr 'P' and was originally valid for 85c. It was issued in booklets of ten, No. SB545, originally sold for $8.50.

1038 Mike Myers

(Des Kosta Tsetsekas, Mike Savage and John Belisle (Signals). Litho C.B.N)

2014 (29 Aug). Great Canadian Comedians. T **1038** and similar horiz designs. Multicoloured. Two fluorescent bands.

(a) Self-adhesive. Die-cut perf 13.
3068	(85c.) Type **1038**	1·40	1·60
	a. Booklet pane. Nos. 3068×6 and Nos. 3069/3072	11·00	
	b. Booklet pane. Nos. 3068, 3069×6 and 3070/3073	11·00	
	c. Booklet pane. Nos. 3068/3069, 3070×6 and 3071/3072	11·00	
	d. Booklet pane. Nos. 3068/3070, 3071×6 and 3072	11·00	
	e. Booklet pane. Nos. 3068/3071 and 3072×6	11·00	
3069	(85c.) Martin Short	1·40	1·60
3070	(85c.) Olivier Guimond	1·40	1·60
3071	(85c.) Jim Carrey	1·40	1·60
3072	(85c.) Catherine O'Hara	1·40	1·60
3068/3072 Set of 5		6·00	7·00

(b) Ordinary gum. Perf 12½×13.
MS3073 131×96 mm. As Nos. 3068/72 .... 7·00 8·50

Nos. 3068/3072 and the stamps within **MS**3073 were inscr 'P' and were originally valid for 85c.
Nos. 3068/3072 were issued in booklets of ten, Nos. SB546/SB550, originally sold for $8.50.

1039 Children in Origami Boat   **1040** Tim Horton (Toronto Maple Leafs)

(Des Paul Haslip (HM and E Design). Litho Lowe-Martin)

2014 (29 Sept). Canada Post Community Foundation. Self-adhesive. Fluorescent frame. Die-cut perf 13½.
3074	**1039** (85c.) multicoloured	1·40	1·60
	a. Booklet pane. No. 3074×10	11·00	

No. 3074 was issued in booklets of ten, No. SB551, originally sold for $8.50.

(Des Avi Dunkelman and Joseph Gault (MIX Design Group). Litho Lowe-Martin)

2014 (3 Oct). Original Six Canadian Ice Hockey Defencemen. T **1040** and similar vert designs. Multicoloured. Fluorescent frames.

*(a) Self-adhesive. Die-cut perf 13½ (3075/3080) or 13½×13 (**MS**3081).*
3075	(85c.) Type **1040**	1·25	1·60
	a. Booklet pane. Nos. 3075/3080	6·50	
3076	(85c.) Doug Harvey (Montreal Canadiens)	1·25	1·60
3077	(85c.) Bobby Orr (Boston Bruins)	1·25	1·60
3078	(85c.) Harry Howell (New York Rangers)	1·25	1·60
3079	(85c.) Pierre Pilote (Chicago Black Hawks)	1·25	1·60
3080	(85c.) Red Kelly (Red Wings and Toronto Maple Leafs)	1·25	1·60
3075/3080 Set of 6		6·50	8·00

MS3081 Six sheets, each 64×90 mm. (a) $2.50 As Type **1040**. (b) $2.50 As No. 3076. (c) $2.50 As No. 3077. (d) $2.50 As No. 3078. (e) $2.50 As No. 3079. (f) $2.50 As No. 3080 (all 52×78 mm) .... 23·00 27·00

(b) Ordinary gum. Perf 12½×13.
MS3082 161×161 mm. (85c.)×6 As Nos. 3075/3080 .... 8·00 9·00

Nos. 3075/3080 and the stamps within **MS**3082 were all inscr 'P' and were originally valid for 85c. each.
Nos. 3075/3080 were issued in booklets of six, No. SB552, originally sold for $5.10.
Nos. **MS**3081(a)/**MS**3081(f) were sold as a pack of six miniature sheets in a foil wrapper for $15.

1041 Winnipeg Jets Ice Resurfacing Machine

(Des Avi Dunkelman and Joseph Gault (MIX Design Group). Litho Lowe-Martin)

2014 (3 Oct). NHL Zamboni Ice Re-surfacing Machines. T **1041** and similar horiz designs. Multicoloured. Fluorescent frames.

(a) Self-adhesive coil stamps. Die-cut perf 8×imperf.
3083	(85c.) Type **1041**	1·60	1·60
3084	(85c.) Ottawa Senators	1·60	1·60
3085	(85c.) Toronto Maple Leafs	1·60	1·60
3086	(85c.) Montreal Canadiens	1·60	1·60
3087	(85c.) Vancouver Canucks	1·60	1·60
3088	(85c.) Calgary Flames	1·60	1·60
3089	(85c.) Edmonton Oilers	1·60	1·60
3083/9 Set of 7		9·50	9·50

(b) Ordinary gum. Perf 13.
MS3090 127×70 mm. (85c.)×7 As Nos. 3083/3089 .... 9·50 12·00

Nos. 3083/3089 and the stamps within No. **MS**3090 were all inscr 'P' and were originally valid for 85c. each.

1042 Wait for Me Daddy (photo by Claude P. Dettloff), 1 October 1940

(Des Susan Mavor (Metaform). Litho Lowe-Martin)

2014 (4 Oct). Wait for Me Daddy (Warren 'Whitey' Bernard and soldiers departing for Second World War). Fluorescent frames.

(a) Self-adhesive. Die-cut perf 13.
3091	**1042**	(85c.) multicoloured	1·60	1·60
		a. Booklet pane. No. 3091×10	13·00	

(b) Ordinary gum. Perf 13.
MS3092 165×240 mm. (85c.) As No. 3091×5........... 7·00   7·50

1043 The Virgin and Child with St John the Baptist (Abraham Janssens van Nuyssen)

1044 Santa answering Letter

(Des Louise Méthé. Litho Lowe-Martin)

2014 (23 Oct). Christmas (1st issue). 350th Anniversary of the Parish of Notre-Dame de Quebec. Self-adhesive. Fluorescent frame. Die-cut perf 13½.
3093	**1043**	(85c.) multicoloured	1·60	1·10
		a. Booklet pane. No. 3093×12	15·00	

No. 3093 was inscr 'P' and was originally valid for 85c. It was issued in booklets of 12 stamps, No. SB554, originally sold for $10.20.

(Des Christiane Beauregard (illustration) and Hélène L'Heureux. Litho Lowe-Martin)

2014 (23 Oct). Christmas (2nd issue). Santa. T **1044** and similar square designs. Multicoloured. Fluorescent frame.

(a) Self-adhesive. Die-cut perf 13.
3094		(85c.) Type **1044**	1·60	1·10
		a. Booklet pane. No. 3094×12	15·00	
3095		$1.20 Flying Santa	2·25	2·25
		a. Booklet pane. No. 3095×6	11·00	
3096		$2.50 Santa in traditional robes of St Nicholas	4·00	4·50
		a. Booklet pane. No. 3096×6	22·00	
3094/6		Set of 3	7·00	7·25

(b) Ordinary gum. Perf 13.
MS3097 85×55 mm. As Nos. 3094/3096.......... 7·00   7·50

No. 3094 was inscr 'P' and was originally valid for 85c. It was issued in booklets of 12 stamps, No. SB555, originally sold for $10.20.

Nos. 3095/3096 were issued in $7.20 or $15 booklets, Nos. SB556/SB557.

1045 Three Rams

(Des Hélène L'Heureux, Susan Scott (illustration) and Ngan Siu-Mui (calligraphy). Litho (3101) or litho and embossed (others) Lowe-Martin)

2015 (8 Jan). Chinese New Year. Year of the Ram. T **1045** and similar square designs. Black, emerald and gold (No. 3101) or multicoloured (others). Fluorescent frame (broken at lower right on $1.85 stamp in No. **MS**3099).

(a) Ordinary gum. Perf 12½.
3098		(85c.) Type **1045**	1·60	1·50

MS3099 118×90 mm. $1.85 Gold horse; $2.50 Deep green and gold ram (transition to Year of the Ram).. 6·00   7·00
MS3100 41×140 mm. $2.50 Deep green and gold ram... 4·25   4·50

(b) Self-adhesive. Die-cut perf 13½.
3101		$2.50 Deep green and gold ram	4·25	4·50
		a. Booklet pane. No. 3101×6	22·00	

No. 3098 was inscr 'P' and was originally sold for 85c.
No. 3101 was issued in $15 booklets, No. SB558.

1046 Sir John A. Macdonald

1047 Nelson Mandela in Canada, 1990 and South African Flag

(Des Paprika and Image Asset Management Ltd (illustration). Litho C.B.N)

2015 (11 Jan). Birth Bicentenary of Sir John Alexander Macdonald (1815–1891, Canada's first Prime Minister 1867–1873, 1878–1891). Self-adhesive. Fluorescent frame. Die-cut perf 13.
3102	**1046**	(85c.) multicoloured	1·60	1·60
		a. Booklet pane. No. 3102×10	13·00	

No. 3102 was inscr 'P' and was originally valid for 85c. It was issued in booklets of ten, No. SB559, originally sold for $8.50.

(Des Ian Drolet. Litho C.B.N)

2015 (30 Jan). Black History Month. Nelson Mandela (1918–2013, President of South Africa 1994–1999) Commemoration. Fluorescent frame.

(a) Self-adhesive. Die-cut perf 13.
3103	**1047**	(85c.) multicoloured	1·60	1·60
		a. Booklet pane. No. 3103×10	13·00	

(b) Ordinary gum. Perf 12½×13.
MS3104 126×88 mm. $2.50 As No. 3103 but 40×41 mm.   4·50   5·00

No. 3103 was inscr 'P' and was originally valid for 85c. It was issued in booklets of ten, No. SB560, originally sold for $8.50.

1048 Canadian Flag

1049 Pansy 'Delta Premium Pure Light Blue'

(Des Kosta Tsetsekas and Defne Corbacioglu (Signals). Litho Lowe-Martin (No. 3105) or C.B.N. (No. **MS**3106))

2015 (15 Feb). 50th Anniversary of Canada's Flag. T **1048** and similar horiz design. Multicoloured. Self-adhesive. Fluorescent frame (No. 3105). Die-cut perf 13×13½ (No. 3105).
3105		(85c.) Type **1048**	1·60	1·60
		a. Booklet pane. No. 3105×10	13·00	

MS3106 141×91 mm. $5 Canadian flag (101×52 mm)..... 8·50   11·00

No. 3105 was inscr 'P' and was originally valid for 85c. It was issued in booklets of ten, No. SB561, originally sold for $8.50.

No. **MS**3104 has a fabric surface.

CANADA

(Des Laurie Koss (illustration), Marcio Morgado and Paul Haslip (HM and E Design). Litho Lowe-Martin).

2015 (2 Mar). Pansies. T **1049** and similar vert design. Multicoloured. Fluorescent frame.

(a) Self-adhesive coil stamps. Size 21×24 mm. Die-cut perf imperf×8.

3107	(85c.) Type **1049**	1·60	1·60
	a. Vert pair. Nos. 3107/3108	3·00	3·00
3108	(85c.) Pansy 'Midnight Glow'	1·60	1·60

(b) Self-adhesive booklet stamps. Size 26×32 mm. Die-cut perf 13½.

3109	(85c.) As Type **1049**	1·60	1·60
	a. Booklet pane. Nos. 3109/3110, each×5	13·00	
3110	(85c.) Pansy 'Midnight Glow'	1·60	1·60

(c) Ordinary gum. Sheet 120×85 mm. Perf 13.

MS3111 As Nos. 3109/10		3·00	3·50

Nos. 3107/3110 and the stamps within **MS**3111 were all inscr 'P' and originally sold for 85c.

Nos. 3107/3108 were issued in rolls of 50 with the two designs in sequence.

Nos. 3109/3110 were issued in booklets of ten, No. SB562, originally sold for $8.50. Booklet pane No. 3109a included ten small stickers.

(Des Stéphane Huot. Litho C.B.N)

2015 (8 Apr). 150 Years of Photography (3rd issue). Multicoloured designs as T **1003**. Fluorescent frame.

(a) Self-adhesive. Die-cut perf 13½.

3112	(85c.) Angels, Saint John Baptiste Day, Montreal, Quebec, 1962 (Sam Tata)	1·50	1·60
	a. Booklet pane. Nos. 3112/3116, each×2	12·00	
3113	(85c.) Southam Sisters, c. 1915–1919 (Harold Mortimer-Lamb)	1·50	1·60
3114	(85c.) Friends and Family and Trips in Front of Simpsons, 1936 (Conrad Poirier)	1·50	1·60
3115	(85c.) Isaac's First Swim, 1996 (Larry Towell)	1·50	1·60
3116	(85c.) Shoeshine Stand, 1974 (Nina Raginsky) (vert)	1·50	1·60
3117	$1.20 Alex Colville on the Tantramar Marshes, 1970 (Geoffrey James)	2·00	2·25
	a. Booklet pane. No. 3117×6	11·00	
3118	$2.50 La Voie Lactée (Geneviève Cadieux)	3·25	4·25
	a. Booklet pane. No. 3118×6	18·00	
3112/3118 Set of 7		11·00	12·00

(b) Ordinary gum. Perf 12½.

MS3119 150×75 mm. As Nos. 3112, 3114/3115 and 3117		6·00	8·00
MS3120 150×75 mm. As Nos. 3113, 3116 and 3118		6·00	8·00

Nos. 3112/3116 were inscr 'P' and were initially valid for 85c. They were issued in booklets, of ten, No. SB564, originally sold for $8.50.

No. 3117 was issued in $7.20 booklets, No. SB563.

No. 3118 was issued in $15 booklets, No. SB565.

1050 Tyrannosaurus rex

1051 Cat wearing Collar and Pot of Sunflowers ('spay/neuter')

(Des Julius Csotonyi (illustration) and Andrew Perro. Litho (Nos. 3121/3125) or recess and litho (No. 3126) Lowe-Martin)

2015 (13 Apr). Dinosaurs of Canada. T **1050** and similar square designs. Multicoloured. Self-adhesive. Fluorescent frame. Die-cut perf 13.

3121	(85c.) Type **1050**	1·60	1·60
	a. Booklet pane. Nos. 3121/3125, each×2	13·00	
3122	(85c.) Tylosaurus pembinensis	1·60	1·60
3123	(85c.) Ornithomimus edmontonicus	1·60	1·60
3124	(85c.) Chasmosaurus belli	1·60	1·60
3125	(85c.) Euoplocephalus tutus	1·60	1·60
3121/5 Set of 5		7·00	7·00
MS3126 160×65 mm. As Nos. 3121/3125		7·00	8·00

Nos. 3121/3125 and the stamps within **MS**3126 were all inscr 'P' and were originally sold for 85c.

Nos. 3121/3125 were issued in booklets of ten, No. SB566, originally sold for $8.50.

(Des Geneviève Simms (illustration) and Lara Minja, Lime Design. Litho Lowe-Martin)

2015 (2 May). Responsible Pet Guardianship. T **1051** and similar square designs. Multicoloured. Fluorescent frame.

(a) Self-adhesive. Die-cut perf 13.

3127	(85c.) Type **1051**	1·60	1·60
	a. Booklet pane. Nos. 3127/3131	13·00	
3128	(85c.) Dog chasing ball ('exercise')	1·60	1·60
3129	(85c.) Dog drinking water ('keep pets cool and hydrated')	1·60	1·60
3130	(85c.) Ginger cat ('vet care')	1·60	1·60
3131	(85c.) Cat wearing collar with ID tag ('identification')	1·60	1·60
3127/31 Set of 5		7·00	7·00

(b) Ordinary gum. Perf 13.

MS3132 148×105 mm. As Nos. 3127/3131		7·00	8·00

Nos. 3127/3131 and the stamps within **MS**3132 were all inscr 'P' and were originally valid for 85c.

Nos. 3127/3131 were issued in booklets of ten, No. SB567, originally sold for $8.50.

1052 Soldier's Silhouette and Crosses in Poppy

(Des q30 design inc. Litho Lowe-Martin)

2015 (3 May). Centenary of Poem In Flanders Fields by John McCrae. Fluorescent frame.

(a) Self-adhesive. Die-cut perf 13×13½.

3133	**1052**	(85c.) multicoloured	1·60	2·00
		a. Booklet pane. No. 3133×10	13·00	

(b) Ordinary gum. Perf 12½.

MS3134 165×241 mm. (85c.) As No. 3133×5		6·50	8·00

No. 3133 and the stamps within **MS**3134 were inscr 'P' and were originally valid for 85c. each.

No. 3133 was issued in booklets of ten, No. SB568, originally sold for $8.50.

No. **MS**3134 was originally sold in a plastic folder for $4.25.

1053 Players and Football

(Des Debbie Adams. Litho Lowe-Martin)

2015 (6 May). FIFA Women's World Cup Football, Canada. Self-adhesive. Fluorescent frame. Die-cut perf 13×13½.

3135	**1053**	(85c.) multicoloured	1·60	1·60
		a. Booklet pane. No. 3135×10	13·00	

No. 3135 was inscr 'P' and was originally valid for 85c. It was issued in booklets of ten, No. SB569, originally sold for $8.50. Booklet pane 3135a also contains ten small football stickers.

1054 Lightning, near Winnipeg, Manitoba

(Des Kosta Tsetsekas and Defne Corbacioglu, Signals. Litho C.B.N)

2015 (18 June). Weather Wonders. T **1054** and similar horiz designs. Multicoloured. Fluorescent frame.

(a) Self-adhesive. Die-cut perf 13.

3136	(85c.) Type **1054**	1·60	1·60
	a. Booklet pane. Nos. 3136/3140, each×2	13·00	
3137	(85c.) Sun dogs, Iqaluit, Nunavut	1·60	1·60
3138	(85c.) Hoar frost covering tree, near Beaumont, Alberta	1·60	1·60
3139	(85c.) Double rainbow, Saint-Gédéon, Quebec	1·60	1·60
3140	(85c.) Early morning fog at Cape Spear Lighthouse National Historic Site, Newfoundland and Labrador	1·60	1·60
3136/3140 Set of 5		7·00	7·00

(b) Ordinary gum. Perf 12½×13.
MS3141 130×95 mm. As Nos. 3136/40............... 8·00 8·50
Nos. 3136/3140 and the stamps within **MS**3141 were all inscr 'P' and were originally valid for 85c.
Nos. 3136/3140 were issued in booklets of ten, No. SB570, originally sold for $8.50.
See also Nos. 3423/**MS**3428.

1055 Hoodoos near Drumheller, Alberta (inscr 'Dinosaur Provincial Park')

1056 Dinosaur Provincial Park, Alberta

(Des Lara Minja, Lime Design. Litho Lowe-Martin)

2015 (3 July–21 Aug). UNESCO World Heritage Sites. T **1055**/**1056** and similar horiz designs. Multicoloured. Fluorescent frame.
(a) Self-adhesive. Die-cut perf 13×13½.
3142	$1.20 Type **1055**	35·00	20·00
	a. Booklet pane. Nos. 3142 and 3144/3145, each×2	55·00	
3143	$1.20 Type **1056** (21 Aug)	2·25	2·50
	a. Booklet pane. Nos. 3143/3145, each×2 (21 Aug)	11·00	
3144	$1.20 Red Bay Basque Whaling Station, Newfoundland	2·25	2·50
3145	$1.20 Wood Buffalo National Park, Alberta/Northern Territories	2·25	2·50
3146	$2.50 Waterton-Glacier International Peace Park, Alberta/Montana	4·25	4·75
	a. Booklet pane. Nos. 3146/3147, each×3	22·00	
3147	$2.50 Kluane/Wrangell-St. Elias/Glacier Bay/Tatshenshini-Alsek, British Columbia/Yukon	4·25	4·75
3142/3147 Set of 5 (excl. No. 3142)		13·50	15·00

(b) Ordinary gum. Perf 12½.
MS3148 130×100 mm. As Nos. 3142 and 3144/3147....... £130 £120
MS3149 130×100 mm. As Nos. 3143/3147 (21 Aug)........ 12·00 15·00
No. 3142 was withdrawn from sale on 6 July 2015, because it depicts a photograph which was not taken within Dinosaur Provincial Park.
Nos. 3142 and 3144/3145 were issued in $7.20 booklets, No. SB571.
Nos. 3143/3145 were issued in $7.20 booklets, No. SB572.
Nos. 3146/3147 were issued in $15 booklets, No SB573.

1057 Alice Munro and Town of Wingham, Ontario (birthplace)

1058 HMS *Erebus* trapped in Ice

(Des Marcio Morgado and Paul Haslip, HM and E Design. Litho Colour Innovations Inc)

2015 (10 July). Alice Munro (writer). Self-adhesive. Fluorescent frame. Die-cut perf 14×13½.
3150	**1057**	(85c.) multicoloured	1·60	1·60
		a. Booklet pane. No. 3150×10	13·00	

No. 3150 was inscr 'P' and was originally valid for 85c. It was issued in booklets of ten stamps, No. SB574, originally sold for $8.50.

(Des Michael Little (illlustration), Elisabeth Wurzinger (map) and Subplot Design Inc. Litho and embossed (85c.) or litho (others) Lowe-Martin)

2015 (6 Aug). 170th Anniversary of the Franklin Expedition. T **1058** and similar multicoloured designs. Multicoloured. Fluorescent frame.
*(a) Ordinary gum. Perf 12½ (3151/3152) or 13 (**MS**3153).*
3151	(85c.) Type **1058**	2·00	2·00
	a. Horiz pair. Nos. 3151/3152	4·00	4·00
3152	(85c.) Map of Arctic region of disappearance of Franklin Expedition	2·00	2·00
MS3153 103×66 mm. $2.50 Plan of HMS *Erebus* (48×24 mm)............		5·00	5·00

(b) Self-adhesive. Die-cut perf 13½×13 (vert) or 13×13½ (horiz).
3154	(85c.) As Type **1058**............	2·00	2·00
	a. Booklet pane. Nos. 3154/3155, each×5	17·00	
3155	(85c.) As No. 3152	2·00	2·00
3156	$2.50 Plan of HMS *Erebus* (48×24 mm)............	5·00	5·00
	a. Booklet pane. No. 3156×6............	26·00	

Nos. 3151/3152 and 3154/3155 were inscr 'P' and were originally valid for 85c. each.
Nos. 3151/3152 were printed together, *se-tenant*, as horizontal pairs in sheetlets of 16 containing 2 blocks of 8 (2×4) separated by a vertical gutter.
Nos. 3154/3155 were issued in booklets of ten, No. SB575, originally sold for $8.50.
No. 3156 was issued in $15 booklets, No. SB576.

1059 Queen Elizabeth II at Canada Day Celebration, Ottawa, 2010 and in 1953

(Des Entro Communications. Litho Lowe-Martin)

2015 (9 Sept). Queen Elizabeth II - A Historic Reign. Self-adhesive. Fluorescent frame. Die-cut perf 13×13½.
3157	**1059**	(85c.) multicoloured	1·75	1·60
		a. Booklet pane. No. 3157×10............	15·00	

No. 3157 was inscr 'P' and was originally valid for 85c. It was issued in booklets of ten, No. SB577, originally sold for $8.50.

(Des Sam Weber (illustrator), Lionel Gadoury and Kammy Ahuja - Context Creative. Litho C.B.N)

2015 (14 Sept). Haunted Canada (2nd series). Horiz designs as T **1033**. Multicoloured. Fluorescent frame.
(a) Self-adhesive. Die-cut perf 13½.
3158	(85c.) Brakeman, Vancouver, British Columbia..	1·60	1·60
	a. Booklet pane. Nos. 3158/3162, each×2 ...	13·00	
3159	(85c.) Ox cart, Red River, Manitoba	1·60	1·60
3160	(85c.) Marie-Josephte Corriveau, Lévis, Quebec	1·60	1·60
3161	(85c.) Caribou Hotel, Carcross, Yukon............	1·60	1·60
3162	(85c.) Halifax Citadel, Nova Scotia	1·60	1·60
3158/62 Set of 5............		7·00	7·00

(b) Ordinary gum. Perf 12½×13.
MS3163 127×73 mm. As Nos. 3158/3162......... 7·00 7·50
Nos. 3158/3162 and the stamps within **MS**3163 were inscr 'P' and were originally valid for 85c.
Nos. 3158/3162 were issued in booklets of ten, No. SB578, originally sold for $8.50.

1060 Girl reading to Young Boy

1061 Ken Dryden, Montreal Canadiens

(Des Marie-Eve Tremblay (illustrator), Lionel Gadoury, Kammy Ahuja and Joanna Poon, Context Creative. Litho C.B.N)

2015 (28 Sept). Canada Post Community Foundation. Self-adhesive. Fluorescent frame. Die-cut perf 13×12½.
3164	**1060**	(85c.) multicoloured	1·60	1·60
		a. Booklet pane. No. 3164×10............	13·00	

No. 3164 was issued in booklets of ten, No. SB579, originally sold for $9.50.

(Des Avi Dunkelman and Joe Gault, Mix Design. Litho or litho and embossed (3172 only) Lowe-Martin)

2015 (2 Oct). Great Canadian NHL Goalies. T **1061** and similar multicoloured designs. Fluorescent frame.
*(a) Self-adhesive. Die-cut perf 13×13½ (Nos. 3165/3170) or 13½×13 (No. **MS**3171).*
3165	(85c.) Type **1061**	1·60	1·60
	a. Booklet pane. Nos. 3165/3170............	7·50	
3166	(85c.) Tony Esposito, Chicago Blackhawks	1·60	1·60

CANADA

3167	(85c.) Johnny Bower, Toronto Maple Leafs		1·60	1·60
3168	(85c.) Lorne 'Gump' Worsley, Montreal Canadiens		1·60	1·60
3169	(85c.) Bernie Parent, Philadelphia Flyers		1·60	1·60
3170	(85c.) Martin Brodeur, New Jersey Devils		1·60	1·60
3165/3170	Set of 6		7·50	7·50

MS3171 Six sheets, each 64×90 mm. (a) $1.80 Ken Dryden, Montreal Canadiens. (b) $1.80 Tony Esposito, Black Hawks. (c) $1.80 Johnny Bower, Toronto Maple Leafs. (d) $1.80 Lorne 'Gump' Worsley, Montreal Canadiens. (e) $1.80 Bernie Parent, Philadelphia Flyers. (f) $1.80 Martin Brodeur, New Jersey Devils (all 52×78 mm)...... 16·00 20·00

(b) Ordinary gum. Perf 12½.

MS3172 160×160 mm. As Nos. 3165/3170........ 7·50 9·00

Nos. 3165/3170 and the stamps within **MS**3172 were all inscr 'P' and were originally valid for 85c. each.

Nos. 3165/3170 were issued in booklets of six, No. SB580, originally sold for $5.10.

Nos. **MS**3171a/**MS**3171f were sold as a pack of six miniature sheets in a foil wrapper for $10.80. They show the six Great Canadian Goalies on the ice during a match.

1062 *Adoration of the Magi* (detail) (Adriaen Isenbrandt)

1063 Moose wearing Hat and Scarf

(Des Louis Méthé. Litho)

2015 (2 Nov). Christmas (1st issue). Self-adhesive. Fluorescent frame. Die-cut perf 13.

3173	**1062**	(85c.) multicoloured	1·60	1·10
		a. Booklet pane. No. 3173×12	15·00	

No. 3173 was inscr 'P' and was originally valid for 85c. It was issued in booklets of 12 stamps, No. SB581, originally sold for $10.20.

(Des Gérard DuBois (illustrator) and Paprika. Litho Lowe-Martin)

2015 (2 Nov). Christmas (2nd issue). Animals. T **1063** and similar square designs. Multicoloured. Fluorescent frame.

(a) Self-adhesive. Die-cut perf 13.

3174	(85c.) Type **1063**	1·60	1·10
	a. Booklet pane. No. 3174×12	15·00	
3175	$1.20 Beaver wearing checked shirt and cap and holding holly in mouth	2·25	2·00
	a. Pane. No. 3175×6	11·00	
3176	$2.50 Polar bear wearing red hat and scarf	4·25	4·50
	a. Pane. No. 3176×6	22·00	
3174/6	Set of 3	7·00	7·00

(b) Ordinary gum. Perf 13½×13.

MS3177 84×54 mm. As Nos. 3174/3176............ 7·00 8·00

No. 3174 was inscr 'P' and was originally valid for 85c. It was issued in booklets of 12 stamps, No. SB582, originally sold for $10.20.

No. 3175 was issued in $7.20 panes of six stamps.
No. 3176 was issued in $15 panes of six stamps.

1064 Sun Wukong the Monkey King from novel *Journey to the West*

(Des Albert Ng and Linna Xu. Litho and embossed (3178/3180) or litho)

2016 (11 Jan–1 Feb). Chinese New Year. Year of the Monkey. Fluorescent frame.

(a) Ordinary gum. Perf 13.

3178	**1064**	(85c.) multicoloured	1·60	1·25

MS3179 118×90 mm. $2.50 Monkey King mask; $2.50 Deep green and gold ram (transition to Year of the Monkey) (1.2)............ 8·00 9·00

MS3180 41×140 mm. $2.50 Monkey King mask (1.2)......... 4·50 4·75

(b) Self-adhesive. Die-cut perf 13½.

3181	**1064**	(85c.) multicoloured	1·60	1·60
		a. Booklet pane. No. 3181×10	13·00	
3182		$2.50 Monkey King mask (1.2)	4·25	4·50
		a. Booklet pane. No. 3182×6	22·00	

Nos. 3178 and 3181 were inscr 'P' and were originally valid for 85c.
No. 3178 was issued in booklets of ten stamps, No. SB584, originally sold for $8.50.
No. 3182 was issued in $15 booklets, No. SB585.

1065 Members of No. 2 Construction Battalion, c. 1917

1066 *Hydrangea macrophylla* 'Endless Summer'

(Des Dennis Budgen (illustration) and Lara Minja (Lime Design Inc). Litho Lowe-Martin)

2016 (1 Feb). Black History Month. Centenary of No. 2 Construction Battalion. Self-adhesive. Fluorescent frame. Die-cut perf 13½.

3183	**1065**	(85c.) multicoloured	1·60	1·60
		a. Booklet pane. No. 3183×10	13·00	

No. 3183 was inscr 'P' and was originally valid for 85c. It was issued in booklets of ten, No. SB586, originally sold for $8.50.

(Des Marie-Élaine Cusson (illustrator), Benny Corrigan and Sputnik Design Partners Inc. Litho C.B.N)

2016 (1 Mar). Hydrangeas. T **1066** and similar vert design. Multicoloured. Fluorescent frame.

(a) Self-adhesive coil stamps. Size 20×24 mm. Die-cut perf imperf×8.

3184	(85c.) Type **1066**	1·60	1·60
	a. Horiz pair. Nos. 3184/3185	3·00	3·00
3185	(85c.) *Hydrangea arborescens* 'Annabelle'	1·60	1·60

(b) Self-adhesive booklet stamps. Size 26×32 mm. Die-cut perf 13.

3186	(85c.) As Type **1066**	1·60	1·60
	a. Booklet pane. Nos. 3186/3187, each×5	13·00	
3187	(85c.) As No. 3185	1·60	1·60

(c) Ordinary gum. Sheet 120×84 mm. Perf 13.

MS3188 As Nos. 3186/3187............ 3·00 3·25

Nos. 3184/3187 and the stamps within No. **MS**3188 were all inscr 'P' and originally valid for 85c. each.

Nos. 3184/3185 were issued in rolls of 50 with the two designs in sequence.

Nos. 3186/3187 were issued in booklets of ten, No. SB587, originally sold for $8.50.

Booklet pane 3186a included ten small circular stickers.

1067 Emblem with Venus Symbol as 'O' and 'T' of 'VOTE'

(Des Tétro. Litho Lowe-Martin)

2016 (8 Mar). Centenary of Women's Suffrage in Canada. Self-adhesive. Fluorescent frame. Die-cut perf 13½.

3189	**1067**	(85c.) black and gold	1·60	1·60
		a. Booklet pane. No. 3189×10	13·00	

No. 3189 was inscr 'P' and originally sold for 85c. each. It was issued in booklets of ten stamps, No. SB588, initially sold for $8.50.

(Des Stéphane Huot. Litho C.B.N)

2016 (13 Apr). 150 Years of Photography (4th issue). Fluorescent frame.

(a) Self-adhesive. Die-cut perf 13.

3190	(85c.) Toronto, 1960 (Lutz Dille)	1·60	1·60
	a. Booklet pane. Nos. 3190/3194, each×2	13·00	
3191	(85c.) Window, 1988 (Angela Grauerholz)	1·60	1·60
3192	(85c.) Freighter's Boat on the Banks of the Red River, MB, 1858 (Humphrey Lloyd Hime)	1·60	1·60
3193	(85c.) Victoria Bridge, Grand Trunk Railway, c. 1878 (Alexander Henderson)	1·60	1·60
3194	(85c.) Sans titre 0310 'La chambre noire, 2005–2010 (Michel Campeau) (*vert*)	1·60	1·60

CANADA

3195	$1.20 Climbing Mount Habel, c. 1909 (Byron Harmon)		2·00	2·25
	a. Booklet pane. No. 3195×6		11·00	
3196	$2.50 Grey Owl (Archibald Belaney 1888–1938), 1936 (Yousuf Karsh) (*vert*)		3·75	4·25
	a. Booklet pane. No. 3196×6		18·00	
3190/3196 Set of 7			12·00	12·00

(b) Ordinary gum. Perf 12½.

MS3197 149×75 mm. As Nos. 3190/3193		5·50	6·50
MS3198 149×75 mm. As Nos. 3194/3196		7·00	8·00

Nos. 3190/3194 were inscr 'P' and were initially valid for 85c. They were issued in booklets, of ten, No. SB590, originally sold for $8.50.

No. 3195 was issued in $7.20 booklets, No. SB589.

No. 3196 was issued in $15 booklets, No. SB591.

1068 Constitution-class Starship USS *Enterprise* NCC-1701

1069 Captain James T. Kirk (William Shatner) and USS *Enterprise*

(Des Signals Design Group. Lenticular Outer Aspect (3208) or litho Lowe-Martin (others). Lenticular Outer Aspect (**MS**3208) or litho Lowe-Martin (others))

2016 (5 May). 50th Anniversary of *Star Trek* (original TV series). T **1068**/**1069** and similar horiz designs. Multicoloured. Fluorescent frame (except **MS**3208).

*(a) As T **1068**.*
(i) Self-adhesive coil stamps. Die-cut perf 8×imperf.

3199	(85c.) Type **1068**		1·60	1·75
	a. Vert pair. Nos. 3199/3200		3·00	3·50
3200	(85c.) Klingon D-7 class battle cruiser		1·60	1·75

(ii) Ordinary gum. Perf 13½×13.

MS3201 126×73 mm. As Nos. 3199/3200		3·00	3·75

*(b) As T **1069**.*
(i) Self-adhesive booklet stamps. Die-cut perf 13×13½.

3202	(85c.) Type **1069**		1·60	1·60
	a. Booklet pane. Nos. 3202/3206, each×2		16·00	
3203	(85c.) Chief Engineer Montgomery 'Scotty' Scott (James Doohan)		1·60	1·60
3204	(85c.) Klingon Commander Kor (John Colicos)		1·60	1·60
3205	(85c.) First Officer Mr. Spock (Leonard Nimoy)		1·60	1·60
3206	(85c.) Chief Medical Officer Leonard 'Bones' McCoy (DeForest Kelley)		1·60	1·60
3202/3206 Set of 5			7·25	7·25

*(ii) Ordinary gum. Perf 13½ (No. **MS**3207) or 14½ (No. **MS**3208).*

MS3207 160×180 mm. (85c.) As Type **1069**; $1 As No. 3204; $1.20 As No. 3206; $1.80 As No. 3203; $2.50 As No. 3205 .... 13·00 15·00

MS3208 140×90 mm. $5 Crew on transporter platform of USS Enterprise; $5 Capt. Kirk and Mr. Spock in time portal *Guardian of Forever* .... 17·00 20·00

Nos. 3199/3206 were inscr 'P' and were originally valid for 85c. each.

Nos. 3199/3200 were issued in rolls of 50 with the two designs in sequence.

Nos. 3202/3206 were issued in booklets of ten, No. SB592, originally sold for $8.50.

Nos. 3199/3200 and stamps as within **MS**3207 were also issued in $19.95 premium booklets, No. SP1.

No. **MS**3207 was created using a lenticular process that makes the images appear to move when the miniature sheet is viewed from different angles.

See also Nos. 3261/3274.

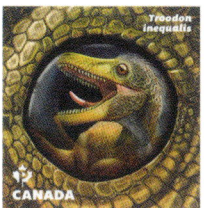

1070 Troodon Inequalis

(Des Sergey Krasovskiy (illustration) and Subplot Design Inc. Litho Lowe-Martin)

2016 (26 May). Dinosaurs of Canada (2nd series). T **1070** and similar square designs. Multicoloured.

(a) Self-adhesive. Die-cut perf 13.

3209	(85c.) Type **1070**	1·60	1·60
	a. Booklet pane. Nos. 3209/13, each ×2	13·00	
3210	(85c.) Cypretherium coarctatum	1·60	1·60
3211	(85c.) Dimetrodon borealis	1·60	1·60
3212	(85c.) Acrotholus audeti	1·60	1·60
3213	(85c.) Comox Valley elasmosaur	1·60	1·60
3209/3213 Set of 5		7·25	7·25

(b) Ordinary gum. Perf 13.

MS3214 159×100 mm. As Nos. 3209/3213		7·25	8·00

Nos. 3209/3213 and the stamps within **MS**3214 were all inscr 'P' and were originally valid for 85c.

Nos. 3209/3213 were issued in booklets of ten, No. SB593, originally sold for $8.50.

1071 Sharp-tailed Grouse (*Tympanuchus phasianellus*) (Saskatchewan)

(Des Keith Martin (illustration), Kosta Tsetsekas, Adrian Horvath, John Belisle and Signals Design. Litho Colour Innovations)

2016 (12 July). Birds of Canada (1st issue). T **1071** and similar vert designs. Multicoloured.

(a) Self-adhesive. Die-cut perf 13½.

3215	(85c.) Type **1071**	2·00	2·00
	a. Booklet pane. Nos. 3215/19, each ×2	16·00	
3216	(85c.) Great Horned Owl (*Bubo virginanus*) (Alberta)	2·00	2·00
3217	(85c.) Atlantic Puffin (*Fratercula arctica*) (Newfoundland)	2·00	2·00
3218	(85c.) Common Raven (*Corvus corax*) (Yukon Territory)	2·00	2·00
3219	(85c.) Rock Ptarmigan (*Lagopus muta*) (Nunavut)	2·00	2·00
3215/3219 Set of 5		9·00	9·00

(b) Ordinary gum. Perf 13.

MS3220 114×92 mm. As Nos. 3215/3219 .... 9·00 10·00

Nos. 3215/3219 and the stamps within No. **MS**3220 were all inscr 'P' and were originally valid for 85c.

Nos. 3215/3219 were issued in booklets of ten, No. SB594, originally sold for $8.50.

See also Nos. 3300/**MS**3305 and 3429/**MS**3434.

(Des Sam Weber (illustrator), Lionel Gadoury and Kammy Ahuja - Context Creative. Litho Colour Innovations, Toronto)

2016 (8 Sept). Haunted Canada (3rd series). Multicoloured. Fluorescent frame.

(a) Self-adhesive. Die-cut perf 13½.

3221	(85c.) Bell Island hag, Newfoundland	1·25	1·40
	a. Booklet pane. Nos. 3221/5, each ×2	10·00	
3222	(85c.) Dungarvon Whooper, New Brunswick	1·25	1·40
3223	(85c.) Lady in white, Montmorency Falls, Quebec	1·25	1·40
3224	(85c.) Winter Garden Theatre, Toronto	1·25	1·40
3225	(85c.) Phantom bell ringers, Kirk of St James, Charlottetown	1·25	1·40
3221/3225 Set of 5		5·50	6·25

(b) Ordinary gum. Perf 13.

MS3226 127×73 mm. As Nos. 3221/3225 .... 5·50 6·50

Nos. 3221/3225 and the stamps within No. **MS**3226 were inscr 'P' and were originally valid for 85c. each.

Nos. 3221/3225 were issued in booklets of ten, No. SB595, originally sold for $8.50.

1072 Sidney Crosby

CANADA

(Des Avi Dunkelman and Joe Gault. Litho Lowe-Martin)

2016 (23 Sept). Great Canadian NHL Forwards. Fluorescent frame.
(a) Self-adhesive. Die-cut perf 13×13½ (3227/3232) or 13½×13 (MS3233a/MS3233f).

3227	(85c.) Type **1072**		1·25	1·40
	a. Booklet pane. No. 3227×6		6·50	
3228	(85c.) Phil Esposito		1·25	1·40
3229	(85c.) Guy Lafleur		1·25	1·40
3230	(85c.) Steve Yzerman		1·25	1·40
3231	(85c.) Mark Messier		1·25	1·40
3232	(85c.) Darryl Sittler		1·25	1·40
3227/3232 Set of 6			6·50	7·50
MS3233 Six sheets, each 64×90 mm. (a) $1.80 Sidney Crosby. (b) $1.80 Phil Esposito. (c) $1.80 Guy Lafleur. (d) $1.80 Steve Yzerman. (e) $1.80 Mark Messier. (f) $1.80 Daryl Sittler (all 48×74 mm)..........			15·00	22·00

(b) Ordinary gum. Perf 12½×13.

MS3234 160×160 mm. As Nos. 3227/3232................... 6·50 8·00

Nos. 3227/3232 and the stamps within No. **MS**3234 were all inscr 'P' and were originally valid for 85c. each.

Nos. 3227/3232 were issued in booklets of six, No. SB596, originally sold for $5.10.

Nos. **MS**3233a/**MS**3233f were sold as a pack of six miniature sheets in a foil wrapper for $10.80. They show the six Great Canadian Forwards on the ice.

1073 Bird with Multicoloured Wings   **1074** Virgin and Child

(Des Andrew Lewis. Litho Lowe-Martin)

2016 (26 Sept). Canada Post Community Foundation. Self-adhesive. Fluorescent frame. Die-cut perf 13½.

3235	(85c.)+10c. multicoloured (blue background) ...	1·40	1·60
	a. Booklet pane. Nos. 3235/6, each ×2	11·00	
3236	(85c.)+10c. multicoloured (green background)	1·40	1·60

Nos. 3235/3236 were inscr 'P+10' and were originally valid for 85c. They were issued in booklets of ten, No. SB597, originally sold for $9.50, which includes a 10c. charity premium on each stamp.

(Des Louise Méthé. Litho CBN)

2016 (1 Nov). Christmas (1st issue). Self-adhesive. Fluorescent frame. Die-cut perf 13.

3237	**1074**	(85c.) multicoloured	1·60	1·25
		a. Booklet pane. No. 3237×12	15·00	

No. 3237 was inscr 'P' and was originally valid for 85c.

No. 3237 was issued in booklets of 12 stamps, No. SB598, originally sold for $10.20.

1075 Santa and Tree

(Des Rolf Harder (illustration) and Hélène L'Heureux. Litho CBN)

2016 (1 Nov). Christmas (2nd issue). T **1075** and similar vert designs. Multicoloured. Fluorescent frame.

(a) Self-adhesive. Die-cut perf 13.

3238	(85c.) Type **1075**	1·60	1·25
	a. Booklet pane. No. 3238×12	15·00	
3239	$1.20 Christmas tree wearing Santa hat	2·00	2·50
	a. Pane. No. 3239×6	10·00	
3240	$2.50 Peace dove and Christmas tree with red lights	10·00	4·75
	a. Pane. No. 3240×6	17·00	
3238/3240 Set of 3		6·25	7·00

(b) Ordinary gum. Perf 12½.

MS3241 85×54 mm. As Nos. 3238/3240......................... 6·50 8·00

No. 3238 was inscr 'P' and was originally valid for 85c. It was issued in booklets of 12 stamps, No. SB599, originally sold for $10.20.

No. 3239 was issued in $7.20 panes of six stamps.

No. 3240 was issued in $15 panes of six stamps.

1076 Rooster

(Des Albert Ng (calligraphy) and Paprika. Litho and embossed (**MS**3243) or litho (others) Lowe-Martin)

2017 (9 Jan). Chinese New Year. Year of the Rooster. T **1076** and similar square designs. Multicoloured. Fluorescent frame or partial fluorescent frame.

(a) Ordinary gum. Perf 12½×13 or 13×12½ (3242) or 12½ (MS3243/3244).

3242	(85c.) Type **1076**	1·75	1·60
	a. Perf 13×12½	1·50	1·40
MS3243 118×90 mm. $2.50 Head of rooster; $2.50 Monkey King mask (transition to Year of the Rooster)..		7·00	8·00
MS3244 40×140 mm. $2.50 Head of rooster................		3·75	4·50

(b) Self-adhesive. Die-cut perf 13½.

3245	(85c.) As Type **1076**	1·50	1·40
	a. Booklet pane. No. 3245×10	12·00	
3246	$2.50 Head of rooster	3·50	4·00
	a. Booklet pane. No. 3246×6	17·00	

Nos. 3242 and 3245 were inscr 'P' and were originally valid for 85c. each. No. 3242 was printed in panes of 25, perforated 12½×13, in which the stamps were laid upright, sideways left, sideways right and inverted. Individual stamps were therefore perforated 12½×13 (No. 3242) or 13×12½ (No. 3242a) according to how they were laid in the pane.

No. 3245 was issued in booklets of ten, No. SB600, originally sold for $8.50.

No. 3246 was issued in $15 booklets, No. SB601.

1077 Mathieu da Costa   **1078** Scene from *Filumena*, Act II Scene 9

(Des Ron Dollekamp (illustration) and Andrew Perro. Litho CBN)

2017 (1 Feb). Black History Month. Mathieu da Costa (17th-century interpreter). Self-adhesive. Fluorescent frame. Die-cut perf 13.

3247	(85c.) multicoloured	1·50	1·40
	a. Booklet pane. No. 3247×10	12·00	

No. 3247 was inscr 'P' and was originally valid for 85c. It was issued in booklets of ten, No. SB603, which were originally sold for $8.50.

(Des Peter Strain (illustration) and Parcel Design. Litho Colour Innovations)

2017 (4 Feb). Canadian Opera. T **1078** and similar horiz designs. Multicoloured. Self-adhesive. Fluorescent frame*.

(a) Self-adhesive. Die-cut perf 13½.

3248	(85c.) Type **1078**	1·90	1·90
	a. Booklet pane. Nos. 3248/3252, each×2	16·00	
3249	(85c.) Gerald Finley (bass-baritone)	1·90	1·90
3250	(85c.) Adrianne Pieczonka (soprano)	1·90	1·90
3251	(85c.) Irving Guttman (director)	1·90	1·90
3252	(85c.) Scene from opera *Louis Riel* Act III Scenes 3 and 6..	1·90	1·90
3248/3252 Set of 5		8·50	8·50

(b) Ordinary gum. Perf 13.

MS3253 175×60 mm. As Nos. 3248/3252......................... 8·50 9·00

Nos. 3248/3252 and the stamps within No. **MS**3253 were inscr 'P' and were originally valid for 85c. each.

Nos. 3248/3252 were issued in booklets of ten, No. SB604, originally sold for $8.50.

Nos. 3248/3252 and the stamps within No. **MS**3253 had a fluorescent frame around the five designs, giving No. 3248 a fluorescent frame at top, left and bottom, No. 3252 a fluorescent frame at top, right and bottom and Nos. 3249/3251 a fluorescent frame only at top and bottom.

CANADA

1079 Fleabane
(*Erigeron speciosus*)

(Des Debbie Adams. Litho Lowe-Martin)

2017 (1 Mar). Daisies. T **1079** and similar vert design. Multicoloured. Fluorescent bands at left and right.

(a) Self-adhesive coil stamps. Die-cut perf 8.
3254	(85c.) Type **1079**	1·40	1·40
	a. Horiz pair. Nos. 3254/5	2·75	2·75
3255	(85c.) Lakeside Daisies (*Tetraneuris herbacea*) (yellow daisies)	1·40	1·40

(b) Self-adhesive booklet stamps. Die-cut perf 13½.
3256	(85c.) Type **1079**	1·40	1·40
	a. Booklet pane. Nos. 3256/7, each ×5	11·00	
3257	(85c.) Lakeside Daisies (*Tetraneuris herbacea*) (yellow daisies)	1·40	1·40

(c) Ordinary gum. Perf 13.
MS3258	120×84 mm. As Nos. 3254/3255	2·75	3·25

Nos. 3254/3257 and the stamps within No. **MS**3258 were all inscr 'P' and originally sold for 85c. each.
Nos. 3254/3255 were issued in rolls of 50 with the two designs in sequence.
Nos. 3256/3257 were issued in booklets of ten, No. SB605, originally sold for $8.50. Booklet pane No. 3256a included ten small circular stickers.

1080 Statue and Twin Pillars of Canadian National Vimy Memorial

(Des Susan Scott and Sarah Bougault. Recess and litho (**MS**3260) or litho (other) Colour Innovations)

2017 (8 Apr). Centenary of Battle of Vimy Ridge, France. T **1080** and similar horiz design. Multicoloured. Fluorescent frame.

(a) Self-adhesive. Die-cut perf 13½.
3259	(85c.) Type **1080**	1·90	1·60
	a. Booklet pane. No. 3259×10	15·00	

(b) Ordinary gum. Perf 13.
MS3260	130×85 mm. $2.50 As Type **1080**; $2.50 *Canada Bereft* statue of cloaked woman and flags of France and Canada (both 35×27 mm)	11·00	11·00

No. 3259 was inscr. 'P' and issued in booklets of ten, No. SB606, originally sold for $8.50.
Stamps of a similar design were issued by France.

1081 *Galileo* Shuttlecraft

1082 Admiral James T. Kirk v Khan Noonien Singh

1083 Borg Cube

(Des Adrian Horvath and Kosta Tsetsekas (Signals Design Group). Litho Lowe-Martin)

2017 (27 Apr). *Star Trek* (2nd series). Horiz designs as Types **1081**/**1083**. Multicoloured. Fluorescent frame (except No. 3274).

(a) Self-adhesive.
*(i) T **1081**. Die-cut perf 8×imperf (No. 3261) or 13 (No. 3262).*
3261	(85c.) Type **1081**	2·00	2·00
3262	(85c.) Type **1081**	2·00	2·00
	a. Booklet pane. No. 3262	4·50	
3261/3267	Set of 5		

*(ii) Booklet stamps as T **1082**. Die-cut perf 13×13½.*
3263	(85c.) Type **1082**	2·00	2·00
	a. Booklet pane. Nos. 3263/7, each ×2	16·00	
3264	(85c.) Captain Jean-Luc Picard v Locutus of Borg	2·00	2·00
3265	(85c.) Captain Benjamin Sisko v Dukat	2·00	2·00
3266	(85c.) Captain Kathryn Janeway v the Borg Queen	2·00	2·00
3267	(85c.) Captain Jonathan Archer v Commander Dolim	2·00	2·00
Set of 6		9·00	9·00

(b) Ordinary gum.
*(i) As T **1082**. Perf 13½.*
3268	(85c.) As No. 3263	2·00	2·00
	a. Booklet pane. No. 3268×3	3·75	
	b. Booklet pane. Nos. 3268/72	9·50	
3269	$1 As No. 3267	1·60	1·75
	a. Booklet pane. Nos. 3269/72	8·00	
3270	$1.20 As No. 3266	1·90	2·00
3271	$1.80 As No. 3265	2·50	3·00
3272	$2.50 As No. 3264	3·50	4·00
3268/3272	Set of 5	10·00	10·00
MS3273	160×210 mm. Nos. 3268/3272	12·00	14·00

*(ii) T **1083**. Perf 13.*
3274	$5 Type **1083**	9·00	10·00
	a. Booklet pane. No. 3274	10·00	

Nos. 3261/3268 were inscr. 'P' and were originally valid for 85c.
No. 3261 was issued in coils of 50.
Nos. 3263/3267 were issued in booklets of ten, No. SB607, originally sold for $8.50.
Nos. 3262 and 3274 were only issued in $21.95 booklets, No. SB608.
Nos. 3268/3272 were issued in booklet No. SB608, and in **MS**3273.

1084 Sir Jackie Stewart

(Des Marie Bergeron (illustration) and Paprika. Litho Colour Innovations)

2017 (16 May). 50th Anniversary of Formula 1 Motor Racing in Canada. T **1084** and similar vert designs. Fluorescent frame.

(a) Self-adhesive. Die-cut perf 16½.
3275	(85c.) Type **1084**	1·40	1·40
	a. Booklet pane. Nos. 3275/3279, each ×2	11·00	
3276	(85c.) Gilles Villeneuve	1·40	1·40
3277	(85c.) Ayrton Senna	1·40	1·40
3278	(85c.) Michael Schumacher	1·40	1·40
3279	(85c.) Lewis Hamilton	1·40	1·40
3275/3279	Set of 5	6·25	6·25

CANADA

(b) Ordinary gum. Perf 13.
MS3280 162×201 mm. As Nos. 3275/3279...................... 6·25 7·00

Nos. 3275/3279 and the stamps within No. **MS**3280 were inscr. 'P' and were originally valid for 85c. each.

Nos. 3275/3279 were issued in booklets of ten, No. SB609, originally sold for $8.50.

1085 Pointed Arch, Crescent Moon and Star

1086 Habitat 67 Complex by Moshe Safdie, Expo 67, Montreal

(Des Doreen Colonello and Erin Enns (Entro Communications). Litho Colour Innovations).

2017 (24 May). Eid. Self-adhesive. Fluorescent frame. Die-cut perf 13½×13.
3281 (85c.) multicoloured .... 1·40 1·40
     a. Booklet pane. No. 3281×10 .... 11·00

No. 3281 was inscr 'P' and was originally valid for 85c. It was issued in booklets of ten, No. SB610, originally sold for $8.50.

(Des Subplot Design Inc. Litho Lowe-Martin)

2017 (1 June). 150th Anniversary of the Confederation of Canada. T **1086** and similar maple-leaf shaped designs. Multicoloured. Fluorescent frame.

(a) Self-adhesive. Die-cut in shape of maple-leaf.
3282 (85c.) Type **1086** .... 2·00 2·25
      a. Booklet pane. Nos. 3282/3291 .... 18·00
3283 (85c.) Trans-Canada Highway, completed
            1971 .... 2·00 2·25
3284 (85c.) Inuit woman (creation of Nunavut
            territory), 1999 .... 2·00 2·25
      a. Booklet pane. No. 3284×8 .... 12·00
3285 (85c.) Flag (Marriage Equality), 2005 .. 2·00 2·25
      a. Booklet pane. No. 3285×8 .... 12·00
3286 (85c.) Paul Henderson scoring goal (Canada–
            USSR ice hockey Summit Series), 1972. 2·00 2·25
3287 (85c.) Terry Fox running Marathon of Hope,
            1980 .... 2·00 2·25
3288 (85c.) Canadarm, 1981 .... 2·00 2·25
3289 (85c.) Arms (Constitution Act, 1982) ... 2·00 2·25
3290 (85c.) Alexandre Bilodeau (gold medal,
            men's moguls, 2010) (Olympic Games
            in Canada, 1976, 1988, 2010) .... 2·00 2·25
3291 (85c.) Skier Lauren Woolstencroft (five
            paralympic golds, 2010) (Paralympic
            Games in Canada, 1976, 2010) .... 2·00 2·25
3282/3291 Set of 10 .... 18·00 20·00

(b) Ordinary gum. Perf 14.
MS3292 155×211 mm. As Nos. 3282/3291 .... 18·00 22·00

Nos. 3282/3291 and the stamps within No. **MS**3292 were inscr. 'P' and were originally valid for 85c. each.

Nos. 3282/3291 were issued in booklets containing the ten designs, No. SB613, originally sold for $8.50.

Nos. 3284/3285 were also sold in separate booklets of eight, Nos. SB611/SB612, originally sold for $6.80.

No. **MS**3292 contains ten circular 45 mm diameter stamps containing maple-leaf designs as T **1086**.

(Des Stéphane Huot. Litho CBN)

2017 (4 July). 150 Years of Photography (5th issue). Multicoloured designs as T **1003**. Fluorescent frame.

(a) Self-adhesive. Die-cut perf 13½.
3293 (85c.) Ti-Noir la jeunesse, la violoneux aveugle,
            1972 (Clare Beaugrand-Champagne).... 1·25 1·50
      a. Booklet pane. Nos. 3293/3297, each ×2 10·00
3294 (85c.) Enlacées, Montréal, 1994 (Gilbert
            Duclos) (vert) .... 1·25 1·50
3295 (85c.) Ontario, Canada, 1989 (Robert
            Bourdeau).................................. 1·25 1·50
3296 (85c.) Construction of the Parliament
            Buildings, Centre Block, circa 1862
            (Samuel McLaughlin) .... 1·25 1·50
3297 (85c.) Sir John A. Macdonald, circa 1883
            (William James Topley) (vert) .... 1·25 1·50
3293/3297 Set of 5 .... 5·50 6·50

(b) Ordinary gum. Perf 12½.
MS3298 150×75 mm. As Nos. 3293 and 3295/3296........ 3·25 4·00
MS3299 150×75 mm. As Nos. 3294 and 3297................ 3·00 4·00

Nos. 3293/3297 and the stamps within Nos. **MS**3298/**MS**3299 were inscr. all 'P' and were originally valid for 85c. each.

Nos. 3293/3297 were issued in booklets of ten, No. SB614, originally sold for $8.50.

(Des Keith Martin (illustration) and Mike Savage (Signals Design). Litho CBN)

2017 (1 Aug). Birds of Canada (2nd issue). Vert designs as T **1071**. Multicoloured. Partial fluorescent frames.

(a) Self-adhesive. Die-cut perf 13.
3300 (85c.) Osprey (*Pandion haliaetus*) (Nova
            Scotia)...................................... 2·00 2·00
      a. Booklet pane. Nos. 3300/3304, each ×2 16·00
3302 (85c.) Blue Jay (*Cyanocitta cristata*) (Prince
            Edward Island) .... 2·00 2·00
3301 (85c.) Gyrfalcon (*Falco rusticolus*) (Northwest
            Territories)................................. 2·00 2·00
3303 (85c.) Great Grey Owl (*Strix nebulosa*)
            (Manitoba) .... 2·00 2·00
3304 (85c.) Common Loon (*Gavia immer*) (Ontario) 2·00 2·00
3300/3304 Set of 5 .... 9·00 9·00

(b) Ordinary gum. Perf 13.
MS3305 114×92 mm. As Nos. 3300/3304....................... 9·00 10·00

Nos. 3300/3304 and the stamps within No. **MS**3305 were inscr. 'P' and were originally valid for 85c. each.

Nos. 3300/3304 were issued in booklets of ten, No. SB615, originally sold for $8.50.

1087 Diwali Lamp

(Des Doreen Colonello, Entro Communications. Litho Lowe-Martin)

2017 (21 Sept). Diwali. T **1087** and similar vert design. Multicoloured. Partial fluorescent frame (at sides and foot).

(a) Self-adhesive. Die-cut perf 13½.
3306 (85c.) Type **1087** .... 1·50 1·50
      a. Booklet pane. Nos. 3306/3307, each ×5 11·00
3307 (85c.) Diwali lamp (*different*).............. 1·50 1·50

(b) Ordinary gum. Perf 13.
MS3308 75×100 mm. $2.50 As Type **1087**; India 25r. as
      No. 3307 (sold at $3)............................... 5·00 6·00

Nos. 3306/3307 were inscr. 'P' and were originally valid for 85c.
Nos. 3306/3307 were issued in booklets of ten, No. SB616, originally sold for $8.50.

The miniature sheet No. **MS**3300 contains a $2.50 Canada stamp and a 25r. India stamp. India Post issued 5r. and 25r. stamps in the same designs on the same day, and also a miniature sheet containing the two 5r. and 25r. stamps. This India miniature sheet was also sold by Canada Post for 60c.

1088 Cats inside Cat   **1089** Maurice Richard, Montreal Canadiens

(Des Andrew Lewis. Litho Lowe-Martin)

2017 (25 Sept). Canada Post Community Foundation. T **1088** and similar square design. Multicoloured. Self-adhesive. Fluorescent frame. Die-cut perf 13½.

3309	(85c.)+10c. Type **1088**	2·00	2·00
	a. Booklet pane. Nos. 3309/3310, each ×5	14·00	
3310	(85c.)+10c. As Type **1088** but green background	2·00	2·00

Nos. 3309/3310 were inscr. 'P+10' and were originally valid for 85c. They were issued in booklets of ten, No. SB617, originally sold for $9.50, a $1 charity premium.

(Des Avi Dunkelman and Joseph Gault (MIX Design Group). Litho (**MS**3318 also embossed) Colour Innovations)

2017 (28 Sept). Canadian Hockey Legends. T **1089** and similar multicoloured designs. Multicoloured.

(a) Self-adhesive. Die-cut perf 13×13½ (3311/16) or 13½×13 (MS3317).

3311	(85c.) Type **1089**	1·75	1·50
	a. Booklet pane. Nos. 3311/3316	6·50	
3312	(85c.) Jean Béliveau, Montreal Canadiens	1·75	1·50
3313	(85c.) Gordie Howe, Detroit Red Wings	1·75	1·50
3314	(85c.) Bobby Orr, Boston Bruins	1·75	1·50
3315	(85c.) Mario Lemieux, Pittsburgh Penguins	1·75	1·50
3316	(85c.) Wayne Gretzky, Edmonton Oilers	1·75	1·50
3311/3316	Set of 6	9·50	8·00
MS3317	Six sheets, each 64×91 mm. (a) $1.80 Maurice Richard, Montreal Canadiens. (b) $1.80 Jean Béliveau, Montreal Canadiens. (c) $1.80 Gordie Howe, Detroit Red Wings. (d) $1.80 Bobby Orr, Boston Bruins. (e) $1.80 Mario Lemieux, Pittsburgh Penguins. (f) Wayne Gretzky, Edmonton Oilers (all 52×78 mm)	16·00	20·00

(b) Ordinary gum. Perf 12½×13.

MS3318 160×160 mm. As Nos. 3311/3316 .... 6·50 8·00

Nos. **MS**3317a/**MS**3317f were sold as a pack of six miniature sheets in a foil wrapper for $10.80. They show the six Canadian Hockey Legends with the Lord Stanley's Cup trophy.

Nos. 3311/**MS**3318 commemorate the Centenary of the National Hockey League.

Nos. 3311/3316 and the stamps within **MS**3318 were all inscr 'P' and were originally valid for 85c. each.

Nos. 3311/3316 were issued in booklets of six, No. SB618, originally sold for $5.10.

No. **MS**3318 was originally sold for $5.10.

1091 Toronto Maple Leafs   **1092** Toronto Maple Leafs Centenary Logo and '100'

(Des Lionel Gadoury and Dave Hurds (Context Creative). Litho Lowe-Martin (No. 3322) or Colour Innovations (Nos. 3323/**MS**3324))

2017 (24 Oct). Centenary of the Toronto Maple Leafs (ice hockey team). Silver, deep blue and black (Nos. 3322/3323) or multicoloured (No. **MS**3324).

*(a) Self-adhesive coil stamps as T **1091**. Die-cut.*

3322	(85c.) Type **1091**	1·40	1·50

*(b) Self-adhesive booklet stamps as T **1092**. Die-cut perf 13½.*

3323	(85c.) Type **1092**	1·40	1·50
	a. Booklet pane. Nos. 3323×10	11·00	

(c) Ordinary gum. Perf 13×13½.

MS3324 140×95 mm. $5 Fabric Toronto Maple Leafs crest on Ted 'Teeder' Kennedy's sweater (100×72 mm) .... 8·00 9·00

Nos. 3322/3323 were inscr. 'P' and were originally valid for 85c. each.

No. 3323 was issued in booklets of ten, No. SB620, originally sold for $8.50.

No. **MS**3324 had a fabric Toronto Maple Leafs crest applied to the miniature sheet and was only issued in a folder.

1090 Modern Pond Hockey Player

(Des Roy White (Subplot Design Inc.) and Brad Pickard (retouching). Litho Lowe-Martin)

2017 (20 Oct). History of Hockey. T **1090** and similar vert design. Multicoloured. Fluorescent frame (around *tête-bêche* pair).

(a) Self-adhesive. Die-cut perf 13½×13.

3319	(85c.) Type **1090**	1·40	2·00
	a. Booklet pane. Nos. 3319/3320, each ×5	11·00	
3320	(85c.) Pond hockey player, 1930s/1940s	1·40	2·00

(b) Ordinary gum. Perf 13.

MS3321 130×90 mm. As Nos. 3319/3320 .... 4·00 4·50

Nos. 3319/3320 and the stamps within No. **MS**3321 were inscr. 'P' and were originally valid for 85c. each.

Nos. 3319/3320 were issued in booklets of ten, No. SB619, originally sold for $8.50.

Nos. 3319/3320 and the stamps within No. **MS**3321 were laid in *tête-bêche* pairs within the booklet and miniature sheet. The fluorescent frame was around the *tête-bêche* pair, giving stamps with a fluorescent frame on three sides.

Similar stamps were issued by the United States of America.

1093 The Adoration of the Shepherds (oil on panel) (attr. Tommaso di Stefano Lunetti)   **1094** Polar Bear

(Des Louise Méthé. Litho Lowe-Martin)

2017 (3 Nov). Christmas (1st issue). Self-adhesive. Fluorescent frame. Die-cut perf 13½.

3325	(85c.) multicoloured	1·40	1·25
	a. Booklet pane. No. 3325×12	12·00	

No. 3325 was inscr. 'P' and was originally valid for 85c. It was issued in booklets of 12, No. SB621, originally sold for $10.20.

(Des Christiane Beauregarde (illustration) and Hélène L'Heureux. Litho Colour Innovations)

2017 (3 Nov). Christmas (2nd issue). T **1094** and similar vert designs. Multicoloured. Fluorescent frame.

(a) Self-adhesive. Die-cut perf 13.

3326	(85c.) Type **1094**	1·40	1·25
	a. Booklet pane. No. 3326×12	12·00	
3327	$1.20 Red Cardinal	1·90	2·25
	a. Pane. No. 3327×6	10·00	
3328	$2.50 Caribou	3·75	4·00
	a. Pane. No. 3328×6	18·00	
3326/3328	Set of 3	6·25	6·75

(b) Ordinary gum. Perf 13½×13.

MS3329 85×54 mm. As Nos. 3326/3368 .... 6·25 8·00

No. 3326 was inscr 'P' and was originally valid for 85c. It was issued in booklets of 12 stamps, No. SB622, originally sold for $10.20.

No. 3327 was issued in $7.20 panes of six stamps.

No. 3328 was issued in $15 panes of six stamps.

CANADA

1095 Front Page of *The Halifax Herald* and *Mont-Blanc* (ship carrying munitions) before Collision with *Imo*

1096 Menorah

(Des Mike Little (illustration) and Larry Burke and Anna Stredulinsky (Burke & Burke). Litho Colour Innovations)

2017 (6 Nov). Centenary of Halifax Explosion. Self-adhesive. Fluorescent frame. Die-cut perf 13½.

3330	**1095**	(85c.) multicoloured	1·50	1·50
		a. Booklet pane. No. 3330×10	12·00	

No. 3330 was inscr. 'P' and was originally valid for 85c. It was issued in booklets of ten stamps, No. SB623, originally sold for $8.50.

(Des Angela Carter (Entro Communications). Litho Lowe-Martin)

2017 (20 Nov). Hanukkah. Self-adhesive. Partial fluorescent frame (at sides and foot). Die-cut perf 13×13½.

3331	**1096**	(85c.) multicoloured	1·50	1·50
		a. Booklet pane. No. 3331×10	12·00	

No. 3331 was originally valid for 85c. It was issued in booklets of ten, No. SB624, originally sold for $8.50.

A version of this booklet showing a Star of David on the cover was withdrawn before the issue date of 14 November 2017, but it is believed that a few were sold to collectors. No. SB624 is the redesigned version showing the Menorah cover, which was issued on 20 November 2017.

1097 Dog (Pekinese) on Lantern

(Des Meimei Mao (illustration) and Subplot Design Inc. Calligraphy by Albert Ng. Litho (Nos. 3332/**MS**3334 also embossed) Lowe Martin)

2018 (15 Jan). Chinese New Year. Year of the Dog. T **1097** and similar square designs. Multicoloured. Fluorescent frame (85c.) or fluorescent frame on three sides (left, right and foot) ($2.50).

(a) Ordinary gum. Perf 12½.

3332	(85c.) Type **1097**	1·50	1·50
MS3333	119×90 mm. $2.50 Dog (Saluki-type) on lantern; $2.50 Head of rooster	7·00	8·00
MS3334	40×140 mm. $2.50 Dog (Saluki type) on lantern	4·00	4·50

(b) Self-adhesive. Die-cut perf 13½.

3335	(85c.) As Type **1097**	1·50	1·50
	a. Booklet pane. No. 3335×10	12·00	
3336	$2.50 Dog (Saluki type) on lantern	4·00	4·50
	a. Booklet pane. No. 3336×6	18·00	

Nos. 3332 and 3335 were inscr 'P' and were originally valid for 85c. No. 3332 was issued in booklets of ten, No. BS625, originally sold for $8.50.
No. 3336 was issued in $15 booklets, No. SB626.

1098 St John's (Newfoundland and Labrador)

1099 Hopewell Rocks (New Brunswick)

1100 MacMillan Provincial Park (British Columbia)

1101 Parc National de l'Île–Bonaventure-et-du-Rocher-Percé, Quebec

1102 Prince Edward Island National Park

1103 Tombstone Territorial Park, Yukon

1104 Athabasca Falls, Jasper National Park, Alberta

1105 Quttinipaaq National Park, Nunavut

1106 Mahone Bay, Nova Scotia

1107 Little Limestone Lake, Provincial Park, Manitoba

1108 Abraham Lake, Alberta

1109 Athabasca Sand Dunes Provincial Park, Saskatchewan

1110 Herschel Island-Qikiqtaruk Territorial Park, Yukon

1111 French River, Prince Edward Island

1112 Îles de la Madeleine, Quebec

1113 Pisew Falls, Provincial Park, Manitoba

1114 Castle Butte, Big Muddy Badlands, Saskatchewan

1115 Carcajou Falls, Northwest Territories

1116 Point Pelee Provincial Park, Ontario

1117 Smoke Lake, Algonquin Provincial Park, Ontario

1118 Carcajou Falls, NWT

1119 Nááts'įhch'oh National Park Reserve, NWT

1120 Mingan Archipelago National Park Reserve, Quebec

CANADA

1121 Swallowtail Lighthouse, Grand Manan Island, New Brunswick

1122 Arctic Bay, Nunavut

1123 Iceberg Alley, near Ferryland, Newfoundland

1124 Cabot Trail, Cape Breton Island, Nova Scotia

(Des Stéphane Huot. Litho Lowe-Martin)

2018 (15 Jan)–**20**. From Far and Wide. Fluorescent frame.

(a) Self-adhesive coil stamps. Die-cut perf 13½ ($1, $1.05, $1.07) or 8×imperf (others).

3337	**1098**	(85c.) multicoloured	1·50	1·50
		a. Vert strip of 5. Nos. 3337/3341	6·75	6·75
3338	**1099**	(85c.) multicoloured	1·50	1·50
3339	**1100**	(85c.) multicoloured	1·50	1·50
3340	**1101**	(85c.) multicoloured	1·50	1·50
3341	**1102**	(85c.) multicoloured	1·50	1·50
3342	**1103**	(90c.) multicoloured (14.1.19)	1·50	1·50
		a. Vert strip of 5. Nos. 3342/3346	6·75	6·75
3343	**1104**	(90c.) multicoloured (14.1.19)	1·50	1·50
3344	**1105**	(90c.) multicoloured (14.1.19)	1·50	1·50
3345	**1106**	(90c.) multicoloured (14.1.19)	1·50	1·50
3346	**1107**	(90c.) multicoloured (14.1.19)	1·50	1·50
3347	**1108**	(92c.) multicoloured (13.1.20)	1·50	1·50
3348	**1109**	(92c.) multicoloured (13.1.20)	1·50	1·50
3349	**1110**	(92c.) multicoloured (13.1.20)	1·50	1·50
3350	**1111**	(92c.) multicoloured (13.1.20)	1·50	1·50
3351	**1112**	(92c.) multicoloured (13.1.20)	1·50	1·50
3352	**1113**	$1 multicoloured	1·60	1·75
3353	**1114**	$1.05 multicoloured (14.1.19)	1·60	1·75
3354	**1115**	$1.07 multicoloured (13.1.20)	1·60	1·75
3355	**1116**	$1.20 multicoloured	2·00	2·50
3356	**1117**	$1.27 multicoloured (14.1.19)	2·25	2·50
3357	**1118**	$1.30 multicoloured (13.1.20)	2·25	2·50
3358	**1119**	$1.80 multicoloured	3·50	4·00
3359	**1120**	$1.90 multicoloured (14.1.19)	3·75	4·25
3360	**1121**	$1.94 multicoloured (13.1.20)	3·75	4·25
3361	**1122**	$2.50 multicoloured	4·00	4·25
3362	**1123**	$2.65 multicoloured (14.1.19)	4·25	4·50
3363	**1124**	$2.71 multicoloured (13.1.20)	4·25	4·50
3337/3362 Set of 18				

(b) Self-adhesive booklet stamps. Die-cut perf 13½ (Nos. 3364/3379) or 9×imperf (others).

3364	**1098**	(85c.) multicoloured	1·50	1·50
		a. Pane. Nos. 3364/3368, each ×2	12·00	1·60
		b. Booklet pane. Nos. 3364/3368, each ×6	35·00	1·60
3365	**1099**	(85c.) multicoloured	1·50	1·50
3366	**1100**	(85c.) multicoloured	1·50	1·50
3367	**1101**	(85c.) multicoloured	1·50	1·50
3368	**1102**	(85c.) multicoloured	1·50	1·50
3369	**1103**	(90c.) multicoloured (14.1.19)	1·50	1·50
		a. Booklet pane. Nos. 3369/3373, each ×2	12·00	1·50
3370	**1104**	(90c.) multicoloured (14.1.19)	1·50	1·50
3371	**1105**	(90c.) multicoloured (14.1.19)	1·50	1·50
3372	**1106**	(90c.) multicoloured (14.1.19)	1·50	1·50
3373	**1107**	(90c.) multicoloured (14.1.19)	1·50	1·50
3374	**1108**	(92c.) multicoloured (13.1.20)	1·50	1·50
3375	**1109**	(92c.) multicoloured (13.1.20)	1·50	1·50
3376	**1110**	(92c.) multicoloured (13.1.20)	1·50	1·50
3377	**1111**	(92c.) multicoloured (13.1.20)	1·50	1·50
3378	**1112**	(92c.) multicoloured (13.1.20)	1·50	1·50
3379	**1116**	$1.20 multicoloured	2·00	2·50
		a. Pane. No. 3379×6	10·00	2·50
3380	**1117**	$1.27 multicoloured (14.1.19)	2·25	2·50
		a. Pane. No. 3380×6	11·00	2·50
3381	**1118**	$1.30 multicoloured (13.1.20)	2·25	2·50
3382	**1119**	$1.80 multicoloured	3·50	4·00
		a. Pane. No. 3382×6	17·00	4·00
3383	**1120**	$1.90 multicoloured (14.1.19)	3·75	4·25
		a. Pane. No. 3383×6	18·00	4·25
3384	**1121**	$1.94 multicoloured (13.1.20)	3·75	4·25
3385	**1122**	$2.50 multicoloured	4·00	4·25
		a. Pane. No. 3385×6	20·00	4·25
3386	**1123**	$2.65 multicoloured (14.1.19)	4·25	4·50
		a. Pane. No. 3386×6	21·00	4·50
3387	**1124**	$2.71 multicoloured (13.1.20)	4·25	4·50
		a. Pane. No. 3387×6	21·00	4·50
3364/3386 Set of 16			32·00	35·00

(c) Ordinary gum. Perf 13.

MS3388 150×75 mm. (85c.)×9 Types **1098**/**1102**, **1113**, **1116**, **1119** and **1122**		14·00	16·00
MS3389 150×75 mm. (90c.)×9 Types **1103**/**1107**, **1114**, **1117**, **1120** and **1123** (14.1.19)		14·00	16·00
MS3390 150×76 mm. (92c.)×5, $1.07, $1.30, $1.94, $2.71 Types **1108**/**1112**, **1115**, **1118**, **1121** and **1124** (13.1.20)		19·00	21·00

Nos. 3337/3341, 3364/338 and five of the stamps within No. **MS**3388 were inscr 'P' and were originally valid for 85c. each.

Nos. 3342/3346, 3369/3373 and five of the stamps within No. **MS**3389 were inscr 'P' and were originally valid for 90c. each.

Nos. 3347/3351, 3375/3379 and five of the stamps within No. **MS**3390 were iscr 'P' and were orginally valid for 92c. each.

Nos. 3364/3368 were issued in panes of ten originally sold for $8.50 and booklets of 30, No. SB627 originally sold for $25.50.

Nos. 3369/3373 were issued in panes of ten originally sold for $9.

Nos. 3375/3379 were issued in panes of 10 originally sold for $9.20.

1125 Nancy Greene (alpine skier)

(Des Subplot Design Inc. Litho Colour Innovations)

2018 (24 Jan). Women in Winter Sports. T **1125** and similar horiz designs. Multicoloured. Fluorescent frame.

(a) Self-adhesive. Die-cut perf 13×13½.

3391		(85c.) Type **1125**	1·50	1·50
		a. Booklet pane. Nos. 3391/3395	12·00	
3392		(85c.) Sharon and Shirley Firth (cross country skiers)	1·50	1·50
3393		(85c.) Danielle Goyette (ice hockey player)	1·50	1·50
3394		(85c.) Clara Hughes (speed skater)	1·50	1·50
3395		(85c.) Sonja Gaudet (wheelchair curler)	1·50	1·50
3391/3395 Set of 5			7·50	7·50

(b) Ordinary gum. Perf 13.

MS3396 160×180 mm. As Nos. 3391/3395 .... 7·50   8·00

Nos. 3391/3395 and the stamps within **MS**3396 were all inscr 'P' and were originally valid for 85c.

Nos. 3391/3395 were issued in booklets of ten, No. SB628, originally sold for $8.50.

1126 Kay Livingstone

1127 *Nelumbo nucifera* (Sacred Lotus)

(Des Tétro. Litho Lowe-Martin)

2018 (1 Feb). Black History Month. T **1126** and similar vert design. Multicoloured. Self-adhesive. Fluorescent frame. Die-cut perf 13½×13.

3397		(85c.) Type **1126**	1·50	1·50
		a. Booklet pane. No. 3397×10	12·00	
3398		(85c.) Lincoln M. Alexander	1·50	1·50
		a. Booklet pane. No. 3398×10	12·00	

Nos. 3397/3398 were both inscr 'P' and were originally valid for 85c. They were issued in separate booklets of ten, Nos. SB629/SB630, originally sold for $8.50.

(Des Eunike Nugroho (illustration) and Parcel. Litho Lowe-Martin)

2018 (1 Mar). Lotus. T **1127** and similar vert designs. Multicoloured. Fluorescent frame around each stamp (Nos. 3399/400) or fluorescent frame around each pair of stamps (others).

(a) Self-adhesive coil stamps as T **1127**. Die-cut imperf×8.

3399		(85c.) Type **1127**	1·50	1·50
		a. Horiz pair. Nos. 3399/3400	3·00	3·00
3400		(85c.) *Nelumbo lutea* (American lotus)	1·50	1·50

CANADA

*(b) Self-adhesive booklet stamps as T **1127** but 25×28 mm. Die-cut perf 13½.*

3401	(85c.) As Type **1127**...	1·50	1·50
	a. Booklet pane. Nos. 3401/3402, each ×5	12·00	
3402	(85c.) As No. 3400	1·50	1·50

(c) Ordinary gum. Perf 13.

MS3403	121×85 mm. As Nos. 3401/3402........................	3·50	4·00

Nos. 3399/3402 and the stamps within **MS**3403 were all inscr 'P' and originally sold for 85c. each.

Nos. 3399/3400 were issued in rolls of 50 with the two designs in sequence.

Nos. 3401/3402 were issued in booklets of ten, No. SB631, originally sold for $8.50.

Booklet pane 3401a included ten small circular stickers.

1128 *Best Friends* (Anita Kunz), *circa* 2012

(Des Lime Design. Litho Lowe-Martin)

2018 (5 Apr). Great Canadian Illustrators. T **1128** and similar multicoloured designs. Multicoloured. Reversed L-shaped fluorescent bands (at right and foot).

(a) Self-adhesive. Die-cut perf 13½.

3404	(85c.) Type **1128**	1·50	1·50
	a. Booklet pane. Nos. 3404/3408	12·00	
3405	(85c.) Untitled Harlequin book cover, 1987 (Will Davies 1924–2016)............................	1·50	1·50
3406	(85c.) *Stage Fright* (Blair Drawson), *circa* 1990	1·50	1·50
3407	(85c.) *It's Not a Stream of Consciousness* (Gérard DuBois), 2015 (30×30 mm)........	1·50	1·50
3408	(85c.) Untitled from 1966 Redbook feature on hair fashion (James Hill 1930–2004) (30×30 mm)	1·50	1·50
3404/3408	Set of 5	7·50	7·50

(b) Ordinary gum. Perf 12½.

MS3409	112×92 mm. As Nos. 3404/3408........................	7·50	7·50

Nos. 3404/3408 and the stamps within **MS**3409 were all inscr 'P' and originally sold for 85c. each.

Nos. 3404/3408 were issued in booklets of ten, No. SB632, originally sold for $8.50.

1129 Princess Elizabeth, July 1951 (photo by Yousuf Karsh)

1130 *Bombus affinis* (Rusty-patched Bumblebee)

(Des Paprika. Litho Lowe-Martin)

2018 (20 Apr). 65th Anniversary of the Coronation of Queen Elizabeth II. Self-adhesive. Fluorescent frame. Die-cut perf 13½×13.

3410	(85c.) black, grey and gold	1·50	1·50
	a. Booklet pane. No. 3410×10	15·00	

No. 3410 was inscr. 'P' and was originally valid for 85c. It was issued in booklets of ten, No. SB633, originally sold for $8.50.

Examples of No. 3410a have been reported printed on the wrong side of the paper, so that the self-adhesive gum is on the backing paper rather than the stamps.

(Des Dave Murray (illustration) and Andrew Perro. Litho CBN)

2018 (1 May). Bees. T **1130** and similar square design. Multicoloured. Self-adhesive. Fluorescent frame. Die-cut perf 13.

3411	(85c.) Type **1130**	1·50	1·50
	a. Booklet pane. Nos. 3411/3412, each ×5	14·00	
3412	(85c.) *Agapostemon virescens* (metallic green bee)..	1·50	1·50

Nos. 3411/3412 were both inscr. 'P' and were originally valid for 85c. each. They were issued in booklets of ten, originally sold for $8.50.

1131 Regina Pats Players of 1919 and 2018 and Memorial Cup

(Des Louis Hébert (illustration) and Paprika. Litho Lowe-Martin)

2018 (18 May). 100th Memorial Cup of Ontario Hockey Association. Self-adhesive. Fluorescent frame. Die-cut perf 13×13½.

3413	(85c.) multicoloured	1·50	1·50
	a. Booklet pane. No. 3413×10	12·00	

No. 3413 was inscribed 'P' and was originally valid for 85c. It was issued in booklets of ten, No. SB635, originally sold for $8.50.

1132 Milky Way

(Des Irene Laschi (illustration) and Parcel Design. Litho Colour Innovations)

2018 (29 June). 150th Anniversary of the Royal Astronomical Society of Canada. T **1132** and similar horiz design. Multicoloured. Fluorescent frame.

(a) Self-adhesive. Die-cut perf 14.

3414	(85c.) Type **1132**	1·50	1·50
	a. Booklet pane. Nos. 3414/3415, each ×5	12·00	
3415	(85c.) Northern Lights (Aurora borealis)...........	1·50	1·50

(b) Ordinary gum. Perf 13.

MS3416	90×100 mm. As Nos. 3414/3415........................	3·00	3·25

Nos. 3414/3415 and the stamps within **MS**3416 were inscr 'P' and were originally valid for 85c.

Nos. 3414/3415 were issued in booklets of ten, No. SB636, originally sold for $8.50.

1133 *Carcharodon carcharias* (Great White Shark)

(Des Julius Csotonyi (illustration) and Andrew Perro. Litho Lowe-Martin)

2018 (13 July). Sharks. T **1133** and similar square designs. Multicoloured. Fluorescent frame.

(a) Self-adhesive. Die-cut perf 13½.

3417	(85c.) Type **1133**	1·50	1·50
	a. Booklet pane. Nos. 3417/3421, each ×2	12·00	
3418	(85c.) *Cetorhinus maximus* (Basking Shark)	1·50	1·50
3419	(85c.) *Prionace glauca* (Blue Shark)....................	1·50	1·50
3420	(85c.) *Somniosus microcephalus* (Greenland Shark)..	1·50	1·50
3421	(85c.) *Isurus oxyrinchus* (Shortfin Mako Shark)	1·50	1·50
3417/3421	Set of 5	7·50	7·50

(b) Ordinary gum. Perf 12½.

MS3422	122×78 mm. As Nos. 3417/3421........................	7·50	7·50

Nos. 3417/3421 and the stamps within **MS**3422 were inscr 'P' and were originally valid for 85c.

Nos. 3417/3421 were issued in booklets of ten, No. SB637, originally sold for $8.50.

CANADA

1134 Northern Lights (Aurora borealis)

(Des Entro Communications. Litho Lowe-Martin)

2018 (26 July). Weather Wonders (2nd issue). T **1134** and similar horiz designs. Multicoloured. Fluorescent frame.

(a) Self-adhesive. Die-cut perf 13×13½.

3423	(85c.) Type **1134**	1·50	1·50
	a. Booklet pane. Nos. 3423/3427, each ×2	12·00	
3424	(85c.) Waterspout	1·50	1·50
3425	(85c.) Lenticular cloud	1·50	1·50
3426	(85c.) Light pillars	1·50	1·50
3427	(85c.) Moon halo	1·50	1·50
3423/3427	Set of 5	7·50	7·50

(b) Ordinary gum. Perf 12½.

MS3428	158×93 mm. As Nos. 3423/3427	7·50	7·50

Nos. 3423/3427 and the stamps within No. **MS**3428 were all inscr 'P' and were originally valid for 85c.

Nos. 3423/3427 were issued in booklets of ten, No. SB638, originally sold for $8.50.

(Des Keith Martin (illustration), Kosta Tsetsekas and Mike Savage (Signals Design). Litho CBN)

2018 (20 Aug). Birds of Canada (3rd issue). Vert designs as T **1071**. Multicoloured. Partial fluorescent frames.

(a) Self-adhesive. Die-cut perf 13.

3429	(85c.) *Poecile atricapillus* (Black-capped Chickadee) (New Brunswick)	2·00	2·00
	a. Booklet pane. Nos. 3429/3433, each ×2	15·00	
3430	(85c.) *Grus americana* (Whooping Crane)	2·00	2·00
3431	(85c.) *Branta canadensis* (Canada Goose)	2·00	2·00
3432	(85c.) *Bubo scandiacus* (Snowy Owl) (Quebec)	2·00	2·00
3433	(85c.) *Cyanocitta stelleri* (Steller's Jay) (British Columbia)	2·00	2·00
3429/3433	Set of 5	9·00	9·00

(b) Ordinary gum. Perf 13.

MS3434	114×92 mm. As Nos. 3429/3433	9·00	9·50

Nos. 3429/3433 and the stamps within No. **MS**3434 were inscr. 'P' and were originally valid for 85c. each.

Nos. 3429/3433 were issued in booklets of ten, No. SB639, originally sold for $8.50.

2018 (20 Aug). International Ornithological Congress, Vancouver. No. **MS**3434 with emblem and 'INTERNATIONAL ORNITHOLOGICAL CONGRESS VANCOUVER. CANADA. AUGUST 19-26, 2018' on upper left sheet margin.

MS3435	114×92 mm. As Nos. 3429/3433	9·00	9·50

1135 Canadian Armed Forces

(Des Shiro Nishiguchi (illustration) and William Lam Design. Litho Colour Innovations)

2018 (14 Sept). Emergency Responders. T **1135** and similar horiz designs. Multicoloured. Fluorescent frame.

(a) Self-adhesive. Die-cut perf 13½.

3436	(85c.) Type **1135**	2·00	2·00
	a. Booklet pane. Nos. 3436/3440, each×2	15·00	
3437	(85c.) Firefighters	2·00	2·00
3438	(85c.) Paramedics	2·00	2·00
3439	(85c.) Police officers	2·00	2·00
3440	(85c.) Search and Rescue Experts	2·00	2·00
3436/3440	Set of 5	9·00	9·00

(b) Ordinary gum. Perf 13.

MS3441	160×180 mm. Nos. 3436/3440	9·00	9·50

Nos. 3436/3440 and the stamps within No. MS3441 are all inscribed 'P' and were originally valid for 85c. each.

Nos. 3436/3440 were issued in booklets of ten, No. SB640, originally sold for $8.50.

No. **MS**3441 was sold in a plastic folder for $4.25.

1136 Boy seeing Shapes in Clouds   **1137** Peace Dove over Barbed Wire

(Des Julie Morstad (illustration) and Matthew Warburton (Emdoubleyu Design). Litho Lowe-Martin)

2018 (24 Sept). Canada Post Community Foundation. Multicoloured. Self-adhesive. Fluorescent frame. Die-cut perf 13½.

3442	**1136**	(85c.)+10c. multicoloured	1·50	1·50
		a. Booklet pane. No. 3442×10	12·00	

No. 3442 was inscr 'P+10' and was originally valid for 85c. It was issued in booklets of ten, No. SB641, originally sold for $9.50, a $1 charity premium.

(Des Jillian Ditner (illustration) and Larry Burke and Anna Stredulinsky, Burke & Burke Design. Litho Lowe-Martin)

2018 (24 Oct). Centenary of the Armistice. Fluorescent frame.

(a) Self-adhesive. Die-cut perf 13½×14.

3443	**1137**	(85c.) multicoloured	1·50	1·50
		a. Booklet pane. No. 3443×10	12·00	

(b) Ordinary gum. Perf 13×12½.

MS3444	161×209 mm. (85c.) As No. 3443×5	6·50	7·50

No. 3443 and the stamps within No. **MS**3444 were iscr 'P' and were originally valid for 85c. each.

No. 3443 was issued in booklets of ten, No. SB642, originally sold for $8.50.

No. **MS**3444 was originally sold in a plastic folder for $4.25.

1138 The Nativity   **1139** Socks

(Des Daniel Robitaille (illustration) and Paprika. Litho Colour Innovations)

2018 (2 Nov). Christmas (1st issue). *Away in a Manger.* Self-adhesive. Fluorescent frame. Die-cut perf 13.

3445	**1138**	(85c.) multicoloured	1·50	1·60
		a. Booklet pane. No. 3445×12	14·00	

No. 3444 was inscr 'P' and was originally valid for 85c.

It was issued in booklets of 12, No. SB643, originally sold for $10.20.

(Des Daniel Robitaille (illustration) and Paprika. Litho Colour Innovations)

2018 (2 Nov). Christmas (2nd issue). Warm and Cozy. T **1139** and similar vert designs. Multicoloured. Fluorescent frame.

(a) Self-adhesive. Die-cut perf 13.

3446	(85c.) Type **1139**	1·50	1·25
	a. Booklet pane. No. 3446×12	14·00	
3447	$1.20 Toque (hat)	1·75	2·00
	a. Pane. No. 3447×6	9·00	
3448	$2.50 Mittens	3·50	4·00
	a. Pane. No. 3448×6	17·00	
3446/3448	Set of 3	6·00	6·50

(b) Ordinary gum. Perf 13½×13.

MS3449	85×54 mm. As Nos. 3446/3448	6·50	7·50

No. 3446 was inscr 'P' and was originally valid for 85c. It was issued in booklets of 12 stamps, No. SB644, originally sold for $10.20.

No. 3447 was issued in $7.20 panes of six stamps.

No. 3448 was issued in $15 panes of six stamps.

1140 Zhu Bajie (Pigsy) in Armour carrying Nine-toothed Rake

CANADA

(Des Seung Jai Paek (illustration) and Albert Ng. Calligraphy by Albert Ng. Litho (Nos. 3450/**MS**3352 also embossed) Colour Innovations)

2019 (18 Jan). Chinese New Year. Year of the Pig. T **1140** and similar square designs. Multicoloured. Fluorescent frame.

(a) Ordinary gum. Perf 13.
3450	(90c.) Type **1140**	1·50	1·50
MS3451	118×90 mm. $2.50 Dog (Saluki type) on lantern; $2.65 Zhu Bajie in red robes holding nine-toothed rake	7·00	8·00
MS3452	40×140 mm. $2.65 Zhu Bajie in red robes holding nine-toothed rake	4·50	5·00

(b) Self-adhesive. Die-cut perf 13½.
3453	(90c.) As Type **1140**	1·50	1·50
	a. Booklet pane. No. 3453×10	12·00	
3454	$2.65 Zhu Baije seated on ground	4·00	4·50
	a. Booklet pane. No. 3454×6	20·00	

Nos. 3450 and 3453 were inscr 'P' and were originally valid for 90c.
No. 3453 was issued in booklets of ten, No. SB645, originally sold for $9.
No. 3454 was issued in $15.90 booklets, No. SB646.

1141 Albert Jackson   **1142** Gardenia

(Des Ron Dollekamp (illustration) and Andrew Perro. Litho Lowe-Martin)

2019 (25 Jan). Black History Month. Albert Jackson (letter carrier). Self-adhesive. Fluorescent frame. Die-cut perf 13½×13.
3455	**1141**	(90c.) multicoloured	1·50	1·50
		a. Booklet pane. No. 3455×10	12·00	

No. 3455 was inscr 'P' and was originally valid for 90c. It was issued in booklets of ten, No. SB647, which were originally sold for $9.

(Des Chantal Larocque (artwork) and Andrew Conlon and Lionel Gadoury (Context Creative). Litho Lowe-Martin (Nos. 3456/3457) or Colour Innovations (others))

2019 (14 Feb). Gardenia. Multicoloured designs as T **1142**. Multicoloured. Fluorescent frame.

(a) Self-adhesive coil stamp. Die-cut perf 8×imperf.
3456	(90c.) Type **1142**	1·50	1·50
	a. Horiz pair. Nos. 3456/3457	3·00	3·00
3457	(90c.) Three Gardenia flowers	1·50	1·50

(b) Self-adhesive booklet stamp. Size 24×29 mm. Die-cut perf 13½.
3458	(90c.) Three Gardenia flowers	1·50	1·50
	a. Booklet pane. Nos. 3458/3459, each×5	12·00	
3459	(90c.) As Type **1142**	1·50	1·50

(c) Ordinary gum.
MS3460	122×73 mm. As Nos. 3458/3459	3·00	3·25

Nos. 3456/3459 and the stamps within No. **MS**3460 were all inscr 'P' and originally valid for 90c. each.
Nos. 3456/3457 were issued in rolls of 50 containing the two designs.
Nos. 3458/3459 were issued in booklets of ten, No. SB648, originally sold for $9. Booklet pane 3458a included ten small circular stickers.

1143 Elsie MacGill (1905–1980, aeronautical engineer) and Hawker Hurricane Fighters

(Des Ivan Novotny (Taylor|Sprules Corporation). Litho Lowe-Martin)

2019 (27 Mar). Canadians in Flight. T **1143** and similar horiz designs. Multicoloured. Self-adhesive. Fluorescent frame.

(a) Self-adhesive. Die-cut perf 13×13½.
3461	(90c.) Type **1143**	1·50	1·50
	a. Booklet pane. No. 3461/3465, each×2	12·00	
3462	(90c.) William George Barker, VC (1894–1930, World War One fighter pilot)	1·50	1·50
3463	(90c.) C. H. Punch Dickins (1899–1995, World War One pilot and bush pilot)	1·50	1·50
3564	(90c.) Avro CF-105 Arrow	1·50	1·50
3465	(90c.) Ultraflight Lazair	1·50	1·50
3461/3465	Set of 5	6·75	6·75

(b) Ordinary gum. Perf 12½.
MS3465a	160×180 mm. As Nos. 3461/3465	7·50	7·50

Nos. 3461/3465 and the stamps within No. **MS**3465a were all inscr 'P' and were originally valid for 90c.
Nos. 3461/3465 were issued in booklets of ten, No. SB649, originally sold for $9.
No. **MS**3465a was sold for $4.50 (face value).

1144 Blueberry Grunt   **1145** Team on Baseball

(Des Mary Ellen Johnson (illustration) and Subplot Design Inc.. Litho CBN)

2019 (17 Apr). Sweet Canada. T **1144** and similar free-form shapes. Multicoloured. Self-adhesive. Fluorescent frame. Die-cut perf 13½.
3466	(90c.) Type **1144**	1·50	1·50
	a. Booklet pane. Nos. 3466/3470, each×2	12·00	
3467	(90c.) Butter Tart (24×26 mm)	1·50	1·50
3468	(90c.) Sugar Pie (28×28 mm)	1·50	1·50
3469	(90c.) Nanaimo Bar (27×25 mm)	1·50	1·50
3470	(90c.) Saskatoon Berry Pie (34×24 mm)	1·50	1·50
3466/3470	Set of 5	6·75	6·75
MS3471	127×90 mm. Nos. 3466/3470	7·00	8·00

Nos. 3466/3470 and the stamps within No. **MS**3471 were all inscr 'P' and originally valid for 90c.
Nos. 3466/3470 were issued in booklets of ten, No. SB650, originally sold for $9.

(Des Subplot Design Inc.. Litho Colour Innovations)

2019 (25 Apr). Vancouver Asahi (Japanese Canadian amateur baseball team). Self-adhesive. Fluorescent frame. Die-cut.
3472	**1145**	(90c.) multicoloured	1·50	1·50
		a. Booklet pane. No. 3472×10	12·00	

No. 3472 was inscr 'P' and originally sold for 90c. It was issued in booklets of ten, No. SB651, originally sold for $9

 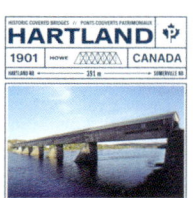

1146 *Clemmys guttata* (Spotted Turtle)   **1147** Hartland Bridge, New Brunswick

(Des Sarah Still (illustration) and Adrian Horvath. Litho CBN)

2019 (23 May). Endangered Turtles. T **1146** and similar vert design. Multicoloured. Self-adhesive. Fluorescent frame. Die-cut perf 13½.
3473	(90c.) Type **1146**	1·50	1·50
	a. Booklet pane. Nos. 3473/3474, each×5	12·00	
3474	(90c.) *Emydoidea blandingii* (Blanding's Turtle)	1·50	1·50
MS3475	82×85 mm. Nos. 3473/3474	3·00	4·00

Nos. 3473/3474 and the stamps within No. **MS**3475 were all inscr 'P' and were originally valid for 90c.
Nos. 3473/3474 were issued in booklets of ten, No. SB652, originally sold for $9.

(Des Paprika. Litho CBN)

2019 (17 June). Historic Covered Bridges. T **1147** and similar square designs. Multicoloured. Fluorescent frame.

(a) Self-adhesive. Die-cut perf 13.
3476	(90c.) Type **1147**	1·50	1·50
	a. Booklet pane. Nos. 3476/3480, each×2	12·00	
3477	(90c.) Powerscourt (Percy) Bridge, Québec	1·50	1·50
3478	(90c.) Félix-Gabriel-Marchand Bridge, Québec	1·50	1·50
3479	(90c.) West Montrose Bridge, Ontario	1·50	1·50
3480	(90c.) Ashnola No. 1 Bridge, British Columbia	1·50	1·50
3476/3480	Set of 5	7·50	7·50

(b) Ordinary gum. Perf 12½.
MS3481	134×86 mm. As Nos. 3476/3480	7·00	8·00

Nos. 3476/3480 and the stamps within No. **MS**3481 were all inscr 'P' and were originally valid for 90c.

Nos. 3476/3480 were issued in booklets of ten, No. SB652, originally sold for $9.

1148 Command Module *Columbia* and Earth

(Des Mack Sztaba (illustration) and Matthew Clark (Subplot Design Inc.). Litho Lowe-Martin)

2019 (27 June). 50th Anniversary of First Manned Moon Landing. T **1148** and similar vert design. Multicoloured. Fluorescent frame.

(a) Self-adhesive. Die-cut perf 13½.
3482	(90c.) Type **1148**	1·50	1·50
	a. Booklet pane. Nos. 3482/3483, each×5	12·00	
3483	(90c.) Lunar module *Eagle* and Moon	1·50	1·50

(b) Ordinary gum. Perf 13½.
MS3484	160×180 mm. As Nos. 3482/3483, each×3	8·00	8·00

Nos. 3482/3483 and the stamps within No. **MS**3484 were all inscr 'P' and were originally valid for 90c.

Nos. 3482/3483 and the stamps within No. **MS**3484 had a fluorescent frame around the vertical pair, which was laid *tête-bêche*.

Nos. 3482/3483 were issued in booklets of ten, No. SB654, originally sold for $9.

No. **MS**3484 was issued in a folder and sold for $5.40 (face value).

1149 *Ursus americanus* (American Black Bear)

(Des Andrew Perro. Litho Lowe-Martin)

2019 (24 July). Bears. T **1149** and similar square designs. Multicoloured. Fluorescent frame.

(a) Self-adhesive. Die-cut perf 13½.
3485	(90c.) Type **1149**	1·50	1·50
	a. Booklet pane. Nos. 3485/3488, each×2	11·00	
3486	(90c.) *Ursus maritimus* (Polar Bear)	1·50	1·50
3487	(90c.) *Ursus americanus* (Kermode Bear)	1·50	1·50
3488	(90c.) *Ursus arctos* (Grizzly Bear)	1·50	1·50
3485/3488	Set of 4	5·50	5·50

(b) Ordinary gum. Perf 13½.
MS3489	160×180 mm. As Nos. 3485/3488	6·00	6·00

Nos. 3485/3488 and the stamps within No. **MS**3489 were all inscr 'P' and originally sold for 90c.

Nos. 3485/3488 were issued in booklets of eight, No. SB655, originally sold for $7.20.

No. **MS**3489 was issued in a folder and sold for $3.60 (face value).

1150 Cohen

(Des Paprika. Litho Lowe-Martin)

2019 (21 Sept). Leonard Cohen (1934–2016, singer, songwriter, poet and novelist) Commemoration. T **1150** and similar vert designs. Multicoloured. Fluorescent frame.

(a) Self-adhesive. Die-cut perf 13½×13.
3490	(90c.) Type **1150**	1·50	1·50
	a. Booklet pane. Nos. 3490/3492, each×3	12·00	
3491	(90c.) Leonard Cohen (standing)	1·50	1·50
3492	(90c.) Leonard Cohen as older man (sitting)	1·50	1·50
3490/3492	Set of 3	4·00	4·00

(b) Ordinary gum. Perf 12½.
MS3493	160×180 mm. As Nos. 3490/3492; $1.27 As Type **1150**; $1.90 As No. 3491; $2.65 As No. 3492	13·00	13·00

Nos. 3490/3492 were inscr 'P' and were originally valid for 90c. They were issued in booklets of nine stamps, No. SB655, originally sold for $8.10.

1151 Ice cream and Lolly holding hands   **1152** Three Wise Men

(Litho CBN)

2019 (23 Sept). Canada Post Commmunnity Foundation. T **1151** and similar square design. Multicoloured. Self-adhesive. Fluorescent frame. Die-cut perf 13½.
3494	(90c.)+10c. Type **1151**	1·50	1·50
	a. Booklet pane. Nos. 3494/3495, each×5	12·00	
3495	(90c.)+10c. As Type **1151** but blue ice cream in cone and figure wearing mauve	1·50	1·50

Nos. 3494/3495 were inscr 'P+10' and were originally valid for 90c. They were issued in booklets of ten, No. SB656, originally sold for $10, which includes a 10c. charity premium on each stamp.

> **NOTE.** Canada Post distributed a (90c.) stamp to employees in November 2020. The stamp shows a post van as a rocket with a rainbow-coloured tail and is inscribed 'THANKS/MERCI'.

(Des Michael Little (illustration), Liz Wurzinger and Timothy King (Subplot Design). Litho Lowe-Martin)

2019 (4 Nov). Christmas (1st issue). The Magi. Self-adhesive. Fluorescent frame. Die-cut perf 13½.
3496	**1152** (90c.) gold and ultramarine	1·50	1·50
	a. Booklet pane. No. 3496×12	16·00	

No. 3496 was inscr. 'P' and was originally valid for 90c. It was issued in booklets of 12, No. SB657, originally sold for $10.80.

Booklets containing No. 3496 exist with stamps printed on the wrong side of the paper, so the self-adhesive gum is on the paper, rather than the stamps.

1153 Reindeer

(Des Andrew Lewis Design. Litho CBN)

2019 (4 Nov). Christmas (2nd issue). Shiny and Bright. T **1153** and similar vert designs. Multicoloured. Fluorescent frame.

(a) Self-adhesive. Die-cut perf 13.
3497	(90c.) Type **1153**	1·50	1·50
	a. Booklet pane. No. 3497×12	16·00	
3498	$1.27 Three dancers	1·75	2·00
	a. Pane. No. 3498×6	9·00	
3499	$2.65 Partridge	4·00	4·50
	a. Pane. No. 3499×6	20·00	
3497/3499	Set of 3	6·50	7·25

(b) Ordinary gum. Perf 12½.
MS3500	85×54 mm. As Nos. 3497/3499	6·50	7·50

No. 3497 was inscr 'P' and was originally valid for 90c. It was issued in booklets of 12 stamps, No. SB658, originally sold for $10.20.

No. 3498 was issued in $7.62 panes of six stamps.

No. 3499 was issued in $15.90 panes of six stamps.

CANADA

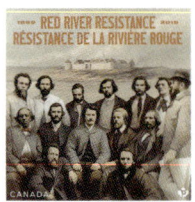 

1154 Red River Resistance   **1155** Candles

(Des Gérard DuBois (illustration) and Paprika. Litho Lowe-Martin)

2019 (6 Nov). 150th Anniversary of the Red River Resistance, 1869–1870. Self-adhesive. Fluorescent frame. Die-cut perf 13½.
3501	**1154**	(90c.) multicoloured	1·75	1·75
		a. Booklet pane. No. 3501×10	12·00	

No. 3501 was inscr 'P' and was originally valid for 90c. It was issued in booklets of ten, No. SB659, originally sold for $9.

(Des Context Creative. Litho Lowe-Martin)

2019 (14 Nov). Hanukkah. Self-adhesive. Fluorescent frame. Die-cut perf 13×13½.
3502	**1155**	(90c.) multicoloured	1·75	1·75
		a. Booklet pane. No. 3502×10	12·00	

No. 3502 was inscr 'P' and originally sold for 90c. It was issued in booklets of ten, No. SB660, originally sold for $9.

1156 Rat Bride on Way to Wedding

(Des Seung Jai Paek and Albert Ng. Calligraphy by Albert Ng. Litho Colour Innovations)

2020 (17 Jan). Chinese New Year. Year of the Rat. Wedding of the Rat's Daughter (traditional story). T **1156** and similar square designs. Multicoloured. Fluorescent frame.

(a) Ordinary gum. Perf 13.
3503		(92c.) Type **1156**	1·50	1·50
MS3504	118×90 mm. $2.65 Zhu Bajie in red robes holding nine-toothed rake; $2.71 Rat bride and groom		4·00	4·50
MS3505	40×140 mm. $2.71 Rat bride and groom		4·00	4·50

(b) Self-adhesive. Die-cut perf 13½.
3506		(92c.) As Type **1156**	1·50	1·50
		a. Booklet pane. No. 3506×10	15·00	
3507		$2.71 Rat bride and groom	4·00	4·50
		a. Booklet pane. No. 3507×6	24·00	

Nos. 3503 and 3506 were inscr 'P' and were originally valid for 92c.
No. 3506 was issued in booklets of ten, No. SB662, originally sold for $9.20.
No. 3507a was issued in $16.26 booklets, No. SB663.

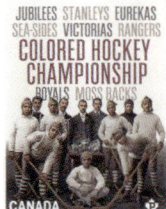 

1157 Halifax Eurekas Coloured Hockey Champion Team Photo, 1904   **1158** Three Dahlias

(Des Ron Dollekamp (illustration) and Lime Design. Litho Lowe-Martin)

2020 (24 Jan). Black History. Coloured Hockey Championship. Self-adhesive. Fluorescent frame. Die-cut perf 13½×13.
3508	**1157**	(92c.) multicoloured	1·50	1·50
		a. Booklet pane. No. 3508×10	15·00	

No. 3508 was inscr 'P' and was originally valid for 92c. It was issued in booklets of ten, No. SB664, originally sold for $9.20.

(Des Lionel Gadoury, Umaymah Motala and Malika Soin (Context Creative). Litho CBN)

2020 (2 Mar). Dahlia. T **1158** and similar vert design. Multicoloured. Fluorescent frame.

(a) Self-adhesive coil stamps. Die-cut imperf×8.
3509		(92c.) Type **1158**	1·50	1·50
		a. Horiz pair. Nos. 3509/3510	3·00	3·00
3510		(92c.) Close-up of Dahlia flower	1·50	1·50

(b) Self-adhesive booklet stamps. Size 26×32 mm. Die-cut perf 13½.
3511		(92c.) Close-up of Dahlia flower	1·50	1·50
		a. Booklet pane. Nos. 3511/3512, each×5	15·00	
3512		(92c.) Type **1158**	1·50	1·50

(c) Ordinary gum. Fluorescent frame. P 12×12½.
MS3513	127×73 mm. As Nos. 3511/3512	3·00	3·50

Nos. 3509/3512 and the stamps within No. **MS**3513 were all inscr 'P' and originally sold for 92c. each.
Nos. 3509/3510 were issued in rolls of 50 with the two designs in sequence.
Nos. 3511/3512 were issued in booklets of ten, No. SB665, originally sold for $9.20.
Booklet pane 3511a included ten small circular stickers.

1159 Eid Mubarak (Have a Blessed Eid) in Calligraphy   **1160** Private Léo Major

(Des Lionel Gadoury, Dave Hurds and Muneeb Khatana (Context Creative). Calligraphy by Nayla Yehia. Litho Lowe-Martin)

2020 (24 Apr). Eid. Self-adhesive. Fluorescent frame on three sides (left, right and foot). Die-cut perf 13×13½.
3514	**1159**	(92c.) multicoloured	1·50	1·50
		a. Booklet pane. No. 3514×10	15·00	

No. 3514 was inscr 'P' and originally sold for 92c. It was issued in booklets of ten, No. SB666, originally sold for $9.20.

(Des Ivan Novotny, Taylor Sprules Corporation. Litho Lowe-Martin)

2020 (29 Apr). 75th Anniversary of Victory in Europe. T **1160** and similar horiz design. Multicoloured. Self-adhesive. Fluorescent frame (broken at right (T **1160**) or left (No. 3516)). Die-cut perf 13×13½.
3515		(92c.) Type **1160**	1·50	1·50
		a. Booklet pane. No. 3515/3516, each×5	15·00	
3516		(92c.) Veronica Foster (munitions worker)	1·50	1·50

Nos. 3515/3516 were inscr 'P' and originally sold for 92c. They were issued in booklets of ten stamps, No. SB667, originally sold for $9.20.

1161 *In the Nickel Belt* (Franklin Carmichael), 1928

(Des Andrew Conlon, Lionel Gadoury and Matthew Killin (Context Creative). Litho Lowe-Martin)

2020 (7 May). Group of Seven 1920–2020. T **1161** and similar horiz designs. Multicoloured. Fluorescent frame.

(a) Self-adhesive. Die-cut perf 13×13½.
3517		(92c.) Type **1161**	1·50	1·50
		a. Booklet pane. Nos. 3517/3523	11·00	
3518		(92c.) *Miners' Houses, Glace Bay* (Lawren S. Harris), circa 1925	1·50	1·50
3519		(92c.) *Labrador Coast* (A. Y. Jackson), 1930	1·50	1·50
3520		(92c.) *Fire-swept, Algoma* (Frank H. Johnston), 1920	1·50	1·50
3521		(92c.) *Québec Village* (Arthur Lismer), 1926	1·50	1·50
3522		(92c.) *Church by the Sea* (J. E. H. MacDonald), 1924	1·50	1·50
3523		(92c.) *Stormy Weather, Georgian Bay* (F. H. Varley), 1921	1·50	1·50
3517/3523	Set of 7		9·50	9·50

(b) Ordinary gum. P 13.
MS3524 160×180 mm. As Nos. 3517/3523...... 11·00 11·00

Nos. 3517/3523 and the stamps within No. **MS**3524 were all inscr 'P' and originally sold for 92c.

Nos. 3517/3523 were issued in booklets of seven, No. SB668, originally sold for $6.44.

No. **MS**3524 was issued as a pane of seven in a clear plastic pack sold for $6.44.

Nos. 3517/**MS**3524 commemorate the Centenary of the first exhibition by the Group of Seven artists, in the Art Gallery of Toronto in May 1920.

1162 Vintage Radio Microphone, 'XWA' (Experimental Wireless Apparatus) and Headphones

1163 James Till and Ernest McCulloch (stem cells)

(Des Oliver Burston (illustrations) and Soapbox Design. Litho Lowe-Martin)

2020 (20 May). History of Radio in Canada. T **1162** and similar horiz design. Multicoloured. Self-adhesive. Fluorescent frame. Die-cut perf 13×13½.
3525 (92c.) Type **1162** .... 1·50 1·50
 a. Booklet pane. Nos. 3525/3526, each×5 15·00
3526 (92c.) Vintage radio box with dials, horn-shaped speaker and three bulbs............ 1·50 1·50

Nos. 3525/3526 were issued in five horizontal pairs throughout the booklet pane, each pair forming a composite background design of circular sound waves.

Nos. 3525/3526 were both inscr 'P' and originally sold for 92c. They were issued in booklets of ten, No. SB669, originally sold for $9.20.

(Des Mike Savage, Dale Kilian, Signals. Litho Colour Innovations)

2020 (10 Sept). Medical Groundbreakers. T **1163** and similar horiz designs. Multicoloured. Self-adhesive. Fluorescent frame. Die-cut perf 13½.
3527 (92c.) Type **1163** .... 1·50 1·50
 a. Booklet pane. Nos. 3527/3531, each × 2 15·00
3528 (92c.) M. Vera Peters (lymphoma and breast cancer)..................................... 1·50 1·50
3529 (92c.) Julio Mantaner (HIV/AIDS treatment and prevention)......................... 1·50 1·50
3530 (92c.) Balfour Mount (palliative care) .... 1·50 1·50
3531 (92c.) Bruce Chown (Rhesus (Rh) disease)...... 1·50 1·50
3527/3531 Set of 5 .... 6·75 6·75

Nos. 3527/3531 were all inscr 'P' and originally valid for 92c. each. They were issued in booklets of ten, No. SB670, originally sold for $9.20.

1164 Animals in Tree

1165 Diwali Lamp and Rangoli Patterns

(Des Isabelle Arsenault (illustration) and Subplot Design Inc. Litho Colour Innovations)

2020 (21 Sept). Canada Post Community Foundation. Self-adhesive. Fluorescent frame. Die-cut perf 13.
3532 **1164** (92c.)+10c. multicoloured .... 1·50 1·50
 a. Booklet pane. No. 3532×10....... 15·00

No. 3532 was inscr 'P+10' and was originally valid for 92c. It was issued in booklets of ten, No. SB671, originally sold for $10.20, which included a 10c. charity premium on each stamp.

(Des Entro Communications. Litho Colour Innovations)

2020 (15 Oct). Diwali. Self-adhesive. Fluorescent frame. Die-cut perf 15.
3533 **1165** (92c.) multicoloured .... 1·50 1·50
 a. Booklet pane. No. 3533×10............. 15·00

1166 *Trenches on the Somme, 1919*

1167 Mary, Joseph and Baby Jesus

(Des Rejean Myette. Litho CBN)

2020 (28 Oct). Mary Riter Hamilton (1867–1954, battlefield artist 1919–1925) Commemoration. Self-adhesive. Fluorescent frame. Die-cut perf 13.
3534 **1166** (92c.) multicoloured .... 1·50 1·50
 a. Booklet pane. No. 3534×10............. 15·00

No. 3534 was originally sold for 92c., and was issued in booklets of ten, No. SB673, originally sold for $9.20.

(Des Sandra Dionisi (illustration) and Soapbox Design. Litho Colour Innovations)

2020 (2 Nov). Christmas. Nativity. Self-adhesive. Fluorescent frame. Die-cut perf 13½.
3535 **1167** (92c.) multicoloured .... 1·50 1·50
 a. Booklet pane. No. 3535×12............. 15·00

No. 3535 was inscr 'P' and was originally valid for 92c. It was issued in booklets of 12, No. SB674, originally sold for $11.04.

1168 *Winter Sleigh Ride, circa early 1960s*

(Des Helene L'Heureux. Litho Colour Innovations)

2020 (2 Nov). Holiday. Folk Art Paintings of Maud Lewis (1901–1970). T **1168** and similar horiz designs. Multicoloured. Fluorescent frames.
(a) Self-adhesive. Die-cut perf 13½.
3536 (92c.) Type **1168** .... 1·50 1·50
 a. Booklet pane. No. 3536×12............. 18·00
3537 $1·20 *Team of Oxen in Winter*, 1967 .... 1·90 2·25
 a. Pane. No. 3537×6............................... 11·00
3538 $2·71 *Family and Sled, circa 1960s* .... 4·00 4·50
 a. Pane. No. 3538×6............................... 22·00
3536/3538 Set of 3 .... 6·75 7·50

(b) Ordinary gum. P 13½×13.
MS3539 112×70 mm. As Nos. 3536/3538........................ 7·25 7·25

No. 3536 was inscr 'P' and was originally valid for 92c. It was issued in booklets of 12, No. SB675, originally sold for $11.04, not yet received.
No. 3537 was issued in $7·80 panes of six stamps.
No. 3538 was issued in $16·26 panes of six stamps.

1169 Menorah

(Des Gerald Querubin, Entro Communications. Litho Colour Innovations)

2020 (5 Nov). Hanukkah. Self-adhesive. Fluorescent frame. Die-cut perf 15.
3540 **1169** (92c.) multicoloured .... 1·50 1·50
 a. Booklet pane. No. 3540×10............. 15·00

No. 3540 was inscr 'P' and was originally valid for 92c. It was issued in booklets of ten, No. SB676, originally sold for $9·20.

CANADA

(Des Paprika. Litho (pane also embossing and foil stamping) Lowe Martin)

2021 (15 Jan). Lunar New Year Cycle. Square designs as Types **933, 954, 976/977, 998, 1023, 1045, 1064, 1076, 1097, 1140** and **1156**. Multicoloured. Fluorescent frame or partial fluorescent frame.

(a) Self-adhesive. Die-cut perf 13½.

3541	(92c.) Rat bride and groom (as No. 3507)	1·50	1·50
	a. Booklet pane. Nos. 3541/3552	18·00	
3542	(92c.) Earthenware cooking pot with ox design by Shu-Hwei Kao (as No. **MS**2582)	1·50	1·50
3543	(92c.) Dragon's head (as Type **977**)	1·50	1·50
3544	(92c.) Jade Snake (as No. 2909)	1·50	1·50
3545	(92c.) Monkey King mask (as No. 3182)	1·50	1·50
3546	(92c.) Head of Rooster (as No. 3246)	1·50	1·50
3547	(92c.) Tiger's head seal (as No. **MS**2644)	1·50	1·50
3548	(92c.) Two white rabbits on medallion (as No. **MS**2703)	1·50	1·50
3549	(92c.) Gold Horse (as No. 2995)	1·50	1·50
3550	(92c.) Deep green and gold ram (as No. 3101)	1·50	1·50
3551	(92c.) Dog (Saluki type) on lantern (as No. 3336)	1·50	1·50
3552	(92c.) Zhu Bajie seated on ground (as No. 3454)	1·50	1·50
3541/3552	Set of 12	16·00	16·00

(b) Ordinary gum. P 12½.

MS3553 160×161 mm. (92c.) Rat Bride on way to wedding (as T **1156**); (92c.) Ox (as Type **910**); (92c.) Tiger seal (as Type **933**); (92c.) White Rabbit (as Type **954**); (92c.) Dragon (as Type **976**); (92c.) Water Snake (as Type **998**); (92c.) Horse (as Type **1023**); (92c.) Three rams (as Type **1045**); (92c.) Sun Wukong the Monkey King from novel *Journey to the West* (as Type **1064**); (92c.) Rooster (as Type **1076**); (92c.) Dog (Pekinese) on lantern (as Type **1097**); (92c.) Zhu Bajie (Pigsy) in armour carrying Nine-toothed rake (as Type **1140**) .... 20·00 22·00

Nos. 3542/3552 and the stamps from **MS**3553 were all inscr 'P' and were originally valid for 92c. each.

Nos. 3542/3552 were issued in booklets of ten, No. SB677, originally sold for $11·04.

1170 Settlers Henry Sneed, Jordan W. Murphy with Great-granddaughter Bernice Bowen, Granddaughter Vivian Harris and Amy Broady and Waggon Train, *circa* 1916 (Amber Valley, Alberta)

1171 Ermine

(Des Rick Jacobson (illustration) and Lara Minja, Lime Design Inc. Litho Lowe-Martin)

2021 (22 Jan). Black History Month. Willow Grove, New Brunswick and Amber Valley, Alberta. T **1170** and similar horiz design. Multicoloured. Self-adhesive. Fluorescent frame. Die-cut perf 13×13½.

3554	(92c.) Type **1170**	1·50	1·50
	a. Booklet pane. Nos. 3554/3555, each ×5	15·00	
3555	(92c.) Settlers Alexander Diggs and Eliza Taylor and sailing ship off Saint John, New Brunswick, 1817 (Willow Grove)	1·50	1·50

Nos. 3554/3555 were both inscr 'P' and originally valid for 92c. They were issued in booklets of ten, No. SB678, originally sold for $9·20.

(Des Adrian Horvath. Illustration Robert Postma (3556), Michelle Valberg (3557), Dennis Fast (3558), Mathilde Poirier (3559), Paul Loewen (3560), backgrounds Michelle Valberg. Litho CBN)

2021 (16 Feb). Snow Mammals. T **1171** and similar multicoloured designs. Fluorescent frame.

(a) Self-adhesive. Die-cut perf 12½×13.

3556	(92c.) Type **1171**	1·50	1·50
	a. Booklet pane. Nos. 3556/3560, each ×2	15·00	
3557	(92c.) Snowshoe Hare	1·50	1·50
3558	(92c.) Arctic Fox (*horiz*)	1·50	1·50
3559	(92c.) Northern Collared Lemming (*horiz*)	1·50	1·50
3560	(92c.) Peary Caribou	1·50	1·50
3556/3560	Set of 5	6·75	6·75

(b) Ordinary gum. Perf 12.

MS3561 129×98 mm. As Nos. 3556/3560 .... 7·50 7·50

Nos. 3556/3560 were all inscr 'P' and originally valid for 92c. They were issued in booklets of ten, No. SB679, originally sold for $9·20.

1172 *Malus Rosseau* (pink blossom)

(Des Marie-Elaine Cusson (illustration) and Sputnik Design Partners Inc. Litho CBN)

2021 (1 Mar). Crabapple Blossoms. T **1172** and similar vert design. Multicoloured. Fluorescent frame.

(a) Self-adhesive coil stamps. Die-cut perf imperf×8.

3562	(92c.) *Malus Maybride* (white blossom)	1·50	1·50
	a. Horiz pair. Nos. 3562/3563	14·00	
3563	(92c.) Type **1172**	1·50	1·50

(b) Self-adhesive booklet stamps. Size 26×32 mm. Die-cut perf 13½.

3564	(90c.) Avro CF-105 Arrow	1·50	1·50
	a. Booklet pane. Nos. 3564/3565, each ×5	14·00	
3565	(92c.) As No.	1·50	1·50

(c) Ordinary gum. Perf 12×12½.

MS3566 120×84 mm. As Nos. 3562/3563 .... 3·00 3·50

Nos. 3562/3563 were issued in rolls of 50 containing the two stamps. Nos. 3564/3565 were issued in booklets of ten, No. SB680, originally sold for $9·20.

Booklet pane No. 3464a included ten small circular stickers.

Nos. 3562/3565 and the stamps within **MS**3566 were all inscr 'P' and were all originally valid for 92c. each.

1173 Redesigned Statuette for 50th Anniversary of JUNO Awards

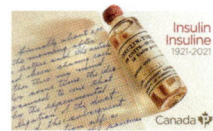

1174 Insulin Vial and Dr Frederick Banting's Notes

(Des Paprika and Amanda Arlotta (illustration). Litho Colour Innovations)

2021 (8 Apr). 50th Anniversary of JUNO Awards (Canadian music awards). Self-adhesive. Fluorescent frame. Die-cut perf 14×13½.

3567	**1173**	(92c.) multicoloured	1·50	1·50
		a. Booklet pane. No. 3567×5	8·00	

No. 3567 was inscr 'P' and was originally valid for 92c. It was issued in booklets of five, No. SB681, originally sold for $4·60.

(Des Subplot Design Inc. Litho Lowe-Martin)

2021 (15 Apr). Centenary of the Discovery of Insulin. Self-adhesive. Fluorescent frame on three sides (top, left and bottom). Die-cut perf 13.

3568	**1174**	(92c.) multicoloured	1·50	1·50
		a. Booklet pane. No. 3568×10	15·00	

No. 3568 was inscr 'P' and was originally valid for 92c. It was issued in booklets of ten, No. SB682, originally sold for $9·20.

1175 Night Sky with Crescent Moon seen through Mosque Window

1176 Fernand Nault (1920–2006, dancer and choreographer)

(Des Lionel Gadoury, Andrew Conlon, and Brad Pyne, Context Creative. Litho Lowe-Martin)

2021 (22 Apr). Eid. Self-adhesive. Fluorescent frame. Die-cut perf 13×13½.
3569 **1175** (92c.) multicoloured .... 1·50 1·50
        a. Booklet pane. No. 3569×10 .... 16·00

No. 3569 was inscr 'P' and was originally valid for 92c. It was issued in booklets of ten, No. SB683, originally sold for $9·20.

(Des Stephane Huot. Litho Colour Innovations)

2021 (29 Apr). Canadian Ballet Legends. T **1176** and similar vert design. Multicoloured. Fluorescent frame.
(a) Self-adhesive. Die-cut perf 13½×13.
3570   (92c.) Type **1176** .... 1·50 1·50
        a. Booklet pane. No. 3570×6 .... 10·00
3571   (92c.) Karen Kain (1951–, dancer and artistic director of Canadian National Ballet) ..... 1·50 1·50
        a. Booklet pane. No. 3571×6 .... 10·00
(b) Ordinary gum. Perf 13.
MS3572 124×90 mm. As Nos. 3570/3571 .... 3·00 3·00

Nos. 3570/3571 were issued in separate booklets of six, Nos. SB684/685, originally sold for $5·52 each.

Nos. 3570/3571 and the stamps within No. **MS**3572 were all inscr 'P' and were originally valid for 92c. each.

1177 John Turner on Sailing Trip through Haida Gwaii, 1985   **1178** *Bluenose* fishing

(Des Paprika. Litho Colour Innovations)

2021 (7 June). John Turner (1929–2020, Minister of Justice 1968–1972, Minister of Finance 1972–1975, Prime Minister of Canada 1984) Commemoration. Self-adhesive. Fluorescent frame. Die-cut perf 13½×14.
3573 **1177** (92c.) multicoloured .... 1·50 1·50
        a. Booklet pane. No. 3573×10 .... 15·00

No. 3573 was inscr 'P' and was originally valid for 92c. It was issued in booklets of ten, No. SB686, originally sold for $9·20.

(Des Dennis Page and Oliver Hill. Illustration Michael Little. Litho Colour Innovations)

2021 (29 June). Centenary of Launch of *Bluenose* (fishing and racing schooner). T **1178** and similar horiz design. Multicoloured. Fluorescent frame around pair.
(a) Self-adhesive. Die-cut perf 13×13½.
3574   (92c.) Type **1178** .... 1·50 1·50
        a. Booklet pane. Nos. 3574/3575, each ×5 15·00
3575   (92c.) *Bluenose* in its first race, International Fishermen's Trophy, 1921 .... 1·50 1·50
(b) Ordinary gum. P 13.
MS3576 105×55 mm. As Nos. 3574/3575 .... 3·00 3·50

Nos. 3574/3575 were inscr 'P' and were originally valid for 92c. They were issued in booklets of ten, No. SB687, originally sold for $9·20.

2021 (29 June). Capex 22 International One Frame Stamp Championship Exhibition, Toronto (1st issue). No. **MS**3577 additionally inscr with CAPEX '22 emblem on lower left sheet margin. Fluorescent frame around pair. Perf 13.
MS3577 105×55 mm. As Nos. 3574/3575 .... 3·00 3·50

1179 Stan Rogers performing at Calgary Folk Festival, early 1980s   **1181** Fireflies

(Des Steven Slipp. Illustration Peter Strain. Litho Lowe-Martin)

2021 (21 July). Stan Rogers (1949–1983, folk singer) Commemoration. Multicoloured. Self-adhesive. Fluorescent frame. Die-cut perf 13½×13.
3578 **1179** (92c.) multicoloured .... 1·50 1·50
        a. Booklet pane. No. 3578×10 .... 15·00

No. 3578 was inscr 'P' and was originally valid for 92c. It was issued in booklets of ten, No. SB688, originally sold for $9·20.

(Des Subplot Design Inc. Illustration Kim Smith. Litho Colour Innovations)

2021 (20 Sept). Canada Post Community Foundation. Self-adhesive. Fluorescent frame. Die-cut perf 13.
3579 **1181** ($1.02) multicoloured .... 1·75 1·75
        a. Booklet pane. No. 3579×10 .... 15·00

No. 3579 was inscr 'P+10' and was originally valid for 92c. It was issued in booklets of ten, No. SB689, originally sold for $10·20, which included a 10c. charity premium on each stamp.

1182 Brian Gable   **1183** Christopher Plummer

(Des Rejean Myette. Litho CBN)

2021 (8 Oct). Editorial Cartoonists. T **1182** and similar square designs. Multicoloured. Self-adhesive. Fluorescent frame. Die-cut perf 13.
3580   (92c.) Type **1182** .... 1·50 1·50
        a. Booklet pane. Nos. 3580/3584, each ×2 15·00
3581   (92c.) Terry Mosher .... 1·50 1·50
3582   (92c.) Duncan Macpherson .... 1·50 1·50
3583   (92c.) Serge Chapleau .... 1·50 1·50
3584   (92c.) Bruce MacKinnon .... 1·50 1·50
3580/3584 Set of 5 .... 6·75 6·75

No. 3580/3584 were inscr 'P' and were originally valid for 92c. each. They were issued in booklets of ten, No. SB690, originally sold for $9·20.

(Des Steven Slipp. Illustrations Spooky Panda. Litho Colour Innovations)

2021 (14 Oct). Christopher Plummer (1929–2021, actor) Commemoration. Multicoloured. Fluorescent frame.
(a) Self-adhesive. Die-cut perf 13.
3585 **1183** (92c.) multicoloured .... 1·50 1·50
        a. Booklet pane. No. 3585×10 .... 15·00
(b) Ordinary gum. Perf 13.
MS3586 160×180 mm. (92c.)×6 Type **1183** .... 9·00 10·00

No. 3595 and the stamps within No. **MS**3596 were all inscr 'P' and were originally valid for 92c. each.

No. 3595 was issued in booklets of ten, No. SB691, originally sold for $9·20.

1184 Rangoli Pattern   **1185** Lionel (Leo) Clarke, Robert Shankland and Frederick William Hall

(Des Seung Jai Paek. Litho Lowe-Martin)

2021 (19 Oct). Diwali. Self-adhesive. Fluorescent frame. Die-cut perf 13×13½.
3587 **1184** (92c.) multicoloured .... 1·50 1·50
        a. Booklet pane. No. 3587×10 .... 15·00

No. 3597 was inscr 'P' and was originally valid for 92c. It was issued in booklets of ten, No. SB692, originally sold for $9·20.

CANADA

(Des Soapbox Design. Illustration Richard Nalli-Petta. Litho Colour Innovations)

2021 (21 Oct). Valour Road. Canadian First World War Recipients of the Victoria Cross. Multicoloured.

(a) Self-adhesive. Die-cut perf 13½×13.

| 3588 | 1185 | (92c.) multicoloured | 1·50 | 1·50 |
| a. Booklet pane. No. 3588×10 | | | 15·00 | |

(b) Ordinary gum. Perf 13×13½.

| **MS**3589 160×180 mm. (92c.) As No. 3588×5 | 7·50 | 8·50 |

No. 3588 and the stamps within **MS**3589 were inscr 'P' and were originally valid for 92c. each.

No. 3588 was issued in booklets of ten, No. SB693, originally sold for $9·20.

1186 Remembrance Poppy

1187 Angel flying over Church

(Des Blair Thomson, Believe in. Litho Colour Innovations)

2021 (29 Oct). The Remembrance Poppy. Self-adhesive. Fluorescent frame. Die-cut perf 13½×13.

| 3590 | 1186 | (92c.) multicoloured | 1·50 | 1·50 |
| a. Booklet pane. No. 3590×10 | | | 15·00 | |

No. 3590 was inscr 'P' and was originally valid for 92c. It was issued in booklets of ten, No. SB694, originally sold for $9·20.

(Des Stephane Huot. Illustration Luc Melanson. Litho CBN)

2021 (1 Nov). Christmas. Angels. Self-adhesive. Fluorescent frame. Die-cut perf 13½×13.

| 3591 | 1187 | (92c.) gold, silver and light grey | 1·50 | 1·50 |
| a. Booklet pane. No. 3591×12 | | | 18·00 | |

No. 3591 was inscr 'P' and originally sold for 92c. It was issued in booklets of 12, No. SB695, originally sold for $11·04.

1188 Santa Claus

(Des Larry Burke and Anna Stredulinsky, Burke & Burke. Illustration Genevieve Godbout. Litho Lowe Martin)

2021 (1 Nov). Holiday Characters. T **1188** and similar square designs. Multicoloured. Fluorescent frame.

(a) Self-adhesive. Die-cut perf 13.

3592	(92c.) Type **1188**	1·50	1·50
a. Booklet pane. No. 3592×12		18·00	
3593	$1.30 Reindeer	2·00	2·00
a. Pane. No. 3593×6		11·00	
3594	$2.71 Elf	4·50	4·50
a. Pane. No. 3594×6		25·00	
3592/3594 Set of 3		7·25	7·25

(b) Ordinary gum. Perf 13.

| **MS**3595 92×54 mm. As Nos. 3592/3594 | 8·00 | 8·00 |

No. 3592 was inscr 'P' and was originally valid for 92c. It was sold in booklets of 12, No. SB696, originally sold for $11·04.

No. 3593 was issued in $7·80 panes of six stamps.

No. 3594 was issued in $16·26 panes of six stamps.

1189 Hanukkujah (Hanukkah Menorah)

1190 Buffy Sainte-Marie, 1992

(Des Joseph Gault and Avi Dunkelman. Litho Lowe-Martin)

2021 (8 Nov). Hanukkah. Self-adhesive. Fluorescent frame. Die-cut perf 13×13½.

| 3596 | 1188 | (92c.) multicoloured | 1·50 | 1·50 |
| a. Booklet pane. No. 3596×10 | | | 15·00 | |

No. 3596 was inscr 'P' and was originally valid for 92c. It was issued in booklets of ten, No. SB697, originally sold for $9·20.

(Des Paprika. Litho Lowe Martin)

2021 (19 Nov). Buffy Sainte-Marie (singer songwriter). Multicoloured. Self-adhesive. Fluorescent frame. Die-cut perf 13×13½.

| 3597 | 1190 | (92c.) multicoloured | 1·50 | 1·50 |
| a. Booklet pane. No. 3597×10 | | | 15·00 | |

No. 3597 was inscr 'P' and was originally valid for 92c. It was sold in booklets of ten, No. SB698, originally sold for $9·20.

1191 Margaret Atwood

1192 Eleanor Collins

(Des Steven Slipp. Litho Lowe-Martin)

2021 (25 Nov). Margaret Atwood (writer). Self-adhesive. Fluorescent frame. Die-cut perf 13½×13.

| 3598 | 1191 | (92c.) multicoloured | 1·50 | 1·50 |
| a. Booklet pane. No. 3598×10 | | | 15·00 | |

No. 3598 was inscr 'P' and was originally valid for 92c. It was issued in booklets of ten, No. SB699, originally sold for $9·20.

(Des Paprika. Illustration David Belliveau. Litho Lowe Martin)

2022 (21 Jan). Black History Month. Eleanor Collins (jazz singer). Self-adhesive. Die-cut perf 13½×13.

| 3599 | 1192 | (92c.) multicoloured | 1·50 | 1·50 |
| a. Booklet pane. No. 3599×6 | | | 8·00 | |

No. 3599 was inscr 'P' and was originally valid for 92c. It was sold in booklets of six, No. SB700, originally sold for $5·52.

1193 Royal Mail Machin Profile of Queen Elizabeth II

(Des Paprika. Litho Colour Innovations)

2022 (7 Feb). Platinum Jubilee. Fluorescent frame.

(a) Self-adhesive. Die-cut perf 13×13½.

| 3600 | 1193 | (92c.) black and silver | 1·50 | 1·50 |
| a. Booklet pane. No. 3600×10 | | | 15·00 | |

(b) Ordinary gum. P 12½×13.

| 3601 | 1193 | (92c.) black and silver | 1·50 | 2·00 |

Nos. 3600 and 3601 were both inscr 'P' and originally valid for 92c.

No. 3600 was issued in booklets of ten, No. SB701, originally sold for $9·20.

No. 3601 was printed in panes of 16.

1194 White Calla

CANADA

(Des Paprika. Illustration Fanny Roy. Litho Colour Innovations)

2022 (1 Mar). Callas. T **1194** and similar vert design. Multicoloured. Fluorescent frame.

(a) Self-adhesive coil stamps.
3602	(92c.) Type **1194**	1·50	1·50
	a. Horiz pair. Nos. 3602/3603	3·00	
3603	(92c.) Pink calla	1·50	1·50

(b) Self-adhesive booklet stamps. Size 25×32 mm. Die-cut perf 13½.
3604	(92c.) Type **1194**	1·50	1·50
	a. Booklet pane. No. 3604/3605, each ×5.	15·00	
3605	(92c.) As No. 3603	1·50	1·50

(c) Ordinary gum. P 13.
MS3606 127×73 mm. As Nos. 3604/3605............ 3·00 3·50

Nos. 3602/3605 and the stamps within No. **MS**3606 were all inscr 'P' and originally valid for 92c.
Nos. 3602/3603 were issued in rolls of 50 containing the two stamps.
Nos. 3604/3605 were issued in booklets of ten, No. SB702, originally sold for $9.20.
Booklet pane No. 3604a included ten small circular stickers.

1195 Donor and Recipient ('Give Life') **1196** Copper Lantern with Pierced Designs

(Des Kristine Do. Illustration: Chris DeLorenzo. Litho Lowe-Martin)

2022 (7 Apr). Organ and Tissue Donation. Self-adhesive. Die-cut perf 13½.
3607	**1195**	(92c.) multicoloured	1·50	1·50
		a. Booklet pane. No. 3607×10............	15·00	

No. 3607 was inscr 'P' and was originally valid for 92c. It was issued in booklets of ten, No. SB703, originally sold for $9.20.

(Des Soapbox Design. Illustration: Richard Nalli-Petta and Irene Laschi. Litho Lowe-Martin)

2022 (12 Apr). Eid. Self-adhesive. Die-cut perf 13½.
3608	**1196**	(92c.) multicoloured	1·50	1·50
		a. Booklet pane. No. 3608×6	8·00	

No. 3608 was inscr 'P' and was originally valid for 92c. It was issued in booklets of six, No. SB704, originally sold for $5.52.

1197 Salome Bey   **1198** *Delphinapterus leucas* (Beluga)

(Des Paprika. Illustration David Belliveau. Litho Lowe-Martin)

2022 (22 Apr). Salome Bey (1933–2020, singer, songwriter and composer) Commemoration. Self-adhesive. Die-cut perf 14×13½.
3609	**1197**	(92c.) multicoloured	1·50	1·50
		a. Booklet pane. No. 3609×6	8·00	

No. 3609 was inscr 'P' and was originally valid for 92c. It was issued in booklets of six, No. SB705, originally sold for $5.52.

(Des Soapbox Design. Illustrations: David Miller. Litho Lowe-Martin)

2022 (20 May). Endangered Whales. T **1198** and similar horiz designs. Multicoloured. Fluorescent frame.

(a) Self-adhesive. Die-cut perf 13½.
3610	(92c.) Type **1198**	1·50	1·50
	a. Booklet pane. Nos. 3610/3614, each×2	15·00	
3611	(92c.) *Eubalaena glacialis* (North Atlantic Right Whale)	1·50	1·50
3612	(92c.) *Balaenoptera musculus* (Blue Whale)	1·50	1·50
3613	(92c.) *Hyperoodon ampullatus* (Northern Bottlenose Whale)	1·50	1·50
3614	(92c.) *Orcinus orca* (Killer Whale)	1·50	1·50
3610/3614	Set of 5	6·75	6·75

(b) Ordinary gum. Perf 13½×14.
MS3615 129×86 mm. As Nos. 3610/3614............ 7·50 7·50

Nos. 3610/3614 and the stamps within No. **MS**3615 were all inscr 'P' and were originally valid for 92c. each.
Nos. 3610/3614 were issued in booklets of ten, No. SB706, originally sold for $9.20.

1199 Mont Tremblant

(Des Paprika. Litho Lowe-Martin)

2022 (9 June). Vintage Travel Posters. T **1199** and similar vert designs. Multicoloured. Fluorescent frame.

(a) Self-adhesive. Die-cut perf 13½.
3616	(92c.) Type **1199**	1·50	1·50
	a. Booklet pane. Nos. 3616/3620, each×2	15·00	
3617	(92c.) *The Royal York*	1·50	1·50
3618	(92c.) *Cruise the Great Lakes*	1·50	1·50
3619	(92c.) *Travel the Canadian*	1·50	1·50
3620	(92c.) *Canada's Picturesque East Coast*	1·50	1·50
3616/3620	Set of 5	6·75	6·75

Nos. 3616/3620 were issued in booklets of ten, No. SB707, originally sold for $9.20.
Nos. 3616/3620 and the stamps within No. **MS**3621 were all inscr 'P' and were originally valid for 92c. each.

(b) Ordinary gum. Perf 12½.
MS3621 117×100 mm. As Nos. 3616/3620............ 7·50 8·50

1200 Marie-Anne Day Walker-Pelletier

(Des Lime Design. Litho Lowe-Martin)

2022 (21 June). Indigenous Leaders. T **1200** and similar multicoloured designs. Fluorescent frame.

(a) Self-adhesive. Die-cut perf 13½.
3622	(92c.) Type **1200**	1·50	1·50
	a. Booklet pane. No. 3622×6	10·00	
3623	(92c.) Jose Kusugak	1·50	1·50
	a. Booklet pane. No. 3623×6	10·00	
3624	(92c.) Harry Daniels	1·50	1·50
	a. Booklet pane. No. 3624×6	10·00	
3622/3624	Set of 3	4·00	4·00

(b) Ordinary gum. Perf 12½.
MS3625 128×94 mm. As Nos. 3622/3624............ 4·50 5·00

Nos. 3622/3624 and the stamps within No. **MS**3625 were all inscr 'P' and were originally valid for 87c. each.
Nos. 3622/3624 were issued in separate booklets of six, Nos. SB708/SB710, each originally sold for $5.25.

1201 Sunflower   **1202** Lakeside Park Carousel

CANADA

(Des Hélène l'Heureux. Litho Lowe-Martin)

2022 (7 July). Help for Ukraine. Self-adhesive. Fluorescent frame. Die-cut perf 13½.
3626 **1201** (92c.) multicoloured .... 1·50 1·50
    a. Booklet pane. No. 3626×10........... 15·00
No. 3626 was inscr 'P' and originally sold for 92c. It was issued in booklets of ten, No. SB711, originally sold for $9.20.

(Des Paprika. Litho Colour Innovations)

2022 (21 July). Vintage Carousels. T **1202** and similar multicoloured designs. Fluorescent frame.

(a) Self-adhesive. Die-cut perf 13.
3627 (92c.) Type **1202** .... 1·50 1·50
    a. Booklet pane. Nos. 3627/3631, each×2 15·00
3628 (92c.) Bowness Carousel................... 1·50 1·50
3629 (92c.) C. W. Parker Carousel No. 119....... 1·50 1·50
3630 (92c.) Roseneath Carousel................. 1·50 1·50
3631 (92c.) Le Galopant .... 1·50 1·50
3627/3631 Set of 5................................. 6·75 6·75

(b) Ordinary gum. 13.
MS3632 90×90 mm. As Nos. 3627/3631............ 7·50 7·50
Nos. 3627/3631 and the stamps within No. **MS**3632 were all inscr 'P' and were originally valid for 92c. each.
Nos. 3627/3631 were issued in booklets of ten, No. SB712, originally sold for $9.20.

1203 Treehouses

1204 Ice Hockey

(Des Joanna Todd (illustration) and Chad Roberts Design. Litho Colour Innovations)

2022 (19 Sept). Canada Post Community Foundation. Self-adhesive. Fluorescent frame. Die-cut perf 13½.
3633 **1203** (92c.) multicoloured .... 1·75 1·75
    a. Booklet pane. No. 3633×10............ 16·00
No. 3633 was inscr 'P+10' and was originally valid for 92c. It was issued in booklet of ten, No. SB713, originally sold for $10.20, which included a 10c. charity premium on each stamp.

(Des Gary Alphonso (illustration) and Jim Ryce. Litho Lowe-Martin)

2022 (21 Sept). Summit Series. Canada's Victory over USSR, 1972. Self-adhesive. Fluorescent frame. Die-cut perf 13½.
3634 **1204** (92c.) multicoloured .... 1·50 1·50
    a. Booklet pane. No. 3634×10............ 15·00
No. 3634 was inscr 'P' and was originally valid for 92c. It was issued in booklet of ten, No. SB714, originally sold for $9.20.

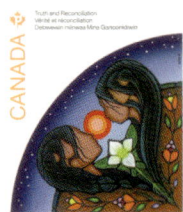
1205 Seeds of Change

1206 Candle

(Des Blair Thomson. Litho Colour Innovations)

2022 (29 Sept). Truth and Reconciliation. T **1205** and similar square designs. Multicoloured. Self-adhesive. Fluorescent frame. Die-cut perf 13½.
3635 (92c.) Type **1205** .... 1·50 1·50
    a. Booklet pane. Nos. 3635/3638, each×2 12·00
3636 (92c.) Woman Lighting Qulliq .... 1·50 1·50
3637 (92c.) Hands and Tears .... 1·50 1·50
3638 (92c.) Beaded Flower Map .... 1·50 1·50
3635/3638 Set of 4................................. 5·50 5·50
Nos. 3635/3638 were inscr 'P' and originally valid for 92c. each.
They were issued in booklet of eight, No. SB715, originally sold for $7.36.

(Des Paprika. Litho Colour Innovations)

2022 (6 Oct). Diwali. Self-adhesive. Fluorescent frame. Die-cut perf 13½.
3639 **1206** (92c.) multicoloured .... 1·50 1·50
    a. Booklet pane. No. 3639×6............. 10·00
No. 3639 was inscr 'P' and originally sold for 92c.
It was issued in booklet of six, No. SB716, originally sold for $5.52.

1207 Violet (Vi) Milstead

(Des Ivan Novotny. Litho Lowe-Martin)

2022 (17 Oct). Canadians in Flight. T **1207** and similar horiz designs. Multicoloured. Fluorescent frames.

(a) Self-adhesive. Die-cut perf 13½.
3640 (92c.) Type **1207** .... 1·50 1·50
    a. Booklet pane. Nos. 3640/3644, each×2 15·00
3641 (92c.) DHC-2 Beaver....................... 1·50 1·50
3642 (92c.) CAE Flight Simulator .... 1·50 1·50
3643 (92c.) Wilbur R. Franks .... 1·50 1·50
3644 (92c.) W. Rupert Turnbull................. 1·50 1·50
3640/3644 Set of 5................................. 6·75 6·75

(b) Ordinary gum. Perf 13.
MS3645 160×180 mm. ($4.60) As Nos. 3640/3644.......... 7·00 7·50
Nos. 3640/3644 and the stamps within No. **MS**3645 were all inscr 'P' and were originally valid for 92c.
Nos. 3640/3644 were issued in booklet of ten, No. SB717, originally sold for $9.20.

1208 Sergeant Thomas (Tommy) George Prince

(Des Blair Thomson. Litho Lowe-Martin)

2022 (28 Oct). Tommy Prince. Fluorescent frames.

(a) Self-adhesive. Die-cut perf 13½.
3646 **1208** (92c.) multicoloured .... 1·50 1·50
    a. Booklet pane. No. 3646×10............ 15·00

(b) Ordinary gum. Perf 13.
MS3647 160×180 mm. ($4.60) As Nos. 3646×5................. 7·00 7·50
No. 3646 and the stamps within No. **MS**3647 were all inscr 'P' and were originally valid for 92c.
No. 3646 was issued in booklet of ten, No. SB718, originally sold for $9.20.

1209 Cardinal

(Des Hambly & Woolley. Litho Colour Innovations)

2022 (1 Nov). Holiday Birds. T **1209** and similar square designs. Multicoloured. Fluorescent frame.

(a) Self-adhesive. Die-cut perf 13.
3648 (92c.) Type **1209** .... 1·50 1·50
    a. Booklet pane. No. 3648×12........... 18·00
3649 $1.30 Blue Jay............................... 2·25 2·25
    a. Pane. No. 3649×6...................... 12·00
3650 $2.71 Evening Grosbeak................... 4·50 4·50
    a. Pane. No. 3650×6...................... 25·00
3648/3650 Set of 3................................. 7·50 7·50

(b) Ordinary gum. Perf 13½.
MS3651 85×54 mm. ($4.60) As Nos. 3648/3650............ 7·00 8·00
No. 3648 was inscr 'P' and was originally valid for 92c. It was sold in booklet of 12, No. SB719, originally sold for $11.04.
No. 3649 was issued in $7.80 panes of six stamps.
No. 3650 was issued in $16.26 panes of six stamps.

CANADA

Booklet pane No. 3659a included ten small circular stickers.

1210 Star   **1211** Coloured Stars

(Des Paprika. Litho Colour Innovations)

2022 (1 Nov). Christmas. Self-adhesive. Fluorescent frame. Die-cut perf 13½.
3652 **1210** (92c.) multicoloured .... 1·50 1·50
         a. Booklet pane. No. 3652×12............. 18·00
No. 3652 was inscr 'P' and originally sold for 92c. It was issued in booklet of 12, No. SB720, originally sold for $11.04.

(Des Andrew Lewis. Litho Lowe-Martin)

2022 (7 Nov). Hanukkah. Self-adhesive. Fluorescent frame. Die-cut perf 13½.
3653 **1211** (92c.) multicoloured .... 1·50 1·50
         a. Booklet pane. No. 3653×6............... 8·50
No. 3653 was inscr 'P' and originally sold for 92c. It was issued in booklet of six, No. SB721, originally sold for $5.52.

1212 Monique Mercure

(Des Underline Studio. Litho Colour Innovations)

2022 (14 Nov). Monique Mercure (Actress). Fluorescent frames.
         (a) Self-adhesive. Die-cut perf 13½.
3654 **1212** (92c.) multicoloured .... 1·50 1·50
         a. Booklet pane. No. 3654×6............... 8·50
         (b) Ordinary gum. Perf 13½.
MS3655 160×180 mm. ($4.60) As Nos. 3654×6................ 7·00 8·00
No. 3654 and the stamps within No. **MS**3655 were all inscr 'P' and were originally valid for 92c.
No. 3655 was issued in booklet of six, No. SB722, originally sold for $5.52.

1213 Chloe Cooley, Slave Resistance Martyr   **1214** Persian Buttercups

(Des Lime Design. Litho Lowe-Martin)

2023 (30 Jan). Chloe Cooley. Self-adhesive. Fluorescent frame. Die-cut perf 13½.
3656 **1213** (92c.) multicoloured .... 1·50 1·50
         a. Booklet pane. No. 3656×6............... 8·00
No. 3656 was inscr 'P' and originally sold for 92c. It was issued in booklet of six, No. SB723, originally sold for $5.52.

(Des Stéphane Huot. Litho Lowe-Martin)

2023 (1 Mar). Persian Buttercup (*Ranunculus Renoncule*). T **1214** and similar multicoloured design. Fluorescent frame.
         (a) Self-adhesive coil stamps. Size 20×23 mm. Die-cut perf 9½.
3657   (92c.) Type **1214** .... 1·50 1·50
         a. Vert pair. Nos. 3657/3658.............. 3·00 3·00
3658   (92c.) Persian Buttercup (*Ranunculus asiaticus*) .... 1·50 1·50
         (b) Self-adhesive booklet stamps. Size 25×32 mm. Die-cut perf 13½.
3659   (92c.) As Type **1214** .... 1·50 1·50
         a. Booklet pane. No. 3659/3660, each ×5. 15·00
3660   (92c.) As No. 3658 .... 1·50 1·50
         (c) Ordinary gum. Perf 13.
MS3661 125×92 mm. (92c.)×2 As Nos. 3659/3660........... 3·00 3·50
Nos. 3657/3660 and the stamps within No. **MS**3661 were all inscr 'P' and originally valid for 92c.
Nos. 3657/3658 were issued in rolls of 50 containing the two stamps.
Nos. 3659/3660 were issued in booklets of ten, No. SB724, originally sold for $9.20.

1215 Bowl   **1216** Sea Otter (*Enhydra lutris*)

(Des Subplot Design. Litho)

2023 (3 Apr). Eid. Self-adhesive. Fluorescent frame. Die-cut perf 13½.
3662 **1215** (92c.) multicoloured .... 1·50 1·50
         a. Booklet pane. No. 3662×6............... 10·00
No. 3662 was inscr 'P' and originally sold for 92c. It was issued in booklets of six, No. SB725, originally sold for $5.52.

(Des Meredith MacKinlay. Litho Lowe-Martin)

2023 (18 Apr). Animal Mothers and Babies. T **1216** and similar square design. Fluorescent frame.
         (a) Self-adhesive. Die-cut perf 13.
3663   (92c.) Type **1216** .... 1·50 1·50
         a. Booklet pane. No. 3663×6............... 10·00
3664   (92c.) Red-Necked Grebe (*Podiceps grisegena*) .... 1·50 1·50
         (b) Ordinary gum. Perf 13.
MS3665 128×86 mm. (92c.)×2 As Nos. 3663/3664.......... 3·00 3·50
Nos. 3663/3664 and the stamps within No. **MS**3665 were all inscr 'P' and were originally valid for 92c.
Nos. 3663/3664 were issued in booklet of six, No. SB726, originally sold for $5.52.

1217 Bear, Fox, Owl and Ant Reading   **1218** King Charles III

(Des John Belisle. Litho)

2023 (1 May). Canada Post Community Foundation. Storytelling. Multicoloured. Self-adhesive. Fluorescent frame. Die-cut perf 13½.
3666 **1217** (92c.+10c.) multicoloured .... 1·75 1·75
         a. Booklet pane. No. 3666×10...... 16·00
No. 3666 was inscr 'P+10' and was originally valid for 92c. They were issued in booklets of ten, No. SB727, originally sold for $10.20, which includes a 10c. charity premium on each stamp.

(Des Paprika. Litho Lowe-Martin)

2023 (8 May). His Majesty King Charles III. Self-adhesive. Fluorescent frame. Die-cut perf 13½.
3667 **1218** (92c.) black and grey .... 1·75 1·50
         a. Pane. No. 3667×10 .... 16·00
No. 3667 was inscr 'P' and originally sold for 92c.
It was issued in pane of ten, originally sold for $9.20.

1219 Royal Canadian Mounted Police   **1220** Thelma Chalifoux

(Des Réjean Myette. Litho Lowe-Martin)

2023 (23 May). 150th Anniversary of the Royal Canadian Mounted Police. Self-adhesive. Fluorescent frame. Die-cut perf 13½.
3668 **1219** (92c.) multicoloured .... 1·50 1·50
         a. Booklet pane. No. 3668×6............... 10·00
No. 3668 was inscr 'P' and originally sold for 92c.
It was issued in booklets of six, No. SB728, originally sold for $5.52.

CANADA

(Des Andrew Perro. Litho Lowe-Martin)

2023 (21 June). Indigenous Leaders. T **1220** and similar multicoloured designs. Fluorescent frame.

(a) Self-adhesive. Die-cut perf 13.

3669	(92c.) Type **1220**	1·50	1·50
	a. Booklet pane. No. 3669×6	10·00	
3670	(92c.) Nellie Cournoyea	1·50	1·50
	a. Booklet pane. No. 3670×6	10·00	
3671	(92c.) George Manuel	1·50	1·50
	a. Booklet pane. No. 3671×6	10·00	
3669/3671 Set of 3		4·00	4·00

(b) Ordinary gum. Perf 12½.

MS3672	128×91 mm. (92c.)×3 As Nos. 3669/3671	4·50	5·00

Nos. 3669/3671 and the stamps within No. **MS**3672 were all inscr 'P' and were originally valid for 92c.

1221 Denys Arcand

1222 Ferry *Spirit of British Columbia*

(Des Paprika. Litho)

2023 (28 June). Denys Arcand (Film director). Self-adhesive. Fluorescent frame. Die-cut perf 13½.

3673	**1221**	(92c.) black and grey	1·50	1·50
		a. Booklet pane. No. 3673×6	10·00	

No. 3673 was inscr 'P+10' and was originally valid for 92c. They were issued in booklets of six, No. SB732, originally sold for $5.52.

(Des Lionel Gadoury, Owen Gabany. Litho Lowe-Martin)

2023 (12 July). Ferries of Canada. T **1222** and similar horiz designs. Fluorescent frame.

(a) Self-adhesive. Die-cut perf 13.

3674	(92c.) Type **1222**	1·50	1·50
	a. Booklet pane. Nos. 3674/3678 each×2.	15·00	
3675	(92c.) Ferry *Chi-Cheemaun*	1·50	1·50
3676	(92c.) Ferry *Trillium*	1·50	1·50
3677	(92c.) Ferry *Alphonse-Desjardins*	1·50	1·50
3678	(92c.) Ferry *Grand Manan V*	1·50	1·50
3674/3678 Set of 5		6·75	6·75

(b) Ordinary gum. Perf 13.

MS3679	170×75 mm. (92c.)×5 As Nos. 3674/3678	7·50	8·00

Nos. 3674/3678 and the stamps within No. **MS**3679 were all inscr 'P' and were originally valid for 92c.

Nos. 3674/3678 were issued in booklet of ten, No. SB733, originally sold for $9.20.

1223 Simonne Monet-Chartrand, 1919–1993

1224 Kamloops Residential School, Kamloops, BC

(Des Paprika. Litho Lowe-Martin)

2023 (28 Aug). Quebec Feminists. T **1223** and similar vert designs. Black. Self-adhesive. Fluorescent frame. Die-cut perf 13½.

3680	(92c.) Type **1223**	1·50	1·50
	a. Booklet pane. Nos. 3680/3682 each×2.	8·00	
3681	(92c.) Madeleine Parent, 1918-2012	1·50	1·50
3682	(92c.) Léa Roback, 1903-2000	1·50	1·50
3680/3682 Set of 3		4·00	4·00

Nos. 3680/3682 were all inscr 'P' and were originally valid for 92c.

Nos. 3680/3682 were issued in booklet of six, No. SB734, originally sold for $5.52.

(Des Blair Thomson. Litho)

2023 (28 Sept). Truth and Reconciliation. Residential Schools. T **1224** and similar vert designs. Multicoloured. Self-adhesive. Fluorescent frame. Die-cut perf 13½.

3683	(92c.) Type **1224**	1·50	1·50
	a. Booklet pane. Nos. 3683/3686 each×2.	12·00	
3684	(92c.) Île-à-la-Crosse Residential School, Île-à-la-Crosse, SK	1·50	1·50
3685	(92c.) Sept-Îles Residential School, Sept-Îles, QC	1·50	1·50
3686	(92c.) Grollier Hall, Inuvik, NT	1·50	1·50
3683/3686 Set of 4		5·50	5·50

Nos. 3683/3686 were all inscr 'P' and were originally valid for 92c.

Nos. 3683/3686 were issued in booklet of eight, No. SB735, originally sold for $7.36.

1225 Donald Sutherland

1226 Willie O'Ree

(Des Paprika. Litho)

2023 (19 Oct). Donald Sutherland (Actor). Self-adhesive. Die-cut perf 13½.

3687	**1225**	(92c.) multicoloured	1·50	1·50
		a. Booklet pane. No. 3687×10	15·00	

No. 3687 was inscr 'P' and was originally valid for 92c. They were issued in booklets of ten, No. SB736, originally sold for $9.20.

(Des Mike McQuade. Litho)

2023 (30 Oct). Willie O'Ree (Hockey player). Self-adhesive. Fluorescent frame. Die-cut perf 13½.

3688	**1226**	(92c.) black, yellow and grey	1·50	1·50
		a. Booklet pane. No. 3688×6	10·00	

No. 3688 was inscr 'P' and was originally valid for 92c. They were issued in booklets of six, No. SB737, originally sold for $5.52.

1227 Mountain Village in Winter

(Des Tim Zeltner and Jocelyne Saulnier. Litho)

2023 (2 Nov). Holiday. T **1227** and similar vert designs. Multicoloured. Fluorescent frame.

(a) Self-adhesive. Die-cut perf 13½.

3689	(92c.) Type **1227**	1·50	1·50
	a. Booklet pane. No. 3689×12	18·00	
3690	$1.30 Skaters on frozen pond	2·00	2·00
	a. Pane. No. 3690×6	11·00	
3691	$2.71 Coastal landscape in winter	4·50	4·50
	a. Pane. No. 3691×6	25·00	
3689/3691 Set of 3		7·25	7·25

(b) Ordinary gum. Perf 13½.

MS3692	127×870 mm. As Nos. 3689/3691	8·00	9·00

Nos. 3689/3691 and the stamps within No. **MS**3692 were all inscr 'P' and were originally valid for 92c.

Nos. 3689 was issued in booklets of 12, No. SB738, originally sold for $11.04.

No. 3690 was issued in $7.80 panes of six stamps.
No. 3691 was issued in $16.26 panes of six stamps.

1228 Madonna and Child

1229 Mona Parsons

(Des Adrian Horforth. Litho)

2023 (2 Nov). Christmas. Self-adhesive. Fluorescent frame. Die-cut perf 13½.
3693 **1228** (92c.) multicoloured .... 1·50 1·50
                a. Booklet pane. No. 3693×12............ 15·00

No. 3693 was inscr 'P' and was originally valid for 92c. They were issued in booklets of 12, No. SB739, originally sold for $11.04.

(Des Larry Burke and Anna Stredulinsky. Litho Lowe-Martin)

2023 (7 Nov). Mona Parsons, 1901-1976. Fluorescent frames.
  (a) Self-adhesive. Die-cut perf 13½.
3694 **1229** (92c.) multicoloured .... 1·50 1·50
                a. Booklet pane. No. 3694×10............ 15·00
  (b) Ordinary gum. Perf 12½.
MS3695 160×180 mm. ($4.60) As No. 3694×5................. 7·00 8·00

No. 3694 and the stamps within No. **MS**3695 were all inscr 'P' and were originally valid for 92c.

No. 3694 was issued in booklet of six, No. SB740, originally sold for $9.20.

1230 Rangoli Pattern **1231** Hanukkah Menorah

(Des Kristine Do. Litho)

2023 (9 Nov). Diwali. Self-adhesive. Fluorescent frame. Die-cut perf 13½.
3696 **1230** (92c.) multicoloured .... 1·50 1·50
                a. Booklet pane. No. 3696×6 .... 10·00

No. 3696 was inscr 'P' and was originally valid for 92c. It was issued in booklets of six, No. SB741, originally sold for $5.52.

(Des Hélène L'Heureux. Litho)

2023 (16 Nov). Hanukkah. Self-adhesive. Fluorescent frame. Die-cut perf 13½.
3697 **1231** (92c.) multicoloured .... 1·50 1·50
                a. Booklet pane. No. 3697×6 .... 10·00

No. 3697 was inscr 'P' and was originally valid for 92c. It was issued in booklets of six, No. SB742, originally sold for $5.52.

1232 Mary Ann Shadd

(Des Natasha Cunningham. Litho)

2024 (29 Jan). Mary Ann Shadd (Publisher), 1823-1893. Self-adhesive. Fluorescent frame. Die-cut perf 13½.
3698 **1232** (99c.) multicoloured .... 1·75 1·75
                a. Booklet pane. No. 3698×6 .... 10·50

No. 3698 was inscr 'P' and was originally valid for 99c. It was issued in booklets of six, No. SB742, originally sold for $5.94.

KIOSK LABELS

In December 2012 Canada Post installed self-service kiosks in 22 locations dispensing self-adhesive labels depicting a multicoloured, stylised Maple leaf and the word 'CANADA', the postal rate and a barcode being printed at the point of purchase. Labels were available at nine different rates, the inland rate initially being 61c. Postal rates changed on 14 January 2013, the inland letter rate rising to 63c. The test ended in early August 2013 and kiosks were withdrawn.

BALDWIN'S 1872

Consign to specialists with over 150 years of auction expertise.

Contact us to
receive a free valuation

www.baldwins.co

The following index is intended to facilitate the identification of Canadian issues *from* **1942**. Portrait stamps are usually listed under surnames only, views under the name of the town or city and other issues under the main subject or a prominent word and date chosen from the inscription. Simple abbreviations have occasionally been resorted to and when the same design or subject appears on more than one stamp, only the first of each series is indicated.

4-H Clubs 1301

A

Abbott, Dr. Maude **MS**1960
Abbott, Sir John J. C. 444
Academy of Arts 972
Acadia 1021, 2364
Aconcagua 2165
Acrotholus Audeti 3212
Adam Brown (locomotive) 1109
Adoration of the Magi 3173
Aerospace Technology 1678
Aeshna canadensis (Dragonfly) 2520, **MS**2522
African Violets 2663, **MS**2665
Africville 2996
Agapostemon virescens (Bee) ... 3412
Agawa Canyon 2145
Agricultural Education 782
AIDS 1682
Air Canada 1251
Air Force 1140, 1623, 1920
Air Training camp 399
Aircraft 399, 438, 509, 540, 556, 636, 966, 996, 1026, 1050, 1251, 1623, 1678, 1920, 1936, 1219, **MS**2357
Alaska Highway 1497
Albani, Emma 983
Alberta 1511, 2362
Alberta and Saskatchewan 481
Alex Colville on the Tantramar Marshes 3117
Alex Fraser Bridge 1653
Alexander, Lincoln M. 3398
Algonkians 723
Algonquin Park 1545
All-Star Games 1963, 2052, 2316
Allan, Sir Hugh 2280
Alouette II (satellite) 570
Alouettes de Montréal 2882, **MS**2883, 2893, **MS**2894
Alpine Club of Canada 2408
American Hellenic Education Progressive Association ... 2201
Amphilex 2002 .... **MS**2157
Angels 1218, 1859, 1949, 2528, 3591
Angels, Saint-Jean-Baptiste Day 3112
Animals 3663
Anka, Paul 2503
Anne of Green Gables 2557
Antique instruments 1001
Apollo 11 3482
Apple Blossom Festival, Nova Scotia 2076
Aquarius 2772
Arbour, Louise 2867, **MS**2871
Arcand, Denys 3673
Archer 845
Archer, Captain Jonathan (*Star Trek*) 3267
Architecture 1275
Arctic 1656
Arctic Hare 2704
Arctic Islands 970
Armbro Flight (Horse) 1906
Armed Forces 3436
Armenian Church 2085
Armistice Centenary 3443
Arms and flowers 543
Art Canada 1289, 1327, 1384, 1421, 1504, 1539, 1589, 1629, 1681, 1721, 1825, 1912, 2011, 2097, 2133, 2355, 2389, 2489, 2551, 2606, **MS**2607, 2686, **MS**2687, 2753, 2839, **MS**2840
Art Déco 2789
Artifacts 1054
Asahi 3472
Ashevak, Kenojuak 1539
Ashnola No. 1 Bridge 3480
Ashoona, Pitseolak 1531
Astronauts 2225
Astronomy 3414
Athabasca (ship) 854
Athabasca River 1433
Athletics World Championships, Edmonton 2087
Atwood, Margaret 3598
Audubon, John J. ... 2195, 2274, 2340
Automobiles **MS**1563, **MS**1611, **MS**1636, **MS**1683, **MS**1684
Autumn 679
Auyuittup National Park, Nunavut 2083
Avro CF-105 Arrow 3464
Avro 540K (aircraft) 1206
Avro Lancaster (aircraft) ... 997, 1577
Avro (Canada) (aircraft) ... 996, 1028

B

Back to God's Country (film) ... **MS**1698
Ballet dancers 3570
Balloons 2388
Banff 885*c*, 1541
Banff Springs Golf Club 1637
Banting, Frederick 1415, **MS**1960
Barbeau, Marcel 1820
Barker, William George 3462
Barkerville, British Columbia ... 2081
Barreau de Québec 1911
Bartlett, Captain R.A. 2628
Baseball 1307, 2073
Basket weaving 1896
Basketball 829, 1454
Bat 1649
Batoche, Battle of 1146
Battle of the Atlantic 2353
Battleford Post Office 1230
Baubles 2698
BC Lions 2875, **MS**2883, 2886, **MS**2894
Be Prepared 515
Bear cub 2715
Beardy, Jackson 1405
Bears 3485
Beau Dommage 2956
Beaugrande-Champagne, Clare 3293
Beaver 473, 1267, 2706*c*
Beaver (ship) 820
Beaver wearing shirt & cap, Holly in mouth 1175
Bed 1061
Bed clothes 1534
Bees 3411
Béliveau, Jean 3312
Bell, Alexander Graham 408, **MS**1984
Bell Canada **MS**1983
Bell Island Hag 3221
Belted Kingfisher 1646
Beneficial Insects 2516, 2517, **MS**2905
Bennett, R. B. 483, 697
Bennett, W. A. C. 1775
Bernard, Warren 3091
Bernier, Joseph E. 893
Berries 1460, 2350
Berthiaume, Treffle 1141
Bethune, Norman 1375
Bey, Salome 3609
Big Ben (Horse) 1905
Big Brothers Big Sisters 2944
Billes, A. J. & J. W. 1722
Binoculars 2200
Biological programme 649
Biotechnology 1680
Bird decoration 765
Birds 407, 443, 474, 479, 495, 539, 620, 638, 906, 977, 1199, 1290, 1432, 1496, 1587, 1646, 1673, 1717, 1756, 1779, 1865, 1974, 2058, 2195, **MS**2236, 2274, 2340, 2350, 2384, 2706*c*, 2710, 2711, 2714*b*, 3648
Birds of Canada 3215, 3300
Bishop, Billy 1609
Bison 1007
Black Bear cub 2715
Black History Month 2600, 2601, 2656, 2750, 2837, 2911, 2912, 3103, 3183, 3247, 3397, 3455, 3508, 3554, 3599
Black, Martha 1748
BlackBerry 2815
Blomidon Park 1555
Blue Heron Route 1813
Blue Jays (baseball team) 2073
Bluenose (schooner) 3574
Blue Poppy 1724
Blue Racer 2422
Blueberry Grunt 3466
Boats 1315, 1377, 1428
Bobak, Bruno 1047*i*, 1825
Bobak, Molly 1503*f*
Bobsleigh 1237, 1485
Bogner's Grocery 3052
Bohemian Waxwing 2276
Bombardier **MS**1984
Bombus affinis (Bumblebee) 3411
Bombus polaris (Bumblebee) 2519, **MS**2522
Bondar, Roberta 2226
Bonsecours Market, Montréal ... 1279
Bookbinding 1887
Books 2510
Borden, Sir R. L. 434, 695
Borduas, Paul-Emile 1012, 1818
Boreal Chickadee 2277
Bouchard, Simone 1138
Boundary Waters Treaty 2617
Bourassa, Henri 627
Bourdeau, Robert 3295
Bourgeoys, Marguerite 805
Bowell, Sir Mackenzie 476
Bower, Johnny 3167
Bowls 921
Boxing 815
Boys and Girls Clubs 2004
Bracken, John 1777
Brakeman 3158
Brant, Molly 1194
Branta canadensis 3431
Breadalbane (Ship) 1249
Brent Goose 2196
Breukelman, Jim 2918
Bridges 2345
British Columbia 503, 685, 1696, 1737, 2567
Brock, Sir Isaac 643, 2872
Brodeur, Martin 3170
Brown Bear 1275
Brown, George 626
Brûlé, Etienne 1232
Brunet, Emile 1667
Brymner, William 1342
Bubo scandiacus 3432
Bubo virginanus 3216
Bumblebee 2519, **MS**2522
Buried Treasure 1448
Burke, Sarah 3000
Burr, Raymond 2563
Burrowing Owl 2706*d*
Burtynsky, Edward 3058
Butchart Gardens 1422, 2075
Buttercup 3657
Butter Tart 3467
Butterflies 1296, 1645, 2385
By, John 943

C

Cabot, John 412, 1210, 1736
Cabot Trail 1738
Cadets 2265
Cadieux, Geneviève 3118
Cains Island 1179
Calgary 812, 2362
Calgary Flames 2964, **MS**2967, 2972, **MS**2975
Calgary Stampede ... **MS**1954, 2864, **MS**2866
Calgary Stampeders (football team) ... 2877, **MS**2883, 2888, **MS**2894
Calla (flower) 3602
Callaghan, Morley 2222
Calling of an Engineer 1987
Campeau, Michel 3194
CANADA 92 1487
Canada 150 3282
Canada Council **MS**1953
Canada Day 944, 1013, 1047*a*, 1090, 1123*a*, 1163, 1203, 1241, 1292, 1323, 1389, 1427, 1503*a*, 1545, 1597, **MS**1642*a*, 1690
Canada Export Month 1337
Canada Games 641
Canada Geese 407, 443, 539, 2710
Canada–China Diplomatic Relations 2372
Canada–Israel 60 Years of Friendship 2666
Canada Post Community Foundation 3532, 3549, 3633,3666
Canadair (aircraft) 966, 1027, 1678
Canadarm 3288
Canadian Amateur Golf Championship 1637
Canadian Broadcasting Corporation 1207, **MS**1953
Canadian Country Artists 3061
Canadian Flag 1630, 2434, 2728
Canadian Flag, 50th anniversary 3105
Canadian Football League Teams ... 2875, **MS**2883
Canadian Forces Postal Service 1198
Canadian Geographic's Wildlife 2679, **MS**2684
Canadian Hockey Legends 3311
Canadian Horse and Newfoundland Pony 2614, 2615
Canadian Indians 721
Canadian International Air Show 1936
Canadian Inventions Spot 2629, 2632
Canadian Labour Congress 2391
Canadian Museum for Human Rights 3067
Canadian National Exhibition ... 2266
Canadian Navy 2673, **MS**2675
Canadian Nurses Association ... 2556
Canadian Opera 3248
Canadian Post, 150 Years 2072
Canadian Postmasters and Assistants Association 2155
Canadian Press 615
Canadian Pride 2728
Canadian Rangers 2200
Canadian Recording Artists 2500, 2618, **MS**2622
Canadian Tire 1722
Canadian Tulip Festival, Ontario 2082
Canadian War Museum 2354
Canadian Wine and Cheese 2415
Canadians in Flight 3461
Canadians in Hollywood 2395, 2560
Canals 1795
Cancer (zodiac) 2765
Candles 745, 2354, 3639
Candy, John 2398
Canoe 1315, 1380
Caouette, Real 1751
Cape Spear Lighthouse 3140
Cape St Mary's Seabird Reserve 1548
Capex '78 .... 907, 914
Capex '87 .... **MS**1212, 1227
Capex '96 .... **MS**1684
Capex '22 .... **MS**3577
Capricorn 2771
Captain Canuck 1664
Carcharodon carcharias (Shark) 3417
Cardinal, Douglas 2494
Caribou 486, 1276*c*, 2708
Caribou Hotel 3161
Carmichael, Franklin **MS**1642*a*
Carol singing 1617
Carousels 3627
Carr, Emily 674, 1421
Carrey, Jim 3071
Cars **MS**1563, **MS**1611, **MS**1684
Cartier, Jacques 1118
Cartography 742
Cartoonists 3580
Casa Loma, Toronto 2208
Casgrain, Therese 1145
Casson, Alfred **MS**1642*c*
Castle Hill 1166
Catherwood, Ethel 1691
Cats 2928, 3127

CANADA **Design Index**

CCM (motorcycle) 2945
Cedar Dunes Park 1547
Census 683
Cetorhinus maximus (Shark) 3418
Chair and Mace 508
Challenger (space shuttle) 1204
Chambly Canal 1800
Champlain, Samuel de 2400, 2550
Charlottetown 642
Charlottetown Conference 557
Charter of Rights and Freedoms 1239
Chasmosaurus belli 3124
Chauliognathus marginatus (Leatherwing) 2519*c*, **MS**2523, **MS**2905
Chemical Industry 489, 2362
Cherry blossom 650
Chevrier, Lionel 1749
Chicora (ship) 853
Chief Justice Robinson (ship) 931
Child 824
Children in origami boat 3074
Children playing 2367
Children reading 3164
Children's paintings 661, 882, 2006
China '99 **MS**1917
China 2009 World Stamp Exhibition **MS**2583
Chinatown Gates 2934
Chinese New Year 1714, 1767, 1862, 1957, 2050, 2116, 2176, 2247, 2314, 2379, 2478, 2538, 2581, **MS**2582, 2643, **MS**2644, 2702, 2826, 2906, 2992, 3098, 3178, 3242, 3332, 3450, 3503
Chinook 1447
Choose adoption 2928
Chown, S. D. 807
Christ in manger 667
Christmas 560, 568, 570, 618, 630, 644, 661, 687, 745, 764, 792, 822, 848, 895, 928, 962, 993, 1023, 1080, 1111, 1137, 1181, 1218, 1254, 1308, 1342, 1405, 1450, 1525, 1572, 1617, 1667, 1711, 1763, 1859, 1949, 2021, 2110, 2172, 2238, 2375, 2376, 2430, 2431, 2526, 2527, 2576, 2579, **MS**2580, 2638, **MS**2641, 2642, 2697, 2698, 2821, **MS**2824, 2825, 2900, 2901, **MS**2904, 2987, 2988, 3093, 3094, 3173, 3174, 3237, 3238, 3325, 3326, 3445, 3446, 3496, 3497, 3535, 3591, 3592, 3652, 3693
Christmas plants 1254
Christmas tree 669, 1023
Chrysochus auratus (Beetle) 2519*d*, **MS**2523
Chrysopha oculata (Lacewing) 2518, **MS**2522, **MS**2905
Church 670, 1111
Churchill River 1587
Churchill, Winston 565, 2554
CIDA **MS**1959
Cinema **MS**1698*a*
Circus 1851
Cirque du Soleil **MS**1954
Citizenship 409
City streets 880
City view 708
Civil aviation 480
Clemmys guttata (Turtle) 3473
Climbers 2408
Climbing Mount Habel 3195
Clown 2098
CN Tower **MS**1985
Coady, Father Moses **MS**1962
Coast and ancient trees 2435
Coat of Arms and flowers 543
Cobalt 60 1295
Cohen, Leonard 3490
Cohen, Lynne 3055
Coin 2555
Colicos, John 3204
Colombo Plan 520
Colophon emerging from Book 2393
Columbia River 1588
Colville, Alex 1047*f*, 2133, 3117
Combine-harvester 404, **MS**1636
Comeau, Napolean Alexandre 1821
Comic Superheroes 1661
Common Murre 2198
Commonwealth Day 1084
Commonwealth Games 908, 918, 1590
Commonwealth Heads of Government Meeting 1253
Commonwealth Parliamentary Association 575
Commonwealth Parliamentary Conference 894
Community Foundation 2895, 2983, 3074, 3164, 3235, 3309, 3442, 3494
Comox Valley Elasmosaur 3213
Conan, Laure 1085
Confederation Bridge 1731
Congresses 741
Consolidated Canso (aircraft) 969
Constitution 1045, 3289
Cook, Dr. J. 808
Cook, James 910
Cooley, Chloe 3656
Corals 2138
Coronation, 50th Anniversary 2203
Coronation, 60th Anniversary 2943
Coronation, 65th Anniversary 3410
Corriveau, Marie-Josephte 3160
Corvus corax 3218
Coteau-du-Lac 1098
Cougar 886, 2372
Count of Frontenac 3047
Countess of Dufferin (locomotive) 1133
Country women 511
CP Class D10a (locomotive) 1135
Crab 2765
Crabapple Blossoms 3562
Cradle 1062
Crate 536
Crèche 2376, 2377
Creighton, Donald G. 1707
Crosby, Sidney 3227
Cross 2354
Crowfoot 1213
Cunard, Sir Samuel 2279
Cupids, Newfoundland 2694
Curling 632, 789, 1282, 2125, 2999
Curtiss (aircraft) 967, 998
Cyanocitta cristata 3302
Cyanocitta stelleri 3433
Cycling 770, 1595, 2224
Cypress Hills Park 1553
Cypretherium Coarctatum 3210

D

D-Day 2281
da Costa, Mathieu 3247
da Silva, Pedro 2204
Dahlia 3509
Daisies 3254
Dalhousie Law School 1110
Dallaire, Jean 1137, 1912
Dan George, Chief 2561
Danaus plexippus 2517
Dance 1340
Dandurand, Senator Raoul **MS**1961
Daoust, Sylvia 2378
Daudelin, Charles 2153
Davies, Robertson 2959
Davies, Will 3405
Dawson 1688
Daylilies 2843, **MS**2847
de Champlain, Samuel 2361
de Gaspé, Philippe Aubert 1195
de Havilland (aircraft) 1026, 1051
de la Gaspésie Park 1546
de Mons, Pierre Dugua 2282
de Saint-Denys Garneau, Hector 2221
de Salaberry, Lieutenant-Colonel Charles-Michel 942, 2949
Deer 2028, 2712
Dempster Highway 1810, 1878
Dentistry Building 2544
Department of Foreign Affairs and International Trade 2616
Desbarats, G.-E. 1243
Desjardins, Alphonse and Dorimène 806, **MS**1962
Desmarteau, Étienne 1692
Desmond, Viola 2838
Destroyer 388
Diamond Jubilee 2830, **MS**2831, 2857, **MS**2858
Dickins, W. H. Punch 3463
Diefenbaker, John G. 982
Dieppe 1523
Difference Makers 2867, **MS**2871
Dille, Lutz 3190
Dimetrodon Borealis 3211
Dinosaur Provincial Park 3142/3143
Dinosaur Trail 1811
Dinosaurs 1568, 3121, 3209
Discovery Trail 1879
Diving 768, 1594, 2359
Diwali 3306, 3533, 3587, 3639, 3696
Doane, Thomas Coffin 2919
Dogs 1303, **MS**2357, 2379, 2547, 2930/2931, 3128
Dollard des Ormeaux 516
Dolls 1385
Doohan, James 3203
Dorchester (locomotive) 1106
Dory 1377
Douglas, Tommy 1772, 2884
Dove **MS**1946, 2201, 2529, 3443
Dragon boat race 2210
Dragonfly 2386, 2520
Drawson, Blair 3406
Dressler, Marie 2562
Dryden, Ken 3165
Drying furs 432
Dubois, Gérard 3407
Duck 495, 1290, 2409
Duck Decoys 2409
Duclos, Gilbert 3294
Duke and Duchess of Cambridge 2795
Dumas, A. 1503*a*
Dumont, Gabriel 1146
Dungarvon Whooper 3222

E

Early morning fog and lighthouse 3140
Eaton, Timothy 1583
Edmonton 2938
Edmonton Eskimos 2876, **MS**2883, 2887, **MS**2894
Edmonton Oilers 2961, **MS**2967, 2970, **MS**2975
Education 522
Edwards, Henrietta 1002
Eid 3281, 3514, 3569, 3608, 3662
Elbrus 2160
Electric oven 2816
Electric wheelchair 2817
Electron microscope 1294
Elizabeth II 410, 450, 463, 512, 527, 559, 579, 613, 700, 759, 855, 867, 1161, 2464, 2830, **MS**2831, 2857, **MS**2858, 2943, 3157, 3410
Elizabeth II and Duke of Edinburgh 440, 500
Emergency Responders 3436
Emergency Services 1441
Empress of Ireland (liner) 3041
Emydoidea blandingii 3474
Endangered Species 2420, 2511, 2569, **MS**2573
Endangered Turtles 3473
Energy 1790
Engineering Institute 1240
Erebus HMS 3151
Erickson, Arthur 2493
Ericsson (ship) 1250
Erigeron speciosus 3254
Ermine 3556
Esposito, Phil 3228
Esposito, Tony 3166
Euoplocephalus tutus 3125
Excavators 913
Exercise (Dog) 3128
Exploration 1208, 1232, 1285, 1319
Expo '67 611, 3282
Expo '86 1192, 1196
Expo 2005, Aichi, Japan 2335

F

Fafard, Joe 2839, **MS**2840
Fairchild (aircraft) 1050
Fairclough, Ellen 2358
Falardeau, Antoine-Sébastien 2430
Falco rusticolus 3301
Family group 785, 825
Famous Canadians 3640
Farm scene 382, 401
Fawn 2712
Félix-Gabriel-Marchand Bridge 3478
Feminists 3680
Fencing 814
Fenerty, C. 1242
Ferries 3674
Ferron, Marcelle 1819
Ferry 587
Fessenden, R. A. 1241
FIFA U-20 World Cup 2499
FIFA Women's World Cup 3135
Films 1338
Filumena 3248
FINA World Championships, Montréal 2359
Finley, Gerald 3249
Fire Service 1443, 2202
Firefighters 3437
Fireflies 3579
Fireworks 2540
First Land Route 538
First Non-stop Flight 636
First Powered Flight in Canada 2602
Firth, Sharon 3392
Firth, Shirley 3392
Fisgard Lighthouse 1129
Fish 976, 1727, 1784
Fisherman 433
Fishing 491
Fishing Flies 1784, **MS**2328
FitzGerald, Lionel 1047*l*, **MS**1642*c*
Flag 944*a*, 1328, 1350, 1389, 1630, 2364, 2728, 3105
Flag and Canada 578
Flamenco at 5.15 (film) 3029
Fleming, Sir Sandford 893, 2170
Fleur de Lys 1665
Flower and buildings 838
Flowers 543, 650, 856, 978, 1019, 1422, 1680, 2234, 2303, 2336, 2384, 2470 2530, 2541, 2645, **MS**2652, 2843, **MS**2847, 2913
Flying Squirrel 1261
Fog and lighthouse 3140
Fokker (aircraft) 1052
Folk Art 3536
Folk Songs 1564
Folktales 1445
Football 831, 2289
Forest 702, 1328, 1394
Forest, Michel 2376
Forestry 441
Formula 1 Motor Racing 3275
Forrester, Maureen 2425
Fort Anne 1164
Fort Beauséjour 1099
Fort Chambly 1096
Fort Erie 1168
Fort Frederick 1172
Fort George (haunted) 3048
Fort Henry 1090
Fort Lennox 1170
Fort No. 1, Point Levis 1097
Fort Prince of Wales 1094
Fort Rodd Hill 1092
Fort Walsh 1169
Fort Wellington 1093
Fort Whoop Up 1167
Fort William 1091
Fort York 1175
Fortes, Joe 2911
Fortin, Marc-Aurele 1011
Fossils 1390, 1417
Foster, Harry Red 1824
Founding members and Registry Roll 2509
Four Indian Kings (painting) 2667, **MS**2671
Fox 1265, 2026, 2423, 2707
Fox, Michael J. 2870, **MS**2871
Fox, Terry 1044, **MS**1959, 3287
Fram (polar research ship) 2263
Francophone Summit 2575
Francophonie Games 2066
Franklin, Benjamin 839, 2948
Franklin Expedition, 170th anniversary 3151
Franklin, Sir John 1320
Franklin the Turtle 2859, **MS**2863
Frappier, Armand **MS**1960
Fraser River 1558
Fraser, Simon 1287
Fratercula arctica 3217
Frechette, Louis-Honoré 1330
Free Press 501
Freestyle aerials (skiing) 2126
Freighter's Boat on the Banks of the Red River 3192
French, Commissioner 751
French River 1585

Design Index CANADA

French Settlement in North America 2282, 2361, 2400, 2508, 2550
Friends and Family and Trips in Front of Simpsons..............3114
Frobisher, Sir Martin 537
Frog..2512
From Far and Wide 3337
Frontenac, Governor 720
Frontier College...........................1941
Frosted tree.................................3138
Frye, Northrop **MS**1970
Fuller, Thomas................................975
Fundy...884

G

G as Beaver enclosing 50..........2414
Gadbois, Abbé Charles-Emile... 1723
Gagnon, C. A.................................795
Games, flags 641
Gannet...474
Gardenias 3456
Gardens...........................1422, 2384
Garneau, Marc 2225
Gateway 922
Gatineau Park, Québec.............2209
Gaudet, Sonja 3395
Gauvreau, Pierre..........................1817
Gavia immer..................................3304
Gélinas, Gratien **MS**1972
Gemini 2774
Geography 744
Geological Survey 1509
Geology 743
George VI 375, 389, 414
Gérin-Lajoie, Marie-Josephine...1530
Gesner, Abraham **MS**1984
Ghost Bride 3044
Ghost Train 3046
Gibraltar Point..............................1131
Gifts..2238
Gilbert, Sir Humphrey 1102
Girl Guides...............515, 1175, 2693
Girl watching Beluga Whale 2402
Gisborne, F. N. 1244
Glacier..884
Glass blowing...............................1889
Glasses of Wine............................2415
Glen Abbey Golf Club 1639
Globe 510
Goat kid.......................................2709*b*
Goin' Down the Road (film) **MS**1698*a*
Gold Rush 1685, 2081
Golf 1637
Goslings 2710
Gould, Glenn **MS**1952
Gouthro, S. 1503*d*
Governor-General 2128, 2267
Goyette, Danielle 3393
Graham, Rodney 2923
Grain elevator 379, 589
Grand Chief of the Mi'kmaq 2508
Grauerholz, Angela 3191
Great Bear Lake 402
Great Blue Heron 1199
Great Canadian Comedians.....3068
Great Canadian Goalies............3165
Great Canadian Illustrators 3404
Great Canadian NHL Forwards ... 3227
Great Cormorant..........................2197
Great Horned Owl 1201
Great Peace of Montréal 2096
Greek figure.......................2201, 2288
Greene, Lorne 2395
Greene, Nancy 3391
Greetings stamps...........1580, 1654, 1988, 2020, 2045, 2099, 2388, 2480, 2540, 2599, 2752
Grenfell..563
Gretzky, Wayne............................3316
Grey Cup 1260, 2885, **MS**2894, 2905*a*
Grey Jay...620
Grey Owl (Archibald Belaney)...3196
Griffith, Harold.............................1416
Grizzly Bear 1758
Gros Morne National Park 3002
Group of Seven 660, **MS**1642, 3517
Grove, Frederick Philip................940
Grus americana............................3430
GT Class E3 (locomotive)...........1134
Guevremont, Germaine 847
Guide Dogs 2547
Guimond, Olivier..........................3070
Guttman, Irving............................3251
Gymnastics 830
Gyrfalcon 2199
Gzowski, Sir Casimir......................535

H

Hadfield, Chris 2228
Haliburton, Thomas C. 1710
Halifax.................................413, 1095
Halifax Citadel..............................3162
Halifax Explosion centenary 3330
Halifax Public Gardens...............1426
Hamilton (ship) 1247
Hamilton, Mary Riter 3534
Hamilton, Lewis...........................3279
Hamilton Tiger-Cats... 2880, **MS**2883, 2891, **MS**2894
Hands enclosing Globe 2391
Hanlan, Ned 985
Hansen, Rick 2868, **MS**2871
Hanson Boorne............................1324
Hanukkah.............3331, 3502, 3540, 3596, 3653, 3697
Harlequin...............................**MS**1972
Harmon, Byron 3195
Harris, Lawren 1344, **MS**1642*a*
Harris, Robert 972
Harrison, T. 1503*j*
Hartland Bridge...............1652, 3476
Harvey, Doug 3076
Harvie, Eric Lafferty..............**MS**1973
Haunted Canada....3044, 3158, 3221
Haunted Fort George.................3048
Haut-fond Prince 1178
Hawker Hurricane (aircraft)........ 999
Head-Smashed-In Buffalo Jump..............2150, 3010, 3036
Healing from Within **MS**1969
Health Professionals...................1805
Hearne 682, 1319
Hébert, Anne................................2220
Hébert, Louis................................1173
Hébert, P. 973, 1047*b*
Help for Ukraine..........................3626
Hémon, Louis 804
Henderson, Alexander...............3193
Hen Hop! (film) **MS**1698
Henday, Anthony.........................1285
Henderson, Alexander...............1325
Hens 977
Henson, Josiah.............................1104
Hepburn, Audrey.........................2553
Heraldry 1697
Heritage 1054
Herschel Island Park 1552
Herzog, Fred 3052
High Jump....................................1593
Highland Games 1742
Highway...................584, 1737, 1876
Highway safety 572
Hiking 771, 2788
Hill, James.....................................3408
Hime, Humphrey Lloyd 3192
Hippodamia convergens (Beetle)...............2516, **MS**2522
Historic Covered Bridges 3476
History of Hockey 3319
HMS Erebus *3151*
Hnatyshyn, Governor General Ramon..................2262
Hoary Bat......................................1649
Hockey.......................957, 2316, 3319
Hockey Night **MS**1954
Hogan's Alley...............................2997
Holgate, Edwin **MS**1642*c*, 2433
Holidays 3689
Holocaust 1672
Home Children 2695
Home hardware 2275
Hong Kong...................................1459
HONG KONG Stamp Exhibitions ...**MS**1716, **MS**2249
Hoodless, Adelaide 1529
Hopkins, Frances Ann 1313
Horse-drawn sleigh 661
Horses 1903
Horton, Tim..................................3075
Hot air balloons...........................2106
Hot Properties #1..........................2918
Hotels..1540
Houses..1826
Houses of Parliament 870
Housser, Yvonne McKague.......2431
Howe, Gordie 3313
Howe, Joseph.................................755
Howell, Harry................................3078
Hoy, C. D.......................................3056
Hudson, Henry.............................1211
Hudson's Bay Company......**MS**1983
Hughes, Clara 3394
Hughes, E, J. 1503*b*
Humphrey, John Peters 1856
Hunter, Tommy 3064
Hunting 898
Huntsman.............................**MS**1982
Hurdling 811
Hyalophora cecropia (Moth) 2521, **MS**2522
Hydrangea arborescens.............3185
Hydrangea macrophylla.............3184
Hydrangeas..................................3184
Hydrological Decade....................623

I

I remember 656
Ice Age artifacts...........................1208
Ice Fields and Fjord 2434
Ice Hockey... 485, 1216, 1484, 1516, 1533, 1746, **MS**1954, 1963, 2052, 2118, 2127, 2178, 2546, 3075, 3165, 3634
Ice re-surfacing machines 3083
Ice skate 764, 2238
Iceberg **MS**2490
Iceberg and boatman 477
Icefields Parkway 2144
Icons 1308
Identification (Cat) 3131
Ile Verte 1130
IMAX **MS**1955
Imperial Penny Postage 1791
In Flanders Fields...........................3133
Indian (motorcycle) 2946
Indians of the Pacific Coast 725
Indians of the Plains 721
Indigenous Leaders 3622, 3669
Industrial Design.........................1741
Infantrymen.................................2219
Information Technology 1679
Inglis, Charles 1312
Innovations...................................2814
Inside Passage, British Columbia 2206
Insulin 675, 3568
International Civil Aviation Organisation 1612
International Co-operation Year 562
International Francophone Summit 1252
International Jazz Festival, Montréal 2259
International Labour Organisation 635
International Literacy Year 1399
International Ornithological Congress, Vancouver....**MS**3435
International Peace Year 1215
International Polar Year 2481
International Women's Year 813
International Year of Astronomy........2608, **MS**2610
International Year of Chemistry 2820
International Year of Older Persons 1881
International Year of the Family **MS**1596
International Year of the Forest..............................2767
International Youth Year............1142
Interparliamentary Union...........................566, 1174
Inuit hunter......................................477
Inuits 898, 924, 958, 989, 1047, **MS**1969
Inukshuk of Five Rocks 2335
Ironwork.......................................1888
Iroquoians 729, 739
Isaac's First Swim 3115
Isenbrandt, Adriaen....................3173
Isurus oxyrinchus (Shark) 3421

J

Jackman, Captain William.........1506
Jackson, A..............1047*a*, **MS**1642*a*
Jackson, Albert.............................3455
Jacques-Cartier River 1435
Jamboree..482
James, Geoffrey...........................3117
Janeway, Captain Kathryn (*Star Trek*).............................3266
Jasper National Park...................2506
Jelly Shelf......................................2489
Jellyfish...2482
Jesous Ahatonhia 895
Jesuits 1235
Jet airliner...................540, 556, 1028
Jewellery making.........................1895
Jigsaw 1699
Jobin, Raoul 2426
Jogging 769
Joggins Fossil Cliffs 3004
Johnny Canuck............................1662
Johnson, E. Pauline. 518
Johnson, Edward. 2429
Johnston, Frank.................**MS**1642*b*
Jones, J. Walter.............................1778
Jones, Oliver 2912
Judo..816
JUNO Awards 3567

K

Kane, Paul 686
Karsh, Yousuf.........2551, 2924, 3196
Katannilik Park.............................1556
Kayak..........................956, 1317, 1429
Keena 2377
Keep pets cool and hydrated...3129
Kelley, DeForest...........................3206
Kelly, Red 3080
Kelsey, Henry..................................654
Kerosene.......................................1292
Kerr 1047*j*
Kilimanjaro...................................2163
Killam Legacy........................**MS**1973
Killer Whale..................................1271
King Charles III............................3667
King Eider 2481
King, W. L. MacKenzie 435, 696, 1666
Kings Landing..............................2147
Kingsway Skoal (Horse) 1904
Kinnear, Helen.............................1532
Kirk, Admiral James T. (*Star Trek*)..............................3263
Kites..1942
Klein, George........................**MS**1984
Klondike Gold Strike..................1685
Kluane..885
Kluane/Wrangell-St. Elias/Glacier Bay/Tatshenshini-Alsek...3147
Knights of Columbus..................1743
Knowles, Dorothy......... 1047*g*, 2389
Komagata Maru...........................3028
Koo-tuck-tuck 2922
Kraken..1401
Kreighoff, Cornelius.......... 749, 2011
Kunz, Anita..................................3404
Kurelek, William...........................1437

L

L'Anse aux Meadows............**MS**1971
L'Arrive d'un Train en Gare (film) **MS**1698
La Francophone 1671
La Mauricie...................................885*e*
La Presse 1141
la Salle, Cavelier.............................571
La Soiree du Hockey **MS**1954
La Verendyre..................................504
La ville de Québec en hiver......3054
La Voie Lactée 3118
Labelle, Father Antoine 1105
Labour 2014
Labrador (ship)...............................934
Lacewing 2518
Lachapelle, Dr. Emmanuel-Persillier 1000
Lachine Canal..............................1801
Lacrosse 625, 1591, 2407
Lady Beetle 2516
Lady in White 3223
Lafleur, Guy..................................3229
Lagopus muta..............................3219
Lake Placid 971
Lakes 402, 1993
LaMarsh, Judy 1750
Lamb 1047*e*
Lambeth, Michel..........................3053
Lampman, Archibald..................1329
Land Mines **MS**1961
Landscapes 584, 704, 1047*a*
Lang, K.D. 3065
Laporte, Pierre 691
Launching 386
Laurence, Margaret.....................1706
Laurier, W. 694

CANADA Design Index

Law Society of Alberta 2510
Law Society of Saskatchewan 2509
Law Society of Upper Canada 1726
Lawn Bowls 1590
le Blanc, Romeo 2657
Leach's Storm Petrel 2195
Leacock, Stephen Butler 646
Leatherworking 1894
Leaves 875
Leclerc, Felix **MS**1952
Leduc, Fernand 1815
Leduc, Ozias 1289
Leg braces 2367
Legendary Creatures 1400
Léger, Jules 1043
Leggo, W. 1243
Lemelin, Roger **MS**1970
Lemieux, Jean Paul 792, **MS**1123
Lemieux, Mario 3315
Leo 2766
Leopard 2373
Les Bons Debarras (film) **MS**1698
Les Hospitalieres de Québec **MS**1962
Les Ordres (film) **MS**1698
Lesage, Jean 1770
Lest We Forget 2636, **MS**2637
Liberation 1627
Libra 2768
Lifesaving Society 2566
Lightfoot, Gordon 2500
Lighthouses 1128, 1176, 2152, 2437, 3140
Lightning 3136
Lilacs 2484
Lincoln's Sparrow 2278
Lion (symbol of Governor-General) 2128
Lismer, Arthur **MS**1642
Literacy 1699
Livernois, Jules-Ernest 1326
Livingstone, Kay 3397
Log Driver's Waltz (cartoon) 3032
Lombardo, Guy **MS**1952
London 2010 Festival of Stamps **MS**2672
London Conference 573
Longboat **MS**1969
Loon 1756, 2711
Lord Strathcona's House 2024
Lotus 3399
Louis R. Desmarais (ship) 1677
Louis Riel (opera) 3252
Louis, Spyros 2283
Louisbourg 1128, 1631
Love Your Pet 3127
Lower Fort Garry 1163
Loyalists 1124
Lumberers Regatta 2491
Lumbering 405
Lunar New Year 3540
Lunenburg Academy 1643
Lutheran World Federation Assembly 2215
Lynx 1268

M

MacDonald, Angus 1774
MacDonald, J. E. H. 756, **MS**1642*b*
MacDonald, Sir John Alexander 693, 3102, 3297
MacDonald Stewart Foundation **MS**1973
MacGill, Elsie 3461
MacKenzie, Sir Alexander 445, 658
MacKenzie River 1586
Maclean, Steve 2227
Maclean's Magazine 2349
Macleod, James 1214
Macoun, John 1018
Macphail, Agnes 1404
Madonna and Child 2430
Magazine covers 2349
Magdalen Islands, Québec 2213
Maggs, Arnaud 2924
Magnolias 2913
Mail boxes 1989
Mail coach 438
Mail delivery 2786
Mail trains 436
Mail van 1382
Main River 1436
Mammals 1261
Mammals (prehistoric) 1613
Mance, Jeanne 754
Mandela, Nelson 3103
Manic Dams **MS**1985
Manitoba 647, 1644, 1877
Manning, Ernest 1776
Maple leaf quilt 1690
Maple leaves and trees 542, 555, 558, 677, 684, 1030, 1427, 1597, 1783, 1836, 2029, 2233
Maps 536, 970, 1013, 1679, 2275, 2406
Marathon of Hope 1044, **MS**1959, 3287
Marco Polo (ship) 1874
Marconi, Guglielmo 796, 2171
Margaree River 1492
Marie de l'Incarnation 1009
Marie-Victorin, Frère 1017
Marine Life 2676, **MS**2678
Marmot 1006
Marquette, Father 1234
Marriage Equality 3285
Martel, Renée 3062
Mask 2394
Mason, Bill 1823
Massey Foundation **MS**1973
Massey, Vincent 633, 889
Masson, H. 793
Matonabbee 1319
Matthew (ship) 412
McAdam Railway Station 1278
McCain Foods **MS**1982
McClelland & Stewart 2393
McClung, Nellie 761
McCrae, John 628, 3133
McIndoe, V. 1503*c*
McKenzie, R. T. 801
McKinney, Louise 1003
McLaughlin, Sam 2568
McLaughlin, Samuel 3296
McLuhan, Professor Marshall **MS**1970
McNair, John 1771
Meals and Friends on Wheels **MS**1959
Medical Pioneers 1413, 3527
Meighen, Arthur 519
Membertou, Chief 2508
Memorial Cup (hockey) 3413
Menorah 3540
Mental Health 2574, 2633, 2696, 2818, **MS**2819
Mercure, Monique 3654
Merritt, Willilam 797
Merry Christmas 993, 1023
Messier, Mark 3231
Meteorology 621
Michener, Daniel Roland 1520
Microscope 502
Migratory Wildlife 1645
Miguasha National Park 3005
Milky Way 3414
Millennium **MS**1946, **MS**1952, 1956, **MS**1959
Milne, David 1047*h*, 1139, 1504
Miner 499, 912
Minerals 1509, 1790
Miss Supertest III (hydroplane) 2812, **MS**2813
Mississauga (Chinese Centre gate) 2940
Mississauga Interchange 1651
Mitchell, Janet 1503*g*
Mitchell, Joni 2501
Mitchell, W. O. **MS**1972
Mol, Leo 2154
Molson, John 1222
Mon Oncle Antoine (film) **MS**1698, 3031
Monarch Butterfly 1645, 2521
Monkey King 3178
Montferrand, Jos 1508
Montgomery, Lucy Maud 803, 2557
Montmorency-Laval, Francois de 750
Montpetit, Edouard 1700
Montréal 1487, 2146, 2935
Montréal Botanical Gardens 1425
Montréal Canadiens (Ice hockey team) 2364, **MS**2635, 2963, **MS**2967, 2969, **MS**2975
Montréal Children's Hospital 2278
Montréal Museum of Fine Arts 1180
Montréal Symphony Orchestra 1117
Moodie, Geraldine 2922
Moodie, Susanna 2223
Moon Landing, 50th anniversary 3482
Moose 448, 1291, 2714
Moose wearing hat and scarf 3174
Moriyama, Raymond 2495
Morrice, James Wilson 1190
Morrisseau, Norval 1406
Mortimer-Lamb, Harold 3113
Mosher, Aaron R. 1022
Moth 2522
Motorcycles 2945
Mount Everest 2162
Mount Logan 2167
Mount McKinley 2166
Mount Robson Park 1549
Mountain biking 2370
Mountain Goat 487, 2709*b*
Mounted Police 751, 1687, 1806, 2207
Mousseau, Jean-Paul 1816
Mowat, Sir Oliver 659
Multiculturalism 1381
Munday, Phyllis 1822
Munitions factory 387
Munro, Alice 3150
Murphy, Emily 1144
Murray, Anne 2502
Museum of Anthropology, BC 1873
Museum of Civilisation 2394
Mushrooms 1331
Music 1341
Musical Instrument 1001
Musk Ox 478, 1272
Muskrat 1263
Myers, Mike 3068

N

Nahanni National Park 3003
Nanaimo Bar 3469
Nanogak, Agnes 1503*l*
Narwhal 622
National Film Board **MS**1953, 3029
National flag 564, 578, 1328, 1630, 2728, 3002
National Gallery of Canada 2496
National Hockey League 2316, 2960
National Parks 2350, 2434
Nativity 848, 1080, 2527
NATO 510, 1940
Neatby, Professor Hilda Marion **MS**1970
Neighbours (film) 3033
Nelligan, Emile 941
Nelson-Miramichi Post Office 1228
Nelumbo lutea 3400
Nelumbo nucifera 3399
Nelvana 1663
Neptune (ship) 819
Neptune Story **MS**1971
New Brunswick 1121, 1812
Newfoundland 1102, 1125, 1522, 1879
Newfoundland Marten 2420
NFB (National Film Board) 3029
Niagara Falls, Ontario 2212
Niagara River 1495
Niagara-on-the-Lake 1020, 2079
Nickel 1103
Nimoy, Leonard 3205
No. 2 Construction Battalion 3183
Nonsuch (ship) 624
Noorduyn Norseman (aircraft) 1053
Normandy 1621
Norris, J. 1503*b*
Northcote (ship) 851
Northern Dancer (Horse) 1903
Northern development 517
Northern Light (ship) 933
Northern lights 2148, 3415
Northwest Territories 648, 1878
Notman, William 1323, 3057
Nova Scotia 508, 1738
Nunavut Territory 1880, 2083, 3284
Nurse 506, 1725, 2556

O

O Canada 980
O'Brien, Lucius 974
O'Hara, Catherine 3072
Ocean Technology 1677
Ogopogo 1403
Oil and Gas Industry 2548
Oil wells 431, 590
Old Town, Lunenburg 3011, 3035
Olympic Games, Athens 2288
Olympic Games, Barcelona 1498
Olympic Games, Beijing 2565
Olympic Games, Canada 3290
Olympic Games, London 2874
Olympic Games, Montréal 762, 768, 786, 798, 809, 814, 829, 833, 842
Olympic Medal Winners 1691
Oncopeltus fasciatus (Milkweed Bug) 2519*b*, **MS**2523
Ontario 1739
Ontario Science Centre 2495
Opera 3248
Opera Singers 2425
Orchestre Symphonique de Québec 2175
Orchids 1883, **MS**1917, 2306, 2530
Order of Canada 890, 1519
O'Ree, Willie 3688
Original Six (ice hockey) 3075
Organ donation 3607
Ornithomimus edmontonicus 3123
Orphan Boy 1446
Orr, Bobby 3077, 3314
Osler, Sir William 637
OSM 50 MSO 1117
Ottawa as Capital 2491
Ottawa (Chinatown gate) 2939
Ottawa Redblacks 3050
Ottawa River 1494
Ottawa Senators 2966, **MS**2967, 2971, **MS**2975
Ottawa University 1835
Ouellette, Gerald 1694
Owl chicks 2706*c*
Oyster Farming 1890

P

Pablum baby food **MS**1982
Pacem in Terris 541
Pacemaker 2814
Pacific Cable 2170
Paintings **MS**1123, 1137, 1289, 1421, 1503*a*/*1503l*, 1504, 1539, 1629, 2340, 2389, 2431
Palliser, John 1288
Pan-American Games (5th) 614
Pan-American Games (13th) 1913
Pandion haliaetus 3300
Pansies 3107
Papal Visit 1126
Papineau, Louis-Joseph 681, 2919
Paralympic Glory 3291
Paramedics 3438
Parent, Bernie 3169
Parks Canada 2788
Parliament Buildings 383, 567, 870, 1147, 1174, 2358, 2491
Parrot 2929
Parsons, Mona 3694
Passport (ship) 852
Pasztor, Andor 2921
Payette, Julie 2232
Peace Bridge 891
Peace Dove **MS**1946, 3443
Peace Garden 1423
Peaceful Uses 574
Pearson, Lester B. 698, **MS**1961
Peggy's Cove 2152
Pelee Passage 1177
Pellan, Alfred 1629
Penfield, Wilder 1414
Peonies 2541
Peregrine Falcon 906
Peterson, Oscar 2365
Petro-Canada 2015
Petroleum 507
Phantom Bell Ringers 3225
Phantom Ships 3045
Pharmaceutical Sciences Congress 1173
Philatelic Exhibition 1037
Phillips, Walter 1721
Photogrammetry 741
Photography, 150 Years of 1323, 2918, 3052, 3112, 3190, 3293
Picard, Captain Jean-Luc (*Star Trek*) 3264
Pickford, Mary 2397

Design Index **CANADA**

Picture Postage 1988, 2020, 2045, 2099, 2217, 2509*a*
Pieczonka, Adrianne 3250
Pier 21 ..... **MS**1971
Pilot and Snowbirds 2403
Pilote, Pierre 3079
Pine tree 585
Pinky (boat) 902
Pintail 1648
Pisces 2773
Plains of Abraham 514
Plaskett 1047k
Platinum Jubilee 3600
Plough 1060
Plummer, Christopher 3585
Poecile atricapillus 3429
Poets 1329
Point Pelée 855*d*
Pointer 1378
Poirier, Conrad 3114
Polanyi, John 2820
Polar Bear 447, 705, 1757, 2211, 2436, 2713
Polar Bear wearing hat and scarf 3176
Pole vaulting 809, 2087
Police 1442
Police officers 3439
Polio Vaccination 2367
Polistes fuscatus (Paper Wasp) 2518*a*, **MS**2523, **MS**2905
Pontiac **MS**1969
Porcupine 1262, 2709
Porpoise 1273
Port Carling Canal 1797
Port-Royal 2361
Post Office 776
Postal Code 938
Postal History 2948
Postman 777
Postmark 2284
Potts, Jerry 1505
Pour la Suite du Monde (film) **MS**1698
POW's 1626
Power station 403
Powerscourt Bridge 3477
Prairie 1328*b*
Pratt, C. 1047*c*
Pratt, E. J. 1086
Pratt, Mary 2489
Praying hands 576
Prehistoric Canada 1390, 1417, 1568, 1613
Preserve the Polar Regions and Glaciers 2611, **MS**2613
Prevent Fires 490
Prince Edward Island 757, 1813
Prince George, Birth of 2985
Prince, Tommy 3646
Prince's Gate 2266
Princess Marguerite (ship) 1246
Princess of Wales' Own Regiment 2927
Prionace glauca (Shark) 3419
Pronghorn 1270
Province House, Charlottetown 2214
Provincial and Territorial Parks 1545
PTTI Congress 1744
Public Pensions 2159
Public Services International World Congress 2158
Puffin 2714*b*
Pulp and Paper 488
Puncak Jaya 2161

Q

Quadra (ship) 821
Québec 505, 1543, 1876
Québec Bridge 1650
Québec Carnival 935
Québec City 2204
Québec in Bloom 1724
Queen Elizabeth II 2241, 2464, 2830, **MS**2831, 2857, **MS**2858
Queen Elizabeth II 80th Birthday 2381, **MS**2392
Queen Elizabeth II. A Historic Reign 3157
Queen Elizabeth II Coronation 2203, 2943, 3410
Queen Elizabeth II Diamond Jubilee 2830, **MS**2831, 2857, **MS**2858
Queen Elizabeth II Golden Jubilee 2115
Queen Elizabeth the Queen Mother 2003
Queen's University, Kingston 1449
Quilting 1892

R

Rabbit 2702
Raccoons 2705
Radio Canada 684
Radisson 1233
Raginsky, Nina 3116
Railcuts: #1 3058
Railway line 2362
Railway locomotives 1106, 1132, 1185, 1223
Rainbow 3139
Ram's head 2762
Rat Bride 2538, 3503
Recording Artists 2500, **MS**2504, 2618, **MS**2622, 2798, **MS**2806, 2954
Red Bay Basque Whaling Station 3144
Red Cross 442, 1120
Red Deer 2351
Red Fox 1265, 2707
Red River 1560
Red River Ox cart 3159
Red River Resistance 3501
Red River Settlement 523, 2856
Regatta 1049
Regiments 1114, 1335, 2024
Regina 1048
Rehabilitation 979
Reid, Bill 1408, 1681
Reindeer 2526
Remembrance Poppy 3590
Rescue Service 1444
Reservoir 403
Resources for Tomorrow 521
Responsible Government 411
Responsible Pet Guardianship 3127
Rhine Crossing 1628
Rhododendron 2603, **MS**2605
Ribbons and Confetti 2480
Richard 1047*d*
Richard, Maurice 3311
Rideau Canal 1798, 3008, 3039
Riel, Louis 657
Riopelle, Jean-Paul 1814, **MS**2236
River Scene 588
River Valley Drive 1812
Rivers 1432, 1492, 1558, 1584, 1993
Riverside Country Club 1638
Roadside Attractions 2623, **MS**2627, 2688, **MS**2692, 2807, **MS**2811
Robarts, John 1769
Robinson, A H. 1345
Rocky Mountain Bighorn Sheep 1761*a*
Rocky Mountains 3006
Rogers Pass **MS**1985
Rogers, Stan 3578
Rogers, Ted **MS**1955
Roman Catholic Church (Newfoundland) 1125
Roméo LeBlanc 2657
Rooster 3242
Rose 1019, 2091, 3023
Rosenfeld, Fanny 1693
Rotary International 2685
Roue, William J. 1809
Rowing 799
Roy, Gabrielle 1708
Royal Agricultural Winter Fair 1766
Royal Architectural Institute 2493
Royal Astronomical Society of Canada 3414
Royal Botanical Gardens 1424
Royal Canadian Academy of Arts 973, **MS**1953
Royal Canadian Army Cadets 2270
Royal Canadian Golf Association 1637
Royal Canadian Legion 828, 2114
Royal Canadian Mint 2555
Royal Canadian Mounted Police 3668
Royal Canadian Navy 1189
Royal Military College 840, 2086
Royal Montréal Golf Club 1641
Royal Ontario Museum 3020
Royal Visit 440, 512
Royal Wedding 2780, 2795
Ruby-crowned Kinglet 2279
Running 810, 919, 2088
Runnymede Library, Toronto 1277
Rush 2955
Rutherford, Erica. 1503*k*
Rutherford, Lord 676

S

Sackville (ship) 1857
Safdie, Moshe 2496
Sagittarius 2770
Saguenay Fjord 2151
Saguenay River 1584
Sailing 800
Sailors 2219, 2353
Sainte-Marie, Buffy 3597
Saint Maurice Ironworks 1302
Saint-Jean 1004
Salaberry, Lieutenant-Colonel Charles-Michel de 942, 2949
Salamander 2387, 2421
Salvation Army 1046
Sampson, J. E. 2432
Samson (locomotive) 1108
San Juan (ship) 1248
Sans titre 0310/ La chambre noire 3194
Santa Claus 665, 766, 822, 1450, 3094, 3592
Santa Claus Parade 1181
Sapling 2215
Saskatchewan 987, 1740, 2363
Saskatchewan Roughriders (football team) 2878, **MS**2883, 2889, **MS**2894
Saskatoon Berry Pie 3470
Sasquatch 1400
Satellite 570, **MS**2357
Sault Ste Marie Canal 1804
Saunders, Sir Charles **MS**1982
Sauvé, Jeanne 1582
Savard, Felix-Antoine 1709
Schmirler, Sandra 2999
Schumacher, Michael 3278
Scorpio 2769
Scotia (locomotive) 1132
Scott, Barbara Ann 2998
Scottish settlers 758
Scouting 1100, 2507
Sculpture 1681, 2153, 2839
Search and Rescue **MS**2357, 3440
Second World War 1346, 1409, 1456, 1521, 1576, 1621, 1625, 2286
Secord, Laura 1507, 2950
Segwun (ship) 1245
Selye, Dr. Hans **MS**1960
Senna, Ayrton 3277
Series of the Century 1746
Service 1120
Service, Robert W. 846
Seventh-day Adventist Church 2005
Sgang Gwaay (BC) 3009, 3038
Shadd, Mary Ann 3698
Shadbolt, Jack 2097
Shaman **MS**1969
Sharks 3417
Shatner, William 3202
Shawinigan (ship) 1858
Shearer 2560
Sheep 449, 703
Shelter 958
Shepherd 767
Shepherd, R. 1503*e*
Ships 386, 406, 412, 437, 818, 851, 902, 931, 1119, 1245, 1677, 1857, 1874, 2268, 2284, 2353, 2400, 2550, 3041
Shipwrecks 1247
Shoeshine Stand 3116
Shooting 493
Short, Martin 3069
Shriners (charitable organisation) 2098
Signal Hill, St John's, Newfoundland 2084
Signs of the Zodiac 2762
Sikhs 1882
Silver Dart (aircraft) 509
Simoneau, Léopold 2427
Sisko, Captain Benjamin (*Star Trek*) 3265
Sisters Islets 1176
Sitting Bull and Buffalo Bill 3057
Sittler, Darryl 3232
Skateboarding 2369
Skating 692, 788, 823, 1483, 2068, 2998
Ski Patrol 1441
Skiing 494, 664, 787, 1217, 1258, 1281, 1486, 2126
Ski jumping 1259, 1482
Skyscrapers 707
Sled 2383
Sleigh 1063
Small Basement Camera Shop 2923
Smallwood, Joseph 1773
Smellie, Elizabeth **MS**1961
Smith, Sir Donald Alexander 673
Snow Goose 1200
Snow, Hank 3061
Snow Mammals 3556
Snowbirds Demonstration Team 2403
Snowboarding 2371
Snowflake 687
Snowmen 663, 2262, 2375, 2431
Snowplough 1203
Society of Graphic Designers 2414
Softimage **MS**1955
Somniosus microcephalus (Shark) 3420
South Nahanni River 1432
South Saskatchewan River 1496
Southam Sisters 3113
Space Programme 1143, 1514, **MS**1985
Spay/neuter (Cat) 3127
Speed skating 1236, 2124, 2382
Spinning wheel 1063
Spirits 989
Spitfire (aircraft) 1205
Spring 677
Spruce Grouse 1202
Spruce Woods Park 1551
St Andrews 1544
St John Ambulance 1087
St John River 1562
St John's 1125, 1300
St Joseph's Convent School 3053
St Joseph's Oratory 2263
St Laurent, Louis 699
St Lawrence Seaway 513, 1122, 1561
St Mary's Church 2494
St Ours Canal 1796
St Ours Post Office 1229
St Peters Canal 1795
St Roch (ship) 932
Stable and star 662
Stadium 918
Stained glass windows 848, 1763
Stampin the Future 2006
Stamps 439, 525, 907, 914, 1037, 2364
Stanley Cup 1533
Stanley Park 2149
Star 3652
Star Trek 3199, 3261
Statuette 3567
Steamships 437, 1245
Stefansson, Vilhjalmur 1322
Stella 2951
Stephenson, Sir William **MS**1955
Stewart, Sir Jackie 3275
Stove 1064
Stowe, Emily 1005
Stratford Festival **MS**1971
Striped Skunk 1266
Strix nebulosa 3303
Sturgeon 2513
Sub-Arctic Indians 727
Sugar Bushes, Québec 2078
Sugar Pie 3468
Summer 678
Summit of the Americas, Québec 2074
Summit Series (ice hockey) 3286
Sumo wrestling 1792
Sun Dogs and settlement 3137
Sunflowers 2757, 3626
Superman 1661, 2976
Supernatural 1752
Supreme Court 817, 1986
Sutherland, Donald 3687
Suzor Côté 634, 1343
Sweet Canada 3466

CANADA Design Index

Swimming....492, 798, 2360
Szilasi, Gabor....2921

T

Tall Ships' visit....1119, 2012
Talon, Jean....524
Tank....384
Tata, Sam....3112
Taurus....2763
TD Bank Building....2339
Teaching = enseignment....2168
Teasdale, Dr. Lucille....**MS**1959
Technology....1677
Tecumseh, Chief....2873
Tekakwitha, Kateri....1008
Telephone....783, 1193
Terra Nova National Park....2505
Tetraneuris herbacea....3255
Textile Industry....462
Textiles (hand-crafted)....1534
Thauberger, D.....1503*i*
The Apprenticeship of Duddy Kravitz (film)....**MS**1698
The Atlas of Canada....2406
The Black Watch of Canada....2896, **MS**2899
The Forks, Winnipeg....2080
The Globe....626
The Grand Theatre....2105
The Grey Fox (film)....**MS**1698
The Guess Who....2957
The Hastings and Prince Edward Regiment....2984
The Holocaust....1672
The Kitchen Sink....2920
The Landscape of Grand Pré....3007, 3037
The Railrodder (film)....3030
The Rocks Park....1554
The Royal Hamilton Light Infantry....2897, **MS**2899
The Royal Philatelic Society of Canada....**MS**2905
The Royal Regiment of Canada....2898, **MS**2899
The Tragically Hip....2954
The World's in Edmonton 2001....2087
Theatre....1339
Théâtre du Nouveau Monde....2104
Théâtre du Rideau Vert....1864
Thirsk, Robert....2229
Thompson, David....496
Thompson, Sir John....475
Thomson, Tom....887, 1384
Tickets....2407
Tisseyre, Pierre....**MS**1972
Titanic....2848, **MS**2852
Todd, R. C.....794
Topley, William James....3297
Toronto....617, 1542, 1557, 2934
Toronto (locomotive)....1107
Toronto (Lutz Dille)....3190
Toronto Argonauts....2881, **MS**2883, 2892, **MS**2894, 2905*m*
Toronto Maple Leafs....2962, **MS**2967, 2974, **MS**2975
Toronto Maple Leafs centenary....3322
Toronto Post Office....1227
Toronto Stock Exchange....2169
Totem Pole....446
Tourist Attractions....2075, 2143, 2262
Towards the Summits....2160
Towell, Larry....3115
Toys....962, 2239, 2278
Toyshop....668
Trades....1887
Traill, Catherine Parr....2223
Train ferry....406
Trains....436, 1197, 2271
Trans-Canada Highway....526, 3283
Transatlantic Flight....636
Travel....924
Travel posters....3616
Travers, Mary....1610
Traversée Internationale du Lac St-Jean....2265
Trees....827, 1467, 2777
Trees and sledge....672
Trent-Severn Waterway....1799
Tripp, Charles....2549
Troodon inequalis....3209
Troopship....1625
Trout, Jennie....1413
Trudeau, Pierre....2089
Truro....1480
Truth and Reconciliation....3635, 3683
Tryggvason, Bjarni....2230
Tsimshian Frontlet....1327
Tulip Festival, Ottawa....2082, 2134
Tulips....**MS**2157
Tupper, Sir Charles....484
Turner, John....3573
Turtle....936, 2514
Twain, Shania....3063
Tylosaurus pembinensis....3122
Tympanachus phasianellus....3215
Tyrannosaurus Rex....3121
Tyrell, Joseph....1321

U

Ukrainian Immigration....1437
Ultraflight Lazair....3465
UNESCO World Heritage Sites....3002, 3035, 3142
UNICEF....1711
Unidentified Chinese man....3056
United Empire Loyalists....1124
United Nations....655, 1666
Universal Declaration of Human Rights....1856
Universiade 83....1088
Universities....2129, 2190, 2276, 2333, 2419, 2487, 2493, 2544
UPU....497, 790, 1919
Uranium....988
Ursus americanus (American Black Bear)....3485
Ursus arctos (Grizzly Bear)....3488
Ursus maritimus (Polar Bear)....3486

V

Vachon....**MS**1983
Vallée, L. P.....3054
Valour Riad....3588
Vancouver....2937
Vancouver Aquarium....2402
Vancouver Asahi....3472
Vancouver Canucks....2960, **MS**2967, 2968, **MS**2975
Vancouver, George....1286, 2497
Vanier, Governor-General....616
Vanier, Pauline....**MS**1961
van Nuyssen, Abraham....3093
Varley, Frederick....1010, 1589, **MS**1642*b*
Varying Hare....1264
Verelst, John (painter)....2667, **MS**2671
Vet care....3130
Vial and notes....3568
Vickers, Jon.....2428
Vickers Vedette (aircraft)....968
Victoria, BC....525, 1481, 1540, 2941
Victoria Bridge, Grand Trunk Railway....3193
Victoria Golf Club....1640
Victorian Order of Nurses....1725
Victory in Europe....3515
Viking ships....1209
Villeneuve, Gilles....1733, 3276
Vimy Monument....629
Vimy Ridge, Battle of....3259
Vinson Massif....2164
Vintage Radios....3525
Virgin and Child....928, 3093
Virgo....2767
Voltigeurs de Québec....2025
Volunteers....1238
Votes for Women....612
Voyageur Waterway....1434

W

Wait for Me Daddy....3091
Walcheren....1624
Wall climbing....2368
Wallenberg, Raoul....2910
Walrus....472, 1269
Walters, Angus....1314
Wapiti....1274, 2715*b*
War of 1812....2872, 2949
Ware, John....2837
Waterton-Glacier International Peace Park....3146
Waterton Lakes....884*c*, 2350
Watkins, Margaret....2920
Watson, Homer....2355
Watt-Clouthier, Sheila....2869, **MS**2871
Weather observation....1398
Weather Wonders....3136, 3427
Weaving....1891
Welder....2548
Werewolf....1402
West (Eliot) River....1493
West Montrose Bridge....3479
Weston....**MS**1983
Whales....622, 937, 1276, 2016, 2402, 2511, 3610
Wheat....1293
Wheelchair race....1592
White, James....2406
White Pass and Yukon Route....2077
White, Portia....**MS**1952
White-winged Crossbill....2280
Whooping Cranes....479
Wigwam and furs....432
Wilberforce Falls, Nunavut....2205
Wildlife....2704
Wildlife Conservation....1290
Willan, Healey....984
William D. Lawrence (ship)....818
Williams, Dave....2231
Williams, James Miller....2549
Williams, Percy....1695
Window (Angela Grauerholz)....3191
Wine Route....1739
Winnie the Pooh....1701
Winnipeg....775, 2080, 2936
Winnipeg Blue Bombers....2879, **MS**2883, 2890, **MS**2894
Winnipeg Jets....2965, **MS**2967, 2973, **MS**2975
Winter....680
Winter Garden Theatre....3224
Winter landscape....586
Winter Olympic Games, Albertville....1482
Winter Olympic Games, Calgary....1191, 1216, 1236, 1258, 1281
Winter Olympic Games, Innsbruck....832
Winter Olympic Games, Salt Lake City....2124
Winter Olympic Games, Turin....2382
Winter Olympic Games, Vancouver....2584, **MS**2589, 2590, **MS**2598, 2653, **MS**2655, 2658, **MS**2659, 2660, **MS**2662
Wireless Telegraphy....2171
Witched Canoe....1445
Wolf....1273, 2027
Wolverine....1270*c*
Woman with Arms outstretched....2363
Women are Persons (sculpture)....**MS**1962
Women in Winter Sports....3391
Women's ice hockey....2127
Women's Suffrage, centenary....3189
Wood Buffalo National Park....3145
Woodchucks....2706
Woodworking....1893
World Communications Year....1083
World Council of Churches....1101
World Cycling Championships....784
World Figure Skating Championships....692, 2068
World Health Day....719
World Lacrosse Championships....2407
World Road Congress....1650
World Rowing Championships....1918
World Youth Day....2156
Worsley, Gump....3168
Wrapped present....2752
Wray, Fay....2396
Writing-on-Stone Park....1550

Y

Year of Asia Pacific....1745
Year of the Child....965
Year of the Dog....2379, 3332
Year of the Dragon....1957, 2826
Year of the Horse....2116, 2992
Year of the Monkey....3178
Year of the Ox....1714
Year of the Pig....2478, 3450
Year of the Rabbit....1862
Year of the Ram....3098
Year of the Rat....2538, 3503
Year of the Rooster....2314, 3242
Year of the Snake....2050, 2906
Year of the Tiger....1767
Yellowhead Highway....1877
Yellowknife....1116
YMCA....2113
York Boat....1379
York Redoubt....1171
Yorkton....1476
Youth Sports....2368
Youville, Marguerite d'....923
Yukon....1810
Yukon Gold Rush....1685
Yukon Quest (race)....2143
Yukon River....1559
Yzerman, Steve....3230

Z

Zamboni ice re-surfacing machines....3083
Zelus luridus (Assassin Bug)....2519*a*, **MS**2523
Zodiac....2762

NEWFOUNDLAND 1938 SG268

Explore an extensive collection of
stamps and postal history
curated by philatelic experts

www.stanleygibbons.com

For Commonwealth enquiries please contact Andrew Mansi
amansi@stanleygibbons.com

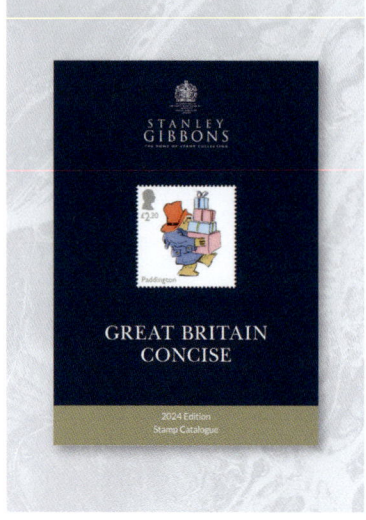

Publications

To view more of our range of catalogues
visit stanleygibbons.com/shop/publications

Visit our website **www.stanleygibbons.com**, call us on **+44 (0)1425 472 363** or email **support@stanleygibbons.com** to order

/StanleyGibbonsGroup @StanleyGibbons @StanleyGibbons @StanleyGibbons1856

Stamp Booklets CANADA

STAMP BOOKLETS

Booklet Nos. SB1/SB60 are stapled.
All booklets up to and including No. SB41 contain panes consisting of two rows of three (3×2).

B1

1900 (11 June). Red on pink cover. Two panes of 6×2c. (No. 155bba).
SB1   25c. booklet. Cover as Type **B1** with English
         text.. £2250

1903 (1 July). Red on pink cover. Two panes of 6×2c. (No. 176a).
SB2   25c. booklet. Cover as Type **B1** with English
         text.. £2500

1912 (Jan)–**16**. Red on pink cover. Two panes of 6×2c. (No. 201a).
SB3   25c. booklet. Cover as Type **B1** with English
         text.. £100
         a. Cover handstamped 'NOTICE Change
            in Postal Rates For New Rates See
            Postmaster'.. £110
         b. French text (4.16).. £225
         ba. Cover handstamped 'AVIS
             Changement des tarifs Postaux Pour
             les nouveaux tarifs consulter le maitre
             de poste'.. £150

1913 (1 May)–**16**. Green on pale green cover. Four panes of 6×1c. (No. 197b).
SB4   25c. booklet. Cover as Type **B1** with English
         text.. £600
         a. Containing pane No. 199a........................... £160
         ab. Cover handstamped 'NOTICE Change
             in Postal Rates For New Rates See
             Postmaster'.. £180
         b. French text (28.4.16).................................. £700
         ba. Containing pane No. 199a......................... £225
         bb. Cover handstamped 'AVIS
             Changement des tarifs Postaux Pour
             les nouveaux tarifs consulter le maitre
             de poste'.. £800

1922 (Mar). Black on brown cover. Two panes of 4×3c. and two labels (No. 205a).
SB5   25c. booklet. Cover as Type **B1** with English
         text.. £400
         a. French text.. £750

1922 (July–Dec). Black on blue cover. Panes of 4×1c., 4×2c. and 4×3c. each. (Nos. 246aa, 247aa, 205a) and two labels.
SB6   25c. booklet. Cover as Type **B1** with English
         text.. £350
         a. French text (12.22)..................................... £700

1922 (Dec). Black on orange cover. Four panes of 6×1c. (No. 246ab).
SB7   25c. booklet. Cover as Type **B1** with English
         text.. £250
         a. French text.. £300

1922 (Dec). Black on green cover. Two panes of 6×2c. (No. 247ab).
SB8   25c. booklet. Cover as Type **B1** with English
         text.. £600
         a. French text.. £700

1923 (Dec). Black on blue cover. Panes of 4×1c., 4×2c. and 4×3c. each. (Nos. 246aa, 247aa, 248aa) and 2 labels.
SB9   25c. booklet. Cover as Type **B1** with English
         text.. £275
         a. French text.. £650

1923 (Dec)–**24**. Black on brown cover. Two panes of 4×3c. (No. 248aa) and two labels.
SB10   25c. booklet. Cover as Type **B1** with English
         text.. £250
         a. French text (5.24)....................................... £450

B2

1928 (16 Oct). Black on green cover. Two panes of 6×2c. (No. 276a).
SB11   25c. booklet. Cover as Type **B2** with English
         text.. 65·00
         a. French text.. £225

1928 (25 Oct). Black on orange cover. Four panes of 6×1c. (No. 275a).
SB12   25c. booklet. Cover as Type **B2** with English
         text.. £120
         a. French text.. £325

1929 (6 Jan). Plain manilla cover. Three panes of 6×1c., two panes of 6×2c. and one pane of 6×5c. (Nos. 275a, 276a, 279a).
SB13   72c. booklet. Plain cover £500
         a. With 'Philatelic Div., Fin. Br. P.O. Dept.,
            Ottawa' circular cachet on front cover..   £2000
         b. With '1928' in the centre of the circular
            cachet.. £1600

1930 (17 June). Black on green cover. Two panes of 6×2c. (No. 290a).
SB14   25c. booklet. Cover as Type **B2** with English
         text.. £130
         a. French text.. £225

1930 (17 Nov). Black on red cover. Two panes of 6×2c. (No. 291a).
SB15   25c. booklet. Cover as Type **B2** with English
         text.. 55·00
         a. French text.. £150

1931 (13 July). Black on red cover. Two panes of 4×3c. (No. 293a) and two labels.
SB16   25c. booklet. Cover as Type **B2** with English
         text.. 85·00
         a. French text.. £140

1931 (21 July). Black on green cover. Four panes of 6×1c. (No. 289b).
SB17   25c. booklet. Cover as Type **B2** with English
         text.. £140
         a. French text.. £250

1931 (23 July). Black on brown cover. Two panes of 6×2c. (No. 292a).
SB18   25c. booklet. Cover as Type **B2** with English
         text.. £150
         a. French text.. £450

1931 (13 Nov). Black on blue cover. Panes of 4×1c., 4×2c. and 4×3c. each. (Nos. 289db, 292ba, 293a) and 2 labels.
SB19   25c. booklet. Cover as Type **B2** with English
         text.. £325
         a. French text.. £650

1933 (22 Aug–13 Nov). Black on red cover. Two panes of 4×3c. (No. 321b) and two labels.
SB20   25c. booklet. Cover as Type **B2** with English
         text (13.11).. 90·00
         a. French text (22.8)....................................... £225

1933 (7 Sept). Black on brown cover. Two panes of 6×2c. (No. 320a).
SB21   25c. booklet. Cover as Type **B2** with English
         text.. £250
         a. French text.. £500

1933 (19 Sept–5 Dec). Black on blue cover. Panes of 4×1c., 4×2c. and 4×3c. each. (Nos. 319b, 320b, 321b) and two labels.
SB22   25c. booklet. Cover as Type **B2** with English
         text.. £200
         a. French text (5.12)....................................... £300

1933 (28 Dec)–**34**. Black on green cover. Four panes of 6×1c. (No. 319a).
SB23   25c. booklet. Cover as Type **B2** with English
         text.. £160
         a. French text (26.3.34).................................. £250

B3

1935 (1 June–8 Aug). Red on white cover. Two panes of 4×3c. (No. 343a) and two labels.
SB24   25c. booklet. Cover as Type **B3** with English
         text (8.8).. 65·00
         a. French text (1.6)... £110

1935 (22 July–1 Sept). Blue on white cover. Panes of 4×1c., 4×2c. and 4×3c. each. (Nos. 341b, 342b, 343a) and two labels.
SB25   25c. booklet. Cover as Type **B3** with English
         text.. £150
         a. French text (1.9.35).................................... £190

CANADA Stamp Booklets

1935 (19 Aug–18 Oct). Green on white cover. Four panes of 6×1c. (No. 341a).
SB26   25c. booklet. Cover as Type **B3** with English text.................... 90·00
        a. French text (18.10) £130

1935 (16–18 Mar). Brown on white cover. Two panes of 6×2c. (No. 342a).
SB27   25c. booklet. Cover as Type **B3** with English text.................... 70·00
        a. French text (18.3)........................... £120

B4

1937 (14 Apr)–**38**. Blue and white cover. Panes of 4×1c., 4×2c. and 4×3c. each. (Nos. 357a, 358a, 359a) and two labels.
SB28   25c. booklet. Cover as Type **B3** with English text.................... 85·00
        a. French text (4.1.38) £150
SB29   25c. booklet. Cover as Type **B4** with English text 57 mm wide............... 85·00
        a. English text 63 mm wide £120
        b. French text 57 mm wide (4.1.38)............. 95·00
        ba. French text 63 mm wide £190

1937 (23–27 Apr). Red and white cover. Two panes of 4×3c. (No. 359a) and two labels.
SB30   25c. booklet. Cover as Type **B3** with English text (27.4).................... 50·00
        a. French text (23.4)............................. 65·00
SB31   25c. booklet. Cover as Type **B4** with English text 57 mm wide (27.4)............ 10·00
        a. English text 63 mm wide .... 65·00
        b. French text 57 mm wide (23.4)............ 13·00
        ba. French text 63 mm wide £180

1937 (18 May)–**38**. Green and white cover. Four panes of 6×1c. (No. 357b).
SB32   25c. booklet. Cover as Type **B3** with English text.................... 60·00
        a. French text (14.10.38)................... 75·00
SB33   25c. booklet. Cover as Type **B4** with English text 57 mm wide............... 50·00
        a. English text 63 mm wide .... 75·00
        b. French text 57 mm wide (14.10.38)............ 50·00
        ba. French text 63 mm wide £170

1938 (3 May)–**39**. Brown and white cover. Two panes of 6×2c. (No. 358b).
SB34   25c. booklet. Cover as Type **B3** with English text.................... 60·00
        a. French text (3.3.39)......................... 85·00
SB35   25c. booklet. Cover as Type **B4** with English text 57 mm wide............... 40·00
        a. English text 63 mm wide .... 85·00
        b. French text 57 mm wide .... 50·00
        ba. French text 63 mm wide £120

1942 (20–29 Aug). Red and white cover. Two panes of 4×3c. (No. 377a) and two labels.
SB36   25c. booklet. Cover as Type **B4** with English text.................... 12·00
        a. French text (29.8).......................... 16·00

1942 (12–14 Sept). Violet and white cover. Panes of 4×1c., 4×2c. and 4×3c. each. (Nos. 375a, 376a, 377a), each with two labels.
SB37   25c. booklet. Cover as Type **B4** with English text (14.9).................. 50·00
        a. French text (12.9).......................... 90·00

1942 (6 Oct)–**43**. Brown and white cover. Two panes of 6×2c. (No. 376b).
SB38   25c. booklet. Cover as Type **B4** with English text.................... 55·00
        a. French text (6.4.43)....................... 70·00

1942 (24 Nov)–**46**. Green and white cover. Four panes of 6×1c. (No. 375b).
SB39   25c. booklet. Cover as Type **B4** with English text.................... 18·00
        a. French text (16.2.43).................... 24·00
        b. Bilingual text (8.1.46)................... 50·00

1943 (3 May)–**46**. Orange and white cover. One pane of 6×4c. (No. 380a).
SB40   25c. booklet. Cover as Type **B4** with English text.................... 10·00
        a. French text (12.5.43).................... 20·00
        b. Bilingual text (8.1.46)................... 24·00

1943 (28 Aug)–**46**. Purple and white cover. Two panes of 4×3c. (No. 378a) and two labels.
SB41   25c. booklet. Cover as Type **B4** with English text.................... 14·00
        a. French text (7.9.43)...................... 35·00
        b. Bilingual text (8.1.46)................... 28·00

B5

1943 (1 Sept)–**46**. Black and white cover. Panes of 3×1c., 3×3c. and 3×4c. each. (Nos. 394a, 395a, 396a) (3×1).
SB42   25c. booklet. Cover as Type **B5** with English text.................... 55·00
        a. French text (18.9.43).................... 70·00
        c. Bilingual text (23.1.46)................. 65·00

B6

1947 (24 Nov). Brown on orange cover. Panes of 6×3c. and 6×4c. each. (3×2) and two panes of 4×7c. (2×2) (Nos. 378b, 380a, 407a).
SB43 $1 booklet. Cover as Type **B6** with English text.................... 55·00
        a. French text .... 60·00

1950 (12 Apr–18 May). Purple and white cover. Two panes of 4×3c. (No. 416a) and two labels (3×2).
SB44   25c. booklet. Cover as Type **B4** with English text.................... 12·00
        a. Bilingual text (18.5)...................... 12·00

1950 (5–10 May). Orange and white cover. One pane of 6×4c. (No. 417a) (3×2).
SB45   25c. booklet. Cover as Type **B4** with English text.................... 45·00
        a. Stitched... 60·00
        b. Bilingual text (10.5)...................... 55·00

1950 (18 May). Black and white cover. Panes of 3×1c., 3×3c. and 3×4c. each (Nos. 422bba, 423a, 423bba) (3×1).
SB46   25c. booklet. Cover as Type **B5** with English text.................... 60·00
        a. Bilingual text .... 80·00

1951 (2 June). Orange and white cover. One pane of 6×4c. (No. 417bba) (3×2).
SB47   25c. booklet. Cover as Type **B4** with English text.................... 10·00
        a. Stitched... 18·00
        b. Bilingual text .... 18·00

1951 (25 Oct)–**52**. Black and white cover. Panes of 3×1c., 3×3c. and 3×4c. each (Nos. 422bba, 423a, 423cca) (3×1).
SB48   25c. booklet. Cover as Type **B5** with English text.................... 48·00
        a. Bilingual text (9.7.52)................... 65·00

1953 (6 July–19 Aug). Orange cover. One pane of 6×4c. (No. 453a) (3×2).
SB49   25c. booklet. Cover as Type **B4** with English text.................... 9·00
        a. Bilingual text (19.8)...................... 14·00

1953 (17 July–20 Oct). Purple cover. Two panes of 4×3c. (No. 452a) and two labels (3×2).
SB50   25c. booklet. Cover as Type **B4** with English text.................... 5·50
        a. Bilingual text (20.10).................... 24·00

1953 (12 Aug). Grey cover. Panes of 3×1c., 3×3c. and 3×4c. each (Nos. 458a, 459a, 460a) (3×1).
SB51   25c. booklet. Cover as Type **B5** with English text.................... 24·00
        a. Bilingual text .... 48·00

All the following booklets are bilingual

1954 (1 Apr–Nov). Blue cover as T **B4**.
SB52   25c. booklet containing pane of 5×5c. and
        one label (No. 473a) (3×2) .... 3·50
        a. Stitched (11.54) .... 4·25

1954 (14 July–Nov). Blue cover as T **B4**.
SB53   25c. booklet containing pane of 5×5c. and
        one label (No. 467a) (3×2) .... 4·00
        a. Stitched (11.54) .... 8·00

1955 (7 July). Violet cover as T **B4**.
SB54   25c. booklet containing pane of 6×4c. (No.
        466a) (3×2) .... 8·00

B7

1956 (1 June). Red and white cover as T **B7**.
SB55   25c. booklet containing two panes of 5×1c.
        and 5×4c., each with one label (Nos.
        463a, 466b) (3×2) .... 6·50

1956 (July). Blue and white cover as T **B7**.
SB56   25c. booklet containing pane of 5×5c. and
        one label (No. 467a) (3×2) .... 6·00

B8

1963 (May)–**67**. Blue and white cover as T **B7**.
SB57   25c. booklet containing pane of 5×5c. and
        one label (No. 531a) (3×2) .... 8·00
        a. Cover Type B8 (1.67) .... 25·00

1963 (15 May). Red and white cover as T **B7**.
SB58   25c. booklet containing two panes of 5×1c.
        and 5×4c., each with one label (Nos.
        527a, 530a) (3×2) .... 10·00

1967 (Feb). Red cover as T **B8**.
SB59   25c. booklet containing two panes of 5×1c.
        and 5×4c., each with one label (Nos.
        579a, 582a) (3×2) .... 3·00

1967 (Mar). Blue cover as T **B8**.
SB60   25c. booklet containing pane of 5×5c. and
        one label (No. 583a) (2×3) .... 6·00

B9

1968 (Sept). Brown and cream cover, 70×48 mm, as T **B9**.
SB61   25c. booklet containing se-tenant pane of
        5×1c. and 5×4c. (No. 598a) (2×5) .... 1·75

1968 (Sept). Red and cream cover as T **B9**.
SB62 $1 booklet containing pane of 25×4c. and
        two labels (No. 599a) (3×9) .... 6·50

1968 (Sept). Blue and cream cover, 82×48 mm, as T **B9**.
SB63 $1 booklet containing pane of 20×5c.
        (No. 600a) (2×10) .... 4·50

1968 (Oct). Orange and cream cover, 70×48 mm, as T **B9**, but without border.
SB64   25c. booklet containing se-tenant pane of
        1×1c., 4×6c. and one label (No. 598b)
        (2×3) .... 2·00

B10 (Illustration reduced. Actual size 128×60 mm)

1968 (15 Nov). Christmas. Red and green cover as T **B10**.
SB65 $1 booklet containing two panes of
        10×5c. (No. 630a) (5×2) .... 4·50
        p. Phosphor (No. 630pa) .... 6·00
Nos. SB65/SB65p exist with left or right opening (i.e. with selvedge at left or right of pane).

1969 (Jan). Orange-red on cream cover as T **B9**, but without border.
SB66 $1.50, booklet containing pane of 25×6c. and
        two labels (No. 601a) (3×9) .... 10·00

1969 (8 Oct). Christmas. Red cover size as T **B10**.
SB67 $1 booklet containing two panes of
        10×5c. (No. 644a) (5×2) .... 3·00
        p. Phosphor (No. 644pa) .... 5·00

1970 (Jan). Black on cream cover as T **B9**, but without border.
SB68 $1.50 booklet containing pane of 25×6c. and
        two labels (No. 602a) (3×9) .... 16·00

1970 (Aug). Black on cream cover, 70×48 mm, as T **B9**, but without border.
SB69   25c. booklet containing pane of 4×6c. (No.
        603a) (2×2) .... 12·00

1970 (Aug). Black on cream cover, as T **B9**, but without border.
SB70 $1.50 booklet containing pane of 25×6c. and
        two labels (No. 607a) (3×9) .... 22·00

1970 (26 Oct). Indigo on cream cover, 70×50 mm. Inscr 'CANADIAN POSTAGE STAMPS ... MADE EXPRESSLY FOR OPAL MANUFACTURING CO. LIMITED'.
SB71   25c. booklet containing 4×2c. and 4×3c.
        (No. 580b) (2×2) with gutter margin
        between .... 1·75
No. SB71 was produced by the Canadian Bank Note Co for use in the private stamp-vending machines owned by the Opal Manufacturing Co Ltd, Toronto. To cover the cost of manufacture and installation these booklets were sold at 25c. each. They were not available from the Canadian Post Office.

1970 (Nov). Black on cream cover, 70×48 mm, as T **B9**, but without border.
SB72   25c. booklet containing pane of 4×6c. (No.
        608a) (2×2) .... 4·00

1971 (30 June). Green on cream cover, 70×48 mm, as Type **B9**, but without border.
SB73   25c. booklet containing se-tenant pane of
        one 1c., one 3c., three 7c. and 1 label
        (No. 604b) (2×3) .... 4·00
This exists with or without a black sealing strip inside the cover.

1971 (30 June). Green and buff cover, 82×47 mm, as Type **B9**, but without border.
SB74 $1 booklet containing se-tenant pane of
        four 1c., four 3c. and 12 7c. (No. 604a)
        (2×10) .... 17·00

1971 (1 Aug). Booklet No. SB73 with label affixed giving the new contents. Sold as an experiment in Toronto for 50c.
SB75   50c. booklet. Contents as No. SB73, but
        containing two panes .... 9·00
The experiment was later continued by the use of machines which issued two 25c. booklets for 50c.

CANADA Stamp Booklets

1971 (30 Dec). Grey on cream cover, 70×48 mm, as Type **B9**, but without border.
SB76   25c. booklet containing *se-tenant* pane of three 1c., one 6c. and two 8c. (No. 604c) (2×3) .... 1·50
    f. White fluorescent paper (No. 604fa)...... 1·75
    q. With fluorescent bands (No. 604qc)...... 2·00
    r. With fluorescent bands on white fluorescent paper (No. 604gfa) .... 2·50

1971 (30 Dec). Grey on cream cover, 77×48 mm, as Type **B9**, but without border.
SB77 $1 booklet containing *se-tenant* pane of six 1c., one 6c. and 11 8c. (No. 604d) (2×9) .... 6·50
    q. With fluorescent bands (No. 604qd)...... 5·00

B11

1972 (1 Mar). As No. SB76, but with brown on cream illustrated covers as Type **B11**. Ten different designs showing Mail Transport: (a) Post Office, 1816; (b) Stage Coach, *c* 1820; (c) Paddle Steamer, 1855; (d) Rural postman, *c* 1900; (e) Motor car, 1910; (f) Ford Model T, 1914; (g) Curtis 'JN4', 1918; (h) Mail truck, 1921; (i) Motorcycle, 1923; (j) Horse-drawn mail wagon, 1926.
SB78   25c. booklet. Contents as No. SB76 (*any cover*) .... 1·50
    f. White fluorescent paper........................ 1·75
    q. With fluorescent bands .... 2·00
    r. With fluorescent bands on white fluorescent paper .... 2·50
Set of 10 *different cover designs* (No. SB78) .... 13·00
Set of 10 *different cover designs* (No. SB78q) .... 18·00

1972 (1 Aug). Ten cover designs as No. SB78, but in blue on cream.
SB79   50c. booklet (*any cover*) containing *se-tenant* pane of one 6c., four 1c. and five 8c. (No. 604e) (2×5) .... 4·50
    q. With fluorescent bands (No. 604qe) ...... 4·50
Set of 10 *different cover designs* (No. SB79) .... 42·00
Set of 10 *different cover designs* (No. SB79q) .... 42·00
This exists with black or white sealing strip inside the cover.

1974 (10 Apr). Red on cream covers as Type **B11**. Ten different designs showing aircraft: (a) Gibson 'Twin-plane'; (b) Burgess Dunne seaplane; (c) Nieuport 'Scout'; (d) Curtiss 'HS-2L'; (e) Junkers 'W-34'; (f) Fokker 'Super Universal'; (g) 'Mosquito'; (h) 'Stranraer' flying-boat; (i) 'CF-100 Canuck'; (j) 'Argus'.
SB80   25c. booklet (*any cover*) containing *se-tenant* pane of three 1c., one 6c. and two 8c. (No. 693a) (3×2) 75
Set of 10 *different cover designs* .... 6·50

B12

1975 (17 Jan). Violet on cream cover as Type **B12**.
SB81 $1 booklet containing *se-tenant* pane of six 1c., one 6c. and eleven 8c. (No. 693b) (9×2) .... 2·25

1976 (1 Sept). Violet on cream cover. Designs as No. SB80.
SB82   50c. booklet (*any cover*) containing *se-tenant* pane of two 1c., four 2c. and four 10c. (No. 693c) (5×2) .... 1·50
Set of 10 *different cover designs* .... 14·00

1977 (1 Nov). Brown on cream covers, similar to Type **B11**, but vert. Ten different designs showing flowers or trees: (a) Bottle Gentian; (b) Western Columbine; (c) Canada Lily; (d) Hepatica; (e) Shooting Star; (f) Lady's Slipper; (g) Trembling Aspen; (h) Douglas Fir; (i) Sugar Maple; (j) Rose, Thistle, Shamrock, Lily and Maple leaf.
SB83   50c. booklet (*any cover*) containing *se-tenant* pane of four 1c. and four 12c. (No. 862a) (3×2) .... 3·25
Set of 10 *different cover designs* .... 29·00

1978 (1 Apr). Green on cream covers. Designs as No. SB83.
SB84   50c. booklet (*any cover*) containing *se-tenant* pane of four 2c., three 14c. and one label (No. 863a) (4×2) .... 2·75
Set of 10 *different cover designs* .... 25·00

B13

1978 (13 Nov). Black on cream covers as Type **B13**. Five different designs showing postcode publicity cartoons: (a) Talking post box; (b) Woman throwing letter to man; (c) Running letters; (d) Letter running to post box; (e) Woman with letter and laughing post box.
SB85 $3.50 booklet (*any cover*) containing pane of 25 14c. and two labels (No. 868ba) (9×3) .... 7·50
Set of 5 *different cover designs* .... 32·00

1979 (28 Mar). Blue on cream covers. Designs as No. SB83.
SB86   50c. booklet (*any cover*) containing *se-tenant* pane of one 1c., three 5c. and two 17c. (No. 870a) (3×2) .... 2·50
Set of 10 *different cover designs* .... 23·00

1979 (3 July)–**81**. Violet on cream covers. Designs as No. SB85.
SB87 $4.25 booklet (*any cover*) containing pane of 25 17c. and two labels (No. 869ab) (9×3) (cover without wavy lines) .... 8·00
SB88 $4.25 booklet (*any cover*) containing No. 869ab (horizontal wavy lines across cover) (4.2.81) .... 11·00
Set of 5 *different cover designs* (No. SB87) .... 35·00
Set of 5 *different cover designs* (No. SB88) .... 48·00

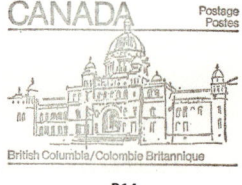

B14

1982 (1 Mar). Black on cream covers as Type **B14**. Ten different designs showing provincial legislature buildings: (a) Victoria, British Columbia; (b) Fredericton, New Brunswick; (c) Halifax, Nova Scotia; (d) Charlottetown, Prince Edward Island; (e) Quebec; (f) Edmonton, Alberta; (g) Toronto, Ontario; (h) Regina, Saskatchewan; (i) Winnipeg, Manitoba; (j) St. John's, Newfoundland.
SB89   50c. booklet (*any cover*) containing *se-tenant* pane of two 5c., one 10c., one 30c. and two labels (No. 1033a) (3×2) ... 2·50
    a. Containing pane No. 1033ab.................. 2·75
    b. Containing pane No. 1033ba.................. 8·00
    c. Containing pane No. 1033bb.................. 8·00
Set of 10 *different cover designs* (No. SB89).............. 22·00

Stamp Booklets CANADA

B15 Parliament Buildings, Ottawa

1982 (30 June). Black on cream cover as Type **B15**.
SB90 $6 booklet containing pane of 20 30c.
        and 1 label (No. 1032ab) (7×3)................ 15·00

1983 (15 Feb)–**85**. Indian red on cream covers as Type **B14**. Designs as No. SB89.
SB91   50c. booklet (*any cover*) containing *se-tenant* pane of two 5c., one 8c., one 32c. and two labels (No. 1033c) (3×2) ... 4·00
     a. Indian red on surfaced yellow cover (3.4.85) .... 4·00
Set of 10 different cover designs (No. SB91).................... 35·00
Set of 10 different cover designs (No. SB91a).................. 35·00

1983 (8 Apr). Indian red on cream cover as Type **B15**.
SB92 $8 booklet containing pane of 25 32c.
        and two labels (No. 1032bb) (9×3) .... 16·00

1983 (30 June). Canada Day. Multicoloured cover, 100×78 mm, showing location map of various forts.
SB93 $3.20 booklet containing *se-tenant* pane of ten 32c. (No. 1090a) (5×2)...................... 3·50

1984 (15 Feb). Cover as Type **B15**, but additionally inscribed '1984' below 'POSTES'.
SB94 $8 booklet containing pane of 25 32c.
        and 2 labels (No. 1032bd) (9×3) .... 22·00

1985 (21 June). Reddish brown on grey-brown covers similar to Type **B14**. Ten different designs showing architectural or ornamental details from Parliament Buildings, Ottawa: (a) Clock from Peace Tower; (b) Library entrance; (c) Gargoyle from Peace Tower; (d) Indian mask sculpture; (e) Stone carving at Memorial Chamber entrance; (f) Door to House of Commons; (g) Stone ornament at House of Commons main entrance; (h) Carved head, Senate Chamber; (i) Windows, Centre Block; (j) Window and war memorial, Peace Tower.
SB95   50c. booklet (*any cover*) containing *se-tenant* pane of three 2c., two 5c. and one 34c. (No. 1148a) (2×3)........................ 4·00
     a. 'R' on bottom left-hand corner of back cover... 4·00
Set of 10 different cover designs (No. SB95).................... 35·00
Set of 10 different cover designs (No. SB95a).................. 35·00

1985 (28 June). Canada Day. Black, pale brown and pale grey-brown cover, 100×78 mm, showing location map of various forts.
SB96 $3.40 booklet containing *se-tenant* pane of ten 34c. (No. 1163a) (5×2)...................... 3·25

B16 Parliament Buildings, Ottawa (*Illustration reduced. Actual size 120×70 mm*)

1985 (1 Aug)–**86**. White on agate cover as Type **B16**.
SB97 $8.50 booklet containing pane of 25 34c.
        (No. 1155a) (5×5) .... 13·00
     a. Containing pane No. 1155ba (4.7.86) .... 26·00

B17 (*Illustration reduced. Actual size 121×61 mm*)

1985 (23 Oct). Christmas. Rosine and emerald cover as Type **B17**.
SB98 $3.20 booklet containing pane of ten 32c.
        (No. 1181a) (5×2) .... 4·25

B18 (*Illustration reduced. Actual size 150×72 mm*)

1986 (29 Oct). Christmas. Black and brown-red cover as Type **B18**.
SB99 $2.90 booklet containing pane of ten 29c.
        (No. 1218a) (1×10) .... 4·50
     a. Containing pane No. 1218ba.................. 50·00

1987 (30 Mar–1 Oct). Ten cover designs as No. SB95 but in blackish olive on grey-brown.
SB100   50c. booklet (*any cover*) containing *se-tenant* pane of two 1c., two 6c., one 36c. and one label (No. 1147a) (2×3) ...... 9·00
     a. Containing pane No. 1147ba (1.10.87) . 7·50
Set of 10 different cover designs (No. SB100)................... 80·00
Set of 10 different cover designs (No. SB100a)................. 65·00

1987 (30 Mar). Yellow-orange on agate cover similar to Type **B16**, but 48×74 mm.
SB101 $3.60 booklet containing pane of ten 36c.
        (No. 1156ba) (2×5) .... 12·00

1987 (19 May). Yellow-orange on agate cover as Type **B16**.
SB102 $9 booklet containing pane of 25 36c.
        (No. 1156bb) (5×5) .... 27·00

1987 (2 Nov). Christmas. Christmas Plants. Black and magenta cover as Type **B18**, but 148×80 mm.
SB103 $3.10 booklet containing pane of ten 31c.
        (No. 1254a) (2×5) .... 8·00

B19

1988 (5 Jan). White and black on bright green cover as Type **B19**.
SB104 $3.70 booklet (49×73 mm) containing pane of ten 37c. (No. 1157ab) (2×5).................. 13·00
SB105 $9.25 booklet (120×73 mm) containing pane of 25 37c. (No. 1157ae) (5×5).................. 27·00

1988 (15 Jan). Covers as Type **B19**, but inscribed 'LUNCH SAVER'.
SB106 $3.70 booklet (49×73 mm) containing pane of ten 37c. (No. 1157ab) (2×5).................. 13·00
SB107 $9.25 booklet (120×73 mm) containing pane of 25 37c. (No. 1157ae) (5×5).................. 27·00

CANADA Stamp Booklets

1988 (3 Feb). Deep blue on grey-brown covers as Type **B14**. Ten different designs as No. SB95.
SB108   50c. booklet (*any cover*) containing se-tenant pane of one 1c., two 6c., one 37c. and two labels (No. 1147bb) (2×3)   3·25
Set of 10 different cover designs .... 27·00

1988 (27 Oct). Christmas. Icons. Multicoloured cover as Type **B18**, but 150×80 mm, showing stamp illustration on the front.
SB109 $3.20 booklet containing pane of ten 32c. (No. 1308a) (2×5) .... 2·50

B20 (*Illustration reduced. Actual size 79×152 mm*)

B21 (*Illustration reduced. Actual size 79×152 mm*)

1988 (29 Dec)–**89**. Multicoloured stamps on bright scarlet and violet-blue covers (Type **B20**) or on scarlet with white inscr (Type **B21**).
SB110 $2.20 booklet containing pane of five 44c. and one label (No. 1269ab) (2×3)
             (18.1.89).. 6·00
         a. Cover Type **B21** (17.3.89) .... 6·00
SB111 $3.80 booklet containing pane of ten 38c. and two labels (No. 1157ca) (3×4) .... 6·00
         a. Cover Type **B21** (17.3.89) .... 6·00
SB112 $3.80 booklet containing pane of ten 38c. and two labels (No. 1162bd) (3×4) .... 6·50
         a. Cover Type **B21** (17.3.89) .... 6·50
SB113 $3.80 booklet containing pane of five 76c. and one label (No. 1275ab) (2×3)
             (18.1.89).. 8·50
         a. Cover Type **B21** (17.3.89) .... 8·50

SB114 $9.50 booklet containing pane of 25 38c. and two labels (No. 1157cb) (3×9).......... 15·00
         a. Cover Type **B21** (17.3.89) .... 15·00
Booklet Nos. SB110/SB114 each exist with either 'Lunch Savers' or 'Would it be more convenient' advertisement on the reverse.
Booklet Nos. SB110a/SB114a also exist with 'Your 'Rush' Connection' advertisement on the reverse.

1989 (18 Jan). Brown-purple on grey-brown covers as Type **B14**. Ten different designs as No. SB95.
SB115   50c. booklet (*any cover*) containing se-tenant pane of three 2c., one 6c., one 38c. and one label (No. 1148ba) (2×3) .. 5·50
Set of 10 different cover designs .... 50·00

B22 (*Illustration reduced. Actual size 85×155 mm*)

1989 (30 June). Multicoloured cover as Type **B22**.
SB116 $5 booklet containing pane of 12 self-adhesive 38c. (No. 1328a) (6×2) .... 14·00
    Two types of cover exist for No. SB116 with one being the mirror image of the other.

1989 (26 Oct). Christmas. Paintings of Winter Landscapes. Multicoloured covers as Type **B21**.
SB117 $2.20 booklet containing pane of five 44c. and one label (No. 1344a) (2×3) (*cover 60×155 mm*).. 13·00
SB118 $3.30 4 booklet containing pane of ten 33c. (No. 1342a) (2×5) (80×155 mm) .... 9·00
SB119 $3.80 booklet containing pane of ten 38c. (No. 1343ab) (5×2) (80×155 mm)........... 32·00
SB120 $3.80 booklet containing pane of five 76c. and one label (No. 1345a) (2×3) (60×155 mm)... 22·00

1989 (28 Dec). Multicoloured covers as Type **B21**.
SB121 $3.90 booklet containing pane of ten 39c. and two labels (No. 1354a) (4×3) .... 11·00
SB122 $9.75 booklet containing pane of 25 39c. and two labels (No. 1354b) (9×3)............ 24·00

B23 Park Corner, Prince Edward Island

1990 (12 Jan). Multicoloured cover as Type **B23**.
SB123 50c. booklet containing *se-tenant* pane
of one 1c., two 5c. and one 39c. (No.
1350a) (2×2) (Perf 13½×14)........................ 1·40
  a. Containing pane No. 1350ba (Perf
  12½×13) .... 40·00

1990 (12 Jan). Multicoloured covers as Type **B21**.
SB124 $2.25 booklet containing pane of five 45c.
and one label (No. 1270ab) (2×3) .... 9·00
SB125 $3.90 booklet containing pane of ten 39c.
and two labels (No. 1162cb) (3×4) .... 19·00
SB126 $3.90 booklet containing pane of five 78c.
and one label (No. 1276ab) (2×3) .... 11·00

1990 (8 Feb). Multicoloured cover as Type **B22**, showing wheatfield.
SB127 $5 booklet containing pane of 12 self-
adhesive 39c. (No. 1328ba) (2×6)............ 14·00
Two types of cover exist for No. SB127 with one being the mirror image of the other.

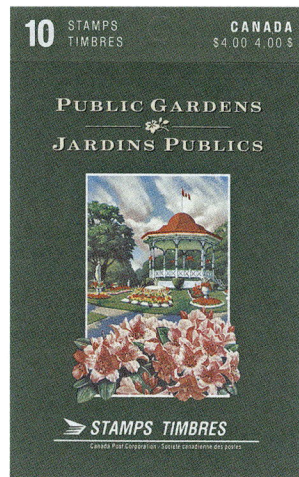

B25 (*Illustration reduced. Actual size* 80×125 mm)

B24 (*Illustration reduced. Actual size* 170×100 mm)

1990 (3 May). 'Moving the Mail'. Multicoloured cover as Type **B24**. Booklet contains text and illustrations on labels attached to the panes and on interleaving pages. Stitched.
SB128 $9.75 booklet containing two panes of eight
39c. (No. 1382a) (2×4) and one pane of
nine 39c. (No. 1382b) (3×4) .... 24·00

1990 (25 Oct). Christmas. Native Art. Multicoloured covers as Type **B21**.
SB129 $2.25 booklet containing pane of five 45c.
(No. 1407a) (2×3) (*cover* 60×155 mm)... 4·25
SB130 $3.40 booklet containing pane of ten 34c.
(No. 1405a) (2×5) (80×155 mm) .... 6·00
SB131 $3.90 booklet containing pane of ten 39c.
(No. 1406a) (2×5) (60×155 mm) .... 8·00
SB132 $3.90 booklet containing pane of five 78c.
(No. 1408a) (2×3) (60×155 mm) .... 9·00

1990 (28 Dec). Multicoloured cover as Type **B23**, but showing Point Atkinson, British Columbia.
SB133 50c. booklet containing *se-tenant* pane
of two 1c., one 5c. and one 40c. (No.
1350c) (2×2)... 2·00
The face value of No. SB133 included 3c. Goods and Service Tax.

1990 (28 Dec). Covers as Type **B21** showing multicoloured stamps on scarlet background with white inscriptions.
SB134 $2.30 booklet containing pane of five 46c.
and one label (No. 1270cc) (2×3) .... 12·00
SB135 $4 booklet containing pane of ten 40c.
and two labels (No. 1162da) (3×4) .... 13·00
SB136 $4 booklet containing pane of five 80c.
and one label (No. 1276cc) (2×3) .... 9·00
SB137 $4 booklet containing pane of ten 40c.
and two labels (No. 1355a) (4×3) .... 11·00
SB138 $10 booklet containing pane of 25 40c.
and two labels (No. 1355b) (9×3)............ 26·00

1991 (11 Jan). Multicoloured cover as Type **B22**, but showing coastal scene.
SB139 $5.25 booklet containing pane of 12 self-
adhesive 40c. (No. 1328ca) (2×6) .... 16·00
Two types of cover exist for No. SB139 with one being the mirror image of the other.

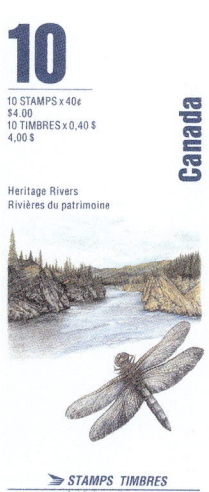

B26 (*Illustration reduced. Actual size* 64×156 mm)

1991 (22 May). Public Gardens. Multicoloured cover as Type **B25**.
SB140 $4 booklet containing *se-tenant* pane of
ten 40c. (No. 1422a) (5×2)......................... 4·50

1991 (20 Aug). Canadian Rivers (1st series). Multicoloured cover as Type **B26**.
SB141 $4 booklet containing *se-tenant* pane of
ten 40c. (No. 1432a) (10×1) .... 7·00

B27 (*Illustration reduced. Actual size* 150×81 mm)

CANADA Stamp Booklets

1991 (16 Oct). 150th Anniversary of Queen's University. Multicoloured cover as Type **B27**. Booklet contains text and illustrations on labels attached to the pane and on interleaving pages. Stitched.
SB142 $4 booklet containing pane of ten 40c.
          and two labels (No. 1449a) (4×3) ....   6·50

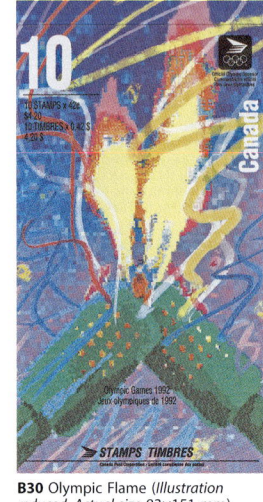

B30 Olympic Flame (*Illustration reduced. Actual size 83×151 mm*)

B28 Christmas Tree   **B29**

1991 (23 Oct). Christmas. Multicoloured covers as Type **B28**.
SB143 $2.30 booklet containing pane of five 46c.
          and one label (No. 1452a) (2×3) ....   6·25
SB144 $3.50 booklet containing pane of ten 35c.
          (No. 1450a) (2×5) (punch bowl and
          candles cover design, 80×155 mm) ....   8·00
SB145 $4 booklet containing pane of ten 40c.
          (No. 1451a) (2×5) (Christmas stocking
          cover design) ....   8·00
SB146 $4 booklet containing pane of five
          80c. and one label (No. 1453a) (2×3)
          (Christmas presents cover design) ....   8·00

1991 (27 Dec). Covers as Type **B29** showing multicoloured stamps on scarlet background with Olympic logo in black.
SB147 $2.40 booklet containing pane of five 48c.
          and one label (No. 1467ab) (2×3) ....   8·00
SB148 $4.20 booklet containing pane of five 84c.
          and one label (No. 1475ab) (2×3) .... 13·00
SB149 $4.20 booklet containing pane of ten 42c.
          (No. 1162ea) (2×5) .... 12·00
SB150 $4.20 booklet containing pane of ten 42c.
          (No. 1356a) (2×5) .... 15·00
SB151 $10.50 booklet containing pane of 25 42c.
          and two labels (No. 1356b) (3×9) .... 27·00
SB152 $21 booklet containing pane of 50 42c.
          and two labels (No. 1356c) (4×13) .... 60·00

The cover of booklet No. SB152 is made up of two $10.50 covers rouletted down the centre. It was issued in connection with a Canada Post special offer of a $1 coupon towards the cost of its purchase.

1992 (28 Jan). Multicoloured cover as Type **B22**, but showing mountain peaks.
SB153 $5.25 booklet containing pane of 12 self-
          adhesive 42c. stamps (No. 1328da)
          (2×6) .... 22·00

Two types of cover exist for No. SB153 with one being the mirror image of the other.

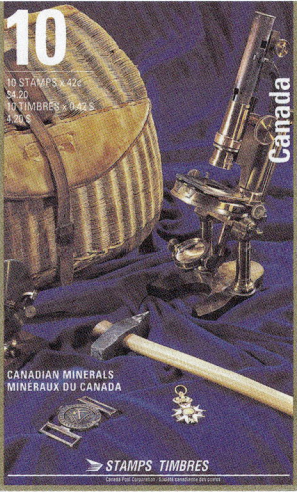

B31 Prospecting Equipment (*Illustration reduced. Actual size 90×151 mm*)

1992 (7 Feb). Winter Olympic Games, Albertville. Multicoloured cover as Type **B30**.
SB154 $4.20 booklet containing se-tenant pane of
          ten 42c. (No. 1482a) (5×2) ....   7·00

Two types of cover exist for No. SB154 with one being the mirror image of the other.

1992 (22 Apr). Canadian Rivers (2nd series). Multicoloured vert cover as Type **B26**.
SB155 $4.20 booklet containing se-tenant pane of
          ten 42c. (No. 1492a) (5×2) .... 13·00

1992 (15 June). Olympic Games, Barcelona. Multicoloured cover as Type **B30**, but showing Olympic flag.
SB156 $4.20 booklet containing se-tenant pane of
          ten 42c. (No. 1498a) (5×2) ....   9·00

Two types of cover exist for No. SB156 with one being the mirror image of the other.

1992 (21 Sept). 150th Anniversary of Geological Survey of Canada. Multicoloured cover as Type **B31**.
SB157 $4.20 booklet containing se-tenant pane of
          ten 42c. (No. 1509a) (5×2) .... 15·00

Stamp Booklets CANADA

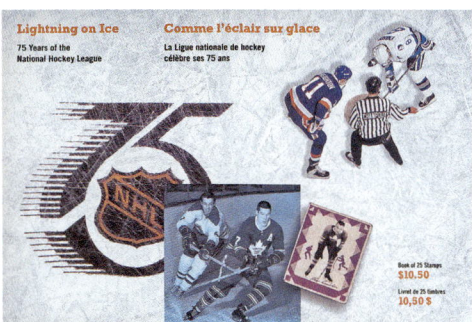

B32 Hockey Players (*Illustration reduced. Actual size* 171×105 mm)

1992 (9 Oct). 75th Anniversary of National Ice Hockey League. Multicoloured cover as Type **B32**. Booklet contains text and illustrations on labels attached to the pane and on interleaving pages. Stitched.

SB158	$10.50 booklet containing 25 42c. stamps in two panes of eight and one label and one pane of nine (Nos. 1516a, 1517a, 1518a) (each 3×3)	28·00

1992 (13 Nov). Christmas. Multicoloured covers as Type **B33**.
SB159	$2.40 booklet containing pane of five 48c. and one label (No. 1527a) (2×3)	8·00
SB160	$3.70 booklet containing pane of ten 37c. (No. 1525a) (2×5) (candle and cookies cover design, 80×156 mm)	8·00
SB161	$4.20 booklet containing pane of ten 42c. (No. 1526ab) (2×5) (hobby horse cover design)	9·00
SB162	$4.20 booklet containing pane of five 84c. and one label (No. 1528a) (2×3) (Christmas tree cover design)	9·00

1992 (30 Dec). Multicoloured covers as Type **B29**, but without Olympic symbol at top right.
SB163	$2.45 booklet containing pane of five 49c. and one label (No. 1468ba) (2×3)	9·00
SB164	$4.30 booklet containing pane of ten 43c. (No. 1162fa) (2×5)	16·00
SB165	$4.30 booklet containing pane of ten 43c. (No. 1357a) (2×5)	12·00
SB166	$4.30 booklet containing pane of five 86c. and one label (No. 1476ba) (2×3)	18·00
SB167	$10.75 booklet containing pane of 25 43c. and two labels (No. 1357b) (3×9)............	30·00

1993 (15 Feb). Multicoloured cover as Type **B22**, but showing lake.
SB168	$5.25 booklet containing pane of 12 self-adhesive 43c. stamps (2×6) (No. 1328ea)..	14·00

Two types of cover exist for No. SB168 with one being the mirror image of the other.

1993 (30 Apr). Hand-crafted Textiles. Multicoloured cover as Type **B34**.
SB169	$4.30 booklet containing *se-tenant* pane of ten 43c. (5×2) (No. 1534a).........................	6·50

B33 Hand Bell

B34 Hand-crafting Techniques
(*Illustration reduced. Actual size* 81×156 mm)

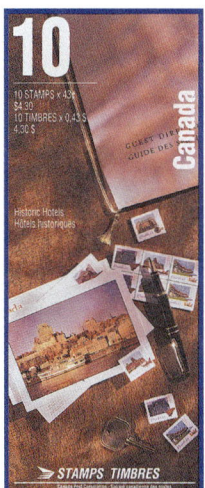 

B35 Postcards and Stamps   **B36** Rabbit and Present
(*Illustration reduced. Actual size* 60×155 mm)

1993 (14 June). Historic Hotels. Multicoloured cover as Type **B35**.
SB170	$4.30 booklet containing *se-tenant* pane of ten 43c. (5×2) (No. 1540a).........................	4·50

1993 (10 Aug). Canadian Rivers (3rd series). Multicoloured vert cover as Type **B26**.
SB171	$4.30 booklet containing *se-tenant* pane of ten 43c. (10×1) (No. 1558a)..........................	6·00

1993 (4 Nov). Christmas. Multicoloured covers as Type **B36**.
SB172	$2.45 booklet containing pane of five 49c. and one label (2×3) (No. 1574a)	4·50
SB173	$3.80 booklet containing pane of ten 38c. (2×5) (No. 1572a) (wooden puppet cover design, 80×156 mm)	6·00
SB174	$4.30 booklet containing pane of ten 43c. (2×5) (No. 1573a) (angel cover design).	6·50
SB175	$4.30 booklet containing pane of five 86c. and one label (2×3) (No. 1575a) (kangaroo cover design)	6·50

CANADA Stamp Booklets

B37

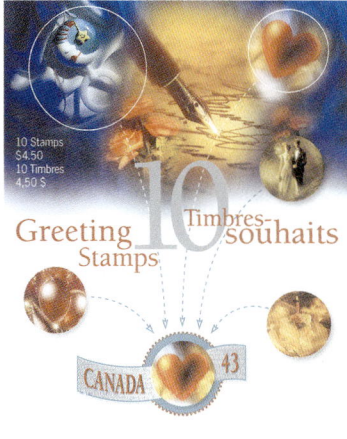

B38 (*Illustration reduced. Actual size* 106×157 mm)

| | a. Containing pane No. 1477ba (three fluorescent bands) (Perf 13) (14.11.94) | 17·00 |
| | b. Containing pane No. 1477ca (three fluorescent bands) (Perf 14½×14) (27.3.95) | 19·00 |

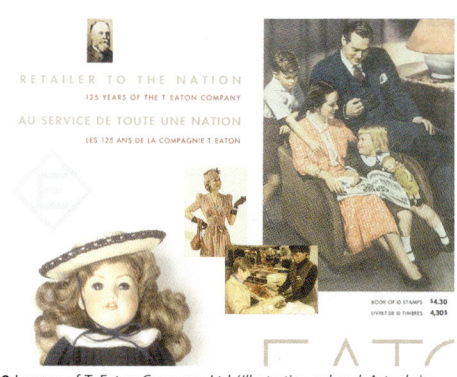

B39 Images of T. Eaton Company Ltd (*Illustration reduced. Actual size* 151×101 mm)

1994 (17 Mar). 125th Anniversary of T. Eaton Company Ltd. Multicoloured cover as Type **B39**. Booklet containing text and illustrations on label attached to the pane and on interleaving pages. Stitched.
SB184 $4.30 booklet containing ten 43c. stamps and two labels (No. 1583a) (6×2) .... 5·00

1994 (22 Apr). Canadian Rivers (4th series). Multicoloured vert cover as Type **B26**.
SB185 $4.30 booklet containing se-tenant pane of ten 43c. (No. 1584a) (2×5)..................... 5·00

1994 (7 Jan–14 Nov). Covers as Type **B37**, each showing multicoloured stamps in a continuous pattern on scarlet background.
SB176 $2.45 booklet containing pane of five 49c. and one label (No. 1468a) (2×3) .... 9·00
SB177 $4.30 booklet containing pane of ten 43c. (No. 1162fa) (2×5) .... 10·00
SB178 $4.30 booklet containing pane of ten 43c. (No. 1357ca) (Perf 14½) (2×5) (18.1) .... 10·00
    a. Containing pane No. 1357a (Perf 13½×13) (14.11)............................ 10·00
SB179 $4.30 booklet containing pane of five 86c. (No. 1476a) and one label (2×3) .... 10·00
SB180 $10.75 booklet containing pane of 25 43c. and two labels (No. 1357cb) (Perf 14½) (3×9) (18.1)................................. 24·00
    a. Containing pane No. 1357b (Perf 13½×13) (14.11)............................ 27·00

1994 (28 Jan). Greetings. Multicoloured cover as Type **B38**.
SB181 $4.50 booklet containing pane of ten self-adhesive 43c. (No. 1580a) and 35 circular greetings labels .... 5·00

1994 (25 Feb)–**95**. Covers as Type **B37** showing multicoloured stamps in a continuous pattern on scarlet backgrounds.
SB182 $2.50 booklet containing pane of five 50c. and one label (No. 1469a) (Perf 13) (2×3).. 7·50
    a. Containing pane No. 1469ba (Perf 14½×14) (27.3.95) .... 15·00
SB183 $4.40 booklet containing pane of five 88c. and one label (No. 1477a) (fluorescent frame) (Perf 13) (2×3) .... 11·00

B40 Carol Singer

B41 Fortress Gateway (*Illustration reduced. Actual size 96×157 mm*)

1994 (3 Nov). Christmas. Multicoloured covers as Type **B40**.
SB186	$2.50 booklet containing pane of five 50c. and one label (2×3) (No. 1619a)	4·00
SB187	$3.80 booklet containing pane of ten (38c.) (2×5) (No. 1617a) (chorister wearing ruff cover design, 80×156 mm)	4·50
SB188	$4.30 booklet containing pane of ten 43c. (2×5) (No. 1618a) (pair of singers cover design)	5·00
SB189	$4.40 booklet containing pane of five 88c. and one label (2×3) (No. 1620a) (singer in hat and scarf cover design)	5·00

1995 (5 May). 275th Anniversary of Fortress of Louisbourg. Multicoloured cover as Type **B41**.
SB190	$4.30 booklet containing pane of ten (43c.) (5×2) (No. 1631a)	5·00

1995 (31 July)–**00**. Covers as Type **B37**, each showing multicoloured stamps in a continuous pattern on scarlet background.
SB192	$2.60 booklet containing pane of five 52c. and one label (No. 1470a) (Perf 13) (2×3)	7·00
	a. Containing pane No. 1470ba (Perf 14½×14) (6.10)	13·00
SB193	$4.50 booklet containing pane of ten 45c. (No. 1162ga) (2×5)	23·00
SB194	$4.50 booklet containing pane of ten 45c. (No. 1358a) (Perf 14½) (2×5)	8·00
	a. Containing pane No. 1358ca (Perf 13½×13) (6.10)	12·00
SB195	$4.50 booklet containing pane of five 90c. and one label (No. 1478a) (Perf 13) (2×3)	7·00
	a. Containing pane No. 1478ba (Perf 14½×14) (6.10)	19·00
SB196	$11.25 booklet containing pane of 25 45c. and two labels (No. 1358b) (Perf 14½) (3×9)	16·00
	a. Containing pane No. 1358cb (Perf 13½×13) (6.10)	27·00

Nos. SB192a, SB194a, SB195a and SB196a, together with a new printing of No. SB193 issued on the same date, show a revised back cover layout including a customer service phone number.

1995 (1 Sept). Greetings. Multicoloured cover as Type **B43**.
SB197	$4.70 booklet containing pane of ten self-adhesive 45c. (No. 1654a) and 15 circular greetings labels	4·75

B42 Player and Bunker (*Illustration reduced. Actual size 52×156 mm*)

B43 Fountain Pen (*Illustration reduced. Actual size 78×156 mm*)

1995 (6 June). Centenaries of Canadian Amateur Golf Championship and of the Royal Canadian Golf Association. Multicoloured cover as Type **B42**.
SB191	$4.30 booklet containing se-tenant pane of ten 43c. (5×2) (No. 1637a)	6·00

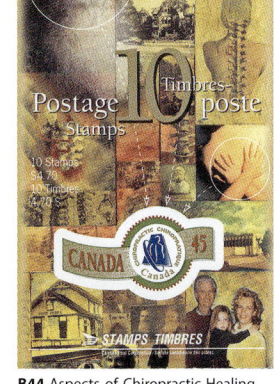

B44 Aspects of Chiropractic Healing (*Illustration reduced. Actual size 78×156 mm*)

CANADA Stamp Booklets

B45 Superman (*Illustration reduced. Actual size 105×169 mm*)

1995 (15 Sept). Centenary of Chiropractic Healing in Canada. Multicoloured cover as Type **B44**.
SB198 $4.70 booklet containing pane of ten self-adhesive 45c. (No. 1654a) and 15 circular commemorative labels .... 4·75

1995 (15 Sept). 50th Anniversary of Arctic Institute of North America. Multicoloured cover as Type **B26**, but showing Inuk woman and Arctic scene.
SB199 $4.50 booklet containing *se-tenant* pane of ten 45c. (No. 1656a) (5×2) .... 6·50

1995 (2 Oct). Comic Book Superheroes. Multicoloured cover as Type **B45**.
SB200 $4.50 booklet containing *se-tenant* pane of ten 45c. (No. 1661a) (5×2) .... 4·50

B47 Binary Codes and Globe (*Illustration reduced. Actual size 90×155 mm*)

1995 (2 Nov). Christmas. Multicoloured covers as Type **B46**.
SB201 $2.60 booklet containing pane of five 52c. and one label (2×3) (No. 1669a) .... 7·25
SB202 $4 booklet containing pane of ten 40c. (2×5) (No. 1667a) (Sprig of holly cover design, 80×156 mm) .... 8·00
SB203 $4.50 booklet containing pane of ten 45c. (2×5) (No. 1668a) (The Nativity cover design) .... 10·00
SB204 $4.50 booklet containing pane of five 90c. and one label (2×3) (No. 1670a) (The Flight to Egypt cover design) .... 10·00

1996 (15 Jan). Greetings. Multicoloured cover as Type **B38**.
SB205 $4.70 booklet containing pane of ten self-adhesive 45c. (No. 1654ba) and 35 circular greetings labels .... 5·50

1996 (15 Feb). High Technology Industries. Multicoloured cover as Type **B47**.
SB206 $5.40 booklet containing pane of 12 45c. (No. 1677a) (2×6) .... 4·75

B46 The Annunciation

B48 Ethel Catherwood (*Illustration reduced. Actual size 95×155 mm*)

B49 Father reading to Children (*Illustration reduced. Actual size 95×155 mm*)

1996 (8 July). Canadian Olympic Gold Medal Winners. Multicoloured cover as Type **B48**.
SB207 $4.50 booklet containing pane of ten 45c.
(No. 1691a) (5×2) .... 8·50

1996 (9 Sept). Literacy Campaign. Multicoloured cover as Type **B49**.
SB208 $5 booklet containing pane of ten 45+5c.
(5×2) (No. 1699a) .... 5·50

B51 Father Christmas

1996 (10 Oct). Canadian Authors. Multicoloured cover as Type **B50**.
SB209 $4.50 booklet containing pane of ten 45c.
(5×2) (No. 1706a) .... 5·50

1996 (1 Nov). Christmas. 50th Anniversary of UNICEF. Multicoloured covers as Type **B51**.
SB210 $2.60 booklet containing pane of five 52c.
and one label (2×3) (No. 1712ab) .... 4·50
SB211 $4.50 booklet containing pane of ten 45c.
(2×5) (No. 1711a) (Child tobogganing
design)... 5·50
SB212 $4.50 booklet containing pane of five 90c.
and one label (2×3) (No. 1713ab)
(Couple ice-skating design) .... 4·50

B50 Canadian Authors (*Illustration reduced. Actual size 80×155 mm*)

B52 Blue Poppy

1997 (4 Apr). Quebec in Bloom International Floral Festival. Multicoloured cover as Type **B52**.
SB213 $5.40 booklet containing pane of 12 45c.
(6×2) (No. 1724a) .... 5·50

B53 Paul Henderson celebrating

B55 Lady Amherst Fly

1997 (20 Sept). 25th Anniversary of the Canada–USSR Ice Hockey Series. Multicoloured cover as Type **B53**.
SB214 $4.50 booklet containing pane of ten 45c. (2×5) (No. 1746a) .... 7·00

1998 (16 Apr). Fishing Flies. Multicoloured cover as Type **B55**.
SB220 $5.40 booklet containing pane of 12 45c. (1×12) (No. 1784a) .... 6·00

B54 The Holy Family **B54a** Flags and Skyscrapers

1997 (3 Nov). Christmas. Stained Glass Windows. Multicoloured covers as Type **B54**.
SB215 $2.60 booklet containing pane of five 52c. (No. 1764ab) .... 3·75
SB216 $4.50 booklet containing pane of ten 45c. (No. 1763ab) (cover showing Regina SSi Rosarii) .... 4·75
SB217 $4.50 booklet containing pane of five 90c. (No. 1765ab) (cover showing Madonna and Child) .... 4·75

1998 (2 Feb–July). Covers as Type **B37**, each showing multicoloured stamps in a continuous pattern on scarlet background.
SB218 $4.50 booklet containing pane of ten 45c. (5×2) (No. 1358da) .... 9·00
       a. Cover as Type **B54a** (7.98) .... 9·00
SB219 $13.50 booklet containing pane of 3 45c. (two blocks of 15 (5×3) separated by vertical margin) (No. 1358db) .... 22·00
       a. Cover as Type **B54a** (7.98) .... 22·00

B56 Ship in Canal Lock

1998 (17 June). Canadian Canals. Multicoloured cover as Type **B56**.
SB221 $4.50 booklet containing pane of ten 45c. and ten labels (No. 1795a) (10×2) .... 7·00

Stamp Booklets CANADA

B57 *Joie Lacustre* (Paul-Emile Borduas) (*Illustration reduced. Actual size* 130×115 mm)

1998 (7 Aug). 50th Anniversary of *Refus Global* (manifesto of The Automatistes group of artists). Multicoloured cover as Type **B57**.
SB222 $3.15 booklet containing pane of seven self-adhesive 45c. (No. 1814a)........................... 5·00

B58 Circus Scenes and VIA Rail Train (*Illustration reduced. Actual size* 182×80 mm)

1998 (1 Oct). Canadian Circus. Multicoloured cover as Type **B58**.
SB223 $5.40 booklet containing *se-tenant* pane of 12 45c. (No. 1851a) (6×2) .... 8·50

B59 Adoring Angel   **B60**

1998 (6 Nov). Christmas. Statues of Angels. Multicoloured covers as Type **B59**.
SB224 $2.60 booklet containing pane of five 52c. and one label (2×3) (No. 1860a) (Perf 13×13½) .... 7·50
    a. Containing pane No. 1860ba (P 13) .... 3·75
SB225 $4.50 booklet containing pane of ten 45c. (2×5) (No. 1859a) (Perf 13) (cover showing Angel blowing trumpet)............... 7·00
    a. Containing pane No. 1859ba (Perf 13×13½) .... 16·00

SB226 $4.50 booklet containing pane of five 90c. and one label (2×3) (No. 1861a) (Perf 13×13½) (cover showing Angel at prayer)... 15·00
    a. Containing pane No. 1861ba (Perf 13)...... 7·50

1998 (28 Dec)–**2000**. Multicoloured covers as Type **B60**.
SB227 $4.60 booklet containing pane of ten 46c. (2×5) (No. 1359a) .... 7·00
SB228 $13.80 booklet containing pane of 30 self-adhesive 46c. (3×10) (No. 1366a) (72×102 mm)................................... 25·00
    a. Additional red on yellow 'Pressure Sensitive Autocollants' inscription on front cover (2000) .... 30·00

B61

B62 Birds' Heads (*Illustration reduced. Actual size* 110×157 mm)

1998 (28 Dec). Multicoloured covers as Type **B61**.
SB229 $2.75 booklet containing pane of five 55c. and one label (2×3) (No. 1836a) .... 8·00
SB230 $4.75 booklet containing pane of five 95c. and one label (2×3) (No. 1838a) .... 11·00

1999 (24 Feb). Birds (4th series). Multicoloured cover as Type **B62**. Self-adhesive.
SB231 $5.52 booklet containing pane of 12 46c. (No. 1869b)....................................... 10·00

B63 *Platanthera psycodes*

1999 (27 Apr). Orchids. Multicoloured cover as Type **B63**.
SB232 $5.52 booklet containing *se-tenant* pane of 12 46c. (No. 1883a) (3×4) .... 6·50

B64 'Big Ben' (show jumper)

1999 (2 June). Canadian Horses. Multicoloured cover as Type **B64**.
SB233 $5.52 booklet containing pane of 12 self-adhesive 46c. (No. 1907a) .... 6·50

B65 Kites

1999 (1 Oct). Stamp Collecting Month. Kites. Multicoloured cover as Type **B65**. Self-adhesive.
SB234 $3.68 booklet containing *se-tenant* pane of eight 46c. (No. 1942a) .... 4·00

B66 Angel with Toys

1999 (4 Nov). Christmas. Victorian Angels. Multicoloured covers as Type **B66**.
SB235 $2.75 booklet containing pane of five 55c. and one label (2×3) (No. 1950a) .... 5·50
SB236 $4.60 booklet containing pane of ten 46c. (2×5) (No. 1949a) (cover showing Angel playing drum)................................. 6·50
SB237 $4.75 booklet containing pane of five 95c. and one label (2×3) (No. 1951a) (cover showing Angel with star).......................... 6·50

2000 (1 Mar). Birds (5th series). Multicoloured cover as Type **B62**. Self-adhesive.
SB238 $5.52 booklet containing pane of 12 46c. (No. 1978a) .... 7·50

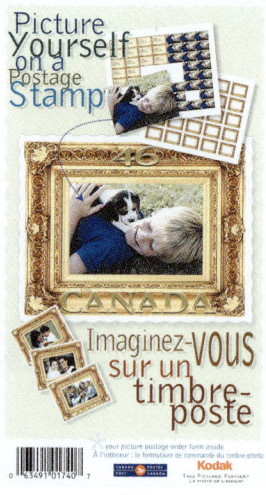

B67

2000 (28 Apr). Picture Postage Greetings Stamps. Multicoloured cover as Type **B67**. Self-adhesive.
SB239 $2.30 booklet containing pane of five 46c. and five greetings labels (No. 1988a) .... 2·50

Stamp Booklets CANADA

B68

2000 (28 Apr). Traditional Rural Mailboxes. Multicoloured cover as Type **B68**.
SB240 $5.52 booklet containing pane of 12 46c. (2×6) (No. 1989a) .... 6·50

B70

2000 (19 July). Tall Ships Race. Multicoloured cover as Type **B70**. Self-adhesive.
SB243 $4.60 booklet containing se-tenant pane of ten 46c. (2×2+2×3) (No. 2012a) .... 4·50

B69

2000 (23 May). Canadian Rivers and Lakes. Multicoloured covers as Type **B69**. Self-adhesive.
SB241 $2.75 booklet containing pane of five 55c. (1×5) (No. 1993a) .... 2·75
SB242 $4.75 booklet containing pane of five 95c. (1×5) (No. 1998a) .... 4·25

B71

2000 (1 Sept). 'Scratch & WIN Instantly!' Game. Multicoloured cover as Type **B71**, incorporating a scratch card as an additional panel. Self-adhesive.
SB244 $13.80 booklet containing pane of 30 46c. (3×10) (No. 1366a) .... 24·00

2000 (13 Sept). 25th Anniversary of Petro-Canada (oil company). Multicoloured cover, 216×105 mm, showing design as No. 2015. Self-adhesive.
SB245 $5.52 booklet containing pane of 12 46c. (4×3) (No. 2015a) and six pages of text   7·00

CANADA Stamp Booklets

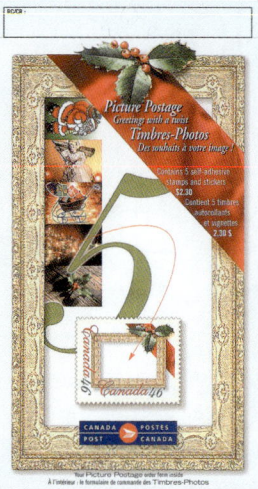

B72

2000 (5 Oct). Picture Postage Christmas Greetings. Multicoloured cover as Type **B72**. Self-adhesive.
SB246 $2.30 booklet containing pane of five 46c.
and five Christmas labels (No. 2020a) ... 2·50

B75 Toronto Blue Jays Emblem, Maple Leaf and Baseball

2001 (9 Apr). 25th Season of the Toronto Blue Jays (baseball team). Multicoloured cover as Type **B75**. Self-adhesive.
SB254 $3.76 booklet containing pane of eight 47c.
stamps (No. 2073a) .... 3·50

B73　　　　　B74

2000 (3 Nov). Christmas. Religious Paintings by Mouth and Foot Artists. Multicoloured covers as Type **B73**.
SB247　$3.30 booklet containing pane of six 55c.
(2×3) (No. 2022a) .... 4·00
SB248　$4.60 booklet containing pane of ten 46c.
(2×5) (No. 2021a) (cover design as 46c.
stamp) .... 5·50
SB249　$5.70 booklet containing pane of six 95c.
(2×3) (No. 2023a) (cover design as 95c.
stamp) .... 7·00

2000 (28 Dec). Multicoloured covers as Type **B74**.
SB250　$4.70 booklet containing pane of ten self-
adhesive 47c. (2×5) (No. 1367a) .... 11·00
SB251　$14.10 booklet containing pane of 30
self-adhesive 47c. (3×10) (No. 1367b)
(72×102 mm)... 30·00
　　　No. SB251 comes with two different back covers, one concerning mail redirection and the other 'Collection Canada 2000'.

2000 (28 Dec). Picture Postage Greetings Stamps. Multicoloured cover similar to Type **B72**. Self-adhesive.
SB252　$2.35 booklet containing pane of five
different 47c. and five greetings labels
(No. 2045a) .... 2·50

2001 (1 Feb). Birds (6th series). Multicoloured cover similar to Type **B62**. Self-adhesive.
SB253　$5.64 booklet containing pane of 12 47c.
(2×6) (No. 2062a) .... 7·00

B76 Details from Stamp Designs

2001 (11 May). Tourist Attractions (1st series). Multicoloured covers as Type **B76**. Self-adhesive.
SB255　$3 booklet containing pane of five 60c.
stamps (No. 2075a) .... 4·25
SB256　$5.25 booklet containing five $1.05 stamps
(No. 2080a) .... 6·25

Stamp Booklets CANADA

B77 Spray of Roses

2001 (1 Aug). Canadian Roses. Multicoloured cover as Type **B77**.
SB257 $5.64 booklet containing pane of 12 self-adhesive 47c. (3×4) (No. 2091a) .... 7·50

2001 (21 Sept). Picture Postage Greetings Stamps. Multicoloured cover similar to Type **B72**. Self-adhesive.
SB258 (–) booklet containing pane of five different domestic mail stamps and five greetings labels (No. 2099a)............. 2·75
No. SB258 was initially sold at $2.35.

 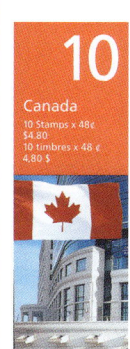

B79 Christmas Lights   **B80**

2001 (1 Nov). Christmas Lights. Multicoloured covers as Type **B79**, each showing a different light pattern.
SB260 $3.60 booklet containing pane of six 60c. (2×3) (No. 2111a) .... 5·50
SB261 $4.70 booklet containing pane of ten 47c. (2×5) (No. 2110a) .... 6·50
SB262 $6.30 booklet containing pane of six $1.05 (2×3) (No. 2112a) .... 6·75

2002 (2 Jan). Multicoloured covers as Type **B80**.
SB263 $4.80 booklet containing pane of ten self-adhesive 48c. (No. 1368a) (any cover)... 11·00
    a. Strip of three booklets showing complete cover design .... 26·00
    b. Slogan and websites added to back cover.. 11·00
    ba. Strip of three booklets showing complete cover design .... 26·00
No. SB263b included the slogan 'From anywhere to anyone' and the Canada Post website address.
No. SB263/SB263b were issued in horizontal strips of three booklets, separated by roulettes, each strip illustrating a complete cover design as No. 1368.

B81

B78 Hot Air Balloons

2001 (1 Oct). Stamp Collecting Month. Hot Air Balloons. Multicoloured cover as Type **B78**. Self-adhesive.
SB259 $3.76 booklet containing pane of eight 47c. (No. 2106a)... 5·00

2002 (28 Feb–27 May). Canadian Universities' Anniversaries. Multicoloured covers as Type **B81**.
SB264 $3.84 booklet containing pane of eight 48c. (4×2) (No. 2129a) .... 4·75
SB265 $3.84 booklet containing pane of eight 48c. (4×2) (No. 2130a) (Université Laval, Quebec) (4.4)...................................... 4·75
SB266 $3.84 booklet containing pane of eight 48c. (4×2) (No. 2131a) (Trinity College, Toronto) (30.4) .... 4·75
SB267 $3.84 booklet containing pane of eight 48c. (4×2) (No. 2132a) (Saint Mary's University, Halifax) (27.5) .... 4·75

CANADA Stamp Booklets

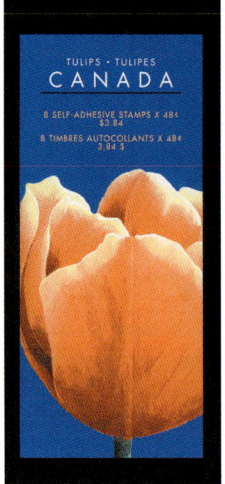

B82 'Ottawa' Tulip

2002 (3 May). 50th Canadian Tulip Festival, Ottawa. Tulips. Multicoloured cover as Type **B82**.
SB268	$3.84 booklet containing eight self-adhesive 48c. (No. 2134a) on which the self-adhesive paper around the stamps was retained..	5·00

2002 (1 June). Tourist Attractions (2nd series). Multicoloured covers as Type **B76**. Self-adhesive.
SB269	$3.25 booklet containing pane of five 65c. (No. 2143a)..	3·50
SB270	$6.25 booklet containing pane of five $1.25 (No. 2148a)..	5·50

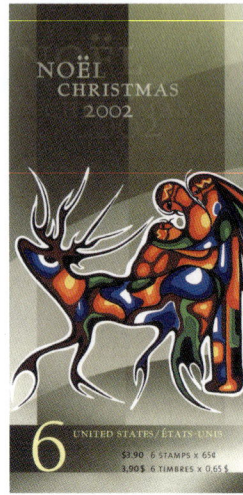

B84 'Winter Travel' (Cecil Youngfox)

2002 (4 Nov). Christmas. Aboriginal Art. Multicoloured covers as Type **B84**.
SB272	$3.90 booklet containing pane of six 65c. (2×5) (No. 2173a)..	4·25
SB273	$4.80 booklet containing pane of ten 48c. (2×3) (No. 2172a) (cover showing 'Genesis' (Daphne Odjig))........................	5·50
SB274	$7.50 booklet containing pane of six $1.25 (2×3) (No. 2174a) (cover showing 'Mary and Child' (Irene Katak Angutitaq))...	6·75

B84a Bishop's University, Quebec

2003 (28 Jan–4 Sept). Canadian Universities' Anniversaries (2nd issue). Multicoloured cover as Type **B84a**.
SB275	$3.84 booklet containing pane of eight 48c. (2×4) (No. 2190a) (Bishop's University, Quebec)..	6·00
SB276	$3.84 booklet containing pane of eight 48c. (2×4) (No. 2191a) (University of Western Ontario, London) (19.3)............	6·00
SB277	$3.84 booklet containing pane of eight 48c. (2×4) (No. 2192a) (St. Francis Xavier University, Nova Scotia) (4.4)...............	6·00
SB278	$3.84 booklet containing pane of eight 48c. (2×4) (No. 2193a) (Macdonald Institute, University of Guelph, Ontario) (20.6)..	6·00
SB279	$3.84 booklet containing pane of eight 48c. (2×4) (No. 2194a) (Université De Montréal) (4.9)...	6·00

B83 Young People

2002 (23 July). 17th World Youth Day, Toronto. Multicoloured cover as Type **B83**. Self-adhesive.
SB271	$3.84 booklet containing pane of eight 48c. (No. 2156a)..	4·25

Stamp Booklets CANADA

B85 John Audubon

2003 (21 Feb). Bird Paintings by John Audubon. Multicoloured cover as Type **B85** Self-adhesive.
SB280 $3.90 booklet containing pane of six 65c.
         (3×2) (No. 2199a) ....   11·00

2003 (12 June). Tourist Attractions (3rd series). Multicoloured covers as Type **B76**. Self-adhesive.
SB281 $3.25 booklet containing pane of five 65c.
         (No. 2205a) ....   5·00
SB282 $6.25 booklet containing pane of five $1.25
         (No. 2210a) ....   8·00

2003 (11 July). Vancouver's Successful Bid for Winter Olympic Games, 2010. No. SB263 with cover optd Vancouver 2010 in red.
SB283 $4.80 booklet containing pane of ten self-adhesive 48c. (No. 2215a) (any cover)...   9·00
         a. Strip of three booklets showing complete cover design ....   23·00

B87 Cyclists in Race

2003 (10 Sept). World Road Cycling Championships, Hamilton, Ontario. Multicoloured cover as Type **B87**.
SB285 $3.84 booklet containing pane of eight 48c.
         (No. 2224a) ....   8·00

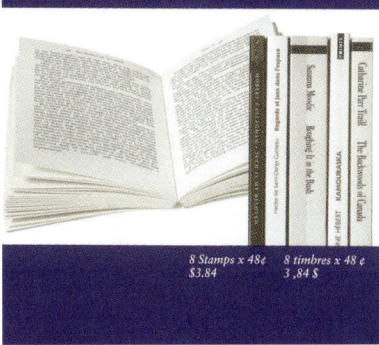

B86 Books

2003 (8 Sept). 50th Anniversary of National Library of Canada. Multicoloured cover as Type **B86**.
SB284 $3.84 booklet containing pane of eight 48c.
         (No. 2220a) ....   5·00

B88 Ice Hockey Player

2003 (4 Nov). Christmas. Multicoloured covers as Type **B88**. Self-adhesive.
SB286 $3.90 booklet containing pane of six 65c.
         (2×3) (No. 2239a) ....   6·75
SB287 $5.76 booklet containing pane of 12 48c.
         (2×6) (No. 2238a) (cover showing skater) ....   7·50
SB288 $7.50 booklet containing pane of six $1.25
         (2×3) (No. 2240a) (cover showing skier)   10·00

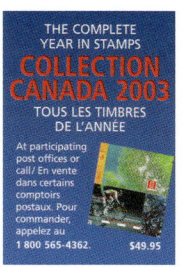

B89

CANADA Stamp Booklets

2003 (19 Dec). Multicoloured cover as Type **B89**. Self-adhesive.
SB289 $4.90 booklet containing pane of ten 49c.
              (No. 1369a)... 11·00

2003 (19 Dec). Multicoloured cover as Type **B89**. Self-adhesive.
SB292 $4.90 booklet containing pane of ten 49c.
              (No. 2241a)... 10·00
        Nos. SB290/SB291 are vacant.
        Folded booklets and flat panes designed to be folded are listed in this catalogue as booklets. Flat panes not designed to be folded have been deleted from this booklet section. These panes are still listed after the stamps they contain.
        Postal forgeries of SB292 are known.

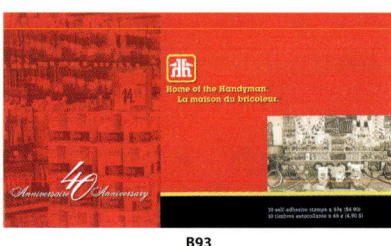

B93

2004 (19 Apr). 40th Anniversary of Home Hardware (co-operative business). Multicoloured cover as Type **B93**. Self-adhesive.
SB299 $4.90 booklet containing pane of ten 49c.
              (4×3) plus a central label (No. 2270a),
              eight pages of text and illustrations
              and a pane of 15 self-adhesive labels ... 8·00

2004 (4 May). 8 May Canadian Universities Anniversaries (3rd issue). Multicoloured covers as Type **B84a**.
SB300 $3.92 booklet containing pane of eight 49c.
              (2×4) (No. 2271a)............................. 5·50
SB301 $3.92 booklet containing pane of eight 49c.
              (2×4) (No. 2272a) (8.5)...................... 5·50

B91

2004 (29 Jan–19 July). Tourist Attractions (4th series). Multicoloured covers as Type **B91**. Self-adhesive.
SB293 $2.94 booklet containing pane of six 49c.
              (No. 2257a)... 5·50
SB294 $2.94 booklet containing pane of six 49c.
              (No. 2258a) (2.4) .... 5·50
SB295 $2.94 booklet containing pane of six 49c.
              (No. 2259a) (1.6)............................... 5·50
SB296 $2.94 booklet containing pane of six 49c.
              (No. 2260a) (18.6)............................. 5·50
SB297 $2.94 booklet containing pane of six 49c.
              (No. 2261a) (19.7).............................. 5·50

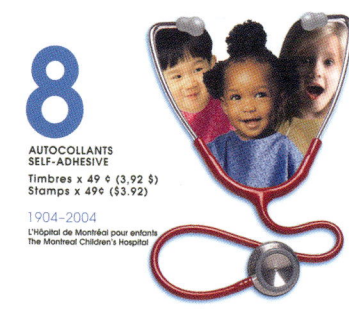

B94

2004 (6 May). Centenary of Montreal Children's Hospital. Multicoloured as Type **B94**. Self-adhesive.
SB302 $3.92 booklet containing pane of eight 49c.
              (No. 2273a)... 6·50

2004 (14 May). Bird Paintings by John Audubon (2nd series). Multicoloured cover as Type **B85** showing face of John Audubon. Self-adhesive.
SB303 $4.80 booklet containing pane of six 80c.
              (No. 2278a)... 11·00

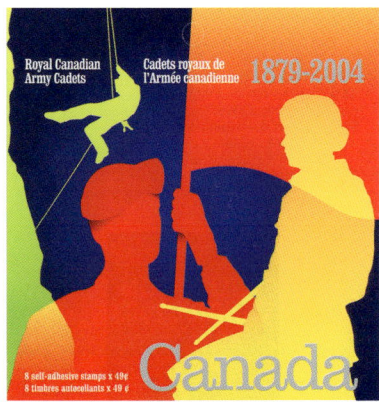

B92

2004 (26 Mar). 125th Anniversary of Royal Canadian Army Cadets. Multicoloured cover as Type **B92**. Self-adhesive.
SB298 $3.92 booklet containing pane of eight 49c.
              (No. 2265a)... 8·00

B95

2004 (2 July). Multicoloured cover as Type **B95**. Self-adhesive.
SB304 $4.90 booklet pane of ten 49c. (No. 1369a) .... 11·00

2004 (27 July). Multicoloured cover as Type **B95**. Self-adhesive.
SB305 $4.90 booklet containing pane of ten 49c.
              (No. 2241a)... 11·00

Stamp Booklets CANADA

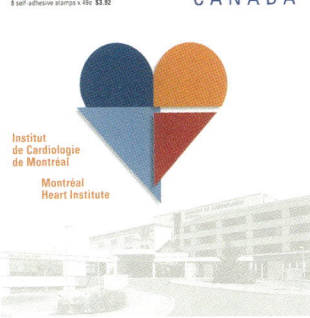

B96

2004 (15 Sept). 50th Anniversary of Montréal Heart Institute. Multicoloured cover as Type **B96**. Self-adhesive.
SB306 $3.92 booklet containing pane of eight 49c.
(No. 2287a) .... 5·75

B101 B100

2004 (20 Dec). Multicoloured covers as Type **B100**. Five different cover designs showing the following advertisements in English and French: (a) 'Picture yourself on a postage stamp!'; (b) 'Looking for a hero?'; (c) 'They'll take you places.'; (d) 'Collect famous masterpieces!'; (e) 'You'll go wild over our stamps!'. Self-adhesive.
SB311 $5 booklet (any cover) containing pane of ten 50c. (No. 1370a) .... 15·00

Nos. SB308 and SB310 are vacant.

In addition to the five different front cover designs No. SB311 comes with five different back covers which reproduce parts of the designs on the stamps, giving twenty-five booklet cover variations.

2004 (20 Dec). Multicoloured covers as Type **B101**. Five different cover designs showing advertisements as No. SB311 but with blue background. Self-adhesive.
SB312 $5 booklet (any cover) containing pane of ten 50c. (No. 2242a) .... 10·00

B97

2004 (1 Oct). Pets. Multicoloured cover as Type **B97**. Self-adhesive.
SB307 $3.92 booklet containing pane of eight 49c.
(No. 2288a) .... 8·00

B98

2004 (2 Nov). Christmas. Multicoloured cover as Type **B98**. Self-adhesive.
SB309 $5.88 booklet containing pane of 12 49c.
(No. 2300a) .... 11·00

B103

2005 (4 Feb). Fishing Flies. Multicoloured cover as Type **B103**. Self-adhesive.
SB315 $4 booklet containing two panes of 50c.
(No. 2329a) .... 8·00

Nos. SB313/SB314 are vacant.

2005 (14 Feb). Canadian Universities Anniversaries (4th series). Multicoloured cover as Type **B84a** (No. SB275) but 90×130 mm. Self-adhesive.
SB316 $4 booklet containing pane of eight 50c.
(No. 2333a) .... 5·75

CANADA Stamp Booklets

B104 White Daffodil with Yellow Trumpet

2005 (10 Mar). Daffodils. Multicoloured cover as Type **B104**. Self-adhesive.
SB318 $5 booklet containing pane of ten 50c.
           (No. 2336a)... 8·00

No. SB317 is vacant.

B105 TD Bank Building in Early 20th Century and Cashier

2005 (18 Mar). 150th Anniversary of TD Bank Financial Group. Multicoloured cover as Type **B105**. Self-adhesive.
SB319 $5 booklet containing pane of ten 49c.
           (5×2) (No. 2339a), eight pages of text and illustrations and a pane of 15 self-adhesive labels .... 7·00

B106 John Audubon

2005 (23 Mar). Bird Paintings by John Audubon (3rd series). Multicoloured cover as Type **B106**. Self-adhesive.
SB320 $5.10 booklet containing pane of six 85c.
           (No. 2344a)... 12·00

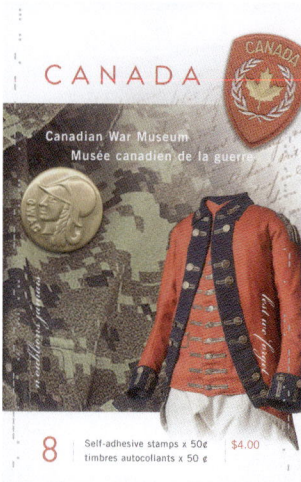

B107 18th-century Uniform and Modern Camouflage Material

2005 (6 May). Opening of New Canadian War Museum Building, Ottawa. Multicoloured cover as Type **B107**. Self-adhesive.
SB321 $4 booklet containing pane of eight 50c.
           (No. 2354a)... 7·00

B108 Mountain Biker, Skateboarder, City and Forest

2005 (1 Oct). Youth Sports. Multicoloured cover as Type **B108**. Self-adhesive.
SB322 $4 booklet containing pane of eight 50c.
           (No. 2368a)... 4·50

B109 Snowman

2005 (2 Nov). Christmas (1st issue). Multicoloured cover as Type **B109**. Self-adhesive.
SB323 $6 booklet containing pane of 12 50c.
         (No. 2375a).. 7·50

B110 Christmas Star   **B111** Balloons

2005 (2 Nov). Christmas (2nd issue). Multicoloured cover as Type **B110**. Self-adhesive.
SB325 $6 booklet containing pane of 12 50c.
         (No. 2376a) (cover 54×138 mm, unfolded)............................ 7·50
No. SB324 is vacant.

2005 (19 Dec). Multicoloured cover as Type **B111**. Self-adhesive.
SB327 $5.10 booklet containing pane of ten 51c.
         (No. 1374ab)...................................... 12·00
No. SB326 is vacant.

B113 Purple Coneflower, other Flowers and American Painted Lady Butterfly

2006 (8 Mar). Gardens. Multicoloured cover as Type **B113**. Self-adhesive.
SB332 $4.08 booklet containing pane of eight 51c.
         (No. 2384a).. 10·00

B115 McClelland and Stewart's Colophon

2006 (26 Apr). Centenary of McClelland and Stewart (publishing house). Slate-blue and grey cover as Type **B115**. Self-adhesive.
SB334 $4.08 booklet containing pane of eight 51c. and eight labels (No. 2393a)..................... 10·00
No. SB333 is vacant.

B112 Queen Elizabeth II

2006 (12 Jan). 80th Birthday of Queen Elizabeth II. Multicoloured cover as Type **B112**. Self-adhesive.
SB331 $5.10 booklet containing pane of 10 51c. and 10 labels (No. 2381a)........................... 8·00
Nos. SB328/SB330 are vacant.

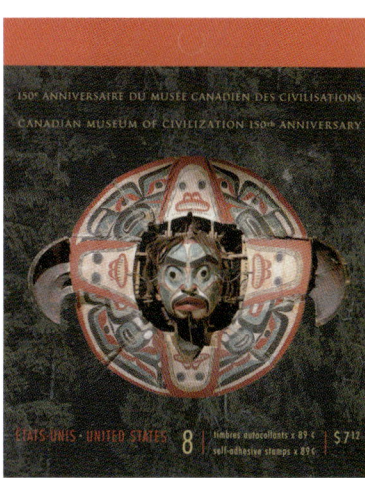

B116 Mid 19th-Century Transformation Mask

CANADA Stamp Booklets

2006 (11 May). 150th Anniversary of Canadian Museum of Civilization, Gatineau, Quebec. Multicoloured cover as Type **B116**. Self-adhesive.
SB335 $7.12 booklet containing pane of eight 89c.
           (No. 2394a) .... 12·00

B120 Arthur Wheeler (founder) and Early and Modern Climbers

2006 (19 July). Centenary of the Alpine Club of Canada. Multicoloured cover as Type **B120**. Self-adhesive.
SB339 $4.08 booklet containing pane of eight 51c.
           (No. 2408a) .... 7·00
No. SB338 is vacant.

B117 Lorne Greene

2006 (26 May). Canadians in Hollywood. Multicoloured covers in four different designs as Type **B117**. Self-adhesive.
SB336 $4.08 booklet containing pane of eight 51c. and eight labels (No. 2395a) (Type
           B117) .... 6·00
           a. Cover showing Fay Wray .... 6·00
           b. Cover showing Mary Pickford ...... 6·00
           c. Cover showing John Candy .... 6·00
The booklet panes in Nos. SB336/SB366c differ in the order of the stamps within the two blocks of four which form the booklet pane.

B121

2006 (23 Aug). Canadian Wine and Cheese. Multicoloured cover as Type **B121**. Self-adhesive.
SB340 $4.08 booklet containing pane of eight 51c.
           (No. 2415a) .... 6·00

2006 (26 Sept). Canadian Universities' Anniversaries (5th series). Multicoloured cover as Type **B84a** (No. SB275) but 90×130 mm. Self-adhesive.
SB341 $4.08 booklet containing pane of eight 51c.
           (No. 2419a) .... 7·00

B118 Beluga Whale

2006 (15 June). 50th Anniversary of Vancouver Aquarium. Multicoloured cover as Type **B118**. Self-adhesive.
SB337 $5.10 booklet containing pane of ten 51c.
           (No. 2402a) .... 6·25

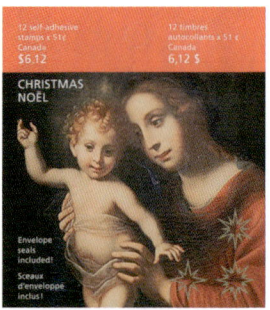

B123 'Madonna and Child' (detail) (Antoine-Sébastien Falardeau)

2006 (1 Nov). Christmas (1st issue). Multicoloured cover as Type **B123**. Self-adhesive.
SB343 $6.12 booklet containing pane of 12 51c.
              (No. 2430a) .... 9·50
No. SB342 is vacant.

B124 'Winter Joys' Christmas Card (J. E. Sampson)

2006 (1 Nov). Christmas (2nd issue). Multicoloured covers as Type **B124**. Self-adhesive.
SB345 $6.12 booklet containing pane of 12 51c.
              (No. 2431a) .... 9·50
No. SB344 is vacant.

B125 River and Forest

2006 (16 Nov)–**07**. Multicoloured cover as Type **B125**. Self-adhesive.
SB347 $5.10 booklet containing pane of ten (51c.) stamps (No. 2434a) (cover as Type **B125**) .... 10·00
SB348 $15.30 booklet containing pane of thirty (51c.) stamps (No. 2434b) (cover Type **B125**) .... 29·00
  a. With barcode on booklet pane (2007).. 29·00
No. SB346 is vacant.
No. 348 has the barcode on the back of the pane.

B129 *Syringa×prestoniae* 'Isabella'

2007 (1 Mar). Lilacs. Multicoloured cover as Type **B129**. Self-adhesive.
SB354 $5.20 booklet containing pane of ten 52c. and ten labels (No. 2484a) .... 8·00
Nos. SB349/SB353 are vacant.

2007 (12 Mar). Canadian Universities' Anniversaries (6th issue). Multicoloured cover as Type **B84a** but 89×130 mm. Self-adhesive.
SB355 $4.16 booklet containing pane of eight 52c.
              (No. 2487a) .... 6·25
SB356 $4.16 booklet containing pane of eight 52c.
              (No. 2488a) (3.4.07) .... 6·25

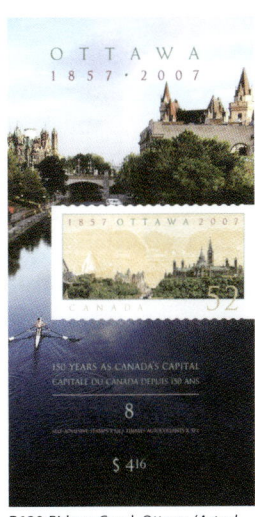

B130 Rideau Canal, Ottawa (*Actual size 89×171 mm*)

2007 (3 May). 150th Anniversary of Ottawa as Capital of Canada. Multicoloured cover as Type **B130**. Self-adhesive.
SB357 $4.16 booklet containing pane of eight 52c.
              (No. 2491a) .... 7·25

CANADA Stamp Booklets

B131 Gordon Lightfoot

2007 (29 June). Canadian Recording Artists. Multicoloured covers in four different designs as Type **B131**. Self-adhesive.
SB358 $4.16 booklet containing pane of eight 52c.
and eight labels (No. 2500a) (Type
B131) .... 8·50
a. Cover showing Joni Mitchell .... 8·50
b. Cover showing Anne Murray .... 8·50
c. Cover showing Paul Anka .... 8·50
The booklet panes in Nos. SB358/SB358c differ in the order of the stamps within the two blocks of four which form the booklet pane.

B134 Scouts of 2007 and 1907

2007 (25 July). Centenary of Scouting. Multicoloured cover as Type **B134**. Self-adhesive.
SB361 $4.16 booklet containing pane of eight 52c.
(No. 2507a) .... 7·25

B135 Reindeer

2007 (1 Nov). Christmas (1st issue). Multicoloured cover as Type **B135**. Self-adhesive.
SB363 $6.24 booklet containing pane of 12 (52c.)
stamps (No. 2526a) .... 11·00
No. SB362 is vacant.

B132 Seashore, Terra Nova National Park   **B133** Elk, Jasper National Park

2007 (6 July). 50th Anniversary of Terra Nova National Park, Newfoundland. Multicoloured cover as Type **B132**. Self-adhesive.
SB359 $5.20 booklet containing pane of ten 52c.
(No. 2505a) .... 10·00

2007 (20 July). Centenary of Jasper National Park, Alberta. Multicoloured cover as Type **B133**. Self-adhesive.
SB360 $5.20 booklet containing pane of ten 52c.
(No. 2506a) .... 10·00

B136 Nativity

2007 (1 Nov). Christmas (2nd issue). Multicoloured cover as Type **B136**. Self-adhesive.
SB365 $6.24 booklet containing pane of 12 (52c.) stamps (No. 2527a) .... 11·00
No. SB364 is vacant.

B142 Guide Dog 'Luke'

2008 (21 Apr). Guide Dogs. Multicoloured cover as Type **B142**. Self-adhesive.
SB377 $5.20 booklet containing pane of ten 52c. (No. 2547a)....................... 12·00
No. SB377 also commemorates the Centenary of the Montreal Association for the Blind.

B139 Peonies 'Elgin' and 'Coral'n Gold'

2008 (3 Mar). Peonies. Multicoloured cover as Type **B139**. Self-adhesive.
SB373 $5.20 booklet containing pane of ten 52c. and ten labels (No. 2541a).......... 9·00
Nos. SB366/SB372 are vacant.

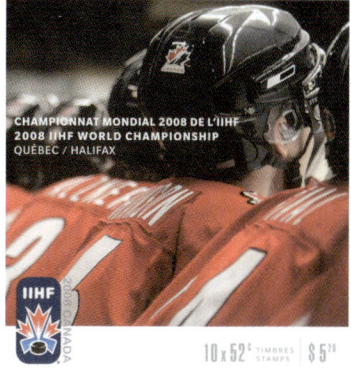

B141 Team Canada Players

2008 (3 Apr). International Ice Hockey Federation World Championship, Halifax and Québec. Multicoloured covers as Type **B141**. Self-adhesive.
SB376 $5.20 booklet containing pane of ten 52c. (No. 2546a)........................ 9·00
    a. Cover showing ice hockey players and stadium .... 9·00
Nos. SB374/SB375 are vacant.
No. SB376 also commemorates the Centenary of the International Ice Hockey Federation.

B143 Sambro Island Lighthouse, Nova Scotia   **B144** Welder working on Pipeline

2008 (1 May). Lighthouses. Multicoloured cover as Type **B143**. Self-adhesive.
SB378 $15.60 booklet containing pane of 30 (52c.) (No. 2439b)....................... 42·00

2008 (2 May). Oil and Gas Industry. Multicoloured cover as Type **B144**. Self-adhesive.
SB379 $5.20 booklet containing pane of ten 52c. (No. 2548a)........................ 10·00

CANADA Stamp Booklets

B145 Audrey Hepburn

2008 (21 May). Art Canada. Birth Centenary of Yousuf Karsh (portrait photographer). Multicoloured covers as Type **B145**. Self-adhesive.
SB380 $7.68 booklet containing pane of eight 96c.
         (No. 2553a) (Type **B145**) .... 14·00
SB381 $12.80 booklet containing pane of eight
         $1.60 (No. 2554a) (cover showing
         Winston Churchill)... 25·00

B147 Anne

2008 (20 June). Centenary of Publication of *Anne of Green Gables* by Lucy Maud Montgomery. Multicoloured cover as Type **B147**. Self-adhesive.
SB383 $5.20 booklet containing pane of ten 52c.
         (No. 2557a)... 9·00

2008 (30 June). Canadians in Hollywood (2nd series). Multicoloured cover as Type **B117**. Self-adhesive.
SB384 $4.16 booklet containing pane of eight 52c.
         and eight labels (No. 2560a) (cover
         showing Norma Shearer .... 9·00
         a. Cover showing Chief Dan George .... 9·00
         b. Cover showing Marie Dressler .... 9·00
         c. Cover showing Raymond Burr .... 9·00
    The booklet panes in Nos. SB383/SB383c differ in the order of the stamps within the two blocks of four which form the booklet pane.

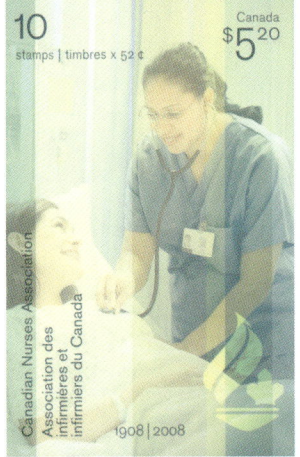

B146 Nurse with Patient

2008 (16 June). Centenary of Canadian Nurses Association. Multicoloured cover as Type **B146**. Self-adhesive.
SB382 $5.20 booklet containing pane of ten 52c.
         (No. 2556a) .... 10·00

B148 Athletes parading with Canadian Flag

2008 (18 July). Olympic Games, Beijing. Multicoloured cover as Type **B148**. Self-adhesive.
SB385 $5.20 booklet containing pane of ten 52c.
         (No. 2565a) .... 12·00

B149 Lifeguards

2008 (25 July). Centenary of Lifesaving Society. Multicoloured cover as Type **B149**. Self-adhesive.
SB386 $5.20 booklet containing pane of ten 52c.
(No. 2566a) .... 9·00

2008 (1 Oct). Endangered Species (3rd series). Multicoloured cover, 120×155 mm. Self-adhesive.
SB387 $4.18 booklet containing pane of eight 52c.
(No. 2569a) .... 12·00

B151 Infant Jesus (crèche figure by Antonio Caruso) (*Illustration reduced. Actual size 70×125 mm*)

2008 (3 Nov). Christmas (1st issue). Multicoloured cover as Type **B151**. Self-adhesive.
SB389   ($6.24) booklet containing pane of 12 (52c.) stamps (No. 2576a) .... 12·00

B150 Woman with Megaphone (*Illustration reduced. Actual size 60×127 mm*)

2008 (6 Oct). Mental Health. Multicoloured cover as Type **B150**. Self-adhesive.
SB388 $6.20 booklet containing pane of ten 52+10c. (No. 2574a) .... 11·00

B152 Child Skiing (*Illustration reduced. Actual size 75×135 mm*)

CANADA Stamp Booklets

B153 Bobsleigh

2008 (3 Nov). Christmas (2nd issue). Winter Fun. Multicoloured covers as Type **B152**. Self-adhesive.
SB391 ($6.24) booklet containing pane of 12 (52c.) stamps (No. 2577a) .... 10·00
No. SB390 is vacant.

2009 (12 Jan). Winter Olympic Games, Vancouver, 2010. Olympic Sports. Multicoloured covers as Type **B153**. Self-adhesive.
SB393 ($16.20) booklet containing pane of 30 (54c.) stamps (No. 2584b) .... 35·00
No. SB392 is vacant.

B155 Nebula

2009 (2 Apr). International Year of Astronomy. Multicoloured cover as Type **B155**. Self-adhesive.
SB395 $5.40 booklet containing pane of ten 54c. and ten labels (No. 2608a) .... 10·00

B154 Rhododendron Flowers

2009 (13 Mar). Rhododendrons. Multicoloured cover as Type **B154**. Self-adhesive.
SB394 $5.40 booklet containing pane of ten 54c. and ten labels (No. 2603a) .... 10·00

B156 Newfoundland Pony

2009 (15 May). Canadian Horse and Newfoundland Pony. Multicoloured cover as Type **B156**. Self-adhesive.
SB396 $5.40 booklet containing pane of ten 54c. (No. 2614a) .... 15·00

B157 Robert Charlebois

2009 (2 July). Canadian Recording Artists. Multicoloured cover as Type **B157**. Self-adhesive.
SB397 $4.32 booklet containing pane of eight 54c. and eight labels (No. 2618a) (Type **B157**) .... 7·00
  a. Cover showing Edith Butler .... 7·00
  b. Cover showing Stompin' Tom Connors ..... 7·00
  c. Cover showing Bryan Adams .... 7·00

The booklet panes in Nos. SB397/SB397c differ in the order of the stamps within the two blocks of four which form the booklet panes.

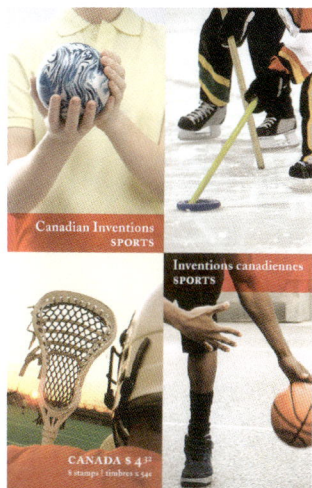

B159 Five-pin Bowling, Ringette, Lacrosse and Basketball

2009 (10 Aug). Canadian Inventions. Sports. Multicoloured cover as Type **B159**. Self-adhesive.
SB399 $4.32 booklet containing pane of eight 54c. and eight labels (No. 2629a).................... 10·00

B158 Signpost

2009 (6 July). Roadside Attractions. Multicoloured cover as Type **B158**. Self-adhesive.
SB398 $4.32 booklet containing pane of eight 54c. and eight labels (No. 2623a)..................... 10·00

B160 Tree and River inside Human Head and Sun breaking through Clouds

2009 (14 Sept). Mental Health. Multicoloured cover as Type **B160**. Self-adhesive.
SB400 ($6.64) booklet containing pane of ten (54c.)+10c. (No. 2633a)................................ 12·00

CANADA Stamp Booklets

B161 Detail from Maurice Richard's Hockey Sweater

2009 (17 Oct). Centenary of Montreal Canadiens (ice hockey team). Multicoloured cover as Type **B161**. Self-adhesive.
SB401 ($5.40) booklet containing pane of ten (No. 2634a) .... 11·00

B162 Soldiers and Horses (detail from National War Memorial)

2009 (19 Oct). Lest We Forget. Multicoloured cover as Type **B162**. Self-adhesive.
SB402 ($5.40) booklet containing pane of ten (No. 2636a) .... 12·00

B163 Madonna and Infant Jesus

2009 (2 Nov). Christmas (1st issue). Multicoloured cover as Type **B163**. Self-adhesive.
SB403 ($6.48) booklet containing pane of 12 (54c.) (No. 2638a) .... 12·00

B164 Christmas Tree

2009 (2 Nov). Christmas (2nd issue). Multicoloured cover as Type **B164**. Self-adhesive.
SB404 ($6.48) booklet containing pane of 12 (54c.) (No. 2642a) .... 12·00

B165 Watson's Mill, Manotick, Ontario

2010 (11 Jan). Mills. Multicoloured cover as Type **B165**. Self-adhesive.
SB405 ($17.10) booklet containing pane of 30 (57c.) (No. 2445b) .... 45·00

Stamp Booklets CANADA

B166 Inukshuk, Whistler Mountain

2010 (12 Jan). Winter Olympic Games, Vancouver. Multicoloured cover as Type **B166**. Self-adhesive.
SB406 $5.70 booklet containing pane of ten 57c.
and ten small stickers (No. 2653a) .... 12·50

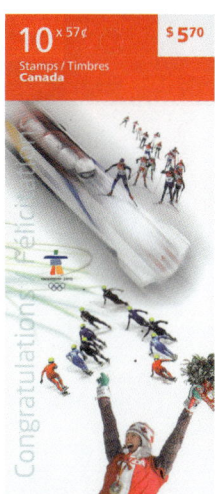

B168 Chandra Crawford, Speed Skaters, Bobsleigh and Skiers

2010 (14 Feb). Olympic Winter Games, Vancouver. Canada's First Olympic Gold on Canadian Soil. Multicoloured cover as Type **B167**. Self-adhesive.
SB407 $5.70 booklet containing pane of ten 57c.
(No. 2658a).. 12·50

2010 (22 Feb). Olympic Winter Games, Vancouver. Multicoloured cover as Type **B168**. Self-adhesive.
SB408 $5.70 booklet containing pane of ten 57c.
(No. 2660a).. 12·50

B167 Gold Medal

B169 African Violet 'Picasso'

2010 (3 Mar). African Violets. Multicoloured cover as Type **B169**. Self-adhesive.
SB409 ($5.70) booklet containing pane of ten (57c.)
and ten labels (No. 2663a)......................... 12·50

209

B170 Figures forming Maple Leaf and Star of David

2010 (14 Apr). Canada–Israel, 60 Years of Friendship. Multicoloured cover as Type **B170**. Self-adhesive.
SB410 $10.20 booklet containing pane of six $1.70
      (No. 2666a).. 25·00

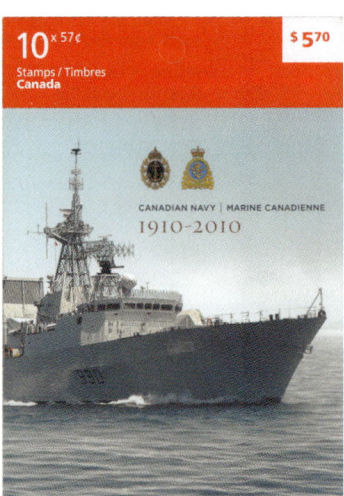

B171 HMCS *Halifax*

2010 (4 May). Centenary of the Canadian Navy. Multicoloured cover as Type **B171**. Self-adhesive.
SB411 $5.70 booklet containing pane of ten 57c.
      (No. 2673a).. 15·00

B172 Sea Otter

2010 (13 May). Marine Life: Sea Otter and Harbour Porpoise. Black, dull ultramarine and new blue cover as Type **B172**. Pane attached by selvedge.
SB412 $4.56 booklet containing pane of eight 57c.
      (No. 2676a).. 11·50

B173 Wildlife

2010 (22 May). Canadian Geographic's Wildlife Photography of the Year. Multicoloured cover as Type **B173**. Self-adhesive.
SB413 $5.70 booklet containing pane of ten 57c.
      (No. 2679a).. 14·00

B174 Rotary Badge

2010 (18 June). Centenary of Rotary International. Multicoloured cover as Type **B174**. Self-adhesive.
SB414 $4.56 booklet containing pane of eight 57c.
      (No. 2685a).. 10·00

2010 (5 July). Roadside Attractions (2nd series). Multicoloured cover as Type **B158**, but showing signpost with star and arrow. Self-adhesive.
SB415   ($4.56) booklet containing pane of eight (57c.) and eight small stickers (No. 2688a).. 11·00

Stamp Booklets CANADA

B175 Guide

2010 (8 July). Centenary of Girl Guides of Canada. Multicoloured cover as Type **B175**. Self-adhesive.
SB416 ($5.70) booklet containing pane of ten (57c.) and ten small stickers (No. 2693a).......... 12·50

B177 'Our Lady of the Night' (sculpture by Antonio Caruso)

2010 (1 Nov). Christmas (1st issue). Multicoloured cover as Type **B177**. Self-adhesive.
SB418 ($6.84) booklet containing pane of 12 (57c.) (No. 2697a)... 15·00

B176 Sun and Tree growing on Mountain Summit

2010 (7 Sept). Mental Health. Multicoloured cover as Type **B176**. Self-adhesive.
SB417 ($6.70) booklet containing pane of ten (57c.)+10c. (No. 2696a) .... 12·50

B178 Red Baubles

2010 (1 Nov). Christmas (2nd issue). Baubles. Multicoloured cover as Type **B178**. Self-adhesive.
SB419 ($6.84) booklet containing pane of 12 (57c.) (No. 2698a)... 15·00

CANADA Stamp Booklets

B179 Canadian Flag on Hot-air Balloon

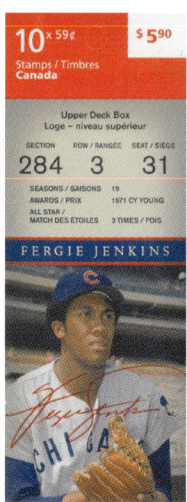

B181 Fergie Jenkins

B182 Pow-wow, 1969

2011 (17 Jan). 'Canadian Pride'. Multicoloured cover, 60×135 mm, as Type **B179**. Self-adhesive.
SB420   ($17.70) booklet containing pane of 30 (59c.)
    (No. 2728b).. 35·00

2011 (1 Feb). Black History Month. Fergie Jenkins. Multicoloured cover, 55×145 mm, as Type **B181**. Self-adhesive.
SB422 $5.90 booklet containing pane of ten 59c.
    (No. 2951a).. 11·00

2011 (21 Feb). Art Canada. Paintings by Daphne Odjig. Multicoloured covers as Type **B182**. Self-adhesive.
SB423 $6.18 booklet containing pane of six $1.03
    (No. 2755a) (cover Type **B182**, 50×118
    mm).. 14·00
SB424 $10.50 booklet containing pane of six
    $1.75 (No. 2756a) (cover 66×142
    mm showing detail from 'Spiritual
    Renewal').. 22·00

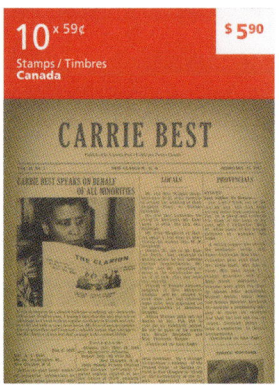

B180 Carrie Best (founder) reading *The Clarion* Newspaper

B183 Sunflower 'Sunbright'

2011 (1 Feb). Black History Month. Carrie Best. Multicoloured cover, 76×100 mm, as Type **B180**. Self-adhesive.
SB421 $5.90 booklet containing pane of ten 59c.
    (No. 2750a).. 11·00

2011 (3 Mar). Sunflowers. Multicoloured cover, 80×120 mm, as Type **B183**. Self-adhesive.
SB425   ($5.90) booklet containing pane of ten (59c.)
    (No. 2759a).. 12·50

Stamp Booklets CANADA

B184 Ram

2011 (21 Mar)–**00**. Signs of the Zodiac. Multicoloured cover, 73×117 mm, as Type **B184**. Self-adhesive.
SB426	($5.90) booklet containing pane of ten (59c.) (No. 2762a)	12·00
SB427	($5.90) booklet containing pane of ten (59c.) (No. 2763a) (21.4)	12·00
SB428	($5.90) booklet containing pane of ten (59c.) (No. 2764a) (20.5)	12·00
SB429	($5.90) booklet containing pane of ten (59c.) (No. 2765a) (22.6)	12·00

B186 Prince William and Miss Catherine Middleton, November 2010

2011 (29 Apr). Royal Wedding. Multicoloured covers, 60×127 mm, as Type **B186**. Self-adhesive.
SB431	($5.90) booklet containing ten (59c.) (No. 2784a)	20·00
SB432	$17.50 booklet containing ten $1.75 (No. 2785a)	48·00

B185 Forest and Silhouettes of Wildlife

2011 (21 Apr). International Year of Forests. Multicoloured cover, 75×110 mm, as Type **B185**. Self-adhesive.
SB430	($4.72) booklet containing pane of eight (59c.) (No. 2777a)	12·00

B187 Hiker, Eagle, Grizzly Bear and Waterfall in Mountain Landscape

2011 (19 May). Centenary of Parks Canada. Multicoloured cover, 75×140 mm, as Type **B187**. Self-adhesive.
SB433	$5.90 booklet containing pane of ten 59c. (No. 2788a)	15·00

CANADA Stamp Booklets

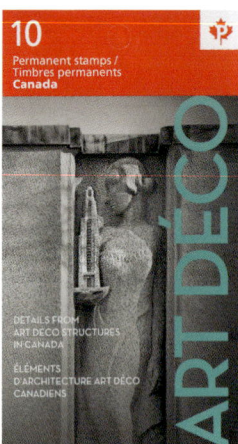

B188 Wall of Cormier House with Stone Carving, Montreal

2011 (9 June). Art Déco. Multicoloured cover, 67×117 mm, as Type **B188**. Self-adhesive.
SB434   ($5.90) booklet containing pane of (59c.) (No. 2789a)... 13·00

B189 Duke and Duchess of Cambridge in State Landau

2011 (22 June). Royal Wedding (2nd issue). Multicoloured cover, 60×127 mm, as Type **B189**. Self-adhesive.
SB435   ($5.90) booklet containing pane of ten (59c.) (No. 2795a)... 16·00

B190 Ginette Reno

2011 (30 June). Canadian Recording Artists (3rd series). Multicoloured covers, 103×98 mm, as Type **B190**. Self-adhesive.
SB436   ($4.72) booklet containing pane of eight (59c.) and eight labels (No. 2798a) (Type **B190**)............................. 10·00
  a. Cover showing Bruce Cockburn............. 10·00
  b. Cover showing Robbie Robertson .... 10·00
  c. Cover showing Kate and Anna McGarrigle... 10·00
The booklet panes in Nos. SB436/SB436c differ in the order of the stamps within the two blocks of four which form the booklet panes.

2011 (7 July). Roadside Attractions (3rd series). Multicoloured cover as Type **B158**, but showing red signpost with circular arrow. Self-adhesive.
SB437   ($4.72) booklet containing pane of eight (59c.) and eight small stickers (No. 2807a)... 12·00

B191 Cockpit of *Miss Supertest III*

2011 (8 Aug). *Miss Supertest III* (hydroplane, winner of Harmsworth Trophy 1959, 1960 and 1961). Multicoloured cover, 75×145 mm, as Type **B191**. Self-adhesive.
SB438   ($5.90) booklet containing pane of ten (59c.) (No. 2812a)... 14·00

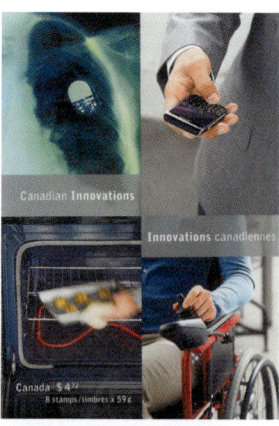

B192 Cardiac Pacemaker, BlackBerry, Electric Oven and Electric Wheelchair

2011 (17 Aug). Canadian Innovations. Multicoloured cover, 76×109 mm, as Type **B192**. Self-adhesive.
SB439 $4.72 booklet containing pane of eight 59c. (No. 2814a)... 11·00

Stamp Booklets CANADA

B193 'The Puzzle' (Miriane Majeau)

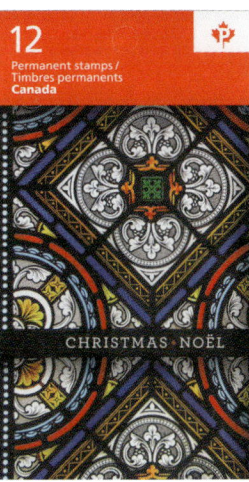

B195 Stained Glass

2011 (6 Sept). Mental Health. Multicoloured cover, 61×127 mm, as Type **B193**. Self-adhesive.
SB440   ($6.90) booklet containing pane of ten
        (59c.)+10c. (No. 2818a) .... 14·00

2011 (1 Nov). Christmas (1st issue). Multicoloured cover, 70×125 mm, as Type **B195**. Self-adhesive.
SB442   ($7.08) booklet containing pane of 12× (59c.)
        (No. 2821a) .... 14·00

B196 Holly

2011 (1 Nov). Christmas (2nd issue). Multicoloured cover, 72×80 mm, as Type **B196**. Self-adhesive.
SB443   ($7.08) booklet containing pane of 12× (59c.)
        (No. 2825a) .... 14·00

B194

B197 Dragon's Head

B198 View from CCGS *Amundsen* (icebreaker)

2011 (3 Oct). International Year of Chemistry. Multicoloured cover, 77×102 mm, as Type **B194**. Self-adhesive.
SB441   ($5.90) booklet containing pane of ten (59c.)
        (No. 2820a) .... 12·00

215

CANADA Stamp Booklets

2012 (10 Jan). Chinese New Year. Year of the Dragon. Multicoloured cover, 55×86 mm, as Type **B197**. Self-adhesive.
SB444 $10.80 booklet containing pane of six $1.80
          (No. 2829a) .... 16·00

2012 (16 Jan). Canadian Pride. Multicoloured cover, 60×135 mm, as Type **B198**. Self-adhesive.
SB445   ($18.30) booklet containing pane of 30 (61c.)
          (No. 2733b) .... 45·00

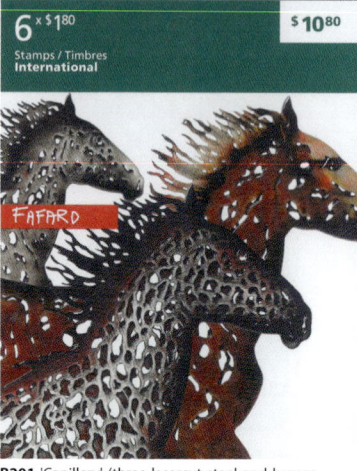

B201 'Capillery' (three lasercut steel and bronze horses)

2012 (23 Feb). Art Canada. Sculptures by Joe Fafard. Multicoloured cover, 98×122 mm, as Type **B201**. Self-adhesive.
SB449 $10.80 booklet containing pane of six $1.80
          (No. 2842a) .... 17·00

B199 Queen Elizabeth II

2012 (16 Jan). Diamond Jubilee. Multicoloured cover, 86×139 mm, as Type **B199**. Self-adhesive.
SB446   ($6.10) booklet containing pane of ten (61c.)
          (No. 2830a) .... 18·00

B200 John Ware

2012 (1 Feb). Black History Month. John Ware and Viola Desmond. Multicoloured covers, 80×147 mm, as Type **B200**. Self-adhesive.
SB447   ($6.10) booklet containing pane of ten (61c.)
          (No. 2837a) (cover Type **B200**) .... 10·00
SB448   ($6.10) booklet containing pane pane of ten (61c.) (No. 2838a) (cover showing Viola Desmond) .... 10·00

B202 Daylily 'Louis Lorrain'

2012 (1 Mar). Daylilies. Multicoloured cover, 79×120 mm, as Type **B202**.
SB450   ($6.10) booklet containing pane of ten (No. 2845a) and ten small labels .... 15·00

Stamp Booklets CANADA

B203 Bow of *Titanic* with Anchor

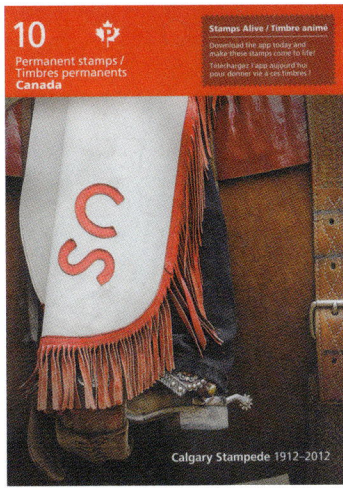

B205 Rider

2012 (5 Apr). Centenary of the Sinking of the *Titanic*. Multicoloured covers as Type **B203**. Self-adhesive.
SB451   ($6.10) booklet containing pane of ten (61c.) (No. 2853a) (cover Type **B203**, 76×148 mm) .... 19·00
SB452 $10.80 booklet containing pane of six $1.80 (No. 2855a) (cover showing *Titanic*, 96×132 mm) .... 32·00

2012 (17 May). Centenary of the Calgary Stampede. Multicoloured covers, 94×128 mm, as Type **B205**. Self-adhesive.
SB454   ($6.10) booklet pane containing ten (61c.) (No. 2864a) (cover Type **B205**) .... 13·00
SB455 $10.50 booklet pane containing ten $1.05 (No. 2865a) (cover showing Guy Weadick, founder of Calgary Stampede) .... 18·00

B204 Franklin the Turtle, Rabbit, Bear, Fox, Beaver and Goose

2012 (11 May). Children's Literature. *Franklin the Turtle*. Multicoloured cover, 83×127 mm, as Type **B204**. Self-adhesive.
SB453   ($7.32) booklet containing pane of 12 (61c.) (No. 2859a) .... 13·00

B206 Louise Arbour

2012 (22 May). Difference Makers. Covers as Type **B206**, 74×117 mm, in colours as stamps. Self-adhesive.
SB456   ($6.10) booklet containing pane of ten (61c.) (No. 2867a) .... 10·00
SB457   ($6.10) booklet containing pane of ten (61c.) (No. 2868a) .... 10·00
SB458   ($6.10) booklet containing pane of ten (61c.) (No. 2869a) .... 10·00
SB459   ($6.10) booklet containing pane of ten (61c.) (No. 2870a) .... 10·00

CANADA Stamp Booklets

B207 Rower and Maple Leaf

2012 (27 June). Olympic Games, London. Multicoloured cover, 83×125 mm, as Type **B207**. Self-adhesive.
SB460 ($6.10) booklet containing pane of ten (61c.) (No. 2874a) .... 10·00

2012 (23 July). Signs of the Zodiac. Multicoloured covers, 75×117 mm, as Type **B184**. Self-adhesive.
SB461 ($6.10) booklet containing pane of ten (61c.) (No. 2766a) (Leo) .... 13·00
SB462 ($6.10) booklet containing pane of ten (61c.) (No. 2767a) (Virgo) .... 13·00
SB463 ($6.10) booklet containing pane of ten (61c.) (No. 2768a) (Libra) .... 13·00
SB464 ($6.10) booklet containing pane of ten (61c.) (No. 2769a) (Scorpio) .... 13·00

B208 BC Lions

2012 (16 Aug). 100th Grey Cup Game. Multicoloured covers, 75×140 mm, as Type **B208**. Self-adhesive.
SB465 ($6.10) booklet containing pane of ten (61c.) (No. 2885a) (Grey Cup and two players) .... 9·00
SB466 ($6.10) booklet containing pane of ten (61c.) (No. 2886a) (Type **B207**) .... 9·00
SB467 ($6.10) booklet containing pane of ten (61c.) (No. 2887a) (Edmonton Eskimos)............. 9·00
SB468 ($6.10) booklet containing pane of ten (61c.) (No. 2888a) (Calgary Stampeders)............ 9·00
SB469 ($6.10) booklet containing ten (61c.) (No. 2889a) (Saskatchewan Roughriders) ...... 9·00
SB470 ($6.10) booklet containing ten (61c.) (No. 2890a) (Winnipeg Blue Bombers)............ 9·00
SB471 ($6.10) booklet pane containing ten (61c.) (No. 2891a) (Hamilton Tiger-Cats)............ 9·00
SB472 ($6.10) booklet pane containing ten (61c.) (No. 2892a) (Toronto Argonauts) .... 9·00
SB473 ($6.10) booklet pane containing ten (61c.) (No. 2893a) (Alouettes de Montréal)................ 9·00

B209 Heart and Circle of Children's Handprints

2012 (17 Sept). Canada Post Community Foundation. Multicoloured cover, 60×127 mm, as Type **B209**. Self-adhesive.
SB474 ($6.10) booklet containing pane of ten (61c.)+10c. (No. 2895a) .... 10·00

B210 The Black Watch (Royal Highland Regiment) of Canada

2012 (11 Oct). 150th Anniversary of the Black Watch of Canada, the Royal Hamilton Light Infantry and the Royal Regiment of Canada. Multicoloured covers, 102×141 mm, as Type **B210**. Self-adhesive.
SB475 ($6.10) booklet containing ten (61c.) stamps (No. 2896a) (Type **B210**) .... 14·00
SB476 ($6.10) booklet containing ten (61c.) stamps (No. 2897a) (Royal Hamilton Light Infantry)... 14·00
SB477 ($6.10) booklet containing ten (61c.) stamps (No. 2898a) (Royal Regiment of Canada) .... 14·00

Stamp Booklets CANADA

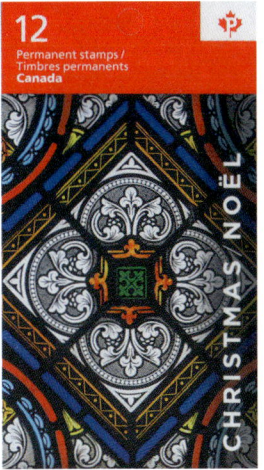

B211 Stained-Glass   B212 Gingerbread Stars

B215 Raoul Wallenberg and Schutz Pass

2012 (15 Oct). Christmas (1st issue). Multicoloured cover, 70×125 mm, as Type **B211**. Self-adhesive.
SB478   ($7.32) booklet containing pane of 12 (61c.)
         (No. 2900a)... 13·00

2012 (15 Oct). Christmas (2nd issue). Gingerbread Cookies. Multicoloured covers, 54×85 mm, as Type **B212**. Self-adhesive.
SB479 $6.30 booklet containing pane of six $1.05
         (No. 2902a) (Type **B212**) .... 13·00
SB480   ($7.32) booklet containing pane of 12 (61c.)
         (No. 2901a) (Gingerbread people).......... 16·00
SB481 $10.80 booklet containing pane of six $1.80
         (No. 2903a) (Gingerbread snowflake).... 16·00

2012 (28 Nov). Victory of Toronto Argonauts in 100th Grey Cup Game. Multicoloured cover, 75×140 mm, as No. SB465 but optd with Toronto Argonauts A emblem as Type **997a**. Self-adhesive.
SB481*a*   ($6.10) booklet containing pane of ten (61c.)
         (No. 2905ab) .... 10·00

2013 (17 Jan). Raoul Wallenberg (Second World War rescuer of Jews) Commemoration. Multicoloured cover, 64×142 mm, as Type **B215**. Self-adhesive.
SB484 $11.10 booklet containing pane of six $1.85
         (No. 2910a)... 16·00

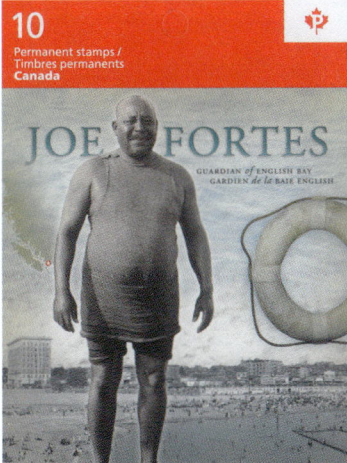

B213 Jade Snake   B214 Muskoka Chairs with Maple Leaf Design on Lakeside Jetty

B216 Joe Fortes

2013 (8 Jan). Chinese New Year. Year of the Snake. Multicoloured cover, 55×85 mm, as Type **B213**. Self-adhesive.
SB482 $11.10 booklet pane of six $1.85 (No. 2909a)... 16·00

2013 (14 Jan). Canadian Pride. Multicoloured cover, 60×134 mm, as Type **B214**. Self-adhesive.
SB483   ($18.90) booklet containing pane of 30 (63c.)
         (No. 2738b).. 45·00

2013 (1 Feb). Black History Month. Joe Fortes. Multicoloured cover, 96×125 mm, as Type **B216**. Self-adhesive.
SB485   ($6.30) booklet containing pane of ten (63c.)
         stamps (No. 2911a) .... 10·00

CANADA Stamp Booklets

B217 Oliver Jones

2013 (1 Feb). Black History Month. Oliver Jones. Multicoloured cover, 71×150 mm, as Type **B217**.
SB486 ($6.30) booklet containing pane of ten (63c.)
(No. 2912a) .... 10·00

2013 (20 Feb). Signs of the Zodiac. Multicoloured covers, 74×117 mm, as Type **B184**. Self-adhesive.
SB487 ($6.30) booklet containing pane of ten (63c.)
(No. 2770a) (Sagittarius) .... 13·00
SB488 ($6.30) booklet containing pane of ten (63c.)
(No. 2771a) (Capricorn) .... 13·00
SB489 ($6.30) booklet containing pane of ten (63c.)
(No. 2772a) (Aquarius) .... 13·00
SB490 ($6.30) booklet containing pane of ten (63c.)
(No. 2773a) (Pisces) .... 13·00

B218 Magnolia 'Eskimo'

2013 (4 Mar). Magnolias. Multicoloured cover, 81×120 mm, as Type **B218**. Self-adhesive.
SB491 ($6.30) booklet pane containing ten (63c.) and ten small stickers (No. 2915a) .... 13·00

B219 Louis-Joseph Papineau, 'The Kitchen Sink' and 'Hot Properties #1'

2013 (22 Mar). 150 Years of Photography. Multicoloured covers as Type **B219**. Self-adhesive.
SB492 ($6.30) booklet containing pane of ten (63c.) (No. 2918a) (Type **B219**, 86×108 mm).. 11·00
SB493 $6.60 booklet containing pane of six $1.10 (No. 2923a) (Basement Camera Shop cover, 55×86 mm).. 10·00
SB494 $11.10 booklet containing pane of six $1.85 (No. 2924a) (Yousuf Karsh cover, 55×86 mm) .... 15·00

B220 Early and Modern Soldiers

2013 (9 Apr). 150th Anniversary of the Princess of Wales' Own Regiment. Multicoloured cover, 102×142 mm, as Type **B220**. Self-adhesive.
SB495 ($6.30) booklet containing pane of ten (63c.) (No. 2927a) .... 13·00

B221 'Coleman'

2013 (22 Apr). 'Adopt a Pet'. Animals from Toronto Humane Society Shelter and Toronto Parrot Sanctuary. Multicoloured cover, 152×101 mm, as Type **B221**. Self-adhesive.
SB496   ($6.30) booklet containing pane of ten (63c.)
           (No. 2928a).. 17·00

B224 Profiles of Girl and Woman Mentor

2013 (14 May). Centenary of Big Brothers Big Sisters of Canada. Multicoloured cover, 59×120 mm, as Type **B224**. Self-adhesive.
SB499   ($6.30) booklet containing pane of ten (63c.)
           (No. 2944a).. 10·00

B222 Temporary Chinatown Gate, built 1882, Victoria

2013 (1 May). Chinatown Gates. Multicoloured cover, 72×85 mm, as Type **B222**. Self-adhesive.
SB497   ($5.04) booklet containing pane of eight
           (63c.) (No. 2934a).. 10·00

B225 Indian Motorcycle, 1914

2013 (5 June). Motorcycles. Multicoloured cover, 80×127 mm, as Type **B225**. Self-adhesive.
SB500   ($6.30) booklet containing pane of ten (63c.)
           (No. 2945a).. 13·00

B223 Diamond Jubilee Portrait by Philip James Richards showing Portrait of Queen Victoria behind Queen Elizabeth II

2013 (8 May). 60th Anniversary of the Coronation. Multicoloured cover, 86×140 mm, as Type **B223**. Self-adhesive.
SB498   ($6.30) booklet containing pane of ten (63c.)
           (No. 2943a).. 13·00

B226 Sailing Ship

CANADA Stamp Booklets

2013 (10 June). 250 Years of Postal History. Multicoloured cover, 80×101 mm, as Type **B226**. Self-adhesive.
SB501 ($6.30) booklet containing pane of ten (63c.)
(No. 2948a) .... 14·00

B229 Robertson Davies

2013 (28 Aug). Birth Centenary of Robertson Davies (writer). Multicoloured cover, 66×106 mm, as Type **B229**. Self-adhesive.
SB507 $6.30 booklet containing pane of ten 63c.
(No. 2959a) .... 10·00

B227 Stella, Sam and Fred the Dog

2013 (5 July). Children's Literature. Stella. Multicoloured cover, 80×127 mm, as Type **B227**. Self-adhesive.
SB502 ($6.30) booklet containing pane of ten (63c.)
(No. 2951a) .... 10·00

B228 The Tragically Hip

2013 (19 July). Canadian Recording Artists (4th series). Vermilion and black (SB506) or multicoloured covers (others), as Type **B228**. Self-adhesive.
SB503 ($6.30) booklet containing pane of ten (63c.)
(No. 2954a) (88×119 mm>, Type **B228**) 10·00
SB504 ($6.30) booklet containing pane of ten (63c.)
(No. 2955a) (80×119 mm, Rush) .... 10·00
SB505 ($6.30) booklet containing pane of ten
(63c.) (No. 2956a) (88×119 mm, Beau Dommage) .... 10·00
SB506 ($6.30) booklet containing pane of ten (63c.)
(No. 2957a) (80×119 mm, The Guess Who) .... 10·00

B230 Vancouver Canucks

2013 (3 Sept). NHL (National Hockey League) Team Jerseys. Multicoloured covers, 90×120 mm, as Type **B230**. Self-adhesive.
SB508 $6.30 booklet containing pane of ten 63c.
(No. 2968a) (Type **B230**) .... 10·00
SB509 $6.30 booklet containing pane of ten 63c.
(No. 2969a) (Montreal Canadiens) .... 10·00
SB510 $6.30 booklet containing pane of ten 63c.
(No. 2970a) (Edmonton Oilers) .... 10·00
SB511 $6.30 booklet containing pane of ten 63c.
(No. 2971a) (Ottawa Senators) .... 10·00
SB512 $6.30 booklet containing pane of ten 63c.
(No. 2972a) (Calgary Flames) .... 10·00
SB513 $6.30 booklet containing pane of ten 63c.
(No. 2973a) (Winnipeg Jets) .... 10·00
SB514 $6.30 booklet containing pane of ten 63c.
(No. 2974a) (Toronto Maple Leafs) .... 10·00

Stamp Booklets CANADA

B231 Cover of Superman Comic

B233 Officers and Soldiers

2013 (10 Sept). 75th Anniversary of Superman. Multicoloured covers, 74×140 mm, as Type **B231**. Self-adhesive.
SB515 ($6.30) booklet containing pane of ten (63c.)
(No. 2977a) (Type **B231**) .... 14·00
   a. Cover showing Superman stopping train .... 14·00
   b. Cover showing the Man of Steel showing 'S' logo .... 14·00
   c. Cover showing Superman (city buildings in background) .... 14·00
   d. Cover showing Superman ('The Man of Steel faces Alien Extinction!') .... 14·00

2013 (18 Oct). 150th Anniversary of the Hastings and Prince Edward Regiment. Multicoloured cover, 102×141 mm, as Type **B233**. Self-adhesive.
SB517 ($6.30) booklet containing pane of ten (63c.)
(No. 2984a) .... 14·00

B232 Floating Adrift (plasticine on board, Ezra Pound)

B234 Duke and Duchess of Cambridge with Prince George

2013 (30 Sept). Canada Post Community Foundation. Winning Entry in Children's Art Competition. Multicoloured cover, 60×126 mm, as Type **B232**. Self-adhesive.
SB516 $7.30 booklet containing pane of ten 63c.+10c. (No. 2983a) .... 13·00

2013 (22 Oct). Birth of Prince George of Cambridge. Multicoloured cover, 76×118 mm, as Type **B234**. Self-adhesive.
SB518 ($6.30) booklet containing pane of ten (63c.)
(No. 2985a) .... 14·00

CANADA Stamp Booklets

B235 *Saint Anne with the Christ Child* (Georges de La Tour)

2013 (22 Oct). Christmas (1st issue). Multicoloured cover, 65×119 mm, as Type **B235**. Self-adhesive.
SB519 $7.56 booklet containing pane of 12 63c.
        (No. 2987a) .... 16·00

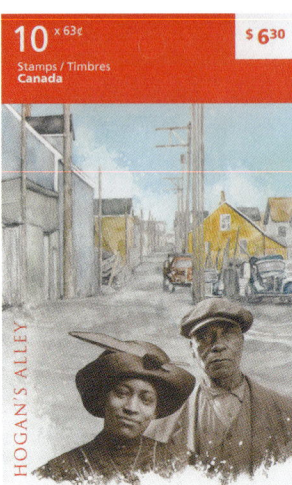

B238 *Nora Hendrix, Fielding William Spotts Jr and Hogan's Alley, Vancouver*

2014 (30 Jan). Black History Month. Africville and Hogan's Alley. Multicoloured covers, 81×129 mm, as Type **B238**. Self-adhesive.
SB524 $6.30 booklet containing pane of ten 63c.
        (No. 2996a) (Africville) .... 10·00
SB525 $6.30 booklet containing pane of ten 63c.
        (No. 2997a) (Type **B238**) .... 10·00

B236 *Flying Reindeer*

2013 (22 Oct). Christmas (2nd issue). Embroidery. Multicoloured covers, 85×55 mm, as Type **B236**. Self-adhesive.
SB520 $6.60 booklet containing pane of six $1.10
        (No. 2989a) (cover Type **B236**) .... 13·00
SB521 $7.56 booklet containing pane of 12 63c.
        (No. 2988a) (cover showing French
        horn) .... 16·00
SB522 $11.10 booklet containing pane of six $1.85
        (No. 2990a) (cover showing Christmas
        tree) .... 16·00

B237 *Horses*

2014 (13 Jan). Chinese New Year. Year of the Horse. Vermilion, bright scarlet and carmine-vermilion cover, 55×85 mm, as Type **B237**. Self-adhesive.
SB523 $11.10 booklet pane of six $1.85 (No. 2995a) ... 16·00

B239 *Barbara Ann Scott*

2014 (3 Feb). Pioneers of Winter Sports. Multicoloured covers, 64×19 mm, as Type **B239**. Self-adhesive.
SB526 $6.30 booklet containing pane of ten 63c.
        (No. 2998a) (Type **B239**) .... 10·00
SB527 $6.30 booklet containing pane of ten 63c.
        (No. 2999a) (Sandra Schmirler) .... 10·00
SB528 $6.30 booklet containing pane of ten 63c.
        (No. 3000a) (Sarah Burke) .... 10·00

Stamp Booklets CANADA

B240 Climber in Banff National Park

2014 (31 Mar). UNESCO World Heritage Sites. Multicoloured cover, 60×134 mm, as Type **B240**. Self-adhesive.
SB529   ($25.50) booklet containing pane of 30 (85c.) stamps (No. 3002b) .... 38·00

B242 Roses

2014 (23 Apr). Roses. Multicoloured cover, 80×120 mm, as Type **B242**. Self-adhesive.
SB531   ($8.50) booklet containing pane of ten (No. 3025a) and ten small labels .... 13·00

B243 Passengers and Steamship Komagata Maru

2014 (1 May). Centenary of the *Komagata Maru* Incident. Multicoloured cover, 54×85 mm, as Type **B243**. Self-adhesive.
SB532 $15 booklet containing pane of six $2.50 (No. 3028a) .... 23·00

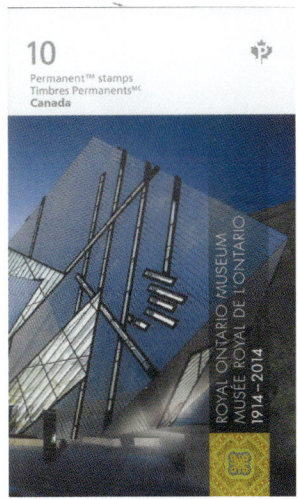

B241 Royal Ontario Museum

2014 (14 Apr). Centenary of the Royal Ontario Museum, Toronto. Multicoloured cover, 86×142 mm, as Type **B241**. Self-adhesive.
SB530   ($8.50) booklet containing pane of ten (85c.) (No. 3020a) .... 13·00

B244 Film Board Emblem

CANADA Stamp Booklets

2014 (2 May). 75th Anniversary of NFB (National Film Board of Canada). Black and pale grey cover, 75×131 mm, as Type **B244**. Self-adhesive.
SB533   ($8.50) booklet containing pane of ten (85c.) stamps (No. 3029a) ....   13·00

B245 Old Town, Lunenburg, Nova Scotia

2014 (16 May). UNESCO World Heritage Sites. Multicoloured covers, 86×55 mm, as Type **B245**. Self-adhesive.
SB534 $7.20 booklet containing pane of six $1.20 stamps (No. 3035a) (Type **B245**)............   11·00
SB535 $15 booklet containing pane of six $2.50 stamps (No. 3038a) (Haida memorial poles, Sgang Gwaay, British Columbia)   22·00

B246 Empress of Ireland

2014 (29 May). Centenary of the Sinking of the Liner *Empress of Ireland*. Multicoloured cover, 80×120 mm, as Type **B246**. Self-adhesive.
SB536   ($8.50) booklet containing pane of ten (85c.) (No. 3041a)..................   15·00

B247 Spectre at Curtained Window

2014 (13 June). Haunted Canada (1st series). Black, grey and grey-brown cover, 74×116 mm, as Type **B247**. Self-adhesive.
SB537   ($8.50) booklet containing pane of ten (85c.) (No. 3044a)..................   13·00

B248 Roughriders Quarterback Russ Jackson and New Redblacks Stadium

2014 (29 June). 'Ottawa Redblacks the CFL returns to Ottawa'. New Canadian Football League Team. Multicoloured cover, 74×140 mm, as Type **B248**. Self-adhesive.
SB538   ($8.50) booklet containing pane of ten (85c.) (No. 3051a)..................   11·00

2014 (7 July). 150 Years of Photography (2nd issue). Multicoloured covers as T **B219**. Self-adhesive.
SB539 $7.20 booklet containing pane of six $1.20 (No. 3057a) (Sitting Bull and Buffalo Bill cover, 54×85 mm)..................   11·00
SB540   ($8.50) booklet containing pane of ten (85c.) stamps (No. 3052a) (St Joseph's Convent School, Untitled and Bogner's Grocery cover, 86×108 mm) ....   12·00
SB541 $15 booklet containing pane of six $2.50 (No. 3058a) (Railcuts: #1 cover, 54×85 mm) ....   20·00

B249 Hank Snow

2014 (31 July). Canadian Country Artists. Multicoloured covers, 94×129 mm, as Type **B249**. Self-adhesive.
SB541*a*   ($8.50) booklet containing pane of ten (85c.) stamps (No. 3061a) (Type **B249**)...........   11·00
SB541*b*   ($8.50) booklet containing pane of ten (85c.) stamps (No. 3062a) (Renée Martel)..   11·00
SB542   ($8.50) booklet containing pane of ten (85c.) stamps (No. 3063a) (Shania Twain) ......   11·00
SB543   ($8.50) booklet containing pane of ten (85c.) stamps (No. 3064a) (Tommy Hunter) ..   11·00

SB544 ($8.50) booklet containing pane of ten (85c.) stamps (No. 3065a) (k.d. lang)................ 11·00

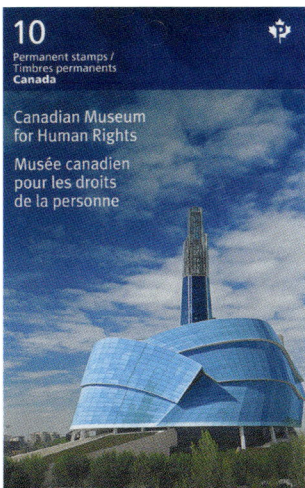

B250 Canadian Museum for Human Rights, Winnipeg

2014 (30 Aug). Canadian Museum for Human Rights, Winnipeg. Multicoloured cover, 90×140 mm, as Type **B250**. Self-adhesive.
SB545 ($8.50) booklet containing pane of ten (85c.) stamps (No. 3067a) .... 11·00

B251 Mike Myers

2014 (29 Aug). Great Canadian Comedians. Multicoloured covers, 64×125 mm, as Type **B251**. Self-adhesive.
SB546 ($8.50) booklet containing pane of ten (85c.) (No. 3068a) (Type **B251**) .... 11·00
SB547 ($8.50) booklet containing pane of ten (85c.) (No. 3068b) (Martin Short) .... 11·00
SB548 ($8.50) booklet containing pane of ten (85c.) (No. 3068c) (Olivier Guimond) .... 11·00
SB549 ($8.50) booklet containing pane of ten (85c.) (No. 3068d) (Jim Carrey) .... 11·00
SB550 ($8.50) booklet containing pane of ten (85c.) (No. 3068e) (Catherine O'Hara) .... 11·00

B252 Children in Origami Boat

2014 (29 Sept). Canada Post Community Foundation. Multicoloured cover, 75×120 mm, as Type **B252**. Self-adhesive.
SB551 ($8.50) booklet containing pane of ten 85c.+10c. (No. 3074a)................................ 11·00

B253 Team Logos

2014 (3 Oct). Original Six Canadian Ice Hockey Defencemen. Multicoloured cover, 90×64 mm, as Type **B253**. Self-adhesive.
SB552 ($5.10) booklet containing pane of six (85c.) (No. 3075a) .... 6·50

B254 Wait for Me Daddy (photo by Claude P. Dettloff), 1 October 1940

2014 (4 Oct). Wait for Me Daddy. Multicoloured cover, 73×140 mm, as Type **B254**. Self-adhesive.
SB553 ($8.50) booklet containing pane of ten (85c.) stamps (No. 3091a) .... 13·00

CANADA Stamp Booklets

B255 The Virgin and Child with St John the Baptist (Abraham Janssens van Nuyssen)

2014 (23 Oct). Christmas (1st issue). 350th Anniversary of the Parish of Notre-Dame de Quebec. Multicoloured cover as Type **B255**. Self-adhesive.

SB554 ($10.20) booklet containing pane of twelve (85c.) stamps (No. 3093a).................... 15·00

B258 Sir John A. Macdonald

2015 (11 Jan). Birth Bicentenary of Sir John A. Macdonald (1815–1891), Canada's first Prime Minister 1867–1873, 1878–1891). Multicoloured cover, 79×142 mm, as Type **B258**. Self-adhesive.

SB559 ($8.50) booklet containing pane of ten (85c.) stamps (No. 3102a)......................... 13·00

B256 Santa

2014 (23 Oct). Christmas (2nd issue). Santa. Multicoloured covers, 85×55 mm, as Type **B256**. Self-adhesive.

SB555 $7.20 booklet containing pane of six $1.20 (No. 3095a) (cover Type **B256**)................ 11·00
SB556 ($10.20) booklet containing pane of twelve (85c.) stamps (No. 3094a) (Santa holding quill pen)......................... 15·00
SB557 $15 booklet containing pane of six $2.50 (No. 3096a) (Santa wearing bishop's mitre).................... 22·00

B259 Nelson Mandela in Canada, 1990

B257 Ram

2015 (8 Jan). Chinese New Year. Year of the Ram. Emerald, black and gold cover, 55×85 mm, as Type **B257**. Self-adhesive.

SB558 $15 booklet pane of six $2.50 (No. 3101a)... 22·00

2015 (30 Jan). Black History Month. Nelson Mandela (1918–2013, President of South Africa 1994–1999) Commemoration. Black and grey cover, 80×125 mm, as Type **B259**. Self-adhesive.

SB560 ($8.50) booklet containing pane of ten (85c.) stamps (No. 3103a)......................... 13·00

Stamp Booklets CANADA

B260 Canadian Flag and Clock Tower of Canadian Parliament Building, Ottawa

2015 (15 Feb). 50th Anniversary of Canada's Flag. Multicoloured cover, 90×131 mm, as Type **B260**. Self-adhesive.
SB561   ($8.50) booklet containing pane of ten (85c.)
            stamps (No. 3105a) ....   13·00

B262 Dinosaur's Eye

2015 (13 Apr). Dinosaurs of Canada. Multicoloured cover, 80×110 mm, as Type **B262**. Self-adhesive.
SB566   ($8.50) booklet containing pane of ten (85c.)
            (No. 3121a) ....   13·00

B263 Cat on Leash

2015 (2 May). Responsible Pet Guardianship. Multicoloured cover, 148×105 mm, as Type **B263**. Self-adhesive.
SB567   ($8.50) booklet containing pane of ten (85c.)
            (No. 3127a) ....   13·00

B261 Pansy 'Midnight Glow'

2015 (2 Mar). Pansies. Multicoloured cover, 80×120 mm, as Type **B261**. Self-adhesive.
SB562   ($8.50) booklet pane containing ten (85c.) and
            ten small stickers (No. 3109a)..................   13·00

2015 (8 Apr). 150 years of Photography (3rd issue). Multicoloured covers as Type **B219**. Self-adhesive.
SB563 $7.20 booklet containing pane of six $1.20
            (No. 3117a) (Alex Colville on the
            Tantramar Marshes cover, 85×55 mm) .   11·00
SB564   ($8.50) booklet containing pane of ten (85c.)
            stamps (No. 3112a) (Angels, Saint John
            Baptiste Day, Isaac's First Swim and
            Southam Sisters cover, 86×108 mm).....   12·00
SB565 $15 booklet containing pane of six $2.50
            (No. 3118a) (La Voie Lactée cover,
            85×55 mm)...   18·00

B264 Soldier's Silhouette and Crosses in Poppy

2015 (3 May). Centenary of Poem In Flanders Fields by John McCrae. Multicoloured cover, 94×120 mm, as Type **B264**. Self-adhesive.
SB568   ($7) booklet containing pane of ten (85c.)
            (No. 3133a) ....   13·00

CANADA Stamp Booklets

B265 Christine Sinclair, Canada

2015 (6 May). FIFA Women's World Cup, Canada. Multicoloured cover, 93×128 mm, as Type **B265**. Self-adhesive.
SB569 ($8.50) booklet containing pane of ten (85c.)
        (No. 3135a).. 13·00

B266 Lightning

2015 (18 June). Weather Wonders. Multicoloured cover, 64×125 mm, as Type **B266**. Self-adhesive.
SB570 ($8.50) booklet containing pane of ten (85c.)
        stamps (No. 3136a)....................... 13·00

B267 Dinosaur Provincial Park, Alberta

2015 (3 July). UNESCO World Heritage Sites. Multicoloured covers, 85×54 mm, as Type **B267**. Self-adhesive.
SB571 $7.20 booklet containing pane of six $1.20 stamps (No. 3142a) (cover showing Hoodoos near Drumheller, Alberta) ...... 38·00
SB572 $7.20 booklet containing pane of six $1.20 (No. 3143a) (cover Type **B267**) (21.8)..... 11·00
SB573 $15 booklet containing pane of six $2.50 stamps (No. 3146a) (cover showing Waterton-Glacier International Peace Park)... 22·00

B268 Alice Munro and Town of Wingham, Ontario (birthplace)

2015 (10 July). Alice Munro (writer). Multicoloured cover, 68×118 mm, as Type **B268**. Self-adhesive.
SB574 ($8.50) booklet containing pane of ten (85c.) stamps (No. 3150a) .... 13·00

B269 HMS *Erebus* trapped in Ice

2015 (6 Aug). 150th Anniversary of the Franklin Expedition. Multicoloured covers as Type **B269**. Self-adhesive.
SB575 ($8.50) booklet containing pane of ten (85c.) (No. 3154a) (Type **B269**) .... 17·00
SB576 $15 booklet containing pane of six $2.50 (No. 3156a) (cover 60×120 mm showing Parks Canada vessel *Investigator* and wreck of HMS *Erebus* discovered on the seabed, 2014)............ 26·00

Stamp Booklets CANADA

B270 Queen Elizabeth II in 1953 and 2010

2015 (9 Sept). Queen Elizabeth II - A Historic Reign. Multicoloured cover, 94×86 mm, as Type **B270**. Self-adhesive.
SB577   ($8.50) booklet containing pane of ten (85c.) stamps (No. 3157a) .... 15·00

2015 (14 Sept). Haunted Canada (2nd series). Multicoloured cover, 75×115 mm, as Type **B247**, showing Raven and Moon. Self-adhesive.
SB578   ($8.50) booklet containing pane of ten (85c.) (No. 3158a) .... 13·00

B271 Girl reading to Young Boy

2015 (28 Sept). Canada Post Community Foundation. Multicoloured cover, 60×126 mm, as Type **B271**. Self-adhesive.
SB579   ($9.50) booklet containing pane of ten (85c.)+10c. stamps (No. 3164a) .... 13·00

B272 Ice Hockey Goalie

2015 (2 Oct). Great Canadian NHL Goalies. Multicoloured cover, 90×64 mm, as Type **B272**. Self-adhesive.
SB580   ($5.10) booklet containing pane of six (85c.) (No. 3165a) .... 7·50

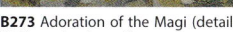

B273 Adoration of the Magi (detail) (Adriaen Isenbrandt)   **B274** Moose wearing Hat and Scarf

2015 (2 Nov). Christmas (1st issue). Multicoloured cover, 65×119 mm, as Type **B273**. Self-adhesive.
SB581   ($10.20) booklet containing pane of twelve (85c.) stamps (No. 3173a)......................... 15·00

2015 (2 Nov). Christmas (2nd issue). Animals. Multicoloured covers, 54×85 mm, as Type **B274**. Self-adhesive.
SB582   ($10.20) booklet containing pane of twelve (85c.) stamps (No. 3174a)......................... 15·00

B275 Rideau Canal Locks

2016 (11 Jan). UNESCO World Heritage Sites. Multicoloured cover, 60×134 mm, as Type **B275**. Self-adhesive.
SB583   ($25.50) booklet containing pane of 30 (85c.) stamps (No. 3007b) .... 38·00

231

CANADA Stamp Booklets

B276 Sun Wukong the Monkey King from novel *Journey to the West*

2016 (11 Jan). Chinese New Year. Year of the Monkey. Multicoloured covers as Type **B276**. Self-adhesive.

SB584	($8.50) booklet containing pane of ten (85c.) stamps (No. 3181a) (Type **B276**, 90×130 mm)	13·00
SB585	$15 booklet containing pane of six $2.50 stamps (No. 3182a) (cover 54×85 mm showing Monkey King mask) (1 Feb)	22·00

B278 *Hydrangea macrophylla* 'Endless Summer' and *Hydrangea arborescens* 'Annabelle'

2016 (1 Mar). Hydrangeas. Multicoloured cover, 80×120 mm, as Type **B278**. Self-adhesive.

SB587	($8.50) booklet pane containing ten (85c.) and ten small stickers (No. 3186a)	13·00

B277 Members and Badge of No. 2 Construction Battalion

2016 (1 Feb). Black History Month. Centenary of No. 2 Construction Battalion. Multicoloured cover, 80×126 mm, as Type **B277**. Self-adhesive.

SB586	($8.50) booklet containing pane of ten (85c.) stamps (No. 3183a)	13·00

B279 Emblem with Venus Symbol as 'O' and 'T' of 'VOTE'

2016 (8 Mar). Centenary of Women's Suffrage in Canada. Black, gold and grey cover, 80×95 mm, as Type **B279**. Self-adhesive.

SB588	($8.50) booklet containing pane of ten (85c.) (No. 3189a)	13·00

2016 (13 Apr). 150 Years of Photography (4th issue). Multicoloured covers as Type **B219**. Self-adhesive.

SB589	$7.20 booklet containing pane of six $1.20 (No. 3195a) (Climbing Mt. Habel cover, 85×55 mm)	11·00
SB590	($8.50) booklet containing pane of ten (85c.) stamps (No. 3190a) (La chambre noir, Victoria Bridge and Window cover, 86×108 mm)	13·00
SB591	$15 booklet containing pane of six $2.50 (No. 3196a) (Grey Owl (Archibald Belaney 1888–1938) cover, 55×85 mm)	18·00

Stamp Booklets CANADA

B280 Captain Kirk, Mr Spock, Scott, McCoy, Commander Kor and USS *Enterprise*

B284 Bird with Multicoloured Wings

2016 (5 May). 50th Anniversary of *Star Trek* (original TV series). Multicoloured cover, 65×140 mm, as Type **B280**. Self-adhesive.
SB592 $8.50 booklet containing pane of ten (85c.)
(No. 3202a).. 16·00

2016 (26 May). Dinosaurs of Canada (2nd series). Multicoloured cover, 90×105 mm, as T **B281**. Self-adhesive.
SB593 ($8.50) booklet containing pane of ten (85c.)
(No. 3209a).. 13·00

2016 (12 July). Birds of Canada (1st issue). Self-adhesive. Multicoloured cover, 60×97 mm, as Type **B282**.
SB594 ($8.50) booklet containing pane of ten (85c.)
(No. 3215a).. 16·00

2016 (8 Sept). Haunted Canada (3rd series). Self-adhesive. Black and grey cover, 75×115 mm, as Type **B247**, showing Skull.
SB595 ($8.50) booklet containing pane of ten (85c.)
(No. 3221a).. 10·00

2016 (26 Sept). Canada Post Community Foundation. Self-adhesive. Multicoloured cover, 74×116 mm, as Type **B284**.
SB597 ($9.50) booklet containing pane of ten
(85c.)+10c. stamps (No. 3235a)................ 11·00

B285 Virgin and Child

B286 Santa and Tree

B283 Guy Lafleur

2016 (23 Sept). Great Canadian NHL Forwards. Self-adhesive. Multicoloured cover, 90×64 mm, as Type **B283**.
SB596 ($5.10) booklet containing pane of six (85c.)
(No. 3227a).. 6·50

2016 (1 Nov). Christmas (1st issue). Self-adhesive. Multicoloured cover, 65×119 mm, as Type **B285**.
SB598 ($10.20) booklet containing pane of twelve
(85c.) stamps (No. 3237a).......................... 15·00

2016 (1 Nov). Christmas (2nd issue). Self-adhesive. Multicoloured cover, 54×92 mm, as Type **B286**.
SB599 ($10.20) booklet containing pane of twelve
(85c.) stamps (No. 3238a).......................... 15·00

CANADA Stamp Booklets

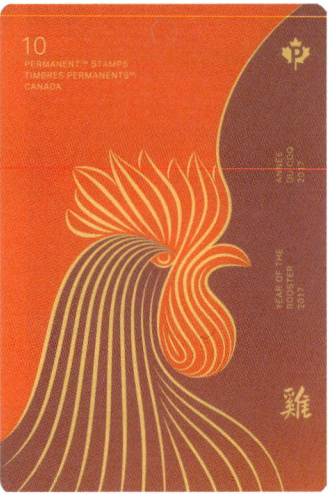

B287 Rooster

2017 (9 Jan). Chinese New Year. Year of the Rooster. Self-adhesive. Multicoloured covers as Type **B287**.
SB600 ($8.50) booklet containing pane of ten (85c.) stamps (No. 3245a) (Type **B 287**, 90×130 mm) .... 12·00
SB601 $15 booklet containing pane of six $2.50 stamps (No. 3246a) (cover 54×85 mm showing head of Rooster) .... 17·00

B289 Mathieu da Costa

2017 (1 Feb). Black History Month. Mathieu da Costa (17th-century interpreter). Self-adhesive. Multicoloured cover, 81×110 mm, as Type **B289**.
SB603 ($8.50) booklet containing pane of ten (85c.) stamps (No. 3247a) .... 12·00

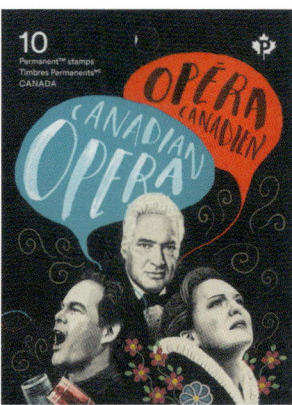

B290 Gerald Finley, Irving Guttman and Adrianne Pieczonka

2017 (4 Feb). Canadian Opera. Self-adhesive. Multicoloured cover, 80×105 mm, as Type **B290**.
SB604 ($8.50) booklet containing pane of ten (85c.) stamps (No. 3248a) .... 16·00

B288 Mistaken Point

2017 (16 Jan). UNESCO World Heritage Sites. Self-adhesive. Multicoloured cover, 60×134 mm, as Type **B288**.
SB602 ($25.50) booklet containing pane of 30 (85c.) stamps (No. 3012b) .... 38·00

B291 Mauve Daisies

234

Stamp Booklets CANADA

2017 (1 Mar). Daisies. Self-adhesive. Multicoloured cover, 80×120 mm, as Type **B291**.
SB605 ($8.50) booklet containing pane of ten (85c.) (No. 3256a) and ten small circular stickers.. 11·00

B292 Statue and Twin Pillars of Canadian Vimy Memorial

2017 (8 Apr). Centenary of Battle of Vimy Ridge. Self-adhesive. Multicoloured cover, 78×91 mm, as Type **B292**.
SB606 ($8.50) booklet containing pane of ten (85c.) stamps (No. 3259a) .... 15·00

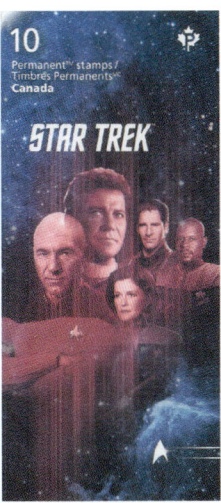

B293 Captains Picard, Kirk, Archer, Sisko and Janeway

2017 (27 Apr). Star Trek. Self-adhesive. Multicoloured cover, 65×141 mm, as Type **B293**.
SB607 ($8.50) booklet containing pane of ten (85c.) (No. 3263a) .... 16·00

B294 Captains Janeway, Picard, Kirk, Sisko and Archer

2017 (27 Apr). Star Trek. Stitched. Multicoloured cover, 172×97 mm, as Type **B294**. Booklet contains text and illustrations on panes and interleaving pages.
SB608 $21.95 booklet containing panes Nos. 3262a, 3268a/b, 3269a and 3274a........................ 30·00
Face value: $22.25

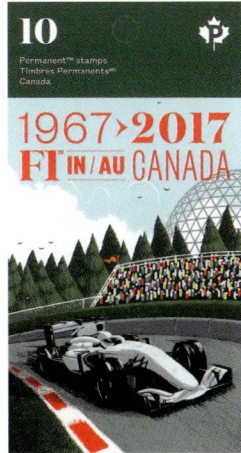

B295 Racing Car

2017 (16 May). 50th Anniversary of Formula 1 Motor Racing in Canada. Self-adhesive. Multicoloured cover, 64×120 mm, as T **B295**.
SB609 ($8.50) booklet containing pane of ten (85c.) (No. 3275a).. 11·00

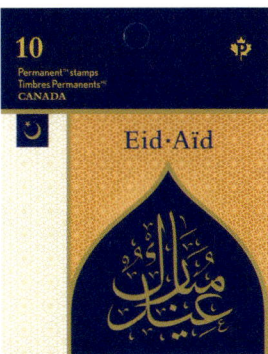

B296 Pointed Arch

2017 (24 May). Eid. Self-adhesive. Multicoloured cover, 74×94 mm, as Type **B296**.
SB610 ($8.50) booklet containing pane of ten (85c.) (No. 3281a).. 11·00

B297 Igloo and Aurora Borealis

CANADA Stamp Booklets

2017 (1 June). 150th Anniversary of the Confederation of Canada. Self-adhesive. Multicoloured covers, 96×99 mm, as T **B297**.
SB611 ($6.80) booklet containing pane of eight (85c.) (No. 3284a) (Type **B297**)............... 12·00
SB612 ($6.80) booklet containing pane of eight (85c.) (No. 3285a) (cover showing flag) 12·00
SB613 ($8.50) booklet containing pane of ten (85c.) (No. 3282a) (cover showing montage of images from stamps)................ 18·00

2017 (4 July). 150 Years of Photography (5th issue). Self-adhesive. Multicoloured covers as Type **B219**.
SB614 ($8.50) booklet containing pane of ten (85c.) (No. 3293a)..................... 10·00

2017 (1 Aug). Birds of Canada (2nd issue). Self-adhesive. Multicoloured cover as Type **B282**.
SB615 ($8.50) booklet containing pane of ten (85c.) (No. 3300a) (cover showing Osprey and Common loon)..................... 16·00

Diwali

B300 Players' Numbers 4, 9, 66 and 99

2017 (28 Sept). Canadian Hockey Legends. Self-adhesive. Multicoloured cover, 90×64 mm, as Type **B300**.
SB618 ($5.10) booklet containing pane of six (85c.) (No. 3311a)................... 6·50

B298 Diwali

2017 (21 Sept). Diwali. Self-adhesive. Multicoloured cover, 74×94 mm, as Type **B298**.
SB616 ($8.50) booklet containing pane of ten (85c.) (No. 3306a)............................... 11·00

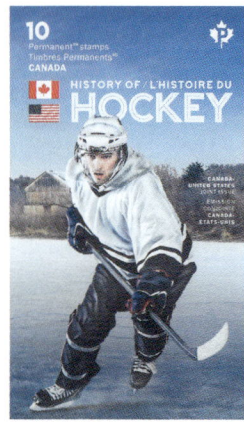

B301 Modern Pond Hockey Player

2017 (20 Oct). History of Hockey. Self-adhesive. Multicoloured cover, 66×110 mm, as Type **B301**.
SB619 ($8.50) booklet pane containing ten (85c.) (No. 3319a)......................... 11·00

B299 Cats

2017 (25 Sept). Canada Post Community Foundation. Self-adhesive. Multicoloured cover, 75×120 mm, as Type **B299**.
SB617 ($9.50) booklet containing pane of ten (85c.)+10c. stamps (No. 3309a)................ 14·00

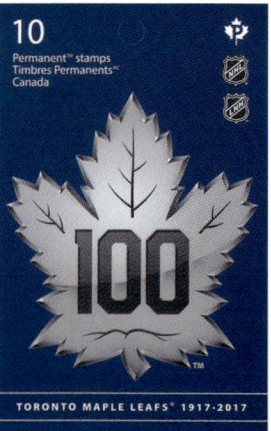

B302 Toronto Maple Leafs Centenary Logo and '100'

2017 (24 Oct). Centenary of the Toronto Maple Leafs (ice hockey team). Self-adhesive. Multicoloured cover as Type **B302**.
SB620 ($8.50) booklet containing pane of ten (85c.) stamps (No. 3323a) .... 11·00

Stamp Booklets CANADA

B303 *The Adoration of the Shepherds* (oil on panel) (attr. Tommaso di Stefano Lunetti)

2017 (3 Nov). Christmas (1st issue). Self-adhesive. Multicoloured cover as Type **B303**.
SB621 ($10.20) booklet containing pane of 12 (85c.) stamps (No. 3325a) .... 12·00

B304 Polar Bear

2017 (3 Nov). Christmas (2nd issue). Self-adhesive. Multicoloured cover, 54×92 mm, as Type **B304**.
SB622 $10.20 booklet containing pane of 12 (85c.) stamps (No. 3326a) .... 12·00

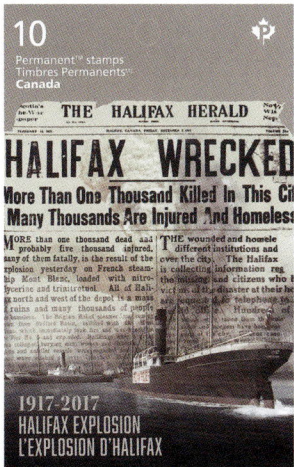

B305 Front Page of *The Halifax Herald* and *Mont-Blanc* (ship carrying munitions) before Collision with Imo

2017 (6 Nov). Centenary of Halifax Explosion. Self-adhesive. Multicoloured cover, 80×125 mm, as Type **B305**.
SB623 ($8.50) booklet containing pane of ten (85c.) stamps (No. 3330a) .... 12·00

B306 Menorah

2017 (20 Nov). Hanukkah. Self-adhesive. Multicoloured cover, 74×94 mm, as Type **B306**.
SB624 $8.50 booklet containing pane of ten (85c.) stamps (No. 3331a) .... 12·00

A version of this booklet showing a Star of David on the cover was withdrawn before the issue date of 14 November 2017, but it is believed that a few were sold to collectors. No. SB624 is the redesigned version showing the Menorah cover, which was issued on 20 November 2017.

B307 Dog (Pekinese) on Lantern

2018 (15 Jan). Chinese New Year. Year of the Dog. Self-adhesive. Multicoloured covers as Type **B307**.
SB625 ($8.50) booklet containing pane of ten (85c.) stamps (No. 3335a) (Type B **307**, 90×130 mm) .... 12·00
SB626 $15 booklet containing pane of six $2.50 stamps (No. 3336a) (cover 54×85 mm showing dog (Saluki-type) on lantern) .... 18·00

237

CANADA Stamp Booklets

B308 Hopewell Rocks

2018 (15 Jan). From Far and Wide. Self-adhesive. Multicoloured cover, 60×134 mm, as Type **B308**.
SB627 ($25.50) booklet containing pane of 30 (85c.)
(No. 3364b)... 35·00

B310 Kay Livingstone

2018 (1 Feb). Black History Month. Self-adhesive. Multicoloured covers, 76×140 mm, as Type **B310**.
SB629 ($8.50) booklet containing pane of ten (85c.)
(No. 3397a) (Type B **310**)............................ 12·00
SB630 ($8.50) booklet containing pane of ten (85c.)
(No. 3398a) (Lincoln M. Alexander)........ 12·00

B309 Tree

2018 (24 Jan). Women in Winter Sport. Self-adhesive. Multicoloured cover, 54×118 mm, as Type **B309**.
SB628 ($8.50) booklet containing pane of ten (85c.) stamps (No. 3391a) .... 12·00

B311 *Nelumbo nucifera* and *Nelumbo lutea*

2018 (1 Mar). Lotus. Self-adhesive. Multicoloured cover, 80×120 mm, as Type **B311**.
SB631 ($8.50) booklet pane containing ten (85c.) and ten small stickers (No. 3401a).................. 12·00

Stamp Booklets CANADA

B312 *It's Not a Stream of Consciousness* (Gerard DuBois), 2015

2018 (5 Apr). Great Canadian Illustrators. Self-adhesive. Multicoloured cover, 82×116 mm, as Type **B312**.
SB632 ($8.50) booklet pane containing ten (85c.)
(No. 3404a) .... 12·00

B313 Princess Elizabeth, 1951 (photo by Yousuf Karsh)

2018 (20 Apr). 65th Anniversary of the Coronation of Queen Elizabeth II. Self-adhesive. Black, grey and gold cover, 67×127 mm, as Type **B313**.
SB633 ($8.50) booklet containing pane of ten (85c.)
stamps (No. 3410a) .... 15·00

B314 *Bombus affinis* (Rusty-patched Bumblebee)

2018 (1 May). Bees. Self-adhesive. Multicoloured cover, 75×111 mm, as Type **B314**.
SB634 ($8.50) booklet containing pane of ten (85c.)
(No. 3411a) .... 14·00

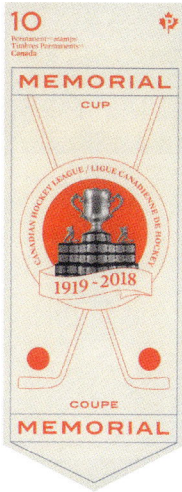

B315 Memorial Cup

2018 (18 May). 100th Memorial Cup of Ontario Hockey Association. Self-adhesive. Multicoloured cover, 58×152 mm, as Type **B315**.
SB635 ($8.50) booklet containing pane of ten (85c.)
stamps (No. 3413a) .... 12·00

B316 Northern Lights

239

CANADA Stamp Booklets

2018 (29 June). 150th Anniversary of the Royal Astronomical Society of Canada. Self-adhesive. Multicoloured cover, 86×100 mm, as Type **B316**.
SB636 ($8.50) booklet containing ten (85c.) stamps (No. 3414a) .... 12·00

B319 Armey RIBs crossing Flood, Forest Fire, Helicopter, Police Car in City and Rescue Helicopter in Rocky Mountains

2018 (14 Sept). Emergency Responders. Self-adhesive. Multicoloured cover, 64×125 mm, as Type **B319**.
SB640 ($8.50) booklet containing pane of ten (85c.) (No. 3436a).. 15·00

B317 Great White Shark

2018 (13 July). Sharks. Self-adhesive. Multicoloured cover, 80×117 mm, as Type **B317**.
SB637 ($8.50) booklet containing pane of ten (85c.) (No. 3417a).. 12·00

B318 Steam Fog

2018 (26 July). Weather Wonders (2nd issue). Self-adhesive. Multicoloured cover, 92×96 mm, as Type **B318**.
SB638 ($8.50) booklet containing pane of ten (85c.) stamps (No. 3423a) .... 12·00

2018 (20 Aug.). Birds of Canada (3rd issue). Self-adhesive. Multicoloured cover as Type **B282**.
SB639 ($8.50) booklet containing pane of ten (85c.) (No. 3429a) (cover showing Black-capped Chickadee and Canada Goose) 15·00

B320 Boy seeing Shapes in Clouds

2018 (24 Sept). Canada Post Community Foundation. Self-adhesive. Multicoloured cover, 69×119 mm, as Type **B320**.
SB641 ($9.50) booklet containing pane of ten (85c.)+10c. stamps (No. 3442a)................ 12·00

Stamp Booklets CANADA

B321 Peace Dove over Barbed Wire

2018 (24 Oct). Centenary of the Armistice. Self-adhesive. Multicoloured cover, 84×120 mm, as Type **B321**.
SB642 ($8.50) booklet containing pane of ten (85c.)
(No. 3443a) .... 12·00

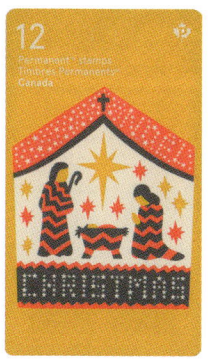

B322 The Nativity

2018 (2 Nov). Christmas (1st issue). *Away in a Manger*. Self-adhesive. Multicoloured cover as Type **B322**.
SB643 ($10.20) booklet containing pane of 12 (85c.)
stamps (No. 3445a) .... 14·00

B323 Socks

2018 (2 Nov). Christmas (2nd issue). Warm and Cozy. Self-adhesive. Multicoloured cover, 54×92 mm, as Type **B323**.
SB644 ($10.20) booklet containing pane of 12 (85c.)
stamps (No. 3446a) .... 14·00

B324 Zhu Bajie (Pigsy) in Armour carrying Nine-toothes Rake

2019 (18 Jan). Chinese New Year. Year of the Pig. Self-adhesive. Multicoloured covers as Type **B324**.
SB645 ($9) booklet containing pane of ten (90c.) stamps (No. 3453a) (Type **B324**, 79×122 mm) .... 12·00
SB646 $15.90 booklet containing pane of six $2.65 stamps (No. 3454a) (cover 85×54 mm showing Zhu Bajie seated on ground).. 20·00

B325 Albert Jackson

2019 (25 Jan). Black History Month. Albert Jackson. Self-adhesive. Multicoloured cover, 69×120 mm, as T **B325**.
SB647 ($9) booklet containing pane of 10×(90c.) stamps (No. 3455a) .... 12·00

241

CANADA Stamp Booklets

B326 Gardenias

2019 (14 Feb). Gardenia. Self-adhesive. Multicoloured cover, 80×120 mm, as T **B326**.
SB648 ($9) booklet pane containing 10×(90c.) and ten small stickers (No. 3458a).......... 12·00

B327 Avro CF-105 Arrow mk. 1

2019 (27 Mar). Canadians in Flight. Self-adhesive. Multicoloured cover, 94×86 mm, as T **B327**.
SB649 ($9) booklet containing pane of 10×(90c.) stamps (No. 3461a) .... 12·00

B328 Box of Recipes

2019 (17 Apr). Sweet Canada. Self-adhesive. Multicoloured cover, 82×127 mm, as T **B328**.
SB650 ($9) booklet containing pane of 10×(90c.) (No. 3466a)........................ 12·00

B329 George Yoshinaka, Koei Mitsui and Kaye Kaminishi

2019 (25 Apr). Vancouver Asahi (Japanese Canadian amateur baseball team). Self-adhesive. Black and carmine-red cover, 77×118 mm, as T **B329**.
SB651 ($9) booklet containing pane of 10×(90c.) (No. 3472a)........................ 12·00

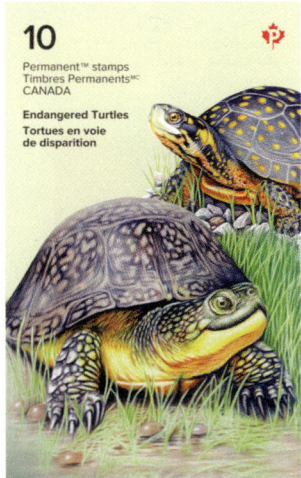

B330 Blanding's Turtle and Spotted Turtle

2019 (23 May). Endangered Turtles. Self-adhesive. Multicoloured cover, 81×128 mm, as T **B330**.
SB652 ($9) booklet containing pane of 10×(90c.) (No. 3473a)........................ 12·00

Stamp Booklets CANADA

2019 (24 July). Bears. Self-adhesive. Multicoloured cover, 86×96 mm, as T **B333**.
SB655 ($7.20) booklet containing pane of 8×(90c.)
(No. 3485a).. 11·00

B331 Historic Covered Bridges

2019 (17 June). Historic Covered Bridges. Self-adhesive. Multicoloured cover, 87×136 mm, as T **B331**.
SB653 ($9) booklet containing pane of 10×(90c.)
(No. 3476a).. 12·00

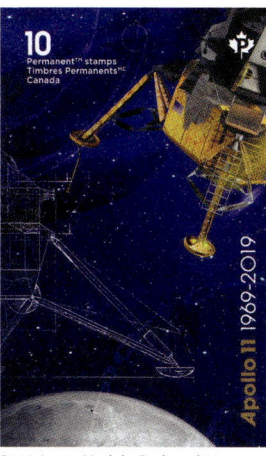

B332 Lunar Module *Eagle* and Moon

2019 (27 June). 50th Anniversary of First Manned Moon Landing. Self-adhesive. Multicoloured cover, 74×117 mm, as T **B332**.
SB654 ($9) booklet containing pane of 10×(90c.)
(No. 3482a).. 12·00

B333 *Ursus arctos* (Grizzly Bear)

B334 Mural of Leonard Cohen, Montreal

2019 (21 Sept). Leonard Cohen (1934–2016, singer, songwriter, poet and novelist) Commemoration. Self-adhesive. Grey, brownish grey and black cover, 90×121 mm, as T **B334**.
SB656 ($8.10) booklet containing pane of 9×(90c.)
stamps (No. 3490a) .... 12·00

B335

2019 (23 Sept). Canada Post Community Foundation.
SB657 ($10.80) booklet containing pane of 12×(90c.)
stamps (No. 3496a) .... 12·00

CANADA Stamp Booklets

B336 The Magi following the Star of Bethlehem

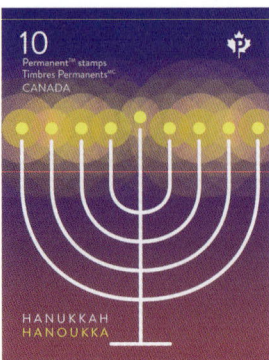

B339

2019 (4 Dec). Christmas (1st issue). The Magi. Self-adhesive. Multicoloured cover, 75×118 mm, as T **B336**.
SB658 ($10.80) booklet containing pane of 12×(90c.) stamps (No. 3496a) .... 16·00

2019 (14 Nov). Hanukkah. Self-adhesive. Multicoloured cover, 74×95 mm, as T **B339**.
SB661 ($9) booklet containing pane of 10×(90c.) (No. 3502a) .... 12·00

B337 Reindeer

2019 (4 Dec). Christmas (2nd issue). Shiny and Bright. Multicoloured cover, 54×92 mm, as T **B337**.
SB659 ($10.80) booklet containing pane of 12×(90c.) stamps (No. 3497a) .... 16·00

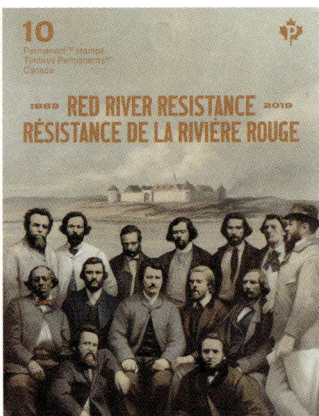

B338

B340 Rat Bride on Way to Wedding

2019 (4 Dec). 150th Anniversary of the Red River Resistance, 1869–1870. Self-adhesive. Multicoloured cover, 88×109 mm, as T **B338**.
SB660 ($9) booklet containing 10×(90c.) stamps (No. 3501a) .... 12·00

2020 (17 Jan). Chinese New Year. Year of the Rat. Self-adhesive. Multicoloured covers as T **B340**.
SB662 ($9.20) booklet containing pane of 10×(92c.) stamps (No. 3506a) (Type **B340**, 89×122 mm) .... 15·00
SB663 $16.26 booklet containing pane of 6×$2.71 stamps (No. 3507a) (cover 85×54 mm showing Rat bride wearing headdress) .... 24·00

Stamp Booklets CANADA

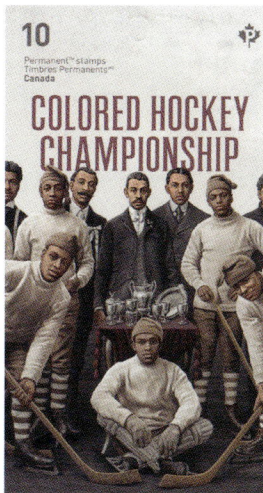

B341 Halifax Eurekas Coloured Hockey Champion Team Photo, 1904

2020 (24 Jan). Black History. Coloured Hockey Championship. Self-adhesive. Multicoloured cover, 80×145 mm, as T **B341**.
SB664   ($9.20) booklet containing pane of 10×(92c.) (No. 3508a) ....   15·00

B342 Two Dahlias

2020 (2 Mar). Dahlia. Multicoloured cover, 80×120 mm, as T **B342**. Self-adhesive.
SB665   ($9.20) booklet pane containing 10×(92c.) and ten small stickers (No. 3511a) ....   15·00

B343 'Eid Mubarak'

2020 (24 Apr). Eid. Multicoloured cover, 74×94 mm, as T **B343**. Self-adhesive.
SB666   ($9.20) booklet containing pane of 10×(92c.) (No. 3514a) ....   15·00

B344 Private Léo Major and Veronica Foster at Work in Munitions Factory

2020 (29 Apr). 75th Anniversary of Victory in Europe. Multicoloured cover, 94×87 mm, as T **B344**. Self-adhesive.
SB667   ($9.20) booklet containing pane of 10×(92c.) (No. 3515a) ....   15·00

B345 Paintings by the Group of Seven

2020 (7 May). Group of Seven 1920–2020. Multicoloured cover, 94×96 mm, as T **B345**. Self-adhesive.
SB668   ($6.44) booklet containing pane of 7×92c. (No. 3517a) ....   11·00

B346 Retro Radio Box, Speaker, Bulbs and Sound Waves

2020 (20 May). History of Radio in Canada. Multicoloured cover, 88×101 mm, as T **B346**. Self-adhesive.
SB669   ($9.20) booklet containing pane of 10×(92c.) (No. 3525a) ....   15·00

CANADA Stamp Booklets

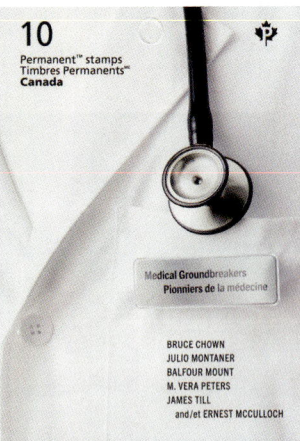

B347 Stethoscope and Lab Coat

2020 (10 Sept). Medical Groundbreakers. Black, white and grey cover, 88×123 mm, as T **B347**. Self-adhesive.
SB670 ($9·20) booklet containing pane of 10×(92c.)
 (No. 3527a)... 15·00

B348 Deer, Rabbit and Red Cardinal

2020 (21 Sept). Canada Post Community Foundation. Multicoloured cover, 80×146 mm, as T **B348**. Self-adhesive.
SB671 ($9·20) booklet containing pane of
 10×(92c.)+10c. stamps (No. 3532a)........ 15·00

B349 Diwali Lamp and Rangoli Patterns

2020 (15 Oct). Diwali. Multicoloured cover, 73×94 mm, as Type **B349**. Self-adhesive.
SB672 ($9·20) booklet containing pane of 10×(92c.)
 (No. 3533a)... 15·00

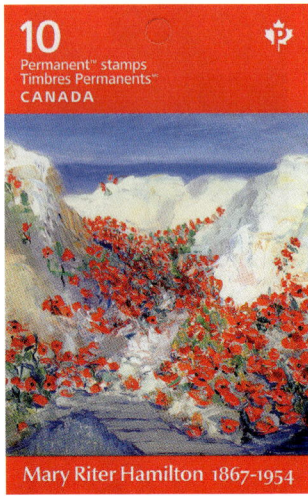

B350 *Trenches on the Somme*, 1919

2020 (28 Oct). Mary Riter Hamilton (1867–1954, battlefield artist 1919–1925) Commemoration. Multicoloured cover, 86×135 mm, as Type **B350**. Self-adhesive.
SB673 ($9·20) booklet containing pane of 10×(92c.)
 (No. 3534a)... 15·00

B352 Winter Sleigh Ride, c. early 1960s

2020 (2 Nov). Holiday: Folk Art Paintings of Maud Lewis (1901–1970). Multicoloured cover, 80×110 mm, as Type **B352**. Self-adhesive.
SB675 $11·04 booklet containing pane of 12×(92c.)
 stamps (No. 3536a)....................................... 18·00

Stamp Booklets CANADA

B353 Menorah

2020 (5 Nov). Hanukkah. Multicoloured cover, 73×94 mm, as T **B353**. Self-adhesive.
SB676 ($9·20) booklet containing pane of 10×(92c.) (No. 3540a) .... 14·00

B355 Settlers Alexander Diggs and Eliza Taylor and sailing ship off Saint John, New Brunswick, 1817 (Willow Grove)

2021 (22 Jan). Black History Month. Willow Grove, New Brunswick and Amber Valley, Alberta. Multicoloured cover, 94×86 mm, as T **B355**. Self-adhesive.
SB678 ($9·20) booklet containing 10×(92c.) stamps (No. 3554a) .... 15·00

B356 Arctic Fox and Peary Caribou

2021 (16 Feb). Snow Mammals. Multicoloured cover, 70×117 mm, as T **B356**. Self-adhesive.
SB679 ($9·20) booklet containing pane of 10×(92c.) (No. 3556a) .... 15·00

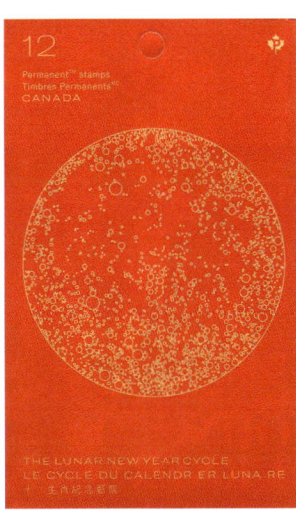

B354 Sun

2021 (15 Jan). Lunar New Year Cycle. Red and yellow cover, 78×125 mm, as Type **B354**. Self-adhesvie.
SB677 ($11·04) booklet containing 12×(92c.) stamps (No. 3541a) .... 18·00

B357 Malus Rosseau

247

CANADA Stamp Booklets

2021 (1 Mar). Crab Apple Blossoms. Multicoloured cover, 80×120 mm, as Type **B357**. Self-adhesive.
SB680 ($9·20) booklet containing pane of 10×(92c.)
(No. 3564a) .... 15·00

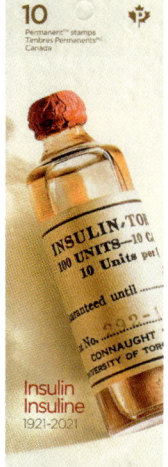

B358 Redesigned Statuette for 50th Anniversary of JUNO Awards   **B359** Insulin Vial

2021 (8 Apr). 50th Anniversary of the JUNO Awards (Canadian music awards). Black and gold cover, 66×124 mm, as T **B358**. Self-adhesive.
SB681 ($4·60) booklet containing pane of 5×(92c.) stamps (No. 3567a) .... 8·00

2021 (15 Apr). Centenary of the Discovery of Insulin. Multicoloured cover, 52×156 mm, as T **B359**. Self-adhesive.
SB682 ($9·20) booklet containing pane of 10×(92c.)
(No. 3568a) .... 15·00

B361 Fernand Nault

2021 (29 Apr). Canadian Ballet Legends. Multicoloured covers, 84×110 mm, as T **B361**. Self-adhesive.
SB684 ($5·52) booklet containing pane of six (92c.)
(No. 3570a) (cover Type **B361**) .... 10·00
SB685 ($5·52) booklet containing pane of six (92c.)
(No. 3571a) (Karen Kain) .... 10·00

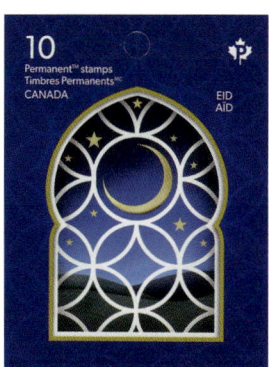

B360 Night Sky with Crescent Moon seen through Mosque Window

2021 (22 Apr). Eid. Multicoloured cover, 74×96 mm, as T **B360**. Self-adhesive.
SB683 ($9·20) booklet containing pane of 10×(92c.)
(No. 3569a) .... 15·00

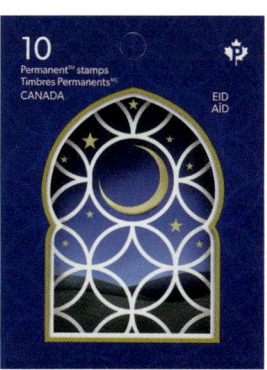

B362 John Turner

2021 (7 June). John Turner (1929–2020) Commemoration. Black and red cover, 88×115 mm, as T **B362**. Self-adhesive.
SB686 ($9·20) booklet containing pane of 10×(92c.)
(No. 3573a) .... 15·00

Stamp Booklets CANADA

B363 *Bluenose*

2021 (29 June). Centenary of Launch of *Bluenose* (fishing and racing schooner). Multicoloured cover, 94×98 mm, as T **B363**. Self-adhesive.
SB687 ($9·20) booklet containing pane of 10×(92c.) stamps (No. 3574a) .... 15·00

B366 Newspaper Headline

2021 (8 Oct). Editorial Cartoonists. Multicoloured cover, 86×135 mm, as Type **B366**. Self-adhesive.
SB690 ($9·20) booklet pane containing 10×(92c.) (No. 3580a) .... 15·00

B364 Stan Rogers

2021 (21 July). Stan Rogers (1949–1983, folk singer) Commemoration. Multicoloured cover, 80×144 mm, as T **B364**. Self-adhesive.
SB688 ($9·20) booklet containing pane of 10×(92c.) (No. 3578a) .... 15·00

B367 Christopher Plummer

2021 (14 Oct). Christopher Plummer (1929–2021, actor) Commemoration. Multicoloured cover, 92×130 mm, as T **B367**. Self-adhesive.
SB691 ($9·20) booklet pane containing 10×(92c.) (No. 3585a) .... 15·00

CANADA Stamp Booklets

B368

2021 (19 Oct). Diwali. Multicoloured cover, 74×94 mm, as T **B368**. Self-adhesive.
SB692   ($9·20) booklet containing pane of ten (92c.)
          (No. 3587a) .... 15·00

B370 Remembrance Poppy

2021 (29 Oct). The Remembrance Poppy. Red and black cover as T **B370**. Self-adhesive.
SB694   ($9·20) booklet of 10×(92c.) stamps (No. 3590a) .... 15·00

B369 Lionel (Leo) Clarke, Robert Shankland and Frederick William Hall

2021 (21 Oct). Valour Road. Canadian First World War Recipients of the Victoria Cross. Multicoloured cover, 85×144mm, as T **B369**. Self-adhesive.
SB693   ($9·20) booklet containing pane of 10×(92c.) stamps (No. 3588a) .... 15·00

B371 Angel flying over Church

2021 (1 Nov). Christmas. Angels. Gold cover, 86×108 mm, as T **B371**. Self-adhesive.
SB695 $11·04 booklet containing pane of 12×(92c.) stamps (No. 3591a) .... 18·00

B372 Santa Claus

B374 Buffy Sainte-Marie playing Guitar

2021 (1 Nov). Holiday Characters. Multicoloured cover, 58×92 mm, as T **B372**. Self-adhesive.
SB696   ($11·04) booklet containing pane of 12×(92c.) stamps (No. 3592a) ....   18·00

2021 (19 Nov). Buffy Sainte-Marie (singer songwriter). Multicoloured cover, 74×105 mm, as T **B374**. Self-adhesive.
SB698   ($9·20) booklet containing pane of 10×(92c.) (No. 3597a) ....   15·00

B373 Hanukkah Candles

B375 Margaret Atwood

2021 (8 Nov). Hanukkah. Multicoloured cover, 74×94 mm, as T **B373**. Self-adhesive.
SB697   ($9·20) booklet containing pane of 10×(92c.) stamps (No. 3596a) ....   15·00

2021 (25 Nov). Margaret Atwood (writer). Black, grey and red cover, 82×143 mm, as T **B375**. Self-adhesive.
SB699   ($9·20) booklet containing pane of 10×(92c.) (No. 3598a) ....   15·00

CANADA Stamp Booklets

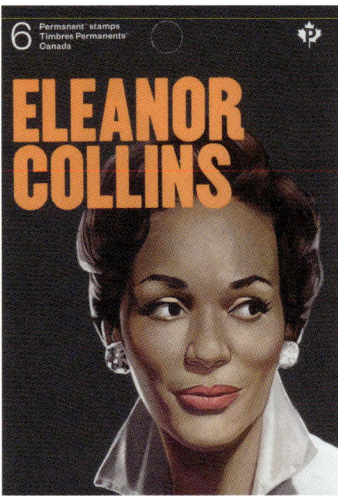

B376 Eleanor Collins

-**2022** (21 Jan). Black History Month. Eleanor Collins (jazz singer). Multicoloured cover, 80×110 mm, as T **B376**. Self-adhesive.
SB700 $5·52 booklet containing pane of 6×(92c.)
            (No. 3599a)... 8·00

B378 Pink and White Callas

2022 (1 Mar). Callas. Multicoloured cover, 80×120 mm, as T **B378**. Self-adhesive.
SB702   ($9·20) booklet containing pane of 10×(92c.)
            (No. 3604a)... 15·00

B377 Queen Elizabeth II

2022 (7 Feb). Platinum Jubilee. Black and silver cover, as T **B377**. Self-adhesive.
SB701   ($9·20) booklet containing pane of 10×(92c.)
            (No. 3600a)... 15·00

B379 Donor and Recipient ('Give Life')

2022 (7 Apr). Organ and Tissue Donation. Multicoloured cover, 88×97 mm, as T **B379**. Self-adhesive.
SB703   ($9·20) booklet containing pane of 10×(92c.)
            (No. 3607a)... 15·00

B380 Copper Lantern with Pierced Designs

2022 (12 Apr). Eid. Multicoloured cover, 66×90 mm, as T **B380**. Self-adhesive.
SB704 ($5.52) booklet containing pane of 5×92c.
(No. 3608a).. 8·00

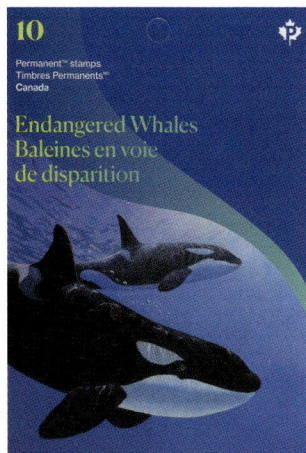

B382 Killer Whales

2022 (20 May). Endangered Whales. Multicoloured cover, 87×123 mm, as T **B382**. Self-adhesive.
SB706 ($9.20) booklet containing 10×(92c.) stamps
(No. 3610a).. 15·00

B381 Salome Bey

2022 (22 Apr). Salome Bey (1933-2020, singer, songwriter and composer) Commemoration. Multicoloured cover, 80×110 mm, as T **B381**. Self-adhesive.
SB705 ($5.52) booklet containing pane of 6×(92c.)
(No. 3609a).. 8·00

B383 *Canada's Picturesque East Coast*

2022 (9 June). Vintage Travel Posters. Multicoloured cover, 86×122 mm, as T **B383**. Self-adhesive.
SB707 ($9.20) booklet containing 10×(92c.) stamps
(No. 3616a).. 15·00

CANADA Stamp Booklets

B384 Marie-Anne Day Walker-Pelletier

2022 (21 June). Indigenous Leaders. Multicoloured cover, No. SB708 100×95 mm, as T **B384**; No. SB709 85×115 mm; No. SB710 84×111 mm. Self-adhesive.

SB708	($5.52) booklet containing 6×(87c.) (No. 3622a) (cover Type **B384**)	10·00
SB709	($5.52) booklet containing 6×(87c.) (No. 3623a) (Jose Kusugak)	10·00
SB710	($5.52) booklet containing 6×(87c.) (No. 3624a) (Harry Daniels)	10·00

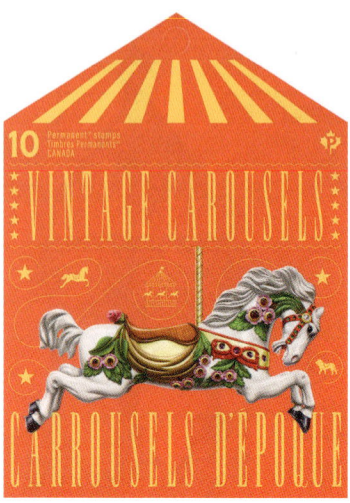

B386 Le Galopant

2022 (21 July). Vintage Carousels. Multicoloured cover, 95×129 mm, as T **B386**. Self-adhesive.

SB712	($9.20) booklet containing 10×(92c.) stamps (No. 3627a)	15·00

B385 Sunflower

(Des)

2022 (7 July). Help for Ukraine. Multicoloured cover, 132×120 mm, as T **B385**. Self-adhesive.

SB711	($9.20) booklet containing 10×(92c.) stamps (No. 3626a)	15·00

B387 Treehouses

2022 (19 Sept). Canada Post Community Foundation. Multicoloured cover, 91×124 mm, as T **B387**. Self-adhesive.

SB713	$10.20 booklet containing 10×(92c.) stamps (No. 3633a)	16·00

Stamp Booklets CANADA

B388 Ice Hockey

B390

2022 (21 Sept). Summit Series. Canada's Victory over USSR, 1972. Multicoloured cover, 88×114 mm, as T **B388**. Self-adhesive.
SB714 ($9.20) booklet containing pane of 10×(92c.)
(No. 3634a)... 15·00

2022 (6 Oct). Diwali. Multicoloured cover, 78×103 mm, as T **B390**. Self-adhesive.
SB716 ($5.52) booklet containing pane of 6×(92c.)
(No. 3639a)... 10·00

B389 Children

B391 DHC-2 Beaver

2022 (29 Sept). Truth and Reconciliation. Multicoloured cover, 82×143 mm, as T **B389**. Self-adhesive.
SB715 ($7.36) booklet containing pane of 8×(92c.)
(No. 3635a)... 12·00

2022 (17 Oct). Canadians in Flight. Multicoloured cover, 93×86 mm, as T **B391**. Self-adhesive.
SB717 ($9.20) booklet containing pane of 10×(92c.)
(No. 3640a)... 15·00

CANADA Stamp Booklets

B392 Sergeant Thomas Prince

B394 Star

2022 (28 Oct). Tommy Prince. Multicoloured cover, 74×119 mm, as T **B392**. Self-adhesive.
SB718   ($9.20) booklet containing pane of 10×(92c.)
           (No. 3646a) ....   15·00

2022 (1 Nov). Christmas. Multicoloured cover, 64×120 mm, as T **B394**. Self-adhesive.
SB720   ($11.04) booklet containing pane of 12×(92c.)
           (No. 3652a) ....   18·00

B393 Cardinal

B395 Stars

2022 (1 Nov). Holiday Birds. Multicoloured cover, 55×101 mm, as T **B393**. Self-adhesive.
SB719   ($11.04) booklet containing pane of 12×(92c.)
           (No. 3648a) ....   18·00

2022 (7 Nov). Hanukkah. Multicoloured cover, 66×124 mm, as T **B395**. Self-adhesive.
SB721   ($5.52) booklet containing pane of 6×(92c.)
           (No. 3653a) ....   8·50

Stamp Booklets CANADA

B396 Monique Mercure

2022 (14 Nov). Monique Mercure. Multicoloured cover, 57×125 mm, as T **B396**. Self-adhesive.
SB722 ($5.52) booklet containing pane of 6×(92c.)
(No. 3654a).. 8·50

B398 Persian Buttercup (*Ranunculus Renoncule*)

2023 (1 Mar). Persian Buttercup (*Ranunculus Renoncule*). Multicoloured cover, 80×120 mm, as T **B398**. Self-adhesive.
SB724 ($9.20) booklet containing pane of 10×(92c.)
(No. 3659a).. 15·00

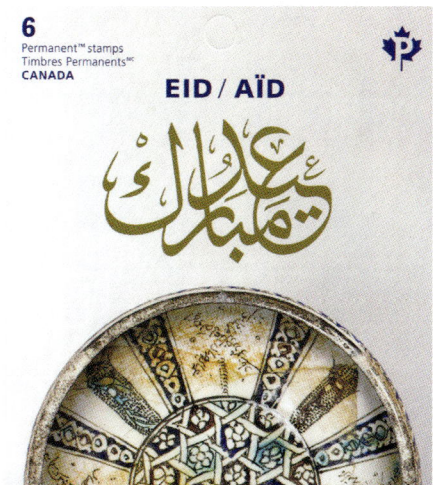

B397 Chloe Cooley

2023 (30 Jan). Chloe Cooley. Multicoloured cover, 100×95 mm, as T **B397**. Self-adhesive.
SB723 ($5.52) booklet containing pane of 6×(92c.)
(No. 3656a).. 8·00

B399 Bowl

2023 (3 Apr). Eid. Multicoloured cover, 95×105 mm, as T **B399**. Self-adhesive.
SB725 ($5.52) booklet containing pane of 6×(92c.)
(No. 3662a).. 10·00

CANADA Stamp Booklets

B400 Sea Otter (*Enhydra lutris*)

2023 (18 Apr). Animal Mothers and Babies. Multicoloured cover, 92×124 mm, as T **B400**. Self-adhesive.
SB726   ($5.52) booklet containing pane of 6×(92c.)
           (No. 3663a) .... 10·00

B402 Mounted Policeman on Horseback

2023 (23 May). 150th Anniversary of the Royal Canadian Mounted Police. Multicoloured cover, 90×90 mm, as T **B402**. Self-adhesive.
SB728   ($5.52) booklet containing pane of 6×(92c.)
           (No. 3668a) .... 10·00

B401 Bear, Fox, Owl and Ant Reading

2023 (1 May). Canada Post Community Foundation. Storytelling. Multicoloured cover, 87×133 mm, as T **B401**. Self-adhesive.
SB727   ($10.20) booklet containing pane of
           10×(92c.+10c.) (No. 3666a) .... 16·00

B403 Thelma Chalifoux

2023 (21 June). Indigenous Leaders. Multicoloured cover, 100×95 mm, as T **B397**, Nos. SB730/SB731 120×95 mm. Self-adhesive.
SB729   ($5.52) booklet containing 6×(92c.) (No.
           3669a) (cover Type **B403**).......................... 10·00
SB730   ($5.52) booklet containing 6×(92c.) (No.
           3670a) (Nellie Cournoyea)........................ 10·00
SB731   ($5.52) booklet containing 6×(92c.) (No.
           36271a) (George Manuel)......................... 10·00

B404 Denys Arcand

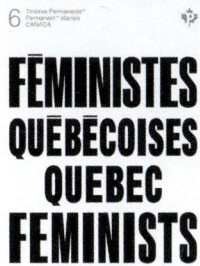

B406

2023 (28 June). Denys Arcand (Film director). Black and grey cover, 140×90 mm, as T **B404**. Self-adhesive.
SB732 ($5.52) booklet containing pane of 6×(92c.)
(No. 3673a) .... 10·00

2023 (28 Aug). Quebec Feminists. Black and grey cover, 150×70 mm, as T **B406**. Self-adhesive.
SB734 ($5.52) booklet containing pane of 6×(92c.)
(No. 3680a) .... 8·00

B405 Flag of Canada

B407 Residential School

2023 (12 July). Ferries of Canada. Multicoloured cover, 120×80 mm, as T **B405**. Self-adhesive.
SB733 ($9.20) booklet containing pane of 10×(92c.)
(No. 3674a) .... 15·00

2023 (28 Sept). Truth and Reconciliation. Residential Schools. Multicoloured cover, 85×143 mm, as T **B407**. Self-adhesive.
SB735 ($7.36) booklet containing pane of 8×(92c.)
(No. 3683a) .... 12·00

B408 Donald Sutherland

B410 Mountain Village in Winter

2023 (19 Oct). Donald Sutherland (Actor). Multicoloured cover, 68×154 mm, as T **B408**. Self-adhesive.
SB736 ($9.20) booklet containing pane of 10×(92c.)
(No. 3687a).. 15·00

2023 (2 Nov). Holiday. Multicoloured cover, 81×148 mm, as T **B410**. Self-adhesive.
SB738 ($11.04) booklet containing pane of 12×(92c.)
(No. 3689a).. 18·00

B409 Willie O'Ree

B411 Madonna and Child

2023 (30 Oct). Willie O'Ree (Hockey player). Multicoloured cover, 76×120 mm, as T **B409**. Self-adhesive.
SB737 ($5.52) booklet containing pane of 6×(92c.)
(No. 3688a).. 10·00

2023 (2 Nov). Christmas. booklet containing pane of 12×(92c.) (No. 3693a).
SB739 ($11.04) booklet containing pane of 12×(92c.)
(No. 3693a).. 15·00

Stamp Booklets, Premium Booklet CANADA

B412 Mona Parsons

2023 (7 Nov). Mona Parsons, 1901-1976. Multicoloured cover, 90×128 mm, as T **B412**. Self-adhesive.
SB740 ($9.20) booklet containing pane of 10×(92c.)
(No. 3694a)... 15·00

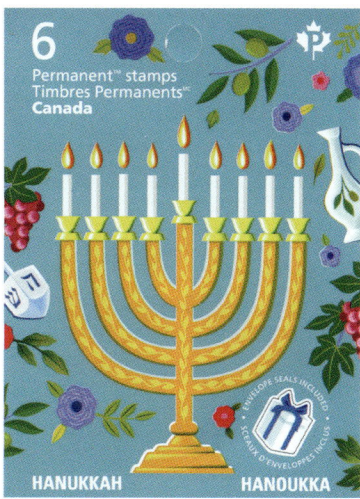

B414 Hanukkah Menorah

2023 (16 Nov). Hanukkah. Multicoloured cover, 70×93 mm, as T **B414**. Self-adhesive.
SB742 ($5.52) booklet containing pane of 6×(92c.)
(No. 3697a)... 10·00

B415 Mary Ann Shadd

2024 (29 Jan). Mary Ann Shadd (Publisher), 1823-1893. Multicoloured cover, 72×160 mm, as T **B415**. Self-adhesive.
SB743 ($5.94) booklet containing pane of 6×(99c.)
(No. 3698a)... 10·50

PREMIUM BOOKLET

The following booklet was sold at a premium over the face value of the stamps.

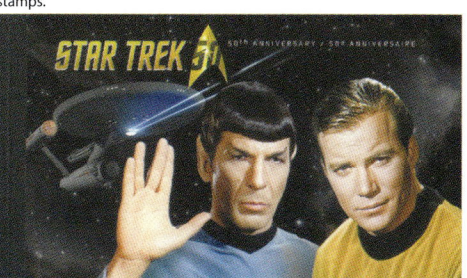

P1 Captain Kirk (William Shatner), Mr. Spock (Leonard Nimoy) and USS *Enterprise*

B413 Rangoli Pattern

2023 (9 Nov). Diwali. Multicoloured cover, 95×118 mm, as T **B413**. Self-adhesive.
SB741 ($5.52) booklet containing pane of 6×(92c.)
(No. 3696a)... 10·00

CANADA Premium Booklet, Registration Stamps, Special Delivery Stamps

2016 (5 May). 50th Anniversary of *Star Trek* (original TV series). Multicoloured cover, 170×95 mm, as Type **P1**. Booklet contains text and illustrations on panes and interleaving pages. Stitched.

SP1	$19.95 booklet containing five panes as follows: Ordinary gum as **MS**3207-(85c.) As No. 3202×4; $1.20 As No. 3206, $1.80 As No. 3203, $2.50 As No. 3205; $1 As No. 3204; (85c.) As Type **1069**, $1 As No. 3204, $1.20 As No. 3206, $1.80 As No. 3203, $2.50 As No. 3205; Self-adhesive As Nos. 3199/200 but die-cut perf 13½	35·00

Face value: $18.95

REGISTRATION STAMPS

R1

(Eng and recess-printed British-American Bank Note Co, Montréal and Ottawa)

1875 (15 Nov)–**92**. White wove paper.

(a) Perf 12 (or slightly under). Perf 12.

R1	R1	2c. orange (1876)	75·00	3·25
R2		2c. orange-red (1889)	80·00	8·00
R3		2c. vermilion	£125	10·00
		a. Imperf (pair)	†	£4500
R4		2c. rose-carmine (1888)	£180	75·00
R5		5c. yellow-green (12.1.76)	£150	3·50
R6		5c. deep green	£100	3·00
		a. Imperf (pair)	£950	
R7		5c. blue-green (1889)	£110	3·00
R7a		5c. dull sea-green (1892)	£150	6·00
R8		8c. bright blue	£500	£300
R9		8c. dull blue	£450	£275

(b) Perf 12×11½ or 12×11¾. Perf 12×11½ or 12×11¾.

R10	R1	2c. orange	£400	75·00
R11		5c. green (*shades*)	£1200	£180

SPECIAL DELIVERY STAMPS

PRINTERS. The following Special Delivery and Postage Due Stamps were recess-printed by the American Bank Note Co (to 1928), the British American Bank Note Co (to 1934), and the Canadian Bank Note Co (1935 onwards).

S1

1898–**1920**. Perf 12.

S1	**S1**	10c. blue-green (28.6.98)	90·00	18·00
S2		10c. deep green (12.13)	70·00	18·00
S3		10c. yellowish green (8.20)	80·00	22·00

The differences between Types I and II (figures '10' with and without shading) formerly illustrated were due to wear of the plate. There was only one die.

S2   **S3** Mail Carrying, 1867 and 1927

1922 (21 Aug). Perf 12.

S4	**S2**	20c. carmine-red	42·00	10·00

No. S4 exists in two slightly different sizes due to the use of 'wet' or 'dry' printing processes. See note below No. 195.

1927 (29 June). 60th Anniversary of Confederation. Perf 12.

S5	**S3**	20c. orange	25·00	28·00

No. S5 exists imperforate, imperf×perf or perf×imperf (*Price, in each instance, £250 per pair, unused*).

S4

1930 (2 Sept). Perf 11.

S6	**S4**	20c. brown-red	45·00	18·00

1932 (24 Dec). As T **S4**, but inscr 'CENTS' in place of 'TWENTY CENTS'. Perf 11.

S7		20c. brown-red	45·00	26·00

No. S7 exists imperforate (*Price per pair £700, unused*).

S5 Allegory of Progress

(Des A. Foringer)

1935 (1 June). Perf 12.

S8	**S5**	20c. scarlet	6·00	10·00

No. S8 exists imperforate (*Price per pair £850, unused*).

S6 Canadian Coat of Arms

1938–**39**. Perf 12.

S9	**S6**	10c. green (1.4.39)	24·00	10·00
S10		20c. scarlet (15.6.38)	45·00	40·00

Nos. S9/S10 exist imperforate (*Price £800, unused, for each pair*).

(S7)

1939 (1 Mar). Surch with T **S7**.

S11	**S6**	10c. on 20c. scarlet	10·00	25·00

S8 Coat of Arms and Flags

S9 Lockheed L.18 Lodestar

1942 (1 July)–**43**. War Effort. Perf 12.

(a) Postage.

S12	**S8**	10c. green	14·00	4·00

(b) Air.

S13	**S9**	16c. ultramarine	6·00	4·00
S14		17c. ultramarine (1.4.43)	5·00	4·00

Nos. S12/S14 exist imperforate (*Prices per unused pair* 10c. £750, 16c. £900, 17c. £900).

S10 Arms of Canada and Peace Symbols

S11 Canadair DC-4M North Star

1946 (16 Sept–5 Dec). Perf 12.
(a) Postage.
S15	**S10**	10c. green	13·00	4·00

(b) Air(i) Circumflex accent in 'EXPRÊS'.
S16	**S11**	17c. ultramarine	4·50	18·00

(ii) Grave accent in "EXPRÈS".
S17	**S11**	17c. ultramarine (5.12.46)	12·00	12·00

(ii) Grave accent in 'EXPRÈS'.
S17	**S11**	17c. ultramarine (5.12.46)	12·00	12·00

OFFICIAL STAMPS

Stamps perforated 'O H M S' were introduced in May 1923 for use by the Receiver General's department in Ottawa and by the Assistant Receiver Generals' offices in provincial cities. From 1 July 1939 this use was extended to all departments of the federal government and such stamps continued to be produced until replaced by the 'O.H.M.S.' overprinted issue of 1949.

The perforated initials can appear either upright, inverted or sideways on individual stamps. The prices quoted are for the cheapest version. Stamps perforated with T O1 are only priced used. Only isolated examples are known mint and these are very rare.

A number of forged examples of the perforated 'O.H.M.S.' are known, in particular of T O1. Many of these forged perforated initials were applied to stamps which had already been used and this can aid their detection. Genuine examples, postmarked after the perforated initials were applied, often show the cancellation ink bleeding into the holes.

(**O1**) (Five holes in vertical bars of 'H')

1923 (May). Nos. 196/215 punctured as T **O1**.
(a) Perf 12.
O1	**44**	1c. yellow-green	—	50·00
O2		2c. carmine	—	40·00
O3		3c. deep brown	—	40·00
O4		5c. deep blue	—	60·00
O5		7c. yellow-ochre	—	80·00
O6		10c. reddish purple	—	60·00
O7		20c. olive	—	60·00
O8		50c. sepia	—	80·00
O1/O8 *Set of 8*				£425

(b) Imperf×perf 8.
O8a		3c. brown		£350

1923 (May). 50th Anniversary of Confederation. No. 244 punctured as T **O1**.
O9	**48**	3c. bistre-brown	—	£275

1923 (May)–**31**. Nos. 246/255 and 263 punctured as T **O1**.
(a) Perf 12. Perf 12.
O10	**44**	1c. chrome-yellow (Die I)	—	40·00
		a. Die II (1925)	—	45·00
O11		2c. deep green	—	32·00
		a. Thin paper	—	45·00
O12		3c. carmine (Die I) (12.23)	—	35·00
		a. Die II (1924)	—	50·00
O13		4c. olive-yellow	—	75·00

O14		5c. violet	—	50·00
		a. Thin paper (1924)	—	60·00
O15		7c. red-brown (1924)	—	60·00
O16		8c. blue (1925)	—	£100
O17		10c. blue	—	55·00
O18		10c. bistre-brown (1925)	—	35·00
O19		$1 brown-orange (7.23)	—	£110
O10/O19 *Set of 10*				£500

(b) Perf 12×8. Perf 12×8.
O20	**44**	3c. carmine (Die II) (1931)	—	90·00

1927 (29 June). 60th Anniversary of Confederation. Nos. 266/273 punctured as T **O1**.
(a) Commemorative issue.
O21	**51**	1c. orange	—	75·00
O22	**52**	2c. green	—	£100
O23	**53**	3c. carmine	—	£100
O24	**54**	5c. violet	—	75·00
O25	**55**	12c. blue	—	£275
O21/O25 *Set of 5*				£550

(b) Historical issue.
O26	**56**	5c. violet	—	80·00
O27	**57**	12c. green	—	£250
O28	**58**	20c. carmine	—	£200
O26/O28 *Set of 3*				£475

1928 (21 Sept). Air. No. 274 punctured as T **O1**.
O29	**59**	5c. olive-brown	—	£200

1928–29. Nos. 275/285 punctured as T **O1**.
O30	**60**	1c. orange	—	45·00
O31		2c. green	—	30·00
O32		3c. lake	—	90·00
O33		4c. olive-bistre	—	£110
O34		5c. violet	—	40·00
O35		8c. blue	—	£100
O36	**61**	10c. green	—	35·00
O37	**62**	12c. grey-black	—	£275
O38	**63**	20c. lake	—	75·00
O39	**64**	50c. blue	—	£475
O40	**65**	$1 olive-green	—	£400
O30/O40 *Set of 11*				£1500

1930–31. Nos. 288/297 and 300/305 punctured as T **O1**.
O41	**66**	1c. orange (Die I)	—	45·00
O42		1c. green (Die I)	—	30·00
		a. Die II	—	25·00
O43		2c. green (Die I)	—	£110
O44		2c. scarlet (Die I)	—	35·00
		a. Die II	—	30·00
O45		2c. deep brown (Die I)	—	40·00
		a. Die II	—	32·00
O46		3c. scarlet	—	25·00
O47		4c. yellow-bistre	—	80·00
O48		5c. violet	—	50·00
O49		5c. deep slate-blue	—	42·00
O50		8c. blue	—	90·00
O51		8c. red-orange	—	65·00
O52	**67**	10c. olive-green	—	35·00
O53	**68**	12c. grey-black	—	£200
O54	**69**	20c. red	—	90·00
O55	**70**	50c. blue	—	£150
O56	**71**	$1 olive-green	—	£275
O41/O56 *Set of 15*				£1200

1930 (4 Dec). Air. No. 310 punctured as T **O1**.
O57	**72**	5c. deep brown	—	£300

1931 (30 Sept). No. 312 punctured as T **O1**.
O58	**73**	10c. olive-green	—	50·00

1932 (22 Feb). Air. No. 313 punctured as T **O1**.
O59	**59**	6c. on 5c. olive-brown	—	£250

1932 (21 June). Nos. 314/314a punctured as T **O1**.
O60	**66**	3c. on 2c. scarlet (Die I)	—	50·00
		a. Die II	—	40·00

1932 (12 July). Ottawa Conference. Nos. 315/318 punctured as T **O1**.
(a) Postage.
O61	**76**	3c. scarlet	—	40·00
O62	**77**	5c. blue	—	75·00
O63	**78**	13c. green	—	£300

(b) Air.
O64	**72**	6c. on 5c. deep brown	—	£275
O61/O64 *Set of 4*				£600

1932–33. Nos. 319/325 punctured as T **O1**.
O65	**80**	1c. green	—	25·00
O66		2c. sepia	—	25·00
O67		3c. scarlet (Die I)	—	25·00
		a. Die II	—	25·00
O68		4c. yellow-brown	—	£100
O69		5c. blue	—	45·00

CANADA Official Stamps

O70		8c. red-orange	—	£100
O71	68	13c. bright violet	—	90·00
O65/O71	Set of 7		—	£375

1933 (18 May). UPU Congress Preliminary Meeting. No. 329 punctured as T **O1**.

O72	81	5c. blue	—	£100

1933 (24 July). World's Grain Exhibition and Conference, Regina. No. 330 punctured as T **O1**.

O73	69	20c. red	—	£140

1933 (17 Aug). Centenary of First Trans-Atlantic Steamboat Crossing. No. 331 punctured as T **O1**.

O74	83	5c. blue	—	£100

1934 (1 July). Fourth Centenary of Discovery of Canada. No. 332 punctured as T **O1**.

O75	84	3c. blue	—	£120

1934 (1 July). 150th Anniversary of Arrival of United Empire Loyalists. No. 333 punctured as T **O1**.

O76	85	10c. olive-green	—	£150

1934 (16 Aug). 150th Anniversary of Province of New Brunswick. No. 334 punctured as T **O1**.

O77	86	2c. red-brown	—	£150

1935 (4 May). Silver Jubilee. Nos. 335/340 punctured as T **O1**.

O78	87	1c. green	—	75·00
O79	88	2c. brown	—	90·00
O80	89	3c. carmine-red	—	£100
O81	90	5c. blue	—	£120
O82	91	10c. green	—	£250
O83	92	13c. blue	—	£300
O78/O83	Set of 6		—	£850

1935. Nos. 341/351 and 355 punctured as T **O1**.

(a) Postage.

O84	93	1c. green	—	28·00
O85		2c. brown	—	50·00
O86		3c. scarlet	—	48·00
O87		4c. yellow	—	90·00
O88		5c. blue	—	55·00
O89		8c. orange	—	90·00
O90	94	10c. carmine	—	75·00
O91	95	13c. purple	—	80·00
O92	96	20c. olive-green	—	90·00
O93	97	50c. deep violet	—	60·00
O94	98	$1 bright blue	—	£180

(b) Air.

O95	99	6c. red-brown	—	£250
O84/O95	Set of 12		—	£950

1937 (10 May). Coronation. No. 356 punctured as T **O1**.

O96	100	3c. carmine	—	£100

1937–38. Nos. 357/367, 370 and 371 punctured as T **O1**.

(a) Postage.

O97	101	1c. green	—	5·00
O98		2c. brown	—	6·00
O99		3c. scarlet	—	5·00
O100		4c. yellow	—	20·00
O101		5c. blue	—	14·00
O102		8c. orange	—	35·00
O103	102	10c. rose-carmine	—	40·00
		a. Red	—	45·00
O104	103	13c. blue	—	55·00
O105	104	20c. red-brown	—	65·00
O106	105	50c. green	—	£130
O107	106	$1 violet	—	£225
O97/O107	Set of 11		—	£550

(b) Coil stamp.

O108	101	3c. scarlet	—	£130

(c) Air.

O109	107	6c. blue	—	60·00

1939 (15 May). Royal Visit. Nos. 372/374 punctured as T **O1**.

O110	108	1c. black and green	—	£100
O111	109	2c. black and brown	—	£100
O112	110	3c. black and carmine	—	£100
O110/O112	Set of 3		—	£275

(**O2**) (Four holes in vertical bars of 'H')

1939 (1 July). Air. No. 274 punctured as T **O2**.

O113	59	5c. olive-brown	32·00	22·00

1939 (1 July). Nos. 347/350 and 355 punctured as T **O2**.

(a) Postage.

O114	94	10c. carmine	£120	55·00
O115	95	13c. purple	£130	55·00
O116	96	20c. olive-green	£140	65·00
O117	97	50c. deep violet	£140	55·00

(b) Air.

O118	99	6c. red-brown	£120	90·00
O114/O118	Set of 5		£550	£275

1939 (1 July). Coronation. No. 356 punctured as T **O2**.

O119	100	3c. carmine	£110	70·00

1939 (1 July). Nos. 357/367, 369/370 and 371 punctured as T **O2**.

(a) Postage.

O120	101	1c. green	3·25	1·00
O121		2c. brown	4·00	1·00
O122		3c. scarlet	4·25	1·00
O123		4c. yellow	9·50	5·50
O124		5c. blue	6·00	1·50
O125		8c. orange	23·00	7·50
O126	102	10c. rose-carmine	75·00	4·00
		a. Red	17·00	1·00
O127	103	13c. blue	30·00	3·50
O128	104	20c. red-brown	50·00	4·50
O129	105	50c. green	75·00	15·00
O130	106	$1 violet	£150	50·00
O120/O130	Set of 11		£325	85·00

(b) Coil stamps.

O131	101	2c. brown	£100	65·00
O132		3c. scarlet	£100	65·00

(c) Air.

O133	107	6c. blue	5·50	2·00

1939 (1 July). Royal Visit. Nos. 372/374 punctured as T **O2**.

O134	108	1c. black and green	£130	65·00
O135	109	2c. black and brown	£130	65·00
O136	110	3c. black and carmine	£130	65·00
O134/O136	Set of 3		£350	£170

1942–43. War Effort. Nos. 375/388 and 399/400 punctured as T **O2**.

(a) Postage.

O137	111	1c. green	2·00	50
O138	112	2c. brown	2·00	20
O139	113	3c. carmine-lake	4·50	2·50
O140		3c. purple	3·50	90
O141	114	4c. slate	13·00	4·25
O142	112	4c. carmine-lake	2·50	30
O143	111	5c. blue	4·00	1·25
O144	115	8c. red-brown	16·00	4·25
O145	116	10c. green	11·00	30
O146	117	13c. dull green	17·00	17·00
O147		14c. dull green	18·00	3·00
O148	118	20c. chocolate	25·00	2·25
O149	119	50c. violet	55·00	9·50
O150	120	$1 blue	£120	45·00

(b) Air.

O151	121	6c. blue	7·00	11·00
O152		7c. blue	7·00	3·50
O137/O152	Set of 16		£250	90·00

1946. Peace Re-conversion. Nos. 401/407 punctured as T **O2**.

(a) Postage.

O153	122	8c. brown	48·00	12·00
O154	123	10c. olive-green	5·00	25
O155	124	14c. sepia	17·00	3·50
O156	125	20c. slate	17·00	75
O157	126	50c. green	50·00	22·00
O158	127	$1 purple	85·00	30·00

(b) Air.

O159	128	7c. blue	5·50	5·00
O153/O159	Set of 7		£200	65·00

1949. Nos. 415 and 416 punctured as T **O2**.

O160	136	2c. sepia	4·00	10·00
O161	137	3c. purple	4·00	10·00

O.H.M.S.
(O3)

1949. Nos. 375/376, 378, 380 and 402/407 optd as T **O3** by typography.

(a) Postage.

O162	111	1c. green	7·00	10·00
		a. Missing stop after 'S'	£250	£150
O163	112	2c. brown	12·00	12·00
		a. Missing stop after 'S'	£250	£150
O164	113	3c. purple	6·50	7·00
O165	112	4c. carmine-lake	7·50	6·50
O166	123	10c. olive-green	9·50	20
		a. Missing stop after 'S'	£250	85·00

O167	124	14c. sepia	22·00	11·00
		a. Missing stop after 'S'	£350	£150
O168	125	20c. slate	14·00	2·00
		a. Missing stop after 'S'	£300	£110
O169	126	50c. green	£180	£170
		a. Missing stop after 'S'	£1500	£1200
O170	127	$1 purple	45·00	70·00
		a. Missing stop after 'S'	£12000	£10000

(b) Air.

O171	128	7c. blue	24·00	17·00
		a. Missing stop after 'S'	£275	£150
O162/O171 Set of 10			£275	£275

Forgeries exist of this overprint. Genuine examples are 2.3×15 mm and show the tops of all letters aligned, as are the stops. The serifs are well defined and, in the case of the 'S', they are vertical. The crossbar of the 'H' is slightly above centre. Overprints applied by lithography are forgeries. Only a few sheets of the $1 showed the variety, No. O170a.

MISSING STOP VARIETIES. These occur on R. 6/2 of the lower left pane (Nos. O162a, O163a, O175a and O176a) or R. 10/2 of the lower left pane (O166a, O167a, O168a, O169a, O170a and O171a). No. O176a also occurs on R. 8/8 of the upper left pane in addition to R. 6/2 of the lower left pane.

1949–50. Nos. 414/415, 416/417, 418 and 431 optd as T **O3** by typography.

O172	135	1c. green	6·00	4·50
O173	136	2c. sepia	3·50	7·00
O174	137	3c. purple	2·75	4·25
O175	138	4c. carmine-lake	2·75	50
		a. Missing stop after 'S'	—	—
O176	139	5c. blue (1949)	8·50	4·25
		a. Missing stop after 'S'	£150	75·00
O177	141	50c. green (1950)	60·00	60·00
O172/O177 Set of 6			65·00	70·00

G G G
(O4) (O5) (O6)

Variations in thickness are known in T **O4** these are due to wear and subsequent cleaning of the plate. All are produced by typography. Examples showing the 'G' applied by lithography are forgeries.

1950 (2 Oct)–**52.** Nos. 402/404, 406/407, 414/418 and 431 optd with T **O4** (1c. to 5c.) or T **O5** (7c. to $1).

(a) Postage.

O178	135	1c. green	1·50	10
O179	136	2c. sepia	8·00	9·00
O180		2c. olive-green (11.51)	1·75	10
O181	137	3c. purple	2·25	10
O182	138	4c. carmine-lake	8·00	2·00
O183		4c. vermilion (1.5.52)	3·00	60
O184	139	5c. blue	8·00	3·00
O185	123	10c. olive-green	3·00	10
O186	124	14c. sepia	23·00	16·00
O187	125	20c. slate	60·00	2·25
O188	141	50c. green	25·00	29·00
O189	127	$1 purple	85·00	85·00

(b) Air.

O190	128	7c. blue	24·00	15·00
O178/O190 Set of 13			£200	£130

1950–51. Nos. 432/433 optd with T **O5**.

O191	142	10c. brown-purple	4·00	1·00
		a. Opt omitted in pair with normal	£950	£750
O192	143	$1 ultramarine	90·00	60·00

On a small number of sheets of 10c. the opt was omitted from R. 7/1.

1952–53. Nos. 441, 443 and 446 optd with T **O5**.

O193	153	7c. blue (3.11.52)	2·00	3·50
O194	151	20c. grey (1.4.52)	3·00	20
		a. Opt double	†	—
O195	154	$1 black (2.2.53)	5·50	13·00
O193/O195 Set of 3			9·50	15·00

1953 (1 Sept)–**61.** Nos. 450/454 and 462 optd with T **O4** (1c. to 5c.) or T **O5** (50c.).

O196	158	1c. purple-brown	15	10
O197		2c. green	20	10
O198		3c. carmine	20	10
O199		4c. violet	30	10
O200		5c. ultramarine	30	10
O201	160	50c. deep bluish green (2.11.53)	3·25	6·50
		a. Opt Type **O6** (24.4.61*)	2·50	8·00
O196/O201 Set of 6			3·25	6·50

* Earliest recorded date.

1955–56. Nos. 463/464 and 466/467 optd with T **O4**.

O202	161	1c. purple-brown (12.11.56)	65	20
O203		2c. green (19.1.56)	15	20
O204		4c. violet (23.7.56)	40	1·00
O205		5c. bright blue (11.1.55)	15	10
O202/O205 Set of 4			1·25	1·25

1955–62. Nos. 477 and 488 optd with T **O5**.

O206	165	10c. purple-brown (21.2.55)	70	80
		a. Opt Type **O6** (28.3.62*)	40	2·75
O207	176	20c. green (4.12.56)	2·75	30
		a. Opt Type **O6** (10.4.62*)	6·00	2·75

* Earliest recorded date.

1953. Pictorial stamps optd **G**. Official Stamps.

O207	176	20c. green (4.12.56)	2·75	30
		a. Opt Type **O6** (10.4.62*)	6·00	2·75
O206	165	10c. purple-brown (21.2.55)	70	80
		a. Opt Type **O6** (28.3.62*)	40	2·75
O195	154	$1 black (2.2.53)	5·50	13·00

1963 (15 May). Nos. 527/528 and 530/531 optd as T **O4**.

O208		1c. chocolate	50	9·00
		a. Opt double	£2000	
O209		2c. green	1·00	9·00
		a. Type **O4** omitted (vert pair with normal)	£2500	
O210		4c. carmine-red	60	3·00
O211		5c. ultramarine	50	3·00
O208/O211 Set of 4			2·40	21·00

No. O209a comes from the top row of an upper pane on which the overprint was misplaced downwards by one row. Owing to the margin between the panes the top row of the bottom pane had the overprint at the top of the stamp.

OFFICIAL SPECIAL DELIVERY STAMPS

1923 (May). Nos. S3/S4 punctured as T **O1**.

OS1	**S1**	10c. yellowish green	—	£375
OS2	**S2**	20c. carmine-red	—	£325

1927 (29 June). 60th Anniversary of Confederation. No. S5 punctured as T **O1**.

OS3	**S3**	20c. orange	—	£350

1930 (2 Sept). Inscr 'TWENTY CENTS' at foot. No. S6 punctured as T **O1**.

OS4	**S4**	20c. brown-red	—	£250

1932 (24 Dec). Inscr 'CENTS' at foot. No. S7 punctured as T **O1**.

OS5	**S4**	20c. brown-red	—	£225

1935 (1 June). No. S8 punctured as T **O1**.

OS6	**S5**	20c. scarlet	—	£250

1938–39. Nos. S9/S10 punctured as T **O1**.

OS7	**S6**	10c. green	—	80·00
OS8		20c. scarlet	—	£200

1939 (1 Mar). No. S11 punctured as T **O1**.

OS9	**S6**	10c. on 20c. scarlet	—	£180

1939 (1 July). Inscr 'CENTS' at foot. No. S7 punctured as T **O2**.

OS10	**S4**	20c. brown-red	£300	£250

1939 (1 July). No. S8 punctured as T **O2**.

OS11	**S5**	20c. scarlet	£150	65·00

1939 (1 July). No. S9 punctured as T **O2**.

OS12	**S6**	10c. green	16·00	18·00

1939 (1 July). No. S11 punctured as T **O2**.

OS13	**S6**	10c. on 20c. scarlet	£350	£100

1942–43. Nos. S12/S14 punctured as T **O2**.

(a) Postage.

OS14	**S8**	10c. green	19·00	22·00

(b) Air.

OS15	**S9**	16c. ultramarine	26·00	38·00
OS16		17c. ultramarine	20·00	22·00

1946–47. Nos. S15/S17 punctured as T **O2**.

(a) Postage.

OS17	**S10**	10c. green	18·00	14·00

(b) Air.

OS18	**S11**	17c. ultramarine (circumflex accent)	60·00	50·00
OS19		17c. ultramarine (grave accent)	95·00	90·00

1950. No. S15 optd as T **O3**, but larger.

OS20	**S10**	10c. green	13·00	50·00

1950 (2 Oct). No. S15 optd as T **O4**, but larger.

OS21	**S10**	10c. green	23·00	48·00

The use of official stamps was discontinued on 31 December 1963.

CANADA Postage Due Stamps

POSTAGE DUE STAMPS

PRINTERS. See note under Special Delivery Stamps.

D1   D2

1906 (1 July)–**28**. Perf 12.

D1	**D1**	1c. dull violet	12·00	3·50
D2		1c. red-violet (1916)	21·00	5·00
		a. Thin paper (10.24)	18·00	26·00
D3		2c. dull violet	40·00	1·50
D4		2c. red-violet (1917)	40·00	2·75
		a. Thin paper (10.24)	38·00	26·00
D5		4c. violet (3.7.28)	55·00	65·00
D6		5c. dull violet	48·00	4·25
D7		5c. red-violet (1917)	55·00	7·00
		a. Thin paper (10.24)	24·00	42·00
D8		10c. violet (3.7.28)	35·00	28·00
D1/D8 *Set of 5*			£140	90·00

The 1c., 2c. and 5c. values exist imperforate, without gum (*Price* £375 *for each unused pair*).

Printings up to October 1924 used the 'wet' method, those from mid 1925 onwards the 'dry'. For details of the differences between these two methods, see above No. 196.

1930–32. Perf 11.

D9	**D2**	1c. bright violet (14.7.30)	11·00	11·00
D10		2c. bright violet (21.8.30)	10·00	2·25
D11		4c. bright violet (14.10.30)	20·00	6·50
D12		5c. bright violet (12.12.31)	20·00	42·00
D13		10c. bright violet (24.8.32)	80·00	45·00
D9/D13 *Set of 5*			£120	95·00

No. D13 exists imperf×perf (*Price for vertical pair* £1200, *unused*).

D3   D4

1933–34. Perf 11.

D14	**D3**	1c. violet (5.5.34)	14·00	19·00
D15		2c. violet (20.12.33)	9·50	6·00
D16		4c. violet (12.12.33)	17·00	15·00
D17		10c. violet (20.12.33)	30·00	48·00
D14/D17 *Set of 4*			60·00	80·00

No. D14 exists imperforate (*Price per pair* £400, *unused*).

1935–65. Perf 12.

D18	**D4**	1c. violet (14.10.35)	80	10
D19		2c. violet (9.9.35)	3·75	10
D20		3c. violet (4.65)	8·00	10·00
D21		4c. violet (2.7.35)	1·50	10
D22		5c. violet (12.48)	6·00	8·00
D23		6c. violet (1957)	2·00	1·00
D24		10c. violet (16.9.35)	70	10
D18/D24 *Set of 7*			20·00	17·00

The 1c., 2c., 4c. and 10c. exist imperforate (*Price* £225 *for each unused pair*).

D5

1967–78. Litho. Perf 12½×12 (20c., 24c., 50c.) or 12 (others).

(a) Size 20×17½ mm.

D25	**D5**	1c. scarlet (3.67)	2·00	12·00
D26		2c. scarlet (3.67)	1·50	1·25
D27		3c. scarlet (3.67)	3·25	11·00
D28		4c. scarlet (2.67)	2·75	1·50
D29		5c. scarlet (3.67)	4·25	12·00
D30		6c. scarlet (2.67)	1·60	4·25
D31		10c. scarlet (1.67)	2·00	2·75
D25/D31 *Set of 7*			15·00	40·00

(b) Size 19½×16 mm.

D32	**D5**	1c. scarlet (12.69)	2·25	1·00
		a. White paper (1.74)	75	1·50
		b. White fluorescent paper	4·00	
		c. Perf 12½×12 (*white paper*) (9.12.77)	15	2·00
D33		2c. scarlet (*white paper*) (1973)	1·00	3·00
D34		3c. scarlet (*white paper*) (1.74)	3·50	6·50
		a. White fluorescent paper	5·00	
D35		4c. scarlet (4.69)	2·00	60
		a. White paper (1.74)	60	60
		b. White fluorescent paper	2·00	
		ba. Printed on the gummed side	£750	
		c. Perf 12½×12 (*white paper*) (9.12.77)	30	1·00
D36		5c. scarlet (2.69)	32·00	40·00
		a. Perf 12½×12 (*white paper*) (9.12.77)	30	2·00
D37		6c. scarlet (*white paper*) (1973)	2·75	5·00
		a. White fluorescent paper	5·00	
D38		8c. scarlet (1.69)	30	45
		a. White paper (1.74)	1·25	45
		b. White fluorescent paper	75	
		c. Perf 12½×12 (*white paper*) (28.6.78)	75	1·40
D39		10c. scarlet (4.69)	1·75	45
		a. White paper (1973)	40	45
		b. White fluorescent paper (*white paper*) (9.77)	40	60
D40		12c. scarlet (1.69)	30	50
		a. White paper (1973)	30	1·00
		b. White fluorescent paper	1·00	
		c. Perf 12½×12 (*white paper*) (9.77)	80	1·50
D41		16c. scarlet (*white paper*) (1.74)	5·50	7·00
D42		20c. scarlet (*white paper*) (9.12.77)	30	1·25
D43		24c. scarlet (*white paper*) (9.12.77)	30	1·50
D44		50c. scarlet (*white paper*) (9.12.77)	40	2·00
D32/D44 *Set of 13 (cheapest)*			14·00	27·00

There are no records of dates of issue of the above but supplies were distributed to depots in the months indicated.

The original 1969 printings of the 1c., 4c., 5c., 8c., 10c. and 12c. on ordinary paper, and the 8c. and 12c. on white fluorescent paper (Nos. D38b, D40b), have shiny 'Dextrine' gum. Later issues on white and white fluorescent ('hybrite') papers have PVA gum.

CANADA 1851 SG2 Proof

Explore an extensive collection of
stamps and postal history
curated by philatelic experts

www.stanleygibbons.com

For Commonwealth enquiries please contact Andrew Mansi
amansi@stanleygibbons.com

Stanley Gibbons
Stamp Catalogues

Commonwealth & British Empire Stamps 1840–1970 (126th edition, 2024)

King George VI (9th edition, 2018)

Commonwealth Country Catalogues

Australia with Australian States & Dependencies (12th edition, 2022)
Bangladesh, Pakistan & Sri Lanka (3rd edition, 2015)
Brunei, Malaysia & Singapore (5th edition, 2017)
Canada (8th edition, 2024)
Cyprus, Gibraltar & Malta (6th edition, 2023)
East Africa with Egypt & Sudan (4th edition, 2018)
Eastern Pacific (3rd edition, 2015)
Falkland Islands (8th edition, 2019)
Hong Kong (6th edition, 2018)
India (including Convention & Feudatory States) (6th edition, 2023)
Indian Ocean (4th edition, 2022)
Ireland (8th edition, 2023)
Leeward Islands (3rd edition, 2017)
New Zealand & Dependencies (7th edition, 2022)
Northern Caribbean, Bahamas & Bermuda (4th edition, 2016)
St Helena & Dependencies (6th edition, 2017)
West Africa (2nd edition, 2012)
Western Pacific (4th edition, 2017)
Windward Islands & Barbados (3rd edition, 2015)

Stamps of the World 2024

Volume 1	Abu Dhabi – Charkhari
Volume 2	Chile – Georgia
Volume 3	German Commands – Jasdan
Volume 4	Jersey – New Republic
Volume 5	New South Wales – Singapore
Volume 6	Sirmoor – Zululand

Great Britain Catalogues

2024 Collect British Stamps (75th edition, 2024)
2022 Channel Islands & Isle of Man (31st edition, 2022)
2024 GB Concise (39th edition, 2024)

Great Britain Specialised

Volume 1	Queen Victoria, Part 1 Line-engraved and Embossed Issues (1st edition, 2020)
Volume 2	King Edward VII to King George VI (14th edition, 2015)
Volume 3	Queen Elizabeth II Pre-decimal issues (13th edition, 2019)
Volume 4	Queen Elizabeth II Decimal Definitive Issues – Part 1 (10th edition, 2008)
	Queen Elizabeth II Decimal Definitive Issues – Part 2 (10th edition, 2010)

Foreign Countries

Arabia (1st edition, 2016)
Austria and Hungary (8th edition 2014)
Belgium & Luxembourg (1st edition, 2015)
China (12th edition, 2018)
Czech Republic and Slovakia (1st edition, 2017)
Denmark and Norway (1st edition, 2018)
Finland and Sweden (1st edition, 2017)
France, Andorra and Monaco (2nd edition, 2023)
French Colonies (1st edition, 2016)
Germany (13th edition, 2022)
Italy and Colonies (1st edition, 2022)
Middle East (1st edition, 2018)
Netherlands & Colonies (1st edition, 2017)
North East Africa (2nd edition, 2017)
Poland (2nd edition, 2023)
Portugal and Colonies (1st edition, 2022)
Southern Balkans (1st edition, 2019)
Spain and Colonies (1st edition, 2019)
Switzerland (1st edition, 2019)
United States of America (8th edition, 2015)

We have catalogues to suit every aspect of stamp collecting

Our catalogues cover stamps issued from across the globe - from the Penny Black to the latest issues. Whether you're a specialist in a certain reign or a thematic collector, we should have something to suit your needs. All catalogues include the famous SG numbering system, making it as easy as possible to find the stamp you're looking for.

STANLEY GIBBONS
THE HOME OF STAMP COLLECTING

STANLEY GIBBONS | 399 Strand | London | WC2R 0LX
www.stanleygibbons.com

 /StanleyGibbonsGroup    @StanleyGibbons    @StanleyGibbons   @StanleyGibbons1856

Subscribe & Save Money
on the cover price*

12-Month Print Subscription

UK £57
Europe (airmail) £90

ROW (airmail) £95

12-Month Digital Subscription

GSM Online £32.45

*UK print subscriptions only

Visit stanleygibbons.com/gsm
or call +44 (0)1425 472 363

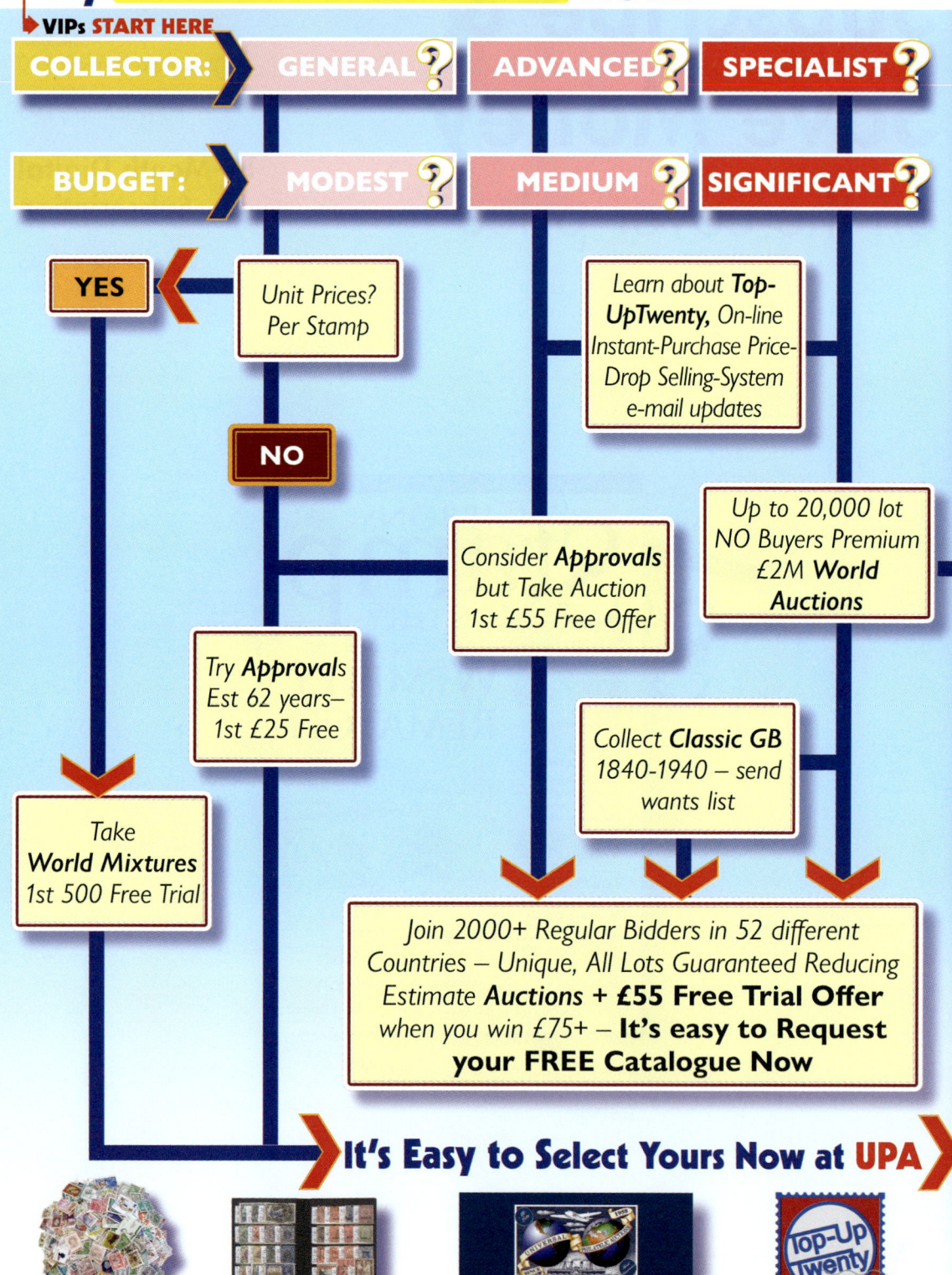